BUILDING A FEDERAL DAM

The
AMERICAN
STORY

RUTH WOOD GAVIAN

WILLIAM A. HAMM

Drawings by P. B. Parsons

D. C. HEATH AND COMPANY

BOSTON

FOREWORD

The *American Story* is intended for the senior high school. Compared with other textbooks in its field it is less difficult and less voluminous and, we believe, more teachable. It avoids difficult words and long sentences. It leaves out the unnecessary details which weary and confuse so many pupils. It focuses attention on the really significant events and issues of American life.

The American Story is more than a political history. It is the story of the American people — how they lived, what they thought, and how they struggled to realize the American dream of equal opportunity for all. The task of writing the Constitution and launching the national government is presented as the great achievement it was. Yet it is recognized that much still remained to be done to bring about a government by and for the people and that in consequence there have always been groups who vigorously demanded and obtained reforms.

The American Story is concerned with American idealism and love of country. It records the public services of our outstanding statesmen and reformers — those whose names are household words and others whose patriotism should not be forgotten. These men and women are portrayed as the leading characters in an inspiring drama.

The ten units cover American history from colonial times to the present. In harmony with the recommendations of the Report on American History in Schools and Colleges, nearly two thirds of the total space is given to the period from 1850 to the present, while more than one fourth of the total space is given to the story of the United States in world affairs.

The organization in the main follows the chronological pattern. However, at times the narrative is halted in order to consider separately some of its important strands. Thus, the topical organization appears in Chapter 2, Making a Living in Colonial Times; Chapter 3, Colonial Society; Chapter 4, Colonial Government; Chapter 17, The Period of Jacksonian Democracy; Chapter 25, The Rise of Big Business; Chapter 26, The Rise of the City; Chapter 27, The Rise of the Labor Movement; and Chapter 28, The End of the Frontier. In Unit VIII, The United States as a World Power, Unit X, The End of Isolationism, and Unit XI, The United States as a World Leader, the treatment is partly topical.

The illustration of *The American Story* has required many months of labor and research. More pictures have been included than in most high school histories. The pictures have been carefully selected for interest and educational value. Contemporary pictures have been used wherever possible. The exact source and date of most of the pictures are given. The maps, especially drawn for this book, were designed for maximum simplicity and usefulness. There are also a number of helpful diagrams.

The teaching aids have been carefully planned. At the end of every chapter there are names to identify, words to explain or define, and questions to help develop full understanding of the text. There is also a list of subjects for oral or written reports. These are intended for the abler students and will enable them to supplement and enrich the text. At the end of every unit practicable group activities are suggested. Each unit also has a bibliography. The titles are those which high school teachers generally have found most usable for collateral reading. Titles suitable for the slower readers are designated. Textbooks and books too difficult for high school pupils were excluded. The Constitution, which appears in the Appendix, has been annotated in order that it may be more intelligible than young people usually find it. Additional teaching helps and suggestions, including lists of source materials and catalogs of visual aids, will be found in the teachers' manual.

TO BOYS AND GIRLS

This is your book. It was planned and written to bring you greater satisfaction and enjoyment in the study of American history. We have worked hard to make it clear and interesting. We believe *The American Story* will help you to understand and take pride in the development of your country. We hope it will inspire you to cherish the American ideals of equal opportunity, liberty, and justice for all.

Criticism and suggestions from teachers and students who read *The American Story* would be of interest and value to the authors.

RUTH WOOD GAVIAN
Assistant Professor, Department of Education
Brooklyn College

WILLIAM A. HAMM
Associate Superintendent, New York City Schools
Formerly Chairman, Social Studies Department
Walton High School, New York City

CONTENTS

Contents

MAPS

CHARTS AND DIAGRAMS

UNIT ONE
OUR COLONIAL HERITAGE

The history of the American nation begins with the settling of the thirteen original colonies. Many kinds of people came to these colonies. Some sought religious or political freedom; others were looking for a chance to earn a better living than they could earn in the old world. The new world was a land of opportunity, but only those with courageous hearts were willing to face its hardships.

The settlers had to tame the wilderness and protect themselves from the Indians. They had to produce nearly everything they used. Men, women, and children worked hard. There was little time for play.

The voters took a lively interest in their government. They expected the legislature to protect their rights and keep a watchful eye on the governors sent from England by the king. The colonial legislatures quarreled continually with the governors and often refused to pay them.

As the colonies grew stronger they saw no need to depend on England for any kind of help. They wanted to make their own laws without interference from Parliament. They finally took up arms to resist British control. The struggle for independence was long and hard, but victory was finally won. A new nation — the United States of America — was born.

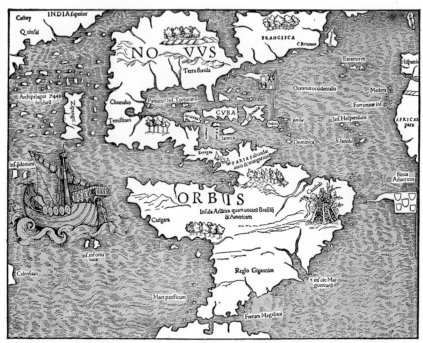

THE MUNSTER MAP *of the New World, 1540. The discovery of the new world fired the imagination of the educated people of Europe. Yet for a long time they had very little idea of what the New World was like. Nearly fifty years after Columbus's first voyage a German geographer named Munster published this map showing the supposed facts about the newly discovered continents. He pictured a cannibal hut in South America, with parts of a human body hanging outside. He imagined Japan (Zipangri) and China (Cathay) as lying just to the west of the New World (Novus Orbis). South of the Strait of Magellan he sketched the northern edges of what might be another continent. Within fifty years explorers found out a great deal more. By 1587 much more accurate maps of the New World had appeared.*

CHAPTER 1

EUROPEANS COME TO LIVE
IN THE NEW WORLD

The period of exploration. The story of the discovery of a "new world" by Christopher Columbus in 1492, while he was trying to find an all-water route to the East, is familiar to every school boy and girl. The discovery started a remarkable series of explorations in the Western Hemisphere. For many years mariners from Spain, Portugal, France, and England searched for a passage through America to India. Finally they realized the vast size of the American continent and its great distance from India. Then they gave up searching for a passage through the American continent. Meanwhile, other explorers, led by tales of wonderful treasures of gold and silver, or by zeal to convert the Indians to Christianity, were making long, dangerous journeys into the heart of the new continent. As a result of daring explorations by sea and by land, continuing for more than a century, Europe gradually learned much about North and South America.

The first settlements. More and more Europeans turned their faces toward this New World in the West. Countless ships crossed the Atlantic to obtain gold and silver from Mexico and Peru, or fish from Newfoundland. Small settlements sprang up. For a long time these were mainly forts, missions, and trading posts.

The Spanish were the most active in the early exploration and settlement of the New World. They started colonies from Florida and California to the Argentine. Later, the Portuguese colonized Brazil. Small numbers of French settled in Canada along the St. Lawrence River. They planted trading posts and mission stations around the Great Lakes and in the Mississippi Valley, and carried on a brisk trade in furs with the Indians. The Dutch settled along the Hudson River, and the Finns and Swedes along the Delaware. But the most numerous settlers in North America were the English. They soon took over the Dutch, Finnish, and Swedish settlements, and later the French as well.

CATHEDRAL AT MEXICO CITY. *The Spanish sent many missionaries to work among the Indians of the New World. These missionaries built many fine churches. This beautiful cathedral was erected at Mexico City in 1573, thirty years before the first English settlers landed in America. The cathedral is beautifully decorated both inside and out.* (Courtesy of F. E. Fanger, Mexico City)

The spread of European culture. The colonization of the Americas meant the spread of European ways of living and of thought. In the Spanish and Portuguese colonies many of the colonists intermarried with the Indians, and there was a mingling of European and Indian culture. In the English colonies there was little intermarriage with the Indians. The red men were steadily pushed back by the advancing settlers, and did not greatly influence the white man's ways of living.

The English colonies. The United States grew from thirteen English colonies scattered along the Atlantic coast from Maine to Georgia. The first colony was started in 1607 by the London Company, at Jamestown, Virginia. Mismanagement, starvation, disease, and hostile Indians created terrible hardships. Of 14,000 persons that the Company sent to Jamestown, only 1232 survived in 1624. In that year the king took away the Company's charter and changed the settlement into a royal colony. (In a royal colony the governor is chosen by the king.) Now that the first lessons of colonization were learned, Virginia grew steadily. The London Company had proved that English settlers could establish themselves in the New World.

ENGLISH WIGWAMS. *The first settlers in Massachusetts built bark houses like those of the Woodland Indians. The Pioneer Village, reconstructed at Salem, Massachusetts, shows us this type of dwelling. The bark rests on a frame of branches. The cracks were daubed with mud.* (Courtesy of the Pioneer Village)

Other English colonies sprang up on the seaboard to the north and south of Virginia. Some were started by commercial companies, others by friends of the king, who made them *proprietors* of immense grants of land in America. There is space here to mention only a few of them.

A little band of Pilgrims landed at Plymouth in 1620. After great suffering they succeeded in creating a permanent settlement. Ten years later the Massachusetts Bay Company started the colony of Massachusetts Bay. This colony grew rapidly. Settlers from Massachusetts soon established branches near by, which became Rhode Island and Connecticut. Another colony was planted in Maryland in 1634. The proprietor, Lord Baltimore, was a Catholic. He welcomed both Catholics and Protestants to his colony, and for a short time it was a home of religious freedom. One of the most interesting colonies was Pennsylvania, founded by the Quaker, William Penn, in 1681. Penn is remembered for his fair treatment of the Indians and his religious tolerance; that is, his willingness to welcome settlers no matter what religion they practiced. The last colony to be established was Georgia, in 1733. Its founder, James Oglethorpe, wished to make it a refuge for debtors confined in English prisons. However, not many debtors ever went there.

The rapid peopling of the English colonies. Unlike the French colonies to the north and the Spanish colonies to the south, the English colonies along the Atlantic seaboard grew rapidly. Their growth was due partly to a high birth rate and partly to immigration.

Why large families were usual. During the colonial period and for a long time afterward, American families were large. Families of eight, ten, or twelve children were rather common. Parents could support numerous children because land was cheap, and a family could build its own house from lumber cut on its own land, grow its own food, and make its own clothing and nearly everything else it required. Children helped in the hard work of the home and the farm, and the more numerous they were, the more likely the family was to get ahead. The custom of early marriage also favored large families. It is true that many children died in infancy, but even so, the average family had more children than does the average family today.

Why immigrants came. Some people came from Europe to America seeking religious and political freedom. Among those coming to escape persecution for their religion were Pilgrims, Puritans, Quakers, Huguenots (French Protestants), Catholics, and Jews. Some individuals came as officials, ministers of the gospel, or missionaries to the Indians, and others came for love of adventure. Far larger numbers came in the hope of making a better living. The custom of giving the newcomer fifty or one hundred acres of land attracted the poor working people and peasants of Europe. Here they could become independent; there it was practically impossible to reach that goal.

Obstacles to immigration. Immigration to America was held back by the cost and dangers of the journey. At best the trip from Europe to America required six to eight weeks; if storms drove the ship from its course, the voyage might last three months. There were no regular lines of ships, no regular dates of sailing, and no laws to regulate fares or protect the safety and health of the passengers. The traveler, after making a bargain with the sea captain for passage, had to wait in port, possibly for several weeks, until the ship was ready to sail and winds were favorable. Meanwhile he was using up his money and the store of food he had bought for the journey.

The ships were small and completely lacking in comfort. Sanitary arrangements were crude. The sick and the well lived, slept, and ate in a crowded hold. The supply of fresh water, always very limited,

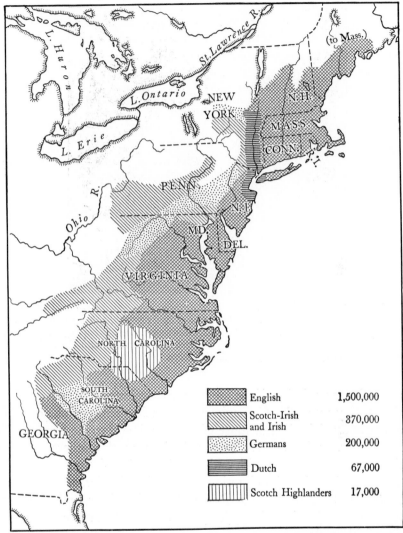

English	1,500,000
Scotch-Irish and Irish	370,000
Germans	200,000
Dutch	67,000
Scotch Highlanders	17,000

NATIONAL ORIGINS OF WHITE SETTLERS IN ENGLISH COLONIES
IN 1775

Before 1700 nearly all the settlers in the English colonies came from England. After 1700 many came from other countries. In this period the largest group of immigrants, next to the English, were the Scotch-Irish. They were among the best frontiersmen and Indian fighters in America and did more than any other group to push the frontier westward over the Appalachians. In addition to the Scotch-Irish there came to America a large number of Germans, many Scotch, Welsh, Irish, Dutch, and French Huguenots (Protestants), some Jews, and at least a few people from nearly every country in Europe. By the time of the Revolution these non-English settlers made up about one third of the total white population of the colonies.

LEONARD CALVERT, *brother of Lord Baltimore and first governor of Maryland. Maryland was founded in 1634. Both Catholics and Protestants were welcomed. In this painting, made by C. Y. Turner in 1902, Governor Calvert is buying land from the Indians. For several years the colonists had friendly relations with the Indians, but later the colony suffered severely from Indian wars.*

became dangerously low if the journey was prolonged by lack of wind or by stormy weather. Contagious diseases frequently broke out. It was not unusual for half or more of those on board to die from smallpox, measles, or dysentery. Young children, weak mothers, and the sick were almost sure to perish under the hardships of a long voyage.

Another obstacle to immigration was religious intolerance. Most of the colonies tried to shut out Roman Catholics, Jews, and Quakers. Only in Pennsylvania and Rhode Island were newcomers of every religious faith made welcome.

Indentured servants. Many farmers and plantation owners were so eager for laborers that they were ready to pay the cost of the voyage for immigrants who would work for them a period of years. In exchange for passage to America adults had to serve from three to seven years; children, until they came of age. The contract between master and servant was known as an *indenture;* this gives us the phrase "indentured servant."

The terms of the indenture were harsh, and the servant little better off than a slave. But when the time of servitude was up, he was free.

WILLIAM PENN *was the son of a wealthy English admiral. This portrait by an unknown painter shows him at the age of twenty-two, dressed as a knight. Soon after, he joined the Quakers and became a missionary and reformer. Six times he was thrown into prison for his beliefs. Later he founded a colony in America where Quakers and all others could enjoy religious and political freedom. The constitution he drew up for his colony was so liberal that Thomas Jefferson called him "the greatest lawgiver the world has produced."* (Courtesy of Historical Society of Pennsylvania. Photo by Philip B. Wallace)

He usually received a suit of clothes from his master. Often he received a small grant of land and managed to become an independent farmer. More often he became a wage earner.

Most indentured servants came here of their own free will, gladly binding themselves to service for a term of years in order to reach America. Entire families often came in this way, each one becoming an indentured servant. Other individuals, both adults and children, were carried here against their will and forced to become servants. The streets of London and other seaports in the British Isles were full of kidnapers. They made a business of hustling their victims into ships bound for America. Upon arrival here the captain delivered his unwilling passengers to whoever would pay him most.

Debtors and criminals. The prisons of England also furnished immigrants to the New World. To avoid the expense of keeping offenders in prison, the authorities frequently sentenced them to be transported to America. Some were in prison because of their religious or political ideas, many because of debts, others because of very minor offenses, a few because of serious crimes. Those sent to America had to serve masters in the colonies for a term of years, usually seven, and were then given their liberty. Some fifty thousand of them were brought to the American colonies.

Negro slaves. Probably one half of all immigrants to the English colonies in America were either indentured servants or Negro slaves. Although Negro slaves were first brought here in 1619, they were less numerous than white indentured servants until after 1700. The colonists from Maryland southward gradually came to depend upon slave labor, especially on the large farms or plantations, as they came to be called. Throughout the 1700's the importation of slaves increased rapidly.

Negro slavery existed in all of the colonies, but three fourths of the slaves were in Maryland, Virginia, North Carolina, South Carolina, and Georgia. Cheap Negro labor drove white labor from the plantations. As indentured servants gained their freedom, and as new immigrants arrived, they avoided the plantation regions. They settled in the northern colonies, or else pushed beyond the plantation area in the South, to make homes on the frontier.

The expansion of the frontier. The coastal plain of eastern North America offered colonists wonderful natural riches. Here were fine harbors, navigable rivers, fertile valleys, abundant wild game, untouched forests, and unexcelled fisheries. By the time the American Revolution began, two and three fourths million people occupied the land east of the Appalachian Mountains, where now some sixty million live. Most of the settlers still lived close to the great bays and navigable streams. In only a few places had settlers moved beyond the first highlands. Yet free land and plentiful wild game beckoned the adventurous westward. They were pushing the frontier back. The westward movement from the Atlantic coast, across the Alleghenies, the Mississippi Valley, the Great Plains, the Rockies, to the Pacific, is the central theme of American history — "the most American thing in all America."

To identify: Lord Baltimore, Huguenots, London Company, James Oglethorpe, William Penn, Scotch-Irish.

To explain or define: charter, indenture, indentured servant, mission station, plantation, proprietor, royal colony, trading post.

THE MASSACRE AT JAMESTOWN, *from a Dutch book of 1634. In 1622 Indians killed three hundred fifty settlers in an attempt to drive out the white men.* (Courtesy of New York Public Library)

A DEBTORS' PRISON IN ENGLAND, *sketched by Hogarth, the famous artist. James Oglethorpe founded the colony of Georgia as a refuge for debtors.* (Courtesy of New York Public Library)

THE BUILDING OF THE *ONRUST. This vessel was built in the Dutch colony of New Amsterdam about 1615. In ships not much larger than this many people crossed the Atlantic, often suffering unspeakable hardships on the way. Note at left the process of sawing the planks by means of a two-man saw, and at right the kettle of pitch used for caulking seams. This drawing by Henry F. Cady was published in* The American Continent, *Philadelphia, 1893.* (Culver Service)

Subjects for Talks or Written Reports

1. The early years of any colony in which you are interested. 2. How William Penn's good ideas helped Pennsylvania. 3. How Rhode Island and Connecticut were started. 4. Good and bad qualities of the Puritans as seen in the Massachusetts Bay Colony. 5. James Oglethorpe's hopes and plans for Georgia and what came of them. 6. The voyage from England to America in colonial times. 7. The treatment of indentured servants in the colonies. 8. The contribution of the Scotch-Irish, or some other one nationality, to colonial America.

Questions for Understanding the Text

1. Give three reasons why the early explorers were interested in North and South America. 2. What nations planted colonies in South America? In North America? 3. (*a*) Where and when was the first English colony started? (*b*) What caused the terrible loss of life during the early years of this colony? (*c*) What did the London Company accomplish? 4. (*a*) Name three proprietors and the colonies they founded. (*b*) For what do we remember each of these proprietors? 5. Why did the English colonies grow so rapidly? 6. (*a*) Give the various reasons which led

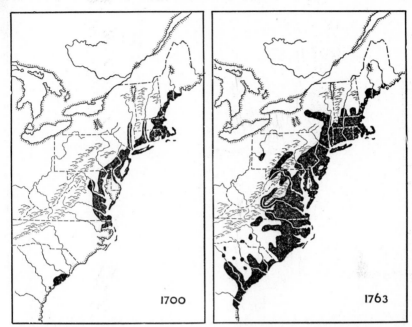

SETTLED PORTIONS OF THE ENGLISH COLONIES IN 1700 AND 1763

The first places to be settled were along the coast and the rivers. By 1763 there were some settlements in the valleys of the Appalachians, and at one place — Pittsburgh — there was a sizable settlement west of the mountains. (From the maps in *America's Economic Growth,* by F. A. Shannon. Courtesy of The Macmillan Company)

people to settle in the colonies. (*b*) Which reason influenced the largest number? 7. (*a*) What countries sent the largest number of immigrants to the English colonies? (*b*) What proportion of the total population was non-English at the time of the Revolution? 8. (*a*) Name two obstacles to immigration to the English colonies. (*b*) Explain each. 9. (*a*) In what way was an indentured servant better off than a slave? (*b*) How long did he have to serve his master? 10. Name three kinds of immigrants who did not come of their own free will. 11. (*a*) When did Negroes outnumber white servants? (*b*) In which colonies did most of the white immigrants settle? Why? 12. What were the natural riches of our eastern coastal plain in colonial times? 13. Why did the early settlers remain near the coast and along the navigable rivers? 14. Name the first important English settlement beyond the Appalachian mountains.

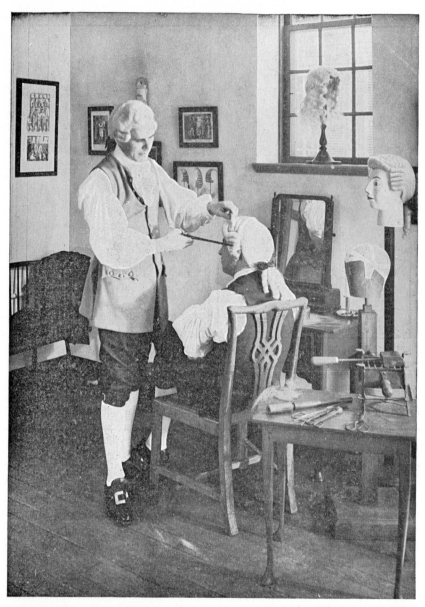

A COLONIAL HAIRDRESSER *curling the hair of his customer's wig. The foundation for a wig may be seen on the wooden form at the right. Throughout the 1600's and until late in the 1700's fashionable men and women wore wigs. The fashion was dying out by the time of the Declaration of Independence, although for some years doctors, lawyers, judges, and prominent officials continued to wear wigs.* (Courtesy of Colonial Williamsburg)

CHAPTER 2

MAKING A LIVING IN COLONIAL TIMES

FARMING IS THE CHIEF OCCUPATION

Importance of farming. For a long time all but a few of the colonists got their living from the land. Each family produced nearly all of its own food, and also provided for most of its other needs.

Clearing the land. Untouched or virgin forest covered the land east of the Mississippi. To clear the land of trees was the first task of the pioneer farmer. If time was short, he might kill the trees by cutting off a girdle of bark ("cutting around" the trees). He could then plant Indian corn or other coarse crops under the leafless branches. The next winter he cut down the dead trees. Then he and his neighbors rolled the giant trunks into piles to be burned. By pouring water through the ashes, his wife obtained potash for making soap.

In New England much of the land was strewn with rocks left by glaciers. To make room for crops, the rocks had to be removed, so they were piled to make walls or rolled into gullies. Each season more stones came to the surface, and the backbreaking toil went on for generations.

Crude tools and poor methods. During the colonial period agriculture was held back by crude tools and poor methods of work. Most of the farmer's tools were the same kind that had been used for thousands of years, including the ax, spade, hoe, fork, sickle, and flail. His plow and harrow were usually made of wood. Because of the lack of improved tools, farm work was very tiring. Oxen were used more generally than horses for farm work. They were cheaper than horses and could stand more hardships. But horses are faster, and for this reason farmers who could afford to do so used horses.

The average farmer had scarcely heard of improved breeds of livestock and improved varieties of plants. He knew little about how to feed livestock in winter. His cows yielded no milk and his hens laid no eggs in winter. A few of the farmers, who had more learning or money than the rest of the farmers, experimented with new tools and methods. Thomas Jefferson was one of these. He developed an iron

A COLONIAL FARM *in one of the Northern colonies. The roomy dwelling, the well in the back yard, the stone wall, and the oxen were common long after the colonial period. Note the long pole, or well sweep, for raising and lowering the wooden bucket.*

plowshare. It did not come into wide use for a number of years because most farmers believed it would poison the land.

Types of farming. In every colony small or family-size farms were the most common. These could be worked by the farmer's family, assisted, perhaps, by one or two indentured servants or Negro slaves. The farmer grew a variety of crops and livestock, chiefly for his family's use. When farm work was slack, the men and boys busied themselves with hunting, trapping, fishing, cutting firewood, making shingles, boiling maple sap, making shoes, and like activities. The women and girls helped with the outdoor work, spun thread and wove cloth, made the family clothes and the household linens, and did scores of other household tasks, most of which are no longer carried on in the home. With all this hard work, the family on the average small farm produced little beyond its own needs and saw little, if any, cash.

Along the seacoast in the South there were many plantations. These were large farms which used gangs of slaves to grow a large quantity of one crop for sale or export. In Virginia and Maryland the cash crop was tobacco; in South Carolina and Georgia it was rice or indigo. The plantations also grew most of their own food.

Although the farms of the Middle Colonies — New York, Pennsylvania, New Jersey, Delaware — were not plantations, some were very large and produced wheat, corn, oats, and barley for sale. Because these colonies grew more cereals than they ate, they are sometimes spoken of as the " Bread Colonies."

The farmer's marketing problem. One of the farm family's hardest problems was to get cash to pay for items not produced at home. The plantation owner solved this problem by growing a "cash crop," such as tobacco. The small farmer might get a little cash by selling furs, shingles, livestock, grain, or whiskey.

Farmers found it difficult to get their products to market, unless they lived on a navigable stream or close to a passable wagon road leading to a town. Otherwise they had to depend on pack horses. Pioneers who settled near the frontier had an especially hard time. They lived so far from the market that they could sell their products only if in a form easy to transport. For this reason they made their extra grain into whiskey, which could be taken to market by pack horse.

The large planters bought the tobacco, rice, or indigo produced by smaller planters in the neighborhood. They shipped what they purchased and what they grew themselves to agents in London and Liverpool. They had to take whatever the buyer across the sea was willing to pay. They had no way of knowing whether their agent returned the full selling price, less his commission, or whether he kept part of it for himself.

OTHER INDUSTRIES DEVELOP

The fishing industry. From the beginning fishing was important to the colonists living near the coast. Close to shore were clams, oysters, scallops, lobsters, smelts, shad, alewives, and sardines. In waters within easy reach of New England harbors was an abundant supply of cod, mackerel, and other kinds of fish. The cod and the mackerel provided the New England colonies with a source of cash income. In 1763 ten thousand New Englanders were occupied as fishermen. Fish caught off the Grand Banks were dried on near-by Newfoundland. The best cured fish were sent to England, Italy, and Spain. Inferior grades were sent to the West Indies to serve as food for slaves.

Whaling became important late in the colonial period. At first many whales were caught near the shores of southern New England. Every village along the coast had watchers to report the appearance of a whale in the waters offshore. In time whales stopped coming in so close, and it was necessary to make long voyages in search of them. Colonial whalers from New Bedford and Nantucket frequently spent months in the Arctic or Antarctic seas.

Shipbuilding. The building of ships for fishing and commerce was a leading industry along the northern coast, especially in New England. Near-by forests provided oak for timbers and boards, fir for masts, and pitch for tar and turpentine. From the farms came hemp for rope, while near-by mines supplied iron for chains and anchors. In scores of busy shipyards swift and beautiful vessels were built, at half the cost of similar ships from English yards. By the 1750's New England was launching some seventy new ships a year, New York and Pennsylvania forty-five, and the colonies to the south, forty.

Why New Englanders turned to the sea. New England, with its stony soil, lack of level land, and long winters, was not well suited to farming. While the bulk of its people were farmers, many turned to the forests and the sea for a living. Sawmills sprang up beside rushing New England streams to supply lumber to the shipyards along the bays. Hundreds of harbors gave safe anchorage to ships. New England had the additional advantage of being nearer to the Grand Banks and to Europe than were the other colonies. For these reasons New England led in shipbuilding, fishing, and commerce.

The growth of manufacturing. As in all new countries, the early settlers spent most of their time in getting food, shelter, and clothing. At first manufacturing was carried on only during the farm slack season, and every farmer had to be a "Jack-of-all-trades." Gradually some began to specialize in making one kind of article. For example, a man who was especially good at making shoes might make them not only for his own family but also for some of his neighbors. Later some began to spend all their time in making things. By the 1700's nearly all the colonies had a variety of small businesses, including gristmills, sawmills, distilleries, tanneries, hat shops, shoe shops, woolen mills, ironworks, and blacksmith shops. The work was usually done by the owner, assisted by one or two indentured servants and perhaps a few young apprentices who worked for their keep. These businesses remained small because of the lack of skilled workers. No free man was satisfied to be a wage earner when he could easily obtain a farm of his own. Therefore manufacturing was on a very small scale, and goods were made mostly for people that lived near by. The worker had a very limited local market for his wares. The better grades of furniture, tools, cloth, and clothing were imported from abroad.

Colonial laws to encourage and regulate manufacturing. The colonial legislatures tried to encourage manufacturing. They offered premiums, or bounties, for the production of iron, salt, silk, and wool.

NEW ENGLAND FISHERMEN *curing cod at Newfoundland. This picture is from a book by Herman Moll, published in 1715.* (Courtesy of Clements Library, University of Michigan)

PROCESSING INDIGO *on a plantation near Charleston, South Carolina. Next to rice, indigo was the most important crop in this colony.* (From A *Compleat History of Drugs,* 1725. Courtesy of New York Public Library)

SAWMILL *near Skenesboro, New York. In the 1700's sawmills, operated by water power, were found in many settlements in the colonies. This picture comes from Thomas Anburey's journal, published in 1793. Note the blockhouse for defense from Indians.* (Courtesy of Clements Library)

They tried to get skilled workmen to migrate here by offering them land grants. They also regulated wages and the prices and quality of manufactured products.

Parliament interferes with manufacturing. Small quantities of American manufactured products gradually began to go from one colony to another, to the West Indies, and to England. In this way they came into competition with goods made in England. When this happened, English manufacturers complained, and Parliament passed laws intended to limit the colonists to the production of raw materials. In 1699 the colonists were forbidden to send woolen goods beyond their own town or county boundaries. In 1732 they were forbidden to export hats or send them from one colony to another. This was done because the colonists could make beaver hats cheaper than the English hatters and were gaining the hat market in England and on the continent of Europe. The growth of the colonial iron industry disturbed English iron makers; to satisfy them Parliament passed an act in 1750 restricting the colonists to the production of crude (pig) iron. These laws were intended to prevent colonial manufactures from compet-

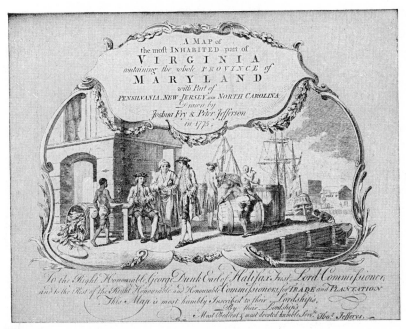

SHIPPING TOBACCO FROM VIRGINIA. *Tobacco was the principal money crop in the Southern colonies. It was shipped in huge casks, which were rolled to the wharves and sent to England. This is a decoration from a map published in 1775.* (Courtesy of Clements Library)

ing with English manufactures in England and abroad and even in the colonies. On the other hand, Parliament sought to encourage colonial production of pig iron and supplies needed by the navy, such as masts, turpentine, tar, and pitch.

COLONIAL COMMERCE BECOMES IMPORTANT

Colonial commerce. Trading towns gradually developed in the colonies. These were located at points where goods could be brought in or sent out by water. The largest commercial centers were Boston and Philadelphia, with a population, in 1760, of 20,000 each; New York, with 10,000; and Charleston, with 9000. There were also many smaller trading centers. In every trading center most of the people earned their living by manufacturing or by trade and commerce.

From the Southern colonies the merchants got tobacco, rice, indigo, pitch, tar, and turpentine; from the Middle and the Northern colonies they got corn, wheat, salt meat, hides, fish, hemp, flax, livestock, furs, lumber, masts, rum, and iron. Merchants loaded these products onto

A BLACKSMITH SHOP OF THE 1700's. *This shop was owned by Elkanah Deane, a maker of coaches and riding chairs. Pieces of iron, after being made white-hot in the forge, were plunged into a tub of water, then shaped on the anvil. Horseshoeing is still done in shops like this.* (Courtesy of Colonial Williamsburg)

THE LANCASTER–PHILADELPHIA TURNPIKE *was the first road in this country to be surfaced extensively with crushed stone. The Conestoga wagon in the background was used for hauling freight. The station wagon in the foreground came into use about* 1795. (Courtesy of United States Bureau of Public Roads)

ships and traded them in the markets of the world. Many of these merchants became wealthy and built fine homes in Newburyport, Salem, Providence, New Haven, Baltimore, Charleston, Savannah, and other colonial ports.

The colonists carried on a lively trade with the West Indies. The West Indian planters specialized in growing sugar, and they imported nearly all their foodstuffs and manufactured goods. American traders brought them great quantities of dried fish, grain, salt meat, and some manufactures, exchanging these for sugar and molasses to be carried to England or made into rum in New England distilleries.

Obstacles to the development of colonial commerce. Colonial commerce would have grown still faster except for three serious obstacles: (1) the difficulty of inland transportation, (2) the lack of money and credit, and (3) English interference.

Difficulty of inland transportation. Travel overland between the early settlements was extremely difficult, if not impossible. Transportation of goods overland for any distance did not pay. In time rough wagon roads were cut through the forests to join the spreading network of settlements. The roads were not hard-surfaced or graded or bridged, and during much of the year they were impassable. To keep them from being overgrown, every settler was required to spend one day a year cutting brush from them. By 1763, in the older settlements, toll bridges had been built over the smaller streams and toll ferries established on the larger ones. A traveler could not go far inland, however, before such signs of progress ceased. Roads tapered off into narrow lanes through the woods, then into Indian trails, and the wagon would have to be abandoned for the saddle horse.

Wagon and stagecoach lines were first started in the early 1700's. Wagons for freight and passengers ran across New Jersey soon after 1700, but their schedule of trips was very irregular. In 1717 a stagecoach line between Boston and Providence was announced. In 1732 a stagecoach line from New York to Philadelphia was started, the journey of ninety miles taking three days. Later Boston and New York were connected by stagecoach. Other short lines were running by the time of the Revolution.

A postal service was established between Boston, New York, and Philadelphia in 1691, but the mails were infrequent, and no one knew when they could be expected. By the middle of the 1700's post roads had been improved, and there were fairly regular mail routes between the larger towns.

Lack of money and credit. Money was scarce in the colonies, and credit was difficult to obtain. Because of the scarcity of money, the colonists fell back on barter, that is, exchanging goods for goods. They also used such articles as wampum, hides, wheat, corn, cattle, and tobacco for money. The great difficulty in using articles like corn and tobacco for money is that they have no fixed value. Uncertainty as to what they are worth delays every transaction. Besides, it is inconvenient to carry these bulky products.

The colonies began to issue paper money in an attempt to get around the difficulties due to the lack of hard money (gold or silver). The paper money was used to pay the expenses of the government. When a large amount of paper money was in circulation, people doubted its value and did not want to take it in exchange for products. Finally Parliament forbade the colonies to issue any more paper money except in case of emergency. The law was not very successful, for many emergencies arose when a colony could not pay the expenses of its government without issuing more paper money.

English interference. A further obstacle to the growth of American commerce was interference by Parliament. The chief interference came from the Navigation Acts and the Sugar and Molasses Act.

The Navigation Acts. Under the laws of the United States today only American ships can carry products from one American port to another. The coast trade is a privilege reserved for American citizens. When Parliament passed similar laws long ago, many Americans were displeased.

Beginning in 1651 Parliament passed an act saying that no ship could carry products from the British colonies to any other part of the British Empire unless it was owned by British citizens. Americans were British citizens, so the act helped those Americans who were shipowners and shipbuilders. But it did not help American exporters, including the farmers who raised things for sale abroad. They had to pay higher freight rates than they would otherwise have had to pay.

Another navigation act passed in 1660 stated that certain exports from the colonies, known as "enumerated articles," could be sent only to places in the British Empire. At first only five products were enumerated. But the list was increased from time to time until finally most of the raw materials produced in the colonies were included. Parliament's purpose was to supply English manufacturers with plenty of raw materials; to increase the business of English merchants; and to raise money, for duties (taxes) had to be paid in England on goods imported from the colonies. The colonists disliked having to ship the enumerated articles to British markets when often they could obtain a better price in a foreign country. They protested vigorously and often disobeyed the law.

The Sugar and Molasses Act. In 1733, in order to benefit the sugar growers of the British West Indies, Parliament passed what is known as the Sugar and Molasses Act. It required Americans to pay a heavy duty on molasses, rum, and sugar imported from the French and Dutch West Indies. Americans thought the Act unreasonable, since the British West Indies did not produce enough sugar and molasses to supply the rum distilleries of New England. The distillers said they could not stay in business if compelled to pay the duties on non-British sugar and molasses. So they took to smuggling. British customs officials in New England did not try very hard to enforce the law; some accepted bribes from the smugglers in return for letting them alone.

Parliament's attitude toward the colonies. In making laws which restricted colonial commerce and manufacturing, the members of Parliament did not feel any ill will toward the colonies. They were guided by an idea held by the officials of every country possessing colonies — the idea that colonies exist for the benefit of the mother country. They thought that the mother country suffered loss if the products of its colonies went to other nations or if the colonies bought from other nations goods which the mother country could supply. It was their plain duty, so they thought, to prevent this loss.

Colonial businessmen enjoyed a number of real advantages under British laws. Several important colonial products were given favored treatment in British markets — that is, smaller duties were charged than on similar products from foreign countries. Also, Parliament paid bounties to the colonists for the production of indigo, masts, pitch, and tar. Then, too, the British navy carried on a continual fight against pirates. Without this protection American commerce with the West Indies and with Europe would have been impossible.

To identify: "Bread Colonies," Parliament.

To explain or define: act, apprentice, barter, cash crop, customs official, distillery, flail, hard money, indigo, pig iron, tannery, virgin forest.

Subjects for Talks or Written Reports

1. Whaling in colonial times. 2. Smuggling in colonial times. 3. Fishing off the Grand Banks in colonial times. 4. Travel overland in colonial times. 5. Postal service in colonial times. 6. Shipbuilding in the colonies. 7. The making of beaver hats in the colonies. 8. Manufacturing and trade in some colonial town which you would like to study.

Questions for Understanding the Text

1. How did the pioneer farmer clear his land of trees? 2. (*a*) Tell about the colonial farmer's tools. (*b*) Why did most farmers use oxen rather than horses? 3. (*a*) Who did the work on the family-size farm? (*b*) What kinds of work were done by the men and boys? By the women and girls? (*c*) What return did the family receive for its labor? 4. (*a*) What is a plantation? (*b*) Where were plantations found? (*c*) What crops did they grow? 5. (*a*) Which colonies raised grain for sale? (*b*) Why did frontier farmers make their extra grain into whiskey? 6. (*a*) How did the planters market their tobacco, rice, or indigo? (*b*) Was this method of marketing satisfactory? 7. (*a*) Why did many New Englanders turn to the sea for a living? (*b*) What did most New Englanders do for a living? 8. (*a*) Name some of the shops common in the colonies in the 1700's. (*b*) Who did the work in these shops? (*c*) Why were these shops so small? 9. (*a*) How did the colonial legislatures encourage manufacturing? (*b*) Outline several acts of Parliament intended to discourage manufacturing in the colonies. 10. (*a*) Name the four largest cities in the colonies. (*b*) How did their people earn a living? 11. (*a*) Name the principal products of the Southern colonies; the Middle and the Northern colonies. (*b*) Describe the trade carried on with the West Indies. 12. (*a*) Describe the difficulties of inland transportation in colonial times. (*b*) What regular stagecoach lines were running in 1763? (*c*) Discuss the mail service. 13. (*a*) Name three ways in which the colonists tried to get around the scarcity of hard money. (*b*) What are the disadvantages of using articles like tobacco for money? (*c*) What was the disadvantage of paper money? 14. (*a*) What was the aim of the first navigation act passed by Parliament? (*b*) How did American exporters feel about it? (*c*) How did American shipowners and shipbuilders feel about it? 15. (*a*) What were the aims of the second navigation act? (*b*) How did the colonists feel about it? Did they obey it? 16. (*a*) What was the purpose of the Sugar and Molasses Act? (*b*) How did the New England distillers feel about it? Did they obey it? 17. What idea was held by the members of the British Parliament concerning the relation of colonies to the mother country? 18. State three advantages which British laws gave to colonial businessmen.

CHAPTER 3

COLONIAL SOCIETY

HOME LIFE IN THE COLONIES

New ways of living. The colonists could not live in the New World just as they had lived in the Old. They had to learn to live in the wilderness without most of the comforts they had known. Colonial society was therefore different in a great many ways from that in Europe.

Colonial homes. The first settlers had to be content for a time with bark houses like those of the Indians. Later the settlers built one-room log cabins. At one end of the cabin a large stone fireplace cooked the meals and furnished warmth and light. Oiled paper let in daylight through one or two wall openings; these were protected at night with heavy wooden shutters. A ladder led to a low loft, where some of the household slept on cornhusk mattresses laid on the floor. As time passed, the more prosperous families built clapboard frame houses with glass windows, either one and one-half or two stories high. The furniture was plain but substantial. The floors were usually bare except for small rugs at the bedside. Tableware consisted of pewter, earthen, and wooden dishes. Among the customary furnishings were a spinning wheel, loom, churn, candle mold, and several sizes of iron kettles.

As time went on, the well to do built better homes. Their houses were beautified with carved staircases and woodwork, and with paint, wallpaper, floor coverings, and upholstered furniture from England. There were silver, china, glass, and fine linens in their dining rooms. But they, too, got along without any plumbing and depended upon open fireplaces for cooking and heating and upon an outdoor spring or well for water.

The grouping of houses. In New England the people lived together in small villages along narrow streets, their fields, pastures, and woodlands surrounding the settlement. Every village had its meetinghouse for worship and for nonreligious gatherings. In the Middle Colonies, also, there were many villages of this description. In the South the plantation, and not the village, was the center of the settlement. The plantations were large, and the homes of the planters were far apart.

THE KITCHEN *of a substantial Massachusetts home in the 1700's. Food was cooked in iron utensils over the open fire. Baking was done in a brick oven heated by building a fire inside. Much of the family's clothing was made from wool spun and knitted or woven at home. The furniture shown here, except for the spinning wheel, was probably homemade. The ironware and pewter were probably bought from near-by craftsmen.* (Courtesy of Essex Institute, Salem)

Many people lived on a plantation, and there were many buildings. Between the plantations, on less desirable land, were scattered a large number of small farms. The small farmers often had to go a long way to find a church or any public building.

Colonial dress. Most of the colonists dressed plainly in coarse, heavy clothing, which was usually made at home out of homespun material. Cotton was little used except by the well to do. Shirts and underwear were made of linen, while breeches, skirts, and work clothes were often of tow — a rough linen fabric. Deerskin, buckskin, and lambskin were also much used for outer garments, particularly on the frontier. Stockings might be knitted from worsted or cotton or made from cloth. Shoes were heavy, with double soles. Most of the farming people went barefoot in summer.

Imported cloth, which was finer than homespun, gradually replaced it among the middle class. Members of the poorer families were likely to have one dress or suit of the finer material, to be worn for church and special occasions.

THE WHITMAN HOUSE *was built at Farmington, Connecticut, about 1660. The casement windows, with small diamond-shaped panes, and the second story overhang are typical of houses built in this period. The long roof line at the rear is found in a great many colonial farmhouses. The big central chimney has several flues, each one leading from a fireplace. This house in some ways resembles the one at Quincy, Massachusetts, where John Adams, our second President, was born.*

From the beginning the well to do ordered fine fabrics (silks, cottons, wool broadcloth, linens), and shoes, suits, hats, and dresses from England. They desired to be in the latest fashion and to possess many changes of costume. Others imitated them in so far as they were able. The love of costly clothes kept many planters in debt to English merchants.

Food and drink. Food was plentiful in colonial households, and the housewife then was acquainted with most of the meats, vegetables, and fruits that we use today. The greatest difficulty was in keeping perishable foods. Except in cold weather, meat and fish had to be used at once, or else smoked, salted, or pickled. In winter fresh fruits and green vegetables could not be obtained. The winter diet was heavy and rather tiresome, consisting of meat, fish, pies, puddings, dried and preserved fruit, pickled or salted vegetables, dried beans and peas, and a few vegetables that can be kept in a storage pit, such as carrots, beets, onions, cabbage. White potatoes did not come into common use until the middle of the 1700's.

The colonists were great hunters and fishermen. Deer, wild turkeys, geese, pigeons, rabbits, and squirrels were always to be found. In the streams and ponds were many kinds of fish, in the bays were oysters, and along the shores were lobsters, crabs, and clams. Because meat and fish were so abundant, several varieties were commonly served at a single meal. At a banquet thirty different meat and fish dishes might be served.

Spices, coffee, tea, cocoa, raisins, lemons, limes, and cane sugar were imported from Europe or the West Indies, but to most families they were luxuries. The small farmer could rarely afford to buy them; for sweetening he depended mainly on maple sugar and honey from wild bees, and for seasoning he used herbs.

The colonists used alcoholic beverages freely. Beer and cider were made in most homes. Apple and peach brandy, cherry cordial, and rum were also widely used. Large quantities of these drinks were served at social gatherings, such as weddings, funerals, house-raisings, and ship launchings. Rum was especially popular among the deep-sea fishermen and others exposed to severe weather.

Care of the sick. Against sickness and death the colonists were almost helpless. Disease germs had not been discovered, and people thought that sickness was due to such things as night air, bad blood, witchcraft, and evil spirits. Nothing was known about correct diet, and very little about hygiene and sanitation. Epidemics were frequent in every community. It is probable that nearly half the children died before reaching their tenth year. Deaths of mothers in childbirth were common. Against these disasters people depended on primitive medicines and on treatments such as sweating and bleeding, which often hastened death. As late as 1799 George Washington, during his last illness, was drained of two quarts of blood.

Physicians had little opportunity in America for training. Many a colonial physician had merely served an apprenticeship to a physician, tending his office, helping him prepare medicines, and going with him sometimes on home visits. After serving the required period, the apprentice set out for himself, usually with very little knowledge of the human body and probably with no books except one giving directions for preparing medicines. There were signs about 1750 of a change in attitude toward medical service in the larger towns, for at this time the physicians in Philadelphia and New York began to take their apprentices into laboratories, where human bodies were dissected. In 1765 a medical school, the first in America, was established in Philadelphia.

BEDCHAMBER *in the palace of the royal governor of Virginia. The beautiful furnishings were doubtless brought from England. Note the carved woodwork on the walls.* (Courtesy of Colonial Williamsburg)

"THE END OF THE FOX HUNT." *Fox hunting was a popular sport among the well to do in the Southern and Middle colonies. This picture, owned by Dr. Wyndham B. Blanton, was painted about 1780 by an unknown American artist.* (Courtesy of Metropolitan Museum of Art)

DR. JOHN CLARK, *a surgeon of early Massachusetts. In his right hand is an instrument for cutting round pieces out of broken skulls to get bone fragments which have been driven in. The portrait, made in 1664 by an unknown artist, is either the first or second oil painting made in the American colonies and belongs to the Boston Medical Library.* (Courtesy of Massachusetts Historical Society)

DUTCH BARBER SURGEON *of the 1600's. In Europe, as well as in America, there were few medical men with training. Most of the surgery was done by barbers. This is an engraving by Wolfgang Killian, who lived from 1581–1662.* (Bettman Archive)

Marriage and family life. In colonial times very few men or women could support themselves except as part of a family group. In most occupations a man could not get ahead without the combined labor of himself, his wife, and his children. A single woman could hardly earn a living, except as a servant. Both men and women married young and remarried promptly if the marriage partner died.

Women did not have much freedom. Courtship was carried on in the presence of the girl's family, and the selection of a husband was often made by the parents. Wives were expected to obey their husbands in small things and large. A woman's property became her husband's when she married. A husband could dispose of any earnings made by his wife as he saw fit. Upon his death a father could, and sometimes did, will away the children from their mother. Divorces were rare, for some churches forbade them, and the courts granted them only in extreme cases.

Children had none of the freedom they enjoy today. While they were probably loved as much then as now, parental love was expressed differently. Caresses were not often given. Everyone believed that "children should be seen and not heard," and "to spare the rod is to spoil the child." Prompt obedience was demanded, and the child had little opportunity to explain an act displeasing to his parents before he was punished.

In most families children were kept busy helping their parents from an early age and had little time for play. When ten or twelve years of age, a boy might be placed as an apprentice to learn a trade, his hours of work and duties being the same as an adult's. At the same age the daughter of poor parents might be placed as a domestic servant, to work all her waking hours in return for her keep.

Social life and recreation. Life in the colonies, except for the wealthy few, was hard and serious. For adults, as for children, there was little time for pleasure. Recreation most often took the form of a change of occupation. For example, the farmer went hunting, trapping, or fishing, or joined his neighbors in a harvesting or husking bee or a barn- or house-raising. The religious ideas of the time were against amusement for its own sake.

Work bees, baptisms, and weddings gave people a chance for feasting, drinking, and seeing each other. Church services, court sessions, and in New England, the annual town meeting, also served to bring people together and enabled them to exchange news and gossip.

The county fairs were important social occasions, although their

DISCOMFORTS OF A CHURCH *built in colonial times. Although this painting shows people dressed in styles of the 1820's, the church is of the colonial period. Note the uncomfortable seats and the use of foot warmers.* (Bettman Archive)

main purpose was trade. They were held in all the colonies once or twice a year, except in New England, where they were frowned upon. The fairs usually lasted three days and featured horse racing, cockfighting, and entertainment by traveling performers such as jugglers, acrobats, and puppeteers.

The planters and other members of the upper class had many social pleasures. Their big houses were often filled with company. They entertained their guests with dining, music, and dancing. They gave elaborate balls and parties. In the South and in New York they often gathered to enjoy fox hunting.

RELIGIOUS AND INTELLECTUAL INTERESTS

Presence of various religious groups. Many persons came to America as a result of religious persecutions. Their coming to a strange, unsettled land shows that they placed a high value on their religion. In New England the leading religious faith was Puritan. The name "Puritan" was gradually replaced by the name "Congregational," because each congregation of worshipers selected its own pastor. In the South most of the people were of the Anglican faith — that is, they were

MISS CAMPION WITH HORN-
BOOK. *This portrait, made in 1661,
shows a richly dressed Puritan girl
holding the hornbook from which she
learned her letters. The plumed hat
on the table belongs to a grownup.*
(From Tuer, History of the Hornbook, *London, 1896*)

members of the Church of England. In the Middle Colonies there was
no one leading religion. The Dutch settlers of the Hudson Valley
were members of the Dutch Reformed Church; the Germans of Pennsylvania and New York were mostly Lutherans, Moravians, and Men-
nonites; the Scotch-Irish were Presbyterian. There were many
Quakers and some Roman Catholics in the Middle Colonies and in
Rhode Island.

Importance of the church. In both New England and the South
there was a union of church and state. That is, the church was supported by taxation, and only church members could vote and hold office. In New England the clergy were powerful. They controlled
education, both public and private. They secured the passage of laws
forbidding labor and amusement on the Sabbath and saw that these
were enforced. In these and in other ways they showed their political
power. Religion and government were connected so closely in New
England that it is difficult to say where one ended and the other began.

In New England church attendance was required of all. There
were no fires in the meetinghouses, and in winter women and children
used small foot stoves to warm their feet. The sermons frequently

lasted two or three hours and were followed by lengthy prayers, during which the worshipers had to stand. At noon those who lived at a distance gathered under the trees or visited friends until time for the afternoon service. This was a pleasant interval in what must have been a rather dreary day.

After a while, especially in the older settlements, the influence of the churches grew less. The colonists became more worldly in outlook and less willing to accept religious rules that limited luxuries and amusements. Compulsory church going could no longer be enforced. The New England clergy lost much of their earlier political power.

Religious intolerance. The same religious intolerance that was common in Europe existed in most of the English colonies. It was particularly strong in Massachusetts, where those who did not fully accept Puritan beliefs were likely to be expelled. Quakers were not tolerated because they insisted on worshiping according to their own "inner light" instead of according to Puritan ideas.

Roger Williams was banished from Massachusetts in 1635 because he insisted that the government should not interfere with religion. After a terrible winter in the wilderness he started a settlement, to which he gave the name of Providence, in what is now Rhode Island. Here church and state were wholly separate, and there was complete religious freedom. While Roger Williams did not accept Quaker teachings, he allowed no persecution of Quakers in his colony. He was one of the few colonial leaders who befriended Jews; he not only allowed them to settle in the colony but also welcomed them as citizens.

Religious liberty also existed in Pennsylvania, which had been founded as a home for Quakers. Maryland had been founded by Lord Baltimore in the hope that it would be a refuge for Roman Catholics, but religious tolerance there was short-lived. Catholics were welcome nowhere in the colonies except in Pennsylvania and Rhode Island.

Books and libraries. During the early colonial period books were not common. The colonists were too much occupied with conquering the wilderness to have much time for reading. The only books possessed by the average family were the Bible or Book of Common Prayer, a cookbook, and an almanac. Clergymen and a few of the more cultured merchants and planters imported and read books and sometimes had a library of fifty to one hundred volumes. At this time a planter's home library usually contained the Bible, some books of sermons, and a few books written in Latin.

In the 1700's the sale of books increased in the older settlements, and importers and sellers of books prospered. Poetry, history, essays, and some works of fiction were read. The first subscription library in the colonies was started in Philadelphia in 1732; anyone might read there, and those who helped support it might take books out. Similar subscription libraries were opened in other cities. By the time of the Revolution several cities had public libraries.

Colonial newspapers. During the 1600's the only newspapers seen in the colonies were occasional papers brought from London. In 1704 a weekly newspaper of four small pages began to appear in Boston. It was not long before papers appeared in other towns. They were usually owned and printed by the same person. For foreign news they depended on personal letters from abroad supplied by their readers. Most of the space was given to essays copied from English publications. Poor and dull as they were, the colonial newspapers had a wide influence.

Almanacs. A kind of publication familiar to nearly all the colonists was the almanac, a curious combination of facts about history and the sun, moon, and tides, observations on the weather, jokes, puzzles, interest tables, and advice on farming. It became the custom of some newspaper owners to publish an almanac yearly. Few families were too poor or too far from town to have at least one. The most famous of the colonial almanacs is Franklin's *Poor Richard's Almanac*, prized for its witty sayings, proverbs, and common-sense advice.

Colonial schools. Most of the colonists either had no book learning at all or only a very scant knowledge of reading, writing, and keeping accounts. In the back country near the frontier, schools were almost unknown. In the older, settled regions along the coast, schools were numerous, although scarcely any of them were free.

Three different ideas of education existed in the colonies. In most places in the Middle and the Southern colonies (except Pennsylvania), the aristocratic idea prevailed — education was for the upper class only. The wealthy sent their children to small, private "dame" schools in the neighborhood or employed tutors for them. The older boys attended private high schools here or in England. The larger towns sometimes had "pauper" schools, where poor children received a little instruction. The purpose of the "pauper" schools was to fit pupils to earn a living as early as possible.

According to another view, every church should be responsible for the education of its members' children. In Pennsylvania the Quakers

HARVARD COLLEGE. *The Puritans were so eager to have a place for training young men for the ministry that they opened Harvard College soon after they came to America. This picture was drawn by William Burgis in 1726.* (Courtesy of Harvard College Library)

THE COLLEGE OF WILLIAM AND MARY IN 1740. *This famous college at Williamsburg, Virginia, was the second college in the English colonies. Many of its graduates took part in the independence movement and in launching the United States government. This is the second building; the first, built in 1693, was destroyed by fire.* (Courtesy of The College of William and Mary)

and the Germans established schools in connection with their churches. Some Anglican churches, particularly those in the Middle Colonies, conducted schools.

The view that the community is responsible for seeing that every child has an education was held in Massachusetts and Connecticut. In 1647 the Massachusetts legislature passed what is often called the most important school law in American history. It required every town having fifty families to provide an elementary school, and every town having a hundred families to provide also a Latin grammar school to prepare boys for college. However, some towns did not carry out the requirements for many years. Only part of the expense for schools was met from taxes, and the schools were not free except to those too poor to pay their share. Nevertheless this was the beginning of our present public school system.

Colleges. Colleges were established in several of the colonies. The first was Harvard, founded at Cambridge, Massachusetts, in 1636, and the second was the College of William and Mary, founded at Williamsburg, Virginia, in 1693. Six others were established before the Revolution. All were chiefly interested in preparing young men for the ministry except one -- the Academy of Philadelphia, founded by Benjamin Franklin in 1751. It gave particular attention to English, the sciences, geography, government, and history — subjects which received little or no attention in most of the other colonial colleges.

Science and superstition. In colonial times the people generally followed the changes of the moon in planting their crops and believed firmly in hundreds of other superstitions. Many believed that demons existed and thought that men and women might bargain with them to obtain magic powers. A witch was one supposed to have contact with a demon, who gave her or him the power to cause injury to livestock and to persons. This notion had caused terrible persecutions in Europe for centuries. In 1692 at Salem, Massachusetts, a hundred and fifty persons were accused of witchcraft and imprisoned; twenty of them were executed. Some of the more prominent of the witch hunters later realized their error and made public apology for it. There was no further persecution of witches in the colonies after this outbreak.

Despite the superstitions of the masses, a small number of leading thinkers in Europe and America were devoting their lives to scientific research. Because American colleges neglected science, Americans seeking training in science usually went abroad to study. The most

SALEM, MASSACHUSETTS, BEFORE THE FIRE OF 1774. *In colonial New England the houses and public buildings were closely grouped. This drawing, made by Dr. Joseph Orne, shows the schoolhouse and whipping post facing the public square.* (Courtesy of Essex Institute, Salem)

famous American scientist of the colonial period was Benjamin Franklin. In 1743 he and other learned men founded the American Philosophical Society. Its purpose was to promote the applied sciences and scientific experiment. It opened a library where Americans could consult the latest European works of science, encouraged the opening of museums of natural history, and held conferences of scientists. The world of science and the machine was starting on its way.

To identify: American Philosophical Society, Anglican Church, Book of Common Prayer, Benjamin Franklin, Roger Williams.

To explain or define: almanac, dame school, dissect, epidemic, subscription library, tow.

SUBJECTS FOR TALKS OR WRITTEN REPORTS

1. The appearance of a typical plantation in colonial times. The different buildings and how they were arranged and furnished. The gardens and fields. 2. Social classes in the colonies. How they differed in occupation, dress, and housing. 3. The care of the sick and the training of doctors in the colonies. 4. Different kinds of schools in the colonies and

what each kind was like. 5. The apprentice system in colonial times.
6. Social life and recreation on a plantation (*a*) for the planter's family,
(*b*) for the slaves. 7. Social life and recreation in a New England village.
8. Benjamin Franklin's contribution to science and to the training of
American scientists. 9. The importance of the church in colonial New
England. 10. The life and teachings of Roger Williams.

QUESTIONS FOR UNDERSTANDING THE TEXT

1. (*a*) Describe a typical one-room log cabin. (*b*) Describe the house
a prosperous farmer might build to replace a log cabin. (*c*) Describe the
house a prosperous merchant or planter might build. 2. Describe a
colonial village in New England. 3. (*a*) How did most of the colonists
obtain their clothing? (*b*) What materials were commonly used for clothing? (*c*) How did the well to do obtain their clothing? 4. (*a*) Compare the food of the colonists with ours. (*b*) Name several imported
foods used by all classes today, which were familiar only to the well to do
in colonial times. (*c*) Discuss the use of alcoholic beverages in colonial
times. 5. (*a*) What did the colonists think was the cause of sickness?
(*b*) Name some colonial medicines and treatments. (*c*) How did the
average colonial doctor get his training? (*d*) What improvement was
made in medical training in the larger towns about 1750? 6. Why were
few single men and women found in the colonies? 7. In what ways did
women lack freedom in colonial times? 8. Compare the relationship of
parents and children then and now. 9. (*a*) Why did most of the colonists
seldom enjoy amusement for its own sake? (*b*) How did they meet the
need for sociability? 10. What was the leading religious faith in New
England? In the South? In the Middle Colonies? 11. (*a*) What is
meant by the union of church and state? (*b*) In which colonies was there
a union of church and state? (*c*) Discuss the influence of the New
England clergy. 12. (*a*) Where were Catholics welcome to settle?
(*b*) Where were Jews given a welcome? 13. (*a*) What books were likely
to be found in a colonial home? (*b*) Describe a colonial newspaper.
(*c*) Describe an almanac. 14. What idea of education was held in the
South and in most of the Middle Colonies? In Pennsylvania? In New
England? 15. (*a*) Name the first two colleges in the colonies. (*b*) How
did the Academy of Philadelphia differ from other colonial colleges?

From the pages of an early primer. (Courtesy of Massachusetts Historical Society)

TOWN MEETING *at Boston, December 16, 1773. A large body of citizens, led by Samuel Adams (in the pulpit) and John Hancock (on the stairway), gathered to talk over what was to be done about a shipment of tea which had just arrived in the harbor. The colonists refused to pay the tax on the tea because payment would be a sign that Parliament had the right to lay taxes on them. After hours of discussion which led to no decision, Samuel Adams exclaimed that the meeting could do nothing more to save the country. His words were a signal for a war whoop from a group of "Sons of Liberty" waiting outside. Disguised as Indians they went to the waterfront and threw the tea into the sea. (Mural painting by Charles Hoffbauer. Courtesy of New England Mutual Life Insurance Company)*

CHAPTER 4

COLONIAL GOVERNMENT

Progress of the English people toward self-government. Before America was settled, the English people had made much progress toward self-government. Their king had been deprived of many of the powers enjoyed by other European rulers, and the people had won a number of important civil rights, such as the right of trial by jury. The struggle for greater political liberty continued during the 1600's and 1700's, both in England and in her American colonies. During this period the people of the colonies, like those in England, advanced far toward full self-government.

The New England town meeting. In New England the town was the unit of local government. The town was a group of small farms and shops gathered around a church, school, and mill. At first all the people living in the town belonged to the same church. The town was really the parish of the church. At this period church and public affairs were almost the same.

The business of the town was discussed by the "town meeting," which all voters were expected to attend. The town meeting levied taxes and decided how they should be spent. It elected a board of selectmen, usually three in number, to carry out its decisions and be responsible for roads and other public property. Often the selectmen were elders of the church. There was one regular town meeting each year; special meetings could be called if necessary. All qualified freemen had equal right to speak and vote in the town meeting. To be qualified, the freeman had to own a certain amount of property and be a member in good standing of the local church. (After a while, as religious tolerance developed and members of other denominations settled in the town, those belonging to approved churches were given the same right.)

The town meeting is an example of *direct* democracy, in which the citizens themselves, rather than their representatives, make the laws.

It is still the method by which the smaller New England communities are governed.

County government in the South. The Southern plantations and the small farms lying between them were too scattered for the type of government possible in the New England town. The county became the unit of local government. Its affairs were managed by a county court made up of justices of the peace. The county court decided how taxes should be spent, supervised the repair of roads and bridges, took care of other county business, and also tried minor cases. The justices and other county officials were appointed by the governor. The voters, who were white men owning property, had little to say about the government. The only question submitted to them was the selection of one or two deputies to represent the county in the colonial assembly.

While ordinary Southern people had but little part in their government, they often knew a surprising amount about it. Many went to the sessions of the county court, which met every three months, to look on. In this way they learned a good deal about the art of government.

Town and county government in the Middle Colonies. In the Middle Colonies the parish was known as a *township*. The powers of local government were divided between the township and the county. In some places town meetings were held, but they had fewer decisions to make than was usual in the New England town meeting.

The general government of the colony. In addition to local government each colony had a general, or over-all, government. At first this was controlled by the commercial company or the proprietor that had founded the colony. As time went on, the king wished to have more to say about colonial affairs; one by one he took back the grants made to companies and proprietors, until eight of the colonies were changed into royal provinces. By the time of the American Revolution only three proprietary colonies — Pennsylvania, Delaware, and Maryland — remained. There were also two so-called self-governing colonies — Rhode Island and Connecticut. The chief difference in the government of the three kinds of colonies was the manner in which the governor was chosen. In the royal colonies he was appointed by the king; in the proprietary colonies he was appointed by the proprietor; and in the self-governing colonies he was elected by the voters. All the colonies were alike in having a *charter*, that is, a written grant of privileges, from the king. This amounted to a constitution, outlining the way in which the colony was to be governed. Each of the colonies gradually developed the spirit and many of the practices of self-government.

The representative assembly. In each of the colonies there was a representative assembly. Its members were chiefly the larger property owners and merchants. The powers of the assembly were not strictly defined by the king. In time the assemblies claimed the right of laying taxes, appropriating all money, raising troops, issuing currency, fixing the salaries of royal officers, and making laws.

The laws passed by the assembly had to be approved by the governor's council. Thus the council was practically an upper house of a two-house legislature. Except in Massachusetts, Rhode Island and Connecticut this upper house was not elected by the voters and therefore did not consider it necessary to please them.

The governor and his powers. The governor had great powers. He was commander in chief of the armed forces. He appointed the military officers, the judges, and the colony and county officials. He appointed and could remove the members of his council. He could call the assembly together, and also dismiss it, whenever he saw fit. Except in Rhode Island and Connecticut, he could veto the laws passed by the assembly. And only in those two states was he elected by the voters rather than appointed by king or proprietors.

The appointed governors were, as a rule, sent from England. They did not expect to remain many years in the colonies, and most of them were more interested in gaining riches here than in promoting the welfare of the people. Accompanying them from England were swarms of job hunters, seeking appointment to the many positions which the governor had power to fill. Some of the positions, as in the land office, gave a dishonest appointee the chance to line his pockets. Other positions carried a good salary and practically no duties. Some governors sold political jobs. Permanent residents in the colonies objected to the whole system by which political jobs went to Englishmen instead of to Americans.

Contests between the governor and the assembly. The assembly passed laws which expressed the wishes of the voters, but again and again an act passed by the assembly was not approved by the governor's council. If the council approved it, the governor himself sometimes vetoed it. The governors usually vetoed laws which they thought might be displeasing to the king or to Parliament. As a result the assemblies had many bitter quarrels with the governor and his council.

THE TRIAL OF JOHN PETER ZENGER, 1734. *The young editor would have been convicted had not Andrew Hamilton, speaker of the Pennsylvania Assembly, suddenly appeared in his defense. Before Hamilton could be halted, he made to the jury a moving plea for freedom of the press.*

The assemblies had one important weapon which they could use to curb governors who went too far — the power of the purse. They had claimed the right of voting taxes for all purposes, including the governor's salary. If the governor refused to approve laws which the assembly thought necessary, it might keep back all or part of his salary. Under threat of such action many a governor gave in.

The right to criticize the government. The appointed governors saw no reason why they should allow the public to criticize their actions. A governor did not have to answer to the voters, but only to the king or the proprietor who appointed him. For a newspaper to publish a criticism of the governor placed the owner and editor in danger of arrest. In 1734 John Peter Zenger, publisher of the *New York Weekly Journal*, printed an article condemning an action of the governor of New York. As a result he was arrested and put on trial for libel. The judge maintained that whoever wrote the article was guilty of libel; all the jury had to decide was whether or not Zenger had written the article. The defense maintained that the jury also had the right to decide whether the article was libelous — that is, false and malicious. The jury decided that the article was not false or malicious, so they found Zenger not guilty. This helped to establish the principle that

GOVERNOR ALEXANDER SPOTSWOOD OF VIRGINIA, *one of the best-known and best-liked royal governors. He carried on a vigorous fight against pirates, encouraged friendly relations with the Indians, and worked hard to promote a postal system.* (From the painting by Charles Bridges. Courtesy of Virginia State Library)

the press has the right to discuss public questions fully and to find fault with officials. In the struggles between the royal governors and the assemblies this right was important. It was still more so in cases where the colonies disagreed with the actions of the king and his ministers across the sea.

Relations between the colonies and the British government. Parliament, as well as the colonial assemblies, passed laws affecting the colonies. In case a law passed by Parliament conflicted with a law passed by an assembly, which law was to be obeyed? In the royal colonies the power to decide belonged to the king. In the other colonies it was not clear who had the power to decide.

During the first century of colonization neither the king nor Parliament showed much interest in the internal affairs of the colonies, and conflicts between a colony and the British government were few. The colonies were left pretty much to themselves, and this enabled them to develop the practice of self-government. Later, when attempts were made to bring them under firmer control, they protested vigorously. For the most part they agreed, however, that their laws should not conflict with those of England and that the king had a right to veto those which did. During the 1700's it became the custom for each colony to have an agent in England. The agent's duty was to keep the British government informed of the needs of the colony.

Political struggles between social classes in the colonies. The assemblies were controlled by the wealthier and older families of the coast settlements. The laws tended to favor their interests and to neglect those of the small farmer, the wage earner, and the people close to the frontier, few of whom had enough property to qualify for voting. Most frontier regions, furthermore, were not represented in the assembly.

In 1676 a conflict between the privileged and unprivileged classes occurred in Virginia. An Indian massacre had led the frontier settlers to call on Governor Berkeley for military protection. He did not provide it, and his opponents claimed that because he made money from the Indian fur trade, he was unwilling to fight the Indians. Five hundred frontiersmen, small farmers, and wage earners gathered under the leadership of Nathaniel Bacon. They marched on Jamestown, the capital, where Bacon demanded that a new assembly be elected, chosen by all freemen, regardless of whether or not they owned property. To this and certain other reforms the governor agreed. He also gave Bacon permission to lead his force against the Indians.

As soon as Bacon and his men left, the governor declared them to be "rebels." Bacon then decided to return and fight it out with the governor's forces in order to set up a new and more democratic government. The governor was defeated and fled the town. Before Bacon could put his reforms into effect, he was taken ill and died. His leaderless forces were defeated, and Berkeley returned to the capital. He then proceeded to hang or imprison many of Bacon's followers. When news of the disturbance reached England, Berkeley was removed from office, and a number of reforms were ordered. However, a large proportion of the freemen continued to be denied the right to vote.

The struggle for greater political equality continued in Virginia and in the other colonies until the American Revolution, and, in fact, long after. Sometimes it led to outbreaks of violence. It should be remembered that this was a struggle intended to benefit the small farmer and the frontiersman. No one thought of giving political rights to those still lower on the social scale — indentured servants, day laborers, and freed Negroes.

Colonial political practices in force today. Many features of colonial government were continued after the American Revolution, becoming the foundation for the government of the United States.

BACON'S REBELLION.
The frontiersmen of Virginia wanted protection from the Indians and a voice in political affairs. Led by Nathaniel Bacon, the owner of a small plantation, they marched to the capital to demand reforms. A modern artist shows them as they faced the haughty royal governor. Governor Berkeley first promised to satisfy them, then declared them to be rebels and ordered the militia to drive them away. Open warfare followed. The rebellion would probably have succeeded if Bacon had not suddenly died. (From the drawing by W. Sheppard in W. A. Crafts, Pioneers in the Settlement of America, Boston, 1876)

Among these have been mentioned a written constitution, a two-house legislature, the veto power of the governor, the control of the purse by the people's representatives, and the freedom of the press.

In addition, the great body of English law known as *common law* was transplanted to the colonies. It became the basis of the law we have today. It consists of legal principles taken from the customs of the people rather than from the acts of a legislature. In deciding a case, judges use the common law to settle points not covered by legislation. These are some of the fundamental principles of the common law: (a) private property is to be protected against individuals and the state, (b) a person suspected of crime is entitled to trial by jury, (c) arrest or search without a warrant is illegal, (d) an arrested person is entitled to a speedy hearing before a judge. These and many other principles of the common law have since been added to our written law.

The separateness of the colonies. Until the Revolution the colonies were not connected to one another by any bonds of government

The difficulties of travel help explain their separateness. Geographic differences, which led to differences in occupation, ways of living, and ideas, were also important. The colonies of New England were very unlike those in the South, while the Middle Colonies, although they resembled the other groups in some things, formed a fairly distinct group of their own. Nevertheless the colonists, for the most part, spoke the same language, inherited the same customs and the same ideas about political justice, and feared common dangers — the French, the Indians, and the loss of their liberties. Would their likenesses in time seem more important than their differences?

The Albany Congress, 1754, and Franklin's Plan of Union. From time to time some of the colonies co-operated briefly in fighting Indians. In 1754, because a great war with the French and their Indian allies seemed to be near, commissioners from seven Northern colonies met at Albany, New York. Their aim was to form an alliance with the six Iroquois Nations and to plan for united military action. They also considered a possible union of the colonies. A plan proposed by Benjamin Franklin for a union of all the colonies for the purpose of defense was unanimously accepted. None of the colonial assemblies approved it. Franklin himself had not been hopeful about its chances for adoption, for he wrote: "It is not likely, in my opinion, that any of them [the assemblies] will act upon it so far as to agree to it, or to propose any amendments to it. Everybody cries, 'A union is absolutely necessary,' but when they come to the manner and form of union, their weak noddles are perfectly distracted."

Nevertheless the French and Indian wars that broke out three years later drove the colonies into close co-operation. A permanent union was not to be long delayed.

A cartoon printed in Benjamin Franklin's Pennsylvania Gazette *in 1754.*

To identify: Bacon's Rebellion, Franklin's Plan of Union.

To explain or define: board of selectmen, common law, direct democracy, justice of the peace, libel, town meeting, township.

Subjects for Talks or Written Reports

1. Governor Berkeley or some other typical colonial governor. His struggles with the assembly. His attitude toward the colony. 2. Nathaniel Bacon and his "rebellion." 3. Franklin's Plan of Union. Why nothing was done about it. 4. The common law. How judges find what it is. 5. Business done at a typical town meeting in a small New England town today. Who attends such a meeting? 6. The "regulators" of North Carolina. Causes for their discontent. What they did. How the disturbance was put down.

Questions for Understanding the Text

1. How did local government in New England differ from that in the South as to (*a*) size of the unit, (*b*) the way in which officials were selected, (*c*) the number of questions submitted to the voters, (*d*) the qualifications required for voting, (*e*) the opportunity of the ordinary citizen to learn the art of government? 2. (*a*) Name the three types of colony government. (*b*) In what way were the three types alike? (*c*) What was the chief difference between them? 3. (*a*) What rights were claimed by the colonial assemblies? (*b*) Why was it difficult for the assembly to have its way? (*c*) How did the assembly often force a governor to carry out its wishes? 4. (*a*) Name the principal powers of a colonial governor. (*b*) How was the governor chosen? (*c*) Where did he usually come from? 5. (*a*) What led to the arrest of John Peter Zenger? (*b*) On what ground did the jury find Zenger not guilty? (*c*) How did this case help the growth of the spirit of self-government? 6. Why did each colony find it desirable to keep an agent in England? 7. (*a*) What groups of people had little influence in the assemblies? (*b*) Name a reform demanded by Nathaniel Bacon. (*c*) Why did Governor Berkeley deserve to be removed from office? 8. Name some of the features of colonial government which are found in our government today. 9. (*a*) What is meant by common law? (*b*) When do judges use it? (*c*) Name some of the fundamental rights which came to us from England in the common law. 10. What conditions kept the colonies separate from one another? 11. What did the people of the different colonies have in common? 12. What was the purpose of the Albany Congress of 1754?

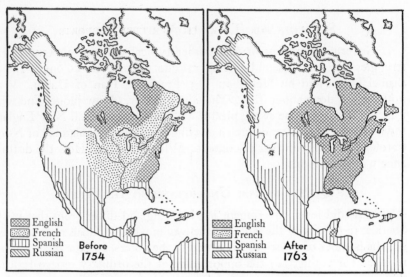

EUROPEAN POSSESSIONS IN NORTH AMERICA BEFORE AND AFTER THE FRENCH AND INDIAN WAR

England and France fought four wars in America. The last one, known in America as the French and Indian War, took place in the years 1754–1763. It began in a struggle for possession of the Ohio Valley. The French wanted to keep the English from settling there or anywhere west of the Appalachians. As a result of the war France gave up all her possessions on the mainland of North America. England received all of North America east of the Mississippi. Spain, which had fought on the French side, received the lands formerly claimed by France west of the Mississippi.

CHAPTER 5

THE COLONISTS RESIST
IMPERIAL CONTROL

The *French colonies in North America.* French settlements were scattered westward along the St. Lawrence River to the Great Lakes, and thence southward along the Mississippi. The French were chiefly interested in the fur trade with the Indians, not in starting permanent homes and communities. Their little settlements were spread thinly, and Indians lived in and around them.

Since the French did not drive the red men away, destroy their hunting grounds, or clear much of the forest, they kept the good will of most of the Indian tribes. Many French missionaries labored to convert the Indians to Christianity, and the activities of these missionaries helped further to strengthen the friendship of the two peoples. Whenever the French and the English were at war, most of the Indians fought on the side of the French. England and France fought four wars in America, and the last one was known here as the "French and Indian War."

The French and Indian War. This final conflict began in a struggle for the possession of the Ohio Valley. English, as well as French, fur traders had entered the area. The French laid claim to it in 1749 and within the next few years built several forts there. Both Virginia and Pennsylvania considered that the land belonged to them. Governor Dinwiddie of Virginia sent George Washington, then twenty-one years of age, to notify the French that they should leave the Ohio Valley. The French did not leave but instead built additional forts. Both sides realized that war was at hand, and early in 1755 France sent an army to Canada, while England sent one, under General Braddock, to Virginia.

Soon after his arrival in Virginia, Braddock led an army of 1500 men westward across the mountains to attack Fort Duquesne, at the place

DEFEAT OF GENERAL BRADDOCK. *The English general led an army to take Fort Duquesne. He failed because he did not understand frontier methods of fighting. Colonel George Washington took part in this battle.* (From C. C. Coffin, *Old Times in the Colonies,* New York, 1880)

now known as Pittsburgh. He was joined by 450 Virginia militiamen commanded by Colonel George Washington. A few miles from the fort the British and colonial forces were suddenly attacked by French and Indians. Braddock kept his men in regular battle formation, an easy target for the enemy. The militiamen fought frontier fashion from behind trees and rocks. Their leader, Washington, showed great skill and courage but could not save the day. Braddock was badly wounded and died during the retreat.

The battle marked the beginning of a fierce struggle between England and France. Most of the Indians sided with the French, carrying on savage attacks against the English frontier communities. The English colonies had no cannon or other war equipment, but they supplied thousands of men, most of them dressed in their own homespun and carrying their own weapons. These colonial fighting men were brave and hardy, but they were not a match for the well-trained and well-equipped French regulars. The French and their Indian allies would easily have won the war in America had it not been for the British army and navy.

The British succeeded in driving the French from the Ohio Valley in 1758. The real climax of the war came the next year with the taking of Quebec and Montreal. The long struggle ended with the signing of the Treaty of Paris in 1763. By this treaty England got all North America east of the Mississippi, including Florida, which had previously belonged to France's ally, Spain. France gave the lands she claimed west of the Mississippi to Spain. The English colonists at last were free from fear of the French.

ENGLAND FACES THE PROBLEM OF GOVERNING THE COLONIES

In the French and Indian War the colonists gained valuable military experience and learned something about co-operating with one another. With the danger from the French removed, they felt that they no longer had much need of British protection. From now on they would insist more than ever on governing themselves.

British leaders, on the other hand, were determined to strengthen their control over the colonies. They thought that the colonies had not done so much as they might have to help the mother country during the war against the French. Even more they resented the fact that during the war the colonies had carried on trade with the French West Indies. To Englishmen it seemed plain that a firmer policy was needed in dealing with the colonies.

Immediate problems to be met. The English government was faced with three immediate problems in regard to the colonies:

1. The Indian problem. The colonists needed stronger defenses against the Indians. In 1763 Pontiac and other chiefs of the Northwestern tribes united in a powerful effort to drive the English from the continent. Fortunately British regulars arrived in time, and two years later Pontiac's war collapsed. But another Indian war might come at any time. Since the colonists did not provide well for their own defense, the English government felt that 10,000 of its regular soldiers should be kept in the colonies. To maintain these men would cost £300,000 ($1,500,000) a year. The mother country thought that a portion of the cost should be paid by the colonists.

2. The question of debt and taxation. The French and Indian War had doubled the British debt. Interest on the debt was a heavy burden. Since the colonists received most of the benefits from the French and Indian War, the English expected them to help bear the expense. This seemed the more reasonable because English landowners were already taxed from 20 to 30 per cent of their income.

3. Enforcement of the trade and navigation acts. The acts regulating trade and navigation in the colonies had never been strictly enforced. (See pages 24–25.) Smuggling was widespread; most English officials in the colonies winked at it, and some accepted a share in the profits. It was reported to Parliament in 1763 that the American revenues from customs amounted to less than £2000 a year, and cost £7000 to £8000 to collect. Parliament thought something must be done to stop this loss.

THE BRITISH PROGRAM FOR THE COLONIES CAUSES PROTESTS

In the ten years following the close of the French and Indian War the leaders of the English government tried hard to meet these three problems. The details of the laws enacted need not concern us here. Their importance in history lies in the fact that the colonists objected to them, resisted them, and finally went to war with the mother country because of them.

The Grenville program. In 1763 George Grenville became Chancellor of the Exchequer. Upon his advice Parliament passed a series of acts affecting the colonies. The measures which most displeased the colonists were:

1. The closing of the frontier. To avoid trouble with the Indians, Grenville issued the Proclamation of 1763, forbidding further settlement in lands west of the Appalachians. Pioneers who had settled in the Indian country were "forthwith to remove themselves." Fur traders were to observe such regulations as the ministers in England should make for "the benefit of said trade." The proclamation was most unpopular in the colonies and was not obeyed.

2. The Sugar Act, 1764. To obtain money to help meet the expense of protecting the colonists, Parliament passed the Sugar Act of 1764. New duties were placed on several products that had been duty-free. The number of enumerated articles which could be sold only in England was enlarged. To lessen the temptation for smuggling, the old rates on molasses were reduced. In addition the Act gave customs officials new powers to help them capture smugglers. This made smuggling harder but did not stop it.

3. The Stamp Act. The British ministers hoped that enough revenue would be raised in the colonies to pay at least a third of the cost of the army stationed in America. They proposed a Stamp Act for America, providing that stamps must appear on all legal documents, pamphlets, newspapers, and playing cards. These stamps had been

used for many years in England, and people there were accustomed to them. It was thought that such a tax would fall chiefly upon the more prosperous, and in any case, would not be a heavy burden to anyone.

Grenville told the colonial agents in London that the colonies must raise money to help support the army. He gave them a year to suggest a more satisfactory method than the stamp tax. Franklin, the agent for Pennsylvania, recommended that the colonial assemblies be asked to raise the necessary sum. "Can you agree," asked Grenville, "on the proportions [of the total amount needed] each colony should raise?" As it seemed unlikely that the colonies could so agree, the Stamp Act was passed in 1765.

The colonists force repeal of the Stamp Act. The Stamp Act produced societies called "Sons of Liberty," which were formed in every colony. Stocks of stamped paper were burned. Stamp sellers were threatened with violence, and the homes of some of them were destroyed by mobs. Many people agreed to buy no more English goods until the Act was repealed.

The Massachusetts assembly asked each colony to send delegates to a congress to protest the Stamp Act. The New Hampshire assembly refused to send delegates, and in Virginia, North Carolina, and Georgia the governors refused to call the assembly for the purpose of choosing delegates. Representatives from the remaining nine colonies met in New York City in October, 1765. The meeting was known as the Stamp Act Congress. After eleven days of debate the delegates passed a resolution denying the right of Parliament to tax the colonies without their consent. This action showed that at last the colonies were developing the ability to stand together.

The Stamp Act was not obeyed. Hardly any stamps were sold. Four and one-half months from the time the Act was supposed to go into effect, it was repealed by Parliament. News of the repeal caused loud rejoicing in the colonies. In New York and Virginia statues were erected to George III as a "restorer of liberty."

The Townshend Acts. Parliament's efforts to raise revenue in the colonies began again in 1767 under a new Chancellor of the Exchequer, Charles Townshend. The tariff law was extended to include glass, paper, lead, and tea. To aid in its enforcement, customs officers were given power to search the homes of any colonists suspected of smuggling and to try suspects without a jury. The revenue raised by the Acts was to be used to pay the salaries of governors, judges, and other

The BLOODY MASSACRE perpetrated in King—Street BOSTON on March 5.th 1770 by a party of the 29.th REG.^t

Engrav'd Printed & Sold by Paul Revere Boston

THE BOSTON MASSACRE *aroused great ill will toward England. This sketch was engraved and printed by Paul Revere. It is a good example of propaganda.* (Courtesy of Bostonian Society)

colony officials and thus remove them from the control of the assemblies.

It is hard to say whether the new duties, the method of enforcing the Acts, or the use to be made of the money collected caused the greatest resentment. At any rate the colonies once again flamed with protests, pamphlets, and meetings. Orators told the people that the Acts violated their rights as Englishmen. Samuel Adams of Boston, the most radical of the colonial leaders, was the most active in stirring up opposition. He succeeded so well that customs officers in Boston found it impossible to carry on their work. He organized a nonimportation association among merchants throughout the colonies. The result was that imports of English goods fell to a small fraction of what they had been.

The Boston Massacre. To protect customs officials in Boston and enable them to do their work, two regiments of British soldiers were sent there. This made the citizens of Boston very angry. Whenever soldiers appeared in the streets, hoodlums pestered them by name-calling and sometimes by throwing rubbish at them. This went on for eighteen months, until the constant nagging of the soldiers provoked a riot, called the Boston Massacre (March 5, 1770), in which five citizens were killed. Under the leadership of Samuel Adams a town meeting was held the next day to demand that the governor order the removal of the troops. He did so, but he could not repair the damage done to relations with the mother country. The incident aroused a new storm of indignation throughout the colonies. It went far to convince the average American that his liberties were in danger.

Parliament gives in. On the very day of the Boston Massacre, the British government decided to repeal all the duties imposed by the Townshend Acts, except the tax on tea. This was to be kept as a sign that Parliament had the right to impose taxes on the colonies. The colonists now resumed trade with Britain but formed societies whose members agreed not to drink tea.

Colonial radicals continue to resist. A small group of radicals led by Samuel Adams kept on stirring up opposition to any and all Parliamentary interference with colonial affairs. They now claimed that Parliament had no right to make any laws for the colonies. However, they were not yet demanding complete independence. What they wanted was the right of the colonies to make all their own laws — the kind of independence enjoyed by Canada, Australia, New Zealand, and South Africa today.

The radicals organized committees of correspondence in most of the colonies. The committee members wrote letters to one another in order to inform the public of objectionable actions by British officials. In this way the spirit of resistance was built up.

The radicals openly praised smuggling as a means of getting around the British customs laws. They even approved such violent acts as the burning of the British revenue boat *Gaspee* near Providence (1772), and the destruction of £18,000 worth of tea aboard a ship in Boston Harbor (the Boston Tea Party, December 16, 1773). In fact, Samuel Adams himself directed the destruction of the tea at Boston.

The Intolerable Acts, 1774. As a result of the Boston Tea Party Parliament passed four acts to punish the colonies. Two of the acts affected all the colonies, while two singled out Massachusetts for special punishment. (1) One act provided that British officers in America, accused by the colonists of serious offenses, could be tried in England. The act was intended to make sure that the accused officer would receive a fair trial. The colonists objected to this act because

BURNING OF THE GASPEE. *The British revenue boat* Gaspee *was patrolling the American coast to prevent smuggling when it ran aground near Providence. The townspeople set fire to the vessel, thus showing their sympathy for smugglers and their dislike of the British government.* (From an old print. Courtesy of New York Public Library)

they believed that their complaints against the accused might not be given a full hearing across the sea. (2) Another act gave the governor of any colony power to force the citizens to quarter (house) soldiers in their homes in case of need. This would make it easier to use troops to compel obedience to the king. (3) A third act made changes in the government of Massachusetts to lessen the people's share in the government. Town meetings, for instance, were forbidden. (4) Finally, the port of Boston was closed to all trade until payment should be made for the tea that had been destroyed. British warships were stationed in the harbor to prevent goods from going in or out; business came to a standstill; widespread unemployment and want followed.

Together these measures were known in the colonies as the "Intolerable Acts." They increased the hard feeling that now existed between the colonies and the mother country.

Resistance to punishment. The Intolerable Acts left the colonists no choice except to resist or submit. Parliament expected that the colonists would soon submit. To make clear that submission was expected, four British regiments were sent to Boston, and their commander, General Gage, was made governor of Massachusetts. The inhabitants showed no sign of yielding. The soldiers were unsafe outside the cover of the fleet and the forts. Fires broke out in stacks of straw intended for their bedding; the planks intended for their barracks were split into useless strips; farmers would not sell them food; workmen refused to build them shelters. After five months Gage advised that the four acts be suspended until a force large enough to conquer the whole of New England could be brought to America. He said that it would take no less than twenty thousand men. King George understood the situation correctly, for he wrote, "The die is cast; the colonists must either submit or triumph."

The demand for an intercolonial congress. The punishment of Massachusetts created a bond of sympathy among the colonies. Cities as far away as Charleston, South Carolina, and Wilmington, North Carolina, sent food and supplies for the relief of Boston's poor. Pamphlets pointing out that Massachusetts was suffering in the common cause appeared everywhere. The day on which the port of Boston was closed (June 1, 1774) was observed in Philadelphia and Virginia as a day of mourning. From newspapers, town meetings, and assemblies went forth a call for a congress to represent the whole continent in discussing what should be done to defend colonial rights.

The First Continental Congress, 1774. On September 5, 1774, delegates from all the colonies, except Georgia, met at Philadelphia. Among the fifty-six delegates were some of the ablest men in America. For seven weeks the discussions went on behind locked doors. Early in the session, in a plea for unity, Patrick Henry exclaimed: "Fleets and armies and the present state of things show that government is dissolved. . . . The distinctions between Virginians, Pennsylvanians, New Yorkers, and New Englanders are no more. I am not a Virginian, but an American."

Two ideas were generally accepted: (1) that there was a united America, and (2) that the Congress should act for it. In regard to what should be done, two plans divided the delegates. One group wished to create a union of the colonies, this union to have a president and the privilege of making its own laws. Had this plan been adopted, and had England allowed it, the colonies would have remained English. A second group favored a declaration of rights and grievances and an Asso-

PATRICK HENRY *speaking before the First Continental Congress. Henry, a Virgin-*
ian, was one of the radical leaders who prepared the way for the Declaration of Inde-
pendence. The painting is by Clyde O. DeLand and hangs in Carpenter's Hall, Phila-
delphia. (Courtesy of American Telephone and Telegraph Company)

ciation to resist England by stopping trade with her. The views of this
group won out.

A famous paper known as the "Declaration of Rights and Grievances" was drawn up. It listed the rights claimed by the colonists and
named thirteen acts of Parliament which violated these rights. Harmony with the mother country could be restored only by the repeal of
the acts named. Congress also adopted an "Association," or agreement,
not to import or use British goods. Congress hoped that by this means
Great Britain would be forced to give in. The Association proved so
effective that in 1775 the import trade from Great Britain was cut
about 95 per cent.

Mixed feelings in England. Early in 1775 a large number of English businessmen begged Parliament to repeal the thirteen acts displeasing to the colonists. Several outstanding English statesmen also spoke
in favor of the colonies, urging Parliament not to drive them further
into rebellion. However, Englishmen agreed that the action of the
Continental Congress in adopting the Association was an act of rebellion. The king and most members of Parliament believed that rebellion should be firmly put down by armed force.

THE BATTLE OF LEXINGTON. *The first blood of the Revolutionary War was shed at Lexington, Massachusetts. Riders carried the news throughout the colonies. Patriots prepared for war, but a great many of the people still hoped for peace.* (From the painting by Henry Sandham. Courtesy of Lexington Historical Society)

ARMED RESISTANCE BEGINS

War appeared likely, and the colonies began to get ready for it. Companies of volunteers began to drill. Committees of safety were organized. Royal governors reported these activities to the home government but were powerless to stop them.

During the winter of 1775 Massachusetts patriots were particularly active. Every town organized a company of militia and appointed officers to train the men. One quarter of each company were "minutemen," pledged to meet at a minute's notice. Stores of provisions and munitions were collected at Worcester and Concord. General Gage decided to seize the stores at Concord and to arrest Samuel Adams and John Hancock, who were hiding in Lexington.

Lexington. On the night of April 18, 1775, a thousand British redcoats left Boston for Lexington. Warned by the midnight ride of Paul Revere and William Dawes, the Lexington militia gathered to meet the foe. When the British entered the town at dawn, their way was barred by sixty men lined up on the village green. The British ordered them to withdraw, but they refused. The little band was quickly swept aside, leaving eight killed and ten wounded.

Concord. The British had reached Lexington too late to capture Hancock and Adams. The troops marched on to Concord in time to destroy a small quantity of military stores. On their way back to Boston they were shot at from every hill and stone wall. The march turned into a disorderly rout.

The news from Lexington and Concord went swiftly from one end of the colonies to the other. Everywhere it produced patriotic demonstrations and increased preparations for war. Militiamen from all over New England gathered outside Boston, ready for battle. Yet a large proportion of the colonists still remained loyal to the king and hoped that war could somehow be avoided.

The Second Continental Congress takes control. On May 10, 1775, three weeks after Lexington and Concord, the Second Continental Congress met in Independence Hall, Philadelphia. It faced a situation which could not be ignored — the people of Massachusetts were in arms against the king's troops. Many delegates urged the Congress to try once more a loyal petition to the king. Many others believed that the time for petitions was past and urged that men and supplies be sent to the camps around Boston. A few recommended that the colonies should declare their independence.

The Congress took a middle course. A respectful petition was sent to the king. (Some called it the "olive-branch" petition.) The Congress also urged the several colonies to prepare to defend themselves. It adopted as its own the army of New Englanders camped in a semicircle around Boston and appointed a Virginian, Colonel George Washington, as commander in chief of the Continental forces.

The Congress provided for a postal system and a system of money and credit. In this and in other ways it began to perform some of the tasks of a central government for all the colonies. Fate was to keep the Congress in session for many years.

The drift toward independence. For months the majority of the members of the Congress waited hopefully for the king's reply to the "olive-branch" petition. There was no answer, except a proclamation that the Americans were rebels. Parliament closed all American ports. As further signs that the British would not yield to colonial demands, the towns of Falmouth, Maine, and Norfolk, Virginia, were burned. These actions convinced many of the colonists that permanent separation from England was the only way out.

In January, 1776, there was published a stirring pamphlet which boldly called for complete independence. This was *Common Sense,*

SAMUEL ADAMS, *leader of the radicals.* (From the painting by John S. Copley, 1770. Brown Brothers)

THOMAS PAINE, *author of the famous pamphlet* Common Sense. (Courtesy of Metropolitan Museum of Art)

by Thomas Paine. It stated the arguments for independence in a simple, lively style and had a powerful effect on public opinion.

Separation from England was now being seriously discussed in colonial assemblies. In April, North Carolina instructed her delegates in Congress to vote for independence if it came to a vote. A month later Virginia told her delegates to propose independence. In June, Richard Henry Lee, of Virginia, placed a motion before Congress saying that "these United Colonies are, and of right ought to be, free and independent states." The motion was adopted.

A committee was then chosen by Congress to draw up the Declaration of Independence. Thomas Jefferson wrote the first draft, which was approved by the other members of the committee with few changes. This famous document, adopted on July 4, 1776, sets forth the reasons for the revolution.

> We hold these truths to be self-evident: That all men are created equal; that they are endowed by their Creator with certain unalienable rights; that among these are life, liberty, and the pursuit of happiness. That, to secure these rights, governments are instituted among men, deriving their just powers from the consent of the governed; that,

whenever any form of government becomes destructive of these ends, it is the right of the people to alter or to abolish it, and to institute a new government, laying its foundation on such principles, and organizing its powers in such form, as to them shall seem most likely to effect their safety and happiness.

In saying that all men are created equal, the framers of the Declaration did not mean that individuals are equal in strength and ability. They were insisting that all citizens, regardless of their rank or wealth, should be treated equally before the law.

Effect of the Declaration. The publication of the Declaration cleared the air. The war was no longer merely an effort to force the British government to recognize American rights but a fight for independence. Every American must now make up his mind whether to support the revolution or the king.

About one third of all the colonists regarded the Declaration as an act of treason to the king. Taking the name of "Loyalists," they refused to have any part in the "rebellion." Most of the Loyalists belonged to the upper, or privileged, class.

Those who received the news of the Declaration with rejoicing came mostly from the underprivileged classes — frontiersmen, small farmers, small tradesmen, wage earners. They hoped that the Revolution would bring them political and economic freedom.

Many others, choosing the American side now that they had to make a choice, were saddened at the cutting of the ties with the mother country. In this group were some members of the privileged class who threw in their lot with the patriots.

❀ ❀ ❀

To identify: Samuel Adams, Boston Massacre, Chancellor of the Exchequer, John Hancock, Intolerable Acts, Loyalists, Thomas Paine, Paul Revere, Sons of Liberty, Stamp Act Congress, Townshend Acts.

To explain or define: militia, minuteman, quartering of troops, revenue.

Subjects for Talks or Written Reports

1. The work of the French missionaries in North America. 2. The fur trade in New France. 3. Pontiac and his war. 4. The Sons of Liberty and what they did. 5. Samuel Adams' part in stirring up the colonists against British rule. 6. The work of the committees of correspondence. 7. Activities of John Hancock in stirring up opposition to the British.

THE DECLARATION OF INDEPENDENCE. *This famous painting by John Trumbull shows the Second Continental Congress receiving the report of the committee appointed to prepare the declaration. John Hancock, president of the Congress, is seated at the table.* (Courtesy of Yale University Art Gallery)

PHILADELPHIA IN THE 1700's. *This city played a large part in the colonists' struggle for liberty. The building in the center foreground of the picture is the courthouse. Note the cobblestone pavements.* (Courtesy of Historical Society of Pennsylvania)

8. Patrick Henry and what he did for American independence.   9. Why George Washington was chosen commander in chief.   10. Activities and training of the minutemen.

Questions for Understanding the Text

1. Why were the French more successful than the English in winning the good will of the Indians?   2. (*a*) Why were the militiamen supplied by the English colonies no match for the French soldiers?   (*b*) How were the French defeated?   3. What old question was settled by the French and Indian War?   4. How did the French and Indian War change the attitude of the colonies toward one another? Toward England?   5. What was the Indian problem in the colonies after 1763 as seen by the English government?   6. Why did the English think the colonists should help pay the war debt resulting from the French and Indian War?   7. (*a*) What was the purpose of the Proclamation of 1763, closing the frontier? (*b*) How was it received by the colonists?   8. What did Parliament hope to accomplish when it passed the Sugar Act?   9. (*a*) What was the Stamp Act?   (*b*) Why did Parliament think this a just law?   (*c*) How did the colonists show their disapproval?   (*d*) What did Parliament do?   10. In what ways were the Townshend Acts objectionable?   11. (*a*) Why were British soldiers sent to Boston in 1768?   (*b*) How were they treated and what was the outcome?   12. Explain the main features of the Intolerable Acts.   13. How did the Intolerable Acts help bind the colonies together?   14. (*a*) What action was taken by the First Continental Congress? (*b*) How did Englishmen feel about this?   15. (*a*) What was the purpose of the British march to Lexington and Concord?   (*b*) What happened?   16. What were the first actions taken by the Second Continental Congress?   17. How did the different groups of colonists receive the news of the Declaration of Independence?

CHAPTER 6

THE WAR FOR INDEPENDENCE

Six years of war. Hostilities between the colonies and the mother country, which started at Lexington and Concord on April 19, 1775, did not end until the surrender of the British at Yorktown on October 19, 1781. These six hard years of war finally convinced England that the colonies were determined to be free.

The unequal resources of the two opponents. To declare independence is one thing; to win it in battle, quite another. The Americans realized that they were no match for the mighty British Empire. Unless they could obtain foreign help, victory could hardly be expected. An American agent was sent to France to seek aid shortly before the Declaration of Independence. He obtained both money and supplies, but not enough to meet the great need.

The British navy ruled the seas, while the Americans had practically no navy. This enabled the British to blockade American ports and prevent shipments by water from one colony to another. The British had a well-equipped, well-trained regular army, led by experienced officers. The colonial troops lacked both training and equipment, and nearly all of their officers were inexperienced.

The British had a strong central government with full authority to raise money and to carry on the war. The Americans had a Continental Congress without any authority. It was really not a legislature but a conference of ambassadors from thirteen independent states. It could not raise money by taxation, and the states usually turned a deaf ear to its requests for money. To purchase supplies for the army, Congress was obliged to issue paper money. Such great quantities were issued that it became nearly worthless.

The British had a large number of factories able to turn out every kind of war material. British restrictions and the scarcity of labor had held back the growth of manufacturing in the colonies, and therefore the Americans were not prepared to produce cannon, bayonets, blan-

THE BATTLE OF BUNKER HILL *and the burning of Charlestown. In this battle heavy losses to the enemy before lack of ammunition forced their retreat. They were Indian War. This picture was sketched by a British officer, who watched the battle*

kets, clothing, and many other items in the quantities needed for war.

Handicaps of the British. While Great Britain had ten times the resources and wealth and three times the population of the colonies, the advantages were not entirely on her side. One of her handicaps was the fact that most Englishmen did not regard the colonists as enemies; when additional troops were needed, few Englishmen volunteered. So the king hired several thousand fighting men from German princes. The Hessians and Brunswickers he obtained in this way had no interest in the war; they deserted in large numbers when the Americans offered them free land. Another handicap resulted from the selection of Sir William Howe as commander in chief of the British forces in America. He had opposed the harsh measures that brought on the war and believed even now that the Americans could be persuaded to give up their demand for independence. He therefore did not try to crush the colonies.

Geographic conditions handicapped the British. It was a difficult task to bring troops and supplies in sailing ships three thousand miles across the ocean. Once here the British soldiers had to fight over a very wide territory. While they could readily seize American shipping and attack the coastal towns, they could not advance far inland

the inexperienced New England militiamen showed their fighting spirit. They caused commanded by Colonel William Prescott, who had seen service in the French and from Beacon Hill in Boston. (Courtesy of New York Public Library)

without being cut off from their base of supplies. When hard pressed, the British could only withdraw to the sea; the Americans could withdraw to the Appalachian Mountains, where they were safe from attack. Had the Americans not possessed geographic advantages, their situation would have been hopeless.

PROGRESS OF THE WAR, 1775–1777

The Battle of Bunker Hill, June 17, 1775. Following the battles of Lexington and Concord, the militia of the New England colonies laid siege to Boston. On June 17 the British attacked the American positions at Bunker Hill. The British advanced boldly up the hill, expecting that the inexperienced Americans at the top would waste their shots at long range and flee when attacked by bayonets. The colonists coolly waited to fire until the enemy was at close range and forced the British back with heavy losses. A second attack was turned back in the same manner. Then the Americans had to retreat because they had no bayonets and had used all their ammunition. The battle proved that the inexperienced American soldiers could hold their own against the seasoned British regulars. When Washington heard of the battle he declared, "The country is safe."

Washington in command. Washington accepted the position of commander in chief with the understanding that he would receive no pay for his services. He took command at Cambridge two weeks after the Battle of Bunker Hill and found the colonial militia "a mixed multitude of people under very little discipline, order, or government." The men were poorly armed and without supplies; they were thinking about going home. Washington began at once to develop them into a real fighting organization. Order reappeared; recruits came in; and supplies arrived from an unexpected source. A small band of patriots, led by Ethan Allen of Vermont, surprised and captured Fort Ticonderoga on Lake Champlain. Without firing a shot, they took possession of a great quantity of ammunition and guns. These were used to equip Washington's forces.

The attempt to capture Canada. The Americans hoped to drive the British soldiers out of Canada and add Canada to the United States. In the fall of 1775 General Richard Montgomery led an expedition northward by way of Lake Champlain. A second expedition under General Benedict Arnold marched overland to help Montgomery take Quebec. In the fierce fighting at Quebec Montgomery was killed and Arnold wounded. In the spring the Americans who were left had to abandon Canada.

The British evacuate Boston. In March Washington seized Dorchester Heights and placed cannon there. Since Boston and the British fleet were in serious danger, Howe decided to quit the city. The entire British army and fleet sailed to Halifax, taking with them some eleven hundred Loyalists.

The British are defeated in the South. Loyalists were numerous in the Carolinas. With their aid the British expected to occupy both colonies and set up governments loyal to the king. A British fleet was on the way, and in February, 1776, some sixteen hundred Loyalists headed toward Wilmington, North Carolina, to join it. They were met and beaten at Moore's Creek by a force of a thousand patriots. When the fleet arrived off Charleston, South Carolina, it was swept with fire from a log fort in the harbor. After one of the severest battles of the war, the fleet withdrew to New York. The South was saved from further invasion for two years.

The campaign around New York, 1776. Howe remained at Halifax until summer, then sailed for New York, where he was met by a fleet commanded by his brother. He now had at his disposal thirty-five thousand men.

GENERAL WASHINGTON
TAKES COMMAND *at Cam-*
bridge, Massachusetts, July 3,
1775. After the Battle of
Bunker Hill, Congress chose
Washington to be commander
in chief of the Continental
armies. His patriotism and
his courage, his justice and de-
votion to his men, won their
complete loyalty. (Mural
painting by Charles Hoffbauer.
Courtesy of New England Mutual Life Insurance Company)

FRANKLIN AT THE COURT OF FRANCE. *Congress sent Franklin to Paris to*
persuade England's old enemy, France, to help the Americans win their independence.
He won the hearts of the French people, rich and poor alike. (From the painting by
Baron Jolly in the collection of Cyrus Curtis, Philadelphia)

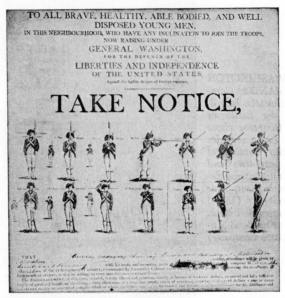

ARMY RECRUITING POSTER *used in the Revolution. Getting men to join the army and keeping them in it after they had volunteered were serious problems. To encourage enlistments this poster promises the recruit money, good clothes, and ample food.* (Courtesy of Historical Society of Pennsylvania)

Washington expected Howe to attack New York and had transferred most of his troops there from Boston. This force was increased by companies of raw recruits from near-by states. It was probably the largest army Washington ever commanded. Between twenty and twenty-five thousand in number, it had little equipment and was poorly prepared for battle. When Howe landed near Brooklyn late in August, Washington had no choice but to withdraw his army as rapidly as possible. Pursued by the British, the Americans retreated, first from Long Island, then from Manhattan, and finally across New Jersey. Thousands were taken prisoner, and thousands more went home because they were discouraged or their terms of enlistment had expired.

Washington appeals for a regular army. Thus far the Americans had no regular army; the fighting was done by state militia who enlisted for terms of three, or at most, six months. By the time they had some experience, their enlistment was over. Many were small farmers who, if their families were not to starve, had to go home from time to time to help with the plowing and harvesting. Others were frontiersmen whose families might be massacred by Indians during their absence. It is not surprising that desertions were common, and that

SURRENDER OF GENERAL BURGOYNE *at Saratoga, 1777. Inability to obtain food from the Vermonters and lack of support from General Howe were the main causes of Burgoyne's defeat. This British disaster proved to be the turning point in the American struggle for independence.* (From the painting by John Trumbull. Courtesy of Yale University Art Gallery)

when the militiaman's brief term of enlistment ended, he usually hurried home. Near the end of 1776 Washington's army had shrunk to three thousand men, and he complained to Congress that his volunteers "come in, you cannot tell how; go, you cannot tell when, and act, you cannot tell where; consume your provisions, exhaust your stores, and leave you at last at a critical moment." He appealed for the organization of a regular army, under the control of Congress and looking to Congress for its pay.

A brilliant victory in a dark hour. Howe had possession of New Jersey. He offered pardon to New Jersey patriots who would declare their loyalty to the king, and twenty-seven hundred accepted. The people of Philadelphia expected their city to be occupied any day, and Congress fled to Baltimore. The patriot cause seemed hopeless.

In this black hour Washington suddenly turned north. Late on Christmas night, with what was left of his army, he crossed the ice-filled Delaware River, and after a quick march, fell upon the Hessians at Trenton. Taken completely by surprise, the enemy was driven from the town with heavy losses. A few days later Washington made a surprise attack on Princeton, where he defeated three British regi-

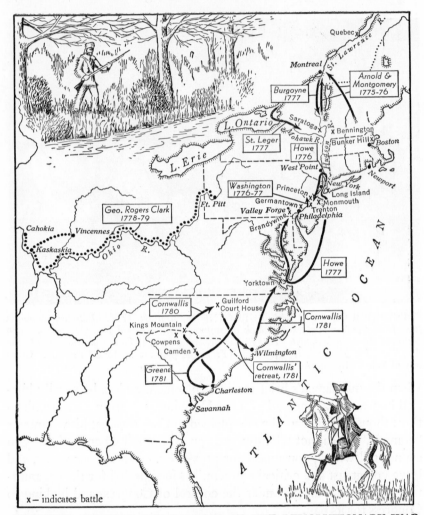

x — indicates battle

PRINCIPAL THRUSTS AND BATTLES OF THE REVOLUTIONARY WAR

Except for the attempt to take Canada at the beginning of the war, the Americans fought only to defend themselves. They did not need to take territory or even to destroy the British forces. They won the war by making the British believe that the effort to crush the rebellion was not worth what it would cost. The British campaigns had three objects: (1) to seize the principal coast cities; (2) to seize the Champlain-Hudson route, thus separating New England from the other colonies; and (3) to detach the four Southern states from the Union. In the main the British accomplished the first. They failed in the second. They came near to succeeding in the third, but were prevented by the skill of American officers like Morgan, Pickens, Marion, and Greene. When Washington, with the help of Rochambeau and De Grasse, trapped Cornwallis at York-town, the British decided to give up the struggle.

ments. The British then left the state of New Jersey, and Washington went into winter quarters at Morristown.

These victories restored American courage and greatly strengthened the country's faith in Washington. Yet try as it might, Congress could not raise an adequate army. By May, 1777, Washington had eleven thousand men, of whom only four thousand were regulars and the remainder state militiamen. For the third time he had to build an army from raw recruits.

The turning point of the war. The year 1777 was to prove the most important of the war. The British worked out a careful plan for driving a wedge through New York State from Canada to the Atlantic. Their purpose was to separate New England from the rest of the states. General Burgoyne, with an army of eight thousand men, was to come down from Canada by Lake Champlain and the upper Hudson Valley. Colonel St. Leger was to advance along the Mohawk Valley and meet Burgoyne at Albany. General Howe was to proceed from New York up the Hudson to join his forces with those of Burgoyne and St. Leger. With New England cut off and the great Champlain-Hudson route in their hands, the rebellion, thought the British, could quickly be brought to an end.

The elaborate scheme ended in complete failure. St. Leger was defeated at Oriskany, New York. Burgoyne's army made painfully slow progress through the rough, wooded country between Lake Champlain and the Hudson River, with the result that his supplies of food ran short. In the vain hope of getting food, Burgoyne sent a detachment to Bennington, Vermont, and in so doing lost eight hundred men. Meanwhile, about twenty thousand Americans, chiefly short-term local militia from New England and New York, gathered to meet him north of Albany. No help was sent from Howe, who had gone to capture Philadelphia at the very time he should have advanced up the Hudson to aid Burgoyne. Burgoyne tried to push on, although his men were on half rations. He suffered heavy losses in several fights. Unable either to retreat or to advance, he surrendered at Saratoga on October 17, 1777. This disaster to the British proved to be the turning point of the struggle, although hard, discouraging years for the patriots still lay ahead.

That autumn, after bitter fighting, the British occupied Philadelphia. Washington went into winter quarters at Valley Forge, some thirty miles away. He and his men experienced terrible suffering all winter. Congress had no funds to pay for supplies and foodstuffs; the

JOHN PAUL JONES *during the famous fight between the American ship,* Bon Homme Richard, *and the* Serapis. *When the* Bon Homme Richard *was sinking and some of its guns had become useless, Jones lashed it to its enemy and won the victory.* (From the painting by Edward P. Moran. Bettmann Archive)

paper money which it had issued was worth only a few cents to the dollar. The neighboring farmers naturally preferred to sell their food-stuffs to the British for gold rather than to Washington for paper bills. Hungry and poorly clad, Washington's army dwindled until fewer than five thousand remained. Once more the American cause appeared to be lost. Nothing but foreign aid could have saved it.

THE REVOLUTION BECOMES PART OF A WORLD WAR

The French Alliance, 1778. Ever since the Declaration of Independence the French and Spanish had been giving secret aid to the Americans. But they were unwilling to go to war with Great Britain until they felt reasonably sure that the Americans could win. When news of Burgoyne's surrender at Saratoga reached Paris in December, the French decided to give the United States open military aid. Early in 1778 France and the United States signed a treaty; each nation promised to make war on the enemies of the other and not to make a separate peace. At once Great Britain and France were at war. The French wanted to help the revolting colonies partly because of the de-

about five thousand French soldiers, was at Newport, Rhode Island. Washington, on learning that Cornwallis was at Yorktown, saw his chance. He sent a swift ship to the West Indies to beg Comte de Grasse to bring the French fleet to Chesapeake Bay. Rochambeau with his army joined Washington on the Hudson, and the two leaders pretended to be making ready to besiege New York City. Then they suddenly marched south and laid siege to Yorktown. The French fleet already had possession of the entrance to Chesapeake Bay and easily drove off the British fleet when it arrived from New York to rescue Cornwallis. Cornwallis' seventy-five hundred men were surrounded by sixteen thousand enemies, nearly half of whom were French. The British outworks were pushed in; then their forces were bombarded. As his situation was hopeless, Cornwallis surrendered on October 19, 1781. Within a few months England agreed to discuss terms of peace.

The Treaty of Paris, 1783. The British government tried hard to arrange a peace without granting American independence. Neither Congress nor any of the states would agree to this, and both France and Holland refused to make peace unless the United States was made independent. Once the British government gave in on this main point, it made generous terms. England acknowledged the thirteen states, each by name, to be free and independent. She recognized the Great Lakes as the northern boundary and the Mississippi as the western boundary of the new nation. The Americans were to continue to share the fisheries on the Newfoundland and Canadian coasts, just as they had as colonists.

Great Britain wanted the United States to arrange for the payment of debts owed by Americans to British merchants for goods bought before the Revolution. She also wanted the property that the states had taken from the Loyalists returned to them. The American commissioners explained that the states controlled these matters and that Congress could do no more than make recommendations to the states in regard to them. The British commissioners accepted this suggestion. The treaty included a promise to remove all barriers to the collection of British debts in American courts, as well as a promise that Congress would advise the states to restore the property of the Loyalists. The British promised, for their part, to restore or pay for all goods and slaves seized by their army during the war.

Great Britain got Florida from Spain at the close of the French and Indian War. Florida was now returned to Spain. The final treaty of

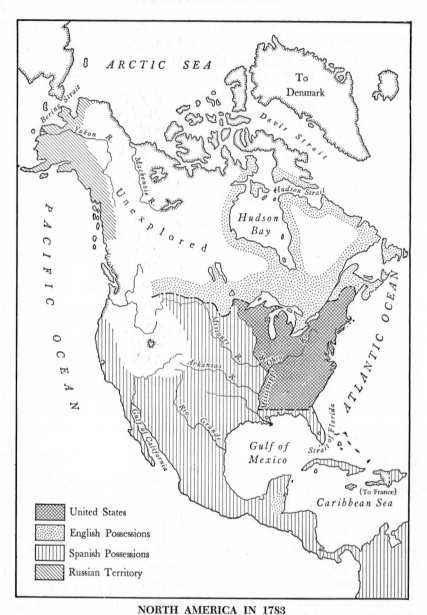

NORTH AMERICA IN 1783

By the Treaty of Paris the United States was declared independent. The Mississippi was established as its western boundary, and the Great Lakes were recognized as its northern boundary. England returned Florida to Spain.

peace was signed at Paris on September 3, 1783, by representatives of the United States, Great Britain, France, Spain, and Holland.

POLITICAL, ECONOMIC, AND SOCIAL CHANGES DURING THE REVOLUTION

Political changes. During the Revolution the thirteen colonies became thirteen independent states. Eleven of the states held conventions to draw up a constitution. Only in Connecticut and Rhode Island, which had been self-governing colonies, were the old charters considered to be a suitable basis for state government. Many of the men who framed the new constitutions had progressive ideas which conservative people of that time thought rather radical. Today we would merely call these ideas democratic. For example, the new constitutions sharply limited the powers of the governor. He was to have no veto power, and except in four states, his term was to be but a single year. In five states he was elected; in the remainder he was appointed by the legislature. The upper house of the legislature, formerly appointed by the king or the governor, was to be chosen either by the people or by the lower house. Frontier sections were to be represented in the legislature. Most of the new constitutions had a "bill of rights," guaranteeing freedom of speech and press, freedom from search and seizure, and trial by jury. Democratic as the new constitutions were in many ways, the privilege of voting was limited chiefly to property holders.

Changes in the land system. Another advance in democracy was the breaking up of many large estates. During the Revolution the states seized the lands of the Crown and of the Loyalists and sold them to farmers in small parcels. The laws of inheritance were changed so that all children might have an equal share in their father's land. (Under the English law the eldest son inherits all his parents' land.)

Other changes emphasizing human rights. The belief that all men are entitled to life, liberty, and the pursuit of happiness brought still other changes. Laws setting the death penalty for minor offenses were repealed. There was a growing belief that slavery was wrong and should be abolished. Nearly all the states put an end to the importation of slaves. Most of the northern states abolished slavery or arranged for the gradual freeing of slaves within their borders.

The growth of manufacturing. After the Declaration of Independence many new shops were started to produce here the articles which had formerly been imported from England. To encourage the manufacture of goods needed for the army and navy, prizes were offered by state legislatures and local committees of patriots. As a result the amount of manufacturing increased. At the war's end, however, many of the new businesses shut down.

Intermingling of people from different states. Before the Revolution, Americans knew but little of one another. Each colony had far more dealings with the mother country than with the other colonies. There was little travel or trade except between seaports. Most people in the interior knew no one outside their own and near-by villages. They were suspicious of those who lived farther away.

In the years just before the Revolution the committees of correspondence began to break down the isolation of one colony from another. The sending of delegates to the Continental Congress also helped to lessen the isolation. Finally, the mingling in the Continental armies of men from all the states, and the sharing of common dangers, drew the people closer together. One sign of this was the growing number of marriages between men and women of different states.

"The birth of a nation." All of these forces — sharing of common dangers and hardships, political changes, and changes in the land system — strengthened the spirit of democracy and brought about a separation from Old World ways. The control of America had passed from the hands of the colonial aristocracy into the hands of the farmers and middle-class people.

The United States in 1783, with a population of three million, five hundred thousand, was a small nation compared with some of the European nations. But the Revolution meant more than the entrance of a small nation into the world. It meant the birth of a nation whose ideals were equal opportunity, individual liberty, and government by the consent of the governed. Although these ideals were not at once or fully put into practice, they were to prove an inspiration for generations to come. The two tasks which now confronted the United States were (1) to win the respect of other nations, and (2) to develop a real central government.

To identify: George Rogers Clark, Hessians, John Paul Jones, Lafayette.
To explain or define: bill of rights, blockade, privateer.

Subjects for Talks or Written Reports

1. Why Burgoyne failed in his drive from Canada. 2. Difficulties in supplying and equipping the American army. 3. Life in Philadelphia during the British occupation. 4. The life of Lafayette. What he did for the cause of American independence. 5. Why we remember John Paul Jones. 6. Why we remember George Rogers Clark. 7. Ways in which the states became more democratic during the Revolution. 8. The weaknesses of the Continental Congress as they appeared during the Revolution. 9. How Robert Morris and Hayme Salomon helped us win the Revolutionary War. 10. The American attempt to take Canada. Why it failed.

Questions for Understanding the Text

1. In what ways were the British better prepared for war than the colonists? 2. What advantages did the colonists have over the British? 3. (*a*) Why did the British hire German fighting men? (*b*) Did the Germans make good fighters? Explain. 4. How did Washington drive the British out of Boston? 5. (*a*) In what ways did Washington find militiamen unsatisfactory as soldiers? (*b*) What solution did he urge? (*c*) Was Congress successful in raising a large regular army? How do you account for this? 6. Explain the difficulties in supplying and equipping the army. 7. (*a*) What was the purpose of the British drive from Canada in 1777? (*b*) Why did the drive fail? 8. (*a*) Why did France decide to help the United States? (*b*) In what ways did France help us? (*c*) How did the French fleet help us win the war? 9. How did foreign gold and silver help us win? What nations supplied it? 10. What are privateers? Discuss their part in the Revolutionary War. 11. How did our frontier settlements suffer during the war? 12. How did George Rogers Clark win the Northwest? 13. (*a*) What did Cornwallis hope to do by his campaign in the South? (*b*) Tell how Cornwallis was trapped at Yorktown. (*c*) What did the French contribute to the victory at Yorktown? 14. What did the peace treaty say regarding (*a*) the thirteen states, (*b*) our northern boundary, (*c*) our western boundary, (*d*) the fisheries on the Newfoundland and Canadian coasts, (*e*) the payment of American debts to British merchants, (*f*) property taken from the Loyalists, (*g*) American goods and slaves seized by the British army? 15. (*a*) When did Great Britain get possession of Florida? (*b*) What was done with Florida at the end of the Revolutionary War? 16. In what ways were the new state constitutions more democratic than the old charters? 17. What changes in the land system occurred as a result of the Revolution? 18. How did the Revolution help unite the people of the different states?

ACTIVITIES FOR UNIT ONE

1. Imagine that you are an indentured servant on a Virginia plantation in the late 1600's or early 1700's. Write a letter to your relatives in England describing your life in the New World.
2. Make a pictorial map showing the ways by which people made a living in colonial times.
3. Prepare a time line (that is, a line on which dates are arranged in order) showing the principal events beginning in 1651 that led to the Declaration of Independence.
4. Develop a panel discussion on social and religious life in the colonies. A good, but difficult, reference is H. J. Carman, *Social and Economic History of the United States*, Vol. I.
5. Draw a cartoon on some aspect of the quarrel between America and England before 1776. Post on the bulletin board in your classroom.
6. Dramatize an argument between Loyalists and patriots soon after the Declaration of Independence.
7. Compose a series of headlines covering the main events of the Revolutionary War.
8. Imagine that you are an American guerrilla fighter fighting in the South under Francis Marion or Nathanael Greene. Write a letter telling of your adventures.
9. Imagine that you are a wealthy Loyalist living in one of the Southern states early in the Revolution. Write a letter to a friend in Canada complaining of your treatment by the patriots.
10. On outline maps show (a) the routes of the principal explorers of the New World in the period 1492–1610, (b) the principal events of the French and Indian War, (c) the principal events of the Revolutionary War. The best map on each subject might be inserted in a classbook of "Maps of American History," to be presented to the school library at the end of the course.

READINGS FOR UNIT ONE

(Stars indicate the easier books)

In the bibliographies in this book the following four abbreviations are used:

(A. L. S.) for *A History of American Life* series, published by The Macmillan Company.

(A. N. S.) for *The American Nation* series, published by Harper & Brothers.

(Chronicles) for *The Chronicles of America* series, published by Yale University Press.

(Pageant) for *The Pageant of America* series, published by Yale University Press.

GENERAL ACCOUNTS

Adams, James T. *Provincial Society, 1690–1763.* (A. L. S.)

Andrews, Charles M. *The Fathers of New England.* (Chronicles)

——. *Colonial Folkways.* (Chronicles)

Becker, Carl L. *Eve of the Revolution.* (Chronicles)

*Carlton, M. M. and Carlton, H. F. *The Story of the Declaration of Independence.* Scribner's.

*Clark, Imogen. *Old Days and Old Ways.* Crowell.

Drinker, Cecil. *Not So Long Ago; a Chronicle of Medicine and Doctors in Colonial Philadelphia.* Oxford University Press.

Dunbar, Seymour. *A History of Travel in America.* Tudor.

Fisher, Sydney G. *The Quaker Colonies.* (Chronicles)

Fiske, John. *The Beginnings of New England.* Houghton Mifflin.

Ford, H. J. *The Scotch-Irish in America.* Princeton University Press.

*Foster, Genevieve. *George Washington's World.* Scribner's.

Gabriel, Ralph H. *Toilers of Land and Sea.* (Pageant)

Goodwin, M. W. *Dutch and English on the Hudson.* (Chronicles)

Gould, John. *New England Town Meeting.* Stephen Daye.

Guerber, H. A. *Story of Our Civilization.* Holt.

Johnston, Mary. *Pioneers of the Old South.* (Chronicles)

Keir, Malcolm. *The March of Commerce.* (Pageant)

Langdon, W. C. *Everyday Things in America, 1607–1776.* Scribner's.

Ogg, Frederic A. *Builders of the Republic.* (Pageant)

*Putney, W. K. *Team-work in Colonial Days.* Wilde.

Rawson, Marion N. *Of the Earth Earthy.* Dutton. (Colonial industry)

Robinson, E. F. and Robinson, T. P. *Houses in America.* Viking.

*Singmaster, Elsie. *The Book of the Colonies.* Doubleday, Doran.

*Weaver, R. B. *Amusements and Sports in America.* University of Chicago Press.

Wertenbaker, T. J. *The First Americans, 1607–1690.* (A. L. S.)

Wissler, Clark, and others. *Adventurers in the Wilderness.* (Pageant)

Wrong, G. M. *The Conquest of New France.* (Chronicles)

——. *Washington and His Comrades in Arms.* (Chronicles)

BIOGRAPHY

*Field, W. T. *Finding the New World.* Ginn. (Short biographies)

*Foote, Anne E. and Skinner, Avery W. *Explorers and Founders of America.* American Book.

*Gray, Elizabeth J. *Penn.* Viking.

Guedalla, Philip. *Fathers of the Revolution.* Putnam.

Harlow, R. V. *Samuel Adams, Promoter of the American Revolution.* Holt.

*Hutchinson, F. W. *The Men Who Found America.* Barse.

*Nicolay, Helen. *The Boys' Life of Lafayette*. Harper.
——. *The Boys' Life of Washington*. Appleton-Century.
*Potter, Edna. *Christopher Columbus*. Oxford University Press.
*Richards, L. E. *Abigail Adams and Her Times*. Appleton-Century.
*Roosevelt, Theodore and Lodge, Henry C. *Hero Tales from American History*. Appleton-Century.
*Tappan, Eva M. *American Hero Stories*. Houghton Mifflin.

FICTION

Bacheller, Irving. *In the Days of Poor Richard*. Bobbs-Merrill.
*Barbour, R. H. *Giles of the Mayflower*. Appleton-Century.
Boyd, James. *Drums*. Scribner's. (The Revolution; John Paul Jones)
Cather, Willa. *Shadows on the Rock*. Knopf. (The French at Quebec)
*Coatsworth, Elizabeth J. *The Golden Horseshoe*. Macmillan. (Colonial Virginia, 1609–1630)
Cooper, James F. *The Spy*. Grosset. (One of Washington's spies)
*Crownfield, Gertrude. *Cristina of Old New York*. Lippincott.
*——. *Strong Hearts and Bold*. Lippincott. (Life in Jamestown, 1670)
*Dix, B. M. *Blithe McBride, Bondservant*. Macmillan.
*Fast, Howard M. *Haym Salomon; Son of Liberty*. Messner.
Ford, P. L. *Janice Meredith*. Grosset. (The Revolutionary period)
*Goss, W. L. *Jack Gregory*. Crowell. (Surrender of Cornwallis)
*Hart, W. S. *A Lighter of Flames*. Crowell. (Life of Patrick Henry)
Johnston, Mary. *The Slave Ship*. Little, Brown. (Early slave trade)
——. *To Have and to Hold*. Houghton Mifflin. (Virginia, 1607–1620)
——. *1492*. Little, Brown. (Columbus)
Lamprey, Louise. *Days of the Commanders*. Stokes. (Short stories)
Mitchell, S. W. *Hugh Wynne*. Appleton-Century. (The Revolution)
Morrow, H. W. *Let the King Beware*. McClelland.
*Oertel, T. E. *Jack Sutherland*. Crowell. (Early settlement in Georgia)
*Rolt-Wheeler, Francis. *The Coming of the Peoples*. Doubleday, Doran. (Exploration and settlement of America, 1492–1700)
*Skinner, C. L. *Silent Scot, Frontier Scout*. Macmillan. (Tennessee)
*Stillman, A. L. *Drums Beat in Old Carolina*. Winston.
Sublette, C. M. *The Bright Face of Danger*. Little, Brown. (Bacon's Rebellion)
*Thomas, Lowell. *The Hero of Vincennes*. Houghton Mifflin.
*Thompson, David P. *The Green Mountain Boys*. Nelson.
Thompson, Maurice. *Alice of Old Vincennes*. Grosset.
*Turner, N. B. *In the Days of Young Washington*. Houghton Mifflin.
*Turpin, Edna. *Littling of Gaywood*. Random House. (Colonial Virginia)
Varble, Rachel. *A Girl from London*. Little, Brown. (Revolution)

UNIT TWO
FORMING A MORE PERFECT UNION

The winning of independence left the young United States with many unsolved problems. The chief problem was the formation of a central government with more power than the weak one which had barely held the nation together during the Revolutionary War. None of the thirteen states was willing to give up any of its powers to a central government. For several years the country struggled along with a government so weak that it was nearly helpless. It could not obtain the respect of foreign nations. It could not even pay its bills. It could not regulate commerce between the states or make them stop quarreling among themselves. In addition, disorders broke out within some of the states, causing thoughtful men to wonder whether republican government was a failure.

In the winter of 1786–1787 conditions became so bad that Congress called a convention to consider making needed changes in the government. The distinguished men who met at Philadelphia decided to write a new constitution. After much argument the Constitution went into effect in 1789. Then the country could enjoy the blessings of a more perfect union.

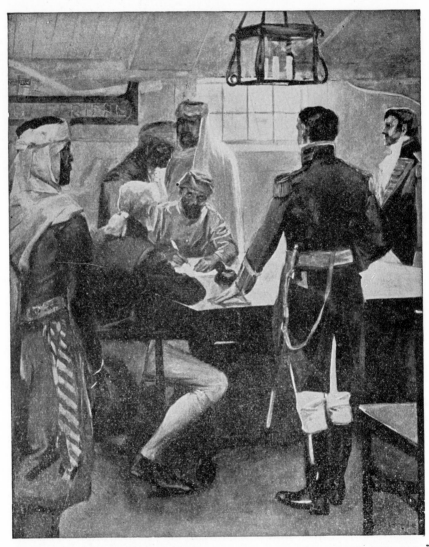

SIGNING A TREATY WITH THE DEY (GOVERNOR) OF ALGIERS, 1805. *After the United States became independent, its merchant ships were no longer protected from pirates by the British navy. Throughout the Critical Period the pirates of Algiers, Tunis, Tripoli, and Morocco preyed on our commerce in the Mediterranean. They continued to make us a great deal of trouble until our navy became strong enough to fight them.* (See page 140.) (From History of the United States Navy, 1894. Courtesy of Boston Public Library)

CHAPTER 7

THE CRITICAL PERIOD

time of weakness. The new republic was like a weak and sickly infant. Few outsiders thought it would live. The years from the end of the war to the adoption of the Constitution in 1788 were the most critical of our nation's history. They are known as the "Critical Period."

Weaknesses of the Confederation government. The thirteen states were bound together in a "league of friendship," or confederation. The Articles of Confederation, which were drawn up in 1777 but not ratified by all the states until 1781, provided for a weak central government. It was headed by a one-house Congress in which each state had an equal voice. Congress had few powers. It could not levy taxes, enlist troops, punish lawbreakers, or compel the states to follow its recommendations. It could not regulate commerce between the states.

Congress had the greatest difficulty in getting funds to support the government and the armed forces. From 1781 to 1783, for example, Congress asked the states for $10,000,000, but they furnished only $1,500,000. Government officials and members of the armed forces seldom received their pay. The interest on the national debt went unpaid. The treasurer borrowed money until no one would lend the government another dollar.

Congressional leaders were not blind to the weaknesses of this "league of friendship." Congress appealed to the states in vain for power to levy a small duty on imports. Congress also begged for power to regulate commerce; this, too, was refused. A change in the Articles required the consent of all the states. To every suggestion that the Articles be amended, one state at least said "no." Because of this situation Washington described the Confederation as "a rope of sand."

Reasons for the failure to create a stronger government. Why were the states so unwilling to strengthen the national government? There were several reasons. *First,* there was the strong loyalty felt by the people of a state to their state government. The state governments had been in operation since the first settlement of the country. The people regarded their state assemblies as their own mouthpiece, for in endless squabbles with royal governors the legislatures had stood for liberty. (See pp. 45–46.) *Second*, there was the fear that the central government might interfere with the people's liberties. The war had been fought to end interference by Parliament; interference by Congress was equally unwelcome. *Third*, there was scarcely any feeling of national unity now that the war had been won. Communication and commerce between the states was slight. Travel was extremely difficult. Most people, except soldiers, still had never been outside their own state. A sense of national unity was needed before the people would wish to strengthen the central government.

Difficulties with foreign nations. The diplomats whom Congress sent abroad met a cold reception. The new republic had hardly a friend in the world. Every European king hoped it would collapse. Even our ally, France, hoped we would remain so weak that we would do as she said.

The Spaniards, who held Florida, the land west of the Mississippi, and the Mississippi's mouth, made no secret of their ill will. They interfered with our use of the Mississippi. Besides, they held posts on American soil, and stirred up the Indian tribes against our Western settlers. Efforts to make an agreement with Spain came to nothing.

Great Britain did not take the trouble to send us an ambassador. She refused to make a trade treaty, saying that thirteen different treaties would be necessary. She also refused to withdraw from military and fur trading posts in the Northwest Territory, pointing out that the states, contrary to the Treaty of Paris, had interfered with the collection of debts owed to English merchants. Congress could not make the states observe the treaty. (See page 83.)

Most shameful of all, the pirates of Algiers, Tunis, Morocco, and Tripoli interfered with our commerce in the Mediterranean, stealing our ships and holding our citizens for ransom. Congress could not stop these crimes, for it was too poor to build a navy. It was plain that the United States could never win the respect of other nations so long as its government had so little power.

Quarrels between the states. The weakness of the Confederation was also shown by quarrels between the states. Connecticut and Pennsylvania nearly went to war over a boundary dispute. An argument over the frontier between Vermont and New York resulted in

SIR WILLIAM PEPPERELL AND FAMILY. *Like many other Loyalists, this family fled the United States during the Revolution, and all their property was seized. As required by the peace treaty, Congress recommended the return of Loyalist property, but the states did not listen. This added to our troubles with Great Britain during the Critical Period.* (From the painting by John S. Copley, 1778)

the calling out of troops. Several states made commercial war upon one another. Connecticut laid duties on imports from Massachusetts. Pennsylvania laid duties on goods from Delaware and New Jersey. New York taxed all imports from other states and charged a fee for every out-of-state boat which landed on her shores. To punish New York, Connecticut businessmen agreed not to trade with New York businessmen for a year, while New Jersey placed a tax on the lighthouse New York City had built at Sandy Hook. Such signs of ill will between the states led to a fear that the Confederation would soon fall apart.

Disorder within the states. Of all the troubles suffered during the years of the Confederation, the one which bothered the most people was the scarcity of money. The paper money issued during the war had become entirely worthless and had ceased to circulate. Most of the small supply of "hard" money — gold and silver — was being sent abroad to pay for imported goods. Money became very scarce and very dear, that is, only a little money could be obtained by selling a large quantity of goods. Prices and wages dropped, and there were three years of hard times.

RHODE ISLAND NOTE *worth two shillings and sixpence, issued in 1786, when the paper-money party had control of the legislature.* (Courtesy American Antiquarian Society, Worcester)

In 1785 and 1786 there was much suffering, especially among small farmers and wage earners. Thousands who owed money lost their property or were imprisoned for failure to pay what they owed. In many cases the money had been borrowed when a dollar was worth little (see page 69); now when dollars were worth a great deal, payment was very difficult. For example, a farmer who had borrowed a hundred dollars when this sum was worth ten bushels of wheat might have to sell a hundred bushels of wheat in order to pay his debt.

The poorer people demanded that the state governments print paper money to revive trade and make easier the payment of their debts. They also asked for laws delaying the collection of debts through the courts. In seven states, where a paper-money party came into power in 1786, paper money was issued. Since no one really knew what it was worth, creditors did not wish to accept it. Some of the states passed laws requiring creditors to take paper money in full payment for debts. Men of wealth complained that these laws were unjust. They wanted to strengthen the central government so that it could protect their interests.

In Massachusetts the legislature refused to issue paper money and to delay the collection of debts through the courts. Farms were being foreclosed daily and sold for very low prices. When the farm brought

DETROIT IN 1794. *At this time the British still held Detroit although the Treaty of Paris had given it to the United States. It was then only a fort and trading post in the wilderness.* (Courtesy of Phelps Stokes Collection, New York Public Library)

less than the mortgage, and the farmer could not pay the balance, he might be sent to jail. In 1786 the farmers in the western part of the state rebelled. They released debtors from prison and broke up sessions of the courts where cases against debtors were being tried. Early in 1787, under the leadership of a Revolutionary captain, Daniel Shays, they tried to break into an arsenal at Springfield in order to get muskets and cannon. The governor sent troops and the uprising was put down. Similar disturbances occurred in Vermont and New Hampshire. Thoughtful men feared that the trouble might spread and that the states might not be able to keep order. They thought the only remedy was to strengthen the central government.

Creation of a national domain. Difficulties with foreign nations, quarrels between the states, and disorders within the states showed the need for a stronger national government. But the event which did most to develop national unity, and so prepared the way for a stronger national government, was the creation of a domain, or territory, belonging to all the states in common.

Seven states claimed land west of the Appalachians and six did not. The states having no claim to western land argued that all such claims should be ceded (given) to the nation, which could then sell the land to pay national debts and support the national government. In 1780

New York agreed to cede its claims. Congress then recommended that all the states having western claims follow this example. Virginia, Connecticut, and Massachusetts gave up their claims, and in 1786 the vast Northwest Territory became a national domain. Common ownership of this rich territory drew the states together with a new feeling of national pride.

The Northwest Ordinance. The most important act passed by the Congress of the Confederation was the Northwest Ordinance (1787) providing for the government of the Northwest Territory. The Ordinance stated that Congress should appoint from the landholders of the region a governor and judges. When there were five thousand free men in the territory, there should also be a governor's council and an elected house of representatives. When there were sixty thousand inhabitants, the voters might adopt a constitution, establish a state, and ask for admission to the Union. The Ordinance stated that "there shall be formed in the said territory not less than three nor more than five states."

This act gave the world a new principle for the government of colonies. The settlers of the West would not remain subjects of the original thirteen states. Instead they would have some share in their own government almost from the beginning, and later would be permitted to form states on a basis of equality with the original thirteen. Carrying out this principle, the thirteen states were to add thirty-five others to the Union. "I doubt," said Daniel Webster, years later, "whether any single law of any lawgiver, ancient or modern, has produced effects of more distinct, marked, and lasting character than the Ordinance of 1787."

The Mount Vernon Conference, 1785. George Washington was one of a small group of Americans who constantly considered the good of the whole Union. He was more interested in the country beyond the Appalachians than most men of his time, for he saw that this region would soon fill with settlers. He pointed out that unless the East and West were connected by ties of trade they might easily break apart. He said, "Let us bind these people to us with a chain that can never be broken."

After returning to his home, Mount Vernon, in 1783, Washington gave most of his time to plans for improving transportation between Virginia and Maryland and the West. In 1785 he became president of a company for extending navigation on the Potomac and James rivers. He would not take any pay for his services, saying that his only pur-

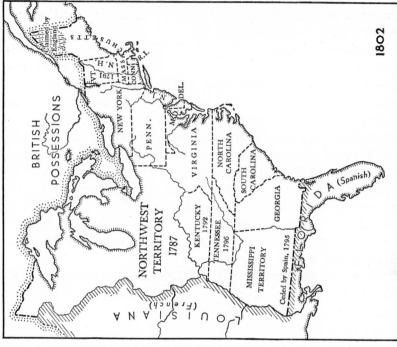

WESTERN LANDS AFTER STATES HAD GIVEN UP CLAIMS

1802

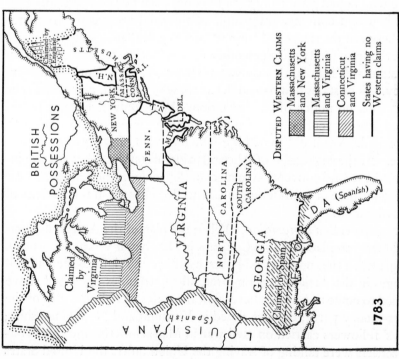

1783

WESTERN LANDS WHEN CLAIMED BY STATES

DISPUTED WESTERN CLAIMS

Massachusetts and New York

Massachusetts and Virginia

Connecticut and Virginia

States having no Western claims

pose was to strengthen the spirit of union by cementing the East and West together.

At Washington's suggestion Maryland and Virginia appointed commissioners to work out an agreement concerning navigation on the Potomac — a matter over which there had long been difficulty. The commissioners met at Mount Vernon. They drew up an agreement which was later approved by the two state legislatures. As Washington's plan included a canal connecting the headwaters of the Potomac with those of the Ohio, and another canal connecting Chesapeake Bay with the Delaware River, Pennsylvania and Delaware would have to be consulted. Washington suggested that the four states might also consult together about reducing the trade barriers between them. The idea grew, and the Mount Vernon Conference ended its work by proposing a convention on navigation and trade to which all the states would be invited to send delegates.

The Annapolis Convention, 1786. A few months later the Virginia assembly invited all the states to take part in a convention at Annapolis to consider trade and navigation problems. General Washington, James Madison, James Monroe, and Alexander Hamilton were among those who hoped great things might come from this convention. Perhaps it would convince the people of the need for greater co-operation between the states and for a stronger central government.

At the appointed time, September 11, 1786, delegates assembled from five states — Virginia, Pennsylvania, Delaware, New York, and New Jersey. Four states had named delegates who failed to come, and four states took no notice of the invitation. With only five states represented, the convention could not accomplish the purpose for which it was called. Yet it did something which proved of far greater importance. At the suggestion of Alexander Hamilton the delegates recommended a second convention to meet in Philadelphia the following year for the purpose of considering much-needed changes in the Articles of Confederation.

Congress calls a convention. When the plan of the Annapolis commissioners was placed before Congress in October, it was not approved. Congress felt that no other body but itself had the right to recommend changes in the Articles. Soon after, all the troubles described above seemed to come to a head. Several of the states were in the grip of the paper-money party; debtors rioted in Vermont and New Hampshire; Shays' followers carried on civil war in Massachusetts; and the Western settlers were talking of leaving the Union unless the United States

WASHINGTON WITH LAFAYETTE AT MOUNT VERNON. *In 1784 the young French nobleman returned to America for a visit as a guest of the nation. He spent some days with the Washingtons at their beautiful home.* (From the painting by T. P. Rossiter and L. R. Mignot. Courtesy of Metropolitan Museum of Art)

government could persuade Spain to give them the free use of the Mississippi. In February the New York legislature dealt the Confederation a heavy blow by blocking an amendment designed to give Congress the power to collect a duty on imports. Among men of wealth and influence there was a growing belief that republican government was a failure. Some of them said openly that the country would be much better off with a king.

In this dangerous hour the Virginia legislature made a bold and statesmanlike move. It chose George Washington as a delegate to the proposed convention at Philadelphia. The news was greeted with joy throughout the land. All at once people began to speak well of the idea of holding a convention. New Jersey, Pennsylvania, North Carolina, and Delaware appointed delegates. Congress decided to fall into line by sending out a formal call for a convention. All the remaining states except Rhode Island then made plans to take part.

To identify: Articles of Confederation, Alexander Hamilton, James Madison, James Monroe, Northwest Ordinance, Daniel Shays.

To explain or define: amendment, cede, convention, Critical Period, dear money, delegate, foreclosure, national domain.

Subjects for Talks or Written Reports

1. The boundary dispute between Vermont and New York. 2. The boundary dispute between Connecticut and Pennsylvania. 3. Trade barriers between the states during the Confederation. 4. Difficulties in the states where the paper-money party came into power. 5. Shays' Rebellion and how it was put down. 6. The Ohio Land Company; how it was formed and how it helped settle the Northwest. 7. How the public land was laid out by surveyors; the size of a section, a township. 8. Piracy in the late 1700's.

Questions for Understanding the Text

1. (a) Why did government officials often go unpaid during the Critical Period? (b) Why did the treasurer of the Confederation find it difficult to borrow money for the use of the government? 2. What occurred when the Confederation Congress tried to obtain additional powers? 3. The Confederation Congress has been called a "conference of ambassadors" rather than a legislature. Is this a good description? Explain. 4. Why were people more loyal to their state government than to the central government? 5. (a) Why was there so little feeling of national unity? (b) How did the national domain help produce a sense of national unity? 6. How did Spain show its ill will toward the United States during this period? 7. (a) Why did Great Britain refuse to make a trade treaty with us? (b) What excuse did she give for keeping the military and fur-trading posts in the Northwest Territory? 8. (a) What navy protected our commerce from pirates until the Revolution? (b) Why did pirates cause us so much trouble after the Revolution? 9. (a) Why was money scarcer than ever during the Critical Period? (b) How did the scarcity of money affect the price of farm products? (c) How did this make it difficult for farmers to pay off old debts? 10. (a) What conditions led to Shays' Rebellion? (b) What did the rebellious farmers do? (c) How did Shays' Rebellion help prepare the way for a stronger central government? 11. From the maps on page 99 can you tell (a) which state made the greatest sacrifice in giving up its claims to land west of the Appalachians, (b) which other states gave up extensive claims? 12. What was the importance of the Northwest Ordinance? 13. How did Washington hope to bind the East and the West together? 14. (a) What was the purpose of the Mount Vernon Conference? (b) What states were represented? (c) What proposal grew out of this conference? 15. (a) What was the purpose of the Annapolis Convention? (b) Why did it not accomplish this purpose? (c) Was the Annapolis Convention a failure? Explain. 16. What action of the Virginia legislature led to the calling of the Philadelphia Convention to revise the Articles of Confederation?

CHAPTER 8

THE MAKING OF THE CONSTITUTION

The Delegates to the Philadelphia Convention. The convention called to revise the Articles of Confederation met at Philadelphia in May, 1787. The states sent their most distinguished citizens.

The majority of the fifty-five delegates were lawyers, most of them with considerable experience in public life. There were also wealthy landowners, planters, moneylenders, and merchants, and a sprinkling of college professors, physicians, and retired ministers. The delegates represented the conservative, propertied class. Small farmers, wage earners, and frontier settlers were not represented.

The convention chose George Washington as its presiding officer. Although he could take no part in the debate, his opinions carried great weight. James Madison of Virginia, a scholar in the field of government, took a leading part in the convention's work, and is often referred to as the "Father of the Constitution." He made careful notes of the proceedings day by day, and these were published after all the delegates had died, as Madison's *Journal of the Constitutional Convention.* Madison's *Journal* is our chief source of information concerning the debates and discussions in the Constitutional Convention. Another well-known delegate was the aged Benjamin Franklin, whose wit and homely common sense kept the members in good humor during the most trying hours. Gouverneur Morris of Pennsylvania, brilliant in writing and debate, was responsible for the final wording and arrangement of the Constitution. Among the delegates were many others of outstanding ability.

A difficult task. Although the convention had been called for the sole purpose of recommending changes in the Articles of Confederation, most of the delegates believed that a new plan of government must be developed. The convention therefore simply threw aside the Articles and decided to write a wholly new constitution. The delegates were well aware that the task would be difficult and that they would often disagree. To make easier the reaching of agreements and to reduce pressure from special interest groups, what went on in the meetings was kept secret.

In a discussion of what sort of constitution would be approved by the people, many of the delegates said that it would have to be a weak one. They thought the people were not ready for a thoroughgoing reform. Washington gravely broke into the discussion to give his own view. In all history few speeches so brief have carried so much weight. "It is too probable," he said, "that no plan we propose will be adopted. Perhaps another dreadful conflict is to be sustained. If, to please the people, we offer what we ourselves cannot approve, how can we afterward defend our work? Let us raise a standard to which the wise and the honest can repair. The event is in the hand of God." These words lifted the tone of the convention from politics to statesmanship.

Points of agreement. On some questions the delegates were sharply divided, but fortunately they agreed on many fundamental points. Most of them believed, for example, (1) that the new government should have the power to defend the country on land and sea, to tax, to coin and borrow money, to regulate commerce, to sell the Western lands, and to secure the return of fugitive slaves and servants; (2) that the public debt should be paid; (3) that property rights should be protected both from mobs and from radical legislation such as that favored by the paper-money party; (4) that a truly *national* government should be established in place of a confederacy; and (5) that this government should have the authority to enforce its laws. The disagreements that arose among the delegates had to do mainly with how these things could be accomplished.

Differences to be harmonized. One of the major disagreements in the convention resulted because the states were unequal in area, wealth, and population. According to the first census (1790), Virginia had three fourths of a million people, while the state with the next largest population, Massachusetts (which then included what is now Maine), had just under half a million. Then came Pennsylvania with 434,000 people, North Carolina with 394,000, and New York with 340,000. The combined population of these five states was almost twice that of the remaining eight. The five with the largest population, together with Georgia, were also the states having the greatest area and land values. It is not surprising, then, that the small states were fearful that the large ones would control the new national government.

A second question dividing the delegates was whether the national

BENJAMIN FRANKLIN *in 1787. He was a truly great man, known on both sides of the Atlantic as a scientist, philosopher, and statesman. His part in the shaping of the Constitution was a fitting climax to a life of public service.* (From the painting by Charles Peale, 1787. Courtesy of Historical Society of Pennsylvania)

government or the states should be supreme. The experiences of the Confederation had shown the necessity for a stronger central government, but many people still believed that each state should be sovereign, that is, supreme. A sovereign state, they thought, should make all its own laws, except on a few matters that could not possibly be handled by each state independently. The small states were more anxious to keep their complete independence than the larger ones, since they feared that they would never have enough influence in the new government to prevent the passage of bills which they thought might injure their interests.

A third difference among the delegates was in their attitude toward democracy. Should the new constitution enable the masses of people to control the government, or should it give control to wealthy land-holders and other men likely to have conservative views? Most of the delegates were afraid of democracy, believing that the masses of people were inclined to be rash and lawless. One delegate, Governor Randolph of Virginia, declared that the troubles of the past few years had been due to the "turbulence and folly of democracy." Alexander Hamilton of New York, arguing in favor of a life term for senators, exclaimed that "all communities divide themselves into the few and the many. The first are rich and wellborn, and the other the mass of people who seldom judge or determine right." This conservative point of view was shown in various decisions of the convention.

The Great Compromise. The differences in the convention appeared in two general proposals of union. These are now called the Virginia and New Jersey plans, or the "large-states plan" and the "small-states plan." James Madison prepared the Virginia plan, which called for a strong central government in which the states should be represented either according to their population or their wealth. Delegates from the small states said that they would never accept this proposal. William Paterson of New Jersey proposed another plan, reserving more power to the states, and giving them equal representation in Congress.

The two plans were debated for days. The most difficult question to settle was how the states were to be represented in the new government. At times there seemed no hope of reaching an agreement. Finally the convention adopted what has come to be known as the "Great Compromise." It was agreed to have two houses in Congress — the House of Representatives, in which the states are represented according to their population, and the Senate, in which the states are represented equally. It was then decided to form a *federal* government — one in which the states keep important powers, while the central government also has much power.

The compromise on the regulation of commerce. Farming was the only industry in the states south of the Potomac — Virginia, North Carolina, South Carolina, and Georgia — while all the other states were interested in commerce as well as in farming. Delegates from the northern states were strongly in favor of giving Congress the power to regulate foreign and interstate commerce. Those from the four southern states feared that if Congress could regulate commerce, it might favor the commercial states. A compromise was arranged which gave Congress the power to regulate commerce, but forbade it (1) to

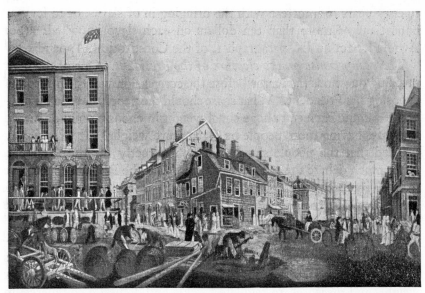

NEW YORK, *already an important commercial city, wanted the federal government to have control over foreign trade and trade between the states. This is the corner of Wall Street and Water Street in 1800.* (Courtesy of New York Historical Society)

impose a tax on articles exported from any state; (2) to give preference to the ports of one state over those of another.

The compromise on taxation. If Congress were given the power to tax, might it not treat large and small states unequally? Delegates from the small states argued that Congress should impose no taxes without a two-thirds vote of its members. As such a rule would enable a small group of Congressmen to hold up any tax bill, it would almost amount to denying Congress the right to lay taxes. The difficulty was overcome by an agreement that (1) all taxes should be the same throughout the United States, and (2) all direct taxes (such as head taxes) should be apportioned among the states according to population. The delegates from the small states then agreed that a tax bill could be passed by a simple majority vote.

The slave-trade clause. Except in the far South slavery had been gradually dying out. In New England it had almost disappeared. In Maryland and Virginia there was a strong party in favor of abolition (doing away with slavery). In North Carolina the abolition movement was gathering strength. But in the rice and indigo swamps of South Carolina and Georgia slavery was still considered necessary. The delegates from these states insisted that Congress be forbidden for twenty years to interfere with the bringing in of slaves, or to levy an import tax of more than ten dollars on each slave imported. (See Article I, Section IX, paragraph 1, of the Constitution, Appendix.)

The compromise on the election of the President. One of the most puzzling questions that came before the convention was the method of choosing the President. What share should the people have in his election? Should each state have equal weight in choosing him or should the states having more people be given more weight? It was quickly decided that the people should not vote directly for the President. After much debate the convention agreed that the President should be selected by electors, chosen as the legislature of each state might think best. To please the large states, the number of electors from each state was made equal to the number of its representatives and senators.

A government of limited powers. The powers of the federal government were carefully listed or enumerated. Among these powers are the right to lay taxes, to borrow money, to coin money, to fix weights and measures, to regulate foreign and domestic commerce, to raise and support an army, and to declare war. Congress was also given the power to "make all laws which shall be necessary and proper for carrying into execution the foregoing powers." (See Article I, Section VIII, paragraph 18, of the Constitution, Appendix.) This is sometimes spoken of as "the elastic clause."

Powers of the states. To prevent confusion, certain powers were denied the states. (See Article I, Section X, Appendix.) The states are not to coin money, to issue bills of credit (that is, paper money), to lay duties on imports, to enter into treaties, or to violate contracts (as, for example, preventing the collection of debts). Many of the difficulties that had arisen during the Confederation were due to these very actions by the states.

The convention intended that all powers not granted to the federal government and not prohibited to the states should be considered as reserved to the states. To make this absolutely certain, the Tenth Amendment was added in 1791. (See page 119.) All the powers of local government were thus left to the states. The states were to decide who should vote and how. The states were to be responsible for schools, local courts, policing, the incorporation of banks and stock companies, the care of bridges, roads, canals, and many other matters.

Despite the care taken by the convention in dividing powers between the nation and the states, many cases have arisen where it was

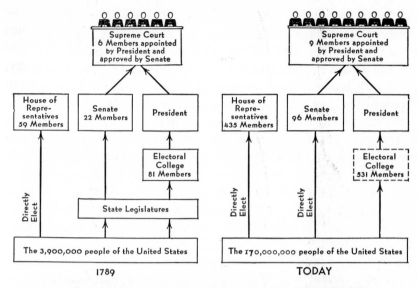

THE FEDERAL GOVERNMENT IN 1789 AND TODAY

The members of the Senate and of the Electoral College are now chosen by the people instead of by the state legislatures. (Courtesy of *Building America*)

not clear whether the power to do a certain thing belongs to the federal or to the state governments. Such cases often come before the Supreme Court for decision.

The separation of powers. The convention decided that the federal government should have three branches — the *legislative*, to make the laws; the *executive*, to see that the laws are carried out; and the *judicial*, to administer justice and safeguard the rights of individuals. The three branches were to be separate; each was to be a check on the others.

The judicial branch is most nearly independent. Yet Congress controls the number of judges and fixes their salaries. The judicial branch checks Congress by deciding what its acts (laws) mean and also by finding whether or not an act is constitutional (allowed by the Constitution). Congress may also be checked by the President, since he has power to veto its acts, and his veto can be set aside only by a two-thirds vote of each house.

The executive branch is subject to many checks by Congress. Without money provided by Congress no agency can continue its work. In filling important offices the President must get the approval of the Senate. The President's power in foreign relations is also limited, for a treaty made with a foreign government requires a two-thirds vote of the Senate to ratify it or make it legal. The President may even be removed from office by Congress. To do this, he is first impeached (that is, charges are brought against him) by the House of Representatives. When impeached, he is tried by the Senate. If found guilty, he may be removed from office. Only one President has ever been impeached, and he was not found guilty. (See pages 327–328.)

Because of the controls that each branch has upon the others, our federal government is often said to be a system of "checks and balances." By creating checks and balances the framers of the Constitution hoped to prevent the government from taking hasty and unwise actions that might be demanded by the masses of people.

The amending process. The delegates realized that the Constitution was not perfect and that changes might become necessary. They provided that an amendment to the Constitution may be proposed either by a two-thirds vote of both houses of Congress or by a constitutional convention, which may be summoned at the request of two thirds of the state legislatures. A proposed amendment becomes part of the Constitution if it is ratified either by the legislatures of three fourths of the states or by specially elected conventions in three fourths of the states. The delegates intended to make the amending process difficult, and they succeeded. A small number of states can block a change desired by the rest. Of the hundreds of amendments which have been proposed, only twenty-two have been adopted.

The convention adjourns. In September, 1787, after nearly four months of wearisome work, the convention held its last meeting. Only three of the delegates present refused to sign. Franklin expressed the views of the others in his usual happy manner. "I confess," he said, "that there are several parts of this Constitution which I do not at present approve, but I am not sure that I shall never approve them." Pointing to the half sun painted in gold on the back of Washington's chair, he remarked, "I have often and often in the course of the session and the vicissitudes [changes] of my hopes and fears as to its issue, looked at that behind the President, without being able to tell whether it was rising or setting; but now, at length, I have the happiness to know it is a rising, and not a setting, sun."

A new method of ratification. According to the Articles of Confederation any change in the government had to be approved (ratified) by the legislatures of all thirteen states. The delegates at Philadelphia thought it unlikely that all the state legislatures would accept their work, so they proposed that each state hold a convention to consider

SIGNING THE CONSTITUTION. *The delegates were solemn as they met to sign the document which they hoped would result in a more perfect Union. They are shown in the beautiful room in Independence Hall, Philadelphia, where they had worked for nearly four months.* (From the mural painting by Albert Herter in the state capitol, Madison, Wisconsin)

the Constitution. When such conventions in *nine* states had given their approval, the Constitution would go into effect for those states, no matter what the other four decided.

Two parties arise. As soon as the Constitution was published, people divided themselves into two groups — the *Federalists,* who wished to ratify the Constitution, and the *Antifederalists,* who opposed ratification. The Federalists were chiefly from the commercial, money-lending, and planting classes, which had tried so long to strengthen the central government. The Antifederalists were chiefly from the debtor and small farmer classes. Both parties had strong, able leaders.

The campaign for ratification. Hot arguments went on wherever people gathered. There were serious questions to be thrashed out. Would the proposed central government oppress the people with heavy taxes? Would it drag them into foreign wars? Might not a President with such powers become a tyrant? Might not the senators become a new aristocracy? Why were the liberties of the people not mentioned — had the convention been more interested in protecting property than human rights? Would the new government reduce the states to mere figureheads? Why did the Constitution begin with the words "We, the people," instead of "We, the states?" These are but a few of the doubts expressed by the Antifederalists.

The country was flooded with pamphlets and newspaper articles.

Some of the ablest articles in defense of the Constitution were written by Alexander Hamilton, James Madison, and John Jay. They were printed in New York newspapers and helped win doubtful New York State to the cause of ratification. They were later gathered together in a single famous volume called *The Federalist*.

The three states in which the contest was closest were Massachusetts, Virginia, and New York. The Federalists won in Massachusetts by a narrow margin after they promised to recommend adding a bill of rights to the Constitution. Massachusetts was the sixth state to ratify. Every state but one which ratified after Massachusetts recommended similar amendments. (This was the origin of the first ten amendments to the Constitution. See pp. 118–119.)

In Virginia the influence of George Washington and James Madison brought victory after a hard struggle. By this time every state but New York, North Carolina, and Rhode Island had ratified. The Constitution was now certain to go into effect. Yet without central and powerful New York the Union might be hopelessly handicapped. When the New York Convention met in June, two thirds of its members were Antifederalists. After a month of fiery argument Alexander Hamilton converted the best speaker on the Antifederalist side. Then other Antifederalists changed sides. New York ratified by the close vote of 30 to 27. North Carolina did not ratify until November, 1789, and Rhode Island held out until May, 1790.

❀ ❀ ❀

To identify: Father of the Constitution, *The Federalist*, Benjamin Franklin, Great Compromise, Gouverneur Morris.

To explain or define: checks and balances, constitutional, elastic clause, elector, executive, federal, impeach, judicial, ratification, sovereign, veto.

Subjects for Talks or Written Reports

1. The contest for ratification in Massachusetts. 2. The contest for ratification in Virginia. 3. The contest for ratification in New York. 4. The attitude of Samuel Adams on ratification. 5. The attitude of Patrick Henry on ratification. 6. Why North Carolina and Rhode Island delayed their ratification so long. 7. Provisions of the Constitution showing a distrust for democracy.

QUESTIONS FOR UNDERSTANDING THE TEXT

1. Name the groups represented at the Philadelphia Convention. What groups were not represented? 2. Name four noted delegates and discuss their contribution to the convention. 3. Why were the proceedings of the convention kept secret? How do we know what went on? 4. Name some important points on which the delegates thought alike. 5. Show that the small states had good reason to fear that they would be overshadowed by the large states. 6. What is meant by a sovereign state? Name several provisions of the Constitution which reflect the desire for state sovereignty. 7. How did many of the delegates feel about democracy? Name several provisions of the Constitution which reflect a distrust of the common people. 8. What was the main difference between the "large-states plan" and the "small-states plan"? How was this settled in the Great Compromise? 9. Which states feared to give Congress the power to regulate commerce? Explain this attitude. What compromise was reached? 10. What differences appeared regarding the power of taxation? What compromise was reached? 11. What is the slave-trade clause? Why was it included? 12. (*a*) Why were the powers of the federal government enumerated? (*b*) Name some of these powers. (*c*) What powers were left to the states? 13. Show that our government is a system of "checks and balances." 14. How may the Constitution be amended? 15. What groups were opposed to ratification? What doubts did they express?

ACTIVITIES FOR UNIT TWO

1. Appoint a committee to begin work on a classbook entitled "American Hall of Fame." Include a picture and a brief biography of each famous person selected by the committee. In writing the biographies emphasize what each individual did for America.

2. Imagine that you were a member of the Confederation Congress in the winter of 1786 when the New York legislature blocked the amendment intended to give Congress power to collect a duty on imports. Write a letter to a friend to show the helplessness of Congress.

3. Make a graph comparing the population of the thirteen states in 1790. The figures can be found in the *World Almanac*.

4. Draw a cartoon illustrating one of the problems faced by the Philadelphia Convention. Post on the bulletin board.

5. Read aloud in class Sections VIII, IX, and X of **Article I of the** Constitution. Be prepared to explain all difficult or unusual terms.

6. Write a radio script giving a discussion which might have taken place in a village store between a little group of Federalists and Antifederalists in 1788.

7. Develop a panel discussion on the questions: Did the makers of the Constitution intend to create a democratic government? Did they do so?
8. Write an article on what the people of the United States owe to the people of Virginia.

READINGS FOR UNIT TWO

(Stars indicate the easier books)

GENERAL ACCOUNTS

Farrand, Max. *The Fathers of the Constitution.* (Chronicles)
——. *The Framing of the Constitution.* Yale University Press.
Fiske, John. *The Critical Period of American History.* Houghton Mifflin.
McFee, I. N. *How Our Government Is Run.* Crowell.
McLaughlin, A. C. *The Confederation and the Constitution.* (A. N. S.)
Ogg, Frederic A. *Builders of the Republic.* (Pageant)
——. *The Old Northwest.* (Chronicles)
*Rexford, F. A. and Carson, C. L. *The Constitution of Our Country.* American Book.
Rodell, Fred. *Fifty-five Men.* Telegraph Press.
*Singmaster, Elsie. *Book of the Constitution.* Doran.
*Tappan, Eva M. *The Story of Our Constitution.* Lothrop.
*Walker, E. E. and Kersey, V. *Our National Constitution; How It Was Framed and How It Works.* Scribner's.
Whipple, Leon. *Our Ancient Liberties.* Wilson. (Origin and meaning of civil and religious liberty in the U. S.)

BIOGRAPHY

*Baldwin, James. *Four Great Americans.* American Book.
*Daugherty, James. *Daniel Boone.* Viking.
*——. *Poor Richard.* Viking.
*Faris, J. T. *Makers of Our History.* Ginn.
*Nicolay, Helen. *The Boys' Life of Alexander Hamilton.* Appleton-Century.
*——. *Boys' Life of Benjamin Franklin.* Appleton-Century.
*Richards, L. E. *Abigail Adams and Her Times.* Appleton-Century.
*Tappan, Eva M. *American Hero Stories.* Houghton Mifflin.
Van Doren, Carl. *Benjamin Franklin.* Viking.
*White, S. E. *Daniel Boone, Wilderness Scout.* Doubleday, Doran.

FICTION

Cooke, Grace. *The Fortunes of John Hawk.* Century. (Life of Loyalists after the Revolution)
Skinner, Constance L. *The White Leader.* (Southwest, 1775–1790)

UNIT THREE
THE NATIONAL GOVERNMENT GROWS STRONGER

The Constitution outlined the new government but left a great many details to be worked out by Congress and the President. Fortunately these details were decided with much wisdom and in a spirit of lofty patriotism. The young Republic was thereby given a good start, although no one then knew whether it would be strong enough to last.

The new government could not give all its attention to affairs at home. Almost from the start it had to deal with difficult foreign problems. It was barely twenty-three years old when it went to war with England. The War of 1812 showed that the United States was determined to be treated with respect and strengthened the feeling of national unity, which remained strong for some ten years after the war. During this ten-year period the central government was greatly strengthened, and the United States showed a new firmness in dealing with other nations. The peak of national feeling came in 1823 when President Monroe announced the famous ideas known as the Monroe Doctrine.

GEORGE WASHINGTON. *The success of the new government depended upon the
kind of men who would first hold the reins of power. Washington seemed the proper
man to give dignity to the new office of President. Responsible men of every section
trusted his fairness, his breadth of view, and his sound judgment. Gouverneur Morris
wrote him in 1787: "Your cool, steady temper is indispensably necessary to give firm
and manly tone to the new government. . . . Among these thirteen horses now about
to be coupled together, there are some of every race and character. They will listen
to your voice, and submit to your control; you therefore must, I say* must, *mount the
seat."* (This portrait, entitled "General Washington at the Battle of Trenton," was
painted by John Trumbull in 1806. Courtesy of Yale University Art Gallery)

CHAPTER 9

LAUNCHING THE NEW
NATIONAL GOVERNMENT

Washington becomes the first President. Arrange. ments were made for launching the new government in the spring of 1789. Washington's name was on everyone's lips, and when the electoral college met, he was chosen unanimously for President. John Adams of Massachusetts was chosen Vice-President.

The meeting of the new Congress and the counting of the votes for President and Vice-President was set for March 4. When the day came, only a few of the congressmen had arrived. The others had been delayed by bad roads or by personal business. Was the country to be left without a government? For some days great anxiety was felt. But one by one the missing congressmen straggled in, and on April 6 the counting of the electoral votes finally took place. Messengers were then sent to give Washington and Adams notice of their election.

Although Washington longed to remain at his beloved Mount Vernon, he accepted the Presidency because of a strong sense of duty. His friends told him that he alone had the confidence of the entire nation and that in the unpopular task of establishing a national government the people would follow him farther than anyone else. His election gave him no happiness. He wrote in his diary: "I anticipated, with a heart filled with distress, the ten thousand embarrassments, perplexities, and troubles, to which I must again be exposed in the evening of a life already nearly consumed in public cares."

In mid-April Washington left his beautiful home on the Potomac to go to New York, the temporary capital. In every village and town the people gathered to cheer him. Children sang by the roadsides, bridges were decorated with evergreens and flowers, banquets were given for him at every halting place. As he approached the city of New York, he was saluted by thirteen guns. On April 30, before a vast throng, he took the oath of office as first President of the United States.

THE NEW GOVERNMENT BEGINS TO FUNCTION

The Constitution provided only the skeleton of the new government. Many details had to be worked out by the first Congress and the first President. Their decisions might determine whether the new government would live or die. The people were divided almost equally for and against the new government, many hoping that the Constitution would prove a failure. Fortunately the supporters of the Constitution had a majority in Congress, and Washington was careful to select for important positions only those who wanted the new government to succeed.

The departments and the cabinet. The Constitution refers to "heads of departments," but leaves Congress to decide what the departments shall be. The first Congress created the Department of State, the Department of War, and the Department of the Treasury. Congress also established the offices of Attorney General and Postmaster General. The heads of the departments and the Attorney General soon came to be known as the President's cabinet. Washington relied heavily upon the advice of the cabinet members. Alexander Hamilton, the first Secretary of the Treasury, and Thomas Jefferson, the first Secretary of State, were to have a lasting influence upon the new government.

The federal judiciary. The Constitution said that the judicial power was to be vested in "one Supreme Court and in such inferior (lower) courts as Congress may from time to time establish." The judges were to be appointed by the President and confirmed by the Senate. In the Judiciary Act of 1789 Congress provided that the Supreme Court should consist of one chief justice and five associate justices — a number which has been changed several times since. The Act also set up three circuit courts and thirteen district courts. Within a year the new national courts were hard at work.

The first eleven amendments. A number of states had ratified the Constitution with strong recommendations for changes. (See page 112.) At first Congress took no notice of these suggestions. Then complaints from the voters forced Congress to act, and finally the first ten amendments — the so-called "Bill of Rights" — were submitted to the states. Among other things these amendments state that Congress shall not interfere with freedom of religion, speech, and the press, or the right of the people to assemble peaceably and petition the government for the redress (righting) of grievances, or their right to

THE INAUGURATION OF WASHINGTON, *April 30, 1789. On this great day, when the first President of the United States took the oath of office, Americans were happy. New York, the temporary capital, was filled with joyful crowds, among them many veterans who had served under Washington during the Revolution.* (Drawn by H. A. Ogden, 1889. Courtesy of New York Public Library)

keep and bear arms. Trial by jury was guaranteed to all persons charged by federal officers with serious crimes. To satisfy further those who feared that the federal government would interfere with the rights of the states and the individual, the Tenth Amendment says that all powers not given to the United States government by the Constitution or withheld by it from the states are to belong to the states or to the people. (See pages 108–109.) The amendments became part of the Constitution in 1791. Seven years later the Eleventh Amendment, written in the same spirit as the Tenth, was ratified. It prohibited the federal courts from hearing any case in which a state was sued by a citizen.

The first tariff act, 1789. The new government needed money to pay its expenses and the interest on the public debt. It owed about twelve million dollars to foreign creditors (French, Dutch, and Spanish), and more than forty millions to its own citizens who had purchased the bonds issued by the Second Continental and the Confederation congresses. To raise funds, Congress passed the first tariff act,

ALEXANDER HAMILTON, *the first Secretary of the Treasury. Hamilton was fourteen years younger than Jefferson and did not agree with the older man's democratic ideas. Hamilton popularized the idea of a strong central government. His masterly reports to Congress helped establish the new Republic on a firm financial foundation. His brilliant career ended when Aaron Burr killed him in a duel.* (Portrait by John Trumbull, about 1792. Courtesy of Frick Art Reference Library, Arthur Iselin Collection)

placing taxes on a number of imports, including molasses, sugar, tea, coffee, boots, and shoes. The revenue from the tariff, amounting to about twenty-two million dollars in the next five years, enabled the government to become well established.

HAMILTON'S FINANCIAL PROGRAM

Hamilton's background. Two months after the passage of the first tariff act, Alexander Hamilton began his remarkable career as first Secretary of the Treasury. He was then thirty-two years old. Born in the West Indies, as a youth he had come to New York, where he completed his education. He had served as Washington's secretary and aide during part of the Revolutionary War, and later, while still a very young man, had become a noted lawyer. The ratification of the Constitution in New York was largely due to his untiring efforts. As first Secretary of the Treasury, Hamilton solved many difficult national problems. He did a great deal to strengthen the new government and win for it the support of men of wealth and influence.

Hamilton's debt proposals. Soon after entering the cabinet Hamilton sent to Congress a brilliant "Report on the Public Credit." In this report he urged (a) the payment of the foreign debt ($12,000,000) in full, (b) the payment of the domestic debt ($40,000,000) in full, and (c) the taking over by the federal government of the unpaid war debts

THOMAS JEFFERSON *was one of the world's leading political thinkers and writers. His great aim was to give men more equal opportunity and a wider liberty. He feared that a strong national government might destroy men's freedom and said frankly, " I am not a friend to a very energetic government."* This portrait by Rembrandt Peale shows Jefferson at the age of sixty, when he was serving his first term as President. (Courtesy of Virginia Conservation Commission)

of the states ($22,000,000). Since the federal government did not have the money to pay this sum, totaling $74,000,000, Hamilton proposed that the treasury issue new bonds to be exchanged for the old bonds and certificates issued by the Confederation Congress and by the states.

Hamilton's recommendation to pay the foreign debt in full met with no objection. A vigorous fight developed over the proposal to pay the domestic debt in full. Most of the certificates were no longer in the hands of the original holders, since speculators had bought them up for as little as fifteen cents on the dollar. Some members of Congress argued that the certificates held by speculators should be redeemed not at their face value but at their market value, which was only one fourth as large. Congress adopted Hamilton's recommendation, amid charges that the new government was being operated in the interests of the wealthy.

The proposal that the federal government assume, that is, take over, the state war debts aroused much discussion. States which had paid little or nothing on their debt were naturally in favor of Hamilton's plan, but not so those which had paid off a large portion of their debt. When the plan was brought to a vote in the House, it failed to carry by two votes. Hamilton would not admit defeat; instead he obtained the necessary votes by means of a clever bargain.

It happened at this time that Congress had before it the question of where to locate the national capital. Virginia, which was against the taking over of the state debts, was eager to have the capital on the Potomac River. Many congressmen from other states were less concerned about the location of the capital than they were about having the federal government take over the state debts. A bargain was made by which the Virginia congressmen voted for "assumption" in return for a promise that the national capital would be on the Potomac.

The excise tax and the Whiskey Rebellion. To help pay the interest on the huge public debt, Hamilton recommended an excise tax of twenty-five cents a gallon on whiskey, to be collected at the stills. Congress adopted this recommendation, and Washington approved it. A storm of opposition immediately broke out in the back country of Pennsylvania, Virginia, and North Carolina, where the farmers commonly made their surplus grain into whiskey. Grain was too bulky to be carried to market on horseback, and to farmers in the back country whiskey was the only source of cash. A tax on whiskey, to be collected at the still, seemed to them most unfair. Then, too, to collect the tax it was necessary for government officers to enter the still owner's property and measure the whiskey on hand — a procedure which was greatly resented. Jefferson was among those who regarded the tax as sure to provoke resistance.

Because of the protests Congress removed the tax from the product of the smallest stills, and this quieted the farmers of Virginia and North Carolina. In Pennsylvania, however, resistance continued. In four western counties the farmers held meetings, refused to pay the tax, appointed committees of safety, and threatened violence to tax collectors and to any who obeyed the law. When federal officers tried, in 1794, to arrest the leaders of the movement, riots occurred in which some of the farmers were wounded and one was killed. Mobs forced a federal officer to flee for his life.

This defiance of the federal government has come to be known as the "Whiskey Rebellion," although it was little more than a disorderly demonstration. The governor of Pennsylvania might have used the militia to put it down but did not wish to make himself unpopular with the voters in the western part of the state by doing so. Washington decided to take stern action. A force of a thousand soldiers could easily have restored order, but the President, strongly urged by Hamilton, wished to show the strength of the federal government. Fifteen thousand militia from Virginia, Maryland, and Pennsylvania were sent

THE BANK OF THE UNITED STATES. *This fine example of classical architecture was built for the main office of the Bank at Philadelphia. The first Bank of the United States was in existence from 1791 to 1811, when its charter expired. Congress chartered the second Bank of the United States in 1816, and its main office was in this same building. The life of the second Bank was twenty years.* (Brown Brothers)

into the rebellious area. Messengers went ahead to persuade the people to submit, and there was no bloodshed. Eighteen leaders were arrested, but only two were convicted, and they were soon pardoned by the President. By taking vigorous action the federal government demonstrated that it had power to enforce its laws.

The first Bank of the United States. The next step in Hamilton's financial program was the establishment of a national bank. In 1789 there were only three banks in the country, one each at Philadelphia, New York, and Boston. Additional banks were needed to care for the needs of the nation's growing industry and commerce. Hamilton believed that there should be a central bank chartered by the federal government, with branches in different parts of the country. In 1791 he persuaded Congress to charter the Bank of the United States for a twenty-year period. Although the government subscribed one fifth of the capital and named some of the directors, the bank was privately owned and managed, with profits passing to the stockholders. The government deposited its funds in the bank and borrowed from it as need arose. Opponents of the plan held that no one bank should have these very profitable privileges. They argued that banks chartered by the states rather than by the federal government would be sufficient.

PRESIDENT WASHINGTON *on a tour of New England in 1789 inspected the Beverly, Massachusetts, cotton mill* (here shown at extreme right). (From a drawing by G. E. Browne. Courtesy of Essex Institute, Salem)

Hamilton advocates a protective tariff. In a famous "Report on Manufactures" Hamilton urged Congress to adopt a protective tariff. American manufacturing was then in its infancy. Its growth should be encouraged, he believed, because it would give employment to women and to children "of a tender age," would attract immigrants, and would create a steady demand for farm products. Hamilton favored placing duties on all foreign goods which could be produced here. The representatives of agricultural sections opposed a protective tariff, because it would raise the price of manufactured goods and thus benefit manufacturers at the expense of consumers. Despite their opposition Congress in 1792 passed a revenue act raising the duties on a number of items. However, Congress did not go so far in this direction as Hamilton wished.

Hamilton's achievements. Hamilton's program made clear to everyone that the United States would pay its debts in full, gave the government all the revenues it needed, established a strong national bank, and encouraged industry and commerce. It won for the national government the support of powerful groups of men in every state, especially manufacturers and bondholders. These men of property now stood strongly behind the new government.

THE RISE OF A NEW PARTY

Jefferson, the spokesman of the masses. Jefferson's ideas were very different from those of Hamilton. He had great faith in the common people and wished the government to be controlled by small farmers, small businessmen, and wage earners. As long as the doors of opportunity were open for every man to own his home and to make a comfortable living by work, he believed the common people could safely be trusted to govern themselves.

Jefferson feared the power possessed by men of wealth. He wanted men to have equal opportunity. He opposed protective tariffs and all other special privileges. He believed the growth of cities and the growth of large factories whose owners could control the lives of their workers should not be encouraged. In turn he had fought for freedom from the king, freedom from control by the church, and freedom from control by big landowners and other men of wealth. He stood, in short, for the ideals known as "the American dream." The common people learned to regard him as their spokesman, while they regarded Hamilton as the spokesman of the rich.

Jefferson wanted to keep the government as close to the people as possible. For that reason he did not favor any further strengthening of the national government.

Two opposing views of the Constitution. Jefferson's view of the powers of the national government was very different from Hamilton's. This was shown in the debate over the Bank of the United States. Jefferson argued that Congress had no power to charter a bank, since the Constitution does not mention any such power. (See Section VIII of Article I, Appendix.) For Congress to use a power not listed was, Jefferson believed, to go contrary to the Constitution. This way of thinking is known as the doctrine of *strict construction*.

In reply to Jefferson, Hamilton pointed out that the Constitution gave to Congress, in addition to those powers that are enumerated, the power "to make all laws which shall be necessary and proper for carrying into effect the foregoing powers." He argued that the chartering of a national bank was a necessary and proper way of using the listed powers of collecting taxes, paying debts, borrowing money, and regulating the currency. He also insisted that Congress had the right to use powers "implied" in the powers actually granted. This is the doctrine of *loose construction* or *implied powers*.

Organization of a new party. After the disagreement over the chartering of the bank, Jefferson resigned from the cabinet. He became

·LADY WASHINGTON'S" RECEPTION. *As wife of the President, Martha Wash-ington entertained with dignity and elegance. Many called her "Lady Washington." Critics ridiculed her elaborate receptions and called the President's New York home the "Republican Court."* (From the painting by Daniel Huntington in the Brooklyn Mu-seum. Courtesy of New York Historical Society)

the leader of a group opposed to further strengthening of the federal government. He called the group the Republican party. It was not the beginning of the present-day Republican party, but rather of the present Democratic party.

The Republican party grew rapidly, especially among the farmers of the South and the Middle states. Societies of party members were formed in the important towns. Each society prepared a list of can-didates for office at each election, worked to obtain new members, and kept in touch with the other societies.

The Federalist party. Hamilton's followers called themselves Fed-eralists. They were chiefly the larger businessmen — merchants, man-ufacturers, bankers — and others who wanted a strong federal govern-ment. As members of prominent families the Federalists were already accustomed to work together. They did not organize societies.

Before the end of Washington's second term the party system had become an accepted feature of our government. Ever since, there have usually been two strong political parties. This was an impor-tant political development not foreseen by the framers of the Constitu-tion, for parties are nowhere mentioned in that document.

To explain or define: doctrine, excise, implied powers, judiciary, strict construction.

SUBJECTS FOR TALKS OR WRITTEN REPORTS

1. Travel and communication in the early years of the Republic. 2. How people made their living in the early years of the Republic (*a*) in New England, (*b*) in the Middle states, (*c*) in the South, and (*d*) on the frontier. 3. City life in the early years of the Republic. Which were the five principal cities in 1790 and what was the population of each? What comforts and conveniences did city people enjoy? What did they do for recreation? 4. The debate over assumption of state debts. 5. The Whiskey Rebellion in Pennsylvania. 6. Hamilton's activities and influence as a member of Washington's cabinet. 7. Washington's attitude toward political parties and toward attacks upon himself in the newspapers. 8. The Post Office Department in the early years of the Republic.

QUESTIONS FOR UNDERSTANDING THE TEXT

1. Why did Washington accept the Presidency? Describe his journey to the inauguration. 2. State some of the problems facing the national government in 1789. 3. What courts did the first Congress establish? Who determines the number of Supreme Court justices? 4. Why were the first eleven amendments added to the Constitution? With what do they deal? 5. What did Hamilton propose regarding the state and federal debts? What opposition developed? What bargain did Hamilton make concerning the location of the national capital? 6. (*a*) Where was whiskey the only source of cash? (*b*) What happened when a tax was imposed at the stills? (*c*) Why did not the governor of Pennsylvania call out the militia? (*d*) What action did Washington take? (*e*) How would the government of the Confederation have solved a similar problem? 7. (*a*) Was the first Bank of the United States a private corporation? (*b*) How did the deposit of government funds help the Bank and its stockholders? (*c*) What control did the government have over the Bank? (*d*) Why did Republicans oppose the Bank? 8. Name Hamilton's principal achievements as Secretary of the Treasury. 9. Contrast Hamilton's and Jefferson's ideas (*a*) about the federal government, (*b*) about the tariff, (*c*) about the desirability of encouraging manufacturing. 10. Explain what is meant by "strict construction" of the Constitution; by the doctrine of "implied powers." 11. Describe the membership of the Federalist party; that of the Republican party. Who led each party?

CHAPTER 10

AVOIDING FOREIGN ENTANGLEMENTS

merican sympathies with the French. A few weeks after Washington's inauguration the first rumblings of revolution rocked France. Americans rejoiced at the news. They felt that the French were following the American example in rising up against tyranny. They thrilled over the great French Declaration of the Rights of Man. When European kings sent armies into France for the purpose of crushing the revolution, Americans watched anxiously, celebrating each victory won by the citizen army of France. Crowds sang French songs in the streets and danced around liberty poles. Hundreds of Jacobin, or Democratic, clubs were organized, like those in France. In Republican circles men laid aside powdered wigs, velvet, and silk to wear simpler clothes, like those of the French revolutionists. It became the fashion among Republicans to drop titles and to speak of "Citizen Smith," "Citizeness Jones," and "Citizen Judge."

As time went on, the revolution in France grew increasingly violent and bloody. The king and queen and thousands of nobles went to the guillotine. Conservative Americans, including Hamilton and his followers, were terribly shocked. They thought the revolution was leading to the overthrow of law and order and to the establishment of the rule of the rabble. They lost all sympathy with the common people of France. This was not true of Jefferson and his followers. They felt that the sacrifice of a few thousand lives was not too high a price to pay for French liberty.

War between France and England. Early in 1793 France declared war on England. Americans quickly took sides. The Federalists wanted England to win; the Republicans hoped for a French victory. Many Republicans thought we should repay our debt to France by going to war with England.

President Washington was neither pro-French nor pro-British. He believed that the United States was too feeble, too much in need of time to set its own house in order, to risk taking part in a foreign war.

He intended to avoid war at all costs. Neutrality was the only sensible policy for a weak and disunited America. In April, 1793, Washington issued a Proclamation of Neutrality declaring that the United States would take no part in the conflict. The Proclamation was a bitter disappointment to the pro-French faction. They criticized the President unmercifully.

By the treaty of alliance with France, made in 1778, the United States was bound to defend the French West Indies. If the United States did so, it would mean war with Great Britain. Fortunately France did not press us to enter the war. We were more useful to her as a friendly neutral than as a powerless ally.

Disputes with England. With a large pro-French faction shouting that we should fight for France, the President found it hard to preserve our neutrality. Neutrality was all the more difficult because of England's attitude toward the United States.

The British still held a chain of military and trading posts on our soil in the Northwest. They had even built one additional fort there. British officials still sold the Indians firewater and firearms and encouraged them to attack American settlers on the frontier. When the United States complained, England replied that we had not carried out the agreement in the Treaty of Paris regarding debts owed by Americans to British citizens. The fact is, however, that the British wanted to keep the valuable fur trade of the Northwest.

To make matters worse, the British began to seize scores of American ships bound for French ports. She threw their crews into foul dungeons or forced them to serve in the Royal Navy. Even Americans with pro-British leanings condemned these actions, while those who were pro-French shouted louder than ever for war.

John Jay is sent to England. By 1794 the country was on the very brink of war. Yet the government, burdened with a heavy war debt, could not raise money to fight another war. Ninety per cent of our imports came from England, and if the revenue from customs duties was cut off by war, the government would be bankrupt. It could no longer pay interest on its debts or even meet its ordinary running expenses. War would be national suicide.

Washington decided to send a special envoy to England. The brilliant John Jay, Chief Justice of the Supreme Court, was selected to go. Hamilton prepared his instructions. Jay was to patch up the differences that had arisen out of the Treaty of 1783. He was to secure payment for ships seized by the British and to arrange for opening the

THE STORMING OF THE BASTILLE. *Because it was used to detain political pris-*
oners, this old fortress and prison was a symbol of royal power. Its capture, July 14,
1789, by the people of Paris marked the beginning of the French Revolution and caused
widespread rejoicing in the United States. (From Collection Complete des Tableaux,
1789)

British West Indies to American ships. If possible, he was to arrange
a long-needed commercial treaty with England.

Jay's treaty with England. Britain was fighting to the death with
France and would give up nothing that might help her win the war.
She refused to stop seizing American ships bound for French ports, although she promised to pay for seized cargoes of foodstuffs. She also
refused to give American ships full privileges of trading with the British West Indies, although she agreed to complete freedom of trade
between the United States and the British Isles and between the United
States and the British East Indies. Most of the differences arising out
of the Treaty of 1783 were to be settled by arbitration (that is, by discussion between British and American commissioners). Britain gave
in on only one matter of real and immediate importance: she promised
to withdraw from the Western posts within two years. She probably
yielded this from fear that otherwise we might fight.

When Jay's treaty was published, a storm of criticism broke out in
Congress and in the press. Angry Republicans burned images of Jay.

THE FRENCH REVOLUTION *stirred the common people of France. Their hope of liberty was expressed in the great patriotic song, "The Marseillaise," written in 1792 by Rouget de Lisle, a young army captain, in a single night. Enthusiastic crowds marched to the song throughout the Revolution. A modern painter Isodore Pils, shows the composer singing his song.* (Erich S. Herrmann, Inc.)

When Hamilton spoke in defense of the treaty in New York, he was stoned. Washington did not like the treaty, but he knew there was no hope of making a better one. He threw his influence behind it, securing the Senate's approval by a bare two-thirds vote. The pro-French faction criticized him, but his action was undoubtedly wise. It postponed war with England for seventeen years and gave the nation time to grow and find its feet.

Trouble with Spain. Settlers beyond the Appalachians had only one way of sending their products to market — to float them down the Mississippi to New Orleans and there transfer them to ocean-going vessels. When the goods reached New Orleans, the Spanish authorities demanded such heavy taxes that there was no profit. As if this was not enough, Spain refused to accept the southwestern boundary of the United States established in the Treaty of Paris. She had posts on our soil and she stirred up the Indians to murder American settlers. The Westerners believed that the people of the East cared nothing for their difficulties, and became so dissatisfied that they talked of setting

TREATY OF FORT GREENVILLE. *While John Jay was in London, General Anthony Wayne defeated the Indians at Fallen Timbers in northwestern Ohio and gained the greater part of Ohio for the United States.* (Courtesy of Chicago Historical Society)

up a government of their own. Washington was well aware of the danger that the West might leave the Union and wrote: "A touch of a feather would turn them [the Western states] either way." In 1795 he sent Thomas Pinckney on a special mission to Spain.

Pinckney's treaty with Spain. Partly because England had shown a new respect for the United States by making the Jay treaty, Spain also decided to listen to American complaints. Pinckney was able to obtain all that he had been sent to ask — everything that Spain had been refusing for the past twelve years. Spain granted the United States the free use of the Mississippi and the right to land goods at New Orleans free of duty while awaiting ocean-going ships. The boundary dispute was settled, and Spain promised not to stir up the Indians along the frontier. The Pinckney treaty was very popular in America. The Senate approved it unanimously.

Washington retires. When Washington took office, half the territory of the United States was under British and Spanish control. Now, by means of the Jay and Pinckney treaties, the United States had full possession of its soil. The new government was fairly launched, and Washington felt he could safely lay down his burdens. Weary of the bitter criticism he had received and of the cares of public office, he refused to be considered for a third term.

As his second term neared its close, he issued his famous Farewell

Address. In this affectionate message he warned his countrymen against sectionalism, saying that the Union should benefit all sections — North and South, East and West. He criticized the violent spirit shown by the pro-British and pro-French factions. Thinking of our alliance with France, he warned against *permanent* alliances with any foreign nation, and said: "We may safely trust to temporary alliances for extraordinary emergencies." He urged the new nation to use its geographic isolation to develop peacefully into maturity and strength. "If we remain one people under an efficient government," he said, "the time is not far off when we may defy injury from any other nation."

The election of 1796. In 1796 John Adams, candidate of the Federalists, was elected President, while Thomas Jefferson, candidate of the Republicans, became Vice-President. The election of a President and Vice-President of opposite parties happened because the Constitution then stated that the man receiving the largest number of electoral votes would become President and the man receiving the next largest, Vice-President.

Adams was a New Englander of great ability and strong character. He had held a number of important public offices. He admired Washington and hoped to continue the same policies. His one term as President was troubled by serious difficulties with France.

French injuries to American commerce. The French were angered by the Jay treaty, since it allowed England to continue seizing food supplies bound from the United States to France. It seemed to the French that we had become a British ally. They refused to receive a minister sent by Washington in 1796. During the next year they captured over three hundred American ships. While England also hurt our commerce, France injured it far more. The Federalists began to shout for war with France. President Adams kept his temper and sent three special envoys to Paris.

The XYZ affair. Talleyrand, the French Secretary of Foreign Affairs, refused to receive the American envoys unless they agreed to make him a personal gift of $250,000 and arrange a large loan to his government. The commissioners replied to his go-betweens, "No, not a sixpence," and left the country. When he heard of this, Adams told Congress, "I will never send another minister to France without assurance that he will be received, respected, and honored as the representative of a great, free, powerful, and independent nation." He did not name the French go-betweens, but called them Mr. X, Mr. Y, and Mr. Z. This episode is known as the XYZ affair.

JOHN JAY. *After many years of patriotic service to his country Jay became the first chief justice of the United States Supreme Court in 1789. Five years later Washington sent him to London to adjust a serious dispute. The treaty Jay brought back was very unpopular in the United States. The Republicans unjustly accused him of selling his country for British gold.* (From the painting by Joseph Wright, 1786. Courtesy of New York Historical Society)

The story of the insult to our commissioners produced a new wave of resentment toward France. Even the Republicans joined in the cry, "Millions for defense, but not one cent for tribute." A new national song, "Hail, Columbia," became popular almost overnight. The people were no longer pro-French or pro-British, but Americans.

The naval war with France, 1798–1800. Congress prepared to protect American rights by force. Washington was called from retirement to head the army. Our little navy was made ready to fight. Congress authorized the capture of armed French ships. An undeclared naval war followed. In the next two years American sailors captured eighty-five French ships, with the loss of only one American ship. Most of them were taken near the West Indies.

Adams puts country above party. The Federalists were getting

JOHN ADAMS, *second President of the United States. Adams had been a member of the first and second Continental congresses, commissioner to France, minister to England, and Vice-President. Completely patriotic and upright, he did what he thought best for his country. This portrait by John S. Copley was painted in England in 1783 and shows Adams in court dress.* (Courtesy of Fogg Art Museum, Harvard University)

ready for a full-dress war with France. Adams knew he would never be elected to a second term if he held them back. But he saw clearly that the United States was too weak to fight. When he heard that France would receive an American minister respectfully, he appointed three commissioners. Hamilton and other prominent Federalists were furious with the President.

While the American envoys were on the way, Napoleon set himself up as dictator of France. He was glad to settle the quarrel with the United States in order to give all his attention to fighting in Europe. Late in 1800 an agreement was completed by which France and the United States canceled the Treaty of Alliance of 1778. The two governments promised to restore all naval vessels captured, and the United States gave up its claim for damages to American commerce. The treaty saved the United States from war and, by making friends with Napoleon, cleared the way for the purchase of Louisiana.

Adams, by his independence of character and personal courage, had done a great service to his country. He was not re-elected. Though he never again held public office, he had no regrets and years later suggested as his epitaph: "Here lies John Adams, who took upon himself the responsibility of the peace with France in the year 1800."

To identify: Jacobin, John Jay, Napoleon, Thomas Pinckney, Talleyrand. *To explain or define:* arbitration, faction, guillotine.

SUBJECTS FOR TALKS OR WRITTEN REPORTS

1. Why the French people rebelled in 1789. Conditions in France at that time. The reforms demanded. 2. Reforms achieved by the French Revolution. 3. The activities of Citizen Genêt, the first minister sent here by the French Republic. 4. Trouble in the Southwest before the Pinckney treaty with Spain. 5. Our foreign trade during Washington's and Adams' administrations. 6. The public service of John Adams. 7. Why Hamilton wanted war with France. How he brought about the defeat of Adams.

QUESTIONS FOR UNDERSTANDING THE TEXT

1. How did Americans feel about the French Revolution (*a*) in its early stages, (*b*) after it became violent? 2. How did each party feel about the war between France and England? Why did Washington issue the Proclamation of Neutrality? 3. Why did France not call upon us to defend the French West Indies? 4. (*a*) What were our grievances against England? (*b*) What led Washington to send Jay to England? 5. (*a*) Why was England unwilling to grant what we asked? (*b*) What valuable concession did she make? 6. (*a*) How was Jay's treaty received in the United States? (*b*) Why did Washington support the treaty? (*c*) Was his action wise? 7. (*a*) Discuss our difficulties with Spain. (*b*) How did Westerners feel about the situation? 8. State the concessions made by Spain in the Pinckney treaty. 9. What great gain had been made in American foreign relations during Washington's administration? 10. Did Washington warn the United States against making any alliances with foreign nations? Explain. 11. How did it happen that a President and Vice-President of opposite parties were elected in 1796? 12. (*a*) What were our grievances against France? (*b*) Describe the undeclared naval war with France. 13. What was the origin of the saying, "Millions for defense, but not one cent for tribute"? 14. (*a*) How did Adams put country above party? (*b*) What were the consequences to him?

CHAPTER 11

THE PRESIDENCY OF THOMAS JEFFERSON

he Republican sweep in 1800. With the almost solid backing of the South and the West and the support of many poor farmers and mechanics in the North, the Republican party easily won the election of 1800. There was a tie vote between Thomas Jefferson and Aaron Burr for highest place. This was settled in the House of Representatives and Jefferson was chosen President.

The election called attention to the need of a change in the manner of electing a President. Congress passed the Twelfth Amendment, which the states promptly ratified. Hereafter the electors were to cast separate votes for President and Vice-President. The strongest party would be able to elect both of these officials.

With the election of 1800 the Federalists lost control of the national government and never regained it. In their twelve years of power they had served the country well. They put the Constitution into operation, created a judicial system, and firmly established the national government. They arranged to pay off the war debt of the national and state governments. They helped build up commerce and industry. They kept the Union together when it seemed that it would fly apart. They also improved our relations with England, France, and Spain.

The Federalists lost control of the government because they did not sympathize with the common people. They followed policies which benefited special interests — the commercial, investing, and manufacturing classes — and they kept the government in the hands of men of wealth. The common people wanted a greater voice in the government. They looked to the Republican party and its leader, Jefferson, to give it to them.

Jefferson's inauguration, 1801. Jefferson was the first President to be inaugurated at Washington. The new national capital was hardly more than a village of shabby houses. Only one wing of the Capitol building was ready for use. The White House was unfinished, the principal staircase not even begun. The streets were rough, muddy roads through swamps and underbrush.

The inaugural ceremony was very simple, as Jefferson wished it to be. The incoming President did not follow the custom of riding in a coach drawn by four or six horses. He walked from his simple boardinghouse to the new Capitol and there took the oath of office.

He delivered one of the greatest inaugural addresses ever made in the United States. The first part was a plea to the Federalists to forget the bitter feelings they had shown during the campaign. He said that good citizens must recognize the right of the majority to rule, but the majority must not oppress the minority. Political intolerance is as bad as religious intolerance. Republicans and Federalists should unite as Americans in preserving the Union and developing the resources of a great country.

In the remainder of the address he stated his program. The country should have a wise and thrifty government. It should preserve the rights of the states and give equal and exact justice to all. It should seek honest friendship with all nations, but entangling alliances with none. The national debt should be paid and public expenditures reduced. Both agriculture and commerce should be encouraged. Education should be widespread. Personal freedom, freedom of the press and of religion, and trial by juries fairly selected should be safeguarded.

Jefferson's simplicity. Jefferson abolished the aristocratic customs so dear to the Federalists. He gave up the formal weekly receptions held by Washington and Adams. He discouraged the use of titles of honor, like "Excellency." He wished the plain people to feel welcome in the White House and in the offices of the government. To him the poorest citizen was as worthy of respect as the highest officer. The White House during Jefferson's occupancy was as open to visitors as his spacious home in Virginia had always been.

A thrifty administration. To quiet Federalist fears that the South would control the new administration, Jefferson chose two department heads and the Postmaster General from New England. He picked a fellow Virginian, James Madison, to be Secretary of State. Albert Gallatin, of Pennsylvania, was appointed Secretary of the Treasury and has gone down in history as one of the ablest men ever to fill that position.

The Republicans had promised to repeal the unpopular excise taxes and to reduce government expenditures. They promptly repealed the excise taxes. As an economy measure Jefferson carried out steps begun by President Adams to reduce the size of the army and navy. Believing that for us a navy was only a toy, he planned to build a dock where

MONTICELLO, *Jefferson's beautiful home at Charlottesville, Virginia, was designed by Jefferson and shows his fondness for the classical style of architecture. The doors of Monticello were always open to visitors. As many as thirty guests sometimes slept there. His hospitality was one of the reasons that Jefferson died a poor man.* (Brown Brothers)

THE WHITE HOUSE IN 1799. *President Washington approved the site for the new capital city in 1791. Although Major L'Enfant, a French architect who had fought in the Revolution, had already drawn up the plans which were to make Washington one of the most beautiful cities in the world, the new city was only a village with muddy streets when the government moved there in 1801. This drawing, done by N. King, shows the White House with three instead of two stories.* (Courtesy of Library of Congress)

it could be "laid up dry and under cover from the sun." This would cut the cost of maintaining it to the lowest figure. Gallatin worked out a budget with a yearly surplus for reducing the national debt. In eight years he cut the debt from eighty million to fifty-two and a half million dollars in addition to providing fifteen million for the purchase of Louisiana. This thrifty policy pleased the people.

Aid to education. Jefferson was America's great champion of liberty, democracy, and public education. He believed that liberty and democracy both depend upon popular education. While Jefferson was President, he signed many bills giving land to the states for the creation of schools and colleges. For example, when Ohio was admitted to the Union in 1803, the federal government gave it one thirty-second of the public land in its borders for educational purposes. A similar gift was made to every state which afterward joined the Union.

The first Republican Congress introduced a custom which helped in the political education of our people. Up to that time newspaper reporters were not permitted to comment on what happened in Congress. One Speaker of the House expelled two newspapermen for reporting speeches. The Republicans gave reporters desks on the floor, with full privileges of reporting everything that went on.

The Tripolitan War. Jefferson always opposed war when it could be avoided, and for this reason his enemies called him a coward. Yet, when necessary, he defended American rights by force. The rulers of the Barbary states — Algiers, Tunis, Tripoli, and Morocco — had long been in the habit of seizing ships which passed their shores. England and other European powers regularly gave handsome presents to these rulers in return for the promise not to seize their ships. The United States was at first too weak to follow a bolder policy. In ten years our State Department had sent over two million dollars to buy off the pirates.

Jefferson determined to try force. But before he could do so, the ruler of Tripoli, dissatisfied with the amount he was receiving, declared war on the United States. Jefferson sent a small squadron of ships to the Mediterranean. For four years (1801–1805) the little navy of the United States struggled bravely with the difficult problems of war in a distant sea. It learned many lessons of naval warfare, and a body of young naval officers received valuable experience. In 1805 the ruler of Tripoli promised that American ships would not be bothered, and the Tripolitan War came to an end. Our victory had a good effect on the rulers of the other Barbary states, for they saw that it was

BOMBARDMENT OF TRIPOLI *by the United States Navy, August 3, 1804. The little American fleet was led by the famous warship,* Constitution. *The attack was indecisive because the enemy had more guns and more ships.* (From the painting by Corne, 1805. Courtesy of United States Naval Academy Museum)

better not to risk war with America. Meanwhile the Republicans looked upon the navy with more favor and increased its strength.

The problem of internal improvements. In the older states private turnpike companies were being chartered to build roads and bridges, with the privilege of collecting tolls from the users. The states usually gave these companies the right of way (the land on which the road was built) and part of the cost of construction. In New York alone, some eighty-eight companies built more than three thousand miles of turnpikes in the years 1800–1807.

The people of Kentucky, Tennessee, and Ohio could not raise enough by taxes to build the needed roads and bridges. Although the population of these states was increasing rapidly, it was still so small that no private company was interested in building toll roads. The settlers therefore looked to the national government for help. Jefferson, always sympathetic to the needs of small farmers, felt that the government should give the desired aid. Gallatin agreed. He realized that improvements would increase the sale of public lands in the West and thus bring revenue to the national treasury.

Gallatin drew up a plan for roads, canals, and river improvements to knit together the East and the West. He recommended that the gov-

OLD TOLLHOUSE *on the Cumberland Road near Frostburg, Maryland. In 1831–1834 Congress turned parts of this national road over to the states through which it passed. The states then collected tolls for its use.* (Courtesy of Public Roads Administration)

ernment spend twenty million dollars to aid in these projects. Congress did not act on much of his plan. However, in 1806 Congress authorized the building of a national road from Cumberland, Maryland, to Wheeling, West Virginia.

The purchase of Louisiana, 1803. Settlers were moving westward in an unending stream. A few thousand had crossed the Mississippi into what was then Spanish territory. By 1800 many Americans believed that sooner or later the United States would acquire the land west of the Mississippi. They knew that Spain was weak and could not long oppose the expansion of the United States. When news came, in 1801, that Napoleon had forced the Spanish government to give the great area called Louisiana back to France, the West was afire with excitement. The mighty Napoleon would be a dangerous neighbor. His plans to build a world empire were well known. By taking possession of Louisiana he would not only block the expansion of the United States beyond the Mississippi, but also would be in a position to seize American territory between the Mississippi and the Appalachians. If he did no more than close the port of New Orleans, he would strike a heavy blow at our Western settlers. Thoroughly alarmed, they demanded action to prevent French occupation of Louisiana; some urged that the United States seize the territory.

FAIRVIEW INN. *Traffic outside the inn near Baltimore in the early 1800's. The Conestoga wagons belong to settlers going west. Note the cattle being driven to market and the stagecoach. This picture was painted by a modern artist.* (Courtesy of Maryland Historical Society)

Jefferson instructed Robert Livingston, our minister to France, to tell the French government that if France took possession of Louisiana, the friendship between the two nations would be destroyed. "There is on the globe," wrote Jefferson, "one single spot the possessor of which is our natural and habitual enemy. It is New Orleans, through which the produce of three eighths of our territory must pass to market. . . . The day that France takes possession of New Orleans . . . we must marry ourselves to the British fleet and nation."

If necessary, Jefferson intended to make an alliance with England. But first he tried to reach a peaceful settlement with France. He told Livingston to find out whether Napoleon would sell New Orleans and any land east of the Mississippi which was included in Louisiana. To impress the French government that the United States was serious, Jefferson sent his friend, James Monroe, to Paris to assist Livingston.

The President's message convinced Napoleon that if he took possession of Louisiana, the United States and England would unite against him. Besides, he was about to renew the war in Europe, and he urgently needed money. Abruptly he offered the United States the whole of Louisiana for fifteen million dollars. Livingston and Monroe were astonished by the offer. They realized that the territory was a wonderful bargain. They had no instructions to buy an empire, but their courage was equal to the occasion, and they accepted.

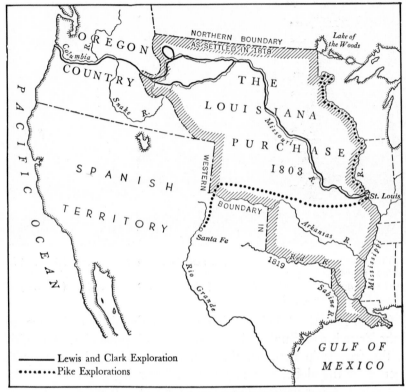

LOUISIANA PURCHASE AND EXPLORATION

The purchase of Louisiana was the most important event in Jefferson's Presidency. He took keen interest in having the new territory explored and chose his secretary, Captain Meriwether Lewis, to head the expedition up the Missouri and down the Columbia River. Pike explored the Mississippi River and the Southwest. Both the Lewis and Clark and the Pike exploring expeditions suffered severe hardships yet brought back valuable information.

According to the agreement with Napoleon, the inhabitants of Louisiana were to be admitted into the Union as soon as possible. This meant that new states would be created by the method provided in the Northwest Ordinance. Angry protests burst from the Federalists. They feared that an increase in the number of Western states would lead to the permanent control of the country by the agricultural rather than the commercial interests and that the Republican party would be able to remain in power forever. They said Louisiana was a worthless wilderness. Forgetting their former interest in loose construction, they claimed that the Constitution gave the government no authority to buy additional territory.

Jefferson was pleased with the amazing bargain made by Livingston and Monroe, but he was also troubled. He believed in a strict interpretation of the Constitution and felt that the federal government was without power to purchase territory. Accordingly, he wrote an amendment to the Constitution authorizing the purchase. His friends told him that passing an amendment would take too much time, since Napoleon might change his mind at any moment. They argued that since the Constitution granted the power of making war and treaties, it implied the power to acquire territory, because territory is frequently acquired by war or treaty. This, of course, was the doctrine of *loose construction,* or *implied powers,* to which Jefferson had been firmly opposed. In spite of his doubts he sent the treaty to the Senate, where it was promptly approved. The amendment to legalize the purchase was never passed. In the general rejoicing that greeted the treaty, few cared whether or not it was constitutional.

How large the new territory was, no one knew. Whether it included West Florida and Texas was not at all clear. According to the treaty of purchase the United States obtained "the colony or province of Louisiana with the same extent that it now has in the hands of Spain, and that it had when France possessed it [prior to 1763], and such as it should be after the treaties subsequently [later] entered into between Spain and other states." Uncertainty as to the boundaries of the land we had bought was to disturb our relations with Spain for years.

The Louisiana Purchase doubled the area of the United States. It gave the nation full possession of the Mississippi Valley, with its great river system and the valuable port of New Orleans. The population of the Louisiana territory at the time of purchase was about fifty thousand; a century later it was four hundred times greater — twenty million. The territory has been the source of immense wealth to the United States. Within a century its farm lands, among the richest in the world, were valued at seven billion dollars — five hundred times the price paid to Napoleon.

Exploring the new territory. Jefferson's interest in science led him years earlier to suggest that the United States explore the vast region beyond the Mississippi River. When he became President, he secured funds from Congress for this purpose and arranged for an expedition of thirty-five men, led by Meriwether Lewis and William Clark (a brother of the Revolutionary hero, George Rogers Clark). In 1804 the expedition went up the Missouri River into what is now North

LEWIS AND CLARK *at Three Forks, where three rivers (which they named the Jef-*
ferson, Madison, and Gallatin) unite to make the Missouri. Sacajawea, the remarkable
Indian woman who served as a guide for the expedition, is shown pointing the way.
(From the painting by E. S. Paxson in the State Capitol, Helena, Montana)

Dakota, where they spent the winter. The next spring they found
passes through the Rocky Mountains and followed the Columbia River
to the Pacific coast. Their explorations gave the United States a claim
to the Oregon country.

Another expedition, led by Lieutenant Zebulon Pike, started out a
few weeks after Lewis and Clark's expedition to trace the Mississippi
and the Red rivers to their sources. Pike discovered the Royal Gorge
of the Arkansas River and the mountain peak in Colorado which bears
his name. Like Lewis and Clark, he brought back with him valuable
observations of the climate, animal and plant life, and the Indian tribes
in the region explored, and a remarkable tale of hardship and adventure.

The re-election of Jefferson, 1804. Throughout his first term as
President Jefferson grew in popularity. He tried to please all sections;
he promoted internal improvements; he protected trade from the Barbary pirates; his Secretary of the Treasury was managing the country's
finances with remarkable skill, and the national debt was being steadily
cut. He got Congress to encourage immigration by a liberal naturalization law. He promoted land settlement by purchasing land from
the Indians and helping them move westward. He made the national
government more democratic. Most pleasing of all, he bought from
France a million square miles of fertile land.

Federalist leaders might grumble that the nation was being ruined by the Republicans, but the people did not believe it. As a matter of fact, Jefferson had continued most of the important policies of Washington and Adams and had kept in office most of the Federalists they had appointed. The country was prosperous; road building was going forward everywhere; a sense of national pride and greater things to come was in the air. In the election of 1804 Jefferson was re-elected by a tremendous majority.

England and France interfere with our commerce. Foreign relations troubled Jefferson's second term. France and England were again locked in a life-and-death struggle. Unable to defeat Napoleon on land, England hoped to blockade him into giving up. She did not recognize the right claimed by neutral countries of trading with her enemies. She ordered all neutral ships bound for France to stop first at a British port and secure a license. No contraband (articles necessary for war) could be carried to France, and contraband included foodstuffs. Napoleon then declared he would seize any ship which touched at a British port or submitted to search by a British warship. America protested, but neither the French nor the English paid any attention.

Both of the warring countries needed American foodstuffs and were willing to pay high prices for them. If one ship in three got to its destination and back again, the profits more than made up for the loss of the other two. In spite of the risks, American trade with France and England increased.

Between 1803 and 1812 the British captured 917 of our ships, while France captured 558. Seizures by the French were fewer than those by the British only because the French had far less sea power. Neither paid any attention to American rights.

The impressment of seamen. Just as irritating as the interference with our trade was the impressment of American sailors. England was in great need of sailors for her navy. Yet the men of her fleet were so ill-fed, ill-treated, and ill-paid that it was impossible to obtain crews by voluntary enlistment. Press gangs went about the ports of Great Britain seizing men to serve in the navy. Many seamen deserted at the first opportunity and were particularly glad to sign up on American ships.

The British claimed the right of searching our vessels anywhere and taking off British subjects. Often their warships cruised just outside American ports, stopping all ships coming in or going out. In many cases it was difficult for British officers to tell whether a sailor was an

Englishman or an American. Moreover, American naturalization papers were not accepted by England, for she insisted that no one born under her flag could become a citizen of another country. The result was that thousands of sailors born in the United States or naturalized in our courts were taken by the British. France also practiced impressment and refused to recognize American naturalization papers. However, hardly any French citizens served on our ships, and France did not find it worth while to search for them.

Popular anger against England was further increased when, in 1807, a British man-of-war, the *Leopard*, stopped an American frigate, the *Chesapeake*, a few miles out of Norfolk, Virginia, claiming that British deserters were aboard. When the American captain denied there were deserters and refused to allow a search, the *Leopard* fired three broadsides into the *Chesapeake*, wounding eighteen sailors and killing three. Officers of the *Leopard* then boarded the *Chesapeake* and took four so-called deserters. The act of firing on an American warship and taking off individuals by force was a serious matter. President Jefferson would have had the American people with him had he immediately asked Congress to declare war. "Never since the battle of Lexington," he wrote, "have I seen this country in such a state of exasperation."

Jefferson's efforts to avoid war. Jefferson was determined to avoid war. Again and again he asked England to give up impressing men from our vessels. He ordered all British warships to remain outside American waters. He urged Congress to keep American goods, ships, and sailors at home. This would prevent incidents likely to lead to war. Also, the cutting off of American trade with both France and England might make these countries give up the practices to which we objected. Accordingly Congress passed the Embargo Act (December, 1807), which stopped all American trade with foreign ports.

Effects of the embargo. The Embargo Act did not have the effect intended. Napoleon looked upon it as helpful to him. Since his navy was so weak that he could not keep American ships from sailing to British ports, he was glad to have the American government do this for him. Napoleon now claimed that any American ships which found their way into European harbors were not American but British ships in disguise. So he captured them. As for Great Britain, the embargo had no effect on her policy; she refused to move from the position she had taken.

The embargo was disastrous to the United States. In 1808 exports

THOMAS JEFFERSON *at the age of seventy-nine. Still a vigorous thinker, he was busy with the establishment of the University of Virginia.* (From the painting by Thomas Sully. Courtesy of United States Military Academy)

dropped to one fifth of what they had been in 1807. Many exporters and shipowners were ruined; others became smugglers. About one hundred and fifty thousand men (mostly sailors, merchants, bookkeeppers, and longshoremen) lost their jobs. Farm prices tumbled because the farmers could not ship their grain, meat, cotton, and tobacco abroad. Hard times spread throughout the country. There was so much opposition that after a year's trial the embargo was repealed.

Jefferson retires. Although Jefferson could easily have been re-elected, he refused a third term. He believed that in a democracy officials should be changed frequently, and wished to follow Washington's example in serving only two terms. Besides, he was heartily weary of office. "Never," he wrote to a friend, "did a prisoner released from his chains feel such relief as I shall on shaking off the shackles of power. Nature intended me for the more tranquil pursuits of science by rendering them my supreme delight."

ROTUNDA OF THE UNIVERSITY OF VIRGINIA. *This beautiful building was de-signed by Thomas Jefferson to be the central building of the university.* (Courtesy of University of Virginia)

After his Presidency Jefferson lived quietly at Monticello, spending much of his time in writing letters and advising government leaders. He corresponded with many learned Europeans regarding scientific matters. He was for many years president of the American Philosophical Society, the most important organization of the time for the promotion of science. He persuaded the Virginia legislature to found the University of Virginia, and he himself laid out its campus, chose the first faculty, and outlined the curriculum. In his old age he wrote the inscription for his tombstone, not mentioning the high offices he had held in the state and national government. It tells us the things by which this great man wished to be remembered. "Here was buried Thomas Jefferson, Author of the Declaration of Independence, of the Statute of Virginia for Religious Freedom, and Father of the University of Virginia."

To identify: William Clark, Albert Gallatin, Meriwether Lewis, Robert Livingston, Zebulon Pike.

To explain or define: broadside, contraband, embargo, impressment, internal improvements, longshoremen, naturalization, press gang, right of way, turnpike.

SUBJECTS FOR TALKS OR WRITTEN REPORTS

1. How Federalist leaders tried to steal the election of 1800. 2. Jefferson's preparation for the Presidency. His influence on the government of Virginia. 3. Jefferson's life after he left the White House. His wide correspondence. His efforts to establish the University of Virginia. 4. Aaron Burr's conspiracy against the United States. 5. The story of the Lewis and Clark expedition; of the Pike expedition. 6. The building of the Cumberland Road, its cost and its value. 7. Why British sailors often deserted and took jobs on American ships. 8. How the Federalists felt about the Embargo Act.

QUESTIONS FOR UNDERSTANDING THE TEXT

1. What improvement was made by the Twelfth Amendment in the manner of electing the President and Vice-President? 2. (*a*) What had the Federalists accomplished in their twelve years in office? (*b*) Why did they lose control of the government? 3. (*a*) How did Jefferson show his democracy in the White House? (*b*) In his support of education? 4. (*a*) What did Jefferson think of our need for a navy? (*b*) What events caused him to change his view? 5. (*a*) What caused the war with Tripoli? (*b*) What did it accomplish? 6. (*a*) Why did Westerners want the national government to help with building roads and waterways? (*b*) What did Gallatin recommend? (*c*) What national road did Congress authorize? 7. (*a*) Describe the circumstances which prompted France to sell, and the United States to buy, the Louisiana Territory. (*b*) What did this purchase have to do with "loose" or "strict" construction? (*c*) Why did the Federalists now adopt the doctrine of strict construction? 8. (*a*) Of what value was the Louisiana Territory to the United States? (*b*) Without this territory could the United States have reached the Pacific? 9. How did the United States establish a claim to the Oregon country? 10. Account for Jefferson's great popularity at the end of his first term. 11. (*a*) How did England and France interfere with our commerce? (*b*) Which captured more of our ships? Why? 12. (*a*) Explain the practice of impressment. (*b*) Why did it cause so much resentment in America? (*c*) Describe the *Chesapeake-Leopard* incident. (*d*) How did it affect American public opinion? 13. (*a*) How did Jefferson seek to avoid war? (*b*) How did the Embargo Act affect (1) British policy, (2) France, (3) American shippers, (4) the price of American farm products? 14. For what three things did Jefferson wish to be remembered?

JAMES MADISON. *Like Washington, Jefferson, and Monroe, Madison was a Virginian. Like them he spent many years in the service of his state and his country. He is described as "a small man, quiet, somewhat precise in manner, pleasant, fond of conversation, with a certain mixture of ease and dignity in his address."* (From the painting by Gilbert Stuart. Courtesy of Bowdoin Museum of Fine Arts)

"DOLLY" MADISON. *Her charm and popularity made her home the center of Washington society. When the British marched on Washington in 1814 and the government fled, she saved some of the White House silver, papers, and other valuables by carrying them with her.* (From the painting by Gilbert Stuart. Courtesy of Pennsylvania Academy of Fine Arts)

CHAPTER 12

THE WAR OF 1812

M*adison becomes President, 1808.* Jefferson used his great influence in the Republican party to secure the nomination of James Madison, his Secretary of State. Madison easily won, for the South and West were loyal to the Republican party. Madison had studious habits and a retiring manner. He never became a great popular leader. He was a lover of peace, and if, like Jefferson, he had been master of his party, there would probably have been no war during his Presidency.

Problems faced by Madison. The new President faced the same difficult foreign problems with which Jefferson had been struggling. Both France and England were seizing many American ships. British ships lay in wait outside our ports, searching every vessel that came out for deserters from the British navy. Sometimes the British took sailors from ships within our harbors. Often they forced native Americans into the hard service of the British navy.

Nonintercourse. Three days before Madison became President, Congress repealed the Embargo Act. A milder measure, the Nonintercourse Act, was passed in its place. This Act permitted American ships to trade with all foreign countries except Great Britain and France. A year later the Macon Act was passed. This Act repealed nonintercourse with the two nations and stated that if either of them would agree to stop interfering with our commerce, we would stop trading with the other.

Napoleon took advantage of this offer, with the idea of leading the United States into war with England. He gave notice that France had removed her restrictions on our trade. Congress then prohibited trade with England. Napoleon did not keep his word. Knowing this, England complained that we had taken Napoleon's side and were no longer neutral. She refused to give up her blockade, since it was her best weapon against France. New Englanders sympathized with England, but Southerners and Westerners, supposing that France had really stopped interfering with our commerce, grew more and more angry with England.

The "War Hawks." In 1810 many Southern and Western papers, dissatisfied with our peaceful policy, urged that stronger representatives be sent to Congress. The voters, too, wanted a change; consequently, over half the next House of Representatives consisted of new men. The Republicans had a very large majority, led by a group of fiery young frontiersmen who wanted war. They had unlimited faith in the future of their country. With youthful enthusiasm they declared that it would be easy for America to overpower England. They hinted at the opportunity of conquering Canada and Florida. John Randolph, a Virginian who had seen long service in Congress, named these warlike young Congressmen the "War Hawks." The leader of the War Hawks was Henry Clay, of Kentucky. When Congress met in November, 1811, Henry Clay was chosen Speaker of the House, a position of great influence. He at once appointed War Hawks to the principal committees.

Portions of President Madison's annual message dealing with our troubles with England were brought to the attention of the House Committee on Foreign Affairs. Most of the members of this committee were War Hawks, and they prepared a warlike report. The report urged the seizing of Canada to make up for the losses inflicted on American shipping and spoke of Canada's wealth, her people's discontent with British rule, and the ease with which Canada could be conquered.

The report accused British fur traders of stirring up the Indians along the frontier and declared that Indian attacks would continue until Canada was ours. Said Grundy, a young Tennessean: "We shall drive the British from our continent — they shall not longer have an opportunity of intriguing with our Indian neighbors and setting on the ruthless savage to tomahawk our women and children."

John Randolph attacked the report in a sarcastic speech. He suggested that the War Hawks had their eyes on the profitable Canadian fur trade. He doubted that the British were responsible for the troubles with the Indians, saying that the frontiersmen had given the red men more than enough cause to fight. He ridiculed the recklessness of the war "boys" and their failure to consider the cost of the war. "It seems this is to be a holiday campaign — there is to be no expense of blood and treasure on our part — Canada is to be subdued by the principle of fraternity."

BATTLE OF TIPPECANOE, *November 7, 1811. Led by an able Shawnee chief,
Tecumseh, the Indians of the Northwest tried to stop the steady advance of the white
race. An army led by General William H. Harrison defeated the red men at Tippecanoe,
but in so doing suffered heavy losses. Because the Indians had obtained arms and ammunition from Canada the settlers of the Northwest blamed England for this bloodshed.*
(From the painting by Alonzo Chappel for *Battles of the United States*, New York,
1858)

Other Federalists were strongly against the report, making it plain
that the Northeast did not want to fight to defend its commerce. Said
Congressman Stowe of New York: "We are told that commerce must
be protected. From whom does this come? Have the shipowners
asked for your assistance? Are there any petitions from merchants on
your tables? No . . . It is remarkable that this spirit of protecting
commerce has come from the interior. It is not from the shipowners,
but from the men furthest removed from ships. When a man rises
in this House you may almost tell how ardent he will be by knowing
how far distant he lives from the sea. . . . But how are we going to
protect commerce? . . . by taking Canada?"

Preparations for war. However, the majority of Congress was for
war. Congress spent the winter of 1812 trying to make the necessary
preparations. Its members were opposed to any new taxes, thinking
the war should be paid for by borrowing money. Nor did they wish
to establish a large regular army, preferring to depend on volunteers
and the state militia. Congress finally authorized an army of thirty-

five thousand regulars, in addition to fifty thousand volunteers **not to** be used beyond the frontiers.

Most Republicans saw no need of enlarging the navy; they wanted to limit the fight with England to a land war. Clay, however, argued for a larger navy. He attempted to win over his fellow Westerners by showing them that warships were needed to protect the mouth of the Mississippi. In spite of his efforts a bill to enlarge the navy was defeated.

When spring came, only the Federalists seemed to realize how little had been accomplished in getting ready for war. The sharp-tongued Randolph again expressed their feelings when he lashed out on May 6: "Go to war without money, without men, without a navy! Go to war when we have not the courage . . . to lay war taxes."

Was war necessary? A few weeks before war was declared, a group of moderate Republicans urged the President to send a special commission to England to make one more try for peace. At first he planned to follow this suggestion, but a more warlike group persuaded him not to do so. Thus he allowed himself to be carried along by the war party, although he did not desire war.

England did not want war with the United States. Weakened by nearly twenty years of war with France, all her strength was needed to bring that struggle to a successful finish. For months her people had been asking their government to give in to the United States. They had suffered severely from our nonintercourse policy, which caused food prices in England to skyrocket. And they were very eager for peace. Finally, on June 16, two days before our declaration of war, the Prime Minister announced that the restrictions to which the United States objected would be repealed. Had there been a cable in those days, war might have been avoided. If Madison had sent special envoys to England when he was urged to do so, there surely would have been no war.

War is declared. On June 18, 1812, Congress declared war on England. The vote showed a sharp division of opinion — 79 to 49 in the House, and 19 to 13 in the Senate. Practically all of those voting for war were Republicans, and practically all of them lived south of New York State. It was perfectly plain that the commercial and shipping interests did not want war.

While the desire for Canada was perhaps the main reason that dragged the country into war, there is no question that the United States had real grievances against Great Britain. Madison stated these

BATTLE OF LUNDY'S LANE, *July 25, 1814. This battle, which took place a mile from Niagara Falls, ended the American effort to take Canada. The English and American troops fought fiercely and both sides lost many men.* (From the painting by Alonzo Chappel for *Battles of the United States*, New York, 1858)

in his war message to Congress: (1) impressment of American sailors, (2) the hovering of British war vessels on our coast, (3) the blockade, (4) the Indian uprising of 1811, which Madison said was prompted by the British. All of these except the last might also have been given as a cause for war with France.

A divided country. News of the declaration of war was greeted enthusiastically in frontier sections. It was received coldly in New Jersey, New York, Connecticut, Rhode Island, and Massachusetts, where opinion was almost solidly against the war. The governor of Massachusetts proclaimed a day of mourning, because the war would help Napoleon. When Congress asked for one hundred thousand militia, Massachusetts and Connecticut refused to furnish their share. The merchants and bankers of the Northeast would not subscribe to the national loans. It was Mr. Madison's war, they said, and he could pay the bills.

Our unready army. When war began, the regular army consisted of only sixty-seven hundred men, mostly located at frontier posts from which they could not be withdrawn. A new army had to be recruited, trained, equipped, and provided with officers. The lack of trained, experienced officers was an enormous handicap. Short enlistments also interfered with developing a trained, seasoned army. Congress repeated most of the mistakes made during the Revolutionary War and made one mistake which had been avoided then — it failed to place one general in supreme command.

The struggle for Canada. The war party thought it would be easy to take Canada. Henry Clay boasted to Congress, "The militia of Kentucky alone are competent to place Montreal and upper Canada at your feet."

Canada had less than five hundred thousand people, while the United States had nearly eight million. But the Canadians did not want to join the United States, and they fought hard. They had the help of several thousand British regulars and several thousand Indians. However, their greatest protection was the wilderness which lay between their settlements and ours.

In 1812 three American expeditions were sent to capture strategic points (places of military value) on the Great Lakes. One column of two thousand men surrendered at Detroit. This gave the British control of the entire Michigan country and left the frontier open to Indian raids. Another column, consisting of four thousand New York militia, failed when three fourths of the men refused to cross the Niagara River into Canada. A third column sent against Montreal also failed because the militia would not leave American soil. The soldiers did not lack courage, but they were poorly equipped and had no confidence in their officers. Then, too, they believed that militia could not be called upon to serve outside the United States.

William Henry Harrison now took command of a new and much larger force. In the fall of 1813 he recaptured Detroit and pursued the British a short distance into Canada. This success was made possible when Commodore Oliver Perry, with ships built by his men on the spot, cleared Lake Erie of British warships. Another expedition sent against Montreal that autumn accomplished nothing. A final attempt to invade Canada in the summer of 1814 also failed.

The war on the high seas. At the beginning of the war the American navy consisted of sixteen ships; and the British navy, of six hundred. American naval officers and seamen were among the best in the world. In a series of brilliant single-ship actions, the Americans defeated equal or heavier British vessels. They destroyed or captured two hundred fifty-four naval and merchant ships before the war ended. The navy was assisted by nearly five hundred privateers, which cap-

THE *CONSTITUTION* DEFEATS THE *JAVA*. *This engagement took place off the coast of Brazil near the close of 1812. The success of the* Constitution *in withstanding enemy fire gave it the familiar nickname of "Old Ironsides."* (From the painting by Carlton T. Chapman, 1897. Courtesy of New York Historical Society)

THE BATTLE OF LAKE ERIE. *Captain Oliver Perry was given the responsibility of building a fleet and clearing Lake Erie of British warships. On September 10, 1813, after a fierce battle, Perry was completely victorious and sent the famous message, "We have met the enemy, and they are ours." This battle gave the Americans control of Lake Erie, enabled General Harrison to recapture Detroit, and kept the Northwest Territory under the flag of the United States.* (From the painting by Thomas Birch, Courtesy of Pennsylvania Academy of Fine Arts)

tured over thirteen hundred prizes, valued at thirty-nine million dollars.

The British blockade. In the end the British navy drove the American navy off the seas and established a tight blockade of our coast. Our commerce practically stopped. The entire country felt the effects. The farmers grew crops which they could not sell and paid very high prices for the necessities which they bought. Receipts from customs duties fell to almost nothing, and the United States government could not pay its bills. As a result of the blockade merchants and ship-owners became more strongly opposed to the war than ever. Federalist leaders in the Northeast talked openly of joining the British in order to stop the war.

The British offensive. Napoleon was overthrown in 1814. The British were then able to send re-enforcements to Canada. In August ten thousand veterans started from Montreal, expecting to invade the United States by way of Lake Champlain, just as Burgoyne had done in 1777. (See page 77.) The British and the Americans each had a small fleet on the lake. The British commander expected an easy victory, since his ships had double the fighting strength of the American ships, due to larger guns. But he was no match for the young American commander, Captain Thomas MacDonough. MacDonough won a complete victory and destroyed the British squadron. With the waterway in American hands the British army had to retreat. MacDonough's brilliant success caused an outburst of joy throughout the United States.

The British had full control of our coast, being able to land raiding parties almost anywhere they liked. They raided a number of coastal villages and forced others to give ransom. They "annexed" eastern Maine to Canada. In August, 1814, a British fleet entered Chesapeake Bay and landed an army of four thousand men. The army advanced inland to Washington without meeting serious opposition. No preparations had been made to defend the capital. The government fled, and the British burned the public buildings in revenge for American destruction of public buildings in Toronto a year earlier. The British then embarked and moved on Baltimore. Here they met determined and well-organized resistance. After bombarding the city and landing troops, they were forced to give up the attempt to seize it. It was during this battle that Francis Scott Key was inspired to write the "Star-Spangled Banner." After this the British made ready to attack New Orleans.

The United States almost bankrupt. A visitor who saw President Madison in the fall of 1814 described him as miserably shattered and unhappy. The situation of the country might have made any American feel gloomy. The Secretary of War reported that the army ranks could be filled only by a draft, while Congress insisted that a free nation must rely on volunteers. The Secretary of the Treasury announced that the government could not pay the interest on its debts and that the treasury was empty. Government bonds were selling for fifty or sixty cents on the dollar. Since it looked as though the United States would be unable to defend itself, the states began building state armies. Most alarming of all, a convention of delegates met at Hartford in December, 1814, to consider a separate peace for the New England states. Their meeting is known in history as the "Hartford Convention."

With the Union showing signs of breaking up, with British squadrons commanding the entrance to our ports, with much of Maine and part of western New York under British rule, and with a large army of British veterans preparing to attack New Orleans, there were good reasons for wanting to make peace. Fortunately the British, too, desired peace. After twenty-two years of war in Europe, they were thoroughly tired of fighting.

The Treaty of Ghent. Early in the war Madison sent a commission abroad to be ready to make peace whenever it had an opportunity. In August, 1814, the American representatives met British representatives at Ghent. The two peace commissions disagreed on almost everything except that both wanted peace. After five months of discussion, they arranged a "peace without victory." The American commissioners could not obtain a settlement of the questions of impressment, search, and blockades, but trusted, now that England and France were at peace, that these difficulties were over. The British abandoned the United States territory that their armies occupied and gave up their demand for a neutral Indian country between the United States and Canada. The treaty was signed at Ghent on Christmas Eve, 1814. News of the signing arrived in the United States forty-nine days later.

Jackson's victory at New Orleans. Two weeks after peace was made at Ghent, the greatest battle of the war was fought at New Orleans. General Andrew Jackson, a Tennessean and a noted Indian fighter, was in charge of defending New Orleans. He had a force of forty-five hundred frontiersmen hastily summoned from the South-

NEW ORLEANS *soon after it became part of the United States. When the British attacked the city in 1815, the citizens defended it with vigor. Louisiana pirates, led by Jean Lafitte, also fought the British. The battle helped make General Andrew Jackson famous.* (Painted by Boqueta de Woisseri. Courtesy of American Geographical Society, New York)

west. His men threw up breastworks, while eight thousand British veterans advanced from the coast across the swamps. On January 8, 1815, as the British charged over open ground before the city, they met withering rifle fire. Twice they rallied, and each time they were driven back. That day the British lost two thousand killed and wounded, while the Americans lost only sixty-three. Jackson's great victory made him the hero of the war. It caused Americans to forget the many defeats on land and the blunders which had caused them. It showed that Americans could defeat some of the best-trained soldiers in the world. Finally, it gave the Westerners new pride in themselves and encouraged them to seek a greater share in the national government.

Results of the war. According to the peace treaty, nothing had been changed by the War of 1812. The grievances that led the United States to declare war were not so much as mentioned. Yet the war had important results. Americans gave up the hope they had held ever since the Declaration of Independence that Canada would become part of the United States. They also gave up the notion that the United States had no need for a navy and a regular army. The war had shown

CHAPTER 13

THE TRIUMPH OF NATIONALISM

A*nation free to work out its own destiny.* The War of 1812 marks the close of a period in American history. From 1789 to 1815 the national government had been greatly concerned with foreign affairs. As we have seen, the long struggle between France and England had created many problems for the young United States and had finally led to war against England. The overthrow of Napoleon and the close of the War of 1812 left our nation free to turn its back on Europe and occupy itself mainly with home affairs.

The Republicans become nationalistic. The "revolution of 1800," which had brought Jefferson into power, was based on distrust of a strong central government. But events since 1800, especially the war with England, had taught the Republicans that a strong central government was necessary and that it need not destroy liberty. The old Republicans had considered the army and navy as useless and destructive of liberty; now everyone agreed that the nation should be armed. The spirit of nationalism had triumphed over the spirit of localism and states' rights.

The change in Republican ideas could be seen in Madison's annual message to Congress in 1815. This former upholder of states' rights called for new warships, a standing army, national aid for building roads and canals, a protective tariff, and the re-establishment of a national bank. Congress carried out these recommendations. As a New England congressman remarked, the Republicans were "out-Federalizing Federalism."

Adoption of a protective tariff. During the war the tariff had been doubled in order to raise funds, with the understanding that a year after the war the rates would be cut to their old level (about 10 per cent). After the war the manufacturers called on Congress to continue the wartime rates in order to discourage imports from abroad. The Republicans, who had once firmly opposed a protective tariff (see pages 124–125), now thought the government should encourage manufacturing in order to make the nation self-sufficient. They hoped that factories would soon spring up in all parts of the country. Meanwhile, the growth of manufacturing would mean larger cities and a better market for farm products. So they supported a bill to continue the wartime tariff rates. Even Jefferson was for it. He wrote: "We must now place the manufacturer by the side of the agriculturalist. . . . He who is now against domestic manufacture must be for reducing us either to dependence . . . or to be clothed in skins and to live like wild beasts in the dens of caverns."

Henry Clay, of Kentucky, argued for the bill as part of an "American system" of high tariffs and internal improvements (roads, canals, and the like). He wanted the revenue from the tariff to be used for road building in the West. He thought more manufacturing would mean higher prices for farm products and that the "American system" would benefit all sections of the country. However, New England importers and shipowners were against the tariff bill, since it would reduce trade between the United States and Europe. In spite of their opposition the Tariff Act of 1816 passed with a large majority.

The second Bank of the United States. The new attitude of the Republicans was clearly shown when they chartered the second Bank of the United States. The first Bank of the United States was established in Washington's administration after bitter debate between the followers of Hamilton and Jefferson. (See page 123.) When its charter ran out in 1811, the Republicans refused to issue a new charter, since they favored state-chartered banks. During the next few years the banking business was in the hands of three hundred state banks, which flooded the country with paper money. Merchants found it hard to carry on business because the value of the paper currency was so uncertain. The Republicans now realized that state banks could not provide the nation with a uniform currency (one having the same value in all parts of the country). In 1816 Congress authorized the second Bank of the United States. The charter was for twenty years, and in return for it the Bank was to pay the government one million, five hundred thousand dollars.

The question of internal improvements. To strengthen the nation and tie all parts of it together, roads, bridges, and canals were greatly needed. Everyone agreed on the need. The question was: Should internal improvements be paid for by the federal government or by the states and local communities? Many of the older Republicans thought that the federal government had no power to make internal improvements. The younger Republicans did not accept this view.

FORT ROSS *was built near San Francisco Bay in 1809 by the Russian-American Fur Company as a base for fur traders.* (From a sketch made in 1843)

Jefferson and Madison favored an amendment to the Constitution giving Congress the right to build roads, canals, and the like. In his last message to Congress, Madison strongly urged such an amendment. A few days later John C. Calhoun, of South Carolina, introduced a bill to provide federal funds for roads and canals. He said:

> Let us conquer space. . . . The mails and the press are the nerves of [our country]. . . . We are great and rapidly — I was about to say fearfully — growing. This is our pride and our danger, our weakness and our strength. . . . If we permit a low sectional spirit to take possession of this House, this happy scene will vanish. We will divide; and in consequence will follow misery. . . .

Congress passed the bill by a close vote. In his last day in office Madison vetoed it. While he was in favor of it, he thought it went beyond the powers of Congress.

The incoming President, James Monroe, told Congress that a constitutional amendment was needed to give Congress the power to make internal improvements. Opposition from the East, particularly New England, prevented such an amendment, and for many years the building of canals and roads was left to the individual states and to private companies. However, work on the National Road, authorized in 1806, was continued. (See page 142.)

The "Era of Good Feeling."   The country was pleased with the new Republican program of nationalism, and the Republicans easily won the election of 1816, when James Monroe became President. There was almost no opposition party during his Presidency (1817-1825). For this reason these years are known as the "Era of Good Feeling." This phrase came from the *Boston Sentinel*, a Federalist paper which had appeared with a black border the day of Jefferson's inauguration in 1801. Now, in the very heart of Federalism, it praised the Republican leader, James Monroe. This striking change of attitude showed the new feeling of national unity.

Now that the Republicans had become so much like the early Federalists, political parties seemed to be a thing of the past. The absence of party feeling was shown in the presidential election of 1820. Monroe, running for a second time, received all the electoral votes but one. That was cast by an elector who felt that only one man, Washington, deserved the honor of a unanimous vote for President.

Nationalism and the Supreme Court.   Meanwhile the Supreme Court was encouraging the spirit of nationalism. Chief Justice Marshall was a Federalist who had been appointed by President Adams. Marshall believed in a strong central government. Although he was but one member of the Court, his logic and his powers of persuasion were so great that he soon won the other members to his way of thinking. Jefferson appointed Republicans to the bench, hoping to offset the influence of Marshall's nationalistic views. It did not work. In time the Republican judges became "Marshallized," and were just as nationalistic as Marshall himself.

In a series of decisions Marshall firmly established the power of the Supreme Court. The first outstanding case was that of Marbury *vs.* Madison, decided in 1803. The Court ruled that it could pass upon the acts of Congress and the President, and might declare a particular act to be "unconstitutional." This is the principle (or idea) of *judicial review*. In two other decisions Marshall carried this principle still further. In Fletcher *vs.* Peck, decided in 1810, Marshall applied the principle to the act of a state legislature. He declared that one of the laws of Georgia was contrary to the Constitution of the United States and was therefore without force. Six years later, in another case, Marshall ruled that the Supreme Court has the right to hear appeals from the state courts. In these three decisions Marshall set the Supreme Court over Congress, over the legislatures of the states, and over the state courts.

JOHN MARSHALL, *the great Virginian who was chief justice of the Supreme Court in its formative period, 1801–1835. He was a nationalist and his decisions helped make the United States government powerful.* (From the portrait by Henry Inman. Courtesy of Virginia Conservation Commission)

JAMES MONROE, *the fourth and last of the "Virginia dynasty" of Presidents. The years of his administration (1817–1825) are known as the "Era of Good Feeling." His name is world famous because of the Monroe Doctrine.* (From a copy of the painting by Thomas Sully in the Virginia State Capitol)

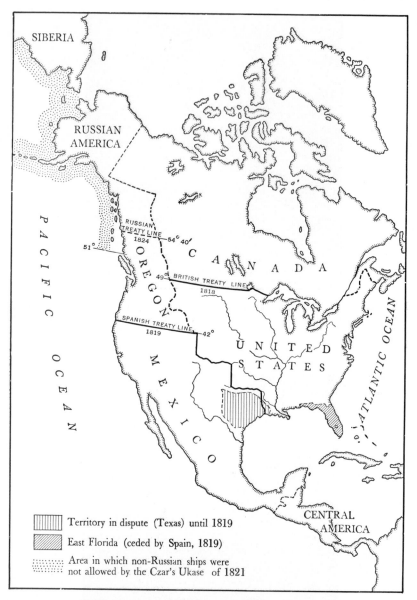

SIBERIA

RUSSIAN
AMERICA

PACIFIC OCEAN

RUSSIAN
TREATY LINE
1824 — 54° 40'

51°

OREGON

49° BRITISH TREATY LINE
1818

SPANISH TREATY LINE
1819 — 42°

CANADA

UNITED
STATES

ATLANTIC OCEAN

MEXICO

CENTRAL
AMERICA

	Territory in dispute (Texas) until 1819
	East Florida (ceded by Spain, 1819)
	Area in which non-Russian ships were not allowed by the Czar's Ukase of 1821

TERRITORIAL PROBLEMS SOLVED — 1819, 1824

In 1819 Spain at last agreed to sell Florida to the United States. At the same time the United States gave up its doubtful claim to Texas. In 1824 Russia signed a treaty with the United States in which Russia gave up all claim to territory south of the parallel 54° 40'. The settlement of these problems was a sign of the new American spirit of nationalism.

In McCulloch *vs.* Maryland (1819) the problem of whether the Bank of the United States was constitutional came before the Supreme Court. The Court decided that Congress has the right to charter a bank. By this decision the Court approved of the broad, or loose, construction of the Constitution for which Hamilton had argued long before. The Court denied that a state could tax the Bank of the United States, ruling that a state may not weaken the power of the national government by taxing one of its agencies. By these and other decisions Marshall strengthened the power of the national government and weakened the power of the states.

Extending the nation's boundaries. The Republicans showed the spirit of nationalism not only in domestic affairs but in their attitude toward foreign nations. Thus they continued to push the Indians off their lands, forcing them from one place to another — always toward the West and away from the lands the white man wanted. Also, they pressed Spain to sell East and West Florida; finally, in 1819, seeing that she could not defend the territory, Spain consented to sell. In return for the Floridas, the United States agreed to pay five million dollars and to give up its claim to Texas.

The Oregon country was claimed by both the United States and England. It was a vast territory extending from Spanish California to Russian Alaska. American and British fur-trading companies were beginning to enter it. In 1818 the United States and England agreed to occupy the territory together (jointly) for ten years. In 1828 they agreed to continue the period of joint ownership indefinitely. Sooner or later, of course, they would divide the territory between them.

Checking the Russian advance. The farsighted saw that the United States must have an outlet upon the Pacific. They now became alarmed because of Russian advances in North America. Russian fur traders had pushed through Siberia and across Bering Strait into Alaska late in the 1700's. During the War of 1812 the Russian-American Fur Company built a fortified village on Spanish territory near San Francisco Bay. In 1821 the Czar announced that the Pacific coast as far south as the parallel of 51° was Russian territory. Neither the United States nor England was willing to accept the Russian claim, and each sent a strong note of protest to the Czar. In a letter to the Russian ambassador in July, 1823, the Secretary of State announced that "the American continents are no longer subjects for any new European colonial establishments." The Russian question was settled a year later. (See page 172.)

Fear of European interference in Latin America. More alarming than the Russian advance was the danger that European nations might interfere in Latin America. Between 1810 and 1823 all the Spanish colonies in America (except Cuba and Puerto Rico) had declared their independence and set up republics. European rulers were alarmed at the growth of the republican spirit in the world. They knew that if it was allowed to grow unchecked, their crowns would soon be in danger. Austria, France, Prussia, and Russia formed a league to put down republican uprisings everywhere. They were considering a plan to aid Spain to reconquer its American colonies. France would take the leading part in such an expedition and might obtain lands for herself in the New World.

The people of the United States felt great sympathy for the patriots of Latin America, wanting them to keep their hard-won independence. Besides, Americans hoped to trade with Latin America, and if Spain reconquered her former colonies, she would not permit them to trade with other countries. For the same reason of trade Great Britain desired to see the new republics remain independent.

The Monroe Doctrine. The problem of protecting the Latin-American republics was discussed many times by Monroe and his cabinet. Monroe also consulted Jefferson, Madison, and prominent members of Congress. As a result of these talks, an American point of view was agreed upon. In his message to Congress in December, 1823, the President stated this point of view, which became known as the *Monroe Doctrine.* The purpose of the Monroe Doctrine was to keep the American continents for the Americans. It included the following ideas: (1) the Western Hemisphere was not open to further colonization by European powers; (2) European powers were warned not to interfere with the political affairs of any portion of the Western Hemisphere, for such interference would be regarded as "dangerous to our peace and safety"; (3) the United States would not interfere with the internal concerns of any European power.

The Monroe Doctrine was a success. This was largely due to the fact that England supported it. Under threat of war England compelled France to promise not to attack the Spanish colonies. Austria, Russia, and Prussia could not make war in Latin America without the help of the French fleet, so they gave up the idea. The following year Russia signed a treaty with the United States in which she gave up all claims to territory south of the parallel 54° 40'. The Monroe Doctrine had accomplished the purpose for which it was announced.

INDEPENDENCE MOVEMENT IN LATIN AMERICA

Inspired by the American and French revolutions, the Latin-American nations fought and won their independence. Venezuela was the first Latin-American country to declare itself independent, but the revolution was put down. Simon Bolivar and José de San Martin carried on the fight for freedom until by 1825 nearly all of Latin America was independent.

The Monroe Doctrine was not a law. It was merely an opinion expressed by the President of the United States. Yet it has survived to this day as a basic part of American foreign policy. It was the high-water mark of the new nationalism which grew out of the War of 1812. It showed how far American pride, self-confidence, and independence had developed.

To identify: American system, John Calhoun, John Marshall, James Monroe, Monroe Doctrine.

To explain or define: internal improvements, joint occupation, judicial review, localism, nationalism, protective tariff, stable currency.

Subjects for Talks or Written Reports

1. How the national defenses were strengthened soon after the War of 1812. 2. Jackson's invasion of Florida in 1818 and how it contributed to Spain's decision to part with Florida. 3. Russian activities on the Pacific coast of North America to 1824. 4. Why did the United States not join with England in warning Europe not to interfere in Latin America? 5. Why we remember John Marshall. 6. The agreement between the United States and England in 1818 regarding fishing rights and our northern boundary. 7. The westward rush after the War of 1812 and how it increased the demand for roads and canals. 8. American and British fur traders in the Oregon country.

Questions for Understanding the Text

1. In what way did the War of 1812 mark the close of a period in our history? 2. What Federalist principles were adopted by the Republicans after the War of 1812? 3. (*a*) What groups favored and opposed the Tariff of 1816? (*b*) How did Henry Clay think the tariff would benefit all sections of the country? 4. (*a*) Why was the charter of the first national bank allowed to expire? (*b*) What was the effect on business? (*c*) When and for how long was the second national bank authorized? 5. (*a*) What was Calhoun's argument for a national program of internal improvements? (*b*) Why did President Madison veto Calhoun's bill? (*c*) Why was the Constitution not amended to authorize Congress to make internal improvements? 6. (*a*) What was meant by the term "Era of Good Feeling"? (*b*) How did Monroe's re-election show the absence of partisanship? 7. (*a*) Who appointed John Marshall as chief justice? (*b*) Why and how did Jefferson try to lessen Marshall's influence? (*c*) How did Marshall's decisions affect the powers of the Supreme Court? Those of the state governments? 8. State four ways in which the spirit of nationalism was shown in foreign affairs during this period. 9. (*a*) What conditions led to the writing of the Monroe Doctrine? (*b*) How was it issued? 10. (*a*) Outline the main points of the Monroe Doctrine. (*b*) What made the success of the Monroe Doctrine possible?

ACTIVITIES FOR UNIT THREE

1. Read aloud portions of *The Patriots*, a historical drama by Sidney Kingsley, showing the conflict between the followers of Hamilton and those of Jefferson.
2. Make a graph to show the American foreign debt, domestic debt, and the debts of the individual states in 1790.
3. Make a chart to show the basic differences between the beliefs of Hamilton and Jefferson.
4. Continue work on the classbook, *American Hall of Fame*, preparing biographies of famous Americans in the period covered by this unit.
5. Draw cartoons on important incidents of the French Revolution. You may take either a favorable or an unfavorable view.
6. Appoint a committee to begin work on an illustrated history of your own community. The facts should be carefully checked before the final write-up. The sources of all facts should be given in footnotes. At the end of the year present the volume to your school library.
7. Develop a panel discussion to show the sectional differences in 1812 on the question: Should war be declared on England? Let two members of the panel take the part of planters; two, Kentucky and Maine frontiersmen; two, New England shipowners; and two, Pennsylvania and New York farmers.
8. Write a news article on the Hartford Convention for a Boston newspaper.
9. On outline maps show (a) the states that went Federalist and those that went Republican in the presidential elections of 1796, 1800, 1804, 1808, 1812, and 1816, and (b) the principal events of the War of 1812.
10. Imagine that you are to paint some historical murals for a public building. Make one or more drawings to picture the triumph of nationalism.

READINGS FOR UNIT THREE

(Stars indicate the easier books)

GENERAL ACCOUNTS

Corwin, E. S. *John Marshall and the Constitution.* (Chronicles)
*Davis, Julia. *No Other White Men.* Dutton. (The Lewis and Clark expedition)
Fish, C. R. *The Rise of the Common Man, 1830–1850.* (A. L. S.)
Ford, H. J. *Washington and His Colleagues.* (Chronicles)
*Fraser, C. C. *Boys' Book of Sea Fights.* Crowell.
Johnson, Allen. *Jefferson and His Colleagues.* (Chronicles)
Paine, R. D. *The Fight for a Free Sea.* (Chronicles)
*Stevens, W. O. *The Boy's Book of Famous Warships.* McBride.

BIOGRAPHY

Adams, James T. *The Living Jefferson.* Scribner's.

Bowers, Claude G. *Jefferson and Hamilton; the Struggle for Democracy in America.* Houghton Mifflin.

Chinard, Gilbert. *Honest John Adams.* Little, Brown.

Dana, Richard Henry. *Two Years Before the Mast.*

Hebard, Grace R. *Sacajawea.* Clark.

Mayo, Bernard, editor. *Jefferson Himself.* Houghton Mifflin.

*Moses, Belle. *John Marshall.* Appleton-Century.

*Nicolay, Helen. *The Boys' Life of Thomas Jefferson.* Appleton-Century.

*Roosevelt, Theodore and Lodge, Henry C. *Hero Tales from American History.* Appleton-Century.

*Seymour, Flora W. *Meriwether Lewis, Trail-Blazer.* Appleton-Century.

*Tappan, Eva M. *American Hero Stories.* Houghton Mifflin.

FICTION

Atherton, Gertrude. *The Conqueror.* Stokes. (Alexander Hamilton)

*Darby, Ada C. *Gay Sourette.* Stokes. (Life in Louisiana before its purchase)

*Eaton, Jeannette. *Daughter of the Seine.* Harper. (France before and after the Revolution)

Ellsberg, Edward. *"I Have Just Begun to Fight!"* Dodd, Mead. (John Paul Jones)

*Finger, Charles J. *When Guns Thundered at Tripoli.* Holt. (War with Tripoli)

Hewes, Agnes. *The Codfish Musket.* Doubleday, Doran. (Meriwether Lewis; Thomas Jefferson)

*Lamprey, Louise. *Days of the Commanders.* Stokes.

*Marshall, B. G. *Old Hickory's Prisoner.* Appleton-Century. (War of 1812)

*Mason, A. B. *Tom Strong, Junior.* Holt. (Life in the United States when our government was young)

*Meigs, Cornelia L. *As the Crow Flies.* Macmillan. (Louisiana Purchase; exploration)

*——. *The Scarlet Oak.* Macmillan. (Effects of the French Revolution on America)

*——. *Clearing Weather.* Little, Brown. (Shipping in the early 1800's)

*Seawell, M. E. *Decatur and Somers.* Appleton-Century. (War with Tripoli)

*——. *Imprisoned Midshipmen.* Appleton-Century. (War with Tripoli)

*Stackpole, E. A. *Privateer Ahoy!* Morrow. (War of 1812)

UNIT FOUR

NATIONALISM AND SECTIONALISM

The willingness to put the welfare of the nation before that of any state or section — that is, the spirit of nationalism *— flourished for a few years after the War of 1812. Then sectional interests began to seem more important than national interests to most people. Congressmen worked chiefly to get advantages for their own sections, and few considered the needs of the nation as a whole; this is the spirit of* sectionalism.

Until about 1850 nationalism and sectionalism were both in evidence — nationalism in the urge to obtain new territories and extend the nation's boundaries, and sectionalism in the quarrels over the tariff, the Bank of the United States, and the making of internal improvements at federal expense.

During this period of nationalism and sectionalism the West developed in population and influence. In 1828 for the first time it sent one of its sons, General Andrew Jackson, to the White House. From that time on many of our Presidents were to come from the West.

The period is also known for the spread of democratic ideas and for reforms which benefited the common people. The reform movement was based on the American belief that there should be equal opportunity for all.

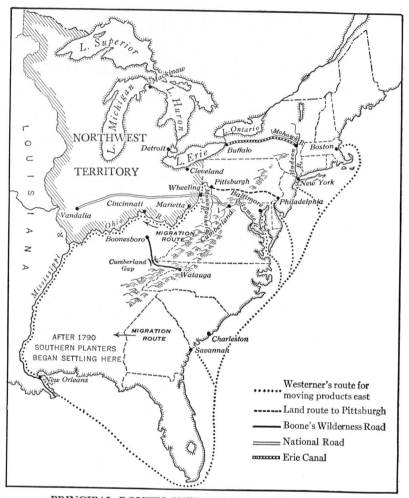

PRINCIPAL ROUTES USED BY WESTERN SETTLERS

The earliest route to the West was the Wilderness Road, which went through Cumberland Gap. The next route to become important went up the Potomac and Monongahela rivers to Pittsburgh, and then down the Ohio River. There was also a land route to Pittsburgh, which started at Philadelphia. The National Road, beginning at Cumberland, played an important part in the westward movement. After 1814, when hostile Indians in Georgia and Alabama were defeated, many settlers went around the southern end of the Appalachians. After 1825 the Erie Canal became the principal route to the West. The Western settlers shipped their products to market down the Ohio and Mississippi rivers to New Orleans, and from there to seaports on the Atlantic coast.

CHAPTER 14

THE GROWING INFLUENCE OF THE WEST

THE EARLY WESTWARD MOVEMENT

Crossing the Appalachians. Even before the Revolution Americans had begun to settle beyond the Appalachians, most of them going through Cumberland Gap, a pass on the border between Kentucky and Tennessee. Daniel Boone blazed a trail through this passage, following a path made by buffalo. His trail become the famous Wilderness Road.

A second gateway through the mountains was by way of the Potomac and Monongahela valleys to Pittsburgh. After the Revolution this became the principal route to the West. From Pittsburgh the settlers went down the Ohio River on boats, often crude flatboats made by themselves. In a single year, 1787, it is recorded that more than 900 boats floated down the Ohio, carrying 18,000 persons, 12,000 head of livestock, and 650 wagons. Many of these people were going to northern Kentucky, others to Ohio and Indiana.

A third gateway was through the Hudson-Mohawk Valley to Lake Erie. With the completion of the Erie Canal in 1825 this became the main route to the West. Another way of going west was through Georgia, around the southern end of the Appalachians. Hostile Indians blocked this passage until Andrew Jackson defeated them in 1814. This route was much used by planters moving from worn-out soil in the Carolinas and Georgia to the rich, unused land of Alabama, Mississippi, and Louisiana.

Going west over the National Road. In 1818 the United States government completed the National, or Cumberland, Road from Cumberland on the Potomac to Wheeling on the Ohio. It was carefully graded and had a surface of crushed stone and gravel. There were then few improved roads and most of these were toll roads. The National Road was free to all. In the next twenty years it was extended through central Ohio, Indiana, and Illinois, nearly to St. Louis. It was soon crowded with settlers going west.

Many settlers used the canvas-covered Conestoga wagon for that part of the journey which could be made by land. The wagon was

A FLATBOAT ON THE OHIO RIVER. *In the years from 1810 to 1820 an average of eight or nine flatboats went down the river every day. On reaching its destination the flatboat was sold for lumber.*

drawn by four or six oxen or horses. In it the travelers stowed their provisions, clothing, blankets, kettles, tools, seeds, medicines, and everything that they expected to need and for which they could find room. The men and boys walked beside the wagon, often driving a cow and a few sheep. Once they reached the Ohio they either paid for passage down the river or built a boat (usually a flatboat or a raft) to carry the party and their belongings to the promised land.

Some could not afford a large wagon with four or six animals to draw it. Instead they used a cart drawn by two horses or oxen, or even one. Some had only a pack horse. Others went on foot, their few belongings in a wheelbarrow, in a handcart, or in a pack on their backs.

The journey at best was long and hard. Bad weather, an accident to the horses or to members of the party, illness, or hostile Indians might make it a nightmare. As a rule several families traveled together for safety's sake and for companionship. At night the travelers usually camped by the roadside. The more prosperous slept in taverns when possible, although the accommodations were often very poor and the traveler might have to share a bed with two or three strangers or even sleep on the floor.

THE WHITMAN MISSION *in the Walla Walla Valley. Dr. Marcus Whitman estab-lished the mission in 1836 after a long trip by wagon from the East. In 1847 he, his wife, and twelve others were killed by Indians at the mission.* (Courtesy of Oregon Historical Society)

Growth of population in the West. Between the first census in 1790 and that of 1830 the population of the United States grew from about four million to nearly thirteen million. In 1790 less than two hundred thousand American settlers lived west of the Appalachians, but by 1830 about one third of the entire population lived there. By 1850 half the population lived west of these mountains.

Where the settlers came from. Nearly all of the early settlers in the West were native-born Americans. Some had been poor wage earners and day laborers back East, but most of them were farmers who went west in search of richer land. A great many were from Virginia and the Carolinas. After 1840 the stream of settlers included numerous immigrants from Europe, particularly from Germany.

Easterners complain of the westward movement. When conservative Easterners realized that a great many industrious heads of families were going west, they complained of "plots to drain the East of its best blood." Pamphlets were distributed far and wide describing the hardships of frontier life and advising people not to go west. But nothing could stop the westward movement so long as there was good, cheap land to be had at the end of the journey.

DANIEL BOONE *did more than any other one man to encourage the settlement of Kentucky.* (From the engraving by Chappel. Reproduced from *The Pageant of America.* Copyright Yale University Press)

"THE TRAPPER AT WORK." *Trappers were the first settlers in the wilderness. When neighbors settled near and wild animals grew scarce, the trapper moved farther west.* (From the sketch by E. W. Deming)

Whole communities were emptied of people. This caused a New Englander to lament:

> Our dwellings, our schoolhouses, and churches will have mouldered to ruins, our graveyards will be overrun with shrub oak; and [there will be left] but here and there a wretched hermit, true to his paternal soil, to tell the tale of other times.

The movement from many places farther south was equally alarming.

How the settlers got their land. At first the government sold its Western lands only in large tracts to land companies and wealthy individuals. These purchasers resold the land in small parcels, usually at a price much higher than they had paid the government. In 1796 Congress provided that government lands could be sold in tracts of 640 acres (one square mile) at $2.00 an acre. Few settlers could raise the money for a tract of this size, so in 1800 Congress provided for the sale of tracts of 320 acres, with four years to pay. These terms could still not be met by the average settlers. The demand for a more liberal policy led in 1820 to an act permitting the sale of parcels of 80 acres at

$1.25 an acre. Many settlers could now afford to buy land directly from the government, and the westward movement grew.

Squatter's rights. Some frontiersmen saw no reason why they should pay a land company or the government for the land they needed. Others were too poor to pay for land. Many a man became a "squatter"; that is, he simply marked off a few acres in the wilderness, built a cabin, and cleared some land for crops. Sooner or later the government or other owner of the land would sell it, and the squatter would have to move on.

The squatter considered that he had a better right to his clearing than anyone else. Had he not spent endless labor on it while in constant danger from the Indians? Squatters often fought those who tried to remove them from their homes. To check such lawlessness Congress sometimes gave *pre-emption* rights to settlers already there when a new area was opened for sale. This meant that a squatter had the first chance of buying his holding and could buy it for the minimum price of $1.25 an acre. In 1830 Congress provided that pre-emption rights should be given every time that government lands were placed on sale.

LIFE OF THE WESTERN SETTLERS

Three kinds of settlers. There were three main groups of settlers in any region. The firstcomers were pioneers. Many of them were single men. The pioneer lived mainly by hunting and trapping. He was a squatter and did not expect to stay long in one place. He was satisfied with a miserable cabin. He usually had a small garden patch, a pig or two, and sometimes a cow. When he could hear the sound of a neighbor's gun, he felt that the country was getting too crowded, so he moved on. Such men blazed the trails, held back the Indians, and prepared the way for the second group.

The next arrivals were farmers, and they had families. Instead of a cabin they built a log house with glass windows, a good chimney, and two or three rooms. Instead of using a spring they dug a well. They bought land and cleared field after field. They and their neighbors made roads, put up rough bridges over the streams, and organized local government. They sometimes hired a teacher and opened a school. Traveling preachers came now and then to hold church services for them. By this time the settlement was no longer on the frontier, for the frontier had fewer than six people to the square mile.

As the community grew more thickly settled and land values rose, the earlier settlers sold out and moved westward, making way for the third group. The last comers included storekeepers, mechanics, lawyers, doctors, preachers, and politicians, as well as a more prosperous class of farmer. The farmers were most important. They built larger barns than the earlier settlers, then better houses of brick or boards. They farmed more skillfully. Soon the village grew into a town with stores, a blacksmith shop, a flour mill, churches, and a school. The town might become a thriving city. Chicago, for instance, which was only a village in 1830, became one of the largest and richest cities in the world before some of its first settlers died.

Scarcity of money. Money was always very scarce in newly settled areas. Because transportation was so difficult, the settlers could get few or none of their products to market. Lacking a cash income, they had to live on what they could produce themselves — that is, they had to be self-sufficient.

One of the hardest problems the settlers faced was getting enough cash to pay interest and installments on their debts. Nearly all the settlers were in debt for their land, either to the government or to private sellers. Of those who bought land from the government on time payments, very few were able to make their payments when due. To avoid further trouble, Congress in 1820 decided to do away with selling land on credit. But private owners continued to sell land on credit; when the settler could not pay the interest or installments, he lost his farm.

The influence of the frontier. The frontier has had a great influence upon American ideas and American customs. Here are some of the attitudes of the frontiersman which are still noticeable among Americans today:

1. Equality. On the frontier all men were independent; no man had to work for somebody else. All were considered equal if they could swing an ax, plow a field, or shoot Indians. A man's ancestry or nationality was of little importance; what mattered was his own ability and character. There were no fixed social classes; every individual was free to make the most of himself.

2. Optimism. The frontier, with its unused soil and untouched mineral resources, was a land of opportunity. The poorest man might get ahead. Indeed, some poor men became wealthy through the discovery of minerals on their land. Many were able to retire in middle age with a comfortable income because land they had bought for a dollar or two an acre reached a value of fifty dollars or more an acre.

A LOG CABIN *left from pioneer days in Missouri. This cabin is in the Meramec State Park near St. Louis.* (Courtesy of State Historical Society of Missouri)

Westerners were optimistic, filled with hope for the future, sure that the hard worker would succeed, confident that their children would be better off than their parents.

3. Rugged individualism. Because they believed that if they worked hard they would succeed, the Western settlers were ambitious and energetic. They were impatient of anything that might limit a man's chances to make money; they wanted freedom from government regulation. This is the idea of "rugged individualism."

4. Democracy. The Western settler hated aristocracy and special privilege. He believed in the rule of the people. He thought every white man should have the privilege of voting and holding office. As the states west of the Appalachians came into the Union, most of them gave these two privileges to all white men. By so doing they attracted many settlers from the East. To check the migration of their people, the Eastern states finally had to repeal the laws which limited voting and officeholding to property owners. (See page 199.)

5. Nationalism. The Western settlers had a strong feeling of nationalism. Coming from many different states and from European nations, they felt no strong sense of loyalty to the state in which they had settled. It was the national government which sold them land on easy terms and gave them protection until they were ready for state-

hood. It was the national government to which they looked for aid in solving the problem of transportation. In time to come they would look to it for help in solving many other problems. They would have little sympathy with the idea that such help would interfere with the rights of the states.

The influence of the frontier is still felt. It shows itself in our dislike of every kind of special privilege and of fixed social classes. It shows itself in our hatred for "red tape" and other kinds of government regulation. At the same time it is responsible for the strong national government we have today.

The plantation system also moves west. The equality of the frontier soon disappeared in those parts of the Southwest suited to plantations. Beginning about 1815 cotton planters moved into the rich valleys of Alabama, Mississippi, Louisiana, and Arkansas. Most of them came from plantations farther east, bringing a class system along with their hundreds of slaves, herds of horses and cattle, and long wagon-trains of goods. They bought land already cleared. The frontiersmen from whom the land was bought moved farther west or settled on rougher lands not suited to plantations.

The demands of the West. During the first half of the 1800's the West was eager for more people. It wished a liberal land policy so that every settler could easily obtain a farm. It wished to encourage immigration from Europe. It wished to drive the Indians off their remaining lands and leave them only land of no value to white men.

The West wanted better transportation and cheap freight for its farm products, so it urged that roads and canals be built with federal funds. It wanted cheap credit and plenty of paper money, so it favored state banks and opposed the Bank of the United States.

The West also wanted greater influence in the national government. Why should the older states along the seacoast continue in control? Were Presidents to be chosen only from Virginia and Massachusetts? Why should not a President come from the West? The Westerners would not be satisfied until one of them was in the White House. In 1828, for the first time, a Westerner, Andrew Jackson, was elected President.

IMPROVEMENTS IN TRANSPORTATION

The coming of the steamboat. The great need of the West was improved transportation. For decades the Westerners floated their products to market on rafts or flatboats. At New Orleans the boats

CHAPTER 15

THE NORTH BECOMES
A MANUFACTURING CENTER

T*he Industrial Revolution comes to the United States.* The change from making goods by hand to making goods by machine and from production in the home to production in the factory is known as the *Industrial Revolution.* This change began in England in the middle 1700's with the invention of machines for spinning and weaving and the development of a workable steam engine. By 1775 England's Industrial Revolution was well under way.

England tried to keep her new manufacturing methods to herself. She prohibited the export of machines or plans and models of machines, and she refused to allow workmen familiar with the machines to leave the country. But she could not prevent the spread of the new methods of manufacture.

Several English mechanics managed to come here and set up from memory the spinning jenny and the power loom. The most famous of these immigrants was Samuel Slater, who in 1790 built a mill in Rhode Island for manufacturing cotton thread. Slater is called "the father of the American factory system." Other spinning mills were soon started, and by 1812 there were almost three hundred, nearly all of them in New England.

The first power loom in the United States was built by Francis Lowell in 1814. It was an improvement on the power looms already in use in England. That same year Lowell started a cotton factory at Waltham, Massachusetts. It was the first factory in the world where spinning and weaving were done under the same roof. Similar factories were soon erected at Lowell, Nashua, Lawrence, and Manchester on the Merrimac River and on scores of smaller streams in New England and eastern New York.

The factory system was soon applied to the manufacture of woolens, silk, carpets, clocks, firearms, and farm implements. But the use of

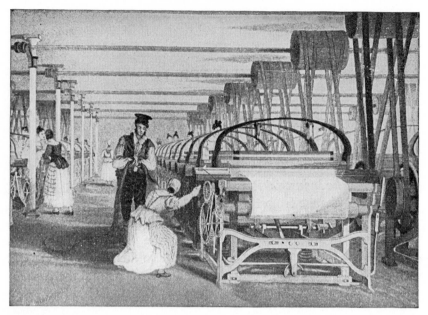

WEAVING ROOM *in Slater's factory. The designs for these machines were drawn from memory by Samuel Slater, an English immigrant.* (Bettmann Archive)

machinery did not stop manufacture at home and in small shops using hand methods. In 1820 two thirds of all the cloth produced in the United States was still made in the home. As late as the middle of the century a great deal of manufacturing was still carried on by hand methods.

Why the factory system developed in the North. The factory system grew much faster in the North than in the other sections. Perhaps the most important reason was that Northerners had money to invest in factories — money they had made in commerce and banking. Other advantages of the North were abundant water power, a population with much mechanical and business ability, and a labor supply of farm girls and of immigrants from Europe. The first center of the factory system was New England, especially Massachusetts, Rhode Island, and Connecticut. From this section the system spread to eastern New York, New Jersey, and Pennsylvania. Later it developed in Ohio, Indiana, and Illinois.

The growth of immigration. The early factory owners found their labor supply on near-by farms. The farmers' daughters were glad of a chance to earn money, and they were used to long hours and hard work. As more factories opened, the supply of American-born

SHOEMAKER'S SHOP ABOUT 1830. *At this period all shoe manufacturing was carried on by hand in little shops like this one.* (Courtesy of Essex Institute, Salem)

women and children was not enough. Factory owners then began to encourage immigration from Europe.

From 1790 to 1825 the number of immigrants was only about eight thousand a year. These easily found work. By 1830 the number of immigrants reached fifty thousand a year, and by 1840, one hundred thousand. Then famine in Ireland and a revolution in Germany sent a flood of newcomers to our shores. By 1850 three hundred thousand foreigners were coming each year. Most of them entered Northern ports and stayed in the North. They were usually uneducated and very poor. They had spent everything they had to get here, and they had to take any job they could find, regardless of poor wages and working conditions.

New social problems due to industrialization. The factory system brought a number of new social problems.

1. The workman's loss of independence. As factories gradually took the place of small shops, the life of the workman was changed in many ways. The skills he had learned through years of experience were not needed in the factory; even a child could soon learn to run most machines. The workman could no longer look forward to being his own boss; he could not start a factory of his own, for machinery

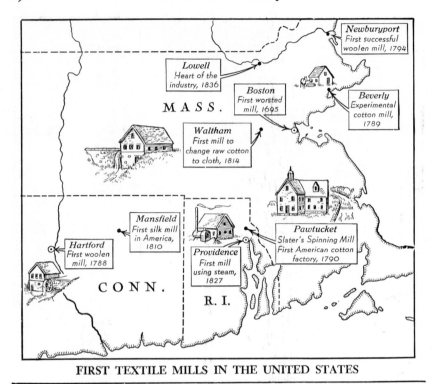

FIRST TEXTILE MILLS IN THE UNITED STATES

The earliest textile mills in the United States were built in New England. The industry soon spread to near-by states.

cost too much. He was dependent for a living on the man or the company owning the factory.

The native-born American hated the thought of working for somebody else. He would prefer to go to the frontier and farm. Many did go west rather than work in a factory. Those who took factory jobs did not expect to stay in the factory long. But many factory workers were unable in a whole lifetime to save enough money to go west with their families and start a farm.

2. Long hours. The hours of work in factories and shops followed the custom of the farm, where everyone labored from sunrise to sunset. The usual workday in a New England mill began at five o'clock in the morning if light permitted. A half hour was allowed for breakfast at eight and for lunch at noon. The day ended when it became too dark to see. Such hours taxed the strength of women and children to the limit.

3. Low wages. Skilled men sometimes got as much as $2.00 a day, but 85 cents to $1.00 was far more common. Women received from $1.50 to $3.00 a week. Children got from 50 cents to $2.00 a week. This wage scale did not change much until after the War between North and South. The single man, who could get a week's board, room, and washing for $2.50, might save money to buy a farm in the West. The man with a family of children found it very hard to make ends meet, even though his wife and some of the children were wage earners.

4. Child labor. Since a man could not support a family on his wages, his wife and children went to work too. Women and children had always worked, and the public did not realize that tending a machine all day in a factory was more tiring and unhealthful than working in the house and on the farm. In one Rhode Island mill in 1801 an observer tells us that he found a hundred girls from six to twelve years of age. They earned from 12 to 25 cents a day and had a "pale, dejected look." At that time most factory workers were children. Nothing much was done about the child-labor problem until late in the century.

5. Industrial accidents. The factory, or industrial, system, as it came to be called, brought new dangers to the worker. Machines then did not have "foolproof" safety devices; in fact they were built without much thought of safety. Artificial lighting was hardly ever used in factories and when used was very poor. Accidents were frequent, particularly to children, who are naturally careless. Some employers gave money to their injured workers, but others did not. Under the common law (see page 49) the employer did not have to pay an injured worker if the worker or any of his fellows was in any way to blame for the accident.

6. Unhealthy living and working conditions. The factory system led to an increase in sickness. Sanitary arrangements were crude, and large numbers of workers in one building favored the spread of infections. Besides, the manufacturing process often created dust, steam, or fumes, causing a high rate of tuberculosis among factory workers. Other health hazards were due to the rapid growth of the factory towns. Few of them had water or sewer systems. Most factory workers crowded into cheap, unhealthy tenements. Poor housing, poor food, and long hours of work under unsatisfactory conditions resulted in a high sickness and death rate, and at this period the city was much less healthful than the country.

IMMIGRANTS *arriving in the United States from Europe. American factory owners and mineowners were eager for additional workers; so the immigrants usually had no difficulty in finding jobs.* (Drawn by A. Berghaus for *Frank Leslie's Illustrated Newspaper,* November 23, 1878. Culver Service)

CHILD WORKERS *in a factory about 1840. At this period, and for many years afterward, most factories hired young children. Children worked the same long hours as adults and received very small wages.* (From a contemporary woodcut. Bettmann Archive)

7. The labor movement develops. Until 1825 it was a crime in England for workers to organize and strike for higher wages. American judges followed the English practice and put many workers in jail for attempting to strike. There were a few workmen's societies in America, but they were powerless. After 1825 the labor movement finally got a start. Many trade unions were organized. In 1828 the trade unions of Philadelphia combined in a federation. Similar federations were soon formed in other cities. By 1834 a national federation of trade unions was established.

Then, as now, labor unions struggled to improve wages, hours, and working conditions. In these matters they at first had little success. Strikes usually failed, for there were many immigrants who could fill the strikers' jobs. Besides, public opinion did not approve of strikes and in most cases took the side of the employer. Since strikes rarely succeeded, the labor organizations of this period put most of their efforts into getting better laws.

Workingmen win the right to vote. Most of the new Western states permitted all white men to vote. The older states limited the vote to property owners. This caused such discontent among wage earners that in the 1820's and 1830's all the states except Rhode Island decided to let any white man vote, whether or not he owned property. From now on political parties had to pay more attention to the needs of the working class. The winning of the right of all men to vote was a big forward step for American labor.

Labor organizations now worked to elect men friendly to labor. In 1828, for example, they joined with the farmers to elect Andrew Jackson President. They also asked for laws to improve the position of working men and women and to give them greater opportunity. They called for free public schools, equal rights for women, free homesteads for Western settlers, abolition of imprisonment for debt, abolition of slavery, laws establishing a ten-hour day, and other reforms.

Labor wins some of its demands. The labor movement won some solid gains. The ten-hour day was established in several of the skilled trades. Cities and states adopted the ten-hour day for government workers, and in 1840 President Van Buren declared ten hours to be a legal workday on government construction jobs. In 1843 Massachusetts prohibited the employment of children under twelve for more than ten hours a day.

The effort to obtain free public schools was successful. (See pages 225–226.) So was the effort to end compulsory militia service. The

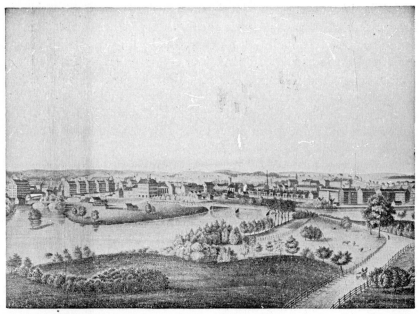

LOWELL, MASSACHUSETTS, IN 1834. *Cotton mills were built in Lowell in 1822;*
thus it is one of the oldest manufacturing cities in the country. Its water power at-
tracted textile mills. The early millowners wanted to make it a model city. (From
the lithograph by Pendleton. Courtesy of American Antiquarian Society, Worcester)

abolition of debtors' prisons was another victory for the labor movement. In 1829 it was estimated that about seventy-five thousand Americans were imprisoned for debt every year, many of them for debts
of a dollar or two. Five sixths of the prisoners in city jails were poor
debtors. In the 1830's one state legislature after another did away
with imprisonment for debt. Few reforms have done more for the
poor and unfortunate.

Demands of the industrialists. The growth of the factory system
not only created a laboring class but also a small and powerful group
of factory owners, or industrialists. These captains of industry believed that laws which helped manufacturing would help the whole
nation. They wanted a high protective tariff. They wanted sound
money and a national bank. They wanted to encourage immigration
in order to increase the labor supply.

At first the factory owners wished to discourage the westward
movement because it took laborers away from manufacturing districts.
They did not favor free homesteads for Western settlers or any other
plans for helping the poor man get a farm in the West. As time passed

NEW ENGLAND SAILING SHIPS *at Mocha, Arabia, in 1824. At this period New Englanders carried on a brisk trade with foreign lands. Their fast sailing vessels could be seen on every ocean.* (Courtesy of Peabody Museum of Salem)

they gradually changed their minds about this, for they saw that the West would furnish a market for manufactured products.

The commercial interests take a back seat. The commercial interests — merchants, importers, shipbuilders, shipowners — had long been the most important group in the North. For many years the gifted Daniel Webster, of Massachusetts, spoke for their interests in Congress. In 1816, for example, he protested strongly against the adoption of a protective tariff. Again, in 1824, when a new tariff bill was being considered, he spoke against any increase in the duties. By 1828, however, he believed that manufacturing had become more important to his section than commerce, so he voted in favor of a high protective tariff. His action was a sign that the commercial interests of the North would soon lose their control. From now on Congress would pay increasing attention to the demands of the manufacturers.

To identify: Industrial Revolution, Francis Lowell, Samuel Slater, Daniel Webster.

To explain or define: debtors' prison, factory system, industrialization, power loom, protective tariff, spinning jenny.

SUBJECTS FOR TALKS OR WRITTEN REPORTS

1. The history of manufacturing in your own community or any community in which you are interested. 2. The story of the development of a practical steam engine, beginning with the toy engines of the ancient Greeks. 3. The history of spinning from early times until now. 4. The history of weaving from early times to the invention of the power loom. 5. Difficulties which immigrants of the period 1800–1850 experienced on the voyage to the United States and upon their arrival here. 6. Strikes in the United States before 1825. Why they were called. What they accomplished. 7. Dorr's Rebellion — the struggle of Rhode Island workingmen for the right to vote. 8. Imprisonment for debt in the United States. 9. Conditions in an early factory and the surrounding town.

QUESTIONS FOR UNDERSTANDING THE TEXT

1. What changes were brought about by the Industrial Revolution? 2. How did England try to prevent the spread of the Industrial Revolution? 3. Tell about the beginnings of power spinning and weaving in the United States. 4. Factory methods of manufacture were first used in producing what kinds of goods? 5. State four advantages of the North in the development of the factory system. 6. How do you account for the fact that most immigrants entered Northern ports? Stayed in the North? 7. Name some of the new social problems connected with the growth of factories. 8. Why were the following conditions more serious in the factory than on the farm: (*a*) long hours, (*b*) low wages, (*c*) child labor? 9. What health problems arose with the growth of the factory system? 10. Why did the labor movement in the United States make little headway until after 1825? 11. (*a*) Why did labor unions turn to politics? (*b*) What reforms did they ask for? (*c*) What kind of candidates did they vote for? 12. What progress was made in shortening the workday during the 1840's? 13. (*a*) During what years were debtors' prisons abolished? (*b*) Did this reform benefit a large number of people? Explain. 14. What is meant by the term "commercial interests"? When and why did they lose their control? 15. Compare the demands of the factory owners with those of the commercial interests. 16. How and why did the factory owners change their minds about the westward movement?

CHAPTER 16

JACKSONIAN DEMOCRACY

The end of the old Republican party. In 1824 John Quincy Adams of Massachusetts was elected President. He was the son of John Adams, the second President. He had great ability and a noble character, but he was never popular with the masses, perhaps because they did not understand him. Adams was a nationalist. He recommended that the government build roads and make other internal improvements. He believed that the government should encourage science and urged Congress to found a national university and observatories where astronomers might study the stars and planets. But states' rights men in Congress were able to block nearly everything he suggested.

Adams had a merciless enemy in General Andrew Jackson, whom he had defeated for the Presidency. No sooner was Adams elected than the fiery-tempered Jackson began a four-year campaign to succeed him. Jackson and his friends fought Adams at every turn, calling him an aristocrat and a foe of the people. They split the Republican party in two. The Jackson group took the name *Democratic Republicans,* or Democrats, while those who supported Adams called themselves *National* Republicans.

Jackson's election, 1828. Jackson had been the idol of the West ever since the Battle of New Orleans. (See pages 161–162.) The frontiersmen lovingly called him "Old Hickory." He was also popular among city wage earners. He was one of the plain people, and the plain people throughout the nation wanted him for President. All the Western and Southern states gave their electoral votes to Jackson, and so did Pennsylvania. Adams trailed far behind, receiving electoral votes only from New England and the Middle States.

The election of 1828 is often spoken of as a revolution. It was a greater overturn by far than that which had placed Jefferson in the White House in 1800. (See page 137.) Jefferson, though a believer in democracy, was a man of deep culture and learning and not one of the common people. Jackson was the first man of the people, and also the

JOHN QUINCY ADAMS, *sixth President of the United States. He was respected for his stern devotion to duty and his complete honesty. Yet he did not win the public's affection and support. After his single term in the White House he served eighteen years in the House of Representatives — the most glorious years of his whole career.* (From the painting by Stuart and Sully. Courtesy of Fogg Art Museum, Harvard University)

first Westerner, to be chosen President. His election was possible because in 1828 more of the common people could vote than ever before.

Jackson's background and personality. Jackson was born in poverty. His father, a poor Scotch-Irish weaver, came to the Carolina frontier in 1765 and cleared a little farm. Two years later he died, shortly before Andrew's birth. Andrew's mother supported herself and her three small children by doing housework for a brother-in-law. Andrew knew what it meant to be a poor relation, and this may explain his lifelong sympathy for the poor.

As a lad he served in the Revolutionary War. His two brothers and his mother died in the service of their country. After the war Jackson entered a lawyer's office, and three years later, when not quite twenty, he received the right to practice law. He moved to Nashville, a frontier settlement in Tennessee, where he was soon appointed pros-

ANDREW JACKSON, *the frontiersman who became one of the most popular Presidents the United States has ever had. He served two terms, 1829–1837, giving the country remarkably strong presidential leadership.* (From the painting by Thomas Sully. Courtesy of Corcoran Gallery of Art)

ecuting attorney for a large district. He had to travel almost constantly over bad roads and through the forests, swimming his horse across the streams and often sleeping in the woods alone, rifle in hand. He had to be on guard against prowling Indians and wrongdoers who threatened to get even with him. Fearless, conscientious, honest, and just, he became the best-known man in western Tennessee.

When Tennessee was getting ready to become a state (1796), Jackson was chosen to help write its constitution. After serving a few months in Congress, he spent six years as a judge in the supreme court of Tennessee. Then he resigned his judgeship and bought a small plantation near Nashville, where he bred race horses and raised crops. He also carried on a general store, bought and sold land, and traded in horses and slaves. He never knew what his farm products would bring. Like his neighbors, he came to hate the Eastern bankers who

THE "HERMITAGE," *Andrew Jackson's stately home at Nashville. Now owned by the state of Tennessee, it has become an American shrine. "Old Hickory's" tomb is in the garden.*

controlled credit and, he thought, caused prices to rise and fall. However, he made money. He was famous for his hospitality, and guests flocked to the "Hermitage," as he called his handsome brick house. But he made enemies as well as friends, for he was very quarrelsome. He had a fighting record, including fighting duels and fighting Indians.

Jackson was the first President since John Adams who had not served as Secretary of State. When he took office, he knew little about the problems of running a government and dealing with foreign countries. Yet he made one of our most outstanding Presidents. He had great courage and independence of character, was perfectly honest and sincere, and his heart was completely with the common people.

Jackson's inauguration. When the day came for the inauguration (March 4, 1829), ten thousand visitors crowded into Washington, some from hundreds of miles away. Eager crowds watched the tall, erect, gray-haired veteran pass on foot from his tavern to the Capitol. After the ceremony a witness said, "Countrymen, farmers, gentlemen, mounted and dismounted, boys, women, children, black and white," rushed pell-mell to the White House to greet their hero. It was the people's day, and they joyfully packed the President's home. Jackson was pushed against a wall, and those nearest him had to link arms to prevent him from being crushed. People stood in muddy

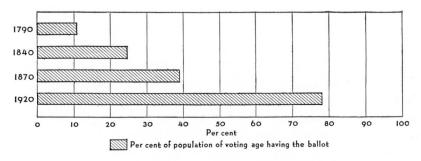

Per cent of population of voting age having the ballot

EXTENSION OF SUFFRAGE SINCE WASHINGTON'S DAY

The election of Jackson was possible because more of the common people could vote than ever before. In 1790 scarcely more than 10 per cent of the people of voting age had the right to vote. By 1840 the removal of property and religious qualifications for voting increased the proportion to about 25 per cent. Adoption of the Fifteenth Amendment in 1870 gave the ballot to Negroes. Adoption of the Nineteenth Amendment in 1920 extended the suffrage to women, at one stroke doubling the number of adults who may vote. Some adults are not permitted to vote because they cannot read and write, because they are not naturalized citizens, or because they have not paid poll taxes.

boots on the satin-covered furniture trying to get a glimpse of him. They upset refreshment tables laden with cut glass and china. "I never saw such a mixture," wrote Justice Story. "The reign of King Mob seemed triumphant."

The spoils system. Most of the people who flocked to the inauguration were looking for government jobs. One of them said: "I am ashamed of myself, for I feel as if every man I meet knew what I came for." "Don't distress yourself," said another, "for every man you meet is on the same business." All those who had worked for Jackson's victory wanted a reward for their services. The party bosses, or managers, declaring that "to the victors belong the spoils," asked the President to replace all federal job holders with his own followers.

Jackson thought that one man had as much right to public office as another. He favored short terms in order to give more persons a chance to hold office and in order to prevent the growth of an official class. He thought that officeholders did not need special training and experience. These opinions were shared by most of the common people, especially the frontiersmen.

During his first year in office Jackson removed about two thousand officeholders, replacing them with men who had helped in his election. He stopped far short of the clean sweep desired by the party managers, but he went much further than any earlier President had gone. The spoils system was already well known in some of the states; from now on it was to be followed in the national government.

Jackson is a "strong" President. Jackson gave the nation remarkably strong presidential leadership. He believed he should carry out the people's wishes as he understood them, without regard to the opinions of Congress or even those of the Supreme Court. He fought vigorously for what he thought the people wanted. He often vetoed acts of Congress. Thus he made the office of President far more important than it had been before. Like Theodore Roosevelt, he is remembered as a "strong" President. While he was much criticized for his vigorous leadership and his enemies called him "King Andrew," the common people approved of his methods.

Calhoun urges nullification. In 1828, a few months before Jackson's election, a new tariff bill was passed raising duties to an average of 49 per cent. This was the highest tariff the country had ever had and was certain to result in higher prices for manufactured goods. The South was solidly opposed to this "tariff of abominations." Southerners protested that they would go in homespuns rather than pay more for cloth made in Northern mills. Some asked whether it was worth while to stay in a Union in which one section could oppress another.

At this time the South Carolina legislature approved a statement called the "South Carolina Exposition and Protest." The writer of the statement (later known to be Vice-President Calhoun) claimed that the federal Union was a compact (an agreement) between the states and that the United States government was merely an agent or servant of the states. He argued that if Congress passed a law which hurt some of the states, those states had a right to nullify (disregard or disobey) the law within their own borders. These ideas were not new. Several states in the North as well as in the South had already threatened to nullify an act of Congress or even to secede (withdraw) from the Union.

Calhoun was one of the great public men of his time. He had stood for nationalism during and after the War of 1812 but had now swung around to sectionalism. For the rest of his life he was to fight for states' rights and the interests of the South. He believed the Union could be held together only by preventing one section from taking advantage of another.

The Webster-Hayne debate (1830). Early in 1830 much sectional feeling was shown in debating a proposal to stop for a time the survey

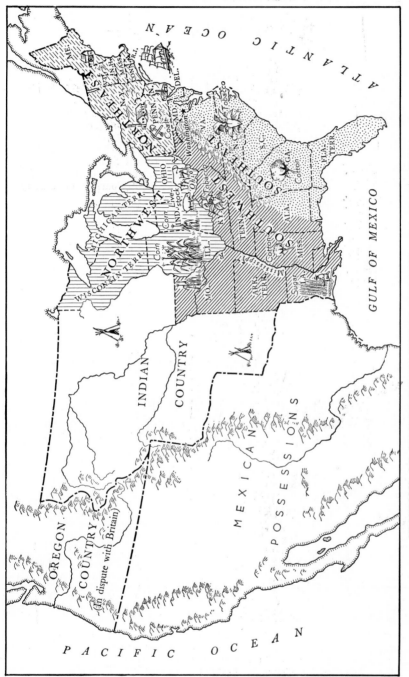

SECTIONS OF OUR COUNTRY WHEN JACKSON WAS PRESIDENT

BORN TO COMMAND.

OF VETO MEMORY.

HAD I BEEN CONSULTED.

KING ANDREW THE FIRST.

"KING ANDREW." *Jackson's enemies accused him of being a tyrant. A cartoonist of the period shows him dressed as a king, clutching a veto in his hand and trampling on the Constitution, the charter of the Bank of the United States, the program of internal improvements, and the judiciary.* (Courtesy of Library of Congress)

WEBSTER'S REPLY TO HAYNE. *This famous speech was given in the Senate chamber late in January, 1830. Webster was known as a wonderful speaker and the galleries were packed with visitors. He denounced the idea that a state had the right to nullify a law passed by Congress.* (From the painting by G. P. A. Healey in Faneuil Hall, Boston. Courtesy of Massachusetts Historical Society)

and sale of Western lands. Western senators objected to the proposal, claiming that its supporters were self-seeking Eastern manufacturers. Southern senators sided with the Western senators on this matter and suggested that the South and West also band together on the tariff question. Senator Hayne of South Carolina made a speech which attracted attention throughout the country. He declared it was unconstitutional for Congress to pass a law harmful to one section or intended to build up one section at the expense of another, and he said he agreed with Calhoun on the right of a state to nullify any act of Congress which the state considered to be unjust.

A few days later Senator Daniel Webster made reply. His speech, which took two days, was the greatest of his career and is considered one of the greatest ever made. He denounced nullification, saying that if first one state and then the other could ignore this or that law to suit its own convenience, the government of the United States would be powerless. If a state should prevent the federal government from enforcing a law within its borders, the result would be civil war.

In closing Webster spoke in high praise of the Union: "While the Union lasts we have high, exciting, gratifying prospects spread out before us, for us and our children." He expressed the fear that before his death the country would be drenched in the blood of civil war, and pleaded that Americans take as their motto "Liberty and Union, now and forever, one and inseparable."

South Carolina nullifies the Tariff of 1832. For a time Southerners hoped that Congress would make a new tariff with much lower rates, so Calhoun and the nullifiers kept quiet. In 1832 Congress passed an act reducing the duties to an average of 36 per cent. It was still a high tariff, and the South was greatly disappointed. South Carolina passed an act declaring the new tariff law to be unconstitutional and stating that it would not be obeyed in South Carolina after February 1, 1833. If the United States should use force to collect duties within South Carolina's borders after that date, the state would leave the Union. The governor called for volunteers, and companies began to drill.

Jackson prepares to use force against South Carolina. Jackson was a strong states' rights man, but he was determined to preserve the Union. In a proclamation to the people of South Carolina he said:

> The laws of the United States must be executed. . . . Those who told you that you might peaceably prevent their execution deceived you; they could not have deceived themselves. Disunion by armed force is treason.

HENRY CLAY (1777–1852). *For over thirty years this distinguished Kentuckian tried to hold the Union together. Like Calhoun and Webster, he failed to gain the Presidency, partly because he said what he believed even though it would cost him votes. Once he made the often-quoted remark, "I would rather be right than be President."* (Courtesy of Corcoran Gallery of Art)

DANIEL WEBSTER (1782–1852). *Beginning public life as a champion of his own section, New England, by 1830 Webster had become the champion of the entire Union. He fought every proposal that might divide North and South. His slogan, "Liberty and Union, now and forever, one and inseparable," is famous the world over.* (Courtesy of New York Historical Society)

Jackson sent warships to Charleston and ordered troops to be ready to go if necessary. He asked Congress for a "force bill" giving him power to use the army and navy to enforce the tariff bill. At his suggestion Congress then passed a new tariff, which provided for reducing the duties gradually until they were the same as in the Tariff of 1816. South Carolina had got what she wanted, so she repealed the act of nullification. She passed another act nullifying the force bill just to show that the nullifiers had not changed their minds.

Jackson removes the Indians to the West. The fate of the Indians was still unsettled when Jackson took office. Thomas Jefferson had believed we should civilize the red men and let them keep part of their land. This policy was not tried in the old Northwest, for there the white settlers advanced along a single wide front, pushing the Indians steadily westward. But in the old Southwest, where the white men settled chiefly along the great rivers, five powerful tribes were left on the lands in between. These tribes were accepting the Christian religion and taking up most of the white men's ways. They were known

"THE GREAT TRIO" *is the name often given to the three statesmen, Calhoun, Clay, and Webster. All three were born poor and had to struggle to get an education. All loved their country deeply, spending their lives in public service. All were great orators. Their influence shaped the history of the United States.*

JOHN C. CALHOUN (1782–1850) *of South Carolina. Entering Congress in 1811, Calhoun at once became a leader of the "War Hawks," who were urging war with England. When the war was over, wanting to strengthen the national government, he supported Clay's "American system," based on a protective tariff and government aid for roads, canals, and other internal improvements. His views gradually changed, and by 1828, in the "South Carolina Exposition and Protest," he put forward the idea that a state has the right to nullify (disobey) an act of Congress. He became the leading champion of the South. Almost his last words were, "The South — the poor South; God knows what will become of her now."* (From the painting by Charles B. King, 1822. Courtesy of Corcoran Gallery of Art)

as the "Five Civilized Tribes." The Cherokees, for example, were excellent farmers and stock raisers, living in neat wooden houses surrounded by orchards. They built roads, kept inns, and made cotton and woolen cloth. They had an alphabet and kept written records. They had a constitution and a government much like ours. The United States had recognized them in treaties as an independent nation.

The people of Georgia wanted the Cherokee lands, so the state authorities announced that the Indians must move. The Cherokees appealed to the courts. The Supreme Court, under John Marshall, ruled that the Cherokees were a nation and that the laws of Georgia did not apply to them. Georgia refused to obey the Supreme Court and began to remove the Indians by force. This action was just as serious as South Carolina's refusal to obey the tariff law. Yet President Jackson did nothing about it. Like other frontiersmen, he had no respect for Indians, and believed they should be driven to places set aside for them in the West, that is, to *reservations.* He is reported to have said, "John Marshall has made his decision; now let him enforce it."

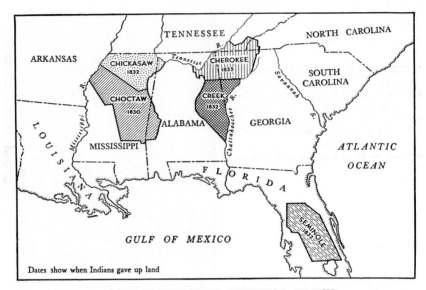

Dates show when Indians gave up land

LANDS OF THE FIVE CIVILIZED TRIBES

Alabama and Mississippi followed Georgia's example by taking steps to get rid of the Indians. Since the President would not protect them, the red men had to give in. They sold their land to the federal government. Congress gave them a large reservation in what is now Oklahoma, promising that it should never be taken from them. By 1837 most of the Indians east of the Mississippi had been moved to reservations in the West.

Opposition to the Bank of the United States. The second Bank of the United States opened its doors on January 1, 1817, with a federal charter good for twenty years. When Jackson was President, the Bank had branches in twenty-nine cities. It was privately owned, and its profits went to the stockholders. All funds of the national government were deposited with the Bank. The Bank had the power to issue notes (promises to pay) which were used as money. Congress had chartered the Bank in the hope that it would give the country a uniform and stable (steady) currency.

The Bank of the United States could not supply enough bank notes to meet the country's needs. Since the states were forbidden by the Constitution to issue money, they chartered state banks, which in turn issued bank notes that were used as money. By 1833 there were five hundred state banks. Most of them were small and had inexperienced

CHICAGO IN 1833. *When Jackson became President, Chicago was a little frontier village. When his second term ended, Chicago had 4000 people and was on its way to becoming the leading city of the West.* (Courtesy of Chicago Historical Society)

directors. Not knowing whether a state bank could make good on its notes, creditors often refused to accept them. On the other hand everyone felt sure of the notes of the Bank of the United States, and these were cheerfully accepted throughout the nation.

Friends of the state banks were jealous of the Bank of the United States and called it the "monster." They argued that it was unfair for the government to put all its money in a single bank and that the Bank had too much power and might attempt to control the government. Westerners pointed out that most of the Bank's stockholders lived in the East and in Europe, while most of its profits came from lending money in the West. They thought it unfair for wealthy Easterners and Europeans to make money from poor Western farmers. They did not realize that the lending of money was a valuable service to the West and that it must be paid for.

Jackson declares war on the Bank. Jackson knew what it meant to be in debt. He and his farmer neighbors had suffered from the scarcity of money and lack of credit in the West — difficulties which they blamed on the Eastern "money power." He thought he could strike a blow at the money power by destroying the Bank of the United States. Although its charter would not run out for seven years, he attacked the Bank mildly in his first message to Congress. A year later he declared the Bank unconstitutional and dangerous to liberty. He was not blind to the need for a central bank, for he asked Congress to establish a new bank owned and controlled by the government. However, Congress did not think well of the idea.

In 1832 the officers of the Bank asked Congress to renew the charter. It was the year of the presidential election, and they thought the President would not veto a bank bill for fear of angering the Northeastern commercial states, whose votes he needed for re-election. They did not understand Jackson. A bill to recharter the Bank passed both houses of Congress. The President vetoed it in a ringing message, declaring that the Bank was meddling in politics.

The election of 1832. The presidential campaign was fought on the question of rechartering the Bank. Henry Clay, nominated by the National Republicans, supported the Bank. Jackson, renominated by the Democrats, thundered against the Bank and the "money power." Jackson won a sweeping victory.

Jackson removes deposits from the Bank. The Bank had fought Jackson's re-election, and he took revenge. Although its charter would not run out until 1836, he ordered the gradual removal of government money. The Bank was crippled. Jackson's victory over it seemed to most people another proof that "Old Hickory" was on the side of the common man and against wealth and privilege.

A period of speculation. The early and middle 1830's were years of unusual prosperity. Many people were moving west. Immigrants by the hundreds of thousands came here from Europe. The factory system grew rapidly. In the East railroad building went forward. Roads and canals were being built in all parts of the country. Sales of government land increased by leaps and bounds, and by 1836 a large surplus was in the treasury.

Prices were going up. This led many people to buy land as a speculation (that is, in the hope of selling it soon at a higher price). Most of the speculators borrowed money to pay for their purchases.

The state-chartered banks did nothing to discourage speculation and too much borrowing. Instead they encouraged both by issuing more and more paper money. Prices soared still higher. Becoming alarmed, Jackson tried to check the speculation in land and the issue of bank notes. He instructed the government land agents to take nothing but gold and silver in payment for public lands. Land sales fell off at once. The bright bubble of speculation was about to burst.

The election of Van Buren, 1836. Jackson was in his seventieth

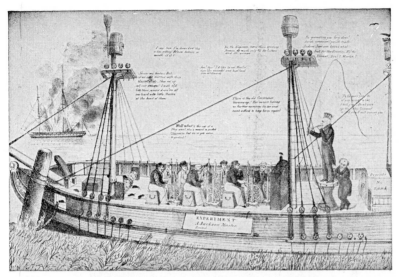

A. JACKSON, SHIPMASTER. *This cartoon shows Jackson with a crown on his head and a whip in his hand. His friend Van Buren, just behind him, says "Don't give up the ship, General, or I shall not succeed you."* (Courtesy of Library of Congress)

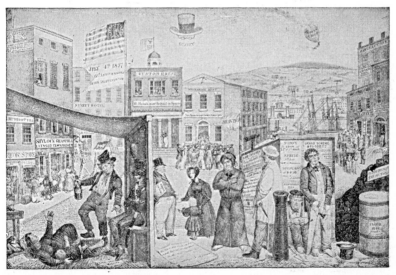

HARD TIMES IN 1837. *One cause of this panic, which lasted until 1843, was gambling in land. The panic caused great suffering to wage earners and to farmers in the South and West. The cartoonist shows idle workmen and miserable women and children. In the background people are trying to get their money from a closed bank* (Courtesy of Library of Congress)

MARTIN VAN BUREN *followed Andrew Jackson in the White House. Because hard times made him unpopular, Van Buren served only one term, 1837–1841.* (From the painting by Henry Inman. Courtesy of Metropolitan Museum of Art)

year. Though he was more popular than ever, he was eager to go home to the Hermitage. He supported Martin Van Buren of New York as his successor, and Van Buren easily won the election.

The rise of the Whigs. Those who opposed Jackson and Van Buren formed a new party called the Whigs. This party included the National Republicans, the nullifiers of South Carolina, and other groups having little in common except dislike for Jackson. The most prominent of the Whigs were senators Henry Clay of Kentucky, John Calhoun of South Carolina, and Daniel Webster of Massachusetts. These three had spent their lives in public service. They were men of great ability. While they disagreed on many questions, they were united against Jackson and Van Buren.

The panic of 1837. In the early months of 1837 the country entered a period of hard times. Hundreds of banks failed. Speculators were ruined as prices dropped. Money became very scarce. The demand for luxuries and manufactured products fell. Mills and factories closed. Work on canals and railroads stopped. Unemployment brought terrible suffering to Eastern wage earners. The Democrats had no plan for restoring prosperity, and the hard times lasted for several years,

CAMPAIGN FLAG, *used in 1840, giving two reasons for voting for William Henry Harrison. Such use of the flag is now forbidden by law. The original flag is in the Clements Library, University of Michigan.* (Courtesy of Clements Library)

The election of Harrison, 1840. The panic of 1837 made Van Buren and the Democrats unpopular, giving the Whigs their chance to elect a President. The managers of the Whig party looked around for a candidate who would please the common people. They turned aside from Henry Clay, the real leader and founder of the party. They preferred someone whose views were less well known because such a candidate would satisfy more groups of voters. They wanted a Westerner, for they needed to attract the farm vote. They knew that a military hero always appeals to the voters. So they selected General William Henry Harrison of Ohio. Harrison had beaten the Indians at Tippecanoe in 1811 and had served with honor in the War of 1812. His political opinions were hazy, and for this reason he would not offend any important group of voters. To catch Southern votes the Whigs nominated John Tyler of Virginia for Vice-President. Tyler was a Democrat, but this fact did not worry the Whig leaders. They had no idea he would shortly become President.

A prominent banker advised the Whig managers: "Let him [Harrison] say not one single word about his principles or his creed — let him say nothing — promise nothing. Let no committee, no convention, no town meeting ever extract from him a single word about what he thinks now or will do hereafter." This advice was followed. The Whig leaders did not prepare a party platform. They simply offered General Harrison to the country as a man of the people, pretending that he lived in a log cabin. At every political meeting they displayed a log cabin, a jug of cider, and a coonskin cap to show their candidate's love of the simple life. They treated the crowds from barrels of hard cider. "Oh, know ye the farmer of Tippecanoe?" sang the crowds.

> With an arm that is strong and a heart that is true,
> The man of the people is Tippecanoe.

The Whigs accused Van Buren of being a wealthy man "who eats with gold spoons and dresses himself before costly French mirrors." They said he had lordly manners and even put cologne on his whiskers. By such means the Whigs turned the tables on the Democrats. The people elected Harrison by a huge majority. They seemed to forget that the Whig party was supported by the rich and wellborn, the Eastern "money power" which they hated. Their old leader, Jackson, watched the campaign anxiously from the Hermitage and did what he could to help Van Buren. He felt that Van Buren's defeat was the defeat of Jacksonianism.

An empty victory. Just one month after his inauguration President Harrison died — worn out from the strain of meeting the swarms of office seekers, who gave him no rest. For the first time in our history a Vice-President stepped into the vacant office of the President. He was John Tyler, a Democrat with ideas like Thomas Jefferson. He believed firmly in states' rights. He was against a high tariff and against any attempt to create a new Bank of the United States. He was, in fact, opposed to most of the measures the Whig leaders were hoping to adopt.

The Whig leaders found themselves in a curious situation. They had expected to pull the strings for the easygoing Harrison; instead they had to deal with a strong-willed Virginian who disliked their policies. The Whigs had a majority in Congress, but President Tyler vetoed most of the bills Congress passed. Harrison's death had robbed the Whigs of their victory.

To identify: Cherokees, Five Civilized Tribes, Old Hickory, old Northwest, old Southwest, South Carolina Exposition and Protest, "tariff of abominations," Webster-Hayne debate, Whigs.

To explain or define: nullify, oppress, reservation, secede, speculation, spoils system, states' rights, survey.

SUBJECTS FOR TALKS OR WRITTEN REPORTS

1. The life of Andrew Jackson until he became President. 2. The civilization of the Cherokee Indians before their removal to the West. 3. The removal of the Five Civilized Tribes to the West. 4. Why his enemies called Jackson "King Andrew." 5. The canal-building boom. 6. The life of Henry Clay. 7. The life of Daniel Webster. 8. The life of John Calhoun. 9. The life of John Quincy Adams.

QUESTIONS FOR UNDERSTANDING THE TEXT

1. For what do we remember the Presidency of John Quincy Adams? 2. Why is the election of 1828 considered a revolution? 3. How did Andrew Jackson's preparation for the Presidency differ from that of earlier Presidents? 4. What did the common people think about the need of government officials for special training and experience? 5. Did Andrew Jackson create the spoils system? Explain. 6. How did President Jackson increase the importance of his office? 7. Why did Southerners oppose the Tariff of 1828? 8. (*a*) What arguments were set forth in the South Carolina Exposition and Protest? (*b*) Who wrote it? 9. How did the sections line up in the debate over stopping the survey and sale of Western lands? 10. State two ideas expressed by Senator Hayne in his famous debate with Daniel Webster. 11. Give Webster's argument against the doctrine of nullification. 12. (*a*) When did South Carolina decide to nullify the tariff law? (*b*) Why was action delayed until this time? (*c*) What did South Carolina intend to do in case the United States insisted on enforcing the tariff law within her borders? (*d*) What did Jackson do? (*e*) What did Congress do? (*f*) Did South Carolina give up the idea of nullification? 13. Compare Jefferson's idea with Jackson's idea of the proper method of treating the Indians. Which idea won out? 14. (*a*) Tell how Georgia defied the Supreme Court in removing the Cherokees. (*b*) Why did Jackson permit Georgia to disobey the Supreme Court? 15. (*a*) What is meant by "a uniform and stable currency"? (*b*) Could state banks give the country a uniform currency? Explain. (*c*) Do we now have uniform currency? Stable currency? 16. (*a*) State the arguments for doing away with the Bank of the United States. (*b*) Why was President Jackson opposed to it? (*c*) Did he believe that state banks could meet all our banking needs? Explain. 17. Describe the boom leading to the panic of 1837. 18. Show why the Whigs chose General Harrison rather than Henry Clay as their candidate for President in 1840. 19. Who was the first Vice-President to complete the unexpired term of a President?

THE CITY OF WASHINGTON *when Jackson was President. The Capitol is the domed building in the background.* (From a painting by G. Cooke. Bettmann Archive)

HORSE RACING *was a popular sport in the early 1800's. Like many Southern planters, Andrew Jackson raised race horses on his estate in Tennessee.* (From a lithograph by C. Severin. Courtesy of Gallery of Fine Arts, Yale University)

CHAPTER 17

THE PERIOD OF JACKSONIAN DEMOCRACY

The Jacksonian Period. In 1828, as we have seen, the common people elected a President, Andrew Jackson. During the next twenty years, which we shall speak of as the "Jacksonian Period" or "Era," they made other important gains. The people established public schools and abolished imprisonment for debt. They attacked the drink evil. They made their churches more helpful. They began to enjoy some of the new comforts and conveniences made possible by invention.

A period of economic opportunity. America was a land of opportunity. There was an abundance of good land, forests, and mineral deposits to be had for very little money. A man needed only $100 to buy land for a small farm, because after 1820 anyone could buy land from the government at $1.25 an acre, in a parcel as small as 80 acres. Of course he also needed money for tools, livestock, wagons, building materials, home furnishings, and perhaps transportation from the East. Yet the single man could, if he was healthy and thrifty, save enough from a few years of wage earning to make a start in farming. Once he began to farm, he was pretty sure of a good living not only for himself but for a family, although the work was hard and the hours long. In time he would be able to sell his farm for much more than it had cost him.

The Western frontier was not the only one. To dwellers on the northeastern coast, the sea was another frontier. Fishing vessels were small and were often owned by their crews, each man receiving a share in the catch. After a few seasons many a fisherman was able to buy a boat of his own. Another frontier was in business. It was the day of the little businessman. A man did not need much money to start a crossroads store, a country inn, a ferry, a gristmill, a shoe factory, or a coal mine. And the country was growing so rapidly that thousands of new businesses were needed every year.

In this period Americans came fairly near to having equal economic opportunity, that is, equal opportunity to earn a living and to get ahead.

COUNTRY SCHOOL. *The Jacksonian Period saw the beginning of the struggle for free public schools. Most of the schools established at this time were one-room schools like the one pictured here. In recent years many of these little schools have been consolidated into large modern schools.* (From the painting by E. L. Henry, 1890, in the Garvan Collection, Yale University. Bettmann Archive)

A Frenchman who visited the United States in 1831 said that nothing struck him "more forcibly than the general equality of conditions among the people." The great majority of people were farmers; they handled little cash, but they were sure of food, shelter, and clothing, and they owned their land. A small planting class in the South and a small class of successful merchants, bankers, shipowners, and factory owners in the Northern cities were well to do, yet their fortunes would not be considered large today. Many of those who made a success in business started at the bottom.

The new political and social equality. The near equality of economic opportunity made for political and social equality. The privileges of voting and holding office were no longer limited to property owners. Members of the aristocracy no longer held all the important places in the government. Americans told their sons that any boy might become President. Had not President Andrew Jackson been a penniless orphan with almost no schooling? Might not any other boy by effort and ability rise to high office?

The old separation between social classes was growing less. This

BOSTON LATIN SCHOOL, *founded in 1635 to prepare boys for Harvard College. This school has always had a high scholastic rating. Massachusetts led in the establishment of public high schools. By 1850 it had sixty-four of them — probably more than all the other states combined.* (From a drawing made about 1848. Courtesy of Massachusetts Historical Society)

was shown in dress and manners. By 1830 gentlemen no longer wore knee breeches and lace-trimmed shirts. They dressed every day much as workingmen did on Sundays. Manners, too, were becoming simpler and more democratic. The old idea that good manners were only for aristocrats was changing. Every boy could become a gentleman if he chose, and this encouraged many to learn the courtesies of speech and conduct which had once been practiced only by aristocrats.

A new interest in social reform. Thoughtful people realized that equal opportunity did not yet exist. Except in the Northeast most children had no chance to attend school. Child laborers in the factories did not have the same chances for a good start in life as did other children. The blind and other handicapped persons found the door of opportunity tightly closed. Women were in no way equal to men. These and other inequalities challenged the democratic spirit. A new interest in social reform was one of the products of the Jacksonian Period.

The fight for free public schools. The founders of the United States saw the need for public schools and colleges. They realized that a republic could succeed only if the voters were informed. Thomas Jefferson planned a great system of public education for Virginia and tried all his life to get it established. George Washington advised Congress to found a national university where the youth of the nation might receive the highest training under American — not foreign — surroundings, and under national — not local or sectional — influences. To prove his earnestness, he left in his will $25,000 for a university at Washington. Jefferson and Washington were ahead of their times. In most parts of the country the taxpayers objected to spending public funds to provide schools and colleges. However, most New England communities had free elementary schools long before the Revolution. Outside of New England the children of the common people seldom went to school unless they belonged to a church having a school for its members.

During the Presidency of Andrew Jackson the people began to demand free public schools. Labor organizations led the demand. The struggle for free public schools continued throughout the 1830's and 1840's. Many towns established free elementary schools for the first time. Rural dwellers formed school districts and built schools. The large cities opened public high schools. The idea that every child in the United States should have an education at public expense was rapidly gaining ground.

The educational awakening leads to better schools. A better quality of education and a longer school term were urgently needed. The schools were open only three or four months of the year, for most children were kept busy on the farm, except in winter. The school buildings were usually crude, unhealthful, and uncomfortable. Many teachers had little education; none had special training for teaching. The public thought that the duties of a teacher could be handled by any honest, industrious person. Learning meant memorizing out of books; the work of the teacher was to hear pupils recite their lessons and whip them when they could not. The dunce's stool, the fool's cap, and the birch rod were in daily use. In fact these instruments of punishment and a few old textbooks were the only teaching aids found in most classrooms.

The influence of Horace Mann. There were signs of an educational awakening during the 1820's. It really got under way in 1837 with the passage of a bill in Massachusetts creating a state board of education. A lawyer named Horace Mann was chosen as secretary of the new board, a post which he held for twelve years. Through his eager-

HORACE MANN. *As secretary of the Massachusetts Board of Education, Mann was one of the leaders of the educational awakening in the United States.* (Courtesy of American Antiquarian Society, Worcester)

ness and tireless efforts he strengthened the schools of Massachusetts in a most remarkable manner. His influence was felt all over the United States.

Mann constantly argued that education should be universal — reaching all children — and free. Girls as well as boys should be trained, and the poor should have the same opportunity as the rich. The aims of education should be sound character and efficiency in everyday living. In discussing the courses to be given, he wrote that he failed to see any reason "why algebra, a branch which not one man in a thousand ever has occasion to use in the business of life, should be studied by more than twenty-three hundred [grammar school] pupils, and bookkeeping, which every man, even the day laborer, should understand, should be attended to by only a little more than half that number."

Mann held that teachers should be trained to understand child nature. He said that lessons should be made attractive and interesting. Brutality was out of place in the classroom; teachers should always treat pupils with kindness. He persuaded the Massachusetts legislature in 1838 to establish three normal schools for the training of teachers. These were the first public normal schools in the United States and succeeded from the start.

Mann realized that better school buildings and equipment were needed. He published a special report calling attention to the unhealthful conditions in many schools. He worked hard to convince the public that school buildings should be clean, well lighted, well ventilated, and equipped with seats suitable for children. He got the state legislature to provide funds for school libraries. He pointed out the need for better textbooks. He organized a state teachers' association. He campaigned for higher salaries for teachers and a longer school term. In these and countless other ways he showed the people of Massachusetts how to improve their schools.

The influence of Henry Barnard. Mann was only one of the leaders of the educational awakening. Another was Henry Barnard, who greatly improved public education in Connecticut and Rhode Island. Barnard's greatest work, however, was in telling the people of the United States about educational progress in Europe. New methods of teaching were being tried in Germany, France, Switzerland, and England — methods based on a new understanding of children and a new respect for them. Barnard visited the leading schools of these countries. In 1854 he established the *American Journal of Education* to tell teachers about educational progress here and abroad. He gave most of his time to this journal for many years and spent his entire personal fortune of $50,000 upon it. Barnard worked hard to get Congress to create the office of United States Commissioner of Education. This was done in 1867, and Barnard was the first person appointed.

The educational awakening was not limited to New England. By 1850 half of the states had created the office of state superintendent of education, and several had established normal schools. These changes show (1) that education was now considered too important to be left wholly to the local community or school district, and (2) that teaching was being recognized as a profession.

Higher education. Higher education had once been only for the rich. But now the common people wanted it for their sons. The years from 1830 to 1850 saw the opening of eighty colleges. Most of them were supported by religious groups, chiefly for training ministers. The principal subjects were religion and ancient and modern languages. There was very little science taught. The most interesting of the new colleges was Oberlin, founded in 1833. It was the first college in the world to admit women on the same basis as men.

The first state universities were established in the South. By 1850 fifteen state universities had been started. None of them had free tuition and none admitted women students.

HENRY BARNARD, *the first United States Commissioner of Education. He and Horace Mann led the great public school awakening that began in the Jacksonian Period.* (Courtesy of United States Office of Education)

LADIES' HALL AT OBERLIN COLLEGE. *This was probably the first dormitory for college women in the United States. Oberlin was the first coeducational college in America. It was also one of the first to admit Negroes.* (Courtesy of Oberlin College)

EMMA WILLARD, *pioneer teacher of women, began teaching in a district school when only sixteen. She wrote textbooks and gave lectures. All her life she worked for better public schools and for the higher education of women.* (From *Emma Willard, Daughter of Democracy,* by Alma Lutz, Houghton Mifflin Company)

MARY LYON, *a pioneer in the education of women. Her enthusiasm for higher education for women resulted in the founding of Mount Holyoke. This daguerreotype was made a few years before her death in 1849. In 1905 her statue was placed in the Hall of Fame.* (Courtesy of Mount Holyoke College)

The education of women. In colonial times most people thought women were better off without schooling. Few girls went to school, and those who did got only a smattering of reading, writing, and figuring. Girls did not go to grammar schools and academies. After the Revolution private academies began to admit girls, and some academies were opened especially for girls. The girls who attended academies were from well-to-do families. Usually they were taught little except music, embroidery, religion, and French. No college admitted women, but here and there a rich girl studied college subjects with a tutor.

There were a few women leaders who insisted that girls ought to have the same educational opportunities as boys. Among them were Emma Willard and Mary Lyon. In three years Emma Willard traveled eight thousand miles on packet boats, canal barges, and stagecoaches, speaking for the cause. In 1821 she opened an academy for girls at Troy, New York, where girls could have really solid training. This academy is now called the Emma Willard School.

Mary Lyon, while still a school girl, vowed she would start a seminary or college for women as good as those open to men. When she was sixteen, she began teaching school for seventy-five cents a week with board. Since no college would admit her, she studied college subjects in her spare time. For years she tried to interest prominent people in starting a college for women. She was ridiculed on every side, but finally collected sixty-eight thousand, five hundred dollars with which to build Mount Holyoke Female Seminary, later known as Mount Holyoke College. When it opened in 1837, eighty girls filled the only building and others were turned away for lack of room. The next year more than four hundred girls were turned away for the same reason. In 1836, the Georgia Female College at Macon, now known as Wesleyan College, was chartered. It was the first college in the world to grant degrees to women. A third college for women was opened at Elmira, New York, in 1851.

Education of the handicapped. The needs of the blind, deaf, and disabled were naturally neglected at a time when many normal boys and girls had no chance for schooling. Yet here and there were individuals eager to provide schools for the handicapped. The first school for the deaf was opened by a minister at Hartford, Connecticut, in 1817. The first state school for the deaf was started by Kentucky five years later. In 1832 the first schools for the blind were opened privately in Boston and New York. In 1848 Michigan founded a school for the deaf and the blind. Other states gradually established similar schools. In this way democratic opportunity was opened to one more portion of the population.

Prison reform. One of the evils which urgently needed reform was the treatment of prisoners. It was customary to place prisoners together in large rooms without regard to their crimes. Young and old, sick and well, hardened criminals and first offenders, and sometimes both sexes were thrown together. Prisons were usually crowded, dark, and dirty — hotbeds of crime and disease. Any place of confinement was thought good enough. For example, an abandoned copper mine was used as a prison in a Connecticut town for more than fifty years.

In the 1830's and 1840's reformers attacked these conditions. Pennsylvania built a prison in which each inmate lived in a separate cell. New York built the Auburn State Prison, in which the prisoners slept in separate cells but went to large workshops during the day. However, this method of housing prisoners was expensive and did not become common for a long time.

Prison associations were formed in Massachusetts and New York to study how imprisonment could be used to reform as well as punish criminals. During this period imprisonment for debt was gradually abolished. (See page 200.) The number of crimes punishable by death was reduced. The lashing and branding of prisoners was made unlawful in most of the states.

Dorothea Dix. Dorothea Dix was a Massachusetts Quakeress who spent most of her life trying to improve the treatment of prisoners, paupers, and the insane. Beginning in 1841 she visited prisons and poorhouses in all parts of the country, describing the terrible conditions which she found. She condemned the cruel practice of keeping insane persons in chains and cages. She pleaded for the separation of the incurably insane from those who might get well if given proper care. She appealed to the wealthy for money. As a result numbers of insane asylums were reorganized and some new ones were built. In eight years she traveled over sixty thousand miles, visiting all the states but three. She addressed state legislatures, securing reforms simply by picturing the conditions in prisons, poorhouses, and insane asylums which she had visited. Not only America but also Europe and Asia benefited from her work. Dorothea Dix was undoubtedly one of the most influential women our country has produced.

The temperance movement. At this period hard drinking was usual among all classes and occupations. Whiskey was considered a necessity for those engaged in physical labor. Drunkenness was common.

The churches began a crusade against drinking. By 1830 the temperance movement was well under way. It was strongest in New England and in states like Ohio, where many New Englanders had settled. Ohio was the first state to restrict the sale of liquor (1830), and Maine was the first to prohibit its sale entirely (1846). Within a dozen years thirteen states followed Maine's example by passing laws which strictly regulated or prohibited the sale of liquor.

One argument against strong drink was the injury it did to the human system. Another argument — that it reduced the workman's efficiency — was first heard about 1830. That year the superintendent in charge of building the Baltimore and Ohio Railroad told his workmen not to drink — an action which attracted much attention. The most common argument against drinking, however, was the religious one. Drinking led people into sin. The drinker had his feet on the downward path. It was better to give up liquor entirely than to lose one's soul.

DOROTHEA DIX, *the noted Quaker reformer.* (From a painting in 1871. From *Dorothea Dix,* by Helen F. Marshall, University of North Carolina Press)

WOMEN PLEADING WITH A SALOONKEEPER. *Hundreds of temperance societies were organized in the 1830's and 1840's. Women had an active part in the temperance movement.* (From a drawing by C. S. Reinhart in *Harper's Weekly,* March 14, 1874)

"FATHERS TOIL *in the nursery while mothers enjoy public life." This cartoon making fun of the women's rights movement appeared in* Harper's Weekly.

The women's rights movement. Women wanted an active part in all the reform movements of the time. They soon discovered they were not wanted. For example, in 1840 eight American women were sent as delegates to an antislavery convention in London. Admittance to the convention was refused merely because they were women. Even in the United States there was strong opposition to giving women any part in public affairs. Such women as Dorothea Dix, Emma Willard, and Mary Lyon had to put up with much ridicule.

Custom and the common law kept women in an inferior position. Girls were ruled by their fathers. When they married, they were ruled by their husbands. The husband could do as he pleased with his wife's property; he had a right to any wages she might earn and to any other income she might receive. He had complete authority over their children.

In the Jacksonian Era women rebelled against their lack of freedom. Two things made their rebellion possible: (1) the rise of the factory system, which enabled women to become self-supporting, and (2) the rise of public schools, which gave them a chance for an education. Their new opportunities made girls and women more independent and less willing to be ruled by their fathers or husbands. They asked for greater educational opportunities and for changes in the laws regarding property. In 1839 Mississippi granted married women control over their own property. By 1851 seven states had passed similar laws.

In 1848 a woman's rights convention was held at Seneca Falls, New York, the first in the history of the world. Among its leaders were Lucretia Mott of Philadelphia and Elizabeth Cady Stanton of New York. The convention issued a Woman's Declaration of Independence, which said that men *and women* are created equal, and which asked equality with men in education, in earning a living, in voting, and in the eyes of the law. The newspapers belittled the declaration with scornful headlines such as "The Reign of Petticoats" and "Insurrection among Women." Most men either laughed or cursed at the whole movement, but such men as Whittier, Emerson, William Lloyd Garrison, and Wendell Phillips supported it. The Seneca Falls Convention of 1848 was the opening gun in a struggle that was to last a century. Even today women do not have full legal equality with men, and only a small number have succeeded in reaching high positions in politics, government, and business.

The abolition movement. The goal of every reform was a better and freer life for the individual. Reformers could not close their eyes to the existence of slavery, which denied liberty and opportunity to millions of Negroes. Throughout this period the antislavery movement was gaining strength.

Religion and the people. The people of this period had a keen interest in religion. In most places the Sabbath was strictly observed, and people attended church at least once a week. Though churches no longer received public funds, they were better supported than ever before. Thousands of new chapels and churches were built. People flocked to revival meetings. Many churches held yearly camp meetings which lasted for days. Even the smallest frontier settlements were reached by circuit-riding ministers, each of whom served a number of scattered churches.

Protestant missions multiplied during this period. American missionaries went to India, China, Africa, and Hawaii, and worked among the American Indians. Wherever they worked, the missionaries put the language of the natives into writing and translated the Scriptures into the native tongue. They also started schools and hospitals as rapidly as they could get funds. In 1848 Bishop Doane of Albany expressed the spirit of his time in a stirring hymn:

CAMP MEETING. *At these religious meetings the people usually became very emotional.* (From the painting by A. Rider. Courtesy of Robert Fridenberg Galleries, New York)

> Fling out the banner! Heathen lands
> Shall see from far the glorious sight,
> And nations crowding to be born,
> Baptize their spirits in its light.

Before this period Quakers were the only denomination to show much interest in social reform. Now other denominations began to be interested in social questions. Preachers and their congregations took an increasing part in the temperance movement, the effort to improve the care of prisoners and the insane, and — in the North — the antislavery crusade. Preachers sometimes lost their places as a result of taking too strong a stand on a public question. Congregations often split over these questions.

The churches took on new activities. They established Sunday schools and young people's societies. City churches built parish houses for social gatherings. Some denominations built hospitals, orphanages, and homes for the aged. Thus the churches were developing the idea of social service and were becoming concerned with the care of the body and the mind as well as with the care of the soul. The new emphasis on Christian social service led to the founding in 1844 of the Young Men's Christian Association, and many years later of the Young Women's Christian Association.

Literature and the people. In 1820 an English critic exclaimed, "In the four corners of the world who reads an American book?" Ameri-

"THE VERDICT OF THE PEOPLE." *Election day brings joy to the winning party, gloom to the losers.* (From the painting by Bingham. Courtesy of Boatmen's National Bank of St. Louis)

cans had been too busy taming the wilderness to have much time for writing or reading. Most books in America were imported from England.

Yet by 1820 the English critic might have seen signs of a change. Londoners were even then reading Washington Irving's *Sketch Book*. Irving's tales of "Rip Van Winkle" and "The Legend of Sleepy Hollow" showed the world that America, too, had interesting folklore. James Fenimore Cooper was already at work on his series of Leatherstocking Tales. He wrote about the experiences of pioneers and Indians in the wilderness of central New York where he grew up. English readers were to greet his novels as eagerly as did American readers. Already America had a promising young poet, William Cullen Bryant. His "Thanatopsis," written when he was about seventeen, is the first great poem written in America. His "To a Waterfowl," published in 1817, was called by two English critics the best short poem in the English language.

Irving, Cooper, and Bryant were the beginners of an American literature which the people gladly read. Soon other American writers were rising to fame, among them Emerson, Thoreau, Longfellow, Whittier, Hawthorne, Lowell, Poe, and the historian, William Prescott. American readers would no longer need to depend completely on books from England. In fact English readers would find pleasure in American books.

WASHINGTON IRVING AND HIS FRIENDS *at Irving's home near Tarrytown, New York. Irving is seated facing the reader. The historian, William Prescott, is seated at his right, and Ralph Waldo Emerson at his left. Among the standing figures are Nathaniel Hawthorne, Henry Wadsworth Longfellow, and William Cullen Bryant.* (Courtesy of New York Public Library)

A PAGE OF FASHIONS *from* Godey's Lady's Book, 1844. *This famous monthly magazine was started in 1830. Its colored fashion plates are now prized by collectors.* (Courtesy of Boston Public Library)

The reading habit grows. When Jackson was elected President, only a small number of Americans had the habit of reading. But before twenty years had passed, the people were reading as they had never done before. In part this resulted from the growing number of free schools. In part it was due to the increasing use of whale oil lamps, which made it easier for people to read in the evening after work was done. In part it was due to improved methods of printing and cheaper newspapers and magazines.

In 1833 Benjamin A. Day, a printer in New York City, decided to publish a newspaper which workingmen could afford and would wish to read. Other daily papers sold for eight to ten dollars a year, a price beyond the reach of most people. Day planned to sell his paper, the *New York Sun,* for a cent a copy. He saw that he could make money only if the paper had a large enough circulation to attract advertisers. So he made his paper interesting to ordinary people having little education. Within three years the *Sun* had a daily sale of twenty-seven thousand copies, while the most successful of the older New York papers had a sale of only seventeen hundred copies.

Day's plan was quickly copied by other editors. Within two years James Gordon Bennett started the *New York Herald.* In 1841 a Vermont printer's boy, Horace Greeley, founded the *New York Tribune.* Ten years later the *New York Times* made its bow. By this time penny papers were being printed in the smaller cities as well, and Americans were becoming a nation of newspaper readers.

As the demand for reading matter grew, hundreds of weekly and monthly magazines appeared. Many lasted for only a few months. As one died, another sprang up in its place. The most popular and successful magazine of the period was *Godey's Lady's Book,* which was published for some forty years. In addition to magazines that were light and entertaining, there were a great number of serious magazines devoted to religion, temperance, abolition, labor, science, or some other special interest. Most of them were inexpensive, and some were given away. Before long there was scarcely a home which did not take at least one magazine.

Before Jackson's time an American writer could hardly support himself with his pen. But as the army of readers grew, hundreds found it possible to earn a living from writing. Many who wrote regularly for newspapers and magazines turned to the writing of books in their spare time.

New comforts and conveniences. In the 1830's and 1840's the coun-

YANKEE PEDDLER. *Most families lived far from stores and eagerly awaited the coming of a traveling peddler.* (From the painting by J. W. Ehninger in the Newark Museum)

try enjoyed better transportation than ever before. Thousands of canal packet boats and river steamboats carried the nation's products to market. Short rail lines linked neighboring cities. Stagecoaches and freight wagons connected places not within reach by steamboat or railroad.

Cities were growing rapidly and city life was becoming safer and healthier. Gas lamps replaced whale oil lamps on the city streets. Water mains and hydrants were replacing the well and the rain barrel. Some cities had started sewerage systems.

Homes, too, were improving. New methods of heating were coming into use. All through the Northeast, kitchen fireplaces had been closed and iron ranges had taken their places. In cities coal was replacing wood as a fuel. By 1850 hot-air furnaces were frequently found in public buildings, churches, and the houses of the well to do.

Lighting was also improved. It is said that this generation was born by candlelight and died by oil lamps. The lamps burned whale oil or lard, for petroleum had not yet come into use. In some cities gaslights were used in private homes as well as for lighting the streets. Whether candles, oil lamps, or gaslights were used, by 1850 they were generally lighted by matches instead of the clumsy flint or steel.

AN EARLY SEWING MACHINE. *Elias Howe invented the first practical sewing machine to be marketed. It was patented in 1846 and began to be widely used during the War between North and South.* (Bettmann Archive)

The kitchen was changed not only by the cookstove but by new kitchenware. In place of heavy copper and iron utensils tinware made its appearance. It was so cheap that most housewives could now afford a good supply of pots and pans. Because these utensils were light in weight, they made kitchen work easier.

Wallpaper, once found only in the homes of the well to do, was now made cheaply in American factories. As a result it was coming into common use. Carpets, too, were now made in America at a price that middle-class people could afford. They were rapidly taking the place of homemade rag rugs. The doorbell was taking the place of the door knocker. The invention of photography enabled the poor as well as the rich to have their portraits made. By 1850 homes often contained photographs of members of the family.

A number of extremely important inventions were made during this period. Among them were the reaper (1834), the telegraph (1837), the process of vulcanizing rubber (1844), the sewing machine (1846), and the rotary printing press (1847). Each was to help produce startling changes in ways of working and living. However, it was some time before any of these was widely used. None of them had much effect on everyday life during the Jacksonian Era.

To identify: Henry Barnard, William Cullen Bryant, James Fenimore Cooper, Dorothea Dix, Horace Greeley, Washington Irving, Mary Lyon, Horace Mann, Lucretia Mott, Elizabeth Stanton, Emma Willard.

To explain or define: camp meeting, circuit rider, normal school, packet boat, revival meeting, seminary, temperance movement.

Subjects for Talks or Written Reports

1. The life and work of one of the following: Henry Barnard, Dorothea Dix, Mary Lyon, Horace Mann, Lucretia Mott, Wendell Phillips, Elizabeth Cady Stanton, Emma Willard. 2. The life, writings, and influence of one of the following: William Cullen Bryant, James Fenimore Cooper, Ralph Waldo Emerson, Horace Greeley, Nathaniel Hawthorne, Henry Wadsworth Longfellow, James Russell Lowell, Edgar Allan Poe, William Prescott, Henry Thoreau. 3. The story of the invention and introduction of one of the following: photography, the process of vulcanizing rubber, the reaper, the rotary printing press, the sewing machine, the telegraph. 4. The struggle for women's rights.

Questions for Understanding the Text

1. What is meant by the "Jacksonian Period"? 2. (*a*) Show that in the Jacksonian Period America was a land of opportunity. (*b*) Did everyone have equal economic opportunity? Explain. 3. Show that the different social classes were becoming more alike at this period. 4. (*a*) What group led the fight for free public schools? (*b*) What were the arguments for education at public expense? 5. Discuss conditions in the public schools before Horace Mann began his work. What reforms did he call for? 6. Why did Henry Barnard found the *American Journal of Education?* 7. What were the principal subjects taught in colleges during the Jacksonian Period? 8. Why were state universities demanded? 9. Why is the founding of Mount Holyoke Seminary considered an important milestone in education? 10. (*a*) Show the need for prison reforms. (*b*) What changes were made at this period in the treatment of criminals? 11. (*a*) To what did Dorothea Dix devote her life? (*b*) How did she go about it? 12. (*a*) Where was the temperance movement strongest? (*b*) State the arguments against the use of strong drink. 13. (*a*) What new conditions led women to demand more freedom? (*b*) Why do we remember the Seneca Falls Convention of 1848? (*c*) How long did the struggle for equal rights continue? 14. How did people of this period show their interest in religion? 15. Name several American writers of the Jacksonian Period. For what kind of writing is each best known? 16. What changes helped make the United States a reading nation? 17. How did the *New York Sun* differ from earlier newspapers? 18. In what ways were cities becoming safer and healthier? 19. In what ways were homes becoming more comfortable? 20. Account for the growing use of wallpaper and carpets.

CHAPTER 18

EXPANSION TO THE PACIFIC

T*he opening of the Far West.* The settling of the vast country west of the Mississippi is a colorful story. One of its first episodes has to do with the exploring expedition which Jefferson sent all the way to the Pacific under two young army officers, Meriwether Lewis and William Clark. (See pages 145–146.) Setting out in 1804, the explorers went up the Missouri River, crossed the Rockies, and went down the Columbia River to its mouth. They carefully mapped and described the country. Their records awakened American interest in the Far Northwest.

The expedition opened up a vast new section to American fur traders. Immediately after his return from Oregon, Clark helped organize the Missouri Fur Company. Soon afterward John Jacob Astor established branches of his American Fur Company in the Northwest. He sent a ship around Cape Horn to set up a trading post, Astoria, at the mouth of the Columbia (1811). A few years later a St. Louis fur trader, William Ashley, organized the Rocky Mountain Fur Company. This was the first fur company to employ trappers rather than depend on buying furs from the Indians. One of Ashley's men was the famous scout and Indian fighter, Kit Carson.

The Far Southwest was part of Mexico. Americans did not enter it to any extent until after 1821, when Mexico won her independence from Spain. The next year an energetic Missouri trader, William Becknell, got together a pack train, which he led eight hundred miles over rough, dangerous country from Independence, Missouri, to Santa Fe, New Mexico. He sold his goods to the Mexicans at a handsome profit. The next year he took a wagon train to Santa Fe. Other traders soon followed his example. Trade over the Santa Fe Trail soon awakened American interest in the Southwest.

American missionaries in the Northwest. The Indians on the Columbia River, after learning something about the Christian religion from British fur traders, sent four men all the way to St. Louis (1831)

ASTORIA IN 1811. *This trading post, built by John Jacob Astor at the mouth of the Columbia River, was the first permanent settlement in the Oregon country.* (Courtesy of Oregon Historical Society)

to ask that preachers be sent them. The Methodist Church was first to answer their call. Quickly raising funds, it sent two ministers and a teacher to the Northwest. They built a mission house in the fertile and beautiful Willamette Valley. Before many years there were missionaries throughout the Oregon country. Besides preaching, the missionaries showed the Indians how to raise crops and build homes. The missionaries wrote enthusiastic letters to their friends in the East, describing the rich soil and fine climate of Oregon. This led many Easterners to move there.

The Oregon Trail. Explorers, fur traders, and missionaries who journeyed from the Missouri River to the Columbia followed a route which came to be known as the Oregon Trail. (See map on page 246.) Starting at Independence on the Missouri, it led across plains and mountains, then down the Columbia, a total distance of some two thousand miles. A party of settlers, numbering about one hundred twenty, successfully made the long, dangerous journey over the trail in 1842. In 1843, about a thousand settlers, with their covered wagons and herds, gathered at the Missouri. Led part of the way by the missionary Marcus Whitman, they, too, crossed over the dry plateaus and trackless mountain ranges to reach their goal in the Oregon country. During the next few years the number of settlers grew rapidly.

CARAVAN ON ITS WAY TO SANTA FE. *Americans carried on a profitable trade with the far Southwest long before this region became part of the United States.* (From the painting by Frederic Remington. Courtesy of P. F. Collier and Son)

Settlers bound for Oregon over the trail traveled in ox-team caravans. On good days they might cover twenty-five miles; on bad days, five to ten. The long lines of covered wagons got into motion at dawn. At nightfall they camped in a circle, the wagons on the outside, the people and animals within. All night long guards watched for prowling Indians and wild beasts. The journey from Independence required five or six months. Often oxen and mules wore out and prized possessions had to be left by the way. The feeble died on the journey and were buried in unmarked graves.

Some settlers preferred to go by sea. They could go around Cape Horn, a voyage taking six or seven months, or could go by sea to the Isthmus of Panama. The trip across the isthmus was made partly by land and partly by water. It was only sixty miles but required a week. Many who attempted this trip died of tropical diseases before they could take a ship for Oregon.

Deciding the ownership of Oregon. Although thousands of Americans were settling in Oregon, it did not yet belong to the United States. Since 1818 the United States and Great Britain had owned the region together. (See page 171.) There had been several attempts to divide the territory, but the two nations could not agree on the boundary. The United States wished the dividing line to be the

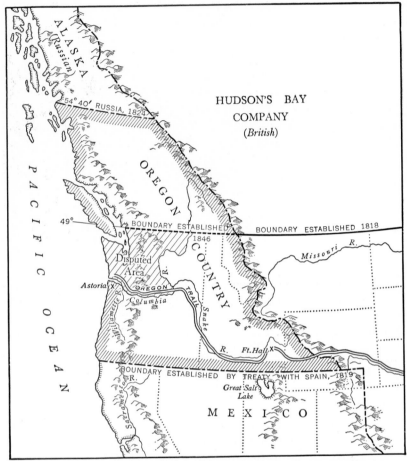

OREGON BOUNDARY DISPUTE AND SETTLEMENT

In 1846 the United States and Great Britain agreed to divide Oregon between them along the 49° parallel. This settled the Oregon question permanently.

49th parallel, while Great Britain wished it to be the Columbia River. For years the question was allowed to drift, but now that the territory was being settled, it had to be decided.

By 1843 there were three or four thousand Americans in Oregon, most of them in the Willamette Valley. That year they held a mass meeting in a barn and organized a government. They adopted laws to be in force until such time as the United States of America should take over the territory. This action caused Congress to debate the Oregon question. The Western congressmen wanted to make Oregon part of the United States. Eastern and Southern congressmen were cool to the proposal. Some feared it might lead to war with England. Others thought that a territory so far away as Oregon could not become a state but must remain a colony. A senator from South Carolina asked: "What do we want with this territory? . . . To talk about constructing a railroad to the western shore of this continent shows a wild spirit of adventure which I never expected to hear . . . in the Senate of the United States." The wealth of the Indies, he added, would not build a railroad across the deserts and mountains lying between the Mississippi and the Pacific.

By 1844 the Democratic party made up its mind that Oregon should be part of the United States. In the presidential campaign that year the Democrats took as their slogan, "Fifty-four forty or fight." This was a demand for *all* of Oregon, as far north as Alaska. The Democrats won the election, and James K. Polk of Tennessee became President. After the election the Oregon question was peaceably settled. England agreed to accept the 49th parallel as the boundary, and a treaty was signed in 1846. The Northwest was disappointed that part of Oregon was to belong to England, but the rest of the country was satisfied.

The Mormons settle Utah. Soon after the Oregon question was decided, the Mormans settled in Utah. The Mormons were a religious denomination started in 1830 by Joseph Smith, a youth of upper New York. He called his organization the "Church of Jesus Christ of Latter Day Saints" and rapidly won a large number of followers in America and Europe. Settling in Illinois, the Mormons built a prosperous city, Nauvoo. They founded a university and commenced to erect a great temple. When their leaders married more than one wife, a mob of non-Mormons killed Smith and his brother. Soon after, the Mormons were driven from Illinois. In 1847, led by Brigham Young, they moved into the Great Salt Lake valley.

Here the Mormons found a healthful climate and land that was fertile but dry. They dug irrigation ditches up and down the valley and soon began to prosper. For their capital they built beautiful Salt Lake City. They sent missionaries to the Eastern states, to Great Britain, and to Europe, to win converts who would settle in Utah. Within three years there were eleven thousand people in the Salt Lake district, and Utah was organized as a territory of the United States.

Expansion into Texas. As we have noted, the boundaries of the Louisiana Purchase were extremely uncertain. (See page 145.)

SALT LAKE CITY. *At first there was suffering in this Mormon settlement, but soon the colony enjoyed abundance.* (*Harper's Weekly,* July 11, 1857)

Americans claimed that Texas was included, but Spain denied this. In 1819, when the United States persuaded Spain to sell Florida, the State Department agreed to a western boundary which gave up our doubtful claims to Texas. This action angered many Westerners; they resolved to get the Texas country back whenever it could be done "with peace and honor."

A few months after this treaty with Spain, an American, Moses Austin, got permission from the Spanish authorities to bring three hundred American families to Texas. A thriving community was soon established, the settlers coming chiefly from Louisiana, Mississippi, and Tennessee. Soon after, Mexico became free from Spain. The Mexican government, wishing to speed up the settlement of Texas, offered large tracts of land to anyone who would agree to bring in at least two hundred families of settlers. The one receiving such a grant was known as an *empresario*. Soon nearly all of Texas had been parceled out, mainly to Americans. The empresarios sold land for 12½ cents an acre, while the cheapest land in the United States was then $1.25 an acre. Within ten years about twenty thousand Americans settled in Texas. Most of them came from the Southern states and usually brought slaves with them.

The Texas Revolution. The Mexican government was inefficient, feeble, and constantly changing. Presidents, congresses, and dicta-

THE MISSOURI RIVER

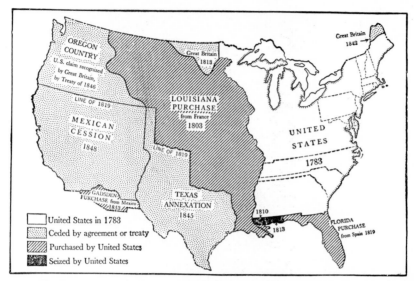

TERRITORIAL GROWTH OF THE UNITED STATES, 1783–1853

tors appeared and disappeared. A policy adopted by one government was ignored by the next. But every Mexican government wanted to keep Texas.

As Americans continued to move into Texas, the Mexican authorities tried to restrict immigration. They also tried to put an end to slavery. In 1829 the Mexican president declared that slavery was abolished. The Texans protested so vigorously that they were allowed to keep their slaves. The next year Mexico prohibited further immigration and further importation of slaves; however, the Mexican government was too weak to enforce either law in Texas.

Texans paid little attention to Mexican laws. They expected that Texas would soon become part of the United States, for they knew that the United States had been trying to purchase the territory. In 1827 President Adams offered Mexico a million dollars for it, and in 1829 President Jackson offered five million dollars. Each offer was refused, but the Texans saw no reason to be discouraged.

In 1835 a new Mexican ruler, Santa Anna, did away with the state governments of Mexico. This was too much for the Texans, and they promptly rebelled. In two months they drove the last Mexican soldier across the border. Santa Anna then swept northward with an army, determined to teach the Texans a lesson. Meeting small bands of armed revolutionists, he crushed one after another. The Texans

SAM HOUSTON. *He did more than any other man to free Texas from Mexico.*
(From a miniature made about 1836. Courtesy of Sam Houston Memorial Museum)

were beginning to lose heart when a heroic event restored their courage. The old fort of the Alamo at San Antonio was held by 188 Texans commanded by Colonel Travis. Three thousand Mexicans led by
Santa Anna closed in around them. Travis and his men refused to
surrender. After a thirteen-day siege all but six had fallen at their
posts. They were shot by Santa Anna. Texas was now aroused and
united. Its battle cry became "Remember the Alamo!"

Under General Sam Houston the little Texan army took revenge.
In the Battle of San Jacinto they almost destroyed Santa Anna's forces,
and Santa Anna himself was captured. When he signed a treaty agree-
ing to the independence of Texas, he was allowed to return to Mexico.
Sam Houston was then elected president of the new "Lone Star
Republic."

Should Texas be annexed? Texas soon sent a petition to Washington asking to be annexed. It was 1836, the year of a presidential election, and President Jackson held back. If annexed, Texas would be
slave territory, so the North was against annexation. While Jackson
wished to annex Texas, he did not wish to stir up a sectional quarrel
which might prevent the election of his friend Van Buren. President

THE ALAMO. *In this old mission at San Antonio, Texas, the entire garrison met death rather than surrender to the Mexicans.*

Van Buren let the question ride. He did not favor adding new slave states to the Union, and, besides, he would not risk war with Mexico. His successor, William H. Harrison, felt the same way. But John Tyler, who became President upon Harrison's death, strongly favored annexation. When Tyler felt that the time was ripe, he had a treaty of annexation drawn up.

This treaty was sent to the Senate early in 1844. A bitter debate followed. Some senators felt that annexation would lead to war with Mexico. Others thought that annexation was a Southern scheme to extend slave territory, with the expectation of adding several new slave states to the Union. The annexationists replied that they only wished to increase the size of the nation. They said the Texans were really our own people who needed our protection, and without it would surely be reconquered. They argued that it was "manifest destiny" (something that had to be) for the United States to control the continent to the Pacific, including Texas and much more besides.

The South was deeply disappointed when the Senate did not ratify the treaty of annexation. Why should the North grow continually stronger by the addition of new free states, while the South was not permitted to grow? Rather than be controlled by a Congress in which the North had the majority, should the South not secede from the Union? A leading South Carolina newspaper declared in a headline, "Disunion, the only remedy." The cry was taken up in many Southern communities. But Calhoun, the best-known Southern leader, advised patience.

The campaign of 1844. The year 1844, in which the Senate turned down the treaty, was a presidential election year. The Democrats boldly declared for the "reoccupation of Oregon and the reannexation of Texas." This was intended to satisfy both North and South. It was thought that the Northerners would be satisfied if the boundaries of the country expanded in the Northwest at the same time as in the Southwest, for one would balance the other. Southerners, of course, would be well pleased by securing Texas.

The Democrats had some difficulty in choosing a candidate. The problem was to find someone who could win votes in both the North and South, for by this time the slavery question had made the two sections unfriendly. The nomination finally went to a "dark horse" (that is, a candidate but little known), former Governor Polk of Tennessee, a friend of Jackson.

The Whigs found the choice of a candidate easy, for all the delegates wanted the great Kentuckian, Henry Clay. The party managers decided to take no stand on the question of expansion. It was soon plain that they had made a mistake, for the common people wanted both Texas and Oregon. When he realized this, Clay tried to explain away his earlier opposition to annexing Texas. He wrote a famous letter saying that he would be glad to see Texas annexed if that was what the people wanted and if it could be done without going to war.

The popular vote was very close. However, Polk received a majority of the electoral votes. For the third time the brilliant Clay was defeated for the Presidency. Polk's victory showed that the country wanted annexation, and early the next year Congress voted to make Texas a territory of the United States. As we have seen, the Oregon question was settled a year later. (See page 247.)

War with Mexico. In spite of the treaty signed by Santa Anna while he was a prisoner of the Texans, Texas was still claimed by Mexico. When Congress voted to annex Texas, the Mexican government called home its minister at Washington and broke off relations with our government. Mexico announced that making Texas a part of the United States would be regarded as a declaration of war.

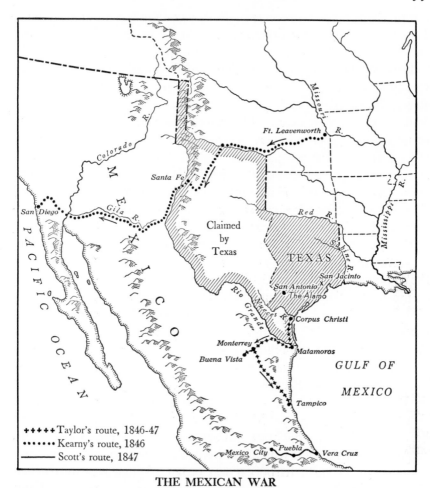

THE MEXICAN WAR

The area of Texas is shown as it was when Texas was a state in Mexico. When Texas became independent, it claimed much additional territory. These claims were the direct cause of our war with Mexico.

Meanwhile many Americans were hoping to gain California and New Mexico. The region belonged to Mexico, but the Mexican government did nothing for it and had no real control over it. Mexican leaders, in fact, had talked of selling the region to Great Britain. In the fall of 1845 Polk sent a special minister to Mexico, instructing him to settle the Texas boundary, and to offer twenty-five million dollars for New Mexico and California. The United States was so unpopular with the Mexican people because of the annexation of Texas that our minister was not even received. Polk accomplished nothing by sending him except to cause additional ill feeling between the United States and Mexico.

It was the boundary question that actually led to war. When Texas had been a state in Mexico, her southern boundary was the Nueces River. Now Texas claimed the Rio Grande as her boundary, and Polk supported that claim. He ordered General Zachary Taylor to occupy the disputed territory between the two rivers. When Taylor did so, Mexico sent troops across the Rio Grande to attack him. A skirmish took place between the Mexicans and a small force of Americans. Soon after this, Polk sent a war message to Congress saying that Mexico had invaded our territory and shed American blood. Congress declared war on May 12, 1846.

We take possession of New Mexico and California. Colonel Stephen Kearny was instructed to occupy New Mexico and California. In the summer of 1846 he made the long march from Fort Leavenworth on the upper Missouri to Santa Fe. After ten weeks on the way he and his small force entered Santa Fe. Kearny set up a temporary American government. Then with three hundred men he hurried across the desert to California. On the way he met Kit Carson bearing news that California was already conquered. Carson explained that in the spring the Americans in the Sacramento Valley had revolted and proclaimed the Republic of California — the "Bear Republic." When they learned that the United States and Mexico were at war, they took down the bear flag and ran up the Stars and Stripes. They were supported by an American squadron which had been waiting off the coast with instructions to seize the harbors if war began. When Kearny reached California in December, the remaining resistance was quickly put down.

Defeat of the Mexicans. Meanwhile an army commanded by General Zachary Taylor invaded northern Mexico. In September, after a stubborn battle, Taylor captured the fortified city of Monterrey. In February, at Buena Vista, Taylor defeated an untrained Mexican force several times larger than his own.

Early the next spring an army commanded by General Winfield Scott landed near Vera Cruz on Mexico's eastern coast. He captured that seaport and then marched westward through the mountains to the capital. After a hard-fought campaign, he took Mexico City. With the loss of their capital, the Mexican government was ready to make peace.

LANDING OF THE AMERICAN FORCES AT VERA CRUZ, *March 9, 1847. Two young officers, later to become famous, Ulysses S. Grant and Robert E. Lee, were in this army, which was ably commanded by General Winfield Scott.* (Lithograph by N. Currier, 1847. Courtesy of New York Historical Society)

BOMBARDMENT OF VERA CRUZ, *March 22, 1847. When the Mexicans refused to surrender Vera Cruz, the city was bombarded from the land and from the sea. Five days later the city's defenders gave up. General Scott then led his army on a difficult march through the mountains to Mexico City and finally captured the capital.* (From the painting by Castaigne in *History of the United States Navy*, 1894. Courtesy of Boston Public Library)

POST OFFICE AT SAN FRANCISCO *during the gold rush. From all parts of the world strangers poured into San Francisco on their way to the gold fields.* (From painting by H. F. Cox. Courtesy of Gallery of Fine Arts, Yale University)

The peace treaty. When peace was made, the United States obtained Texas, California, and New Mexico. From New Mexico were later formed the states of Nevada and Utah, most of Arizona and New Mexico, and parts of Wyoming and Colorado. In return the United States promised to pay fifteen million dollars, besides taking over the claims of American citizens against Mexico, amounting to about three millions. Mexico agreed that Texas belonged to the United States as far as the Rio Grande. The treaty was signed at Guadalupe Hidalgo in 1848.

Five years later Mexico sold us a strip of land along the border for ten million dollars. We paid much more for this land, called the Gadsden Purchase, than for the land obtained at the end of the war. The purchase rounded out the present boundaries of the United States.

The discovery of gold in California. As a result of the Mexican War, the United States gained an enormous territory. Much of it was desert, and some Americans wondered whether it was worth the price paid for it. Little did they dream at the time that the United States had purchased a treasure house.

WASHING GOLD AT SUTTER'S MILL. *The California gold rush began when gold was found in a millrace belonging to John Sutter of Sacramento. His workmen deserted, his cattle were stolen, and his land was occupied by squatters.* (From the motion picture, *Sutter's Gold.* Universal Pictures Company, Inc.)

Gold was discovered in the Sacramento Valley in January, 1848, just two weeks before the signing of the treaty ending the Mexican War. When they heard the news, Californians dropped whatever they were doing and hurried to the gold fields. By early summer a thousand men were busy washing gold. With nothing but a shovel and a pan a man could make from $10 to $100 a day. One miner made $4500 in a few weeks, and a schoolboy carried home over $3000 after less than two months' work. Sometimes an individual found a single nugget worth thousands of dollars.

A Californian has given us a picture of what happened there in 1848:

> Settlements were completely deserted; houses, farms and stores abandoned. Ships, deserted by their sailors, crowded the bay of San Francisco; soldiers deserted wholesale; churches were emptied; town councils ceased to sit; merchants, clerks, lawyers, and judges and criminals everywhere flocked to the foothills.

The news reached the East in the fall of 1848. At once people from every walk of life prepared to leave for California. The farmer sold his land; the merchant, his business; the minister left his pulpit; the clerk, his desk; the teacher, the schoolroom. Most went overland by the Santa Fe Trail, and soon the deserts were littered with the skeletons of their horses and oxen, their abandoned prairie schooners and baggage, and the graves of those who perished of sickness or thirst. Others took the long journey by boat around South America. Still others went across the Isthmus of Panama.

The greatest rush of gold seekers was in 1849, and the "Fortyniners" are famous in song and story. The following is part of a song celebrating the gold rush.

> I'll scrape the mountains clean, old Girl,
> I'll drain the rivers dry.
> I'm off for California, Susannah, don't you cry.
> Oh, Susannah, don't you cry for me.
> I'm off to California with my washbowl on my knee.

As thousands poured into California, the seaport towns and the mining camps grew like mushrooms. Prices rocketed. Rooms rented for unheard-of prices. In 1849 a tent in San Francisco rented for $40,000 a year; a pick or shovel sold for $10 to $50. In the mining camps flour and potatoes sold for $1.00 a pound, sugar and coffee for $4.00 a pound. Wages were set by the amount of gold one could pan in a day. Carpenters got $20 a day; clerks, from $300 to $500 a month. These high prices and wages continued for several years in the more remote camps.

California had about fifteen thousand people at the beginning of 1848. Two years later it had one hundred thousand people and was admitted to the Union as a state. By that time it had already yielded gold worth several times the price paid for the entire Southwest. The rapid inflow of people wiped away the Spanish customs and laws and changed California from a sleepy Mexican province to a hustling American state.

❁ ❁ ❁

To identify: the Alamo, Santa Anna, John Jacob Astor, Moses Austin, Bear Republic, Kit Carson, Sam Houston, Lone Star Republic, Joseph Smith, Colonel Travis, Marcus Whitman, Brigham Young.

To explain or define: convert, dark horse, denomination, empresario, plateau.

SUBJECTS FOR TALKS OR WRITTEN REPORTS

1. The life of John Jacob Astor. 2. The life and adventures of Kit Carson. 3. Trade and travel on the Santa Fe Trail before the mid-century. 4. The early history of Oregon. 5. A trip over the Oregon Trail in the 1840's. 6. Early history of the Mormons. 7. The early history of Texas. 8. An all-water journey to California in the gold-rush days. 9. Life in the mining camps during the gold rush.

QUESTIONS FOR UNDERSTANDING THE TEXT

1. Name the explorers who opened up the far Northwest. What was their route? 2. (*a*) Name the most famous fur trader of the Northwest. (*b*) What company did he organize? (*c*) How did this company obtain furs? 3. How did Americans become interested in the far Southwest? 4. How did missionaries help in settling Oregon? 5. Describe the journey of an ox-train caravan to Oregon. 6. Why did Eastern and Southern congressmen hesitate to make Oregon part of the United States? 7. (*a*) Give the correct name of the Mormon church. (*b*) Who founded this denomination? (*c*) Why were the Mormons driven from Illinois? (*d*) Who led them to Utah? 8. (*a*) Why did many Americans buy land in Texas rather than in the United States? (*b*) Where did most of them come from? (*c*) Why did the Mexican government decide to resist the immigration of Americans into Texas? Was it successful? (*d*) Why did Texans disobey Mexican laws? 9. (*a*) What caused the Texans to rebel against the Mexican government? (*b*) What did the Mexican ruler do about the rebellion? (*c*) What happened at the Alamo? 10. (*a*) Why did President Jackson not annex Texas? (*b*) Why did President Van Buren not annex Texas? (*c*) Why did the Senate not ratify the treaty of annexation when President Tyler submitted it in 1844? (*d*) How did Southerners feel about the Senate's refusal to annex Texas? 11. Why did the Democratic leaders choose a dark horse for their candidate in 1844? 12. Why do you think the Whig leaders decided to say nothing during the 1844 campaign about annexing Texas and Oregon? 13. What incident resulted in war between the United States and Mexico? 14. State the terms of the peace treaty between the United States and Mexico. 15. (*a*) When was gold discovered in California? What did the Californians do then? (*b*) What happened when the news reached the East? 16. What three routes were open to the Forty-niners? Which would you have chosen? Why?

ACTIVITIES FOR UNIT FOUR

1. Draw a cartoon to show how the Eastern businessman felt at first toward the westward migration. Draw another to show how the Eastern laborer felt about going west.

2. Write an editorial on the desirable and undesirable qualities which develop in the settlers of a frontier community. A good reference is H. J. Carman, *Social and Economic History of the United States,* Vol. I, pages 557–571.
3. Make a chart showing the chief inventions of the Industrial Revolution between 1730 and 1830. Give inventors and dates, and state how each invention was used. Consult *The Pageant of America,* Vol. V, Ch. 3, and W. B. Kaempffert (editor), *A Popular History of American Invention,* Vol. I.
4. Continue work on the classbook, *American Hall of Fame,* and on the history of your community.
5. Appoint committees to prepare an illustrated classbook entitled "Life in the Jacksonian Era." Include sections on travel, art, dress, amusements, education, farming, housekeeping, peddlers, marketing farm products, newspapers and magazines, prisons, drinking and the temperance movement, religion, and so on.
6. Write an editorial on living and working conditions among factory workers in the 1830's and 1840's.
7. On outline maps show (a) the states carried by Jackson and those carried by Clay in 1832, (b) the principal events of the Mexican War, (c) territorial growth of the United States to 1853, (d) admission of states to 1850.
8. Write imaginary interviews with Calhoun, Webster, Clay, and Jackson on the threatened secession of South Carolina.
9. Develop a panel discussion on the question of whether a peacetime President should try to lead the nation or should let Congress take the lead.
10. Prepare an editorial or cartoon for a Mexico City newspaper of that time on the outbreak of war with the United States. Prepare another on the same topic for a South Carolina newspaper.

READINGS FOR UNIT FOUR

(Stars indicate the easier books)

GENERAL ACCOUNTS

Bolton, Herbert E. *The Spanish Borderlands.* (Chronicles)
Brown, Harriet C. *Grandmother Brown's One Hundred Years, 1827–1927.* Blue Ribbon.
*Bush, M. G. and Waddell, J. F. *How We Have Conquered Distance.* Macmillan.
Dunbar, Seymour. *A History of Travel in America.* Tudor.
Fish, Carl R. *The Rise of the Common Man, 1830–1850.* (A. L. S.)

Fraser, H. R. *Democracy in the Making.* Bobbs-Merrill. (The Jackson-Tyler era)
*Holland, R. S. *Historic Railroads.* Macrae-Smith.
Hurlburt, Archer B. *Forty-Niners.* Atlantic.
Kaempffert, Waldemar B., editor. *A Popular History of American Invention.* Scribner's.
Keir, Malcolm. *The Epic of Industry.* (Pageant)
Laut, Agnes C. *Overland Trail.* Stokes.
Ogg, Frederic A. *The Reign of Andrew Jackson.* (Chronicles)
——. *The Old Northwest, a Chronicle of the Ohio Valley and Beyond.* (Chronicles)
Skinner, Constance L. *Pioneers of the Old Southwest.* (Chronicles)
——. *Adventurers of Oregon.* (Chronicles)
Stephenson, Nathaniel W. *Texas and the Mexican War.* (Chronicles)
Vestal, Stanley. *The Old Santa Fe Trail.* Houghton Mifflin.
Weigle, Luther A. *American Idealism.* (Pageant)
White, Stewart E. *The Forty-Niners.* (Chronicles)
Williams, Stanley T. *The American Spirit in Letters.* (Pageant)
Woestemeyer, Ina F. *The Westward Movement: A Book of Readings on Our Changing Frontiers.* Appleton-Century.

BIOGRAPHY

*Britt, Albert. *The Boys' Own Book of Frontiersmen.* Macmillan.
Crockett, David. *Autobiography.* Scribner's.
*Horton, Edith. *A Group of Famous Women; Stories of Their Lives.* Heath.
James, Bessie R. and James, Marquis. *The Courageous Heart.* Bobbs-Merrill. (Life of Andrew Jackson)
James, Marquis. *The Raven.* Blue Ribbon. (Sam Houston)
Jennings, N. C. *A Texas Ranger.* Southwest Press.
Lutz, Alma. *Emma Willard, Daughter of Democracy.* Houghton Mifflin.
Mann, Mary P. *Life of Horace Mann.* National Education Association.
Nevins, Allan. *Frémont: Pathmarker of the West.* Appleton-Century.
*Nicolay, Helen. *Andrew Jackson, the Fighting President.* Appleton-Century.
Seymour, F. W. *Boys' Life of Kit Carson.* Appleton-Century.
*Tappan, Eva M. *American Hero Stories.* Houghton Mifflin.
Vestal, Stanley. *Kit Carson, Happy Warrior of the Old West.* Houghton Mifflin.

FICTION

*Altsheler, J. A. *The Texan Scouts.* Appleton-Century.
*Bacheller, Irving. *A Boy for the Ages.* Farrar & Rinehart. (Lincoln)

*Darby, Ada C. *Keturah Came 'Round the Horn*. Stokes. (Travel by sea to California, 1840–1849)

Edmonds, Walter. *Rome Haul*. Modern Library. (Canal transportation in the 1850's)

Eggleston, Edward. *The Hoosier Schoolmaster*. Grosset. (Life in Indiana about 1850)

Fairbank, Janet A. *Bright Land*. Houghton Mifflin. (Pioneer life in Illinois)

Garland, Hamlin. *Trailmakers of the Middle Border*. Grosset. (Pioneer days in Wisconsin)

*Hanck, Louise P. *The Youngest Rider, a Story of the Pony Express*. Lothrop.

Hough, Emerson. *The Covered Wagon*. Grosset. (The Oregon Trail in 1848)

——. *North of 36*. Grosset. (Texas independence; the Alamo)

Jones, Nard. *Swift Flows the River*. Dodd, Mead. (Pioneer days in Oregon)

*Meadowcroft, Enid L. *By Wagon and Flatboat*. Crowell. (A trip from Pennsylvania to Ohio)

*Medary, Marjorie. *Prairie Anchorage*. Longmans. (Frontier life in Iowa, 1850–1860)

*Morris, Rhoda. *Susan and Arabella, Pioneers*. Little, Brown. (A trip to Oregon)

Nicholson, Meredith. *The Cavalier of Tennessee*. Grosset. (Andrew Jackson)

*Palmer, Elizabeth. *Give Me a River*. Scribner's. (Pioneer days in Minnesota)

Quick, Herbert. *Vandemark's Folly*. Grosset. (Early life in Wisconsin and Iowa, 1840–1860)

Quinn, Vernon. *War-paint and Powder-horn*. Stokes. (The Santa Fe Trail)

Roberts, Elizabeth M. *The Great Meadow*. Viking. (Pioneering in Kentucky, 1780–1800)

*Skelton, C. L. *Riding West on the Pony Express*. Macmillan.

Stewart, George R. *East of the Giants*. Holt. (California, 1837–1848)

Twain, Mark. *Huckleberry Finn*. Harper. (Life along the Mississippi)

Venable, Clark. *All the Brave Rifles*. Reilly & Lee. (David Crockett; Sam Houston)

UNIT FIVE
CONFLICT BETWEEN
THE NORTH AND SOUTH

With the continued growth of manufacturing in the North and of cotton growing in the South, the interests of the two sections grew further and further apart. Each wanted to control the national government so that its own interests might be favored. When the South saw that it was losing strength in Congress, the idea of leaving the Union gained ground.

The victory of the Republican party and the election of Lincoln in 1860 meant that the North had at last gained control of the national government. The states of the deep South promptly seceded from the United States and set up an independent government known as the Confederate States of America. When Lincoln refused to let the Confederate states leave the Union, there began four years of hard fighting. This struggle, which we may speak of as the War of the Confederate States for Independence, or the War between North and South, left the South completely exhausted.

The Southern states were compelled to return to the Union on any terms they could get. President Lincoln wished the terms to be as easy as possible but he was assassinated before he could carry out his plans. Congress then took charge and forced the South to pass through ten terrible years of so-called "reconstruction."

ELI WHITNEY. *This Massachusetts schoolteacher invented the cotton gin and thus helped fasten slavery on the South.* (From the painting by Alonzo Chappel in the possession of Johnson, Fry and Company, Publishers, New York)

CHAPTER 19

THE SLAVERY SYSTEM

The beginning of slavery in America. Slavery had existed in the Old World since the dawn of history. When the Spanish settled in the New World, they began at once to enslave the Indians. The red men were too fierce and proud to make good slaves. Besides, they could not resist the white man's diseases and died in great numbers. The Spanish soon turned to the use of Negro slaves.

Before long many ships were bringing Negroes from Africa to the New World. To increase their business the slave traders were always on the lookout for new markets. Hardly had the English colony of Jamestown become firmly established when a vessel came there with twenty Negroes (1619). These were bought by the planters. It is interesting to note that the Virginians regarded these Negroes as indentured servants, who were to be set free after a few years' service. However, some of the English settlers objected to the presence of free Negroes, and before long it became the custom to keep Negroes in lifelong bondage, just as in the Spanish colonies.

Why slaves were little used in the North. Slavery existed in all the English colonies in North America. Yet our first census, in 1790, showed that of seven hundred thousand slaves in the United States, only forty thousand were in the states north of Maryland. In the North slaves were used chiefly as house servants. Their labor was not profitable on the small Northern farms. Few of them were used in commerce and manufacturing because so many whites objected to working side by side with persons of another race.

Why slaves were chiefly used on plantations. A Southern farm having at least twenty field hands was considered a plantation. Plantations were of various sizes. The most profitable size for growing cotton was thought to consist of a thousand acres of land and a hundred slaves. The plantation usually produced only one crop for sale, which might be cotton, rice, tobacco, or sugar cane. Other crops and live-stock were raised for home use.

THE VISIT OF THE MISTRESS. *The planter's wife often took a kindly interest in the welfare of the slaves.* (From the painting by Winslow Homer. Courtesy of Smith-sonian Institution)

On plantations there was a great deal of work which could be done by groups of unskilled laborers directed by an overseer. Since most slaves were unskilled and did not work well unless watched, they were worth more to planters than to other employers. The planters could therefore pay a higher price for slaves than could other buyers. That is why most of the slaves were found on plantations.

Early attempts to restrict slavery. Slavery did not exist in the British Isles, although some Britishers took part in the slave trade. Perhaps slavery would not have existed in the British colonies had the settlers not needed labor so badly. Massachusetts and Rhode Island early passed laws to restrict slavery. In 1710 Virginia tried to check the slave trade by placing a duty of £5 (about $25) on each slave imported. The royal governor vetoed the bill for the sake of the British slave traders. Other Southern colonies tried to restrict the importation of slaves, but the bills were always vetoed.

Importation of slaves forbidden in 1808. The First Continental Congress passed a law forbidding the importation of slaves, and the law remained in effect throughout the Revolution. During, or soon after, the Revolution every state but South Carolina and Georgia prohibited the bringing in of more slaves. In 1787 the Confederation Congress ruled against slavery in the Northwest Territory. The same year the slavery question was discussed in the Constitutional Convention. Most of the delegates wished to prohibit the importation of slaves, but because the rice planters of South Carolina and Georgia insisted, a clause was included in the Constitution saying that Congress should not interfere with the slave trade for twenty years. When the twenty years had passed (1808), Congress passed a bill to forbid the bringing of slaves into the United States. The law was not strictly enforced, and some smuggling continued until the War between North and South.

The emancipation movement. For many years before the Revolution the Quakers had been urging that the slaves be set free, that is, emancipated. After the Declaration of Independence non-Quakers, too, began to urge the freeing of the slaves. In the Northern states, where the number of slaves was small, the emancipation movement made rapid progress. Vermont led the way in 1777, when she declared slavery illegal. Three years later Massachusetts adopted a constitution saying that "All men are born free and equal," and the courts held that this abolished slavery within the state. The same year Pennsylvania provided that children born to slave parents should be free when they reached twenty-five years of age. By 1804 every state north of Delaware had either abolished slavery or provided for gradual emancipation.

In the early years of the Republic many Southerners joined antislavery societies. The emancipation movement was especially strong in Virginia. Jefferson in writing about slavery said: "I tremble for my country when I reflect that God is just; that his justice cannot sleep forever." Washington said: "Not only do I pray for it [emancipation] on the score of human dignity, but I can clearly foresee that nothing but the rooting out of slavery can perpetuate the existence of our Union." Madison, Monroe, and many other Southern leaders expressed similar feelings.

At this period slaveowners often set free their favorite slaves, and some slaveowners, including Washington and Jefferson, arranged in their wills for the freeing of all their slaves. Yet most white people objected to having many free Negroes in their communities. This feeling was as strong in the North as in the South. In fact the average Northerner was no more kindly toward the Negro than the average Southerner.

The colonization experiment. Some thought the solution to the

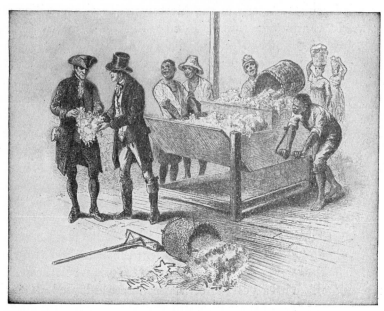

COTTON GIN. *This machine, known at first as the "cotton engine," separated the seeds from the cotton fiber.* (Culver Service)

problem was to send the freed Negroes to Africa. In 1816 the American Colonization Society was formed for this purpose. Congress appropriated $100,000 for the society's work. The society established the Negro republic of Liberia but could persuade few American Negroes to go there. Most of those sent to Liberia soon died of tropical diseases. Plainly colonization in Africa would not solve the problem.

Cotton growing fastens slavery upon the South. Even before the colonization experiment failed, many Southerners lost interest in freeing the slaves. The reason was that cotton had become the leading Southern crop, and cotton planters needed all the slaves they could get.

Cotton had not always been an important crop in the South. There was little sale for it until machines for spinning and weaving came into use in England in the late 1700's. Then English mills began to use large quantities of cotton. Although the price of cotton rose, cotton production in the United States did not increase rapidly, because so much labor was required to separate the cotton fiber from the seed. If someone would invent a machine to do this tiresome work, there would be money in growing cotton. A Northerner, Eli Whitney, became interested in the problem during a visit to the South. In 1793 he invented the cotton gin. With a gin one man could clean three hundred

COTTON *being unloaded from river steamboats in Louisiana.* (Sketched by J. R. Hamilton for *Harper's Weekly,* June 13, 1863)

pounds of cotton in a day — without it, but a single pound. The use of the cotton gin made cotton growing so profitable that production expanded at a startling rate. Between 1790 and 1800 the cotton crop of the United States increased from two million to forty million pounds. By 1820 it was one hundred seventy-five million pounds. Between 1820 and 1860 the cotton crop increased ten times (that is, by 1000 per cent). English and American cotton mills bought the cotton as fast as it could be produced.

The price of slaves goes up. The planting, cultivating, and harvesting of cotton takes a great deal of hand labor, for which groups of slaves could be used. As the demand for cotton grew, so did the demand for slaves. The price of slaves increased rapidly. A first-class field hand could be bought for between $500 and $900 in 1810, but by 1850 he was worth from $1500 to $2000. At these prices few masters could afford to free a slave. If the North should force them to free their slaves, they would be bankrupt.

Slaves most numerous in the lower South. Most of the cotton was grown in the lower or deep South — South Carolina, Georgia, Alabama, Mississippi, and Louisiana. By 1850 more than half the slaves in the United States lived in these five states. Half the people in these states were slaves. Most of the larger plantations were in the river valleys, and here slaves made up nine tenths of the population.

The upper South supplies slaves to the lower South. The land of the upper South — Virginia, Maryland, North Carolina, Tennessee, and Kentucky — was wearing out through continual tobacco growing. For this reason farming there was no longer very profitable. It did not pay to use first-class slaves when they could be sold for high prices in the cotton belt. Besides, the slaves multiplied rapidly, and there was not enough work for all of them in the upper South. The result was that slaveowners in this section sold unneeded slaves to the cotton planters of the lower South. Slaves of the upper South lived in dread of seeing members of their families sold "down the river." Their sorrow comes to us in the words of the old song, "Darling Nelly Gray."

How the planters lived. The planters were fond of good living and of social activities. Their homes were often large and beautiful. They gave many dinners, dances, and house parties. They enjoyed hunting and horse racing. They liked to travel. Most planters managed their own estates, but the richer ones left the management to a hired overseer and spent much time in the city or at fashionable pleasure resorts.

The planter's wife was a gracious hostess, often known for her beauty and charm. Yet she usually had many responsibilities. She trained the house servants and the seamstresses who made clothes for the Negroes. When slaves were sick, she often prescribed medicine for them and saw that they had care. She might even give them religious instruction and teach some of them to read and write.

The planters sent their sons to military schools and later to college in the South, the North, or in Europe. Many of these young men became officers in the United States Army. All young men of the planter class learned to ride and to use arms. A great many of them volunteered for service in the Mexican War. Compared to Northerners of equal wealth, they were not only better trained for military duty but also more interested in it. This caused Southerners to feel that if war came, the Southern armies would be better than those of the North.

Instead of going into business, the well-to-do Southerner went into politics. The planters took great interest in the government and held nearly all the public offices. The small farmers, who far outnumbered the planters, took little part in politics. They looked up to the planters and allowed them to manage public affairs.

A PLANTATION HOME IN SOUTH CAROLINA. *The wealthier planters had spacious dwellings. This one is in the Southern colonial style.* (From "Dixie," one of the Chronicles of America photoplays, copyrighted. Permission of Yale University Press)

SLAVE QUARTERS *on a plantation. These brick cabins appear substantial and comfortable.* (From "Dixie," one of the Chronicles of America photoplays, copyrighted. Permission of Yale University Press)

A BACK COUNTRY CABIN. *In isolated mountain sections of the South the people still live just as their ancestors did a hundred years ago.* (Courtesy of Tennessee Valley Authority)

How the slaves lived. The life of the slaves was very different from that of the planters. The Negroes lived in small log cabins, furnished with an open fireplace, a kettle or two, a chest, and either beds or bunks for sleeping. The cabins often had no window glass and sometimes no floors. In cold weather they were likely to be dark and smoky.

The clothing of the slaves depended upon their duties. House servants dressed neatly, often in clothes discarded by the master's family. Every winter field hands received their year's supply of clothing, consisting of one or two pairs of shoes and a few garments. Slave clothing was as good as that of the poorer white people.

House servants might have food left from the master's table. Other slaves were supplied plain food, chiefly corn meal and salt pork. Usually they prepared their own meals, but on some of the larger plantations there was a central kitchen to cook for all. Many slaveowners encouraged their Negroes to grow vegetables and raise chickens for themselves. If a slave raised more of these than he wanted to eat, he might sell the surplus and keep the money for himself.

A slave was a valuable piece of property, and the slaveowner tried to keep his slaves in good health. Every plantation had a plentiful supply of medicines. On large plantations there was sometimes a doctor

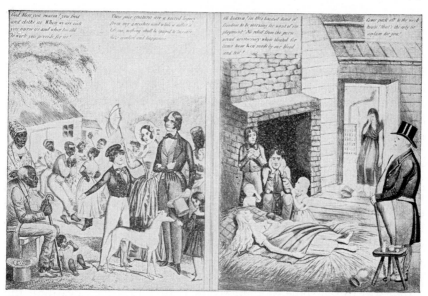

"BLACK AND WHITE SLAVES." *A cartoon drawn in 1844 to show that the lot of the Negro slave was happier than that of the white wage earner.* (Courtesy of New York Historical Society)

who lived there to attend the master's family and look after the health of the Negroes. On any plantation a doctor was called in case a slave was seriously sick.

Slaveowners generally considered it a duty to see that their Negroes went to church service on Sunday. If there was no chapel on the plantation, the services might be held outdoors or the slaves might attend a church off the plantation. There were some Negro churches, but in most places the Negroes sat in the gallery of a church built for whites.

A Mississippi plantation. A careful New York observer has told us how the slaves lived on a first-rate cotton plantation in Mississippi, which he visited during the middle of the 1850's. On this plantation nearly 1400 acres were planted to cotton and corn, and 200 hogs were raised. Of the 135 slaves, about 70 were field hands. Every day but Sunday they worked from dawn to dark, with a brief pause at noon for food and rest. A Negro driver walked among them, urging them on and sometimes letting his lash fall across the back of a slow worker. Every week each received a peck of corn meal and four pounds of pork. They could grow vegetables and poultry if they wished. At Christmas they were given a supply of coffee, tobacco, and calico.

During the winter the work day was shorter, and the women made clothes for their families while the men cut fuel for their cabins from a wood lot on the plantation. On Sundays they could cut lumber for sale, using the money to buy small comforts. The overseer said that the slaves did not often run away because they were almost sure to be caught with the aid of trained dogs kept for the purpose. This was a typical plantation. On some, slaves were treated better, and on others, worse.

Was the slave system cruel? The usual method of punishing a slave was by whipping. In those days, most people did not think whipping cruel. White children were frequently whipped by their parents and schoolteachers. White sailors in the navy and merchant marine were whipped. Harsh punishment of slaves was uncommon unless they rebelled, tried to run away, or were under a brutal overseer.

On small plantations, where the owner personally looked after his slaves, they were usually well treated. Yet even the kindest masters often had to sell some of their slaves. At the master's death all the slaves might be sold. The sale of a slave often meant parting him from his relatives and friends. One of the most tragic experiences in the life of the slave was the separation of parents and children.

The planters' defense of slavery. By 1830 Southerners had stopped apologizing for the slave system. Instead they began to praise it. John C. Calhoun was one of those who led this change of thought. He argued that there never had been an educated society in which part of the people did not live on the labor of the rest. He denied the idea that all men are created equal. In place of it he brought forward the old notion that some men are fit only for hard toil, while a few are fit to manage and to rule. These ideas soon came to be widely held by Southerners of the planter class.

Slaveowners often argued that Negro slaves were better off than white wage earners in the North. The slave was cared for from birth to death and was always sure of food, clothing, shelter, and medicine. He did not have to worry over sickness or old age. He could have a large family of children without fear that they would suffer want. It was to his master's advantage to keep him in good health and see that he was contented.

Wage earners in the North had no security. The employer was not responsible for workers who were injured, sick, or too old to work. The moment business got bad, workers might lose their jobs. Hours of work were so long and wages so small that many a free worker enjoyed no more comfort than a slave. Workmen who made trouble were blacklisted and were often unable to get another job. Under these conditions, said the Southern planter, the freedom of the Northern wage earner was an empty word.

Most Southerners not slaveowners. Only a small proportion of Southerners were slaveowners. In 1850 less than one Southern family in five owned slaves, and half of the slave-owning families had no more than four slaves. Yet at this time nearly every Southerner defended his constitutional right to hold slaves.

Most of the small white farmers lived in the "back country" — the hilly sections back from the coastal plain and the river valleys. They did not raise cotton because they could not get it to market and because their land was rough and not very fertile. They raised corn and livestock. Sometimes they owned one or two slaves or a small family of slaves. If so, they and their children worked side by side with the Negroes.

It was the great ambition of every small farmer to become a slave-owner, not only to make money but to obtain social standing. He dreamed of owning enough slaves to enable him to move to the cotton lands and make a beginning as a planter. He knew that this was the way to wealth and privilege. He believed that slavery was a good thing. He was fiercely proud of being a Southerner, and he resented Northern criticism of the South's "peculiar institution" — the slavery system.

To identify: American Colonization Society.

To explain or define: back country, bondage, emancipate, overseer, plantation.

SUBJECTS FOR TALKS OR WRITTEN REPORTS

1. The business of the African slave trader. 2. The smuggling of slaves into the United States. Efforts made to prevent smuggling. 3. The slave trade within the United States. 4. The life of free Negroes in the South and in the North before the war between the two sections. 5. The Negro republic of Liberia. How it began and how it has prospered. 6. Negro writers in the United States. 7. Negro artists in the United States. 8. The contribution of the Negro to music. 9. The contribution of the Negro to science and industry. 10. Race relations in France and North Africa compared with those in the United States.

QUESTIONS FOR UNDERSTANDING THE TEXT

1. (*a*) How large a farm in the South was considered a plantation? (*b*) What was usually raised on plantations? (*c*) What was considered the best size for a cotton plantation? (*d*) Why was the average slave more valuable on a plantation than anywhere else? 2. Why did the royal governors veto every bill passed by the colonial assemblies which interfered with the importation of slaves? 3. Why did Congress wait until 1808 to forbid the importation of slaves? 4. (*a*) How did leading Southerners feel about slavery in the early years of the Republic? (*b*) Why were not more slaves set free during this period? (*c*) What was the colonization experiment? (*d*) Why did it fail? 5. (*a*) What invention caused the planters to lose interest in freeing the slaves? (*b*) Explain the need for such a machine. (*c*) How did it change the South? 6. (*a*) Name the five states of the lower or deep South. (*b*) How did these states differ from other Southern states in regard to (1) the principal crop, (2) the proportion of slaves in the population, (3) the prices paid for slaves? (*c*) What proportion of all the slaves in the United States lived in these five states? (*d*) Would you expect the people of the lower or the upper South to defend slavery more vigorously? Why? 7. How did Southern men of the planting class compare with Northern men of equal wealth, as to (1) training for military duty, (2) interest in government, (3) interest in business? 8. (*a*) How did slaves obtain spending money? (*b*) Why did slaveowners look carefully after the health of their Negroes? (*c*) Can you see any reason why some planters thought it paid them to have a central kitchen in which cooks prepared food for all the Negroes? 9. (*a*) How did planters defend the slave system? (*b*) Compare the condition of the average Northern wage earner and that of the average slave. 10. (*a*) By 1850 what proportion of Southern families owned slaves? (*b*) How did the average Southerner who had no slaves feel about the slave system? 11. (*a*) Where in the South did most of the small white farmers live? (*b*) Why did they not raise cotton? (*c*) Why did the small farmer dream of owning many slaves? 12. What was meant by the phrase, the South's "peculiar institution"?

CHAPTER 20

SLAVERY IN POLITICS

W*hy the North grew faster than the South.* Since colonial times commerce and manufacturing had been more important in the North than in the South. This was due partly to geographic conditions. Most of the Northeast was poorly suited to crop growing, and its people had to find other ways of making a living. They learned to build and sail ships, to trade, and to manufacture. They made money and year by year expanded their enterprises.

The North had another advantage — a supply of free skilled labor. More and more European immigrants were coming to the United States, and nearly all of them settled in the North. Some of them were highly skilled. Because they were free and not slaves, they cost their employers nothing but their wages. Many a small businessman who could not possibly have bought a slave could afford to hire a free laborer.

While the North grew rapidly in population and wealth, the South lagged behind. One reason for this was the differences in the labor supply of the two sections. The South could not attract white laborers because of its cheap black labor. It lacked money to start industries because nearly all its wealth was in slaves.

Southerners realized that their section was less prosperous than the North. For this many of them blamed the North. The following paragraph, written by an Alabama newspaperman in 1851, shows the way Southerners often felt about Northern wealth and Northern leadership:

At present, the North fattens and grows rich upon the South. . . . Our slaves are clothed with Northern manufactured goods, have Northern hats and shoes, work with Northern hoes . . . are working for Northern more than Southern profit. The slaveholder dresses in Northern goods, rides in a Northern saddle . . . patronizes Northern newspapers, drinks Northern liquors, reads Northern books. . . .

In Northern vessels his products are carried to market; his cotton is ginned with Northern gins . . . his rivers are navigated by Northern steamboats; his mail is carried in Northern stages; his Negroes are fed with Northern bacon, beef, flour, and corn . . . his son is educated at a Northern college, his daughter receives the finishing polish at a Northern seminary . . . his schools are supplied with Northern teachers, and he is furnished with Northern inventions and notions.

Conflicting economic interests of North and South. The economic interests of the South were opposed to those of the North. This was seen in the contest over the protective tariff (see page 208) and again in the contest over the Bank of the United States. (See pages 214–216.) The protective tariff raised the prices of manufactured goods needed by Southerners without raising the prices of the raw products which they had for sale. A central bank, Southerners thought, would place them at the mercy of the Northern "money power." Another conflict arose over the question of federal aid to shipowners. This was favored by the North and opposed by the South, since nearly all shipowners were Northerners.

To protect its own economic interests, each section wanted to control the national government. New states meant additional congressmen, and each section wanted to spread its own economic system into the territories from which new states would be formed. Since the Southern economy rested on slavery, the South wished to increase the number of slave states. Since the Northern economy rested on free labor, the North wished to see more free states created.

Missouri seeks admission to the Union. For a time the admission of slave states kept even pace with the admission of free states. When Missouri applied for admission (1819), there were eleven states in the Northern, or free, section and the same number in the Southern, or slave, section of the country. This meant that each section had an equal number of senators. However, the population of the free states was increasing much faster than that of the slave states, and already the North had more representatives in Congress than the South. This made Southern leaders the more anxious to keep the balance in the Senate.

Slavery suddenly became a burning national question, or issue, when Missouri asked to be admitted as a slave state. Northerners feared that slavery might spread throughout the vast territory bought from France (the Louisiana Purchase). When the bill for the admission of Missouri was introduced, General James Tallmadge, a representative

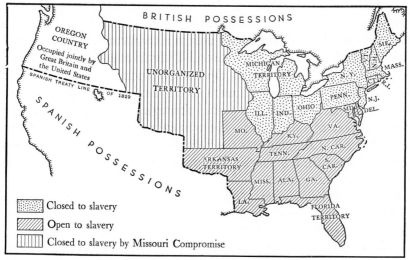

THE MISSOURI COMPROMISE, 1820

The admission of Missouri, a slave state, was delayed until Maine came into the Union as a free state. This kept in the Senate an equal number of senators from slave states and free states. Congress prohibited slavery in most of the remaining territory purchased from France.

from New York, proposed an amendment which would force Missouri to become free. It provided that no more slaves could be brought into the state and that all children of slaves born after the date of admission should be free upon reaching the age of twenty-five. The amendment did not pass, but it caused heated public discussion. To Southerners the amendment proved that the North intended to get control of the Senate and make the South nothing more than a colony. Southerners insisted that every state had the constitutional right to decide whether or not slavery should be allowed within its borders. If Congress interfered with slavery in Missouri, Congress might try next to interfere with slavery in the older states of the South. Indeed Congress might even interfere with other matters that each state had the constitutional right to decide for itself. Therefore, when they attacked the Tallmadge amendment, Southerners felt that they were defending their most sacred constitutional rights. Jefferson said the dispute was a warning of grave trouble to come — a "fire bell in the night that filled with terror." A Georgia senator told Tallmadge he had kindled a "fire which only seas of blood could extinguish."

The Missouri Compromise, 1820. The next year Maine asked for admission to the Union as a free state. This offered a solution to the Missouri question. After a long debate a compromise was arranged: Maine was admitted as a free state and Missouri as a slave state. It was also agreed that in the rest of the territory purchased from France, slavery should be prohibited north of the southern boundary of Missouri. The compromise was passed through the influence of Henry Clay, Speaker of the House. He was ever afterward known as the "Pacificator." Congress was not troubled again by the slavery question for more than ten years. The question then came up because of the abolition movement.

Rise of the abolitionists. At first the antislavery movement was led by men and women of moderate views, who saw the difficulties of freeing the Southern slaves all at once. They favored gradual emancipation, colonization of the freed slaves, and strict enforcement of the laws forbidding the importation of slaves. They had followers in both North and South.

The antislavery movement took a new turn about 1830 when William Lloyd Garrison became its leader. Garrison was born in Massachusetts. He was young, penniless, and fearless. He demanded the immediate freeing of all slaves. He called slavery a crime and slaveholders criminals. Early in 1831 he began to publish a newspaper, the *Liberator*. His spirit is shown by a statement in the first issue:

> I will be as harsh as truth and as uncompromising as justice. On this subject [slavery], I do not wish to think, or speak, or write with moderation. No! No! Tell a man whose house is on fire to give a moderate alarm . . . tell the mother to gradually extricate her babe from the fire into which it has fallen; but urge me not to use moderation in a cause like the present. I am in earnest — I will not equivocate — I will not excuse — I will not retreat a single inch — and I will be heard.

Garrison soon won many followers in New England. Among them were Whittier, Longfellow, Lowell, and Emerson. These writers took up their pens in the cause of abolition.

Nat Turner's Insurrection. Southerners had long dreaded an uprising of the slaves. They reminded one another that there had been a slave uprising on the island of Haiti in 1804, when all the whites had been killed or banished and the Negroes had set up a republic. Since that time Southern white men had feared that something similar might

WILLIAM LLOYD GARRISON. *Garrison had to leave school and go to work when only nine years of age. As a young man he resolved to devote his life to working for the freedom of the slaves. For over thirty years he published a four-page weekly called the* Liberator. *He and his partner had to work sixteen hours a day, often with no food but bread and water, to keep the paper alive.* (Courtesy of American Antiquarian Society, Worcester)

take place in the South, especially in a community where there were more slaves than whites.

A few months after the first issue of the *Liberator,* a Negro preacher named Nat Turner led an uprising against the slaveowners of Southampton County, Virginia. Some fifty white people were killed. Southerners believed that the uprising was due to abolition propaganda. They asked Northern legislatures to forbid abolition societies and to have all abolition literature destroyed. They tried to have Congress pass a law making antislavery literature unmailable. They no longer wanted to permit the discussion of antislavery arguments.

The Southern states passed laws intended to make another slave uprising impossible. Slaves were forbidden to leave their master's land without a pass. They were forbidden to assemble, even for worship, unless white men were present. Negroes were forbidden to preach. Some of the states made it a crime to teach Negroes, whether slaves or free men, to read or write. This law was not strictly enforced. Some states banished their free Negroes; others made it difficult for free Negroes to keep their freedom.

Northern mistreatment of abolitionists and Negroes. Hatred for abolitionists and free Negroes was not confined to the South. Antislavery meetings in the North were frequently broken up and speakers

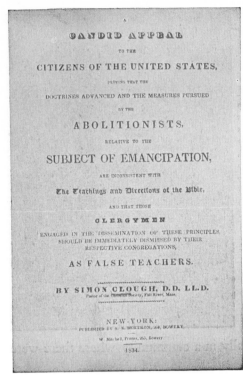

A

ⓒⒶⓃⒹⒾⒹ ⒶⓅⓅⒺⒶⓁ

TO THE

CITIZENS OF THE UNITED STATES,

PROVING THAT THE

DOCTRINES ADVANCED AND THE MEASURES PURSUED

BY THE

ABOLITIONISTS,

RELATIVE TO THE

SUBJECT OF EMANCIPATION,

ARE INCONSISTENT WITH

The Teachings and Directions of the Bible,

AND THAT THOSE

CLERGYMEN

ENGAGED IN THE DISSEMINATION OF THESE PRINCIPLES,
SHOULD BE IMMEDIATELY DISMISSED BY THEIR
RESPECTIVE CONGREGATIONS,

AS FALSE TEACHERS.

BY SIMON CLOUGH, D.D. LL.D.
Pastor of the Christian Society, Fall River, Mass.

NEW-YORK:
PUBLISHED BY A. K. BERTRON, 24, BOWERY.

W. Mitchell, Printer, 265, Bowery

1834.

TITLE PAGE OF AN ANTIABO-
LITION PAMPHLET. *This pamphlet by a Massachusetts minister
was published in 1834. The author
recommends the dismissal of clergymen preaching in favor of abolition.
He declares that the arguments used
by the abolitionists are contrary to
the teachings of the Bible.* (Courtesy of New York Historical Society)

stoned. A Boston mob destroyed the office where the *Liberator* was published and dragged Garrison through the streets. He narrowly escaped death at their hands. In 1837 Elijah Lovejoy, a minister who published an abolition journal in Illinois, was killed by a mob. Violence against Negroes became common in the North. In New York City, for example, mobs attacked Negro quarters, destroying property and taking life. In New Hampshire three hundred men destroyed a Negro schoolhouse. Such outrages strengthened the abolition movement. Thousands joined it because they felt it had become the cause of human liberty.

The "Underground Railroad." During the 1830's abolitionists organized the "Underground Railroad" to help runaway slaves. The houses of trusted persons willing to aid fugitives were known as "stations." The slaves went secretly from station to station until they reached safety in a free state or in Canada. Sometimes "conductors" for the Railroad met them in the South and led them to freedom. The Railroad helped about two thousand runaway slaves each year between 1830 and 1860. Those who aided the fugitives broke a federal law.

They were called "slave stealers" by Southerners. Some of the Southern states made it a crime punishable by death to give help to a runaway.

The "gag" resolution. Abolitionists sent many petitions to their representatives in Congress, most of them asking that slavery be abolished in the District of Columbia. The main purpose of the petitioners was to keep the slavery question before the public — which, of course, the proslavery group wished to avoid. Those favoring slavery would, in fact, have stopped all antislavery talk if they could.

In 1836 the proslavery men got Congress to pass a "gag" resolution providing that antislavery petitions should be laid aside without being read or printed and that no further action be taken on them. This was a clear violation of the First Amendment, which guarantees the right of petition to the government.

John Quincy Adams, formerly President and now a member of the House of Representatives, protested that the gag resolution was unconstitutional. Although not an abolitionist, he fought to have the resolution repealed. The abolitionists sent him petitions by the hundreds, and he presented them all. Whenever the regular hour for petitions arrived, he was at his desk in the House, a pile of petitions before him. He would rise with words like these: "I have a request from citizens of the town of —— praying for the abolition of slavery in ——." The Speaker's hammer would fall and Adams would be declared out of order. He would take another paper from the pile, begin with the same words, and be cut off in the same manner. He stopped only when he reached the bottom of the pile. He kept this up for eight years, until at last the friends of slavery saw that the gag resolution was making friends for the abolitionists. The rule was repealed late in 1844.

The quarrel over annexing Texas. The South soon discovered that the Missouri Compromise was working badly for her. Most of the national domain was north of the compromise line and therefore closed to slavery. South of the line lay only Arkansas, part of what is now Oklahoma, and the territory of Florida. Southern leaders began to look for additional slave territory in order to keep the balance in the Senate between slave states and free states.

Texas won her independence from Mexico in 1836 and applied for admission to the Union as a slave state. The South wanted to annex Texas at once. Texas was large enough to make at least half a dozen slave states. If this happened the South would control the Senate for a long time to come, and perhaps always. Most Northerners were

BURNING OF PENNSYLVANIA HALL, *Philadelphia, May 17, 1838. This hall was built by abolitionists. Their foes destroyed it the day after it was first used for a meeting. Riots continued for three days and many houses where Negroes lived were attacked.* (From a sketch by John Sartain. Courtesy of Historical Society of Pennsylvania)

against annexation. Finally, in 1844, Congress voted to annex Texas. War between the United States and Mexico came the next year. Antislavery groups claimed that we entered the war for no other purpose than to get more slaveholding territory. (See page 251.)

The Wilmot Proviso. In 1846 Congress was considering a bill to appropriate money for use by the President in making peace with Mexico. David Wilmot, of Pennsylvania, offered an amendment to shut out slavery from any territory obtained from Mexico. The amendment is known as the *Wilmot Proviso.* After passing the House, it was defeated in the Senate. The attempt to pass the Wilmot Proviso has been called "the turning point in the history of the slavery struggle." Its passage by the House showed that the North had made up its mind not to permit the extension of slavery.

Should the Southwest be open or closed to slavery? As a result of the Mexican War the United States got California and New Mexico as well as Texas. Slavery did not exist in California and New Mexico, for it had been forbidden by Mexican law. Most of the territory was probably unsuited for slavery, but few Americans knew this at the

"ASHLAND," *the home of the great statesman, Henry Clay, at Lexington, Kentucky. The baylike porch and delicate iron railing over the front door of this stately mansion are often found on houses built in the early 1800's.* (Courtesy of C. Frank Dunn, Lexington, Kentucky)

time. People debated with ever-growing bitterness the question of whether or not slavery should be admitted there.

President Polk wished to divide the new territory according to the old Missouri Compromise. Calhoun, leader of the proslavery group, insisted that the whole territory be open to slavery. Webster led those who wanted the whole territory to be free. Senator Lewis Cass of Michigan suggested that Congress leave the matter to the people of the territory. The question was still unsettled when Polk's term came to an end. As a result neither California nor New Mexico had a territorial government.

General Taylor becomes President. In 1848 General Zachary Taylor, hero of the Mexican War, was elected President by the Whig party. He was a Southerner and a slaveholder. When he took office, sectional feeling was more violent than ever. People doubted that the Union would hold together much longer.

California seeks admission to the Union. After the discovery of gold in 1848 California filled up rapidly. (See pages 256–258.) The settlers needed an orderly government and could not wait for Congress

HENRY CLAY *addressing the Senate on the Compromise of 1850. The great Ken-· tuckian had returned to the Senate in his old age so that he might propose this com- promise. He hoped that it would prevent war between the North and South.* (From a painting by P. F. Rothermel, Shoenfeld Collection. Three Lions)

FUNERAL OF DANIEL WEBSTER *at Marshfield, Massachusetts. Webster died four months after his old friend, Henry Clay. The whole nation mourned the passing of the two great statesmen.* (From *Gleason's Pictorial,* November, 1852. Courtesy of New York Public Library)

to set it up. Late in 1849 they took matters into their own hands. They prepared a constitution which barred slavery. Then they elected a governor and a legislature and asked for admission to the Union. The new Congress would have to take action.

Clay suggests a compromise. The new Congress met in December, 1849. It was a brilliant gathering. In the Senate were the great trio, Daniel Webster, Henry Clay, and John Calhoun, now almost at the end of their lives. Clay was seventy-four years of age. He had won election to the Senate, after an absence of seven years, in order to propose a compromise which he hoped would save the Union. Besides the great trio, a number of rising young leaders were in the Congress, some of them having strong antislavery views.

Early in the session Clay outlined his plan for adjusting the differences between North and South. The most important suggestions were (1) California should be admitted as a free state; (2) Congress should organize territorial governments in New Mexico, leaving the people of the territories to decide whether or not to prohibit slavery; (3) Texas was to be paid ten million dollars for her claim to part of New Mexico; (4) the slave trade (but not slavery) should be abolished in the District of Columbia; (5) Congress should pass an effective fugitive-slave law. For the next seven months Congress, and the entire nation, argued over the proposals.

Calhoun and Webster take opposite sides. Early in March, Calhoun, who was to die of consumption within the month, appeared in the Senate to attack the suggested compromise. He was too ill to speak, and his speech was read for him. He declared that the South was bound to secede unless the North stopped its antislavery propaganda, honestly enforced the fugitive-slave law, and gave the South equal rights in the new territories (that is, allowed slavery in all of them). He pointed out that the cords which held the sections together were fast breaking.

Three days later Calhoun tottered into the Senate to hear Daniel Webster's reply. It was Webster's last great speech. "I wish to speak today," he began, "not as a Massachusetts man, but as an American. . . . The imprisoned winds are let loose, the East, the North, and the stormy South combine to throw the whole sea into commotion . . . I speak today for the preservation of the Union."

Webster charged the abolitionists with being too severe, saying they had done no good and much harm by their violent arguments. He said that the fugitive-slave law ought to be strictly enforced. He declared that slavery would never gain a foothold in New Mexico or California, since their soils and climate were not suited to slavery. At the end he pleaded again, as in his famous "Reply to Hayne," for the preservation of the Union and warned the South that peaceable secession was impossible.

Webster's speech stirred up anger in his own state, Massachusetts, the center of the abolition movement. His support of a stronger fugitive-slave law was hotly condemned. The speech ended Webster's chances of being nominated for President but won votes for the compromise in the Senate.

The Compromise of 1850 is adopted. The debate lasted throughout the spring. President Taylor used his influence against the compromise, for he thought that each point should be decided separately on its own merits. In July, Taylor suddenly died. His successor, Millard Fillmore, actively supported the compromise. In September Congress approved Clay's proposals, and they became law. Clay and Webster, with their followers, had for the time being saved the Union.

Effects of the Compromise of 1850. It was not easy to say which side had the better in the compromise. The admission of California looked like an important gain for the North, since it broke the balance between free and slave states, giving the free states a majority in the Senate. The question whether there would be slavery in New Mexico was left in doubt, but the soil and climate had already decided that slavery would not succeed there. The settlement with Texas meant that New Mexico was larger than it would otherwise have been. The closing of the slave markets in Washington only meant their removal to near-by Virginia. Both sides were satisfied to have this done. The abolitionists could no longer say that the trade in human beings went on under the very shadow of the national Capitol.

The new fugitive-slave act seemed to be an important victory for the slaveholders. They could now use federal courts and federal officers to help them get back a runaway slave. The runaway was denied a jury trial and could not testify in his own defense. Anyone who aided his escape was liable to a heavy fine and six months' imprisonment. In the North many people considered the law unfair. Emerson wrote in his diary, "I will not obey it." The Underground Railroad became more active than ever. The law was soon to prove unenforceable.

In 1850 the average American was satisfied with the compromise and hoped it would end the quarrel between the sections. Northern busi-

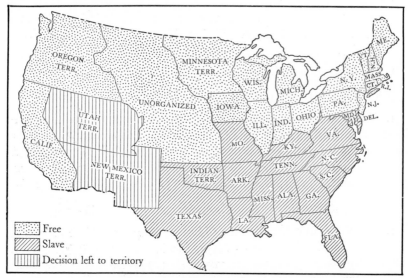

SLAVE AND FREE TERRITORY BY THE COMPROMISE OF 1850

Antislavery men were disappointed because slavery was made possible in the lands obtained from Mexico.

nessmen were particularly pleased that the threatened storm had blown over. Much of their business was done with the South, and they wanted Southern good will.

General Pierce becomes President. The desire for harmony was shown in the election of 1852. The Democrats, who were strongest in the South, praised the compromise and promised to enforce the fugitive-slave law. They had a hard time to agree on a candidate who could please both North and South. Finally, on the forty-ninth ballot, they nominated a man "without a record" and "without an enemy" — General Franklin Pierce of New Hampshire. The Whigs, who were strongest in the North, dared not take a strong stand. They promised to maintain the compromise until time showed changes to be necessary. As their candidate they chose General Winfield Scott of Virginia.

Both Webster and Clay, the principal Whig leaders, died during the campaign. Without them the party began to break up. In the North many antislavery Whigs deserted to join the new Free Soil party. In the South the Whigs lost many of their proslavery members. The Democrats easily won the election.

To identify: Compromise of 1850, Missouri Compromise, Millard Fillmore, William Lloyd Garrison, the *Liberator*, General Franklin Pierce, General Zachary Taylor, Underground Railroad, Wilmot Proviso.

To explain or define: abolitionist, gag resolution.

SUBJECTS FOR TALKS OR WRITTEN REPORTS

1. The life of William Lloyd Garrison. 2. The slave uprising in Haiti in 1804. 3. Nat Turner's Insurrection and its consequences. 4. Mistreatment of abolitionists in the North. 5. Why many Northerners hated the Fugitive-Slave Act of 1850. What they did about it. 6. The work of John Greenleaf Whittier for abolition. 7. The Underground Railroad.

QUESTIONS FOR UNDERSTANDING THE TEXT

1. (*a*) Why, in colonial times, did more people turn to commerce and manufacturing in the North than in the South? (*b*) What conditions helped Northern industries to expand? (*c*) What conditions made it difficult for Southerners to start industries? 2. Name three questions on which the economic interests of the North were opposed to those of the South. 3. (*a*) Why did each section want to control the national government? (*b*) Why did each section want to spread its own economic system into the territories from which new states would be formed? 4. (*a*) What was the Tallmadge Amendment? (*b*) Why were Southerners so angry over it? 5. How did Henry Clay win the name of "Pacificator"? 6. Contrast the views of early leaders of the antislavery movement with those held by the abolitionists. 7. What event stopped the discussion of antislavery arguments in the South? Why did it have this effect? 8. (*a*) Were abolitionist leaders safe in the North? Explain. (*b*) How did mistreatment of abolitionists affect the growth of the abolition movement? 9. Tell about the Underground Railroad. 10. (*a*) What was the gag resolution? (*b*) How did John Quincy Adams bring about the repeal of the gag resolution? 11. (*a*) Why were Southern leaders eager to annex Texas at once? (*b*) Why did many Northerners oppose annexation? 12. (*a*) What was the Wilmot Proviso? (*b*) Did it pass? (*c*) Why is it considered important? 13. (*a*) What was remarkable in Henry Clay's election to the Senate in 1849? (*b*) Give the main points of his plan to save the Union. 14. Was Calhoun willing to let the people in each territory decide whether or not slavery should be allowed there? 15. (*a*) Did Webster want to bar slavery from New Mexico and California? Why or why not? (*b*) What did Webster sacrifice in order to support Clay's proposals? Explain. 16. Why did the Democrats choose a dark horse to run for President in 1852? Who was he? 17. Why did the Whigs lose members in the North? In the South?

CHAPTER 21

THE STATES OF THE DEEP SOUTH SECEDE

Ten years of mounting ill will. The public was tired of the quarrel between the North and the South. Yet the peace which followed the Compromise of 1850 did not last long. One thing after another kept the quarrel brewing until finally the Union broke apart. As we look back at this period from 1850 to 1860 we can see how the trouble grew.

Uncle Tom's Cabin. There were millions of Northerners who knew or cared little about the hard lot of the slave. In 1852 a book was published which brought them a tragic story of human suffering and jarred them out of their indifference. This was *Uncle Tom's Cabin,* by Harriet Beecher Stowe. It painted a dark and not wholly true picture of the slave system. Perhaps no other book in the world has ever aroused such a storm of emotion. Years later Lincoln spoke of it as one of the leading causes of the War between North and South.

The book had a large sale; three hundred thousand copies were sold the first year. It was translated into twenty-three different languages. Changed into a play, it stirred huge audiences here and abroad. The characters of Uncle Tom, Eliza, and Topsy became familiar in every Northern household and created a new sympathy for the slave.

The Kansas-Nebraska Act. In 1854 the old question of slavery in the territories came up again. People were already settling in the region now included in the states of Kansas and Nebraska. Under the Missouri Compromise this region was closed to slavery. However, Missouri slaveowners objected to having Kansas organized as a free territory. They thought runaway slaves would seek safety there. Also, Missouri would then have three free neighbors and might soon become a free state. Already it had a strong antislavery movement. Acting for the slaveowners, Missouri congressmen blocked various efforts to set up the territory of Kansas.

Then Stephen Douglas, a senator from Illinois, introduced a bill to organize Kansas and Nebraska. Douglas' bill provided for repeal of the Missouri Compromise and left the people of each territory to de-

THE KANSAS–NEBRASKA ACT, 1854

Free
Slavery
To be settled by popular sovereignty

cide whether the territory should enter the Union as a free or a slave state. Douglas and his followers called this method of handling the slavery question by the attractive name of "popular sovereignty," which means "rule by the people." After a hard fight Congress passed the bill.

The Kansas-Nebraska Act caused great anger in the North. Northerners feared that slavery would now spread into all the territories. If this happened, the slave party might gain permanent control of the national government. Protest meetings were held all over the North. Douglas said he could travel from Washington to Chicago by the light of fires built to burn him in effigy.

"*Bleeding Kansas.*" Proslavery and antislavery men struggled for the control of Kansas. Hordes of slaveowners from Missouri went there. Often they had two homes — one in Kansas for voting and fighting and another in Missouri where they actually lived. New England antislavery men organized the Emigrant Aid Society to help settle Kansas with people pledged to keep it free soil. Kansas was not well adapted to slavery, and the free-soil settlers were soon in a majority. However, so many proslavery men crossed the river from Missouri to cast illegal votes in Kansas that a proslavery legislature was elected. The free-soil men then drew up a government of their own. Guerrilla fighting broke out. Before this little civil war was stopped, two hundred lives were lost. The events in "bleeding Kansas" were watched anxiously in both North and South. Far from solving the problem of slavery in the territories, popular sovereignty had only made the problem worse.

Northerners refuse to obey the Fugitive-Slave Act. Northerners felt that the bargain made in the Compromise of 1850 had been broken by the passage of the Kansas-Nebraska Act. Many refused, therefore, to obey the hated Fugitive-Slave Act. Runaway slaves arrested in the North were often seized by mobs and taken to places of safety. News of such happenings caused angry protests from the South.

Ten Northern states passed "personal liberty" laws, which had the effect of nullifying the Fugitive-Slave Act. These "personal liberty" laws forbade state officials to help capture runaway slaves, prohibited the use of state and local jails for confining them, and provided that they should have a jury trial before removal from the state. By this time antislavery feeling in the North had become so strong that a jury was unlikely to send a captured Negro back to his master.

Birth of the Republican party. Opposition to the Kansas-Nebraska Act led to the forming of the present Republican party. Although its leaders were not abolitionists, they opposed any extension of slavery. The party was organized at a convention in Michigan in 1854, and two years later nominated a candidate for President. While the Democratic candidate, James Buchanan, won the election, the Republican party showed strength in the North and West. Republican leaders looked forward hopefully to the campaign of 1860.

The Dred Scott Case. Buchanan had been in the White House only two days when the Supreme Court handed down a remarkable decision — a milestone in the great antislavery struggle. The decision concerned the famous Dred Scott case. Dred Scott was a slave whose master had taken him into territory where slavery was forbidden by the Missouri Compromise. After two years Scott was brought back to Missouri. With the approval of his owner and with the aid of antislavery lawyers, Scott sued for his freedom, claiming that residence in free territory had made him free. (This idea, or principle, was accepted in the British Isles. In 1772 the highest British court decided that as soon as a slave set foot on the soil of the British Isles, he became free. To have the principle recognized here would be a triumph for the antislavery movement.)

The courts of Missouri denied Scott's plea, saying that he was not a citizen and had no right to bring suit. Then his owner sold him to a citizen of New York in order that he might bring suit in the federal courts, since the federal courts may try cases between citizens of different states. After several years the case reached the Supreme Court. In a seven to two decision, the Supreme Court ruled that Scott was not a citizen and could not bring suit and that a slave did not become free when taken into free territory. Going still further, the Court ruled that neither Congress nor a territorial legislature could prohibit slavery in a territory. Therefore the Missouri Compromise had been unconstitutional.

Southerners rejoiced over the Court's findings. Northerners refused to accept the decision. "Hereafter," wrote the poet-editor, William Cullen Bryant, "if this decision shall stand for law, slavery, instead of being what the people of the slave states have hitherto called it, their peculiar institution, is a Federal institution . . . the shame of all the states; . . . wherever our flag floats, it is the flag of slavery . . . it should be dyed black. . . . Are we to accept these new readings of the Constitution. . . ? Never, never!"

Abraham Lincoln runs for senator in Illinois. In 1858 the author of the Kansas-Nebraska Act, Stephen Douglas, stood for re-election as senator from Illinois. He was a Democrat, a noted speaker, and one of the outstanding men of his time. To run against him, Republican leaders in Illinois chose Abraham Lincoln. Although he had served eight years in the state legislature and two years in Congress, he was not nationally known. While in Congress (1847–49), he had opposed the Mexican War and voted for the Wilmot Proviso (see page 284) but had attracted very little attention.

Lincoln became famous in the Midwest through a speech made in Illinois in 1854. Speaking of the Kansas-Nebraska Bill and the repeal of the Missouri Compromise, he said that repeal was wrong, for all national laws should carry out the idea held by the fathers of the Republic — that slavery was to be restricted and finally abolished. He declared that popular sovereignty as applied to slavery was wrong, for slavery in a territory was the concern of the entire United States. He could appreciate what the South said about the difficulty of getting

THE GOVERNOR'S HOUSE AT LECOMPTON, *Kansas Territory. For a time the territory had two rival governments, one favoring slavery and one opposed to it.* (From *Harper's Weekly,* June 6, 1857)

rid of slavery where it was already established. "I surely will not blame them [the Southerners] for not doing what I should not know how to do myself."

When Lincoln accepted the nomination as senator, he made another great speech. Every American is familiar with a portion of it:

A house divided against itself cannot stand. I believe this government cannot endure permanently half slave and half free. I do not expect the Union to be dissolved — I do not expect the house to fall — but I do expect it will cease to be divided. It will become all one thing or all the other.

The Lincoln-Douglas debates. Lincoln was unattractive to look at, poor, and a failure in his political career. Yet he dared to challenge his distinguished opponent, Douglas, to a series of debates to be held in different parts of the state. Each debate drew crowds of people, many riding for miles to hear "Honest Abe" and the "Little Giant."

Lincoln spoke out plainly against any extension of slavery. Douglas hoped to run for President in 1860 and needed to please the South. He called Lincoln's words "abolition ravings." He still favored popular sovereignty in the territories and said, "I do not care whether slavery is voted up or voted down."

LINCOLN RIDING THE CIRCUIT. *Lawyers went with the circuit court to obtain cases.* (From *Collier's Weekly,* February 13, 1909, after a drawing by Rollin Kirby. Courtesy of New York Public Library)

In one of the debates, Lincoln asked Douglas whether the people of a territory could lawfully bar slavery within their boundaries before they had a state constitution. If he said "yes," his answer would be in conflict with the Dred Scott decision and would anger the South. If he said "no," he would turn his back on his own principle of popular sovereignty and would anger his Northern friends who refused to accept the Dred Scott decision. Douglas avoided saying "yes" or "no." He answered that slavery had a legal right in the territories, but that it could not exist where the people did not want it, since their legislatures would not pass laws giving it police protection. This offended the South and cost Douglas any chance of being elected President two years later. However, he won the senatorship by a narrow margin. While Lincoln lost the senatorship, the debates with Douglas made him known throughout the nation.

John Brown's Raid. Year by year ill will between the sections grew. Late in 1859 an act of violence by a Northern abolitionist brought the

South close to the breaking point. John Brown, an elderly New Englander who had taken part in the fighting in Kansas, decided that the
time had come for the slaves to strike for their freedom. He planned
to set up a Negro republic on American soil. With eighteen followers
he seized the arsenal at Harpers Ferry, Virginia, and offered arms to
the slaves in the surrounding countryside. He was quickly captured
by a small federal force. After a fair trial Brown was condemned and
hanged for treason. He died willingly for what he believed, bearing
himself to the very end with remarkable dignity. The antislavery
party hailed him as a martyr and a hero. Southerners were horrified
by Brown's act. They feared that other abolitionists would come into
the South to set the slaves against their masters. They were angrier
against the North than ever before.

The presidential campaign of 1860. When the Democratic convention met in 1860, the members were sharply divided. Southern extremists, led by Senator Jefferson Davis of Mississippi, wanted the party
to ask Congress to guarantee slavery in any territory where the territorial legislature refused to give it police protection. Such a demand
was a strange one to come from the party of states' rights. Douglas
led the fight against the proposal, for it would force slavery upon the
people of a territory against their will. The convention split in two.
The Northern delegates nominated Douglas, and the Southern delegates nominated John Breckinridge of Kentucky.

The Republicans were determined that slavery should spread no farther. They selected Lincoln as their candidate. They framed their
platform carefully to please as many groups as possible. It promised a
protective tariff (to please manufacturers), a better banking system (to
please merchants and financial interests), free homesteads for settlers
(to please Westerners and land-hungry Easterners), a Pacific railway
and federal aid for improving rivers and harbors (to please everybody
in the North and West). It was the Whig program and the program
of Hamilton all over again — the program which the South had always
opposed. It meant a strong central government and government aid
to industry and commerce. This economic program alarmed the
South as much as the demand that slavery be kept out of the territories.
Southern leaders said openly that if the Republicans won the election,
the South would secede.

A new party, the Constitutional Union, was organized for this campaign. It nominated John Bell, of Tennessee, on a platform urging
that the Union be preserved. It won a large number of votes in every

LINCOLN DEBATES WITH SENATOR DOUGLAS, 1858. *Lincoln hoped to be elected senator in the place of the "Little Giant." He and his opponent took part in a series of debates which made Lincoln known to the whole nation.* (Brown Brothers)

THE CAPTURE OF JOHN BROWN. *After trying unsuccessfully to rouse the slaves at Harpers Ferry to rebel, Brown and his band were surrounded in a little building called the engine house. Colonel Robert E. Lee made the capture.* (From a drawing in *Leslie's Weekly*. Three Lions)

Southern state, particularly in those areas where the small white farmers lived.

Lincoln received 1,866,000 popular votes, Douglas 1,376,000, Breckinridge 859,000, and Bell 588,000. While Lincoln got but 40 per cent of the popular votes, he had more than half of the electoral votes and so won the election. Breckinridge, the only candidate favoring secession, received less than 20 per cent of the popular votes. This showed that the people of the South were not eager to secede.

South Carolina and the Gulf States leave the Union. Had the people of the South been asked to vote on secession, it is probable that the majority would have voted "no." They were not asked. A group of extremists were largely responsible for secession. They believed that if one state should secede and ask for the support of its neighbors, it could not be refused. The South Carolina legislature was in session when the news of Lincoln's election flashed over the wires. It called immediately for a special convention, and the convention voted to secede (December 20, 1860). Leaders in scme of the neighboring states protested that this step should not have been taken by one state acting alone. However, within six weeks Georgia, Florida, Alabama, Mississippi, Louisiana, and Texas also seceded. In February, at a convention held in Montgomery, Alabama, the seven seceding states formed the "Confederate States of America" and selected Jefferson Davis as President. A constitution was adopted which was strikingly similar to that of the United States, except that it gave less power to the central government and more to the individual states.

Reasons for secession. It should not be thought that slavery was the main reason for secession. The Republican platform pledged the party not to interfere with slavery where it already existed. Lincoln had said again and again that he had no intention of interfering with slavery in the slave states. If Congress wanted to abolish slavery, it could do so only by a constitutional amendment. Since an amendment must be approved by three fourths of the states, the South could easily block it. It is clear, then, that slavery did not stand in any danger from the national government.

Secession was really the result of a long struggle for control of the national government by two sections with opposing economic interests. The triumph of the Republican party meant that at last the North had gained control. By stopping the spread of slavery into the territories, it would prevent the formation of any new slave states. Southern leaders feared that in the future the North would always hold the

JEFFERSON DAVIS, *President of the Confederate States of America. A graduate of West Point, who had served with distinction as a colonel in the Mexican War and later as Secretary of War, Davis hoped to become the commander of the Confederate forces in the field. Instead (February, 1861) he was elected President of the newly formed Confederacy. He had always stood for the rights of the states, but now he discovered that a war could not be carried on successfully if each state were going to do as it pleased. He began to take more and more power into his own hands. For this he was savagely criticized. In spite of criticism he worked with great zeal and energy for the Southern cause.* (Courtesy of United States Signal Corps)

reins of the national government. Rather than give in, they preferred to form an independent nation. They saw a bright future for the Confederacy. They did not expect war with the North, but if it came, they felt sure of an early victory. Later they hoped to obtain new territories by conquering Cuba, Mexico, and Central America. They dreamed of a great Confederate empire circling the Gulf of Mexico.

Would slavery in time have been abolished without a war? If the South were to abolish slavery, its economic interests would gradually become more like those of the North. The sectional quarrel would then disappear. It is interesting to try to guess whether or not the South might have freed its slaves had there been no War between North and South.

Economists believe that slavery would have died out. It had already been abolished in every other civilized nation except Brazil. Slavery was profitable in the South only on rich land suited to cotton, and by 1860 the limits of slavery expansion had been reached. In the upper South slavery had been dying out for years. The demand for slaves came entirely from the lower South. Should slavery cease to be profitable there, the price of slaves would drop until they no longer had any value. Then slaveowners would lose nothing by setting their slaves free. There would still be the problem of training the Negro to take his place in the community as a freeman. Who can doubt that if left alone, the South would in time have solved the problem and done it better than was possible after war had laid the region in ruins?

To identify: John Brown, James Buchanan, Jefferson Davis, Stephen Douglas, Emigrant Aid Society, Dred Scott, Harriet Beecher Stowe.

To explain or define: popular sovereignty.

SUBJECTS FOR TALKS OR WRITTEN REPORTS

1. The life of Harriet Beecher Stowe. 2. The life of Stephen Douglas. 3. The life and death of John Brown. 4. How Northerners nullified the Fugitive-Slave Act of 1850. 5. The history of the Republican party to the election of Lincoln. 6. The Presidency of James Buchanan. 7. The life of Lincoln to his election as President. 8. The convention at Montgomery, Alabama, in February, 1861. 9. The life of Jefferson Davis. 10. Opposition to the Confederate government in the South itself.

QUESTIONS FOR UNDERSTANDING THE TEXT

1. How did *Uncle Tom's Cabin* help cause the War between North and South? 2. Why did Missouri congressmen block efforts to organize the territory of Kansas? 3. (*a*) State the two main provisions of the Kansas-Nebraska Act. (*b*) Why did it cause anger in the North? 4. (*a*) How did the antislavery men work to keep Kansas free soil? (*b*) How did proslavery men from Missouri work to get control of Kansas? 5. How did it happen that Kansas had two different territorial governments at the same time? 6. Give the main points of the personal liberty laws. 7. (*a*) What led to the formation of the Republican party? (*b*) Were its members abolitionists? Explain. 8. (*a*) What did antislavery leaders hope to accomplish by having Dred Scott sue for his freedom? (*b*) Why did the courts of Missouri refuse to hear his case? What did his owner do then? (*c*) What were the rulings of the Supreme Court in this case? (*d*) How did proslavery men feel about the decision? Antislavery men? 9. Why was Lincoln opposed to the repeal of the Missouri Compromise? 10. Why did he oppose the principle of popular sovereignty? 11. (*a*) Why did Douglas answer neither "yes" or "no" to Lincoln's question as to whether the people of a territory could bar slavery within their borders? (*b*) Give Douglas' answer. Do you agree with him? 12. (*a*) Tell the story of John Brown's Raid. What were his plans? (*b*) How did Southerners feel about Brown's action? 13. What proposal made at the convention in 1860 caused the Democratic party to split? 14. (*a*) Give the main planks in the Republican platform of 1860. (*b*) How did the South feel about this program? 15. What evidence is there for the statement that the majority of the Southern people probably did not want to leave the Union? 16. (*a*) Show that slavery was in no danger from the national government. (*b*) Why, then, did the states of the deep South secede? 17. Why do economists think that slavery would soon have died out in the South?

CHAPTER 22

THE WAR OF THE CONFEDERATE
STATES FOR INDEPENDENCE

THE BEGINNING OF THE WAR

period of doubt and indecision. The winter of 1861, before Lincoln took office, was a time of doubt and indecision. Should force be used to bring the seven seceded states back into the Union, or should the North follow the advice of the abolitionists, and let them go in peace? The country's best-known editor, Horace Greeley, wrote in the *New York Tribune:*

> If the cotton states shall decide that they can do better out of the Union than in it, we shall insist on letting them go in peace. . . . We hope never to live in a republic where one section is pinned to the residue [the other sections] by bayonets.

Meanwhile men searched feverishly for a compromise that might save the Union. Several compromises were proposed to Congress. The most important was a plan for an amendment to the Constitution running the Missouri Compromise line to the Pacific and giving federal protection to slavery in all territory south of that line. The Republicans turned down this plan. While they were ready to protect slavery where it existed, they were not willing to let it spread to any new territory.

Seizure of federal property by the Confederacy. During the winter the seceded states took over the forts, arsenals, post offices, and other United States property within their borders. President Buchanan made no effort to stop them. He told the country that neither he nor Congress had any power to force a state to stay in the Union. Many people in both North and South agreed with him.

In taking over federal property, Confederate officials met no resistance except at Fort Sumter in Charleston harbor, where the commander, Major Anderson, refused to give it up. He asked Buchanan for re-enforcements, and a small merchant ship was sent with men and supplies. When Confederate guns at the harbor entrance fired upon

INAUGURATION OF LINCOLN, *March 4, 1861. Lincoln was accompanied by President Buchanan.* (Drawn for *Frank Leslie's Illustrated Newspaper,* March 16, 1861)

the ship, it turned back. Buchanan took no further action. Northerners showed surprisingly little anger over the incident. They seemed discouraged and leaderless.

The deciding step is taken. The whole country waited anxiously to learn what the incoming President, Lincoln, intended to do. His inaugural address left no room for doubt. He declared that no state had the right to secede and that he would maintain the Union. He said he would "hold, occupy, and possess the property and places belonging to the government and collect the duties and imposts." He promised not to interfere with slavery in the states where it existed and to work for the enforcement of the fugitive-slave law. He closed with an appeal to the Southern people:

In your hands, my dissatisfied fellow countrymen, and not in mine, is the momentous issue of civil war. The government will not assail you. You can have no conflict without being yourselves the aggressors. You have no oath registered in heaven to destroy the government, while I have the solemn one to "preserve, protect and defend it."

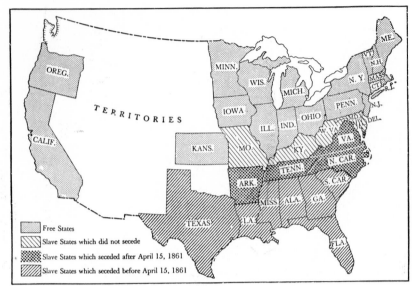

STATES OF THE NORTH AND THE SOUTH IN 1863

A month later Lincoln notified the governor of South Caroiina that he was sending supplies to Fort Sumter by sea. The Confederate government called on Major Anderson to surrender. When he refused, the fort was shelled. After two days of bombardment, Anderson and his men had to give up. This battle began four years of bloody conflict.

The call for volunteers. On April 14, 1861, when the news from Charleston flashed through the North, the people seemed to forget all their differences in a cry for revenge. The next day Lincoln issued a call for volunteers to put down what he called the "insurrection." Men responded quickly and in greater numbers than the President asked. Jefferson Davis also called for volunteers, and thousands rushed to the Confederate colors.

The spread of secession. Up to this time eight slave states in the upper South had not seceded. In each of them two parties were struggling for control — the Secessionists and the Unionists.

Once it became clear that Lincoln would use force against the seceded states, the middle slave states — Arkansas, Tennessee, North Carolina, and Virginia — joined the Confederacy. At first North Carolina voted against secession, but changed its mind when Virginia seceded. There was a bitter division of opinion in Virginia, and the western counties refused to follow the rest of the state. They organized the

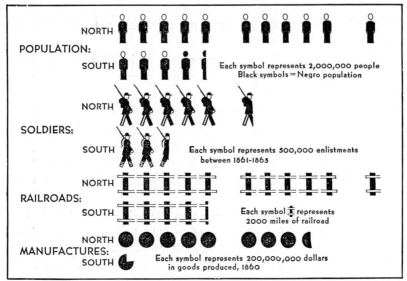

RELATIVE STRENGTH OF NORTH AND SOUTH IN 1861

state of West Virginia, which was admitted to the Union in 1863. Lincoln approved this action as a war measure, although the Constitution forbids the division of a state without its consent.

Four slave states are saved to the Union. In Missouri the Unionists and Secessionists fought a civil war of their own, but the state did not secede. The governor of Kentucky declared that his state would take no part in the war — that is, it would remain "neutral." Lincoln's tact kept Kentucky in the Union, and tens of thousands of her citizens enlisted in the Union army. However, several thousand Kentuckians served in the Confederate army. In fact every border state and every Confederate state furnished men to both sides.

In Maryland the Secessionist party was strong. If Maryland seceded, Washington would be surrounded and might become the Confederate capital. One Confederate leader said publicly that before May 1, 1861, the Confederate flag would float over Washington. However, United States military authorities occupied Baltimore and Annapolis, where they arrested Secessionist leaders. The secession movement collapsed. Maryland was saved for the Union, and with it Delaware.

Advantages of the North. The eleven Confederate states, with their nine million people (more than one third of whom were slaves), were lined up against twenty-three states having twenty-two million white people. In man power, then, the North was vastly superior. In fact the North had more than three times as many white men of military age as the South.

The North had another great advantage in her industries. Practically all the iron, steel, textile, and munitions plants in the country were in the North. Then, too, it was easy for the North to expand its industries, for it had experienced manufacturers and trained workmen. After the first year of the war the North produced nearly everything needed for its army and navy. While the South had a few factories at the outset and managed to start some new ones during the war, it could not produce anywhere near enough clothing, equipment, and medical supplies for its army.

The North possessed far better transportation facilities than the South. At the beginning of the conflict it had twenty-two thousand miles of railroad; the South had nine thousand miles. Most of the Northern lines had been connected into systems. This was not true in the South, where most of the lines were short and disconnected. When Southern railroad equipment wore out under heavy wartime use, it could not be replaced. The rails of less important lines were sometimes torn up to mend the more important ones. The Confederacy was also inferior to the North in canals, river steamboats, and improved highways. This bothered the invaders as well as the defenders. Northern supply wagons and artillery moved with difficulty over the wretched Southern roads. "Have I been through Virginia? Yes, in several places" was a familiar Yankee witticism that might have been made of any state where armies went.

The North had another important advantage in its control of the sea. Practically all the warships and the merchant ships of the United States were in Northern hands. This made possible a tight blockade of Southern ports.

Advantages of the South. Not all the advantages were on the side of the North. When war began, the South felt sure of victory. The Confederacy had stores of arms and ammunition obtained by seizing federal forts and arsenals. It had many able officers of high rank, who resigned from the United States Army to serve the Confederacy. The South was also better supplied with minor officers than the North, for the men of the planter class were used to command.

An attacking force must be larger than a defending force, so the Confederate army did not need as many men as the Union army. It did not have to invade and conquer the North. All it needed to do

PRESIDENT LINCOLN AND HIS YOUNGEST SON, TAD. *Of Lincoln's four sons only one, Robert, lived to grow up. Tad died when he was eighteen.* (National Archives)

LINCOLN'S ADDRESS AT GETTYSBURG, *November 19, 1863. Soon after the Battle of Gettysburg a part of the battlefield was dedicated as a national cemetery. The speech made by President Lincoln will be remembered as long as our language lives.* (From the painting by A. I. Keller for *Harper's Weekly,* February 10, 1900)

was to fight long and hard enough to persuade the people of the North that victory would cost more than it was worth. The North might then decide to let the seceded states go.

The South had a great moral advantage over the North. It was fighting for liberty and independence, and for these it would count no sacrifice too great. The North was fighting to force unwilling states to remain in the Union. This was not a cause to inspire the people to support a long, costly war. Not until the Emancipation Proclamation late in 1862 did the North have a strong reason for fighting.

PROGRESS OF THE WAR

Both sides have to draft soldiers. At first there was a rush of volunteers in both North and South. The early enthusiasm did not last long, however. In August, 1862, when Lincoln called for three hundred thousand volunteers, only eighty-seven thousand responded. Recruiting had already broken down in the Confederacy. Both governments were forced to draft men.

In March, 1863, Congress passed the first national conscription act. It applied to all able-bodied citizens from twenty to forty-five years of age. Names were drawn by lot. Any man whose name was drawn could be excused by paying $300 or by furnishing a substitute. The poor naturally grumbled at a law which enabled the well to do to escape military service. Draft riots broke out here and there. The worst was in New York City, where about five hundred people were killed before order was restored.

The Confederate draft was equally unpopular. It was considered to be an injury to states' rights. Davis was denounced as a foe of liberty. Several governors refused for a time to let draftees leave their states. The governor of Georgia declared that no act of the government of the United States before the secession of Georgia had struck a blow at constitutional liberty so severe as the Confederate draft.

The Northern blockade cripples the South. One of President Lincoln's first acts after the fall of Fort Sumter was to order a blockade of Southern ports. For the task of watching a coast of nearly three thousand miles, the United States Navy had ninety wooden vessels. Only two dozen were steamships, and none of them was protected by armor. The Navy Department hurriedly bought and built ships until it had three hundred on blockade duty. By 1863 the blockade had strangled Southern commerce. This stopped the South from importing the things it needed so desperately, and also stopped the export of cotton, which would have provided money to carry on the war.

THE *MONITOR* AND THE *MERRIMAC*. *The Confederate ship* Merrimac *was defeated in a famous fight near Norfolk. The battle proved the value of ironclad ships and foretold an end to the building of wooden naval vessels.* (Courtesy of Yale University Library)

The South tried to break the blockade by building ironclads. The first one, known as the *Merrimac*, steamed out of Norfolk harbor one day in March, 1862, and destroyed three Northern frigates. Shots from the Northern ships glanced harmlessly off the *Merrimac's* iron sides. News of the arming of the *Merrimac* had already reached the North. When the *Merrimac* returned the next day, she was met by a strange-looking ironclad craft with a revolving gun turret. It was the Northern ship *Monitor*. After a fierce battle the *Merrimac* had to retire. The United States government built many ships like the *Monitor*. This ended Southern hopes of raising the blockade.

All through the war swift ships tried to run the blockade. Leaving the South, they carried cotton; and on the return trip they carried the manufactured goods needed so much by Confederate soldiers and civilians. A ship which made two or three trips before capture gave the owner a handsome profit. Fifteen hundred blockade runners were captured. Toward the end of the war, ship losses were so heavy that blockade running almost stopped.

The war in the East, 1861–62. The Union armies carried on two principal campaigns, one east and one west of the Appalachians. The chief purpose of the eastern campaign was to destroy the Southern forces protecting Richmond, the Confederate capital. The story of this campaign is a long tale of Union blunders and defeats.

CAVALRY CHARGE *by Union soldiers at Gaines's Mill, June 27, 1862. Cavalry tac- tics used in this war are still studied today.* (From *History of the United States Army,* 1894. Courtesy of Boston Public Library)

1. The Confederates win the Battle of Bull Run. The summer of 1861 saw the first attempt to smash the Army of Virginia. Neither side was properly trained or equipped; many soldiers did not even have uniforms. Yet the people of the North were clamoring, "On to Richmond!" To satisfy them, the War Department ordered General Mc-Dowell to lead the Army of the Potomac into northern Virginia. The Battle of Bull Run resulted. After several hours of hard fighting, the Union forces suddenly went to pieces. Throwing away their muskets, the soldiers fled toward Washington in a panic. The North now re-alized that the South could not be conquered without a hard struggle. The South was misled into thinking that Northerners were poor fight- ers and that the war would soon be over.

2. McClellan fails to take Richmond. Lincoln removed McDow- ell and placed General George McClellan in command of the Army of the Potomac. For nine months the cautious McClellan trained his men. Then he took them down the Potomac River in transports and marched them overland toward Richmond. At one time they were so near they could hear the clocks striking in the Confederate capital. Mc- Clellan had twice as many men as his opponent, General Robert E.

"FLYING ARTILLERY — a Hint to General McClellan on how to 'advance on Rich-mond.'" *The title of this amusing contemporary cartoon explains itself.* (Courtesy of New York Public Library)

Lee. After a week of heavy fighting (June 26–July 1, 1862), McClellan drew back and asked for re-enforcements. The public lost confidence in him and demanded a new commander. Lincoln appointed General John Pope, who soon met defeat in the second battle of Bull Run (August 30, 1862). The Union army withdrew to Washington. Pope was removed and McClellan again took command.

3. McClellan stops Lee at Antietam. Lee decided to carry the war into the North in hopes of adding Maryland to the Confederacy. With 60,000 men he marched through that state, calling on the people to rise. Some citizens of Maryland welcomed him, but others refused to sell him provisions. McClellan pursued him with a force of 87,000. At Antietam Lee's advance was stopped (September 17, 1862). This fight, known as the Battle of Sharpsburg by the Confederates, was the bloodiest single day of the entire war, about 23,500 men being killed or wounded. Lee retreated to Virginia, and the North went wild with joy. Because McClellan made no attempt to check Lee's retreat, Lincoln appointed Burnside in his place.

4. Lee wins the Battle of Fredericksburg. Burnside was as bold as McClellan was timid. In December, 1862, he attacked Lee at

THE BATTLE OF MOBILE BAY. *Mobile was the last important Confederate seaport on the Gulf of Mexico. After days of hard fighting Admiral Farragut took it in August, 1864.* (From the painting by William Overend. Courtesy of Wadsworth Atheneum, Hartford)

Fredericksburg in northern Virginia. The Confederate soldiers occupied a strongly fortified position at the crest of a hill. Burnside tried to take the position by a frontal assault in broad daylight. Six times he ordered his men to advance, and six times they were hurled back with frightful losses. Despair settled over the army and the nation. Lincoln replaced Burnside with General Joseph Hooker, who was no more successful.

The war in the West, 1861–62. The Union campaign in the West was far more successful than that in the East. Its aims were (1) to prevent the Confederates from taking Kentucky and Missouri, and (2) to gain control of the Mississippi. During the first year of the war the Confederacy tried to take Kentucky and Missouri, but it was defeated. An attempt to take Kentucky the next year also failed.

General Ulysses S. Grant helped drive the Confederates out of Kentucky in 1861. Early the next year he captured Fort Henry and Fort Donelson near the Tennessee-Kentucky line. The Confederates then had to give up the important city of Nashville, and Union troops advanced to the southern boundary of Tennessee. Here, on April 6 and 7, raged one of the fiercest fights of the entire war – the terrible Battle of Shiloh, or Pittsburgh Landing, in which twenty-five thousand men were killed or wounded. The Confederates fell back to Corinth, a railroad center in northern Mississippi. They were driven out of Corinth a few weeks later.

In April, 1862, a Union fleet commanded by Admiral David Farragut steamed up the Mississippi River. After knocking the river forts to pieces, Farragut captured New Orleans, the largest Confederate city. Next, a fleet of gunboats moving down the Mississippi captured Memphis. By mid-June, Vicksburg was the only point on the Mississippi left in Confederate hands. If Vicksburg could be taken, the entire river would be under Union control, and the Confederacy would be cut in two. The remainder of 1862 brought no important gains to either side.

Abolitionists criticize Lincoln. Lincoln was severely criticized here and abroad because he did not make abolition a war aim. But he knew that to do so would drive the border slave states from the Union. Besides, thousands of Union soldiers and some of the highest Union commanders were opposed to abolition. So he patiently waited. In August, 1862, in reply to an editorial by Horace Greeley complaining of his hesitating attitude toward slavery, Lincoln stated his position:

> My . . . object in this struggle is to save the Union, and is not either to save or destroy slavery. If I could save the Union without freeing *any* slaves, I would do it; and if I could save it by freeing *all* the slaves, I would do it; and if I could save it by freeing *some* and leaving others alone, I would also do that. What I do about slavery and the colored race I do because I believe it helps to save this Union.

The Emancipation Proclamation. At the time his letter to Greeley was printed, Lincoln had already written the Emancipation Proclamation. He was waiting for a favorable time to make it public. After the Union victory at Antietam in September, 1862, Lincoln published the Proclamation. It stated that on January 1, 1863, the slaves would be free *in all parts of the Confederacy still in rebellion.* The Proclamation did not apply to slave states in the Union. It was a military order which could be enforced only in occupied territory. It would have no standing when peace came.

The Proclamation had three aims: (1) to weaken the South through the loss of the slaves, (2) to gain the support of the abolitionists, who up to this time had opposed the war, and (3) the most important, to win the support of the British people. The Proclamation came in time to help keep the British government from taking steps to break the blockade. Cotton mills in England were closing down for lack of cot-

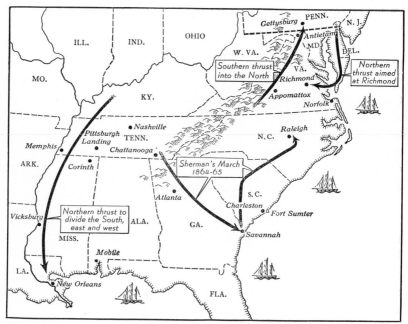

PRINCIPAL THRUSTS IN THE WAR BETWEEN NORTH AND SOUTH

ton, and there was great suffering in the manufacturing districts. The millowners wanted the government to recognize the Confederacy as an independent nation and to insist on trading with it. After the Emancipation Proclamation the British public sided strongly with the Union, refusing to let their government aid the Confederacy.

The tide turns, 1863. In the North the year 1863 opened in deepest gloom. The eastern campaign had led to one defeat after another. Voluntary enlistments had fallen so low that in March Congress was obliged to pass a draft law. (See page 308.) Grant and his men had spent months in Mississippi but seemed to make no progress in the attempt to take Vicksburg. Letters criticizing Grant poured into the White House, and Lincoln said sadly, "I think Grant has hardly a friend except myself." But the tide was about to turn, bringing three important victories — Vicksburg, Gettysburg, and Chattanooga.

Grant captures Vicksburg. In April, with the aid of a fleet of gunboats, Grant succeeded in surrounding Vicksburg. He then began to starve and shell the city into submission. To escape bombardment, the people took refuge in caves and cellars. They killed horses and mules for food. On July 4 the city surrendered. This gave the

Union control of the Mississippi. Texas, Arkansas, and Louisiana were completely cut off from the other Confederate states.

Lee wins at Chancellorsville but loses a great general. While Grant was besieging Vicksburg, the Army of the Potomac prepared to attack Lee once more. Hooker had 130,000 men, while Lee had only half as many. But Lee's military skill and that of his assistant, "Stonewall" Jackson, made up for the smallness of their forces. In the forest around Chancellorsville, Lee sprang a trap on Hooker. After three days of fighting (May 2–5, 1863), Hooker fell back with a heavy loss of men. This was "Stonewall" Jackson's last battle, for he was mortally wounded when his own men fired upon him by mistake. By his death the Confederacy suffered a stunning blow, and Lee lost the man whom he called his "right arm."

Meade defeats Lee at Gettysburg. After the battle of Chancellorsville, Lee decided to invade the North for the second time. His plan was to move swiftly through the Shenandoah Valley into Pennsylvania, seize Harrisburg, then turn east and come down upon Baltimore and Washington. If he succeeded in taking these cities, the North might be willing to make peace.

The Army of the Potomac, now commanded by General George Meade, went north into Pennsylvania. On July 1, it met Lee's army at Gettysburg. The two armies were nearly equal in size. In a desperate three-day battle the Confederate advance was stopped. Of 150,000 men taking part, nearly 50,000 were killed, wounded, or missing. On July 4, the very day that Vicksburg surrendered, Lee's greatly weakened army began its sad retreat. Gettysburg had been the high tide of Confederate hopes; the tide was now clearly running out. However, Lee's army had not been destroyed. General Meade did not interfere with it on its way back to Virginia.

Grant completes the conquest of Tennessee. During the rest of 1863 the heaviest fighting was in southeastern Tennessee. The Union leaders hoped to capture Chattanooga, a busy railroad junction and one of the three most important strategic points in the South (the others being Vicksburg and Richmond). A Union force of 70,000 men led by General W. S. Rosecrans approached Chattanooga early in September. Twelve miles from the city it met a strong Confederate force led by General Bragg. Here the Battle of Chickamauga was fought, 36,000 men being killed or wounded in two days. The Union forces escaped capture by fleeing into Chattanooga. Bragg then laid siege to the city, and Rosecrans called for help. Grant was placed in command

GENERAL ULYSSES S. GRANT. *The military successes which saved the Union were chiefly due to his perseverance and energy.* (Courtesy of United States Signal Corps)

of all the Union forces in the West and sent to the rescue. Assisted by General William T. Sherman, Grant drove the besiegers from their positions on Lookout Mountain and Missionary Ridge. Chattanooga and all of Tennessee were now in Union hands. This gave the Union army control of the mountain passes into Georgia.

THE END OF THE WAR

The last year of the war. Lincoln had finally found the general he was looking for. He put Grant at the head of the Union armies. Grant arrived in Washington for the first time in his life on March 8, 1864, a "short, round-shouldered man in a very tarnished uniform." He took charge of the Army of the Potomac and began to hammer at Lee.

1. Sherman's march to the sea. Grant gave Sherman chief command in the West and ordered him to march from Chattanooga to Atlanta. Atlanta was the principal industrial city in the South; it had numerous rolling mills, ironworks, and munitions plants. It was also a railroad center. Its loss would be greatly felt by the Confederacy.

GENERAL ROBERT E. LEE. (From a portrait made especially for Queen Victoria of England. Courtesy of United States Signal Corps)

Sherman took Atlanta early in September, burning whatever might be of value to the enemy. Then he moved onward to the sea, destroying nearly everything in a belt sixty miles wide. He estimated that the property destroyed was worth one hundred million dollars. Most of this property had no military value.

Just before Christmas, Sherman occupied Savannah. A few weeks later he turned northward through the Carolinas, taking three cities and causing even more destruction than in Georgia. The Confederates were not able to offer any serious resistance to his advance.

2. Lee surrenders to Grant. After a hard campaign lasting nearly a year, Grant forced Lee to abandon Richmond. Lee hoped to take his half-starved army to North Carolina to join another Confederate force. When he reached the village of Appomattox, about 80 miles west of Richmond, he found Grant with 62,000 men directly in his path. Lee had only 27,000 men, of whom less than 10,000 were armed. There was nothing to do but surrender. On April 9, 1865, the two commanders met at Appomattox Courthouse to discuss the terms. The Confederate officers and men were to go free on condition that

GENERAL ROBERT E. LEE *and other Confederate generals. The Confederacy had a greater number of able military leaders than the Union.* (From the mural painting by Charles Hoffbauer. Courtesy of Confederate Memorial Institute)

they should not fight again. Officers were to keep their side arms and horses, and men in the cavalry and artillery who owned their horses were to keep them "for the spring plowing." Grant's generous terms pleased the Southern people. Soon after, the other Confederate armies also surrendered, and the war was over.

Exhaustion of the South. In the final days of the war the Confederacy had but two hundred thousand soldiers in the field. These were half starved, half clad, with the scantiest of arms and munitions. Opposed to them the United States had a million men in the field, well fed, well clothed, and abundantly equipped. Besides, the United States had two million reserves, while the Confederacy had no reserves.

The South was completely exhausted. Great parts of it lay in waste. Some of the chief Southern cities had been burned. Most of the railroads and bridges had been destroyed. Food was scarce, and in Richmond and other cities near the coast civilians were starving. Because of the tight blockade, medical supplies and manufactured goods were almost unobtainable, for either soldiers or civilians. The worthlessness of Confederate bonds and paper money added to all the other hardships. To pay for the war, the government had issued both bonds and paper money exchangeable for cash when victory was won. As the hope of victory faded, this paper became valueless. Toward the end of the war a spool of thread cost $25, a quart of milk $4, a pound of sugar $75, a pair of shoes $150. By the time Lee surrendered, nearly everyone in the South was bankrupt and in want.

The War between North and South cost a million dead and wounded. On the Union side about three hundred sixty thousand soldiers died from wounds or disease during the conflict. On the Confederate side about two hundred fifty-eight thousand soldiers perished. In proportion to its white population, the South lost three times as many men as the North.

The antislavery movement in the South. The war strengthened the antislavery movement in the South as well as in the North. By the early part of 1865 emancipation had been ordered by state conventions in Maryland, Virginia, Missouri, Arkansas, Louisiana, and Tennessee. At this time both General Lee and President Jefferson Davis urged that slaves be taken into the Confederate armies and that they be promised freedom at the end of their service. In the closing weeks of the war the Confederate government offered to free all the slaves in return for aid from England and France.

The Thirteenth Amendment. Soon after the Emancipation Proclamation, Lincoln suggested an amendment to the Constitution to end slavery forever in any part of the United States. After a long dispute Congress approved the measure in January, 1865, and sent it to the states for ratification. It was quickly ratified by all the Union states except Delaware and Kentucky, and by eight former Confederate states. Before the year's end it became the Thirteenth Amendment to the Constitution. Southern slaveowners lost two billion dollars' worth of slave property for which they received no compensation. The slavery question was settled, but in its place was another no less difficult — the race problem — which has troubled the nation ever since.

The Union is supreme. In losing the war the Southern states lost all hope of forming an independent nation. That the Union was supreme over the individual states was no longer in doubt. The questions of whether a state had the right to nullify a federal law or secede from the Union had been settled. The United States had become an "indestructible Union of indestructible states."

❀ ❀ ❀

To identify: Emancipation Proclamation, Ulysses S. Grant, "Stonewall" Jackson, Robert E. Lee, George McClellan, Thirteenth Amendment.

To explain or define: ironclad.

SUBJECTS FOR TALKS OR WRITTEN REPORTS

1. How Republican leaders might have saved the Union without war.
2. Why North Carolina first voted against secession, then changed its
mind. 3. How the state of Virginia tried to save the Union in the winter
of 1861. 4. Opposition to the draft during the War between North and
South. 5. The Copperheads and how they interfered with the war
effort in the North. 6. How the Southern belief in states' rights made
difficulties for the Confederate government. 7. Northern opposition to
President Lincoln during the war. The election campaign of 1864. 8. The
life of General Lee. Why he is honored by North and South alike.
9. The life of General Grant. 10. The care of sick and wounded soldiers
during the war. 11. Conditions among Confederate civilians near end of
the war. 12. British aid to the Confederacy. 13. The Maximilian affair.

QUESTIONS FOR UNDERSTANDING THE TEXT

1. Did the abolitionists favor war to preserve the Union? Explain.
2. What was President Buchanan's attitude toward the seceded states?
3. What led the middle slave states to secede? Name them. 4. Name
four border slave states which remained in the Union. 5. Had Maryland
seceded, what would have happened to Washington? 6. Compare the
Confederate states with the states remaining in the Union as to (*a*) number, (*b*) man power, (*c*) industries, (*d*) railways, (*e*) other transportation
facilities. 7. State the advantages on the side of the South. 8. Why was
the draft unpopular in the North? In the South? 9. How did the Northern blockade of Southern ports shorten the war? 10. What was the aim
of the Union armies in the East? 11. What was Lee's aim in invading
Maryland in the second year of the war? 12. What were the main aims
of the Union campaign in the West? 13. (*a*) Why did Lincoln not
declare that the victory of the Union forces would bring abolition?
(*b*) Was the Emancipation Proclamation intended to end slavery in
the Union? Explain. (*c*) How did the Proclamation help in defeating the
Confederacy? 14. Why were people in the North so gloomy in the
early part of 1863? 15. Why was the capture of Vicksburg so important? 16. (*a*) What was the purpose of Lee's second invasion of the
North? (*b*) What battle ended his advance? 17. (*a*) What was the
object of Sherman's march to the sea? (*b*) Why is this march remembered so bitterly in the South? 18. Describe the condition in the final
months of the war of (*a*) the Confederate armies, (*b*) the civilians in the
states still held by the Confederacy. 19. Show that the war advanced the
antislavery movement in the South. 20. What was accomplished by the
Thirteenth Amendment? When was it ratified? 21. What questions
were settled by the war?

CHAPTER 23

THE TRAGIC ERA OF RECONSTRUCTION

L*incoln's plan of reconstruction.* Throughout the war Lincoln had been studying how to rebuild, or reconstruct, the Union. He saw the difficulties that would face the nation when the war was over. He wanted to restore friendly relations between North and South as quickly as possible. He believed there were people in each seceded state who could be counted on to form a loyal government, if those who had supported secession were removed from power.

Late in 1863 Lincoln announced his plan for bringing the seceded states back into the Union. He would pardon those individuals who had aided the Confederacy if they took an oath of allegiance to the United States. Whenever 10 per cent of the voters of a state had taken this oath and formed a loyal government, he would recognize it. He said that according to the Constitution, Congress should decide when members from the seceded states might resume their seats. Three states — Louisiana, Arkansas, and Tennessee — accepted Lincoln's terms and set up loyal governments during 1864. Congress refused to seat their representatives. Lincoln knew then that he faced a hard struggle. He would need all his powers of persuasion to get Congress to agree to his plan.

In March, 1865, when he gave his second inaugural address, his theme was forgiveness and good will. He spoke as a great statesman. "With malice toward none; with charity for all; . . . let us strive on to finish the work we are in; to bind up the nation's wounds; . . . to do all which may achieve a just and lasting peace. . . ."

Five weeks later Lee surrendered. Once more Lincoln turned to the problems of reconstruction. He felt no ill will toward the Confederacy or its leaders. To someone who told him Jefferson Davis should be hanged, he answered, "Judge not, that ye be not judged." On April 14 he met his cabinet to discuss what was to be done for the South. He expressed the wish that there be no persecution, no bloody work after the war. He spoke kindly of Lee and other Confederate leaders. He rejoiced that Congress was not in session and that he

BRITANNIA PAYS TRIBUTE TO LINCOLN. *This drawing by John Tenniel was published in the English magazine* Punch *shortly after Lincoln's death. It pictures Britannia laying a wreath on the President's bier, beside which Columbia and an ex-slave are weeping.* Punch, *reflecting the view of the British upper classes, had sneered at Lincoln while he lived. Now the editors were remorseful. They published a poem announcing their change of attitude. It said in part: "Yes, he had lived to shame me for my sneer . . . This rail-splitter a true-born king of men . . . Four long-suffering years' Ill-fate, ill-feeling, ill-report, lived through And then he heard the hisses change to cheers . . . Sore heart, so stopped when it at last beat high, Sad life, cut short just as its triumph came."*

would have a chance to restore the states to their proper place in the Union before it met again.

Lincoln's death. On the evening of April 14 the President attended the theater. A half-crazed actor, John Wilkes Booth, stole into the President's box and shot him through the head. Lincoln never spoke again. He died early the next morning. The whole country mourned. As the funeral train bore his body home to Springfield, Illinois, thousands gathered at every stop to pay their respects to the dead President.

The loss to the nation from Lincoln's death can never be estimated. He was the one man who might possibly have curbed the hatred and party selfishness which followed the war. He was the one man who might have reunited North and South with the least delay and the least suffering. Long afterward Jefferson Davis said: "Next to the destruction of the Confederacy, the death of Abraham Lincoln was the darkest day the South has known." Lincoln's death meant more than the loss of his leadership. It meant that the North felt new hatred for the South. Northerners thought his murder was the result of a plot by Confederate leaders to overthrow the United States government. They shouted for revenge.

Andrew Johnson becomes President. The man who took up Lincoln's task was self-educated. Born in a log hut in North Carolina and left fatherless when three years old, he grew up in ignorance and poverty. At the age of ten he became a tailor's apprentice. After running away from his master, he settled in Greeneville, Tennessee, where he worked at his trade. He married, and his wife taught him how to write. In time young Johnson saved enough to start a tailor shop. By his mid-thirties he owned land and slaves and was regarded as Greeneville's first citizen. He became the leader of the small farmers of eastern Tennessee and rose from one political office to another. When the war came, he was a United States senator, the only senator from a seceded state who remained loyal to the Union. Because of his loyalty to the Union, Lincoln appointed him military governor of Tennessee, a difficult and dangerous post. In 1864 he was nominated for Vice-President because Lincoln wanted a Southerner on the ticket. Johnson was honest, fearless, and intelligent. He fought for what he believed to be right, but he had little of Lincoln's skill in managing men and guiding public opinion.

Johnson tried to carry out Lincoln's plans for reconstruction. He appointed a temporary governor for each of the Southern states. He pardoned large numbers of Confederates so that they might take part in forming loyal state governments. Each state held a convention which repealed its act of secession. Then its white citizens elected a governor and a legislature. When the legislature approved the Thirteenth Amendment, Johnson considered the state to be back in the Union. All the states but Texas completed these steps by the time that Congress met in December, 1865. Congress refused to admit their representatives. This action gave notice that Congress meant to take charge of reconstruction.

Why Congress rejected Johnson's program. Congress blocked Johnson's program of reconstruction for a number of reasons. *First,* it wanted to reduce the President's power. Always during a war the President's powers are increased. When the war is over, Congress seeks to regain control. In 1865 Congress felt that the time had come to take the reins again. *Second,* many people in the North believed that Johnson's program was too generous to the former Confederate states — that they should not be allowed to return to the Union without punishment for their disloyalty. *Third,* the Republicans, who had a majority in Congress, feared that with the Democratic Southern states back in the Union, the Democratic party might win the next election. The Republicans would be sure of staying in power if they could shift some of the Southern states into the Republican column. This could be done by giving the vote to the freed slaves, who would naturally support the party that had freed them. Since the President's plan of reconstruction did not give the vote to the freedmen, it would be replaced by a plan which did.

Another reason why Congress rejected Johnson's program was the belief that the Negro needed protection from the Southern whites. The state legislatures created under the Johnson plan had already passed laws defining the privileges and rights of the freed Negroes. These laws varied from state to state. In the main they allowed the Negroes most of the rights of white citizens, such as the right to own and hold property, to sue and be sued, and to make contracts. The laws did not allow the Negro to vote or sit on juries, and they contained restrictions intended to keep the Negroes from becoming tramps and wanderers and to force them to work. At the time the restrictions were probably necessary, for many of the freed slaves thought they no longer had to work.

When the Northerners heard of the "Black Codes," as these laws were called, they grew angry. They feared that the South was planning to make slaves of the Negroes again. For his own protection they thought the Negro should have the privilege of voting and holding office. They demanded that no state be admitted to the Union until it gave the Negro these privileges. They believed that the South should be forced to give full citizenship to the Negroes.

Congress takes control of reconstruction. Congress turned its back upon the President's plan for reconstruction. An amendment to the Constitution was passed, with the understanding that every Southern state must ratify it before seeking admission to the Union again. This, the Fourteenth Amendment, covers the Congressional plan for reconstruction.

The first sentence reads: "All persons born or naturalized in the United States . . . are citizens of the United States and of the State wherein they reside." This simple sentence contains one of the most important results of the war. It declares that there is such a thing as United States citizenship, and that a person born or naturalized in the United States is a citizen of the United States as well as of the state

ANDREW JOHNSON. *Called to the Presidency by the assassination of Lincoln, Johnson faced the most difficult situation a President has ever had to face. In the words of one of his biographers, "No American has ever had a lonelier or more treacherous path to tread."* (L. C. Handy Studio. From the photograph by Brady)

BIRTHPLACE OF ANDREW JOHNSON, *Raleigh, North Carolina. Johnson was born in poverty and never went to school a day in his life.* (Courtesy of State of North Carolina, Department of Conservation and Development)

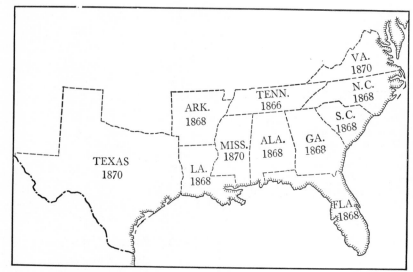

THE READMISSION OF THE CONFEDERATE STATES

wherein he resides. Its chief purpose was to give United States citizenship to Negroes. The Amendment goes on to forbid any state from
interfering with the rights of United States citizens.

The framers of the Amendment feared that the Southern states
would not allow many of the Negroes to vote. The second section
threatens to reduce a state's representation in Congress if the state de-
prives its male citizens of the right to vote. This clause has never
been enforced.

Another section says that no person may hold a federal or state office who has ever held high office and then engaged in rebellion. According to the Northern point of view, this applied to a large number
of Confederate leaders. The people of the South, who did not consider the war as rebellion, felt worse about this section than they did
about the other parts of the Amendment, for they loved many of their
former leaders and wanted their guidance in the hard times ahead.

A fourth section says that the Confederate war debt shall never be
paid and that no payment shall be made to the former owners of emancipated slaves. This was a hard blow to those who had lent everything
they had to the Confederate cause, and to those whose wealth had gone
with the loss of their slaves.

The Amendment was a harsh dose for the South. Believing it must
take the bitter medicine, Tennessee ratified it; Congress then seated

Tennessee's representatives and senators. The other ten Confederate states refused to accept the Amendment. They thought they could block it by holding out, since they were more than one fourth of the total number of states.

Congress compels the South to accept. The Republican majority in Congress dealt harshly with the ten Confederate states which had rejected the Amendment. A severe Reconstruction Act was passed. Johnson vetoed it, but Congress passed it over his veto. It swept away the civil governments built up under the President's guidance and placed the ten unreconstructed states under martial law. The ten states were divided into five military districts, each under a major-general of the United States Army. The generals were to preserve order and supervise the elections. Negroes in the five districts had the right to vote, in spite of the fact that not a single Northern state west or south of New York gave them this privilege. Whites who had aided the Confederacy were not permitted to vote. This clearly meant that the Negroes were to control the elections and the new state governments. When a new state government had been organized, Congress agreed to recognize it if its constitution gave Negroes the vote and if it ratified the Fourteenth Amendment. Under this plan state governments were organized in North Carolina, South Carolina, Florida, Georgia, Alabama, Louisiana, and Arkansas. These seven states were readmitted to the Union in 1868. They had been compelled to accept the Fourteenth Amendment at the point of the bayonet.

Johnson's struggle with Congress. The Republicans in Congress disliked Johnson because he opposed their plan for reconstruction. They went out of their way to shame him. As we have seen, they undid everything he had done to reconstruct the South. Then they took control of the army out of his hands and gave it to General Grant; this action, of course, kept the President from having any authority over the ten states which Congress had placed under military rule. Next, Congress tried to prevent Johnson from removing Edwin Stanton from the position of Secretary of War.

Stanton was in the Cabinet when Johnson became President. He despised the President and continually worked behind his back. When Johnson asked him to resign, he refused. To prevent Johnson from removing Stanton, Congress passed a Tenure of Office Act (1867), making it a "high misdemeanor" for the President to dismiss a federal officer without the consent of the Senate. This robbed Johnson of an important power possessed by every previous President. Johnson thought that the Tenure of Office Act was unconstitutional. He defied Congress by removing Stanton. Johnson's enemies seized upon this action as an excuse for impeaching him — that is, bringing him to trial. They felt sure they could remove him from the Presidency.

The Constitution provides that the President may be impeached for high crimes and misdemeanors in office. In reality Johnson's only offense was his opposition to Congress's program of reconstruction. His enemies drew up a long list of charges against him, and early in 1868 the House of Representatives impeached him. He was then tried before the Senate. If he was found guilty, it would mean that any future President who was unpopular with Congress could be removed.

The trial lasted nearly two months. The President was defended by five distinguished lawyers, including the Attorney General. Johnson did not appear before the Senate, although he was summoned. On the advice of his lawyers he remained at the White House, attending to his official duties. The case against him was purely political. This became more and more clear as the trial went on. The President's enemies tried by bribery and threats to secure the two-thirds majority necessary to convict him. They needed thirty-six votes, but with all their efforts they could obtain only thirty-five. Every Democrat in the Senate voted "Not guilty," but only seven Republican senators had the courage to do so. No other President has ever been impeached. The nation has accepted the principle that a President cannot be removed just because he opposes the majority of Congress.

The election of General Grant, 1868. To succeed Johnson the Republicans nominated General Grant. Though very popular, his only claim to fame was that he had "saved the Union." He had never held public office and but once in his life had taken the trouble to vote. His two terms as President were to prove that "a great general may be a babe in politics."

The Republican platform praised the Reconstruction Acts. The Democratic platform condemned the Reconstruction Acts, demanded an end of military rule in the South, and applauded President Johnson. The election returns showed that the Democrats received more white votes than did the Republicans. However, the Republicans won the election because they obtained the Negro vote in the states under Congressional control.

The Fifteenth Amendment. The strength shown by the Democrats in 1868 alarmed Republican leaders. If the reconstructed states took steps to stop Negroes from voting, the Democrats would win the next election. To prevent this, the Republicans in Congress framed the

THE TRIAL OF PRESIDENT ANDREW JOHNSON. (From a sketch made at the opening of the High Court of Impeachment, for *Frank Leslie's Illustrated Newspaper,* March 28, 1868)

Fifteenth Amendment and sent it to the states. Its purpose was to fasten Negro suffrage (voting) permanently upon the South. At the same time, it gave the ballot to Negroes in twenty Northern states where they did not have it.

The Amendment provides that "the right of citizens to vote shall not be denied or abridged by the United States or any state on account of race, color, or previous condition of servitude." A state might still deny its citizens the right to vote on some other ground — for instance, not paying poll taxes, not owning property, or not passing an educational test. In these ways the Southern whites were later able to keep the majority of Negroes from voting.

When the Fifteenth Amendment was sent to the states, there were still three which had not yet been readmitted — Virginia, Texas, and Mississippi. Congress required them to ratify both the Fourteenth and the Fifteenth Amendments. They did so, being powerless to refuse. The Fifteenth Amendment became part of the Constitution in 1870. The same year Virginia, Texas, and Mississippi were taken back into the Union.

Controlling the Negro voters. Most of the suddenly freed slaves could neither read nor write. They knew nothing of the world outside the plantations on which they worked. They were not in any way prepared to share in the government. Many looked to their old masters for guidance and advice and would have supported the Democratic party, as their masters did, had they been left alone. The Republicans took care to prevent this. They organized the Negroes into secret political clubs called "Union Leagues." By 1868 nearly every freedman belonged to one of these clubs.

The League taught Negroes that their former masters were enemies seeking to re-enslave them. It promised to divide the white men's land among the Negroes. It punished Negroes who went to Democratic meetings or showed Democratic leanings. New members of the League were required to take an oath to vote for League candidates. As a result of League activities, and because the Negroes were grateful to the party which had freed them, most of them have been Republicans to this day.

Carpetbaggers and scalawags. The Union Leagues were led by white politicians willing to use the Negroes for their own purposes. Some were adventurers from the North called "carpetbaggers." They moved into the South after the war to get what pickings they could, and many grew rich at public expense. Some Southern whites also wanted a share in the loot. Most white men despised them as traitors to the South and called them "scalawags."

The rule of the carpetbaggers. For several years after the war the carpetbaggers held most of the high offices in the reconstructed states. They let scalawags and Negroes hold minor offices. The carpetbaggers and their followers used public office as a way of getting rich. Carpetbaggers controlled the state legislatures, in which a large proportion of the members were Negroes. While some Negro legislators were men of education and fine character, many were unfit to govern. It should be said that many of the white legislators were also unfit. The result was perhaps the most corrupt and extravagant government ever known in an English-speaking land.

"Corruption is the fashion," said a carpetbag governor of Louisiana. "I do not pretend to be honest, but only as honest as anybody in politics." In one term he cleaned up half a million dollars. The state debt rose to fifty millions, and what became of the money nobody knows.

The state of Florida decided to build a railroad from Jacksonville to Pensacola. The legislature authorized a bond issue of $2,800,000. After the bonds were sold and various "commissions" had been paid, the state got $1,400,000. When 19 miles of railroad had been built, it was learned that all the money was gone.

South Carolina had a legislature of 155 members, 98 of them Negroes, of whom only 22 could read or write. Once the white speaker took a bribe of $15,000 for his vote. The legislature voted him a gift of $1,000 when they learned he had lost that sum betting on a horse race. This legislature paid bills of $200,000 for $18,000 worth of furniture for the Statehouse. It kept a restaurant and bar in the Statehouse where members could get food, liquor, and cigars free of charge. Among other foolish actions, it voted a loan of nearly $2,000,000 to aid in building the Blue Ridge Railroad. The money went to a ring of carpetbaggers, and the railroad was never built.

Similar stories could be told of all the reconstructed states while they were ruled by carpetbaggers. The state governments borrowed until they could borrow no more. Taxes rose from two to fourteen times what they had been before the war. Thousands of property owners could not meet their taxes and lost their houses and lands. Business staggered beneath the tax burden. The carpetbaggers and scalawags picked the South bare.

The Ku Klux Klan. The Southern whites wanted to regain control of their state and local governments. They wished to drive out the carpetbaggers. Even more they wished to prevent the Negroes from voting or holding office, for in many places the number of Negroes equaled or exceeded the number of whites. As long as Congress kept federal troops in the South to protect Negro voters and support the carpetbag governments, Southern white men could not act openly. So they formed secret societies to frighten the Negroes and discourage them from voting, and also to drive out the carpetbaggers. The most noted of these organizations was the Ku Klux Klan.

The Klan started in Tennessee in 1866, quickly spreading over the entire South. Its leaders were prominent Confederate officers, and most of its members were Confederate soldiers. In 1867 the hundreds of local Klans united in the "Invisible Empire of the South," with General Nathan Forrest as "Grand Wizard." No matter how good its purpose may have seemed to its members, its evil methods cannot be defended. Terror was its weapon. Klansmen, dressed in white robes and hoods, appeared suddenly in the night to punish those who disobeyed its orders. Unruly Negroes were whipped. Carpetbaggers were sometimes tarred and feathered. Weird threats were used. One of these said: "The ghosts of the mighty dead are stirring. The fiends of Hell are loose. You are not wanted here. You are given ten days to clear out. If you fail to obey this warning, then life's fretful fever will come to an end in the cool quiet of the grave. KKK."

Rash, cruel men sometimes got control of local Klans, with the result that moderate men dropped out. Such Klans were often guilty of frightful outrages against defenseless Negroes. Then, too, criminals sometimes took advantage of the hood to rob and murder. General Forrest and other leaders saw that the organization had become dangerous, and in 1869 ordered it to disband. Some of the Klans refused to break up, preferring to continue their violent activities. Congress then passed a series of force bills to stamp out the organization and protect the Negro voters. By 1872 the last remnants of the Klan had disappeared. Other, less violent methods were found to keep the Negroes from voting.

Home rule is restored. It was now clear that Negroes would not be allowed to vote in most Southern communities unless federal troops were kept there to protect them. Northerners were tired of using force. They began to say that the Negro was the Southerner's problem. Liberal-minded Republicans in Congress joined with Democrats to restore home rule in the Southern states. In 1871 Congress gave nearly all the former Confederates the right to vote. The next year Congress restored the right to hold office to all but some five hundred Confederate leaders. In 1875 President Grant refused to send federal troops to Mississippi for the purpose of guarding the Negroes as they cast their ballots; the result was that the Negroes did not vote, and the Democrats came into power. Two years later Grant's successor, President Hayes, removed all the troops from the South. This meant the end of carpetbag rule and "reconstruction." The Southern whites were again in control. Real efforts to rebuild the South could now begin.

The Solid South. Every Southern state which passed through military reconstruction became Democratic as soon as military rule ended. These states have voted Democratic in every presidential election since 1876, with the exception of 1928 and 1952. In those years four of them voted Republican. (See pages 536 and 688.) They were found in the Democratic fold in 1932, 1936, 1940, 1944, and 1948. This devotion to the Democratic party is described by the term "Solid South."

To identify: Black Codes, John Wilkes Booth, General Nathan Forrest, Ku Klux Klan, Solid South, Union League.

To explain or define: carpetbagger, civil government, martial law, military government, misdemeanor, oath of allegiance, scalawag.

Subjects for Talks or Written Reports

1. Vagrancy laws adopted by the Southern states after the War between North and South for the purpose of forcing Negroes to work. How vagrancy was defined. How vagrants were punished. Are these laws still in force? 2. The impeachment and trial of President Johnson. 3. The Presidency of General Grant. Why he is not regarded as a great President. 4. Progress made by the Negro race since the War between North and South. 5. The Presidency of Rutherford B. Hayes. Show that he deserves to be remembered as a patriot and a man of sterling character and fine ideals. 6. The history of the first Ku Klux Klan.

Questions for Understanding the Text

1. What action by Congress prevented President Lincoln from bringing any of the seceded states back into the Union? 2. Why did Jefferson Davis consider Lincoln's death to be a blow to the South? 3. (*a*) Tell about the early life of Andrew Johnson. (*b*) What shows that he was a man of ability? (*c*) Why was he chosen as military governor of Tennessee? (*d*) Why was he nominated for Vice-President? 4. (*a*) Outline Johnson's plan for reconstruction. (*b*) What fault was found with it by Republican leaders in the North? 5. Name the main restrictions placed on the freed Negroes under the Black Codes. 6. (*a*) Read the Fourteenth Amendment to the Constitution and state the purpose or intention of each part. (*b*) What section has never been enforced? 7. (*a*) How did the people of the seceded states hope to prevent adoption of the Fourteenth Amendment? (*b*) What did Congress do to compel these states to ratify? 8. (*a*) Why did President Johnson wish to remove Secretary of War Stanton? (*b*) What did Congress do to prevent Stanton's removal? (*c*) What did Johnson do then, and how did he justify his action? 9. Had Johnson been found guilty by the Senate, how would this have affected future Presidents? (Compare with the Parliamentary system in which the Prime Minister resigns whenever he loses the support of a majority in the legislature.) 10. (*a*) Why were Republican leaders eager to give Negroes the vote? (*b*) Read the Fifteenth Amendment. Has it accomplished it purpose? Explain. 11. (*a*) Why did the Republicans organize the Negro voters into "Union Leagues"? (*b*) How did the League convince Negro voters that they should support the Republican party? 12. Explain the difference between carpetbaggers and scalawags. 13. Why did taxes rise so rapidly in states ruled by carpetbaggers? 14. (*a*) How did Congress protect the carpetbag governments? (*b*) What President brought an end to carpetbag rule? How did he do so? 15. (*a*) Why did Southerners form secret societies to destroy the power of the carpetbaggers? (*b*) Name the most famous of these organizations. Who

led it? (*c*) What were its purposes? Outline its methods. (*d*) Why did its leaders order it to disband? 16. Name the steps by which home rule was restored to the South. 17. Account for the fact that the Southern states have only one important political party.

ACTIVITIES FOR UNIT FIVE

1. Continue work on the classbook, *American Hall of Fame*, and on the history of your community.
2. Draw a series of cartoons dealing with the quarrel over slavery from 1819 to 1860.
3. Select portions of *Uncle Tom's Cabin* to read in class to show how Mrs. Stowe thought that Northerners, as well as Southerners, were unjust to the Negro.
4. On outline maps show (*a*) the states that went for Lincoln in 1860; (*b*) the areas affected by the Missouri Compromise, the Compromise of 1850, and the Kansas-Nebraska Act; (*c*) the principal events of the War between North and South; (*d*) the states which seceded from the Union and the slave-holding states which remained in the Union. Include the best map on each topic in the classbook of historical maps.
5. Make posters which might have been used in the presidential campaigns of 1860 and 1864.
6. Imagine that you are a resident of one of the border states in the spring of 1861. Write a letter to a friend in either the North or the deep South telling which cause you expect to support and giving your reasons.
7. Draw a cartoon on Buchanan's indecision in the winter of 1860–61.
8. Draw a cartoon for a Democratic newspaper, criticizing the Republican administration for its conduct of the war up to the appointment of Grant as head of the Union armies.
9. Imagine that you are a schoolboy or schoolgirl in some part of the South during the last year of the war. Write a letter describing your living conditions.
10. Hold an exhibit of relics and pictures of the War between North and South. Prepare a catalog explaining each item and telling who lent it to you. Invite other classes to view the exhibit.
11. Have the class sing some of the songs of the War between North and South.

READINGS FOR UNIT FIVE

(Stars indicate the easier books)

GENERAL ACCOUNTS

Adams, James T. *American Tragedy.* Scribner's.
Bassett, John S. *Makers of a New Nation.* (Pageant)

Bowers, Claude. *The Tragic Era.* Houghton Mifflin.
Brawley, B. G. *Short History of the American Negro.* Macmillan.
Cole, Arthur C. *The Irrepressible Conflict, 1850–1865.* (A. L. S.)
Dodd, W. E. *The Cotton Kingdom.* (Chronicles)
——. *Expansion and Conflict.* Houghton Mifflin.
DuBois, W. E. B. *The Gift of Black Folk.* Stratford.
Fleming, W. L. *The Sequel of Appomattox.* (Chronicles)
*Foster, Genevieve. *Abraham Lincoln's World.* Scribner's.
Johnson, Gerald. *The Secession of the Southern States.* Putnam's.
Macy, Jesse. *The Antislavery Crusade.* (Chronicles)
Stephenson, N. W. *Abraham Lincoln and the Union.* (Chronicles)
——. *The Day of the Confederacy.* (Chronicles)
Wood, William. *Captains of the Civil War.* (Chronicles)
Wood, William and Gabriel, Ralph H. *In Defense of Liberty.* (Pageant)

BIOGRAPHY

*Adams, Julia. *Stonewall.* Dutton.
*Barton, W. E. *The Great Good Man.* Bobbs-Merrill. (Lincoln)
Bradford, Gamaliel. *Confederate Portraits.* Houghton Mifflin.
——. *Lee, the American.* Houghton Mifflin.
——. *Union Portraits.* Houghton Mifflin.
Charnwood, Lord. *Abraham Lincoln.* Garden City.
*Daugherty, James. *Abraham Lincoln.* Viking.
Dodd, W. E. *Jefferson Davis.* Macrae-Smith.
*Fauset, Arthur H. *For Freedom, a Biographical Story of the American Negro.* Franklin.
*Humphrey, Grace. *Women in American History.* Bobbs-Merrill.
Hunt, Gaillard. *John C. Calhoun.* Macrae-Smith.
Lodge, Henry Cabot. *Daniel Webster.* Houghton Mifflin.
Morse, J. T. *John Quincy Adams.* Houghton Mifflin.
*Moses, Belle. *The Gray Knight.* Appleton-Century. (Robert E. Lee)
*Nicolay, Helen. *The Boys' Life of Abraham Lincoln.* Appleton-Century.
Rogers, J. M. *The True Henry Clay.* Lippincott.
*Roosevelt, Theodore and Lodge, Henry C. *Hero Tales from American History.* Appleton-Century.
Sandburg, Carl. *Abraham Lincoln.* Harcourt, Brace.
*Tarbell, Ida M. *Boy Scouts' Life of Lincoln.* Macmillan.
Tate, Allen. *Stonewall Jackson: the Good Soldier.* Minton, Balch.
Winston, R. W. *Andrew Johnson, Plebeian and Patriot.* Holt.
——. *Robert E. Lee.* Morrow.

FICTION

*Allee, Marjorie H. *Susanna and Tristam.* Houghton Mifflin. (The Underground Railroad)

Bacheller, Irving. *A Man for the Ages.* Grosset. (Lincoln)

Brown, Katherine H. *The Father.* Grosset. (Abolition in Ohio)

DeForest, John W. *Miss Ravenal's Conversion.* Harper. (Life during the war in both North and South)

Ehrlich, Leonard. *God's Angry Man.* Simon and Schuster. (Abolitionist movement; John Brown)

Glasgow, Ellen. *The Voice of the People.* Doubleday, Doran. (Virginia during the Reconstruction period)

*Gray, Elizabeth J. *Jane Hope.* Viking. (Life in Carolina before the war)

*Lamprey, Louise. *Days of the Leaders.* Stokes. (Biographical short stories)

*Long, Laura. *Hannah Courageous.* Longmans. (The Underground Railroad)

Lynn, Margaret. *Free Soil.* Macmillan. (The struggle in Kansas, 1856–1858)

——. *The Land of Promise.* Little, Brown. (Missouri Compromise; slavery controversy, 1850–1860)

Page, Thomas N. *Red Rock.* Scribner's. (Reconstruction; the Ku Klux Klan)

*Swift, Hildegarde H. *The Railroad to Freedom; a Story of the Civil War.* Harcourt, Brace.

UNIT SIX

THE EMERGENCE OF MODERN AMERICA (1865–1900)

The America we know today took shape after the War between North and South, for the war greatly hastened the nation's industrial development. During the next thirty-five years our country made amazing progress. This period marked the rise of the city and the end of the frontier.

The rise of big business was perhaps the most remarkable change that took place in this period. Little factories were combined into the great industries we know today. Short railroad lines were joined in great systems. As the consolidation of business went on, the people feared that big business would rule the nation. They demanded laws to prevent the growth of the trusts, but the laws proved almost useless.

Throughout this period labor conditions were very unsatisfactory. Workingmen tried to win better conditions but made little progress. The farmers, too, were increasingly discontented. In an effort to get the government to pay more attention to their woes, workingmen and farmers united in 1892 to form the Populist, or People's, party. The party grew so rapidly that conservatives became alarmed and in the campaign of 1896 spent money more freely than ever in our history to insure the election of a conservative President, William McKinley. The conservatives won the election and the Populist party was soon almost forgotten.

THE HOME COMING, 1865. *Many a Confederate soldier returning to his home after the war found the dwelling in ruins and his family in want. How could he repair the damage and provide for his loved ones when he, like nearly every other Southerner, was penniless and business in the South was at a standstill? Great obstacles were overcome as the new South gradually arose from the ruin of the war.* (From the painting by a Confederate soldier, William L. Shepherd. Courtesy of Confederate Museum, Richmond)

CHAPTER 24

THE WAR BRINGS ECONOMIC CHANGE

Economic ruin in the South. The Confederate soldiers returned to their homes in despair. Everywhere they saw signs of ruin caused by the war. The entire South was terribly poor. From Virginia to Texas it was dotted with towns partly or completely destroyed. Wide areas in Virginia, the Carolinas, Georgia, Tennessee, and Arkansas had been laid waste. The railroads had broken down. Roads and bridges were almost impassable. Banks had closed their doors. Business was paralyzed. Even the farms were in bad shape — their livestock gone, fences down, tools worn out. Savings invested in slaves and Confederate war bonds had been wiped out. Confederate money was worthless. The commonest necessities were lacking. The future looked bleak. Yet the defeated South turned bravely to the task of economic reconstruction. Within one generation much of the damage was repaired and prosperity partly restored.

The breakup of the plantation system. The planter class was wrecked by the war. The planters no longer had slaves to work their fields or money to pay hired labor. Because of the extravagance and greed of carpetbag officials, taxes were almost unbearable. Thousands of plantations were broken up and sold to pay the taxes. Good land brought only three to five dollars an acre. Many white families came down from the hilly back country to buy land belonging to some planter who had lost everything. A new class of prosperous small farmers developed.

The share-crop system. Many planters divided their land into small parcels, which they rented to poor whites or Negroes. Few of the whites and almost none of the Negroes could pay a cash rent. Instead they paid a share of the crop. Under the share-crop system the landlord furnishes the tenant with a house, land, tools, seed, fertilizer, and mules. The sharecropper gives his labor and receives one third to one half of the crop. The average sharecropper earns very little for his year's work, so little that long before the next harvest he usually has

GEORGE WASHINGTON CARVER *in his laboratory at Tuskegee Institute. After struggling for an education, Dr. Carver devoted his life to teaching and research. He discovered hundreds of new uses for Southern crops. For his distinguished service in the field of science, he received many honors.* (Polk Studio, Tuskegee)

to buy on credit or borrow money to keep his family going. As security he pledges his growing crop — that is, he gives a *lien*, or mortgage, on it to the lender. The one crop on which the average landlord, merchant, or banker is willing to take a lien is cotton, which is more certain of a good yield and a good price than other crops. So the sharecropper grows little else but cotton. Continual cotton-growing wears out the soil and keeps the sharecropper poor. When the crop is sold and his debts are paid, he is lucky to have anything left. Often he remains in debt from one harvest to the next and frequently moves away owing the landlord.

Conditions among the freedmen. During the first two or three years after the war the freed slaves of the deep South were worse off than they had been under slavery. Some of them stayed with their former masters, but thousands took to the roads, wandering aimlessly from place to place, living on what they could find. Other thousands swarmed into the cities, where they lived under horribly crowded conditions. Diseases swept the Negro quarters, and Negro children died like flies. In some communities one fourth to one third of the Negroes died from disease or from starvation within two or three years.

The Negroes of the upper South got along better. There were not so many of them in proportion to the white population. Most of them soon managed to find work, although the wages were miserably low.

The sufferings of the Negroes would have been greater had not Congress in the last days of the war created the Freedmen's Bureau. The Bureau gave food and medicine to the ex-slaves and helped them find work or rent land. Gradually the Negroes settled down and learned to take care of themselves.

The more ambitious Negroes went North or found work in towns, but the vast majority became sharecroppers. Some of the sharecroppers succeeded after a time in buying little farms. Ten years after emancipation one in every twenty freedmen owned the land he farmed; by 1900, one in four did so.

The freedmen were eager for education. Many felt they could die happy if they could only learn to read the Bible. Schools for Negroes, supported by Northern churches, were soon built in most parts of the South. In 1866 one hundred and fifty thousand Negroes of all ages attended school, and every year the number grew. Normal schools and colleges to train Negro teachers soon opened. One of the most interesting of these is Hampton (Virginia) Normal and Agricultural Institute, established in 1870. Its founder, General Samuel Armstrong, had commanded Negro troops during the war and later served as an officer of the Freedmen's Bureau. He believed that the Negro race could rise through vocational education. Before long Hampton graduates proved that with good training Negroes could learn to manage a farm or carry on a business successfully. One of the first graduates of Hampton, Booker T. Washington, founded Tuskegee Institute in Alabama. How this penniless young Negro, with the gifts of other poor Negroes and friendly white people, built a school and made it a great institution for the improvement of his race is an inspiring story.

The Industrial Revolution comes to the South. Under the slavery system men with money put it into slaves rather than into industry. The South bought most of its manufactured goods in the North or in Europe.

In the 1870's Southern manufacturing began to forge ahead. Small cotton mills, flour mills, lumber mills, furniture shops, or tobacco factories were started, mostly beside waterfalls. Rich deposits of coal and iron were uncovered in Tennessee and northern Alabama. Birmingham, which was a cotton field in 1870, became in twenty years the center of a booming iron industry, served by six railroads. By that time the South was producing one fifth of the nation's pig iron. The South also had the largest tobacco factory in the world at Durham, North Carolina. In the 1890's hundreds of new textile and knitting mills were built. Most Southerners still lived by farming, but the South was becoming an important manufacturing region.

Industrial expansion in the North. Instead of ruin the War between North and South brought prosperity to the North. Manufacturing, transportation, and commerce expanded as never before. The use of machinery increased greatly. Almost overnight little businesses grew into big ones. Before the war ended, our modern industrial system had taken shape.

Perhaps the greatest effects of the war were seen in the field of transportation. The movement of hundreds of thousands of troops and the supplies they needed forced rapid improvements in railroading. Small lines were joined to large ones. Connecting links, double tracks, and bridges were built. War needs led Congress in 1862 to vote federal aid for building a transcontinental railroad; however, construction had barely begun when the war ended. The closing of the Mississippi at the start of the war meant that the products of Western farms had to go east instead of south and had to move by railroad instead of by river boat. Chicago suddenly became the great Western shipping center.

The supplying of a great army forced many industries to expand. To make cloth for uniforms, scores of new woolen mills were built. The manufacture of ready-to-wear clothing grew into a huge business during the war — a growth made possible by the sewing machine, invented in 1846. Army orders for millions of shoes caused the shoe business to leave the one-man shop for the factory. Great packing houses were built to fill army orders for meat, with the result that after the war thousands of local slaughterhouses had to close. In spite of fewer men on the farms, farm production increased, for the farmers turned to the use of the reaper and the mowing machine. The farm machinery industry grew enormously but could not keep up with the demand. The need for iron and steel to make machinery, cannon, rails, locomotives, and steamships led to the opening of scores of iron and steel mills. The steel manufacturing district around Pittsburgh got its start during the war.

War also helped the mining industry. The railroads and the war industries demanded large quantities of coal, iron, and copper. Oil was needed for lubrication and for lighting. The first oil well had been

A RAILROAD STATION AND TRAIN *in the 1860's. The scene is Stratford, Connecticut. Note the big smokestack on the wood-burning locomotive.* (From the painting by Edward L. Henry, 1867. Courtesy of Metropolitan Museum of Art)

sunk in 1859 at Titusville, Pennsylvania. Before the war's end western Pennsylvania was dotted with hundreds of derricks, and oil refining was becoming an important business.

Expansion continues after the war. For several years after the war, industry continued its rapid growth. Thousands of businessmen who had made fortunes from army contracts invested their wealth in new factories. Hundreds of thousands of immigrants poured into the country each year, supplying plenty of workers, who also became customers for manufactured products. The West was filling up, creating a demand for farm machinery, manufactures of all kinds, and more railroads. The five years after Appomattox saw more rails laid, more lumber sawed, more houses built, more coal, iron, silver, and copper mined, more flour milled, and more cotton cloth woven than any previous five years in the nation's history.

European critics thought that the return of a million Union soldiers to civilian life in 1865 would cause hard times. They were mistaken. The Union soldiers had little trouble finding jobs. Many went into the factories, oil fields, and mines, or into railroading. Others claimed a free homestead in the West and settled down to farm.

The triumph of industrialism. When it came to power in 1861, the

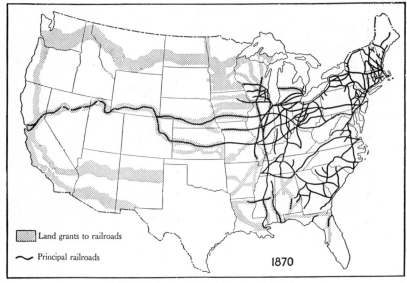

RAILROAD LINES AND GRANTS

Congress gave to railroads large tracts of valuable land in the West. (Based on the map of the American Geographical Society)

Republican party was pledged to a high tariff, land grants to aid railroads, free farms for Western settlers, and a reform of banking and currency. This program could not have been written into laws had the Southern states not seceded and taken their representatives out of Congress. When this happened, Congress speedily adopted the whole program.

1. A high tariff. The tariff rate had been dropping ever since 1832, when South Carolina threatened to nullify the "Tariff of Abominations." (See pages 208–212.) In 1861 Congress passed the Morrill Tariff Act to raise the duties. By the end of the war the average duty had risen from 18 to 47 per cent. This tariff wall protected Northern manufacturers against all competition from abroad. Not until 1913 would there be any real reduction of tariff rates.

2. Free land for homesteaders and railroad companies. In 1862 Congress passed the Homestead Act, which permitted the head of a family to obtain 160 acres of public land merely by building a dwelling on it and working it for five years. Before the good land was gone, several hundred thousand families got a free farm. Under a series of railroad laws Congress voted vast tracts of land as gifts to transconti-

nental railroads. Altogether the railroads got five times as much free land as the homesteaders.

3. A uniform currency. Since the destruction of the Bank of the United States by Andrew Jackson (see pages 214–216), the nation had been without a uniform currency. Banks were chartered by the states, and each issued its own brand of paper money. In 1861 there were seven thousand kinds of bank notes in circulation, besides five thousand kinds of counterfeit notes. Only an expert could tell what a piece of paper money was worth. In 1863 Congress passed a National Banking Act to give the country a sound, uniform currency. Under this law and its amendments any bank choosing to accept federal regulation could get a charter as a "national bank." A national bank could buy government bonds, deposit them with the treasury at Washington, and issue bank notes up to 90 per cent of the value of the bonds. Since the value of national bank notes is never in doubt, they circulated anywhere in the United States. By 1866, 80 per cent of all the banks had accepted federal regulation, and the notes of state banks no longer circulated.

The adoption of the Republican program meant that at last the policies of Hamilton had triumphed over those of Jefferson. What the planters had feared from the Republicans had come to pass. A revolution had taken place — a new class had come to power. Manufacturers and bankers had control of the reins of government. They could keep command as long as they had the support of the Western farmer.

To *identify:* General Samuel Armstrong, Freedmen's Bureau, Homestead Act, Booker T. Washington.

To *explain or define:* homesteader, lien, national bank, sharecropper.

Subjects for Talks or Written Reports

1. The work of the Freedmen's Bureau. 2. The history of Hampton Institute. 3. The life of Booker T. Washington. 4. The history of Tuskegee Institute. 5. The development of the iron industry in the South. 6. The early history of the oil industry. 7. The experiences of some homesteaders. 8. What the railroads did with the free land they received from Congress.

QUESTIONS FOR UNDERSTANDING THE TEXT

1. Describe economic conditions in the South at the close of the War between North and South.   2. How did many farmers from the back country benefit from the breakup of the plantation system?   3. (*a*) How does the share-crop system work?   (*b*) Why is sharecropping more common than renting for cash?   (*c*) Why is sharecropping likely to lead to the wearing out of the soil?   4. Describe conditions among the freed Negroes shortly after the war (*a*) in the deep South, (*b*) in the upper South. 5. Name two famous institutions for training Negro teachers.   6. Name several kinds of manufacturing which became important in the South by 1890.   7. In the North how did the war affect (*a*) transportation, (*b*) the growth of Chicago, (*c*) the clothing and shoe industry, (*d*) the slaughtering industry, (*e*) the farm machinery industry, (*f*) the iron and steel industry, (*g*) the mining industry?   8. How did wartime profits help Northern industry?   9. Was there serious unemployment after the War between North and South?   Why or why not?   10. What situation enabled the Republican party to carry out its program for helping industry? 11. (*a*) How much did Congress raise tariff duties during the war?   (*b*) Were these high rates reduced after the war?   12. How could a homesteader obtain a free farm?   13. How did Congress at this time dispose of a large part of the public lands?   14. What must a bank do to become a national bank?   15. How do we know that any note issued by a national bank is worth its full face value?   16. What is meant by saying that a revolution took place during the War between North and South?   17. Why have our two major political parties tried to please the Western farmers ever since the War between North and South?

CHAPTER 25

THE RISE OF BIG BUSINESS

Hamilton's dream, not Jefferson's, comes true. Hamilton wanted the United States to become a great manufacturing nation. Jefferson dreamed of a great republic filled with farmers, each owning his own land. He hoped the nation would never have a large class of wage earners. For many years Jefferson's dream seemed to be coming true. The nation had a vast area of fertile land still to be settled. Most of its people were independent farmers or small businessmen. Industries grew slowly, and at the beginning of the War between North and South employed but a small part of the population. Yet a change was already setting in. Between 1850 and 1860 the output of American factories doubled in value. Between 1860 and 1880 it doubled again. By 1890 the United States had become the leading manufacturing nation in the world. Hamilton's dream, not Jefferson's, had come true.

THE BASIS OF AMERICA'S INDUSTRIAL GROWTH

Rapid industrial progress of the United States was not an accident. It resulted because we have here everything required for large-scale industries — varied natural resources, an abundant labor supply, money to invest, a market for industrial products, able scientists and inventors, skillful managers, and a government which has been eager to encourage private business.

1. Natural resources. Few nations are so richly blessed with natural resources as the United States. Its stimulating climate, numerous harbors, navigable rivers; its great water power; its forests; its immense stores of coal, oil, natural gas, iron, copper, lead, zinc — all these set the stage for the development of industry.

2. Labor supply. After the War between North and South the population continued to grow rapidly, partly because of the high birth rate and partly because of immigration. Every year we had a million and a quarter more people. They could not all go into farming, for the use of farm machinery reduced the labor needed to grow a given quan-

tity of crops. Most of the additional people went to the cities, where they took work for any wage they could get.

3. Money to invest. The rapid growth of industry demanded capital — that is, money to invest in buildings, machinery, railroads and shipping, and raw materials. Much of the capital needed soon after the War between North and South was supplied by Northern bankers and manufacturers out of the huge profits they made during the war. More of it came from Europe. European investors had faith in the United States and its future. They were willing to lend money to our businessmen at fairly low rates of interest.

4. A market for industrial products. The United States furnished a broad and growing market. High tariffs kept out foreign competition. The businessman had the whole country for his market, for the separate states had no tariff walls to keep out goods from other states.

5. Able scientists and inventors. Americans are a practical people. They have been quick to apply scientific discoveries to everyday affairs. Searching for ways to save labor, they have improved numberless machines and ways of making things. They have probably made more inventions than any other people. A few examples will show how inventions have made big business possible.

In 1837 Samuel F. B. Morse worked out the basic ideas for the telegraph. He could not afford to build a telegraph line, and the public was not interested. Finally, in 1843, he persuaded Congress to pay for building a line from Washington to Baltimore. Within a few years the Western Union and other companies had netted the country with their lines. The telegraph was a great help in buying and selling in distant markets. It also made modern railroading possible.

Builders of telegraph lines soon learned to span rivers and lakes by using cables. In 1850 a cable was laid across the English Channel. A few years later Cyrus Field tried to lay a cable across the Atlantic. After several costly failures the work was completed in 1866. The same year a second Atlantic cable was laid, and soon all the continents were linked by underseas communication. The cable helped greatly in the development of foreign trade. Later it made worldwide news services possible.

In 1876 a Scotch immigrant, Alexander Graham Bell, exhibited the first practical telephone. Two years later a telephone exchange was built at Hartford, Connecticut, and soon after in other cities. Within a few years every store and business office had a phone box, and the streets of large cities were dark with overhead wires. The telephone

ABOARD THE CABLE–LAYING SHIP. *Cyrus Field and his co-workers are eagerly awaiting the result of their work.* (From the painting "Awaiting the Reply," by Robert Dudley, 1866. (Courtesy of Metropolitan Museum of Art)

enabled the businessman to serve customers in a wider area than ever before. Like the telegraph, the telephone promoted the growth of nationwide businesses.

In the 1850's Henry Bessemer in England and William Kelly in the United States invented a new method for making steel. The method became known as the "Bessemer process." Steel had been rare and costly, being used chiefly for knives and fine tools. Soon it became as cheap as cast iron. Steel was far superior to iron for most purposes and soon replaced iron in rails, bridges, and machinery. It is sometimes said that we live in the "Age of Steel."

Improvements in transportation were necessary for the growth of industry. The adoption of the steel rail brought heavier, more powerful locomotives and larger cars. The invention of the air brake, the automatic coupler for joining cars together, and the block system of signals made the railroads safer. The refrigerator car, which came into use in the 1870's, led to remarkable changes in the food business. Milk, butter, meat, and other perishable goods could now be shipped long distances. The result was that packing plants, dairy companies, and chain stores took the entire country for their market.

Other great inventions gave us the electric industry. For years electricity had been little more than a toy, its feeble currents produced by batteries. In 1877 Charles F. Brush, a young Ohio engineer, showed a practical *dynamo*, or generator. It produced current far more cheaply than could batteries. Inventors hastened to work out ways for using electricity for light and power. In 1878 Brush developed an arc light for use on city streets. In 1879 Thomas Edison developed a practical lamp for lighting buildings, boats, and railroad cars. He soon had a factory turning out bulbs in thousands. The electric motor had been designed years earlier, but was little used because of the high cost of current. Now it was put to use in electric locomotives and in the trolley car. Before 1890 about twenty cities had trolley cars running on their streets. The electric industry has continued its rapid progress down to our own day, creating new jobs, new conveniences, and new sources of profit.

6. Skillful managers. To succeed, a business needs skillful management. The good manager must be at once practical and imaginative, careful and daring. He sees and makes use of opportunities which others neglect. Such a man was Cornelius Vanderbilt.

In 1865 Vanderbilt was seventy-one years old, and owned a fleet of steamboats worth ten million dollars. When he died twelve years later, he left one hundred four millions, then an unheard-of fortune. He won it by creating the New York Central Railroad system.

When Vanderbilt went into railroading, the railroads had little, wheezy locomotives which ran over flimsy iron rails and wooden bridges. Great railroad systems did not exist. Freight going from New York to Chicago had to be unloaded seventeen times, carted across town, and reloaded onto other trains. Vanderbilt bought the separate lines and combined them into a single, smoothly operating system. He ripped up the old iron rails and replaced them with steel, put down four tracks where there had been two, erected steel bridges, discarded the old locomotives for more powerful ones, built new, convenient stations, and cut down the hours required for a New York-Chicago trip from fifty to twenty-four. In accomplishing all this he did not hesitate to bribe legislatures and judges, to sell stock to the public for twice its value, or to take advantage of inside information to win huge sums on the stock exchange. His methods were those of a "robber baron," yet he helped to open up a continent. What he did was soon repeated by other railroad leaders in all parts of the country.

7. Government aid. Our government has always tried to encourage private business. For instance, through the patent system an inventor is given complete control of his invention for seventeen years.

During the War between North and South and for many years afterward, business interests were given many advantages by the national government. The tariff was raised again and again. Enormous grants of the public land were made to railroad companies. Large tracts of land covered with timber or known to contain minerals were sold to individuals and companies for a dollar or two an acre. Cattlemen grazed their herds and lumbermen cut trees on the public lands, many growing rich from these valuable privileges.

State and local governments were as eager as the national government to encourage business. They voted gifts of money and land to railroad companies. They gave *franchises* to railroad, water, electric, telephone, and gas companies. (A franchise permits a company to use public highways or streets for its lines, pipes, or other facilities. Once it has a franchise, a company is in a position to make a large profit because it has no competition.) State legislatures issued charters to corporations, giving them various privileges, including the right to do business anywhere in the United States. All these favors helped the rise of big business.

LITTLE BUSINESS BECOMES BIG BUSINESS

Many small companies combine. At the close of the War between North and South most businesses were small. For instance, thousands of companies were drilling oil in Pennsylvania. In that state alone there were more than two hundred oil refineries. Some two hundred companies were making mowers and reapers, seventy-five of them in the state of New York. Fifty companies were making salt in Michigan. Forty years later the picture was very different. Small companies did but a small part of the total business of the country. One giant concern might control an entire industry. For example, the International Harvester Company made almost all the farm implements, while the Standard Oil Company did a large part of all the oil refining.

The *consolidation of business* — that is, the combining of many separate businesses into one large company — began during the 1860's and has continued ever since. One of the main reasons for consolidation is to reduce competition and make possible control over prices. Another reason is to reduce costs. The large business often, but not always, produces at a lower cost per unit than the small business. (The unit may be an article such as a gallon of oil, or it may be a service.) A third reason is the human love for power. Men like Vanderbilt, Rockefeller, McCormick, and Carnegie enjoyed the power which

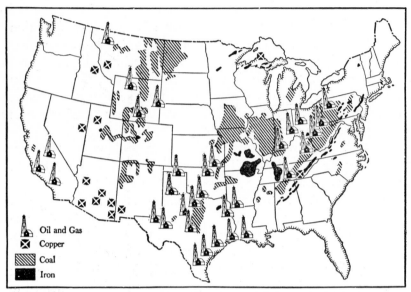

THE UNITED STATES HAS RICH MINERAL RESOURCES

came to them as they bought out their competitors and made themselves the masters of giant enterprises.

The corporation and the trust. In Lincoln's day the typical business was owned by one individual or a *partnership*. A partnership enables several individuals to pool their money and their skill. If the business fails, each partner is *liable* (responsible) for its debts and may lose everything he has.

The *corporation* is a form of business organization better suited than the partnership to large enterprises. It enables any number of individuals to put their money into a business, and, in case the business fails, limits their responsibility for the company's debts to the sum each has put in. The corporation must have a charter granted by a state legislature. Usually the charter gives it the right to do business anywhere in the nation. Corporations did not become numerous until after the War between North and South.

Strictly speaking, the word "trust" means a group of corporations run by a single board of trustees. However, the word is popularly used to mean any large business combination which controls an industry. The first to emerge was the Standard Oil Trust, organized in 1882. Soon there was a trust in nearly every industry. How trusts develop will appear from the story of the oil trust and the steel trust.

OIL CREEK VALLEY, PENNSYLVANIA. *The first well for the commercial production of oil was drilled here in 1859.* (Drawn by F. H. Schell for *Frank Leslie's Illustrated Newspaper,* January, 1865)

The story of the oil trust. At the close of the War between North and South, oil refining was one of the nation's fastest growing businesses. John D. Rockefeller, a young produce merchant of Cleveland, organized an oil refining concern known as Rockefeller, Andrews, and Flagler. He realized that soon the whole world would demand petroleum products, and he made up his mind to gain control of the refining industry. The first step was to build up a strong cash reserve. He advised his partners: "Don't buy new clothes and fast horses; let your wife wear her last year's bonnet. You can't find any place where money will earn what it does here."

In 1870 Rockefeller organized the Standard Oil Company of Ohio. He got the railroads to give his company secret rebates (refunds) on the rates paid for shipping oil; this enabled him to sell oil cheaper than his competitors. He then bought out his competitors one by one. In two years his company had taken over twenty out of twenty-six independent refineries in Cleveland. Then, by similar methods, he gained control of refining in New York, Philadelphia, Pittsburgh, and Baltimore. By 1882 his companies, which refined 90 per cent of the petroleum products produced in the United States, were combined into the Standard Oil Trust. Rockefeller next got control of the principal pipe lines and oil storehouses. This done, the trust entered the business

OIL REFINERY *at Oil Creek, Pennsylvania, about 1864. The oil refining industry had its beginnings during the early 1860's.* (Courtesy of Drake Museum, Titusville, Pennsylvania)

of drilling and pumping oil. Within ten years the trust was master of the oil business from well to consumer. No longer having any competition to speak of, it could set prices to suit itself — it had, that is, become a *monopoly.*

The story of the steel trust. As Rockefeller's name stands out in the story of oil, so does that of Andrew Carnegie in the story of steel. Carnegie, who was born in Scotland in 1835, came to America a poor boy. At thirteen he worked in a cotton mill for one dollar and twenty cents a week. At seventeen he was a telegraph clerk; a few years later he was private secretary to the president of the Pennsylvania Railroad. He was honest, industrious, and wide-awake. His charm of manner won the friendship of prominent railroad men, who helped him get ahead. Before he was thirty he had an income of forty to fifty thousand dollars a year from investments in express and sleeping-car companies, in oil, and in iron.

In 1865 Carnegie decided to put all his money into the iron business. Within a few years he organized, or bought into, companies that made iron bridges, rails, and locomotives. After seeing a Bessemer converter in operation, he said, "The day of iron has passed." He set about building the largest steel mill in the country. Soon it was turning out

MODERN BLAST FURNACES. *The blast furnaces produce pig iron from iron ore In the iron and steel industry big business is supreme.* (Courtesy of Bethlehem Steel Company)

more steel than all the other American mills put together. He sold steel to his railroad friends, and they gave him secret rebates on all his shipments. Gradually he ruined or bought up his rivals. Year by year his holdings grew. He bought coal mines, coke companies, iron mines, and a fleet of steamboats to carry the iron ore from Minnesota to Lake Erie. Where the boats unloaded, he built a port town. Then he built a railroad connecting the port to the mills in Pittsburgh.

Carnegie drew about him skillful managers. He left them to produce steel while he went into the markets to sell it. He inspired the men who worked for him with his own energy and enthusiasm. However large the output of a mill, he called for more. "We broke all records for making steel last week!" a manager wired him. Carnegie replied, "Congratulations. Why not do it every week?"

By 1900 the Carnegie company was producing one fourth of all the steel made in the United States. With the help of high tariffs and secret rebates it made a profit of forty million dollars a year. Yet it had several powerful competitors. To crush them Carnegie threatened to buy new mines, build more freighters, and construct plants for making finished products out of steel. Frightened bankers, with investments in rival steel companies, appealed to J. Pierpont Morgan and Company to buy out Carnegie at his own price. Carnegie was an old man. He really wanted to retire and give away his money. So he agreed to sell his properties for nearly five hundred million dollars. In 1901 the Carnegie and other companies, which together did 60 per cent of the country's steel business, were combined into the United States Steel Corporation. Its bonds and stocks were valued at almost one and a half billion dollars — a sum larger than the total national wealth a hundred years before. Today this huge concern is the greatest producer of steel in the world.

Effects of the consolidation of business. By the turn of the century (1900) most of the nation's manufacturing, mining, transportation, banking, and communications business was done by giant corporations. These made or controlled almost everything the city man ate and wore, the furnishings of his house, his tools, his fuel, lights, telephone, and transportation. The products he used, the services he enjoyed, were better than those of a generation earlier, but for the most part they were no longer produced by local firms. Large numbers of local companies had gone out of business or had been bought by larger competitors. Most city men no longer worked for themselves or someone they knew, but for a distant corporation.

The owners of a corporation are those who hold its bonds and stock. They may be scattered over the entire world. Most of them have no knowledge of how the corporation is run. All they ask is regular payment of interest or dividends. (Dividends are paid on stock.) This system of *absentee ownership* is very different from the local ownership which was customary in the days of small business.

The rise of big business centered vast wealth in the hands of a few men. What is more important, it gave a few men power over millions of workers and consumers. They often used their power to keep wages down and prices up, to crush attempts of labor to organize, and to dictate to state legislatures and even to Congress itself.

The early captains of industry had little regard for public opinion and the law. At the time that Vanderbilt was combining various railroad lines, one of his associates told him that "each and every one" of certain deals he had put through "is absolutely forbidden by the statutes of the state of New York." "John," said the Commodore, "you don't suppose you can run a railroad in accordance with the statutes of the state of New York, do you?" "Law!" he roared on a similar occasion. "What do I care about law? Hain't I got the power?"

The rise of big business had good effects as well as bad. It reduced wasteful competition and so saved money for improved equipment and for research. It made possible mass production at low cost. As a result a wide variety of comforts was brought within the reach of the masses of people. Andrew Carnegie called this "triumphant democracy."

The government steps in. The growth of big business soon brought protests from small businessmen who were being crushed to the wall. As early as 1876 Peter Cooper, running for the Presidency on the Greenback ticket, declared, "The danger to our free institutions now is only less than in the inception [beginning] of the rebellion. . . . There is fast forming in this country an aristocracy of wealth, the worst form of aristocracy that can curse the prosperity of any country."

During the 1880's the public began to complain that the trusts were raising prices and making unreasonable profits. Several state legislatures held investigations and passed laws against monopolies. Some states compelled the trusts to break up. But a trust broken up in one state might incorporate in another where the laws were less strict and go on doing business exactly as before. Federal regulation seemed to be necessary.

In 1888 President Grover Cleveland told Congress that "corporations, which should be carefully restrained . . . and servants of the people, are fast becoming the people's masters." Both the Republican and Democratic parties declared that they were against monopolies. Finally, in 1890, Congress passed the Sherman Antitrust Act.

A way was quickly found to get around the Antitrust Act. The great combinations simply changed their form from trusts to *holding companies.* (A holding company buys a majority of the voting stock of each concern it wishes to control. The American Telephone and Telegraph Company is an example of the holding company.) In 1895 the Supreme Court ruled that the Antitrust Act did not apply to holding companies. Combinations continued to become more numerous and more powerful. When the huge United States Steel Corporation was formed in 1901, it was clear that Congress had failed completely in checking the growth of big business.

To identify: Alexander Graham Bell, Henry Bessemer, Charles F. Brush, Andrew Carnegie, Thomas Edison, Cyrus Field, Cyrus McCormick, John D. Rockefeller, Cornelius Vanderbilt.

To explain or define: absentee ownership, arc light, capital, consolidation of business, corporation, dynamo, franchise, holding company, monopoly, rebate, stock dividend, trust.

SUBJECTS FOR TALKS OR WRITTEN REPORTS

1. The Bessemer process for making steel and the great changes it brought about in modern living. 2. The early years of the electric industry. 3. The principal inventions of Thomas Edison. 4. The life of Cornelius Vanderbilt, John D. Rockefeller, Andrew Carnegie, or Cyrus McCormick. 5. Advantages and disadvantages of giving inventors complete control of their inventions for a long period of years. 6. How a corporation is formed and carried on.

QUESTIONS FOR UNDERSTANDING THE TEXT

1. What remarkable changes took place in the United States in the period 1850 to 1890? 2. (*a*) Where did the money come from which made possible the rapid growth of industry after the War between North and South? (*b*) Where did the laborers come from? 3. How did the large population of the United States and the absence of tariff barriers between the states help the growth of our industries? 4. Name several inventions which assisted the growth of nationwide businesses. 5. Name an invention which brought great changes in the food industry. Name some of these changes. 6. What invention made possible the wide use of electricity? 7. (*a*) What did Vanderbilt do to improve railroading in the Northeast? (*b*) What was his attitude toward the public? Toward government officials? 8. Name ways in which our government has encouraged private business. 9. (*a*) What is a franchise? (*b*) Why is it valuable? (*c*) What kinds of companies need franchises? 10. (*a*) What is meant by consolidation of business? (*b*) When did it begin? (*c*) What are the reasons for consolidation of business? 11. State the chief differences between a partnership and a corporation. 12. Tell the story of the oil trust. 13. How did secret rebates given to Rockefeller force his competitors to sell out to him? 14. Tell the story of how Andrew Carnegie became one of the leaders in the steel industry. 15. (*a*) How did Carnegie in 1900 frighten his competitors into buying him out? (*b*) What large company was then formed? (*c*) What was remarkable about it? 16. What is meant by absentee ownership? Is it better or worse for a community than local ownership of business? 17. (*a*) Name the good effects resulting from the consolidation of business. (*b*) Name the evil effects which sometimes follow. 18. (*a*) What groups protested the growth of the trusts? (*b*) Why did the Sherman Antitrust Act fail to prevent the growth of great combinations?

CHAPTER 26

THE RISE OF THE CITY

How *the cities got their people.* The rapid growth of manufacturing and trade led to a rapid growth of cities, In 1860 only one American in six lived in a place having 10,000 or more people, but by 1900 one in three did so. The cities drew many of their people from the farms. It became the custom for most of the farmers' sons and daughters to go to the city to earn their living. If a farmer had poor land, all his boys and girls were likely to leave home for the city. In this period thousands of farms in the Northeast were given up. Soon nothing remained of them but cellar holes surrounded by clumps of lilac and syringa, tumble-down buildings, scrubby orchards, and pastures growing up into forest. In hilly parts of New England whole villages were gradually abandoned.

The cities also attracted millions of immigrants from Europe. Between 1860 and 1900 over fourteen million foreigners came to the United States, most of them settling in factory and mining towns in the Northeast. Until about 1880 the great bulk of the immigrants came from northwestern Europe, mainly from the British Isles and Germany. These immigrants were much like the people already living here and quickly fitted into our ways. After 1880 we began to receive many immigrants from eastern and southern Europe, especially from Italy, Hungary, and Russia. These people took much longer to learn our language and our customs. By 1890 three fourths of the immigrants entering the United States were from eastern and southern Europe. Soon our big seaport cities had whole sections known by such names as "Little Italy," "Little Hungary," or "Little Bohemia," where the newcomers settled to be near their own countrymen.

IMPROVEMENTS HELP CITIES GROW

The modern city was made possible by new methods of communication, transportation, sanitation, lighting, and fire protection.

Improvements in communication. New methods of communication helped businessmen to reach more customers. As businesses grew bigger, the cities grew bigger also.

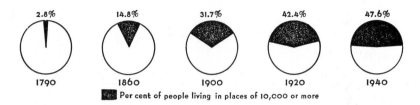

2.8%   14.8%   31.7%   42.4%   47.6%

1790   1860   1900   1920   1940

Per cent of people living in places of 10,000 or more

1. Better postal service.   Until 1863 people went to the post office to get their letters.   In that year free delivery of mail was started in the larger cities.   In 1887 carrier service was given to all towns with ten thousand or more people.   Free rural delivery began ten years later.

2. Invention of the typewriter.   In 1867 a middle-aged printer named C. L. Sholes succeeded in making a practical commercial typewriter.   The first model had many defects.   For six years Sholes and two friends worked to overcome the defects, and by 1873 they had a machine that was good enough to be sold to the public.   Businessmen found the typewriter a great convenience, and it soon came into common use.

3. Invention of the telephone.   A crude telephone was shown at the Philadelphia Exposition in 1876.   Before long it was greatly improved. By 1880 eighty-five cities had telephone exchanges, although only two or three cities were connected by telephone.   By 1900 nearly a million telephones were in use, and most of the larger cities were connected. Telephones were found chiefly in stores and offices; only well-to-do people had them in their homes.

Improvements in local transportation.   The cities needed better transportation even more than they needed faster communication. Until late in the 1880's few American cities had any kind of local transportation except horse-drawn vehicles.

1. Electric railways.   The improvement which helped the average city most was the electric street railway.   A number of short lines were built in the 1880's, and by 1890 there were nearly eight hundred companies in the business.   These early street railway companies were small, having an average of only ten miles of track.   Horse-drawn cars soon disappeared from most cities, although as late as 1920 a very few were still in use.

2. Elevated lines and subways.   The streets of the largest cities were so crowded that some method had to be found to take car lines off the streets.   New York started an elevated steam railway in 1867.   By the 1880's New York had several elevated lines, and Brooklyn and Kan-

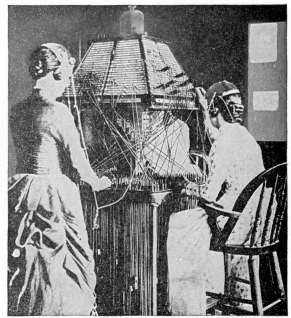

TELEPHONE OPERA-TORS, 1881. *This is a pyramid switchboard at Richmond, Virginia. At first boys were employed as operators, but it was soon found that girls were more satisfactory.* (Courtesy of American Telephone and Telegraph Company)

sas City were also building "els." Chicago opened an elevated line in 1892 and Boston did so in 1901. Electrification of the lines ended the nuisance of cinders and ashes dropping upon people in the streets below.

In the middle 1890's the city of Boston built a subway. New York opened its first subway in 1904. Subways would finally take the place of most of the noisy elevated lines.

3. Paved streets. In the 1880's the streets of even our largest cities were either badly paved or not paved at all. Cobblestones and granite blocks were the favorite paving materials in the East, while wood blocks were popular in the Midwest. Brick, asphalt, and macadam pavements then came into use, and the rough, dirty cobblestone streets were gradually made over into the smooth, clean streets we have to-day. However, many years passed before cities thought it necessary to pave all their streets.

4. Automobiles. Electric railways met the needs of passengers very well. There was great need for a faster, cleaner way to haul goods. Fortunately the autotruck was soon to replace the horse-drawn cart and wagon.

During the 1890's a number of inventors were experimenting with automobiles. No gasoline cars were made for sale until 1896 or later,

A RACING CAR OF 189Ɔ. *Barney Oldfield is at the wheel. Henry Ford stands beside him. The engine had four cylinders. This model has little resemblance to the modern streamlined automobile.* (Brown Brothers)

but by that time several types of electric and steam automobiles were on the market. Buyers eagerly snapped up the first automobiles. By 1899 in New York City alone there were about one hundred taxicabs, twenty motor trucks, and from thirty to fifty private cars. Nearly all of these vehicles were run by electric power from storage batteries.

New York was the first city to undertake the control of traffic. The traffic rules drawn up there in 1903 were copied all over the country.

Improvements in sanitation, lighting, and fire protection. While the city's communication and transportation problems were being solved, a series of changes made the city a healthier and safer place in which to live.

1. Sewerage systems. In 1879 a noted engineer said that proper sewage disposal was "the great unanswered question of the day." At that time nearly all cities had open sewers, which caused foul odors and spread disease. The sewers emptied into near-by lakes, rivers, and harbors. Open sewers have now almost disappeared, but the emptying of sewage into near-by bodies of water is still a common practice.

2. Water systems. City dwellers once got water from wells in their back yards, but by the 1850's or 1860's most cities had water mains serving the majority of their people. At first little attention was given to making the water supply safe. Often the water was piped from a

lake or river into which sewage was poured. Typhoid fever and other diseases carried by dirty water caused much loss of life. Many a city learned the importance of pure water only after suffering a terrible outbreak of disease.

3. Street lighting. City streets were dimly lighted by gas lamps until the arc light came into use in the 1880's. (See page 350.) The brightness of the arc lights made the streets safer and pleasanter and encouraged people to go about after dark.

4. Fire protection. Until the 1880's fire was a constant worry to city dwellers, since it could easily spread over most of a city. In 1871 a large part of Chicago was destroyed by fire. A few years later Boston had a bad fire. After these disasters our city governments gave more thought to fire prevention. Laws were passed requiring builders to use fire-resistant materials and more careful methods of building. Strict rules were drawn up for electric wiring. Factories and office buildings were required to install automatic sprinklers. Fire-fighting methods were improved by adopting the fire alarm signal box, the water tower, the fireboat, and the chemical engine. Most cities that still had volunteer fire departments now hired full-time firemen instead.

CHANGES IN HOME LIFE AND RECREATION

The growth of cities led to many changes in the way people lived. The new ways adopted by city dwellers gradually spread to people living in the little towns and villages.

New comforts and conveniences. After the War between North and South many improvements were made in lighting, heating, and furnishing the home.

1. Lighting. In the 1860's and 1870's kerosene replaced whale oil for use in lamps. In the larger cities the more well-to-do families soon turned to gas for lighting purposes. Before the end of the century gaslights were found in most city homes, while the well to do had changed from gas to electric lights.

2. Heating. When the war ended, the ordinary home was heated by stoves, while the more prosperous homes had hot-air furnaces. Radiators were introduced in the 1870's, being used mostly in office and apartment buildings and in the homes of the very well to do. By the end of the century radiators were finding their way into some middle-class homes.

3. Plumbing. Plumbing was greatly improved during the 1870's and 1880's. The zinc-lined bath tub was replaced by a tub of white

enamel or porcelain. Traps and vent pipes were introduced in order to keep sewer gas out of the house. Bathrooms were no longer expected to be small, dark, unpleasant places, as they had been earlier. But at the end of the century the average city home was still without a bathroom, while in the country, bathrooms were scarcely known. The masses of people took their baths on Saturday night in a wash tub in the kitchen. If they had running water in the kitchen, they thought themselves lucky.

4. Home furnishings. Sewing machines and washing machines became popular in the 1870's and 1880's. The sewing machine was worked by a foot pedal, the washing machine by a rocker or a crank. Washday drudgery was further cut by the clothes wringer and by an improved flatiron with a detachable handle to avoid burning the hands. For many years these conveniences were found only in the more prosperous homes.

The work of preparing meals was lightened by a number of new conveniences, such as the double boiler, Dover egg beater, gas toaster, and cake tins with removable bottoms. Enamelware utensils came into common use in the 1870's and were so cheap that almost every housewife could have a good supply. Aluminum utensils were introduced in the 1890's.

Most furniture was now factory-made. It was lighter in weight and often less beautiful and less lasting than that made by the old-fashioned craftsman. Metal bedsteads came into common use. Instead of carpets covering the entire floor, rugs became popular. Horsehair upholstery went out of style, and so did dark, gloomy wallpaper.

Much drudgery leaves the home. Factories gradually took over much of the work once done in the home. City housewives no longer did any spinning or weaving. While they still did a great deal of sewing, they no longer made their husbands' shirts and suits and seldom made their own coats. City women let the canning factories do at least part of their canning and let the bakeries and biscuit factories do part of their baking. Yet as late as 1900 a good housewife usually made her own pies, cake, and cookies, while some still made all their own bread. By this date commercial laundries were fairly common and served families who could afford to send the washing out.

More leisure for women. Middle-class city women began to have considerable time for their own enjoyment. Many of them used their leisure in church work, many others in women's clubs of various kinds. By 1889 there were so many women's clubs that a national organiza-

CAB STAND *in Madison Square, New York, in the 1890's.* (From the J. Clarence Davies Collection. Courtesy of Museum of the City of New York)

tion — the General Federation of Women's Clubs — was formed to link them together. Club work helped train women to take a more active part in the affairs of the community and the nation, and this in turn led many to feel that women should have the right to vote.

More freedom for women. City life brought women more chances for freedom than they had ever known. Not only were their household cares lighter, but they could find plenty of paid work outside the home. Many women took jobs in clothing factories, laundries, bakeries, restaurants, and food factories, doing the same kind of work they had always done in the home. Others went into new occupations such as typewriting and telephone operating. Some went into business for themselves. A few made their way into professions once open only to men, such as medicine, the law, the ministry, and journalism.

Now that women could support themselves, they had more personal freedom. For instance they were less likely to marry when very young. In fact some chose not to marry at all. Wives were more likely to leave their husbands if their married life was unhappy. Partly for this reason the divorce rate increased, until by 1900 there was one divorce for every twelve new marriages. (By 1940 there was one divorce for every six new marriages.)

Women now had educational opportunities almost equal to those of men. By 1880 half of the colleges were *coeducational* — that is, they took both men and women students. By 1900, 70 per cent of the col-

A CROQUET GAME IN THE 1860's. *Croquet was very fashionable. It was one of the few outdoor sports in which women took part.* (Drawn by Bush for *Harper's Weekly*, September 8, 1866)

leges were coeducational. Several of the famous men's colleges in the East set up near-by women's colleges taught by the same teachers as the men had. Harvard, for example, opened Radcliffe College, and Columbia opened Barnard. Professional schools, such as those for the study of medicine, law, and architecture, gradually opened their doors to women. By using these new opportunities, women were to gain more and more independence and also a greater voice in public affairs.

Growth of commercial amusements. City people had more time for recreation than farm people, and the cities provided a great variety of amusements for those with money to spend. The amusement business — which is now one of our biggest industries — began to grow rapidly soon after the War between North and South.

Many new theaters were opened. Almost every fair-sized city had a stock company which remained at the same theater, giving a long series of different plays. There were also about two hundred road companies which traveled from place to place. The old-fashioned blackface minstrel show was so well liked that in the early 1880's there were thirty or more traveling minstrel companies. The variety, or vaudeville, show, with its succession of songs, dances, acrobatic stunts, trained-animal acts, and the like, became very popular in the 1890's. Musical plays and operettas also drew large audiences.

Circuses were popular in this period, mainly because of new fea-

THE DEATH OF JUMBO, 1885. *P. T. Barnum brought the huge African elephant to America in 1883. Jumbo was killed in a railroad accident.* (Courtesy of Ringling Brothers and Barnum and Bailey Combined Shows, Inc.)

tures introduced by the famous American showman, P. T. Barnum. As part of his show he brought together freaks and curiosities — giants, dwarfs, and strange animals from the ends of the earth. He was the first to conduct the performance in two rings, and the first to transport his show by rail instead of by wagon. His circus was so successful that other circus men copied his ideas. In the 1880's and 1890's there were forty or more different circuses touring the United States.

Commercialized sport was another important branch of the amusement business. Baseball was the first sport to draw great throngs of spectators. A professional ball club was organized in Cincinnati in 1869, and soon after, professional baseball spread over the nation. Horse racing, prize fighting, and football also attracted large numbers of spectators, although none of these was so popular as baseball.

The play movement. Some people were not satisfied just to watch other players. They wanted a chance to take an active part in sports. To help meet this need, the Young Men's and Young Women's Christian Associations built gymnasiums in the larger cities. Business and professional men in cities organized athletic clubs and built clubhouses where they could take part in athletics. Well-to-do families often joined together to provide themselves with a country club for golf, tennis, dancing, and other recreation.

However, many city people could hardly afford to spend anything for play, and, anyway, had no place for play. The city child usually had to play in the streets, in constant danger from carts and carriages. In 1885 a Boston society provided sand gardens where little children might play in safety. By 1900 some twelve other cities had established playgrounds for their children. The time was coming when cities would spend public money freely to provide playgrounds, athletic fields, picnic grounds, and other recreational facilities for all their citizens, grownups as well as children.

To identify: P. T. Barnum.

SUBJECTS FOR TALKS OR WRITTEN REPORTS

1. Bicycling in the 1880's and 1890's. 2. Conditions in the slums of a great city in the 1880's and 1890's. 3. The early history of Hull House, the famous settlement house in the Chicago slums. 4. The story of baseball and how it became our most popular sport. 5. The development of football as a popular sport. 6. The story of P. T. Barnum and his contribution to the amusement industry. 7. The growth of the telephone industry. 8. The history of communications and transportation in my community. 9. The history of the fire department, street lighting, sewage disposal, and water supply in my community.

QUESTIONS FOR UNDERSTANDING THE TEXT

1. In what sections have American cities grown most rapidly? Why? 2. Where did the cities get their additional people in the period 1860 to 1900? 3. Where did most immigrants to the United States come from before 1880? In 1890? 4. Name several improvements in communication made before 1900. How did these help the growth of cities? 5. How was transportation within the city improved during the 1880's and 1890's? 6. Describe conditions in an average city in the 1880's in regard to (*a*) sewage disposal, (*b*) the water supply, (*c*) street lights, (*d*) fire protection. 7. How were most homes lighted in 1900? In the city? In the country? 8. (*a*) How were ordinary homes heated in 1900? (*b*) What methods of heating were found in more prosperous homes? 9. What plumbing was found in an average city home in 1900? 10. Name some of the new household furnishings that gradually came into use after 1865. 11. (*a*) How did middle-class city women get more leisure time? (*b*) How did they use it? 12. (*a*) How did city life bring women greater freedom? (*b*) What was the effect on the age of girls at marriage? On the divorce rate? 13. By 1900 how did educational opportunities for women compare with those for men? 14. Discuss amusements popular in the 1880's and 1890's.

CHAPTER 27

THE RISE OF THE LABOR MOVEMENT

Hardships caused by industrial progress. The growth of industry and the rise of big business produced wealth for a small class, but for a long time brought little benefit to wage earners. They did not share much in the new sources of wealth. In some ways they were worse off than in the old days of small-scale industry. They no longer had personal contact with their employers. They no longer used their own simple tools but worked on costly machines which they could never hope to own. They no longer lived on farms but in big cities; they suffered terribly when hard times closed down the plants where they worked.

Labor conditions in the 1860's. Industry prospered during and after the War between North and South, and prices were almost double what they had been before the war, yet intelligent workmen in the larger cities were glad to get two dollars a day. They generally worked ten hours a day, six days a week. In some trades the hours were a little shorter, in others longer. Drivers of horse cars, stages, and hacks in New York City worked from twelve to sixteen hours a day for two dollars. Women workers earned less; thousands toiled in factories and shops for, at most, three and a half or four dollars a week. In the dry-goods stores of Eastern cities girls worked from half past seven in the morning until nine or ten at night, without seats, rest rooms, or a hot lunch, for a weekly wage of five dollars.

What the public thought about labor conditions. Very few leaders of opinion and very few statesmen gave thought to the troubles of the wage-earning class. Scarcely anybody believed that the government should interfere between employers and employees. The employer had the right to hire and fire workers as he chose and to offer whatever wages he chose. Low wages were thought to be due to an oversupply of workers — a condition which could not be helped. It was thought that unemployment was the workers' own fault, that even in hard times deserving men could always find jobs. Accidents on the

COMING HOME FROM THE FACTORY AT NIGHTFALL. *Many of these workers are Irish immigrants. The place is Lawrence, Massachusetts. A woolen mill may be seen in the background.* (From the drawing by Winslow Homer in *Harper's Weekly,* July 25, 1868)

job were held to be due to the carelessness of the worker. If workers crowded into unhealthy slums, that, too, was their own fault. If they combined in unions and tried to force employers to raise wages, they were thought to be little better than criminals.

Difficulties in organizing American labor. Enormous difficulties stood in the way of organized wage earners. The *first* difficulty was the problem of leadership. As long as free land could be had, the bolder and more capable workmen — those who could lead — were apt to go west and become farmers, leaving other workmen leaderless. The *second* difficulty was public opinion. Those who were not wage earners had little sympathy with unions and frowned on strikes.

A *third* difficulty was the constant flood of immigrants eager for jobs and willing to work for any wages. They were so poor that they could not refuse jobs as strikebreakers. Then, too, they could not be easily organized because of language difficulties, religious differences, and the grudges felt by those of some nationalities toward those of other nationalities. Often it was necessary to form a separate union in each trade for each nationality.

A *fourth* difficulty in organizing labor was the presence of Negro workers and the unfriendly attitude taken toward them by white workers. Skilled white workers generally insisted on keeping Negroes out of their local unions. Frequently white workers called strikes to force the firing of colored workers. As a result Negroes willingly served as strikebreakers when given the chance.

A *fifth* difficulty was the growing number of women workers. They worked for smaller wages than men, even when doing the same work. Employers used them instead of men whenever possible. Yet women took little interest in labor unions, for most of them planned to marry and did not expect to remain wage earners long.

Early craft unions. From the early days of the Republic working-men had tried to organize. For the most part their unions were small, weak, and short-lived. The courts did not recognize the right of labor to organize, and labor leaders were sternly punished. In the 1820's the courts began to change their attitude. It seemed for a time that the common people were coming into their own, and while Andrew Jackson was in the White House, labor unions grew in number and strength. All unions went to pieces when the panic of 1837 threw a great number of men out of work. During the 1850's unions were again started. Four or five trades, or crafts, formed national unions, but only one lasted through the panic of 1857. Early in the 1860's about thirty trades organized national unions. These combined in 1866 to form the "National Labor Union." When a period of hard times set in six years later, this organization crumbled.

The first national industrial union. In 1869 a group of poor garment cutters in Philadelphia launched the "Noble Order of the Knights of Labor." It soon grew into a national organization. In 1878 Terence V. Powderly became its leader, and for ten years he was the outstanding figure in the American labor movement.

The Knights hoped to unite all labor into one big union. They welcomed all toilers — skilled and unskilled; wage earners and farmers; men and women; white and colored. Their purpose was idealistic and rather vague — "to secure to the toilers a proper share of the wealth that they create; more of the leisure that rightfully belongs to them; . . . all of those rights and privileges necessary to make them capable of enjoying, appreciating, defending, and [continuing] . . . good government."

The Knights tried to promote the interests of farmers as well as wage earners. They also tried to establish co-operative businesses owned and managed by workers. They urged government ownership of railways, telegraph lines, water works, and other utilities. They demanded the eight-hour day, the stopping of child labor, equal pay for men and women, the shutting out of Chinese immigrants, and the adoption of income and inheritance taxes. By 1886 the Knights had seven hundred thousand members, most of them unskilled workers. In that year they lost many strikes and the Order began to fall apart. Most of the skilled workers went over to an organization just rising to power — the American Federation of Labor. Within a few years the Noble Order of Knights of Labor was little heard of.

The rise of the American Federation of Labor. The American Federation of Labor is a combination of self-governing trade, or craft, unions. It was started in 1881. Its officers spent their time organizing and strengthening groups of skilled workers. By 1886 the Federation was strong enough to set up an office and employ full-time paid officers. Samuel Gompers was chosen president at a salary of $1000 a year. His first office was a room eight feet by ten, with a kitchen table for a desk and empty tin cans for filing cases. The Federation tried to avoid strikes by persuading employers to bargain peacefully with organized labor. It tried to create a friendly public opinion. Its officers did not urge government ownership or other plans to change the economic system. By 1900 the Federation had 550,000 members. Though small, it was solidly established.

Samuel Gompers. For forty years the man who stood out above all others in the American Federation of Labor was Samuel Gompers. His father was a London cigar maker who came to this country with his family in 1863. Samuel went to work in his father's trade at the age of thirteen, and soon became active in the Cigar Maker's Union. He had no schooling, but in the cigar factory he learned economics and labor history. He wrote long afterwards:

> It was the custom of the cigar makers to chip in to create a fund for purchasing papers, magazines, and books. Then while the rest worked, one of our members would read to us for perhaps an hour at a time, sometimes longer. In order that the reader might not be the loser financially, each one of the other men in the shop gave him a definite number of cigars. I had a habit of saving any interesting magazine or newspaper articles to read to my shopmates. Others did the same. . . . In fact these discussions in the shops were more like public debating societies or what we call these days "labor forums." This practice had a great deal to do with developing the interest of cigar makers in leading economic questions.

Gompers early saw the weakness of existing labor unions — their confused purposes and their lack of funds. When he became president

SAMUEL GOMPERS. *This famous labor leader helped organize the American Federation of Labor and was its president for forty fruitful years.* (Keystone View Company)

JOHN P. ALTGELD, *governor of Illinois. He protected the rights of wage earners at a time when government officials generally took the part of the employer.* (Courtesy of Chicago Historical Society)

of the American Federation of Labor, he gave it practical, hardheaded leadership. He urged each member union to build up a large reserve fund from dues, so it would not go to pieces in case of a strike or a panic. He advised the member unions to put all their efforts into raising wages, shortening hours, and getting better working conditions, rather than into idealistic schemes for making over society. Under his leadership unions of skilled workers won remarkable gains. He served as president of the Federation until his death in 1924. As long as he lived it could be said of him: "The Federation was Gompers, and Gompers was the Federation."

Efforts to crush labor unions. Labor had to fight hard for its gains. By the middle of the 1860's the right to organize had been recognized by the courts but was still not recognized by most employers. Big corporations fought the unions tooth and nail. They hired spies to help crush their employees' efforts to organize. They discharged men who tried to start labor unions, placing their names on a black list, which was sent to other employers in the industry. Once black-listed, a man might never be able to get another job.

During strikes corporations sometimes hired thugs to destroy property and stir up mobs to acts of violence. This was done to turn pub-

lic opinion against the strikers and also to provide an excuse for demanding the use of troops. The result was that many a strike was put
down by soldiers.

The first large-scale strike, 1877. With the rise of big business, labor disputes were apt to affect thousands of workers. The first large-
scale dispute was the railroad strike of 1877. Before the strike firemen
and brakemen on some lines made but $1.35 to $1.75 a day. They averaged only four days' work a week and had to spend a good part of
their wages for room and board at distant stations. When the big Eastern railway lines suddenly ordered a 10 per cent cut in wages, the
workers struck.

The strike soon led to violence. In Baltimore, when strikers tried to
prevent the movement of trains by strikebreakers, the governor called
out the militia. Nine of the strikers and bystanders were killed and
twenty were wounded. A far worse disturbance occurred at Pittsburgh, where militiamen attacked a throng of strikers, killing twenty-
five persons. An angry mob then burned railroad property worth
three million dollars. In Chicago, where the police tried to break up a
meeting of strikers, there was an all-day battle in which nineteen persons were killed. Similar fights between strikers and soldiers or police
took place at some twenty railroad centers. In the end the strike was
broken everywhere, and the workers had to accept the wage cut.

Two famous strikes. Between 1881 and 1900 about twenty-four
thousand strikes and lockouts occurred. Nearly all have long since
been forgotten. Two of them — the Homestead strike and the Pullman strike — are worth our attention as examples of the fierce struggle
between big business and the labor unions. In this struggle the government and the courts generally took the side of the corporations.

The Homestead strike, 1892. In 1892 Henry Frick, Superintendent of the Carnegie Steel Company at Homestead, Pennsylvania, announced a wage cut. The workers refused to accept it and asked him
to make a wage agreement with their union. Frick refused, for he intended to destroy the union. He got ready to operate the plant with
nonunion men, hiring three hundred armed guards to protect them. A
battle resulted between strikers and guards, with deaths on each side.
The governor of Pennsylvania sent eight thousand state militia to the
aid of the steel company, and the plant started up again with nonunion
labor. Carnegie, who was in Scotland, thought that Frick had gone
too far. He wrote to a friend: "Our firm offered all it could offer . . .
but the false step was made in trying to run the Homestead works with

THE HOMESTEAD RIOT. *During the great strike at the Carnegie steel works in Homestead in 1892 there was a pitched battle between strikers and armed guards hired by the company. The steel workers lost the strike and for twenty-five years did not attempt another one.* (Drawn by W. P. Snyder, after a photograph by Dabbs, for *Harper's Weekly*, July 16, 1892)

new men. . . . It is expecting too much of poor men to stand by and see their work taken by others."

Poor labor conditions continued in the steel mills for many years. The workday was twelve hours long and was not reduced until after World War I. The majority of steelworkers were immigrants from eastern Europe, helpless to win better conditions. The steel companies defeated every effort to unionize their workers until 1937.

The Pullman strike, 1894. The winter of 1893–94 was a terrible one for labor. One in every six wage earners was unemployed. Bands of jobless men wandered over the country. Many companies ordered wage cuts because of the hard times. In April, when the Pullman Company ordered a 20 per cent slash of wages in its car works, the men asked the company to arbitrate, that is, to lay the question before a board of judges. This Mr. Pullman refused to do, although the mayors of fifty American cities urged him to consent. A strike in the car works followed.

The American Railway Union called a "sympathetic" strike by ordering its members not to work on trains carrying Pullman cars. In order that the strike should not interfere with the mails, the Union asked the railroad companies not to attach Pullman cars to mail trains.

PULLMAN STRIKE, 1894. *National Guardsmen are firing into the mob in order to prevent interference with the trains.* (Drawn by G. W. Peters for *Harper's Weekly,* July 21, 1894)

However, the companies insisted on attaching Pullman cars to every train carrying mail. The companies hired 3600 armed guards, then used strikebreakers to run their trains. Mobs stopped a number of trains, and some railroad property was destroyed. The strikers claimed that the railroad companies had hired thugs to lead the mobs. The railroad companies promptly asked President Grover Cleveland to send federal troops. The governor of Illinois, John P. Altgeld, who thought the strikers were in the right, insisted that he could restore order by using the militia. The President has no constitutional right to send federal troops into a state without the consent of its governor, but Cleveland decided he must send troops to protect the mails. The troops soon broke the strike.

During the strike the Attorney General of the United States applied the Sherman Antitrust Act in a new way. He claimed that the American Railway Union had violated the Antitrust Act by interfering with interstate commerce. A court order, or *injunction*, was issued forbidding Eugene V. Debs, the head of the Union, to interfere with the operation of the railroads. If he obeyed, the strike would collapse for lack of leadership. Debs disobeyed and was sent to prison for six months. It seemed to the strikers that the federal government had taken the side of the Pullman and the railroad companies. The strike failed and the American Railway Union was ruined.

The injunction becomes a powerful antilabor weapon. After the Pullman strike the injunction was used regularly in labor struggles. The employer would ask a court to forbid the union or its leaders from acting in certain ways likely to injure his business or property. The court would usually issue the requested order, or injunction, forbidding the actions feared by the employer. Anyone who disobeys an injunction is in "contempt of court" and may be sentenced to prison without a jury trial. The injunction could be used to prevent such actions as striking, urging others to strike, collecting money to further a strike, and even the meeting of strikers. In 1932 this powerful weapon against labor was limited by passage of the Norris-La Guardia Anti-Injunction Act.

The creation of government bureaus of labor. The struggles of the unions gradually led the public to take more interest in labor conditions. In 1869 the Massachusetts legislature set up a bureau of labor statistics. A few years later Congress created a federal Bureau of Labor Statistics. By 1900 most states had a similar bureau. All of these bureaus collected and published information on wages, hours, industrial accidents, strikes, and other labor matters. Their publications showed that the growth of industry had produced serious labor problems, among them low wages, unemployment, child labor, a high rate of industrial accidents and industrial diseases, and continual disputes between capital and labor. People began to realize that these conditions were harmful to the whole nation.

The need for labor laws. Labor problems could not be solved by individual employers. An employer could not, for instance, afford to raise wages, shorten hours, or provide unemployment insurance unless his competitors did the same. Labor unions could not accomplish much in improving the condition of the workers, since most of them were unorganized. Laws protecting labor seemed to be needed, yet attempts to pass such laws met fierce opposition. In spite of this a number of states enacted laws to protect labor. Some regulated labor conditions in mines, laundries, and sweatshops (places where women and children did handwork and were paid by the piece, as in the making of artificial flowers). Others required safety devices on power saws and other dangerous machinery. Some regulated housing. The laws were often not enforced, yet they were signs of a new attitude toward labor. They prepared the way for stronger legislation in the twentieth century. (See pages 425-426, 546-549.)

A little progress was made in protecting women and children in in-

CHINESE WORKERS *in a California cigar factory. In the 1860's and 1870's thousands of Chinese immigrants were brought to this country by corporations seeking cheap labor. In some occupations on the Pacific coast white workers were entirely replaced by Chinese. The labor unions demanded that the Chinese be kept out of the United States.* (Courtesy of Bancroft Library)

dustry. By 1900 twelve states limited the number of hours per day or per week that women might be employed. Four states prohibited the employment of women at night. Twenty states prohibited the employment of young children at night, although some of the laws now seem very timid. For instance, one state went no further than forbidding the employment at night of girls under twelve years of age. The real evil of child labor had scarcely been touched, for in 1900 one in every five children between the ages of ten and fifteen was a wage earner.

Labor demands curbs on immigration. By 1880 nearly a third of a million immigrants came here every year. Within a few years the figure rose to nearly a million. The United States, it was thought, had room for all who wished to come. Steamship companies sent agents all over Europe to persuade people to come to America. Western railroad companies, with land to sell, did the same thing. Large corporations made contracts with laborers who wished to come to America. The corporation paid the laborer's fare, and the laborer promised to work for the corporation for a certain period of time. Unskilled Chinese laborers by the tens of thousands were brought in under contract to build railroads in the West.

Labor leaders saw that their efforts to raise wages and improve working conditions would not get far so long as the country was flooded with poor immigrants eager to take any job. The labor unions demanded that the Chinese be shut out, and in 1882 Congress passed the Chinese Exclusion Act.* Next labor unions called on Congress to stop the practice of bringing in laborers under contract. Congress did so in 1885. Still the flood of immigrants increased. Labor then asked that immigrants unable to read and write be shut out. Many employers were against any such restriction. Some liberals opposed it because they wanted America to continue to be a refuge for the ill-treated. Labor did not have its way until 1917, when Congress passed a law requiring immigrants to be able to read or write in some language.

Labor conditions in 1900. At the turn of the century wages and hours were little better than in 1865. According to the census of 1900 two thirds of the male workers received less than $12.50 a week. Only the most highly skilled workers earned as much as $18.00 a week. Of course prices were much lower than they are now. Beef sold for 17 cents a pound, pork for 14 cents, eggs for 21 cents a dozen. A good pair of shoes cost $2.00, and a good suit cost $20.00. Low as these prices seem, most American workers found that their wages would barely support even a small family.

Since the War between North and South the wealth of the nation had increased wonderfully. Yet it was concentrated in a small number of hands. By 1900, 1 per cent of the people owned more than the other 99 per cent put together. However, a large part of the wealth owned by the fortunate 1 per cent was invested in factories, machinery, mines, railroads, steamboats, and other business property. This investment made mass production possible. It would gradually bring about shorter hours of labor and enable the people to enjoy more comforts.

To identify: John P. Altgeld, Anti-Injunction Act, Samuel Gompers, Knights of Labor, Terence V. Powderly.

To explain or define: arbitration, black list, contempt of court, co-operative business, craft union, injunction, strikebreaker, sweatshop, sympathetic strike.

* This Act was repealed in 1943. Now a small number of Chinese may come here every year.

Subjects for Talks or Written Reports

1. The history of the Knights of Labor. 2. The life of one of the following: Terence V. Powderly, Samuel Gompers, John P. Altgeld. 3. Attempts by the Knights of Labor to establish co-operative businesses and why they usually failed. 4. How the American Federation of Labor is governed. 5. The history of the American Federation of Labor. 6. The fight to end the twelve-hour day in the steel industry. 7. The fight for and against the Anti-Injunction Act. 8. The struggle against child labor up to the present day. 9. Immigration to the United States in the period 1860 to 1900.

Questions for Understanding the Text

1. In what ways were wage earners worse off because of the rise of big business? 2. Discuss labor conditions in the 1860's. 3. What was the attitude of the public toward labor unions? Low wages? Industrial accidents? 4. How did the supply of free land affect the growth of labor unions? 5. State the chief difficulties in organizing wage earners in the period 1860 to 1900. 6. Why did labor unions generally go to pieces during hard times? 7. What groups were welcomed by the Knights of Labor? 8. Why was the American Federation of Labor stronger and more successful than the Knights of Labor? 9. How did the big corporations fight labor unions? 10. Whose side did government officials usually take during a strike? 11. For what reason might a big corporation whose men were on strike hire thugs to damage its own property? 12. How did President Cleveland's Attorney General use the Sherman Antitrust Act to break the railroad strike? 13. What is an injunction? How were injunctions used to prevent or crush strikes? 14. What good has come from the formation of government bureaus of labor? 15. Why could the improvement of labor conditions not be left to individual employers? 16. Describe some of the early laws to protect labor. 17. What did businessmen do to encourage immigrants to come to the United States? 18. Why did labor leaders demand laws to curb immigration? 19. How was the wealth created by modern industry distributed among the population? Was this situation good or bad for the nation?

CHAPTER 28

THE END OF THE FRONTIER

he Far West is swiftly settled. In 1860 the region west of the Missouri River was, for the most part, a wilderness. It included half the area of the United States but contained only 1 per cent of the population. Except for a narrow fringe of settlement along some of the river valleys and around Great Salt Lake in Utah, the whole territory was occupied only by Indians. Thirty years later a startling change had taken place. The Indians were shut into reservations, the vast herds of buffalo on which they lived had been wiped out, five railroads had pushed across the prairies and the mountains to the Pacific, five million farmers had settled on the land, and the frontier was gone. This swift change was mainly due to the building of the railroads.

Building the first transcontinental railroad. Beginning with the rush to the California gold fields in 1849, there was much talk of the need for a railroad to the Pacific. To build it, federal aid was necessary, and Congress could not agree on the route. Southerners wanted the road to start from New Orleans, Louisiana, or Memphis, Tennessee. Northerners wanted it to start from some point in the North. After the Confederate states seceded, Congress decided that the road should start from Omaha, Nebraska.

The Pacific Railway Act of 1862 gave charters to two railroad companies — the Union Pacific and the Central Pacific. The Union Pacific was to build westward from Omaha, and the Central Pacific eastward from Sacramento. For each mile of road built Congress promised the companies twenty square miles of the public land along their right of way, and from sixteen thousand to forty thousand dollars per mile according to the roughness of the country.

The two companies raced toward their meeting point to see which could build more miles and collect more of the government bounty. The more crooked the road, the longer the track, so the companies built along the winding rivers rather than in a direct line. In this way they also got valuable lands in the river valleys.

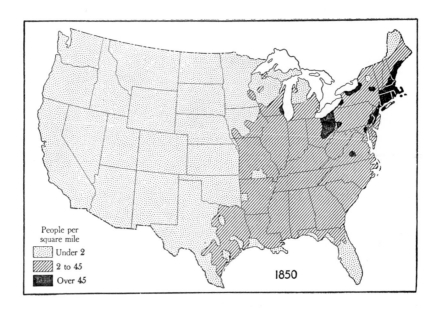

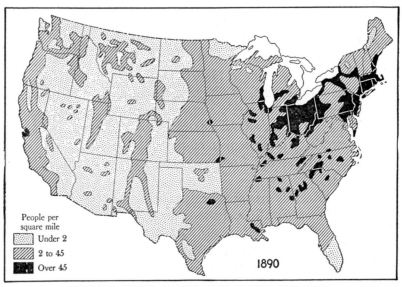

SETTLEMENT OF THE FAR WEST, 1850–1890

In 1850 few white men had settled in the region west of the Missouri. By 1890, there were five million settlers in the region and nearly all the good farm land was privately owned. The rapid settling of the Far West was made possible by the building of railroads.

The Central Pacific company faced harder construction problems than did its rival. In the first 125 miles it had to climb over 7000 feet through the Sierra Nevada mountains. Every rail, car, locomotive, and piece of machinery had to be carried around Cape Horn or over the Isthmus of Panama. Roadways had to be blasted over mountains, and bridges built over gorges. In one sixty-mile stretch in the Sierras fifteen tunnels were bored. These gigantic tasks were carried out with the labor of ten thousand coolies whom the company brought in from China. With these difficulties the Central Pacific built 689 miles of road while the Union Pacific was building 1086 miles.

The Union Pacific was built with the labor of Irish immigrants and ex-soldiers of the Union and Confederate armies. As they crossed the Indian-troubled prairies, the men worked with their rifles in reach. To house them a huge construction camp moved forward as they advanced — a "city on wheels." The engineer in charge has left us an interesting summary of the problems faced:

> At one time we were using at least ten thousand animals, and most of the time from eight to ten thousand laborers. The bridge gangs always worked from five to twenty miles ahead of the track, and it was seldom that the track waited for a bridge. To supply one mile of track with material and supplies required about forty cars, as on the plains everything — rails, ties, bridging, fastenings, all railroad supplies on the entire work — had to be transported from the Missouri River. . . . Our Indian troubles commenced in 1864 and lasted until the tracks joined at Promontary. We lost most of our men and stock while building from Fort Kearney, Nebraska, to Bitter Creek, Wyoming. At that time every mile of road had to be surveyed, graded, tied, and bridged under military protection.

The two lines met in Utah on May 10, 1869, and the entire country celebrated the great event. As the last spike was driven into place, the telegraph carried the strokes to the principal cities of the country. A wonderful feat of engineering had been accomplished. Yet the nation's pride in its first transcontinental railroad was mixed with shame. To build the road the directors of the Union Pacific had organized themselves into a construction company and paid themselves three times as much for the work on each mile as it really cost. To block an investigation they gave bribes to influential congressmen. The directors of the Central Pacific had also formed a construction company, which they paid one hundred twenty-one million dollars for a fifty-eight million dollar job. Both groups of directors loaded their roads

DRIVING THE GOLDEN SPIKE *that completed the first transcontinental railroad.*
(From the Paramount picture, "Union Pacific."   Courtesy of Union Pacific Railroad)

with such heavy debts that the communities served by those roads had
to pay very high railroad rates for many years to come.

Other Far Western railroads.   The first railroad line to the Pacific
was hardly finished before others were planned.   Within fifteen years
seven different lines had entered the Rockies, and three — the Southern
Pacific, the Northern Pacific, and the Santa Fe — had reached the
coast.   All but one of these roads received generous land grants from
the federal government of a value that was often more than the cost
of construction.   In addition the railroads asked for, and received,
gifts of money or land from the states and counties which they crossed.

Destruction of the buffalo.   The buffalo grass on the Great Plains
supported great numbers of buffalo.   It is estimated that just after the
War between North and South there were about fifteen million of
these beasts in the United States.   A train passed through one herd for
a hundred and twenty miles.

The building of railroads across the plains meant the end of the buffalo.   Passengers shot them from the train windows for the pleasure of
seeing them kick.   Professional hunters shot them for their skins.
Even when the price dropped so low that it did not pay to skin the
animals, the destruction went on, most of them being left to lie where
they dropped, food only for coyotes and insects.   Millions were killed
each year during the early 1870's.   By 1881 only a few remained.

MANHATTAN, NEVADA, IN 1900. *A mining rush explains the unfinished buildings and the prospectors' tents.* (Brown Brothers)

The destruction of the buffalo was a tragedy for the Plains Indians, since they got tent coverings, boat coverings, bow strings, clothing, and food from these animals. Starvation now stared the red men in the face. In return for food they had to give up their freedom and accept the terms offered by the federal government.

The Indians are subdued. The settlement of the Great Plains brought on twenty-five years of warfare with the Indians (1862–1886). Again and again the red men were driven from lands that had been promised them in solemn treaties. Always they were pushed onto less desirable lands. If they fought the whites, they were certain to be defeated and savagely punished. Yet fight they did. More than one hundred printed pages were required to list the battles between Indians and federal troops between 1868 and 1882 alone.

A new Indian policy was adopted in 1887 when Congress passed the Dawes Act, giving farms to Indians who stopped living in tribes. More than half the Indians accepted this offer and became naturalized citizens. The remainder were shut up on reservations, where most of them have lived in poverty to this day.

The mining frontier. Mining was the magnet which first drew settlers into the Far West. The gold rush to California was the first of a series of rushes. Another occurred in 1858–59, following the discovery of gold and silver in Nevada. A third rush began a few months later when gold was discovered near Pikes Peak in Colorado. Just after the War between North and South came the Montana and Wyoming gold rushes.

A new discovery of gold or silver anywhere soon brought thousands of fortune hunters. Within a few weeks a city of tents and huts would rise near the "diggings," and the miners would squander their money in its gambling houses, saloons, and dance halls. When the surface deposits gave out, most of the people went away as quickly as they had come, some moving on where rumors of new discoveries called them, others going back, perhaps empty-handed, to the East. Some, realizing that the real wealth of the West was its grass and soil, settled down as cattlemen and farmers.

The cattle frontier. The grasslands of the West stretched from the Rio Grande in the South to the Canadian border in the North, and from Kansas, Nebraska, and the Dakotas into the valleys of the Rockies. The whole wide territory where the buffalo had grazed became a great cattle region.

Cattle raising on a large scale began in Texas. Because of the distance from market, the cattle were grown for hides and tallow (fat) rather than for their meat. About five years before the War between North and South a number of Texas cattlemen began to drive their herds to St. Louis to be shipped east in livestock cars. The "long drive" was a dangerous journey of seven or eight hundred miles. On the way the cowboys had to cross great rivers, defend their herds from cattle thieves, or rustlers, stop stampedes among the frightened cattle, and fight roving bands of Indians. After the war, as the railroads pushed westward, shipping points were established nearer to the cattle country, and the drive became shorter and less dangerous.

Buyers searched Texas for herds of young beef animals, hired cowboys to drive them north in the early spring, and fattened them on free grass. In a good season the cattle sold, after fattening, for four or five times what they had cost. Memories of this colorful business come to us in cowboy songs such as the "Texas Lullaby":

> It's a whoop and a yea, get along my little dogies,
>   For camp is far away.
> It's a whoop and a yea and a-driving the dogies,
>   For Wyoming may be your new home.

Meanwhile stockmen found that they could winter cattle in the North, for the animals would paw through the snow to reach the nour-

THE "LONG DRIVE." *A drove of Texas cattle cross a stream on the way north to a shipping point.* (Drawn by A. R. Wand for *Harper's Weekly,* October 19, 1867)

ishing grass underneath. Cattle raising spread all over the Great Plains and into the mountain valleys. But cattle raising in the North was a risky business. After an unusually heavy snow or a sleet storm that formed a hard crust, the cattle sometimes died by thousands from hunger. In time Northern cattlemen learned that they must provide hay for such emergencies.

In the beginning anyone with a few dollars could start a herd by buying a few cows and calves and turning them out to graze on the public land. Some of the big cattlemen made their start in this way. After a few years the big cattlemen and cattle companies, by fair means or foul, got control of the ranges. They fenced in water holes and streams or fenced huge tracts of the range. In this way they drove out small competitors. They also waged continual war on the sheep raisers, whose flocks ruined the pasture for cattle.

For some twenty-five years the cattlemen ruled the land of the blue sky and the prairie grass. Then small farmers began to settle along the streams on "homesteads" given them by the federal government. (See page 344.) The enraged stockmen tore down the homesteaders' fences and sometimes killed those who insisted on staying. But the homesteaders had the government behind them. President Cleveland ordered the stockmen's fences cut down and the grasslands thrown open for settlement.

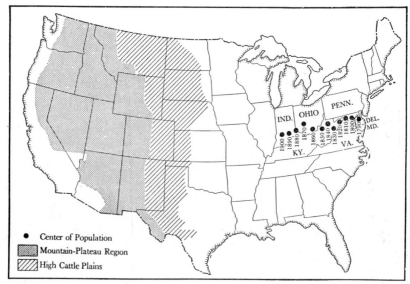

WESTWARD ADVANCE OF CENTER OF POPULATION, 1790–1900

Settlement was hastened by the railroads with lands to sell. Their salesmen and advertising covered the whole of Europe. At one time a single road, the Northern Pacific, sent eight hundred agents abroad to sell land. Immigrants poured into the country. Hamlin Garland wrote that when he went to claim a homestead in Dakota:

> Trains swarming with immigrants from every country of the world were haltingly creeping out upon the level lands. Norwegians, Swedes, Danes, Scotchmen, Englishmen, and Russians all mingled in this flood of land-seekers rolling toward the sundown plain, where a fat-soiled valley had been set aside by good Uncle Sam for the enrichment of every man.

Similar scenes could be observed all along the plains. By 1890 most of the cattlemen and sheepmen had been pushed onto lands too dry for crops. They dug wells and erected windmills to provide water for their stock.

Life on the last frontier. In addition to struggling with the Indian and the cowboy, the settler on the Great Plains had to struggle with nature. The work was harder and the rewards less than on farms in the Ohio or Mississippi valleys. The scorching summer was followed by a long winter of cruel cold, with the temperature dropping to twenty and thirty below zero. In good seasons the rainfall was barely enough for grain; in poor seasons drought killed the crops. Some years plagues of grasshoppers swarmed over the plains, eating every green thing in their path. Prairie fires were a constant threat and once started might sweep across the treeless plains for days.

At first settlers lived in sod houses or in dugouts on the side of a hill. These crude homes were dark and badly ventilated; every rain made puddles on the bare floor. In time some families saved enough to build a small wooden house. Unshaded by trees, the yard bare of flowers and shrubs, the inside without conveniences or comforts, the typical house was as cheerless as it looked. In times of drought, when there was no water to spare for house cleaning or washing or even for baths, the wife of many a settler pleaded with him to go back east. After the drought and grasshopper plague of 1874, thousands left their farms. Sometimes they chalked a message on the sides of their grimy covered wagons — "Going back to our wife's folks" or "In God we trusted; in Kansas we busted."

Loneliness was almost harder to bear than the heat and dust and toil. From one year's end to another the pioneer might see only a dozen faces. In winter, when deep snows blocked the roads for weeks, the farmhouse seemed like a prison. Far from neighbors, a long way from a town, beyond reach of a doctor, the farmer's wife sometimes lost her mind.

The settlement of Oklahoma. In Jackson's time the rich lands of Oklahoma were set aside as a permanent reservation for the civilized Indian tribes. (See pages 212–214.) Fifty years later, when most of the West had been settled, land-hungry white men demanded the right to settle on the Indian lands. The federal government bought most of the territory from the Indians. It was to be thrown open on April 22, 1889. Crowds gathered on the border waiting for the signal to enter. At noon, upon the blast of a bugle, the rush began. On horseback, on foot, and in every kind of vehicle, the people hurried for the best locations. At nightfall on the first day Oklahoma had fifty thousand white settlers. Within one year there were communities with churches, schools, banks, and newspapers. Bit by bit the rest of the reservation was opened to settlers until finally the Indians had only a small strip left.

The end of cheap land. In 1890 the superintendent of the federal Land Office announced that the frontier was gone. It was no longer possible to draw a line between the edge of settlement and the wilderness. The government had no more good farm land to give away.

SOD HOUSES *were used by early settlers on the Great Plains because lumber from the East cost so much.* (Courtesy of North Dakota State Historical Society)

What land it still had was in the mountains or was too dry to farm without irrigation. An important chapter of American history had ended.

THE AGRICULTURAL REVOLUTION

While the frontier was vanishing, great changes were taking place in methods of farming. These changes, known as the "agricultural revolution," are just as remarkable as the changes in manufacturing and transportation known as the "industrial revolution." In both revolutions men turned from hand tools to the use of machinery.

1. Tools used in the Jacksonian Period. When Jackson was President, farmers used cast-iron plows drawn by oxen or horses. They sowed grain by hand and reaped it with the sickle, the scythe, or the cradle. They threshed it either by flail or by the tramping of work animals. They hoed their corn and potatoes by hand. A family could grow no more than eight or ten acres of crops, even though the women and children helped.

2. Improvements in the plow. The plow was the first important tool to be improved. The problem was to make a plow that could cut and turn the soil cleanly, that would not become clogged with earth, and that would not break against stones or roots. Jefferson designed a good plow before 1800. However, it was made of iron and broke

AN EARLY McCORMICK REAPER. *One man drove while another raked the grain from the platform where it fell. Other workers, often women, bound the sheaves.*

easily. In 1837 John Deere of Illinois perfected a steel plow that would break the tough prairie sod, and within twenty years his factory was turning out thousands every year. After the War between North and South the sulky plow and the gang plow came into use. By 1900 a successful steam tractor was developed, which plowed, sowed, and covered the seed in one operation.

3. Improvements in reaping. Improvements which took place in reaping are even more startling. In George Washington's time a farmer using a hand sickle could cut half an acre of wheat a day if he worked hard. With a cradle, which came into use in the early 1800's, he might cut two acres a day. In 1834 Cyrus McCormick of Virginia invented a reaper that could cut five or six acres a day. Realizing that the best market for the machine was in the West, he built a factory in the young prairie town of Chicago. By the start of the War between North and South he had sold a quarter of a million reapers and so helped release many thousands of farmers for service in the Union army.

The reaper was steadily improved. The backbreaking work of gathering up the cut grain and binding it into bundles (sheaves) was done away with by adding a platform on which two men stood and bound the grain as it was cut. Soon came the automatic twine binder (1872). About the same time a threshing machine was perfected. A few years later the reaper and thresher were united in the combine, which reaped, threshed, cleaned, and bagged the grain in one continuous operation. The combine was drawn by twenty horses and could harvest seventy or eighty acres in one day. With a combine four men could do the work done by three hundred in the early days of the Republic.

4. Other new machines. In almost every branch of farming, machinery was introduced. Shortly before the War between North and South the mowing machine, horse-drawn rake, hay drier, and mechanical hay fork came into use, reducing by four fifths the time needed to harvest a ton of hay. After the war the corn planter, potato planter, fertilizer drill, manure spreader, corn sheller, cream separator, and a hundred other machines began to lighten the farmer's toil. Of course, small farmers, and those without money, were slow to adopt machinery, and even today many struggle along using hand tools.

The use of farm machinery made it possible for the farmer to feed a growing number of city dwellers. When Jackson was President, four fifths of the population lived and worked on farms, but by 1900 less than two fifths did so. By 1950 the proportion had shrunk to 15 per cent, which is roughly one seventh.

5. Problems due to the use of farm machinery. The introduction of machinery brought problems that farmers had never known before. Formerly farm equipment was simple and cheap. Often the farmer made it himself. Once he had it, it might last a lifetime. Now the farmer needed expensive equipment, which must be replaced every few years. Without it he could not compete with well-equipped farmers, and must either live in poverty or become a wage earner. Since on small farms machines do not pay for themselves, such farms were constantly being combined into larger ones. Farming had become a business requiring the investment of considerable money. It no longer offered independence and a good living to the poor man.

Science as an aid to agriculture. The agricultural revolution was helped by the growth of agricultural science. Scientists developed better seeds, better breeds of livestock and poultry, improved fertilizers, methods for controlling plant diseases and insect pests, and improved methods of caring for livestock. Their discoveries enabled each farmer, and also each acre of land, to produce more. This resulted in overproduction of some farm products, especially grain and cotton.

The federal and state governments helped to make farming more sci-

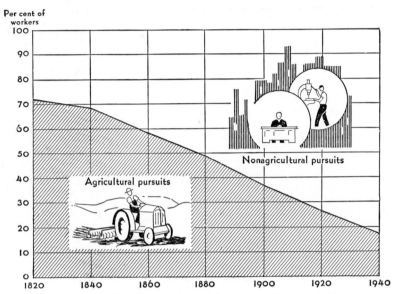

**SHIFT OF WORKERS FROM AGRICULTURAL TO NONAGRICULTURAL
PURSUITS, 1820–1940**

entific. In 1862 Congress set up the Bureau of Agriculture, now the
Department of Agriculture. One of its main purposes is to develop
agricultural science. The same year Congress gave public lands to every state for a college of agriculture and mechanic arts. Twenty-five
years later Congress appropriated money to establish agricultural experiment stations throughout the nation. Every year since, Congress
and the states have set aside large sums for agricultural research.

UNREST AMONG FARMERS

The farmer's discontent. Every year American farmers raised
larger crops. Yet the farmers were not prosperous and happy. Prices
of farm products began to drop soon after the war's end in 1865, and
the drop continued until almost the end of the century. One cause of
the drop was an insufficient supply of money. When money is scarce,
prices fall. Another cause was the great increase in production due to
the settlement of new lands, the use of farm machinery, and the growth
of agricultural science. Businessmen combined to limit production
and keep up prices, but farmers could not do so. Each produced what
he could and sold it for what it would bring.

A GRANGE MEETING *in an Illinois schoolhouse. The officers wear a band over one shoulder.* (Drawn by Joseph B. Beale for *Frank Leslie's Illustrated Newspaper,* January 31, 1874)

While farm prices were falling, the cost of some of the things the farmer bought was rising. High tariffs kept up the price of manufactured articles. Trusts controlled the prices of farm machinery, barbed wire, fertilizer, oil, shoes, and other items important to farmers.

The farmer was also troubled by the high cost of credit. Frequently he had to borrow money to put in his crop or to buy machinery or livestock. He could not get a loan so cheaply as a merchant or manufacturer and often paid from 15 to 20 per cent interest and sometimes more. Many a farmer's family went in rags because the interest on borrowed money took every cent they could earn. Thousands lost their farms every year because they could not keep up the payment of interest on their mortgages.

Farmers who lived far from their market paid high freight rates to the railroads and high charges to the middlemen who helped them market their crops. The powerful corporations which owned the grain elevators, the stockyards, the packing houses, and the railroads could charge what they liked. When corn was selling in the East for a dollar a bushel, the Iowa farmer might get only fifteen cents a bushel.

The Granger movement. Businessmen, bankers, and workmen were organizing. Farmers gradually saw that they too must organize. In 1867 there was formed a national association of farm men and women known as the Grange or Patrons of Husbandry. It was a secret society, and its meetings were given to education, patriotic celebrations, and social festivities. The order grew rapidly during the hard times of the early 1870's. Its greatest strength was in the Middle West.

Many state Granges set up co-operative marketing associations in order to do away with the high profits made by the dealers (middlemen) who handle farm products on their way to the consumers. Some Granges set up co-operative creameries, grain elevators, loan agencies, stores, and factories for making farm machinery. The co-operatives were owned by the members, and any profits made were divided among them. The co-operatives often saved members a great deal of money. The more successful they were, the more fiercely they were fought by their competitors. In the end most of them had to close.

At first the Granges took no part in politics, but as times grew worse, some of the members urged political action. In a number of Midwestern states during the early 1870's Grangers were elected to the legislatures and pushed through laws regulating grain elevators and railroads. The corporations became alarmed. They asked the Supreme Court to declare the "Granger laws" unconstitutional.

The Granger cases. One of the Granger cases is very important. This case had to do with a law passed by the state of Illinois, fixing charges for the storage of grain in warehouses or elevators. Such a warehouse is a *public utility* — that is, a business which is expected to serve all the people in a given area without any competition. The Supreme Court was asked to decide whether a state has the power to fix rates or in other ways regulate public utility companies. The Court gave a historic opinion: When private property is devoted to a public use (as, for example, a railroad, a water works, or a telephone system), it is subject to public regulation. Further, the Court declared that the right to regulate includes the right to fix charges. Following this history-making decision, it became the custom for the states to regulate railroads and other public utilities within their borders.

In another Granger case the Supreme Court ruled that a state may not pass laws which affect interstate commerce. Since most railroad traffic crosses a state line, this means that the states are almost helpless to regulate railroads. By the time this decision was given (1886), the Granger movement had lost its strength. Other farm organizations urged Congress to take action, and the next year the famous Interstate Commerce Act was passed. While this act was very weak, it was at least a beginning in the regulation of public utilities by the federal government. Its passage encouraged those who wanted big business brought under control.

To identify: Central Pacific, John Deere, Granger laws, Interstate Commerce Act, Union Pacific.

To explain or define: agricultural experiment station, agricultural revolution, combine, co-operative, flail, marketing association, middlemen, public utility.

Subjects for Talks or Written Reports

1. The life of William Cody. How he won his nickname, "Buffalo Bill." 2. The building of the Central Pacific Rairoad. 3. Life on an Indian reservation. 4. Life in an early Western mining community. 5. Life in the cattle country in the 1860's and 1870's. 6. The life of the early farmers on the Great Plains. 7. The history of the Patrons of Husbandry. 8. The growth of the agricultural co-operative movement in the United States.

Questions for Understanding the Text

1. Compare conditions west of the Missouri in 1860 with those in 1890. 2. Tell about the building of the first transcontinental railroad. 3. (*a*) How did directors of the Central Pacific and the Union Pacific enrich themselves during the construction of their lines? (*b*) What was the effect on railroad rates? 4. How did the destruction of the buffalo help in subduing the Plains Indians? 5. What happened when rich deposits of gold and silver were found in the West? 6. How did Texas cattlemen get their herds to market before the War between North and South? 7. How did cattlemen make use of the public lands? 8. How did the railroad companies aid in settling the Far West? 9. Describe the settlement of Oklahoma. 10. What announcement was made by the federal Land Office in 1890? 11. What is meant by the "agricultural revolution"? 12. Discuss farming methods at the time when Jackson was in the White House. 13. (*a*) Why is a steel plow so much better than an iron plow? (*b*) When did the steel plow come into general use? 14. Outline the chief improvements in reaping made since George Washington's time. 15. How did the use of farm machinery affect the proportion of the population living on farms? The size of farms? The amount of money needed to start and run a farm? 16. How has the development of agricultural science made farms more productive? 17. How does a co-operative marketing association often save money for its members? 18. Why did the farmers demand that railroads and grain elevators be regulated? 19. Why was it necessary for Congress to undertake the regulation of the railroads?

CHAPTER 29

THE RISE AND FALL OF POPULISM

he Republican party is supreme after the War between North and South. When the long sectional struggle came to an end, the Republican party was popular and strong. It had, so its leaders claimed, saved the Union. It had pleased businessmen and bankers by setting a high tariff, giving generous aid to railroads, creating a system of national banks, and providing the country with uniform and dependable paper money. By passing the Homestead Act it had pleased workmen who wanted free land in the West. It had pleased farmers by creating the Bureau of Agriculture, by helping the states establish agricultural colleges, and most of all by helping the Western railroads. It had pleased Negroes by ending slavery and by giving them the vote. To please the soldiers of the Union army, it soon provided pensions for the disabled and for the widows of soldiers. Thus the party won the gratitude of large groups of people. In addition, it filled the federal offices with loyal party members, as is the custom of the party in power. It is not surprising, then, that the Republicans won every presidential election but two between 1860 and 1912.

The Democratic party recovers. The War between North and South weakened the Democratic party. Its Southern members were blamed for secession. Its Northern members were blamed because many of them, believing that a state had the right to leave the Union, opposed the war. Republican leaders called it the party of disloyalty and took extreme steps to prevent it from returning to power. (See pages 324–330.) In this way the Republicans piled up a large majority for General Grant in the elections of 1868 and 1872.

Yet the Democratic party soon began to recover. In 1876 its candidate for President, Samuel J. Tilden, of New York, won a safe majority of the popular vote. The Democrats claimed he also had a majority of the electoral vote. However, returns from three Southern states were contested and a special electoral committee, voting strictly by party lines, declared the Republican candidate, Rutherford B. Hayes, the winner.

PRESIDENT GROVER CLEVELAND AT THE POLLS. *Our Presidents are careful to carry out the duty of every adult American — to vote.* (Drawn by V. Gribayedoff for *Frank Leslie's Illustrated Newspaper,* November 17, 1892)

President Hayes believed that the Southern states should have control of their own elections. He recalled the last federal troops from the South. After this few Southern Negroes were allowed to vote, and the election returns from the Southern states became solidly Democratic. (See page 332.)

In 1884, for the first time in twenty-four years, a Democrat became President. This was Grover Cleveland, of New York, who was known for his fearlessness and honesty. He said, and sincerely believed, "Public office is a public trust." He displeased the managers of his party by refusing to replace every Republican officeholder with a Democrat and by vetoing bills for unnecessary public buildings. He displeased war veterans by vetoing what he considered a poor pension bill. He displeased manufacturers by urging a lowering of the tariff. It is no wonder that the politicians disapproved of him and that he failed to be re-elected. However, Cleveland won a second term in 1892. No other Democrat was to occupy the White House until the election of Woodrow Wilson in 1912. Although the Democrats rarely elected a President, they often had a majority in the House of Representatives. This showed that their strength was growing.

Both major parties seek to please businessmen. Until 1860 the two major parties had represented two distinct economic groups. One, the Federalist, or Whig, party, appealed chiefly to businessmen and men of wealth; the other, the Democratic party, to small farmers and wage earners. In 1860 the slavery quarrel changed the line-up. Northern businessmen and Western farmers united under the Republican banner to prevent the spread of slavery. After the War between North and South, Republican managers tried to keep the farmers satisfied by choosing presidential candidates from the Midwest. The first five Republican Presidents to follow Lincoln — Grant, Hayes, Garfield, Harrison, and McKinley — were all born in Ohio. All had held high rank in the Union army, a fact which won them many votes.

After the War between North and South the Democratic party was made up chiefly of Northern wage earners and Southern farmers. Nearly every Southern white man was a Democrat, and as Southern manufacturing and commerce grew, the party soon had many members from the business class. In fact the party looked to this class for leadership and for financial support. As a result the usual Democratic stand against national banking and government aid to business was given up. Democratic congressmen might argue in favor of a low tariff, but they usually voted for a high tariff when it gave protection to industries in their districts.

Both parties obtained campaign funds from wealthy businessmen. In return businessmen expected tariff protection and other favors. Big corporations often contributed to both parties. The sugar trust, for example, supported the Democrats in a Democratic state, and the Republicans in a Republican state, expecting that the men elected to office would do what it wanted on questions in which it was interested.

Minor parties demand reforms. While the government was doing so much to help business, it seemed to overlook the sufferings of the farmers and the wage earners. Whether the Republicans or the Democrats were in power made little difference, for business interests had great influence in both parties. From time to time groups of farmers or wage earners tried to start a party which would represent the common people. In each presidential campaign from 1872 on, one or more minor parties appeared. They asked for reforms, such as a larger supply of money, regulation of public utilities, laws to protect wage earners, and inheritance and income taxes. They condemned the old parties as tools of big business.

Most of the minor parties began in a period of hard times and faded away when conditions improved. Their lack of financial backing prevented them from making much headway. Yet throughout the 1870's, 1880's, and early 1890's, there was great unrest among farmers and laborers. The unrest led in 1892 to the formation of the Populist, or People's, party. This was the strongest of all the minor parties up to that time. For four years it gathered strength. Leaders of the two major parties began to fear another revolution such as that which swept Andrew Jackson into the White House. How this party developed and why it failed is told below.

The Greenback Labor party. During the middle 1870's discontented Western farmers (including many Grangers) launched the Greenback party. Farm prices were so low that farmers could scarcely make a living. Since one way of raising prices is to increase the amount of money in circulation, the Greenback party demanded that Congress increase the supply of paper money. Congress decided instead to increase the amount of silver money by coining each month two million dollars' worth of silver. This would help to raise farm prices and at the same time help the owners of silver mines. Neither the farmers nor the silver miners were satisfied; they soon began to ask for unlimited coinage of silver.

At this time there was much unemployment because of the panic of 1873, and wage earners formed several small labor parties to work for reforms. In 1878 these parties joined with the farmers to form the Greenback Labor party. Among other things the platform called for free coinage of silver as a means of raising prices, the stopping of Chinese immigration, and laws to reduce hours of labor. That year a million votes were cast for Greenback candidates, and fifteen Greenbackers were elected to Congress. But when the sun of prosperity began to shine again, the Greenback Labor party melted away. Its demands, however, were soon taken up by other groups.

The Farmers' Alliances. During the late 1880's farm prices reached the lowest level in many years. World markets were flooded with grain, for new grain-growing regions had been opened up, not only in the United States but also in Russia, Australia, and Argentina. Corn was so cheap in the Midwest that farmers burned it for fuel. Southern cotton now had to compete on the world market with cotton from India; the price of cotton fell to half what it had been in the 1870's. Railroad rates, interest rates, and tax rates remained high, and farmers were in despair.

These conditions led to a rapid growth of farmers' clubs. Local clubs united to form two powerful regional organizations known as the Northwestern Farmers' Alliance and the National (or Southern) Farmers' Alliance. Among the reforms called for by the Alliances were free coinage of silver, reduction of the tariff, control of corporations, government ownership of railroads, an income tax, credit for farmers at a low rate of interest, and popular election of United States senators. Conservatives ridiculed these demands, giving Alliance members the name of "hayseed socialists." Yet the Alliances continued to grow; by 1892 they had three million members.

In 1890 Congress gave in to popular pressure by passing two important bills: (1) the Sherman Antitrust Act (see page 357), and (2) the Sherman Silver Purchase Act, which provided for the purchase and coinage of four and a half million ounces of silver a month. Neither Act satisfied the Alliances. They had asked for free coinage of silver and had secured merely a slight increase in the amount to be purchased. They had also insisted on complete control of the monopolies which they believed were crushing them and had received a weak law of uncertain meaning.

That summer and fall a political whirlwind swept the West and South. Nothing like it had been seen in America. Crowds of farmers and wage earners gathered at picnic grounds and in schoolhouses, churches, and public halls to hear Alliance speakers. In Kansas, where the storm was fiercest, the most popular speaker was Mary Lease. She told her audiences:

> Wall Street owns the country. It is no longer a government of the people, by the people, and for the people, but a government of Wall Street, by Wall Street, and for Wall Street. . . . The parties lie to us and the political speakers mislead us. We were told two years ago to go to work and raise a big crop and that was all we needed. We went to work and plowed and planted; the rains fell, the sun shone, nature smiled, and we raised the big crop that they told us to; and what came of it? Eight-cent corn, ten-cent oats, two-cent beef, and no price at all for butter and eggs — that's what came of it. . . . The main question is the money question. . . . We want money, land, and transportation. . . . We want the accursed foreclosure system wiped out. Land equal to a tract thirty miles wide and ninety miles long has been foreclosed and bought in by loan companies of Kansas in a year. . . . The people are at bay; let the bloodhounds of money who have dogged us thus far beware!

"BOSSES OF THE SENATE." *This cartoon bitterly attacks the power of the trusts.* (Drawn by J. Keppler for *Puck,* January 23, 1889)

She expressed the feelings of a multitude of plain people, and they flocked to hear her.

Formation of the People's Party. The elections of 1890 sent a score of Alliance men to Congress and hundreds to the state legislatures. Encouraged by this showing, Alliance leaders decided to invite labor groups to join them in forming a new political party. On Independence Day of 1892 a thousand delegates from all parts of the Union met at Omaha to select a candidate for President and adopt a platform. They took the name "People's party," but were usually known as "Populists." Their platform was considered very radical. It complained that the newspapers were muzzled, that the people's homes were covered with mortgages, that workmen were denied the right to organize, that employers used armed guards to shoot strikers, and that "the fruits of the toil of millions are boldly stolen to build up huge fortunes for the few."

In the presidential election that fall many citizens with Populist leanings voted for the Republican or Democratic candidate rather than throw their vote away on the Populist candidate, whom everybody knew could not possibly be elected. Yet the Populists polled over a million votes. The Democrats won the election, and Grover Cleveland again became President.

PANIC OF 1893. *Many people blamed Cleveland for the depression. This cartoon was labeled "Gone Democratic!"* (Drawn by Gillam for *Judge*, September 2, 1893)

Populism grows stronger. During the next four years various events deepened the popular unrest. Cleveland was hardly in the White House when the country found itself in the grip of the worst panic it had yet had – the panic of 1893. Business firms crashed, banks failed, factories shut down, mortgages were foreclosed. The unemployed walked the streets looking for jobs that did not exist. City soup kitchens served long lines of hungry men, women, and children.

Populists thought the panic resulted from a scarcity of currency. Business leaders thought just the opposite — they blamed it on the large government purchases of silver. Cleveland called a special session of Congress to repeal the Sherman Silver Purchase Act. This convinced the silver supporters that the President was a tool of Wall Street. More loudly than ever they asked for free coinage of silver.

The government took no further action to cure the depression. Cleveland, like other conservative men of his day, thought that the storm had to blow itself out. For two years conditions grew worse. The year 1894 brought still lower farm prices and still more wage cuts and unemployment. Jacob S. Coxey, a well-to-do reformer, thought of a plan to force the country to give attention to the sufferings of the jobless. He led a small army of unemployed to Washington. When he tried to make a speech on the Capitol steps, he was arrested and his

THE ORIGINAL "COXEY'S ARMY." *The cartoonist points out that big manufacturers asking favors from the government could be sure of a welcome from Congress.* (Drawn by W. A. Rogers for *Harper's Weekly,* May 12, 1894)

followers driven away. In a written protest he said that persons seeking favors for trusts and corporations were welcome in the committee rooms of Congress, while the way had been barred to him and the needy unemployed.

The arrest of Coxey led a magazine editor to write: "The 'Industrial Army' composed of manufacturers besieging the government with their clamor for higher duties and higher profits, has prepared the way for the 'Industrial Army' composed mostly of vagabonds marching upon Washington and demanding that the government feed them." Like this editor, most people outside the wage-earning group thought the men of "Coxey's Army" were vagabonds deserving no sympathy. Nothing came of their march to Washington except new bitterness among the jobless.

The same year saw a wave of strikes, most of them due to wage cuts. Cleveland's handling of the Pullman strike (see pages 375–376) aroused fierce resentment among workmen. They were shocked to discover that the Sherman Antitrust Act, which appeared powerless to break up monopolies, could be used to smash strikes.

To soothe popular discontent, Congress levied a 2 per cent tax on incomes above $4000. The next year (1895), by a five to four decision, the Supreme Court declared the tax unconstitutional. To the Populists this seemed clear proof that the Court, like the rest of the government, was on the side of the wealthy. The party faced the presidential election of 1896 strong and determined. This time, they thought, a Populist might win the election.

Anxiety in conservative circles. The spread of labor disputes and other signs of unrest worried the conservatives. They feared that a revolutionary spirit was gaining ground. When Congress passed the income tax law, a Democratic senator from New York said publicly that professors and socialists had caused the people to demand this dangerous kind of tax. A well-known lawyer, arguing before the Supreme Court a few months later, declared that the income tax law was communistic. Mr. Justice Field, speaking in the Court's name, voiced a similar view:

> The present assault upon capital is but the beginning. It will be but the stepping stone to others larger and more sweeping, till our political conditions will become a war of the poor against the rich.

The Republicans nominate McKinley. It was clear to all that the presidential campaign of 1896 would be a struggle between the moneyed class and the plain people. Republican leaders decided to take a firm stand against free coinage of silver and for a higher tariff. The Republican national convention chose as its candidate William McKinley, of Ohio. McKinley was well liked in Congress. The public knew him chiefly as the author of the McKinley tariff of 1890, the highest tariff ever adopted up to that time. His ideas were conservative. He called Populism "a sudden, dangerous, and revolutionary assault upon law and order" and said that nothing is worse than attempts "to array class against class, the classes against the masses, section against section, labor against capital, the poor against the rich, or interest against interest."

McKinley owed his nomination to the efforts of Marcus A. Hanna, a Clevelander said to be "the owner of more oil wells, street railways, aldermen, and legislators than any other man in Ohio." Hanna had gone into politics years before to obtain franchises and other favors for his vast business enterprises. Now he wanted to be a "President-maker." He was a warmhearted man and got real pleasure from promoting his friend McKinley. Hanna spent a year and a half of his time and more than $100,000 of his own money in getting McKinley nominated. He then took charge of McKinley's campaign.

The Democrats nominate Bryan. Many discontented Democrats gave signs of joining the Populists. To prevent this, Democratic lead-

WILLIAM JENNINGS BRYAN. *Three times an unsuccessful candidate for President of the United States — 1896, 1900, and 1908 — he was known for many years as the "Peerless Leader" of the Democratic party. Through his influence Woodrow Wilson won the Democratic nomination in 1912. Wilson accomplished a number of the reforms for which Bryan had fought.* (Photo by Pach Brothers, New York)

ers were willing to adopt a platform pleasing to farmers and wage earners. Most of them thought free silver should be made the chief issue of the campaign, for this would appeal to the most voters. Besides, the silver miners could be counted on for campaign contributions. The only difficulty with this issue was the opposition of President Cleveland and other conservative Democrats from the Northeast. When the convention met, there was an angry debate over the money question. The convention might have broken up had not a great leader appeared.

Among the delegates was a Nebraska lawyer, William Jennings Bryan, then only thirty-six years old. With all his heart he believed in free silver and in the Populist cause. He made a speech to the convention that excited the fifteen thousand delegates to a frenzy and united all but a handful behind the free-silver plank. The fight for free silver, he said, was a "cause as holy as the cause of liberty, the cause of humanity." It was a contest between the idle holders of idle capital and the toiling millions. He pleaded for the little businessman, the wage earner, the miner, the farmer:

> It is for these we speak. We do not come as aggressors. Ours is not a war of conquest. We are fighting in defense of our homes, our families, and our children. We have petitioned and our petitions have been scorned. We have entreated and our entreaties have been disregarded. We have begged and they have mocked when our calamity came. We beg no longer; we entreat no more; we petition no more. We defy. . . . We shall answer their demands for a gold standard

PRESIDENT WILLIAM McKINLEY. *A man of high principles and deep religious feeling, President McKinley was kindly, quiet, and dignified. Enlisting at the age of eighteen, he rose from the rank of private to major in the War between North and South. Later he served seven terms as congressman from Ohio and one term as governor. In 1896 he defeated Bryan for the Presidency. Throughout his first four years in the White House he grew in popularity and in 1900 easily won re-election. Six months later he was killed by an assassin's bullet. The third President to lose his life in this manner, his death shocked the nation.* (Brown Brothers)

by saying to them: You shall not press down upon the brow of labor this crown of thorns. You shall not crucify mankind upon a cross of gold.

The delegates went wild. The hall shook with their cheers. Next day they nominated the young Nebraskan on a platform calling for free silver, an income tax, protective labor laws, and tariff reduction.

The Populists nominate Bryan. The Populists made a fatal mistake by delaying their convention until after those of the two major parties. They expected both parties to endorse the gold standard, leaving them the free-silver issue. When they met, the Democrats had stolen their loudest thunder — free silver. If they threw their support to Bryan, he had a good chance of victory. This would, however, merge their party with the Democratic party. If they nominated a candidate of their own, their party might be kept together, but the silver vote would be split and McKinley would surely be elected. They faced a difficult decision.

Most of the thirteen hundred delegates were poor men. Some had walked a long distance to save railroad fare. Others used up their small store of money before the long convention was over and suffered for want of suitable sleeping places and adequate food. Many had grown old in the service of various reform groups and minor parties. All felt the seriousness of the decision they must make. After days of earnest discussion the convention decided to support Bryan, even at the risk of destroying the party they had worked so hard to build. The result turned out to be the end of their organization.

Bryan, the "Great Commoner." The youthful Bryan was an attractive figure. Taller and broader than most men, with coal-black hair, black flashing eyes, a determined mouth, he looked like one born to command. A great orator, he was also gifted with a beautiful speaking voice. Quick-witted, intelligent, fearless, he won the devotion of millions of plain people. He had grown up on an Illinois farm, attended a country college, and settled in Nebraska to practice law. A faithful Presbyterian, his speeches were rich in quotations from the Scriptures. A plain democrat, sincerely devoted to the public interest as he saw it, he won the title the "Great Commoner."

A history-making campaign. Free silver was the most talked-of issue of the campaign. Yet the real issue was the belief that Bryan stood for the rights of the plain people. Silver and gold were merely symbols — silver, of the prairies and little towns; gold, of big business and the "money power." In one of his speeches Bryan clearly said that "this is not a contest for the supremacy of one of two metals — it is not a miners' campaign." The fight, he added, was to save the people from being controlled by Wall Street.

Like the campaign of 1800 to elect Jefferson and that of 1828 to elect Jackson, this was a struggle between two different economic classes. A modern historian describes it as "a battle between the Western plow-holder and the Eastern bondholder." At the time a committee of leading Populists declared:

> There are but two sides in the conflict that is being waged in this country today. On one side are the . . . monopolies, the money power, great trusts and railroad corporations, who seek the enactment of laws to benefit them and . . . [make the people poor]. On the other side are the farmers, laborers, merchants, and all others who produce wealth and bear the burden of taxation. The one represents the wealthy and powerful classes who want the control of the Government to [rob] the people. The other represents the people [struggling] for equality before the law, and the rights of man. Between these two there is no middle ground.

The campaign was the most bitter, hard-fought, and expensive of any up to that time. Mark Hanna collected between three to seven million dollars from businessmen and bankers who feared the election of "that madman" Bryan. The money provided an army of speakers, an ocean of pamphlets printed in twenty languages, and numberless parades and mass meetings. McKinley stayed at home in Canton, Ohio, speaking from his front porch to the crowds who came on ex-

SETTLERS ON TH

O THE FAR WEST

CARTOON DESIGNED BY SENATOR TILLMAN *for Bryan's 1896 campaign.* *The cow represents the nation's wealth.* *The Western farmers feed her; Wall Street bankers milk her.* *This is one of the most widely circulated cartoons ever printed in America.* (From the *Congressional Record.* Courtesy of Library of Congress)

MARK HANNA IN A DOLLAR–MARK SUIT. *The cartoonist is attacking Hanna for collecting and spending millions to elect McKinley.* (Drawn by Homer Davenport for the *New York Journal.* Courtesy of Clements Library, University of Michigan)

cursion trains to hear him. Bryan spoke of McKinley's listeners as "worshipers at the shrine of the golden calf."

The Democrats, too, employed speakers and published pamphlets, but their campaign fund was only $300,000. In the main they depended on their candidate's own efforts. Bryan went directly to the people. Riding in hot, dusty day coaches, he crisscrossed twenty-nine states, speaking eight and ten times a day. Everywhere he attracted throngs.

The shrewd Hanna, seeing that the election would be close, saved his trump cards to the end. Just before the election, manufacturers put up notices that should Bryan win, they would close their doors, while bankers warned farmers that if Bryan won, their mortgages might not be renewed. Undoubtedly these threats led many of Bryan's supporters to vote for McKinley.

McKinley wins the election. The popular vote was large and close, but McKinley received most of the electoral votes. Besides electing the President, the Republicans won a majority of the seats in the House of Representatives and the Senate. They had control of all branches of the government. They were to keep control for fourteen years.

The tariff is boosted again. In his first inaugural address McKinley urged a higher tariff. He called a special session of Congress, which passed the Dingley tariff. The duties averaged 57 per cent. This was the highest tariff we had yet had. The captains of industry were in the saddle, and they rode forward to greater wealth and power than ever before.

The silver question is forgotten. The great excitement over the silver question was soon almost forgotten. Prosperity gradually returned. This was partly due to a large increase in the world's production of gold. New gold mines were discovered in Alaska, South Africa, and Australia. Besides, a new and cheap process was invented for extracting gold from inferior ore. With the increased gold supply the price of gold fell. This caused the prices of silver, farm products, and other goods to rise. The farmers and miners stopped asking the government to buy silver. The reformers turned their attention to other questions that were perhaps more important in the long run.

The reform movement goes on. Although the People's party had been defeated, the reform movement did not die. Ten years later Theodore Roosevelt was to take up the same fight that the Populists had fought. Even in our own day, the fight is still going on. For example, some of the reforms of the "New Deal" were demanded by the Populists of fifty years ago. The next unit will tell of many reforms made in the twenty years before World War I.

❀ ❀ ❀

To identify: William Jennings Bryan, Jacob S. Coxey, Greenback Labor party, Marcus A. Hanna, William McKinley, Populist party.

To explain or define: communist, gold standard.

Subjects for Talks or Written Reports

1. The disputed presidential election of 1876 and how it was settled. 2. Why we remember President Grover Cleveland. 3. Why so many of our Presidents come from Ohio and New York. 4. The panic of 1893 and the hard times which followed. 5. The march of Coxey's Army. 6. The life of William Jennings Bryan. 7. The story of one of the Farmers' Alliances. 8. The Presidency of William McKinley. 9. The life of Marcus A. Hanna. How he became rich. How he made McKinley President.

Questions for Understanding the Text

1. Explain how the Republican party was able to win every presidential election but two between 1860 and 1912. 2. (*a*) What new groups became important in the Democratic party soon after the War between North and South? (*b*) How did their presence change the earlier Democratic views on government aid to business? 3. Why do big corporations often contribute to both of the major parties? 4. (*a*) Why were several minor parties started in the 1870's, 1880's, and 1890's? (*b*) Name some of them. (*c*) Name the reforms they usually demanded. 5. (*a*) Why did farmers want a larger supply of paper money? (*b*) Why did they join with silver miners in asking for the unlimited coinage of silver money? 6. (*a*) Why were farm prices so low in the late 1880's? (*b*) What farmers' organizations were formed at this period? (*c*) Name some of their demands. 7. (*a*) What groups united to form the Populist or People's party? (*b*) Why did not many Populists vote for the Populist candidate for President? 8. (*a*) How did Populists explain the panic of 1893? (*b*) How did business leaders explain it? (*c*) What did President Cleveland do to cure the depression? 9. (*a*) What was Coxey's purpose in leading an army of unemployed to Washington? (*b*) How were he and his followers received? (*c*) What did the public think about his army? 10. (*a*) What did conservative people think about the income tax law of 1894? (*b*) What became of this law? 11. (*a*) The election of 1896 was a struggle between what classes? (*b*) Who were the candidates? 12. To what individual did McKinley owe his nomination and election? Tell

something of this man's life. 13. (*a*) Why did most of the Democratic leaders want to make free silver the main issue of the campaign of 1896? (*b*) Who united the convention behind this issue? (*c*) Tell about his remarkable speech to the convention and what followed. 14. (*a*) What difficult decision was made by the Populist convention? (*b*) Why did they make it? (*c*) What was the effect on their organization? 15. Why was Bryan so attractive to the plain people? 16. Was free silver the real issue in the campaign of 1896? Explain. 17. (*a*) Contrast the campaign expenditures for McKinley with those for Bryan. (*b*) Compare the methods of campaigning used by McKinley and Bryan. (*c*) How did Hanna make sure that McKinley would win? 18. After the election what was done about the tariff? 19. Why was the silver question soon forgotten? 20. Did the Populists win or lose their fight for reform? Explain.

ACTIVITIES FOR UNIT SIX

1. Appoint committees to prepare a classbook on the progress made by American Negroes since the end of the War between North and South. Include sections on economic conditions, business, education, music, art, literature, and scientific research.
2. Make a class scrapbook on some large industry, such as oil, steel, rubber, or automobile. Cover the story of its development down to the present day.
3. Arrange a class visit to some near-by factory. Ask the manager to tell you how inventions have helped his industry.
4. Write a short history of some local industry. Try to have it published in your school newspaper or local newspaper.
5. Write a short history of the labor movement in your community.
6. Make a class scrapbook on the labor movement. Include clippings on labor unions, working conditions, strikes, labor laws, labor leaders, gains made by labor, and the like. Include both friendly and unfriendly materials.
7. If you live in a farming community, write a short history of each of the local farm organizations. Tell why it was founded and what it has accomplished.
8. Draw campaign posters that might have been used for the presidential election of 1884.
9. Draw a series of cartoons on the rise and fall of Populism.
10. Prepare a classbook on life in the 1890's. Include sections on farm life, city life, dress, travel, amusements, education, home furnishings, architecture, art, literature, politics, new inventions, transportation, and so on.

READINGS FOR UNIT SIX

(Stars indicate the easier books)

GENERAL ACCOUNTS

*Bridges, T. C. *The Young Folk's Book of Invention.* Little, Brown.

Brown, Harriet E. *Grandmother Brown's One Hundred Years, 1827–1927.* Blue Ribbon.

Buck, Solon J. *The Agrarian Crusade.* (Chronicles)

*Bush, M. G. and Waddell, J. F. *How We Have Conquered Distance.* Macmillan.

*Crump, Irving. *Boys' Book of Cowboys.* Dodd, Mead.

De Voto, Bernard. *Mark Twain's America.* Little, Brown.

Dunbar, Seymour. *A History of Travel in America.* Tudor.

Faulkner, H. U. and Starr, Mark. *Labor in America.* Harper.

Garland, Hamlin. *Boy Life on the Prairie.* Harper.

*Gillett, J. B. and Driggs, H. R. *The Texas Ranger.* World Book.

Glasscock, C. B. *Gold in Them Hills.* Bobbs-Merrill.

*Hartman, Gertrude. *Machines.* Macmillan. (Changes in industry)

Hendrick, B. J. *The Age of Big Business.* (Chronicles)

Holbrook, A. H. *Iron Brew.* Macmillan. (A century of American iron)

*Holland, R. S. *Historic Railroads.* Macrae-Smith.

Hough, Emerson. *The Passing of the Frontier.* (Chronicles)

Kaempffert, Waldemar B., editor. *A Popular History of American Invention.* Scribner's.

Keir, Malcolm. *The Epic of Industry.* (Pageant)

Kouwenhoven, J. A. *Adventures of America, 1857–1900.* Harper.

Krout, John A. *Annals of American Sport.* (Pageant)

Moody, John. *The Masters of Capital.* (Chronicles)

——. *The Railroad Builders.* (Chronicles)

Nevins, Allan. *Emergence of Modern America, 1865–1878.* (A. L. S.)

Orth, S. P. *The Armies of Labor.* (Chronicles)

Paxson, F. L. *New Nation.* Houghton Mifflin. (The period 1885–1897)

Schlesinger, Arthur M. *Rise of the City, 1878–1898.* (A. L. S.)

*Swan, O. G., editor. *Frontier Days.* Macrae-Smith.

Tarbell, Ida. *Nationalizing of Business.* (A. L. S.)

Van Metre, T. W. *Trains, Tracks and Travel.* Simmons-Boardman.

Woestemeyer, Ina F. *The Westward Movement; a Book of Readings on Our Changing Frontiers.* Appleton-Century.

BIOGRAPHY

*Bolton, S. K. *Lives of Poor Boys Who Became Famous.* Crowell.

Carnegie, Andrew. *Andrew Carnegie's Own Story for Boys and Girls.* Houghton Mifflin.

*Cody, W. F. *An Autobiography of Buffalo Bill.* Cosmopolitan.

*Davis, R. J. *The Boys' Life of Grover Cleveland*. Harper.
Garland, Hamlin. *A Son of the Middle Border*. Macmillan.
Holt, Rackham. *George Washington Carver*. Doubleday, Doran.
Josephson, Matthew. *The Robber Barons*. Harcourt, Brace.
de Kruif, Paul. *Seven Iron Men*. Blue Ribbon.
*Moore, R. D. *When They Were Girls*. Owen.
*Wade, M. H. *The Master Builders*. Little, Brown. (Hill, Bell,
      B. T. Washington, Goethals, Carnegie, Ford)
Washington, Booker T. *Up from Slavery*. Burt.
Wildman, Edman. *Famous Leaders of Industry*, 2 vol. Page.

FICTION

Aldrich, Bess Streeter. *A Lantern in Her Hand*. Appleton-Century.
      (Pioneer life in Nebraska, 1864–1890)
Bacheller, Irving. *The Handmade Gentleman*. Harper. (New York in
      the time of Vanderbilt and Carnegie)
Cather, Willa. *My Ántonia*. Houghton Mifflin. (Immigrant farmers)
Ferber, Edna. *Cimarron*. Grosset. (The Oklahoma land rush of 1889)
Ford, Paul L. *The Honorable Peter Stirling*. Grosset. (A novel based on
      the career of Grover Cleveland)
*Hall, C. G. *Through by Rail*. Macmillan. (Railroading, 1865–1880)
Howells, William Dean. *The Rise of Silas Lapham*. Houghton Mifflin.
      (The story of a self-made man)
Jackson, Helen Hunt. *Ramona*. Grosset. (Indian missions)
Johnston, Mary. *Michael Forth*. Little, Brown. (Southern conditions)
*Lamprey, Louise. *Days of the Leaders*. Stokes. (Biographical stories)
Lane, Rose W. *Let the Hurricane Roar*. Longmans. (Homesteading)
Norris, Frank. *The Octopus*. Doubleday, Doran. (Farmers *vs.* railroads)
——. *The Pit*. Modern Library. (Big business, 1890–1914)
*Rolt-Wheeler, Francis. *The Book of the Cowboys*. Lothrop.
Rolvaag, O. E. *Giants in the Earth*. Blue Ribbon. (Norwegian settlers in
      South Dakota)
*Rounds, Glen. *Pay Dirt*. Holiday House. (Black Hills gold rush)
*Sterne, Emma G. *The Calico Ball*. Dodd, Mead. (Alabama, 1883–1890)
Stribling, T. S. *The Store*. Doubleday, Doran. (The new South)
——. *The Forge*. Doubleday, Doran. (Beginning of the new South)
Tarkington, Booth. *The Magnificent Ambersons*. Grosset. (Changes in
      a midwestern city)
*Warner, Anna S. *Sidesaddle Ranch*. Bobbs-Merrill. (Ranch life in
      Colorado in the 1870's)
*Wilder, Laura I. *Little House in the Big Woods*. Harper. (Pioneer life
      in Wisconsin, 1870–1880)
Wister, Owen. *The Virginian*. Grosset. (Wyoming, 1874–1890)

UNIT SEVEN
THE PROGRESSIVE MOVEMENT

The period from 1896 to 1916 is often spoken of as the "Age of Reform" or the "Progressive Era." A wave of reform like that in the time of Andrew Jackson swept over the country. Just as in his day, the common people were calling for a greater share in the government. To get it they wanted to destroy the power of the political boss. They also demanded that business be regulated in the public interest. Among other things this meant control over the rates charged by railroad companies, control over labor conditions, and protection for consumers. In addition the people wanted better schools, additional public health services, further opportunities for wholesome recreation, and other things to make life more worth-while.

The reformers turned to their state legislatures with their requests, and many progressive laws were passed. But on some things the states were powerless to take action. Presidents Theodore Roosevelt, William Howard Taft, and Woodrow Wilson saw the need for federal action and got Congress to pass a number of progressive laws. After doing much good, the progressive movement was interrupted by the outbreak of World War I.

ROBERT M. LA FOLLETTE. *As governor of Wisconsin in the early 1900's "Fighting Bob" broke the hold of the railroads on the state, curbed the power of the political bosses, and made Wisconsin the chief example of Progressivism in the nation. Under his leadership and that of the faculty of the state university, Wisconsin adopted a long series of reforms, including strict regulation of railroads, insurance companies, and banks, the direct primary, a workmen's compensation law, creation of a state forest reserve, laws limiting hours of labor for women and children, and graduated income and inheritance taxes. Serving in the United States Senate from 1906 to his death in 1925, he continued to fight for reform and was known as a leader of the Republican Insurgents. (Underwood)*

CHAPTER 30

THE PROGRESSIVE ERA (1896–1916)

POPULISM GIVES WAY TO THE PROGRESSIVE ERA

A *new age of reform.* Bryan called the campaign of 1896 "the first battle." Although that battle ended in the defeat of Populism, it marked the beginning of a new struggle by the common people — a struggle to regain control of their government, to bring business under control, and to obtain a better life. This struggle continued for some twenty years and led to many reforms. The period 1896–1916 is therefore known as the "Age of Reform," or the "Progressive Era."

Voices of the "Progressive Era." The period was one of great discontent — discontent because the common man felt that the American dream of freedom and equal opportunity was not being fulfilled. All around them the people saw poverty, injustice, and political dishonesty. They wanted to know why these conditions had come about and what could be done to remedy them. They were eager to read magazine articles and books on the subject of reform. A new kind of popular literature was called for, and a number of writers accepted the challenge. We can mention only a few.

One of the first was Jacob Riis, a young reporter for the *New York Sun.* His book, *How the Other Half Lives,* appeared in 1890. It pictured the disease, crime, and misery in the overcrowded slums of New York. Newspapermen in other cities made similar reports, and the nation came to realize that city dwellers had grievances just as serious as those of the farmers.

In 1894 a Chicago newspaperman, Henry D. Lloyd, published a volume entitled *Wealth against Commonwealth.* It gave facts about conditions which the public had suspected for a long time, showing how trusts destroyed competitors and bribed public officials.

In the early 1900's several young novelists wrote powerful stories about the evils they saw around them. *The Octopus,* by Frank Norris, published in 1901, told of the struggle between the farmers and the railroads. *The Pit,* published two years later by the same author, showed how the farmers suffered from the activities of speculators in the Chicago grain market. Upton Sinclair's novel, *The Jungle*, exposed the horrible conditions in the Chicago packing plants. Jack London's novels laid bare the miserable working and living conditions endured by sailors and unskilled workers.

During the same years popular magazines began to print articles about dishonesty in business and politics. The first to do so was *McClure's*. In 1902 and 1903 *McClure's* published a series of articles by Ida Tarbell, telling of the ugly methods used by the Standard Oil Company in crushing its rivals. At the same time *McClure's* ran a series by Lincoln Steffens called "The Shame of the Cities." Steffens told how politicians in many cities were growing rich by selling franchises and other favors to public utility companies. The public liked these articles, and other magazine editors hastened to follow *McClure's* lead. For instance, *Everybody's Magazine* brought out a series on the beef trust and another on the stock market. The writers of this type of material came to be known as "muckrakers." However, they did a useful public service in showing the need for reform.

The states point the way. Under our Constitution the states are responsible for local government, education, labor conditions, the regulation of business within state borders, and most other matters of social welfare. In each state the reformers naturally turned to their state legislature for action. Often they found that the legislature was controlled by powerful corporations which opposed reform. Yet when the people became thoroughly aroused and when they had a strong leader, they usually obtained the laws they demanded.

A reform tried in one state was often copied by other states and later, perhaps, by the national government. The states led the way. They also served as training schools for national leaders. Men who cleaned up politics in their own state often were sent to the United States Senate, and sometimes to the White House. Three of our Presidents since 1900 — Theodore Roosevelt, Woodrow Wilson, and Franklin D. Roosevelt — became known as progressives while serving as governors of their states.

POLITICAL REFORMS

Many of the reforms carried out by the states were intended to restrict the political boss and to give the people more control over their government. We will take up briefly the most important of these changes.

The merit system. One way of weakening the political boss is to take away his power over government jobs. This can be done by adopting the *merit system*, which means that government employees are chosen through competitive examination, and once appointed cannot be dismissed except for misconduct or inefficiency. The merit system was adopted first in New York and Massachusetts. In 1883 Congress passed the Civil Service Act, placing fourteen thousand federal employees — about one in every eight — under the merit system. After 1900 the system was rapidly extended, until by 1932 four out of five employees were covered. The system has also been adopted in fourteen states and some three hundred cities.

The Australian ballot. Formerly each party prepared its own ballot. When the voter dropped his ballot into the ballot box, anyone in the polling place could tell what party he was voting for. Those who bought votes could easily make sure that their purchases were delivered. An employer could require his workmen to vote for one party. To make voting secret, Massachusetts in 1888 adopted the Australian ballot. This ballot is furnished by the government and contains the names of the candidates of all parties. No one can tell without opening the ballot what candidates have been voted for. By 1900 nearly all the states used the Australian ballot.

The direct primary. In the old days local candidates were nominated in little meetings held by the party boss of the district. State and national candidates were chosen at conventions by an inner circle, or "ring," of bosses. Unless favored by the inner circle of his party, no one had a chance of being nominated. The remedy was sought in the *direct primary.* Candidates were not to be chosen at secret meetings. Any citizen might run for any office (except President and Vice-President), provided a certain number of voters sign a petition to place his name on the ballot at the primary election. Wisconsin was the first state to adopt the direct primary. By 1918 every state but four had followed Wisconsin's example. Some states have tried the direct primary, been dissatisfied with it, and then returned to the old system.

Direct legislation. In order to restore the government to the people, reformers recommended two devices — the *initiative* and the *referendum* — which give the voters direct control over the passage of new laws. Under the initiative any bill may be placed before the people at an election upon the petition of a certain percentage of the voters. If a majority votes for the bill, it then becomes a law. The initiative is valuable when a legislature or city council refuses to pass a measure favored by the people. The referendum allows citizens who disapprove of an act passed by the legislature to get up a petition against it and require a vote on it at the polls. South Dakota adopted the initiative and referendum in 1898. Nearly half the states and most of the cities have since adopted these devices, but they are not used to any great extent.

The recall. This is another device to give the people more control over the government. It enables them to remove an official before his term expires. Whenever a certain number of voters are dissatisfied with an official, they may sign a petition requiring him to stand for a new election. If defeated at this election, he cannot serve any more of his term. The recall was introduced in the United States in 1903 when Los Angeles wrote it into the city charter. Today the recall is provided for state officers in one fourth of the states and for city officials in more than a thousand cities. However, it is seldom used.

Improvements in city government. Most of our large cities were badly governed when the Progressive Era began. Bosses controlled the elections, appointments to office, purchase of supplies, and every other activity of the city government. They grew rich from graft. City government was so complicated that the voters never knew who was responsible for inefficiency and corruption in the different departments. Reformers said, "Let us elect only a few men and hold them responsible for city affairs." The result was that the council was reduced in size and the mayor given power to appoint all the chief officials. The voters could then hold the mayor to account when any department was poorly run.

Galveston introduced a new type of city government in 1901. A terrible storm had destroyed most of the city, and the citizens decided they must have a strong, efficient government to take charge of reconstruction. So they abolished the mayor and council scheme and put the government of the city in the hands of five commissioners. By 1920 more than four hundred cities had followed Galveston's example. Under the commission type of government, each commissioner has full control of one department, such as public works or public safety. He appoints the officials in his department, and the citizens hold him to blame for any shortcomings in the way the department does its work.

A few years after Galveston's experiment, another type of city government was introduced in Sumter, South Carolina. It is known as the city manager plan. Under this plan the council appoints a city manager to take charge of running the departments. He usually names the

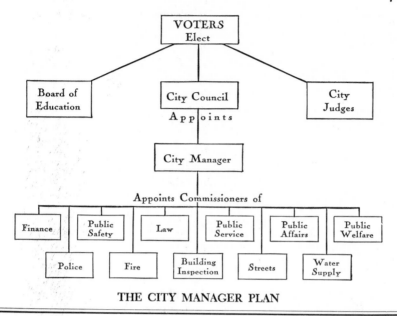

THE CITY MANAGER PLAN

department heads, since he is responsible for the smooth running of every department. He may be discharged at the pleasure of the council. When the voters choose good councilmen, and the councilmen select a competent and honest manager, this plan produces excellent results. It has become very popular.

In order to change its form of government, a city must first get permission from the state legislature. Sometimes the legislature refused its permission and even interfered actively in the city's affairs. This led the cities to try to get "home rule" — the right to make their own charters, or constitutions, and manage their own affairs. Missouri was the first state to give its cities home rule. Eighteen states now allow their cities to write their own charters. This has helped the cities to improve their government.

Woman suffrage. Women took an active part in the reform movement. All over the country they organized women's societies and clubs to work for this or that reform. Some worked for the cause of temperance, that is, for control of the sale of liquor; others for changes in city government, for labor laws, public health, pure food, or prison reform. In most states they made slow progress because they did not have the right to vote. In correcting this injustice the Western states led the way. Wyoming, while still a territory, gave women the right to vote in 1869. On becoming a state twenty years later, Wyoming

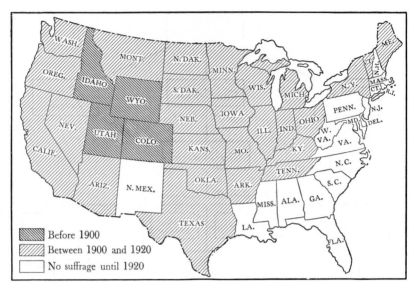

PROGRESS OF THE WOMAN SUFFRAGE MOVEMENT

insisted on keeping woman suffrage in spite of protests in Congress. Colorado gave women the right to vote in 1893, and Idaho and Utah did so three years later. The next victory for woman suffrage was in the state of Washington in 1910. Nearly every year after that, one or more states gave women the ballot. Meanwhile the "suffragists" worked for an amendment to the federal Constitution which would give the women of every state the right to vote. The Nineteenth, or Woman Suffrage, Amendment was added to the Constitution in 1920.

ECONOMIC REFORM

The idea that government should leave business alone (*laissez-faire*) was very popular in the 1800's. The idea became less popular after the rise of big business, for the great corporations seemed indifferent to the rights of consumers and the rights of workingmen. Then, too, they bribed public officials in a shameless manner. Edward Harriman, head of the Union Pacific Railroad, boasted openly that he could buy both legislatures and courts whenever he needed them. This attitude was held by many other heads of big business.

The people saw that the corporations must be brought under control or democracy would die. "We must," said Theodore Roosevelt, "abandon definitely the laissez-faire theory . . . and fearlessly support a system of increased governmental control, paying no attention

WOMAN SUFFRAGE PARADE, *New York City, in 1917. The 20,000 women march-ers were led by Dr. Anna Howard Shaw and Mrs. Carrie Chapman Catt, lifelong workers for women's rights.* (Wide World Photo)

to the cries of worthy people who denounce this as socialistic." The states tried in various ways to bring business under their control. Some of the most important ways are discussed below.

Regulation of the railways. The first attempts to control private enterprise in the public interest began even before the Progressive Era. We have already mentioned the Granger laws. (See pages 395–396.) In 1886 the Supreme Court ruled that the states could not fix the rates of railways crossing state lines. Congress then passed the Interstate Commerce Act — the first effort by the federal government to regulate business.

Regulation of public utility companies. During the Progressive Era most of the states established public utility commissions to regulate the rates and practices of electric light plants, water works, telephone companies, gas companies, and other public utilities. In some states the commissions were fairly successful; in others they proved no match for the powerful companies they were supposed to regulate.

Public ownership of utilities. Some reformers insisted that public ownership of the utilities was the only way to secure fair rates. They argued that regulation did not work well and that the utility companies continued to bribe officials and newspapers. Hundreds of cities bought water works and electric light plants. Most of the city-

"UNCLE SAM'S 'WILD WEST' SHOW." *The Interstate Commerce Commission is
shown trying to control the railroads.* (Drawn by W. A. Rogers for *Harper's Weekly,*
April 9, 1887)

owned utilities were well operated and provided service at low cost.
The utility companies fought government ownership with great clev-
erness. Their arguments were (1) that government should not compete with private enterprise, and (2) that government officials would
not run any business so efficiently as it could be run by private owners.

Regulation of insurance companies. The insurance business also received attention from reformers. The insurance companies were run
purely for private profit, and some showed little regard for the interests of their policyholders. An investigation of the insurance business
in Massachusetts and New York led these states to adopt strict laws to
regulate insurance companies. The other states soon passed laws for
the same purpose.

Tenement house control. Another type of business which seemed
to need regulation was housing. Bad housing was a problem in every
large city. Most people of the laboring class had to live under terrible
conditions. In New York City in 1890 it was found that half a million
persons lived in rickety wooden tenements five or six stories high.
These tenements were dark, poorly ventilated, and filthy. People living in the tenements had a death rate four times that of people living in
the better parts of the city. A typical tenement house had fourteen

rooms to the floor, only four of which had direct sunlight, the remainder either having no windows, or opening upon a narrow air shaft scarcely larger than a chimney. Ten years later conditions were still worse due to the rapid growth of the population. At that time the New York Tenement House Commission declared that New York had "the most serious tenement house problem in the world." To prevent the building of new slums, the New York legislature then passed a special tenement house law. The law regulated the size of rooms, air space, light, and sanitary arrangements for all new buildings in large cities of New York State. Other states quickly passed similar laws.

Workmen's compensation laws. Manufacturers did not long escape regulation. They were the principal group of employers to be affected by the new workmen's compensation laws.

At the beginning of the century some five hundred thousand American workers annually were either killed or injured at their work. Every year the number mounted higher. Employers were hardly ever required to do anything for an injured workman or for the family of a workman killed while at work. (See page 197.) Much of the poverty in cities was due to this very fact.

Maryland was the first state to attack this problem. In 1902 the Maryland legislature passed a Workmen's Compensation Act, setting up an insurance system for the benefit of injured workers. The employer must pay the cost of the insurance. By 1920 forty-two other states had adopted a similar law.

Child labor laws. Child labor had existed in America from the earliest times, but it was given no thought until the coming of the factory. Massachusetts limited the workday of children in factories as early as 1843 (see page 199). After the War between North and South several states prohibited night work for children (see pages 377–378). Most of the evils of child labor had not yet been touched. In fact they were growing worse as more and more children began to work in factories and mines.

About 1900, labor unions, women's clubs, and other organizations took up the problem. The movement was strengthened by John Spargo's book, *The Bitter Cry of the Children*, published in 1906. Spargo wrote of scenes he had actually observed — children kept awake during the long night in a cotton mill by having cold water dashed in their faces; little girls in canning factories "snipping" beans for sixteen hours a day in the rush season; ten-year-old "breaker" boys bent for ten hours a day over a dusty coal chute, picking sharp slate out of the

A TYPICAL TENEMENT *in a big city at the turn of the century. A great number of working people lived in crowded, unhealthful dwellings. This photograph was taken in New York in 1900.* (Brown Brothers)

fast-moving coal. He also pictured boys from orphan asylums and re-form schools losing their health in glass factories, and tots toiling until late at night over artificial flowers in city tenements. Shocked by these facts, the legislatures of many states passed new child labor laws or improved their old laws. By 1914 every state but one had some minimum age limit for child workers. Most states also limited the workday of children employed in factories and prohibited their em-ployment in mines and quarries. Some states still allowed children of twelve to work in factories for as long as ten hours a day, and some states with better child labor laws did not enforce them. In states that were really determined to prevent child labor, factory owners were at a disadvantage, since their labor costs were higher than in states where child labor was permitted. The solution to the child labor problem called for federal action.

Minimum-wage laws. Women and children received low wages, often just a few cents an hour. This led several states to pass minimum-wage laws. Massachusetts pioneered in this field in 1912. By 1938 twenty-two states had legislation concerning minimum wages. Some states did not pass such laws because their businessmen feared compe-tition from businessmen in other states where wages were low. Here again federal action seemed to be necessary.

SOCIAL REFORMS

The common people wanted social changes as well as political and economic changes. They especially wanted more educational opportunities for their children. In the cities they wanted playgrounds and parks and public health services. They also wanted to end drunkenness and the conditions which lead children into crime. In short they were seeking a fuller and happier life. Fortunately many people of wealth and influence were interested in social reforms, and some of them became leaders in the reform movement. This helps explain the rapid progress which was made.

Expansion of educational opportunities. At the close of the nineteenth century the average child attended a one-room school for sixty-eight days a year. He was taught by a young woman who had little if any training beyond the elementary grades and whose salary was about thirty-eight dollars a month. He left school in the seventh or eighth grade. By 1916 the situation was far better. Attendance had improved, the school year was longer, the average salary of teachers had nearly doubled, and thousands of consolidated schools had been formed from one-room schools.

In 1900 few children had a chance to attend high school. In most parts of the country public high schools were found only in the larger towns and cities. High school courses were planned for those who expected to go to college; few high schools offered subjects planned for those who would soon go to work. By the end of the Progressive Era these conditions were being changed. Hundreds of new high schools were built every year. Twice as many children were going to high school, and most high schools gave vocational courses to fit pupils for work. In many places the junior high school had been introduced so that children in the seventh, eighth, and ninth grades might have different teachers for different subjects and a richer program.

The number of students in the colleges was nearly three times as great in 1916 as it had been twenty years before. One in every twenty-five young people of college age was attending college. The idea was growing that every gifted boy and girl should have the opportunity for a college education.

Expansion of public health services. Once people knew the facts about the high death rate in city slums, particularly the high death rate of young children, they demanded action. Public health officials asked for, and obtained, larger powers. About 1897 these officials began to give special attention to the milk supply. One of the first steps was to require regular inspection of dairies. Another step was to require that all cows be tested for tuberculosis. A later step was to forbid the sale of raw milk. In addition to safeguarding the milk supply, many cities established milk depots, where needy mothers could buy milk at low cost. Many cities organized baby clinics, where specialists gave advice to needy mothers on the health of their babies. Day nurseries where working mothers might leave their little ones, visiting nurses, and medical inspection of school children also helped in preventing needless sickness and death. In time some of these health services were started in small towns and villages. The growing attention to public health was one of the greatest achievements of the period.

The recreation movement. One of the most urgent problems of the cities was the increasing crime rate. Boys and girls living in crowded slums, with no place except the streets for play, easily drifted into crime — that is, they became *juvenile delinquents.* Those who studied the problem believed that many young people could be saved from delinquency by giving them more chance for wholesome activities in their leisure time.

Near the close of the century the cities started to open supervised playgrounds, and by 1915 there were over three thousand. The Young Men's Christian Association and many city churches also began to offer leisure-time programs for boys and girls. In 1910 the Boy Scouts of America was organized. It became popular overnight. Within two or three years there were troops in all parts of the country. The success of the Boy Scouts led to the founding of the Campfire Girls and the Girl Scouts in 1912. All of these new recreational opportunities helped promote the health and happiness of young people.

The prohibition movement. By 1900 New York, Buffalo, San Francisco, and other large cities had one saloon to every two hundred people. There was a great deal of heavy drinking, especially among poor people seeking to forget the hardships of their daily life. Drinking made their troubles far worse, for it wasted their money and often led to disease, accidents, and crime. The liquor business was also one of the chief sources of political corruption. Most saloons bribed city officials to let them disregard Sunday closing laws and other regulations.

The Women's Christian Temperance Union, the Anti-Saloon League, and some of the churches carried on a ceaseless campaign in favor of prohibition. By 1900 seven states, all of them rural, were

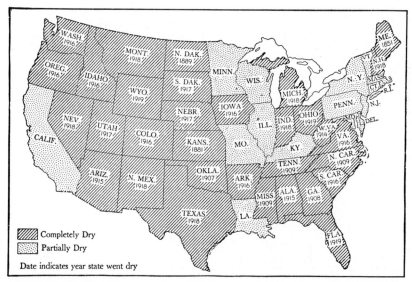

PROHIBITION ON THE EVE OF THE EIGHTEENTH AMENDMENT

In the "local option" states liquor was sold in most of the cities. Persons living in "dry" communities could get liquor from these cities. To stop the sale of liquor altogether, the "Drys" demanded national prohibition.

"dry," while many others had "local option." (Local option means that any town or county in the state may prohibit the sale of alcoholic beverages within its boundaries.) The prohibition movement made rapid headway during the early 1900's. By the time of World War I nearly all rural areas and small towns were dry. In the large cities the liquor interests were still in power. The prohibitionists called for federal action in order to make the whole nation dry. Finally, in 1919, the Eighteenth Amendment was adopted, prohibiting the manufacture, sale, or transportation of intoxicating liquor in the United States. National prohibition did not work well, and in 1933 the Eighteenth Amendment was repealed by the Twenty-first Amendment.

To identify: Anti-Saloon League, Jack London, Nineteenth Amendment, Frank Norris, Jacob Riis, John Spargo, Lincoln Steffens, Ida Tarbell, Women's Christian Temperance Union.

To explain or define: Australian ballot, direct primary, initiative, juvenile delinquent, laissez-faire, local option, merit system, muckraker, prohibition movement, recall, referendum, woman suffrage, workmen's compensation.

SUBJECTS FOR TALKS OR WRITTEN REPORTS

1. The struggle for woman suffrage. 2. How the city manager plan works. 3. The child labor problem today. 4. Minimum-wage laws in my state. The federal minimum-wage law. 5. How my state protects women and children at work. 6. The history of one of the following: Boy Scouts, Girl Scouts, Campfire Girls, Young Men's Christian Association, Young Women's Christian Association, Young Men's Hebrew Association, Young Women's Hebrew Association. 7. The history of the Women's Christian Temperance Union. 8. The growth of the public school system in my community. 9. Reforms led by Robert M. La Follette, Sr.

QUESTIONS FOR UNDERSTANDING THE TEXT

1. (a) What were three aims of the common people during the Progressive Era? (b) Why were the common people so discontented? 2. Name some of the muckrakers and the subjects on which they wrote. 3. Why were reforms usually begun by the state governments rather than the national government? 4. Name three Presidents who were known as progressive state governors. 5. How does the merit system weaken the political boss? 6. How does a candidate get his name on the ballot: (a) where there is a direct primary? (b) where there is not? 7. Under what conditions is each of the following useful: (a) the initiative, (b) the referendum, (c) the recall? 8. How may a city boss use his influence for his own profit? 9. What is the advantage in reducing the number of elected officials in a city government? 10. (a) From whom must a city get permission to change its form of government? (b) What is meant by "home rule" for cities? 11. (a) Where did women first win the right to vote? (b) When was the Constitution amended to give women this right? 12. What caused the idea of laissez-faire to lose its popularity? 13. Name the first industry which Congress tried to bring under control. 14. What kinds of business did the states try to bring under control? 15. Describe the conditions that led New York to pass a tenement house law. 16. Why do we need workmen's compensation laws? 17. (a) What laws did the states pass to control child labor? (b) Why was federal action needed? 18. Why were the states timid about passing strong minimum-wage laws? 19. (a) Describe the educational opportunities of the average child in 1900. (b) How had his opportunities improved by 1916? 20. Name some of the steps taken during the Progressive Era to improve the public health. 21. How did the liquor business produce political corruption? 22. (a) What progress had been made by the prohibition movement by the time of World War I? (b) Why did the prohibitionists want federal control of the liquor business? (c) How long did the United States experiment with national prohibition?

CHAPTER 31

THEODORE ROOSEVELT AND THE "SQUARE DEAL"

A reformer unexpectedly becomes President. Since the War between North and South the federal government had been in the hands of conservative leaders who were friendly to big business. Although many leaders of the people had demanded reform, the Presidents and the majority of Congress paid little attention. Congress, it is true, passed a few progressive laws, such as the Civil Service Act of 1883, the Interstate Commerce Act of 1887, and the Sherman Antitrust Act of 1890. But these laws accomplished little, either because they did not go far enough or were not properly enforced.

President McKinley, who defeated Bryan in 1896 and again in 1900, was a conservative. Republican leaders depended on him to do or say nothing unfriendly to big business. They thought the government need pay no attention to the complaints of farmers and wage earners and to the "crackpot" plans of reformers. They had no idea that a reformer was about to take McKinley's place in the White House.

Six months after beginning his second term, McKinley was shot by a fanatic. Theodore Roosevelt, the Vice-President, became the nation's chief executive. Young, energetic, and progressive, he was to make great changes in national politics.

Theodore Roosevelt's background and personality. Theodore Roosevelt was the youngest of all our Presidents. Born of an old and well-to-do New York family, he was educated at Harvard and at Columbia University Law School. His experiences were remarkably varied. He had lived on a ranch in North Dakota, been a member of the New York legislature, served as head of the New York City police force, and helped manage the Federal Civil Service Commission. He had also been Assistant Secretary of the Navy, led a volunteer regiment, the "Rough Riders," in Cuba during the Spanish-American

War, and been governor of New York. In all of these offices he had distinguished himself by his courage, honesty, and ability. Although he had always been a loyal Republican, party bosses had no use for him because he would not do what they wanted. Boss Platt of New York, wishing to get him out of New York politics, had him nominated for Vice-President. Platt thought he was putting Roosevelt permanently on the shelf, for as Vice-President the voters would soon forget him.

Roosevelt was a cheerful, enthusiastic person, and he had unusual energy. He loved the strenuous life, took part in numerous outdoor sports, and kept himself in fighting trim. A reporter wrote of him, "An electric energy seemed to exude [come] from his body and emphasize his personality."

Roosevelt was interested in everybody and made friends with all sorts of people. He had sympathy for all classes and races — rich and poor, white, yellow, and black. He fearlessly took the part of the "little man." Like Andrew Jackson, he won the trust of the plain people. Soon after he became President, people began to speak of him affectionately as "Teddy" or "T.R.," and children named their toy bears "Teddy" in his honor.

Theodore Roosevelt's ideas about economic reform. Roosevelt was the first President since the War between North and South who understood the discontent of the masses. Like them he believed that government should be supreme over business. "The great development of industrialism," he declared, "means that there must be an increase in the supervision exercised by the government over business enterprise."

Roosevelt was not a radical — he did not want to make over our economic system or to destroy big business. He thought that large-scale business was necessary. He believed that there were good trusts as well as bad ones and said: "We draw the line against misconduct, not against wealth. . . . We do not wish to destroy corporations but we do wish to make them serve the public good."

Roosevelt wanted fair play in business as in politics. The biggest corporation, like the humblest private citizen, must be made to obey the law. By weeding out evil business practices the common man would, he thought, get more of a "square deal."

"Trust-busting." During McKinley's administration, big business grew faster than ever. There was no attempt to enforce the Sherman Antitrust Act, and business leaders thought the Act a dead letter. Al-

PRESIDENT THEODORE ROOSEVELT *talking with a train crew.* "*T.R.*" *was a good mixer. He liked people and quickly won their affection. He established a friendlier relation with labor than any President before him.* (Brown Brothers)

most every week saw the formation of another large holding company. The trusts seemed to be above the law and more powerful than Congress. Years later Roosevelt wrote: "When I became President, the question of the *method* by which the United States government was to control the corporations was not yet important. The absolutely vital question was whether the government had power to control them at all."

Roosevelt made up his mind to bring the corporations under control. Soon after becoming President he declared: "It is idle to tell this people that we have not the power to solve such a problem as that of exercising adequate supervision over the great industrial combinations of today. We have the power, and we shall find out the way."

Early in 1902 Roosevelt ordered the Attorney General to start an antitrust suit against the Northern Securities Company, a powerful railroad holding company. Wall Street was surprised and angry. Had not the Supreme Court already decided that the Sherman Antitrust Act did not apply to a holding company? (See page 357.) Would the Supreme Court now reverse itself? For two years business leaders waited to find out. At last the case reached the Supreme Court. By a vote of five to four the Court declared the Northern Securities Company to be an illegal combination. This was a triumph for democratic government. Roosevelt said of it:

> The Northern Securities suit is one of the great achievements of my administration. . . . Through it we emphasized the fact that the most powerful men in this country were held accountable before the law. . . . The success of the Northern Securities case definitely decided the power of the government to deal with all great corporations.

Roosevelt went on to attack other combinations, among them the oil, tobacco, chemical, and meat-packing trusts. Before his administration closed, no less than forty-four antitrust suits were under way.

Roosevelt steps in to end the coal strike. The President soon took part in another kind of contest with big business, this time against the coal trust. The miners of anthracite (hard) coal had serious complaints. Their wages averaged only $560 a year. Their work was dangerous, and no compensation was paid in case of death or injury. They had to live in company houses and buy at high-priced company stores. In 1902 the United Mine Workers asked for recognition of their union, a nine-hour day, a 20 per cent increase in wages, and guarantees that the coal dug would be fairly weighed. When the mine operators refused to discuss these demands, the miners went on strike. The attitude of the mine operators may be seen in their spokesman's reply to a letter urging him to end the strike. He said that the rights and interests of the laboring man would be protected and cared for, not by the labor organizers, but by the Christian men to whom God had given control of the mines. Churchmen and newspaper editors all over the country attacked this statement.

From May until October the miners did not work. It looked as if the nation would face the winter without fuel. The price of coal rose to thirty dollars a ton. Roosevelt stepped in — not, as Cleveland had done in the Pullman strike, to support the employers — but rather to force them to discuss terms. He said he would send soldiers to take over the mines unless the operators came to an agreement with the miners. The result was that the operators agreed to let a board of arbitration settle the dispute. This satisfied the miners, and they went back to work.

The President's action pleased the people. It showed that the powers of the federal government could be used to protect both sides in an industrial dispute. Newspapermen here and abroad praised the President. The London *Times* said:

> In a most quiet and unassuming way the President has done a very big and entirely new thing. We are witnessing not merely the ending of the coal strike, but the definite entry of a powerful government upon a new sphere of operation. . . . Let the Americans stick to their President and strengthen his hand. If there is any living man who can show them the way out of the dangers threatening them, that man is Mr. Roosevelt.

Railway regulation. Roosevelt's biggest fight was to bring the railroads under control. The railroad companies owned one tenth of the nation's wealth. They were so powerful that neither state legislatures nor Congress had succeeded in regulating them. The Interstate Commerce Commission, created in 1887, had practically no power. (See page 395.) After a hard fight Roosevelt pushed through Congress a number of bills to regulate the railroad companies. The Elkins Act of 1903 prohibited rebates (refunds of freight charges) and made the receiving as well as the giving of a rebate punishable. The Hepburn Act of 1906 greatly strengthened the Interstate Commerce Commission and gave it power to reduce unreasonable rates. The Act also prohibited the railroad companies from giving passes to any persons except their employees. This meant that the companies could no longer bribe public officials and newspapermen by supplying free passes to them and their families. These and other acts passed during Roosevelt's administration gave the government real power over the railroads. The "octopus" was at last being brought under control. Still stronger laws would be passed within a few years.

Food and drug legislation. The food and drug industry was next to feel President Roosevelt's "big stick." For several years chemists in state and federal agencies had been investigating the sale of harmful patent medicines and the adulteration of foods. (A food is *adulterated* when it contains impurities.) They found that harmful substances called *preservatives* were commonly mixed with meat, preserves, milk, and butter, in order to keep them from spoiling. It was also found that injurious coal-tar dyes were often added to candy, baked goods, canned goods, and preserves, and further that many widely advertised medicines contained dangerous drugs. The states were trying to regulate the sale of food and drugs, but the job was too big without help from the federal government. Year after year a pure-food bill had been introduced into Congress, but it had never passed. Big business always had fought the proposal as "socialistic" and "destructive of liberty" and had succeeded in blocking it.

In his annual message to Congress in 1905 Roosevelt urged the passage of a national pure-food and drug act. A bill was introduced to require truthful labeling of food and drugs and to prevent the sale of diseased meat, spoiled food, and food containing harmful preservatives and dyes. The Republican leader of the Senate was among those who tried to defeat the bill. He asked:

> Is there anything in the existing condition that makes it the duty of Congress to put the liberty of all the people of the United States in [danger]? . . . Are we going to take up the question as to what a man shall eat and what a man shall drink, and put him under severe penalties if he is eating or drinking something different from what the chemists of the Agricultural Department think desirable?

His argument was unfair, for the bill did not regulate consumers.

The food and drug bill finally passed in spite of fierce opposition. At the President's urging, Congress also passed the Meat Inspection Act. This says that no meat may be shipped from one state to another unless approved by a federal inspector. The familiar words "Government inspected and passed" stamped on meats and printed on the labels of canned meat are there because of this law.

Conservation and reclamation. Roosevelt was keenly interested in *conservation*, that is, making our natural resources last as long as possible. In his first message to Congress he recommended a far-reaching program to protect the nation's natural resources. A short time later Congress passed the Reclamation Act, providing for irrigation of desert areas at the expense of the federal government. Under this Act work soon began on several irrigation projects in the Far West. During

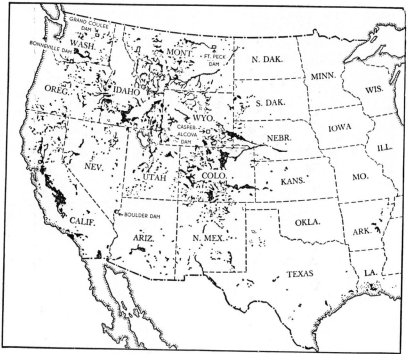

LANDS IRRIGATED UNDER THE RECLAMATION ACT

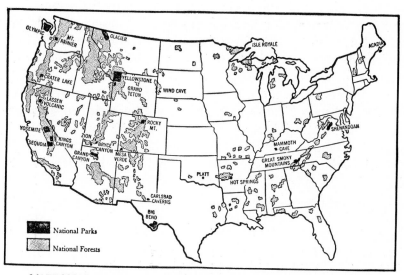

NATIONAL PARKS AND FORESTS OF THE UNITED STATES

ROOSEVELT DAM. *Begun under President Theodore Roosevelt, this great dam in Arizona provides water to irrigate 200,000 acres.* (Courtesy of United States Reclamation Service)

his administration the President set aside one hundred fifty million acres of the public lands to be national forests. This displeased the big lumber companies but was praised by nearly everyone else.

Roosevelt had lawsuits started against those who had obtained government lands by fraud, and as a result the government recovered a number of large tracts of land. He had the Forest Service undertake fire prevention work on a large scale. He started the practice of charging a fair rental for the privilege of grazing sheep and cattle on the public lands. In 1908 he called the state governors to a White House conference on conservation. In these and other ways Roosevelt did a great deal to awaken the public to the need for conservation. This was one of his most valuable and lasting services to the nation.

"T.R." chooses his successor. By 1908 Roosevelt had served two terms — one as McKinley's successor and one in his own right. He had given the country an example of strong presidential leadership. He had voiced the desires of the common people as no President had done since Lincoln. He had vastly strengthened the reform movement. He had won the affection of millions of his countrymen and could doubtless have had another term for the asking. But he decided not to run again. He asked the Republicans to nominate his old friend, William Howard Taft. The Democrats nominated Bryan for the third and last time. With Roosevelt's backing, Taft easily won the election.

Taft as President, 1909–1913. Taft had been in public office since early youth. As a federal judge, then as governor of the Philippines,

"TANGLED." *In writing a tariff bill the various interests pull in different directions.* (Drawn by C. R. MacCauley for the *New York World*, April 5, 1909)

and later as Roosevelt's Secretary of War, he had shown himself able and completely honest. Taft had none of Roosevelt's showmanship. He was cautious, slow-moving, moderate. By contrast with Roosevelt, the public found him too tame.

Taft was eager to continue Roosevelt's policies. In four years his Attorney General brought more suits against the trusts than had been brought in seven and a half years while Roosevelt was President. Taft extended the merit system to many more federal employees. He pushed the conservation program. He supported the Sixteenth Amendment, authorizing an income tax, and the Seventeenth Amendment, providing for the direct election of senators. Congress passed a number of progressive laws which he recommended. Among them were acts increasing the powers of the Interstate Commerce Commission, establishing the parcel-post system and the Postal Savings Bank, creating a separate Department of Labor and a Children's Bureau, and requiring that campaign expenditures of candidates for Congress be made public. Few Presidents have accomplished so much in one term.

In spite of his record, the public came to think of Taft as an extreme conservative and "standpatter." The main reason for this was that the Republican party was splitting into two bitterly hostile groups — the conservatives and the progressives — and Taft tried to co-operate with both. For example, he called a special session of Congress to lower the tariff. Conservative members of the Senate insisted on raising many of the rates and prevented the lowering of any rates that really mattered. The result was the Payne-Aldrich Tariff, which progressives asked the President to veto. Fearing that a veto would split the party wide open, Taft signed the bill and even praised it. This led progressives to call him a tool of selfish business interests. Similar fights between progressives and conservatives occurred throughout his term. Taft's administration was anything but an "Era of Good Feeling."

"T.R." returns from Africa. At the beginning of Taft's term, Roosevelt went abroad — in order, as he said, to give the President a free hand. He spent nearly a year in Africa shooting big game. Then he toured Europe, where he was honored by some of the leading universities and entertained by kings. The American public eagerly read stories of his adventures in the newspapers, which reported everything he did and said. His followers, disappointed in President Taft, began to hope that "T.R." would come back to take up the fight against privilege. A popular ditty expressed this desire:

> Teddy, come home and blow your horn,
> The sheep's in the meadow, the cow's in the corn.
> The boy you left to tend the sheep
> Is under the haystack fast asleep.

The Bull Moose Convention. Early in 1912 Roosevelt announced, "My hat is in the ring," meaning that he would run again for President. He said that Taft was feeble, incompetent, and ungrateful. When the Republican convention met in June, the party steam roller flattened out Roosevelt's supporters and gave the nomination to Taft. Roosevelt called the action "theft."

A few weeks later Roosevelt's followers met again to organize the Progressive party and name him as its candidate. When Roosevelt arrived to accept the nomination, he told reporters he felt like a "bull moose." The new party then took the bull moose as its symbol.

It is said that the Progressive convention was more like a religious revival than a political meeting. Roosevelt ended his speech of acceptance by saying that his party was battling for the Lord. The delegates responded by marching around the hall singing "Onward, Christian Soldiers." The convention closed with another rousing hymn.

The Democrats nominate Woodrow Wilson. The split in the Republican party gave the Democrats an excellent chance of victory. At the Democratic national **convention** conservatives and liberals strug-

WILLIAM HOWARD TAFT. *As President, Taft helped carry many reform measures through Congress. Later he devoted his strength and influence to the promotion of a league to enforce peace. In 1921 he became chief justice of the Supreme Court. His decisions were progressive, for he believed that law is made for man, not man for law.* (Harris and Ewing)

gled for control. Bryan was still the most influential member of the party. Defying conservative Democrats from Wall Street and from Tammany Hall, he threw all his strength to Woodrow Wilson, the liberal governor of New Jersey. Wilson was nominated on the forty-sixth ballot. Bryan, who had never been able to win the Presidency himself, had named the next President.

The campaign of 1912. Of the four parties which took part in the campaign of 1912, three — Progressives, Democrats, and Socialists — had platforms which called for sweeping reforms. Even the Republican platform was more progressive than usual. Of the four candidates, three — Roosevelt, Wilson, and the Socialist, Eugene Debs — were reformers. The fourth candidate, Taft, was, as we have seen, more of a progressive than the public thought. Because of these facts, the campaign has been called "the peak of the Progressive Era."

The campaign was mainly a contest between Roosevelt and Wilson. Wilson received the regular Democratic vote, while the Republican vote was divided between Roosevelt and Taft. Wilson was elected, although he received only 42 per cent of all the votes cast. In addition to winning the Presidency, the Democrats won majorities in both houses of Congress and elected twenty-one state governors. The triumph of the Democratic party in the national election and in so many of the state elections showed that the people were deeply discontented with the party of big business.

Another sign of popular discontent was the large vote for reform candidates. Wilson, Roosevelt, and Debs together obtained over three fourths of the popular vote. Never before in the nation's history had so large a proportion of the voters cast their ballots for reform.

❂ ❂ ❂

To identify: Bull Moose party, Eugene Debs, Meat Inspection Act, Tammany Hall.

To explain or define: adulteration, conservation, preservative, reclamation, standpatter.

SUBJECTS FOR TALKS OR WRITTEN REPORTS

1. Theodore Roosevelt as governor of New York. 2. Theodore Roosevelt as a sportsman and conservationist. 3. Theodore Roosevelt as President. 4. The history of our national forests. 5. The history and work of the national Forest Service. 6. The history of the Bull Moose party. 7. The history of the Children's Bureau. 8. The life and ideas of Eugene Debs. 9. The life of William Howard Taft. 10. The fight for the Sixteenth or Income Tax Amendment.

QUESTIONS FOR UNDERSTANDING THE TEXT

1. How did a reformer first manage to become President? 2. Discuss the qualities that made Theodore Roosevelt so popular. 3. (*a*) Show that Theodore Roosevelt was not a radical. (*b*) Explain what he meant by the "square deal." 4. What was the importance of the Supreme Court decision regarding the Northern Securities Company? 5. Discuss Roosevelt's record as a "trust-buster." 6. (*a*) What conditions led to the coal strike of 1902? (*b*) How did the mine operators feel about the strike? (*c*) What led the operators to agree to let a board of arbitration settle the dispute? 7. (*a*) What evil had resulted from the giving of railroad passes? (*b*) What was done to correct this evil? 8. What was the need for (*a*) the Elkins Act of 1903, (*b*) the Hepburn Act of 1906, (*c*) the Food and Drug Act of 1905, (*d*) the Meat Inspection Act? 9. What argument was used against the passage of the Food and Drug Act? 10. What is meant by the "direct election of senators"? When was this method of election adopted? 11. Show that Taft deserves to be remembered as an able and progressive President. 12. Had Taft followed a less colorful President than "T.R.," do you think he might have been more popular? Explain. 13. (*a*) Tell about the formation of the Bull Moose party. (*b*) How did it lead to the election of a Democratic President? 14. Why has the campaign of 1912 been called "the peak of the Progressive Era"? 15. Wilson was a minority President. What does this mean?

CHAPTER 32

WOODROW WILSON AND THE "NEW FREEDOM"

oodrow Wilson's background and character. Unlike most of our Presidents, Woodrow Wilson was almost a newcomer in politics. He had never held public office until he became governor of New Jersey in 1910. Yet he knew a great deal about government. He had written scholarly books on law and politics. He was an authority on American history and the Constitution, and he had taught these subjects in leading Eastern colleges. He was, perhaps, the greatest scholar our nation has ever chosen for President.

Wilson, who was born in Virginia, came from hardy Scotch-Irish stock. For generations his ancestors had been intellectual men — ministers, teachers, writers. His father was a Presbyterian minister, who brought him up to believe that man's duty is to battle for the right.

After graduating from college and law school, Wilson practiced law for a short time, then decided to be a college teacher. He was a brilliant lecturer, and students flocked to his courses. In 1902 he became president of Princeton. He promptly began to make the university more democratic. His fight against exclusive clubs for rich students attracted public attention. In 1910 he was elected governor of New Jersey and set to work to clean up a corrupt political machine. Up to this time the reform movement had made little progress there. Under Wilson's leadership the legislature passed important reform measures, including a direct primary bill, a workmen's compensation bill, and a plan for regulating public utilities. Liberals throughout the nation applauded his record as governor. They said he would make a good President. When Bryan supported him, Wilson won the Democratic nomination for President.

Wilson's gifted mind, scholarly training, and high ideals lifted him above the common run of men. He was often thought cold and reserved, but his close friends found him warmhearted and deeply interested in people and their problems. He did not try to appeal to peo-

WOODROW WILSON. *In appearance President Wilson was impressive and attractive, "with eyes that shifted suddenly from merriment to severity," and a jaw that expressed his strong will.* (Harris and Ewing)

ple's emotions so much as to their reason. This may explain why he was never so popular as Andrew Jackson and Theodore Roosevelt. Yet he understood ordinary people and believed in them. He hated special privilege. He thought that farmers and working people and little businessmen should have greater influence in the government. Of all our Presidents, he was the most like Thomas Jefferson.

Wilson preaches the "new freedom." Wilson's campaign speeches had a poetic quality like Lincoln's. Those who listened to him felt his sincerity and his fairness. They were inspired by his faith in justice, freedom, and democracy. They were thrilled when he said that the time had come for a "new freedom" of opportunity, and when he promised that his administration would be run in the interest of the many, not the few.

Wilson's inaugural address shows his deep sympathy with working people. He spoke in moving words of the nation's traditions of liberty and of its great wealth, but added:

. . . evil has come with the good. . . . We have been proud of
our industrial achievements, but we have not hitherto stopped thoughtfully enough to count the human cost . . . the fearful physical and
spiritual cost to the men and women and children upon whom the
dead weight and burden of it all has fallen. . . . The great government we loved has too often been made use of for private and selfish
purposes, and those who used it have forgotten the people. . . . We
shall restore, not destroy. . . . This is not a day of triumph; it is a day
of dedication. . . . Men's hearts wait upon us; men's lives hang in the
balance; men's hopes call upon us to say what we will do.

In his speech he listed the things that ought to be changed. He mentioned the high tariff, a banking and money system which failed to provide enough credit, poor labor conditions, and the destruction of natural resources. He declared that the government should be "put at the
service of humanity" in safeguarding the health and welfare of its
people. These were fine-sounding phrases, but could a college professor with little experience in politics manage to get them written
into law?

Wilson's fight for tariff reduction. The President quickly called a
special session of Congress. When it met, he addressed it in person instead of sending a written message to be read by a clerk. This was a
return to the custom followed by Washington and John Adams. Since
Wilson's time most Presidents have not followed his example.

In his first message Wilson urged Congress to reduce the tariff.
Ever since the War between North and South we had had a high tariff.
Both Cleveland and Taft tried to get Congress to lower the duties, and
both failed. Theodore Roosevelt avoided this question altogether.

Following Wilson's message, the House passed the Underwood bill,
which reduced many duties and dropped some altogether. But when
the Senate took up the measure, swarms of lobbyists appeared. A *lobbyist* is a person who tries to persuade members of a legislature to vote
in a certain way. Nearly every large industry sends lobbyists to Washington. When a tariff is being considered, lobbyists from a particular
industry go to work on congressmen from districts where that industry is important. In this way every congressman is made to feel organized pressure from the industries in his district.

Under pressure from the lobbyists, the senators got ready to make
over the Underwood bill so that the duties would be as high as ever.
They used a method called *logrolling* — each senator agrees to vote for
the duties wanted by other senators if these others will vote for the du-

"OUR CHOKED-UP HOME MARKET." *In this cartoon Uncle Sam sits behind a high tariff wall, surrounded by heaps of American products which the home market cannot use, while in the foreground are unemployed American workmen.* (Drawn by Louis Dalrymple for *Puck*, June 5, 1889)

ties he wants. The senators from sugar-growing sections, for example, promise to vote for a high duty on plate glass if the senators from the sections where plate glass is manufactured will vote for a high duty on sugar. In this way each senator gets what he wants for his own district. The resulting tariff bill is pretty sure to place high duties on everything produced in the United States.

Wilson was always a fighter for what he believed to be the right. He did not intend to let the lobbyists write the new tariff bill. He took action in a way no other President had ever tried. He wrote a public letter pointing out that lobbyists were at work to prevent a reduction of the tariff. He said that the people at large have no lobby to protect their interests. The letter was like a bombshell. The Senate felt obliged to appoint an investigating committee. For a while the lobbyists were checked. The Senate then passed the Underwood bill, with few changes. For the first time in over fifty years, the average duty was lowered.

Adoption of the income tax. It was thought that reduction of the tariff might mean some loss of revenue. To make up for this, Congress adopted a tax on incomes. This action was possible because the Sixteenth, or Income Tax, Amendment had been added to the Constitution earlier in the year. The first income tax rates were low, ranging from 1 per cent on incomes of $3,000 a year to 6 per cent on those above $500,000. Yet adoption of the tax was a great victory for the progressive movement. Within a few years the income tax was to furnish most of the revenues of the federal government and give the nation a substantial slice of the vast fortunes created by big business.

Reform of the banking and money system. The system of national banks established during the War between North and South had certain weaknesses. In the first place, most of the nation's bank deposits piled up in New York City, leaving the rest of the country without enough money to supply the needs of businessmen and farmers. In the second place, there was no satisfactory way to expand the currency (that is, to increase the amount of money in circulation) at times when more money was needed. Every fall, when crops were going to market, there was a scramble for money, and interest rates rose sharply. Panics often resulted. For years Western and Southern farmers had been calling for reform, as in their fight for free silver.

The large bankers had a plan for overcoming these difficulties. They wanted a powerful central bank under their own control. Progressives did not like this plan. Bryan, who had led the fight for free silver, insisted that the government ought to control credit. President Wilson sided with him, saying in a message to Congress, "Control must be public, not private . . . so that the banks may be the [servants], not the masters, of business."

After a long debate Congress passed the Federal Reserve Act. It called for twelve Federal Reserve Banks under the control of the government. The country was divided into twelve Federal Reserve Districts, each having one Federal Reserve Bank. The Act gave the South and West better bank services and easier credit than they had ever had. The Act also provided methods for increasing or decreasing the amount of money in circulation whenever such a change is needed. The Democratic party had won a victory over the "money trust" which would have delighted even Andrew Jackson.

New antitrust laws. President Roosevelt and President Taft had tried their best to enforce the Sherman Antitrust Act. In spite of their efforts, big business continued to get bigger. Wilson in a campaign speech said:

"WILSON'S WELCOME."
The cartoonist ridicules Wilson for backing the Underwood Tariff Bill, on the ground that lowering the tariff will flood the United States with cheap foreign goods. (Drawn by Hy Gage for the *Philadelphia Press*, May, 1913)

American industry is not free as it was once free . . . the man with only a little capital is finding it harder to get into the field, more and more impossible to compete with the big fellow. Why? Because the laws of the country do not prevent the strong from crushing the weak.

As soon as Congress completed its work on the tariff and the banking system, President Wilson asked for laws to regulate big business. Congress spent most of 1914 considering this legislation, then passed the Clayton Antitrust Act and the Federal Trade Commission Act.

The Clayton Act made illegal a number of unfair practices likely to prevent competition. It also provided that a person injured by such practices might ask the new Federal Trade Commission to investigate. This made it easier for the small businessman to get help before the large corporation had destroyed his business. The Clayton Act stated that antitrust laws did not apply to labor unions, and it attempted to limit the use of injunctions in labor disputes. However, these parts of the Act were soon weakened by the courts and gave labor almost no protection.

The Federal Trade Commission Act set up a Federal Trade Commission of five members to be appointed by the President. Its duties are to investigate the business practices of corporations (except railroads and banks) doing business across state lines and to hear complaints of unfair methods of competition. The Commission accomplishes most of its work without going to the courts. It has found that most corporations are willing to co-operate with it. By holding conferences with representatives of an industry, it works out rules of fair play to govern business practices in that industry. It then orders firms which break these rules to stop doing so. If the firm continues the unfair practice, the Commission may appeal to the courts. Some of the practices considered unfair by the Commission are misbranding of goods, bribery, adulteration of goods, false advertising, and false statements about competitors. The Commission also disapproves of too close an imitation of a competitor's trade name or package by a rival company.

Labor and farm legislation. Labor and the farmers were not forgotten. Congress passed two laws planned to end child labor in industry, but the Supreme Court declared each of them unconstitutional. The La Follette Seamen's Act of 1915 regulated conditions of labor on American ships, putting a stop to evils under which sailors had always suffered. This Act has been called "a charter of liberties for America's seamen." The Adamson Act of 1916 established an eight-hour day for workers on interstate railroads. The Federal Farm Loan Act (1916) created twelve Federal Land Banks to lend money on farm mortgages. A farmer who borrows money from a Land Bank pays a moderate rate of interest and repays the loan over a long period of years.

Wilson's reform program is halted. Wilson's program of reform could be carried no farther because of the gathering war clouds. In three years he had pushed through more legislation of importance than any President since Lincoln. This achievement was made possible in part because of the groundwork laid by Theodore Roosevelt and by Taft. In part it was made possible by his strong leadership of Congress and of public opinion.

Wilson a "strong" President. Like Andrew Jackson and Theodore Roosevelt, Wilson gave the nation an example of strong presidential leadership. He believed that it is the President's duty to propose legislation and to work actively for its passage. Years before he had written: "The President is at liberty . . . to be as big a man as he can. His capacity will set the limit. He has no means of compelling Congress except through public opinion." How true these words are was shown by Wilson's own term of office.

Results of the progressive movement. The progressive movement reached its height in the early years of Wilson's administration. Then

"GOVERNMENT CARE VS. GOVERNMENT NEGLECT." *The law protects young fish, oysters, lobsters, livestock, and trees; why not young human beings?* (Drawn by Joseph Keppler, Jr. for *Puck,* February 15, 1913)

it was interrupted by World War I and did not regain strength for many years. Let us see what it accomplished in the twenty years between 1896 and 1916, which we have called the "Progressive Era."

First, the progressive movement gave the people more control over the government through such devices as the secret ballot, direct primary, publicity for campaign expenditures, and the popular election of senators. It was now much easier than before for the public to control its officials. The political boss and his political machine did not disappear, but they had to work much harder in order to keep their power.

Second, the progressive movement changed the attitude of big business. Business leaders no longer paid no attention to public opinion, as in the 1880's and 1890's. Instead, they tried to win public approval by showing that they were serving the public and by looking after the welfare of their workers. Some employers provided clubrooms, gymnasiums, athletic fields, medical care, and other benefits for their employees. Many employers established for their workers clubs known as company unions, which were intended to promote good relations with their men and to keep out organizers of independent labor unions.

Third, the progressive movement brought business partly under control. That business could be regulated by government was now an accepted principle. The large corporations had been taught that they

PRESIDENT WILSON *signing the Child Labor Bill.* *The measure was later declared unconstitutional.* (Photo by Harris and Ewing. Reproduced from *The Pageant of America.* Copyright Yale University Press)

could not do as they pleased. Few trusts had been dissolved, but the Federal Trade Commission had begun to correct many abuses in their methods of doing business.

Fourth, city and state governments were promoting the public welfare in many ways scarcely dreamed of before the Progressive Era. The larger cities now used tax money for hospitals, clinics, playgrounds, libraries, evening schools, and other public benefits. The state governments were trying much more earnestly to regulate bad conditions of labor and to protect women and children. The idea was growing that the purpose of government is not just to keep order, but rather to do everything possible to serve the people.

Fifth, the powers of the national government had been increased. This came about because the states could not deal successfully with some of the problems caused by modern industry. It was now understood that the national government should supervise the railroads, the telephone and telegraph companies, and other corporations doing business across state lines, and that it should also control banking and credit. The national government was now taking steps to protect consumers from impure and wrongly labeled foods and drugs, to regulate labor conditions on ships and on railroads, and to provide easier credit for farmers. The old fear of a strong national government seemed to be passing away.

The nation had, indeed, made great strides since the days when the Populists were thought to be dangerous radicals. Many of the reforms demanded by the Populists, and other reforms, too, had been achieved.

To identify: Federal Land Bank, Federal Reserve Act, Federal Trade Commission.

To explain or define: company union, lobbyist, logrolling.

SUBJECTS FOR TALKS OR WRITTEN REPORTS

1. Woodrow Wilson as president of Princeton. 2. Woodrow Wilson as governor of New Jersey. How did he happen to be elected governor? 3. The work of the Federal Trade Commission. 4. Labor conditions at sea before passage of the La Follette Seamen's Act. How the Act improved these conditions. 5. The Federal Land Banks. Where they get their money. How farmers may borrow money from them. How these banks are controlled. 6. Why labor leaders dislike company unions. 7. The ways in which my community promotes the public welfare. The year when each of these services was started.

QUESTIONS FOR UNDERSTANDING THE TEXT

1. In what ways was Woodrow Wilson well prepared for the Presidency? In what ways was he not well prepared? 2. How did Wilson become nationally known before his nomination? 3. What did Wilson mean by the "new freedom"? 4. What do lobbyists do when a tariff bill is being considered? 5. Tell about Wilson's fight for tariff reduction. 6. Give an example of logrolling in Congress. 7. (*a*) For what reason did Congress adopt a tax on incomes? (*b*) Why was this important? 8. (*a*) State two weaknesses of the banking system established during the War between North and South. (*b*) How did the bankers want to overcome these difficulties? (*c*) What did Wilson think of their plan? 9. (*a*) Give the main features of the Federal Reserve System. (*b*) What sections of the country received the greatest benefit? 10. (*a*) Did the Sherman Antitrust Act check the growth of big business? Explain. (*b*) In passing the Clayton Act and the Federal Trade Commission Act did Congress try to break up business combinations or only to regulate big corporations? Explain. (*c*) How did these Acts help the small businessman? 11. Name some of the practices considered unfair by the Federal Trade Commission. 12. During Wilson's administration what was done for labor? For the farmers? 13. (*a*) How did Wilson manage to accomplish so many reforms? (*b*) What halted Wilson's reform program? 14. What is meant by saying that Jackson, Theodore Roosevelt, and Wilson were

"strong" Presidents? 15. Summarize the accomplishments of the progressive movement in regard to the following: (*a*) popular control of the government, (*b*) the attitude of big business toward the public, (*c*) the regulation of business, (*d*) the growth of large corporations, (*e*) the use of tax money by city and state governments, (*f*) the fear of a strong national government.

ACTIVITIES FOR UNIT SEVEN

1. Continue work on the classbook, *American Hall of Fame*, and on the history of your community.
2. In a map talk show the states which were first to adopt various reforms. Does any section of the country seem to be more progressive than other sections? If so, how do you account for it?
3. Write a report on the decline of customs and the repeal of laws that unfairly restrict women.
4. Write a report on the history of any reform in which you are interested.
5. Draw a cartoon for or against one of the following: woman suffrage, a child labor amendment to the Constitution, the city manager plan, minimum-wage laws, a strong food and drugs law, the use of tax money to provide public recreation, public ownership of electric light, gas, and water companies.
6. Draw a series of sketches on the progress of public education since the beginning of the Progressive Era. Write a brief explanation of each sketch.
7. Appoint a committee to interview a sample of the grownups in your community. Ask each one whether or not he or she voted in the last election and if not, why not. Tabulate the results and report in your school or local newspaper.
8. Visit one or more near-by government housing projects. Arrange in advance to meet the manager and discuss the housing situation in your community.
9. Appoint a committee to interview well-informed persons in your community on needed local reforms. You might, for instance, include the mayor, the editor of the local newspaper, your principal, and so on. Report the results to the class and discuss ways in which you could work now, and after you leave school, to bring these reforms about.

READINGS FOR UNIT SEVEN

(Stars indicate the easier books)

GENERAL ACCOUNTS

Antin, Mary. *They Who Knock at Our Gates.* Houghton Mifflin.
Chamberlain, John. *Farewell to Reform.* Dav-

Faulkner, H. M. *Quest for Social Justice*, 1898–1914. (A. L. S.)
Groves, Ernest R., editor. *The American Woman*. Greenberg.
Howland, Harold. *Theodore Roosevelt and His Times*. (Chronicles)
Kent, Frank. *The Great Game of Politics*. Doubleday, Doran.
Ogg, Frederic. *National Progress*. (A. N. S.)
Regier, Cornelius. *The Era of the Muckrakers*. University of North
  Carolina Press.
Riis, Jacob A. *The Battle with the Slum*. Macmillan.
Roberts, Peter. *The New Immigration*. Macmillan.
Steiner, Edward A. *On the Trail of the Immigrant*. Revell.
Sullivan, Mark. *Our Times*. Vols. I and II. Scribner's.

BIOGRAPHY

Addams, Jane. *Twenty Years at Hull House*. Macmillan.
Asbury, Herbert. *Carry Nation*. Knopf. (The crusade for prohibition)
Charnwood, Lord. *Theodore Roosevelt*. Atlantic.
Ford, H. J. *Woodrow Wilson, the Man and His Work*. Appleton.
Fuess, C. M. *Carl Schurz, Reformer*. Dodd, Mead.
*Hagedorn, Hermann. *The Boys' Life of Theodore Roosevelt*. Harper.
Hoover, Ike. *Forty-Two Years in the White House*. Houghton Mifflin.
Pringle, Henry F. *Theodore Roosevelt*. Blue Ribbon.
Riis, Jacob A. *The Making of an American*. Macmillan.
Shaw, Anna Howard. *Story of a Pioneer*. Harper. (Woman suffrage)
Steffens, Lincoln. *Autobiography*. Harcourt, Brace.
Werner, M. R. *Bryan*. Harcourt, Brace.
*Wise, Winifred E. *Jane Addams of Hull House*. Harcourt, Brace.

FICTION

Adams, Henry. *Democracy, an American Novel*. Hall. (Corruption in
  Washington)
Atherton, Gertrude. *Senator North*. Dodd, Mead. (Political problems)
Churchill, Winston. *Coniston*. Macmillan. (A political boss)
——. *Mr. Crewe's Career*. Macmillan. (Corporations in politics)
Quick, Herbert. *The Hawkeye*. Bobbs-Merrill. (Politics in Iowa)
Sinclair, Upton. *The Jungle*. Sinclair. (Picture of misery in Chicago)
Updegraff, R. R. *Captains in Conflict*. Shaw. (Big business, 1890–1914)
White, W. A. *A Certain Rich Man*. Macmillan. (Business, 1890–1914)
Wilson, Charles M. *Rabble Rouser*. Longmans. (Arkansas politics)

UNIT EIGHT
THE UNITED STATES AS A
WORLD POWER

The Spanish-American War brought the United States distant possessions and helped Americans to see that their country was a world power — that is, a power able to influence international affairs. Following the war, the United States worked out ways of governing its new possessions. It also added to its responsibilities as a world power by building the Panama Canal.

For a long time the United States has had a strong interest in Caribbean America and has been determined that no unfriendly nation should set foot there. When the Caribbean countries owed money to European bankers and could not pay their debts, the United States sometimes stepped in to straighten out their affairs. This meddling was meant well but caused our country's small neighbors to fear us. To win their good will, the United States has recently adopted the "Good Neighbor" policy.

Although the United States was a world power, Americans wanted to stay out of European affairs. When war swept over Europe in 1914, the United States tried to be strictly neutral and yet sell war supplies to the Allied nations. Before long, German attacks on American ships forced the United States into the war. America helped the tired Allies win the war; then tried to turn its back on Europe, and, in so doing, lost the peace.

EXPANSION OF THE UNITED STATES, 1867–1916

CHAPTER 33

THE UNITED STATES GAINS AN EMPIRE

T*he purchase of Alaska, 1867.* We had scarcely gained possession of Oregon, California, and the great Southwest when some Americans started looking around for additional territory. But until after the slavery question was settled, no new lands were added to the United States.

William Seward, who served as Secretary of State under Lincoln and Johnson, was eager to add new territory to the United States. He tried unsuccessfully to persuade Congress to buy the Danish West Indies (the Virgin Islands) and the Dominican Republic on the island of Haiti. In the face of strong opposition he did persuade Congress to purchase Alaska from Russia.

At the time, Americans knew nothing of Alaska's rich resources of gold, copper, coal, timber, and fish. They scornfully called the territory "Seward's Icebox" or "Johnson's Polar-Bear Garden." They thought the purchase price of $7,200,000 far too high, although it was less than 2 cents an acre. Most of the newspapers made fun of Mr. Seward. The *New York Herald* published a make-believe advertisement:

> Cash! Cash! Cash! — Cash paid for castoff territory. Best price given for old colonies, North or South. Any impoverished monarchs retiring from the colonization business may find a good purchaser by addressing W. H. S. [Seward], Post Office, Washington, D. C.

Today we know that Seward made a wonderful bargain. Alaska is as large as the thirteen original states, and nearly three-fourths as large as the Louisiana Purchase. It has already yielded gold worth many times the price paid for the territory, and it still contains much gold. Its copper deposits were nearly as valuable as its gold deposits. The fish caught in one year in Alaskan rivers are worth more than Russia received for the territory.

The Samoan Islands. To provide harbors and coaling stations for American ships, the United States Navy sometimes took possession of small islands in the Pacific. In 1867, for instance, an American naval officer took the uninhabited Midway Islands — tiny dots of land a thousand miles west of Hawaii. Five years later another naval commander visited one of the Samoan Islands about five thousand miles southwest of California. He made arrangements with a native chieftain for American control of the splendid harbor of Pago Pago. In 1899 the United States got outright possession of all the Samoan Islands except the two largest.

Annexation of the Hawaiian Islands, 1898. Our interest in the Hawaiian Islands goes back to the 1790's, when ships owned by New England merchants began to stop there on the way to the Far East. In 1820 the first band of American missionaries went to Hawaii, where they won many natives to the Christian faith. Before long hundreds of American whalers were using the islands as a base, and hundreds of American planters were settling there to raise sugar. American influence was so strong that Honolulu became like a New England town. In 1842 the United States announced that the Monroe Doctrine applied to Hawaii and that no foreign power would be allowed to interfere with Hawaiian affairs.

Most Americans knew little about the "Island Paradise," as Hawaii was called, until 1893, when a revolution broke out and Queen Liliuokalani was overthrown. The new Hawaiian government asked to be annexed to the United States. President Harrison had a treaty of annexation drawn up, but before the Senate could ratify it, Cleveland became President a second time. Cleveland was suspicious about the revolution and sent a special commissioner to Hawaii to look into it. The commissioner reported that the revolution had been led by American residents and that they had had the help of United States marines. He also reported that the natives did not wish annexation. Cleveland then withdrew the treaty. Republicans were angered by this action, which they called a "betrayal of American interests." When McKinley became President, he drew up a new treaty, and in 1898, during the Spanish-American War, Hawaii was annexed by the United States.

American interests in Cuba. Before the War between North and South, the Southern planters often talked of some way to get control of Cuba and bring it into the Union as a slave state. In 1848 President Polk offered Spain one hundred million dollars for the island, but Spain refused to sell. After we abolished slavery, the United States lost interest in buying the island. Before long, however, rich Americans be-

WHALING OFF THE HAWAIIAN ISLANDS. *New England whalers in the Pacific often used Hawaii as a base.* (From the painting by Thomas Birch, 1838. Courtesy of Joseph S. Martin, New Bedford)

gan to invest large sums in the sugar and tobacco industries of Cuba. By 1896 they had invested about fifty million dollars there. Trade between the United States and Cuba grew until it amounted to over one hundred million dollars a year. But the United States was interested in Cuba for other reasons than trade and investment. Because of Cuba's position close to our shores we could not let it fall into the hands of a strong power who might use it as a base for attacking us. Our government, therefore, always kept an eye upon it.

Revolution in Cuba. The Spanish government of Cuba was corrupt and cruel. It existed not for the benefit of the people but for the benefit of the ruling class. The people were very poor; they were heavily taxed. They had no voice in their government and were imprisoned if they complained about their rulers. They had to support a large standing army, the purpose of which was to keep them from rebelling against the government.

A revolt broke out in 1868 but was put down after a struggle lasting ten years. Conditions went from bad to worse. In 1895 another rebellion started. The leader of the revolt hoped to force the United States to interfere in order to protect property owned by American investors. He ordered his men to destroy plantations, tear up railways, and burn factories.

A CUBAN CONCENTRA-
TION CAMP IN HAVANA.
*The terrible suffering in these
camps led to protests from the
United States government.*
(Drawn by W. A. Rogers for
Harper's Weekly, April 2,
1898)

In 1896 Spain sent General Weyler to Cuba to put down the rebellion. He locked up thousands of Cuban civilians in concentration camps to keep them from giving aid to the rebels. Most of the prisoners were women and children. The camps were horribly unclean and overcrowded, and the prisoners had little food. Half of them perished from disease and hunger.

American newspapers clamor for war. From the very beginning, Americans sympathized with the Cubans in their struggle for independence. When news came of the suffering in the concentration camps, many felt that the United States should go to the aid of the Cubans. Some of our newspapers demanded that an American army be sent to Cuba.

At the time, Hearst of the *New York Journal* and Pulitzer of the *New York World* were having a race to secure readers. Their reporters hunted for stories to startle and attract the public, and the news was often "doctored" to make it more exciting. The trouble in Cuba seemed made to their order. They played up stories of Spanish cruelty. They made much of the destruction of American property on the island, while glossing over the fact that most of the damage was done by the revolutionists. They called General Weyler a "human hyena," a "mad dog," a "butcher." An example of the sensational style of the news reports from Cuba is the following dispatch printed in the *World:*

> Blood on the roadsides, blood in the fields, blood on the doorsteps, blood, blood, blood! The old, the young, the weak, the crippled — all are butchered without mercy. . . . Is there no nation wise enough, brave enough, and strong enough to restore peace in this blood-smitten land?

Judging from newspaper sales, the American people liked the sensational methods of Hearst and Pulitzer. The circulation of their "yellow journals" climbed and climbed. This led many other papers to imitate their methods and buy their stories. Thus the clamor for war with Spain spread over the whole country.

"Remember the Maine." McKinley became President in March, 1897. Soon after, his Secretary of State sent a note to Spain protesting against Weyler's cruelty and the failure of the Spanish government to protect American lives and property in Cuba. The Spanish government recalled Weyler, sent a more merciful governor in his place, and promised to give Cuba self-government. This did not satisfy the Cubans, for they wanted full independence. However, the new governor set to work to improve conditions in the island, and the revolution seemed to be dying down.

Early in 1898 there was a riot in Havana between revolutionists and loyalists. This led our government to send the battleship *Maine* to Havana harbor on what was described as a friendly visit. The real purpose was to protect American lives and property in case of further rioting. Loyal Spaniards resented the sending of the battleship; it looked to them like a threat from the United States to use force to help the revolutionists.

For several weeks the *Maine* lay at anchor in Havana. Then, on the night of February 15, 1898, she suddenly blew up, with a loss of 260 officers and men. The captain of the vessel, realizing that Americans would think that Spain had blown up the ship, telegraphed to Washington: "Public opinion should [wait] until further report." Public opinion did not wait. The yellow journals flooded the country with war extras. The *Journal* shrieked in big headlines, "The warship *Maine* was split in two by an enemy's secret infernal machine." War fever swept over the country, and Congress unanimously voted fifty million dollars for war preparations.

The facts about the sinking of the *Maine* are still unknown. American investigators, who examined the hull, reported that the explosion was due to an underwater mine, but Spanish authorities insisted that the explosion took place inside the ship. Thirteen years later the hull was raised and examined by American naval experts. Most of them decided that the explosion was caused by a mine, yet several thought that it was due, as the Spaniards said, to some internal cause. We shall probably never know what produced the explosion. Today it seems unthinkable that the Spanish government had anything to do with it, for Spain was trying desperately to avoid war with the United States. It is possible that revolutionists were responsible, believing that destruction of the ship would lead the United States to declare war on Spain. Most Americans at the time thought that Spain had deliberately blown up our battleship. From one end of the country to the other the cry arose, "Remember the *Maine!*" The people demanded war.

Negotiations with Spain. The nation's businessmen, except for the small group who had investments in Cuba, were almost solidly for peace. President McKinley wanted peace. He tried hard to settle the Cuban problem by diplomacy. Three weeks after the sinking of the *Maine* he asked Spain to close the concentration camps and declare an armistice in Cuba. The Spanish cabinet agreed to close the camps immediately and promised to arrange an armistice as soon as Spanish public opinion would allow. Our minister to Madrid cabled, "I hope that nothing will be done to humiliate Spain, as I am satisfied that the present government is going . . . as fast and as far as it can."

The American people were in no mood to wait. They wanted both to free Cuba and to have revenge for the loss of the *Maine*. Bryan and other Democratic leaders urged war. In the President's own party a group of warlike young men taunted him for his patience toward Spain. Theodore Roosevelt is reported to have said, "McKinley has no more backbone than a chocolate eclair." Congressmen of both parties joined in the clamor against Spain. A representative from Maine declared, "Every congressman has two or three newspapers in his district — most of them written in red ink . . . and shouting for blood."

A group of Republican congressmen threatened to turn against the administration if it did not go to war. The pressure for war became so strong that McKinley could no longer resist. All at once he decided to lay the whole question before Congress. He wrote Congress a message asking for authority to use the Army and Navy to restore order in Cuba. The day before sending the message he received a note from

ADMIRAL GEORGE DEWEY *at Manila Bay. Dewey led his little fleet of four cruisers and three smaller ships into the Bay early on May 1, 1898. There he easily destroyed the old-fashioned Spanish ships. This was the first blow struck in the Spanish-American War.* (From the painting by Zogbaum, owned by Mrs. Margaret G. Blue. Courtesy of United States National Museum)

Spain promising to stop the fighting in Cuba, to call a Cuban parliament, and to do practically anything else we might ask. He did not make the note public and barely mentioned it to Congress. For this he has been severely criticized. However, it is very likely that Congress would have gone to war, anyway, to set Cuba free.

War is declared. On April 19, 1898, just a few days after receiving the President's message, Congress passed a joint resolution which (1) declared Cuba free, (2) demanded Spain's withdrawal, (3) directed the President to enforce this demand with the Army and Navy, and (4) stated that the United States had no intention of annexing Cuba. This amounted to declaring war on Spain.

Congressmen were so enthusiastic that groups of them in the lobbies of the Capitol sang "The Battle Hymn of the Republic," "Dixie," and "Hang General Weyler to a Sour Apple Tree as We Go Marching On."

Dewey at Manila. The United States had a navy of moderate size. It was modern and well managed. When war began, the Pacific squadron was at Hong Kong under command of Commodore George Dewey. He promptly received orders to go to the Philippine Islands and destroy or capture Spain's Asiatic fleet. On May 1 Dewey won the Battle of Manila Bay, destroying the Spanish men-of-war with the loss of only one American sailor and with no damage to our ships. He then settled down to blockade Manila. When American troops arrived a few weeks later, they easily captured the city.

The fall of Santiago. Soon after the declaration of war a Spanish fleet commanded by Admiral Cervera started across the Atlantic. Wild rumors spread that American coastal cities might be bombarded. Learning that an American fleet was on the lookout for him, Cervera took refuge in the harbor of Santiago in the southeastern part of Cuba. Soon after, he was blockaded by the American fleet.

In June an American army of seventeen thousand men landed near Santiago. One by one it captured the forts defending the city. Most of the soldiers were regulars, but there was one regiment of volunteer cavalry known as the "Rough Riders." Lieutenant Colonel Theodore Roosevelt won fame when he led this regiment to capture San Juan hill.

Admiral Cervera knew that if Santiago fell, his ships would be bombarded from the heights until they sank. He determined to make a dash for freedom, that the fleet might at least go down fighting. His vessels were completely outclassed by the American vessels and were destroyed one after another as they sailed from the harbor. Ten days later Santiago surrendered. A force under General Miles then occupied Puerto Rico. Spain asked for peace. On August 13 the fighting stopped.

The treaty of peace. The peace treaty was written at Paris. By its terms Cuba was made independent, Puerto Rico and Guam (a small island in the distant Pacific) were given to the United States, and Spain agreed to accept twenty million dollars for the Philippines. Spain did not wish to sell the Philippines; she gave them up under protest, knowing she was too weak to resist.

Many senators denounced the plan to annex the Philippines. They said it was tyranny to take over millions of unwilling people. Besides, it was against the spirit of the Declaration of Independence for the United States to rule lands which must always remain colonies. In addition, they argued, the United States would have to keep up a powerful navy to defend them. This would be expensive and might lead to foreign wars.

Other senators claimed that it was our duty to carry civilization and Christianity to our "brown brothers," the Filipinos. In the spirit of Kipling, they said the United States should

"IF THE WAR BRING NOTH-
ING ELSE, *for This We Are
Thankful."* *The Spanish-American War united the North and
the South and led to very cordial relations with England.*
(From the *New York Herald*)

Take up the White Man's burden,
  Send forth the best ye breed;
Go bind your sons to exile
  To serve your captives' need.

They pointed out, too, that if we returned the islands to Spain, it was likely that either Japan or Germany would soon seize them, and in that case the islanders might never gain their freedom. They also argued that the islands would be a convenient base for trade with China and other parts of the Far East. President McKinley favored annexation.

The Senate debated the treaty for weeks. Ratification looked doubtful. Then William Jennings Bryan came to Washington. He urged his followers to support the treaty so that the United States could end the war, get control of the Philippines, and grant the Filipinos independence. The treaty was finally ratified with only one vote to spare.

Results of the war. The war had a number of important results. *First,* it made the United States an empire. This meant the nation must take on the difficult problem of governing colonies. *Second,* it led to the permanent strengthening of the Army and the Navy, for the United States must be ready to defend its distant possessions. *Third,* the war convinced everybody of the necessity for building a canal across the isthmus connecting North and South America. This was brought home when the battleship *Oregon,* ordered from the Pacific coast to Cuba early in the war, required sixty-eight days to make the journey. *Fourth,* the struggle led to friendlier feelings for Great Britain, since the British celebrated American victories almost as their own, and discouraged other nations from going to the aid of Spain. *Fifth,* the war led Americans to realize that their country was a world power — a power which could play an important part in international affairs.

To identify: Admiral Cervera, Commodore Dewey, Hearst, Pulitzer, Rough Riders, William Seward.

SUBJECTS FOR TALKS OR WRITTEN REPORTS

1. The people and resources of Alaska. 2. The history of Hawaii since Americans began to go there. 3. Life in Samoa. 4. The revolutionary movement in Cuba from 1868 to 1898. 5. The story of the "Rough Riders." 6. How Dewey succeeded in destroying the Spanish fleet. How did it happen that he was ready to sail at once from Hong Kong to Manila? 7. Weaknesses in our army and our supply system shown in the Spanish-American War. What was done to correct them. 8. The battle against tropical diseases in Cuba during the Spanish-American War.

QUESTIONS FOR UNDERSTANDING THE TEXT

1. (*a*) What did most Americans think of Secretary of State Seward's plan for buying the Danish West Indies, the Dominican Republic, and Alaska? (*b*) What part of his plan was carried out? 2. Was Alaska worth the price paid for it? Explain. 3. How did the United States obtain the Midway Islands? Of what use are they? 4. Why did we take control of Pago Pago in Samoa? 5. How did Americans become interested in the Hawaiian Islands? 6. Why was President Cleveland unwilling to annex Hawaii? 7. (*a*) Why did American planters want to get control of Cuba? (*b*) When did we lose interest in buying the island? 8. Give several reasons for American interest in Cuba during the 1880's and 1890's. 9. Why was so much American property in Cuba destroyed during the revolution that broke out in 1895? 10. What conditions helped to arouse American sympathy for the Cubans in 1896? 11. What steps did the Spanish government take in answer to President McKinley's note protesting against conditions in Cuba? 12. (*a*) Why was the battleship *Maine* sent to Havana? (*b*) What happened to it? (*c*) How did this help bring about war with Spain? 13. Do you think the Spanish-American War could have been prevented? Explain. 14. How did we get possession of the Philippines? 15. (*a*) Why did the battleship *Oregon* rush to Cuba? (*b*) How long did the journey take? (*c*) What lesson did this teach? 16. State the terms of the peace treaty with Spain. 17. (*a*) Why did some senators oppose annexing the Philippines? (*b*) What were the arguments for annexation ? 18. State the principal results of the Spanish-American War.

CHAPTER 34

GOVERNING OUR POSSESSIONS

puzzling new problem. When rejoicing quieted down after our easy victory over Spain, Americans realized that almost overnight their country had become an empire. There were puzzling new questions to be decided. What was the United States to do with its far-flung possessions, especially Puerto Rico, Hawaii, and the Philippines? Should they be taken into the Union; should they be kept permanently as colonies; or should they be given their independence? If we kept them, should their people be made citizens of the United States? Were they to have the same liberties and privileges as other United States citizens?

Americans disagreed over these questions. In the presidential campaign of 1900 the leading issue was how we should deal with the islands taken from Spain. Most Republicans thought that we should keep them and govern them as colonies. Bryan, the Democratic candidate, wanted to make all the islands independent as soon as possible. The Democratic platform said that "no nation can long endure half republic and half empire." The Republicans won the election and began working out ways of governing each possession.

Puerto Rico. This beautiful island in the West Indies is smaller than any of our states except Delaware and Rhode Island. It has nearly two million people. About two thirds of them are of Spanish descent, while one third are Negroes. Puerto Rico is one of the most thickly populated places in the world. Most of its people live in extreme poverty.

Puerto Rico accepted the rule of the United States willingly. Congress gave the island a form of government similar in most ways to that of the American territories. All adult citizens who can read and write have the privilege of voting. There is a two-house legislature. The governor is appointed by the President of the United States.

Puerto Rico is an *unincorporated territory*. This means that the island is not a part of the United States but a possession. A few parts of the Constitution do not apply to it. It has the same tariff and tax laws

A BEAUTIFUL SQUARE IN PUERTO RICO. *American occupation has meant modern sanitation, hospitals, schools, and highways.* (Courtesy of United States Department of the Interior)

as the United States and the same money system. The money collected there for federal taxes does not go to the United States Treasury, but is spent on the island for roads, schools, public health, irrigation, and other projects for the benefit of its people.

In 1917 Congress made the Puerto Ricans citizens of the United States. They are proud of being American citizens, yet only one fourth of them are able to speak our language. This is due mainly to their lack of schooling. About half of the grownups never had a chance to go to school and the other half went to school for an average of only three years. In recent years there has been a considerable improvement in educational facilities and opportunities.

The people of Puerto Rico were discontented. They complained that American corporations owned most of the best land, while four fifths of the population was landless. The island's wealth in sugar goes chiefly to American plantation owners and managers. The Puerto Ricans who work for them labor long hours for small wages, and much of the year are unemployed. Because of these conditions Puerto Ricans described the island as "Uncle Sam's sweatshop."

Some Puerto Ricans wanted independence from the United States. Others hoped that Puerto Rico would be made a state of the Union.

THE SPLENDID HARBOR AT HONOLULU, HAWAʼI. *Six miles west at Pearl Harbor, the United States has built one of the strongest naval bases in the world.* (Press Association, Inc.)

But the great majority seemed pleased when Puerto Rico achieved "home rule" on July 4, 1952 and became known as the "Commonwealth of Puerto Rico" under a constitution of their own making.

Hawaii. Mark Twain spoke of the Hawaiian group as "the loveliest fleet of islands that lies anchored in any ocean." The islands are famous for their scenery, pleasant climate, and the good will and hospitality of their people.

The total area of the islands is a little more than that of Connecticut and Rhode Island together. The islands are not crowded, for they have only about four hundred thousand people. While most of the best land is used for sugar and pineapple plantations, there are also a great many small farms. Only a few of the people are very poor.

The inhabitants of Hawaii are of various races — native Hawaiians, Europeans, Filipinos, Chinese, and Japanese — but due to intermarriage they are fast becoming one people. All children born in the islands since annexation (1898) are citizens of the United States. Most of the people can speak English.

Hawaii was annexed at its own request. In 1900 Congress made it an *incorporated* territory. It is, therefore, a part of the United States, and all parts of the Constitution apply to it. While the Hawaiians

would very much like to become a state, they are not seriously discon-
rented with their present form of government.

The Philippines.   Five hundred miles off the coast of China lies a
group of seven thousand islands known as the Philippines.   Most of
them are very small, but the two largest, Luzon and Mindanao, are
about the size of the states of Ohio and Indiana.   The total area of the
islands is nearly equal to that of New York and New England.

The islands have about sixteen million people.   Although they look
very much alike, they speak a variety of dialects.   About nine tenths
of them are Christian, and most of the rest are Mohammedan.   The
Mohammedans are usually spoken of as "Moros"; they are a warlike
group who have never got along well with their Christian neighbors.
Besides the Christians and the Moros there are a small number of pa-
gans who live in the mountains and are only partly civilized.

The Filipino revolt.   Spain ruled the Philippines for four hundred
years.   She did little to improve the lot of the common people, and in
1896 they revolted.   To stop the revolt Spain promised reforms, but
the promises were not kept.   When Admiral Dewey took Manila in
1898, the rebel leaders expected the United States to help the islands
win their independence.   A few months later, when they found that
the United States did not intend to set the islands free, they again took
up their fight for freedom.   Led by the daring Emilio Aguinaldo, they
resisted a force of sixty thousand American troops.   After three years
of fighting, which cost more lives than our war with Spain and nine
times more money than we had paid for the islands, the rebellion was
put down.   Americans who love their own freedom are troubled by
this chapter of our history.   Yet if we had given the Philippines their
independence, it is certain they would soon have been taken over by
either Germany or Japan.

Setting up a Philippine government.   In 1901 the task of setting up
a government for the Philippines was placed in the hands of a commission of five Americans headed by Judge William Howard Taft.   President McKinley told the commission to be guided in all matters by
the best interests of the native people.   The commission carried out its
work with great tact and skill and soon won the co-operation of most
Filipinos.

The next year Congress passed the Philippine Act, creating a regular government for the islands similar to that of Puerto Rico.   The
people were made "citizens of the Philippine Islands," with most of the
rights of American citizens except the right of trial by jury.

"WHAT WILL HE DO WITH IT?" *asks the cartoonist. Most Americans in 1898 were puzzled to learn that the United States had control of the Philippines.* (From the *New York Herald*, June 3, 1898)

When Woodrow Wilson became President, steps were taken to give the Filipinos a larger share in their government. The powers of the legislature were increased. In place of Americans, Filipinos were appointed to nearly all the offices. In these and other ways the people were being prepared for full self-government.

The question of Philippine independence. The Filipinos never forgot their dream of complete independence. The Democratic party repeatedly encouraged them to expect freedom. For instance, in 1916 a Democratic Congress promised independence for the Philippines "as soon as a stable government can be established therein."

The Republicans, who returned to power in 1920, thought that the granting of independence should be postponed. Some felt that the islands were necessary to the United States as a commercial base in the Far East. Others argued that the Philippines were too weak to protect themselves and without American help would soon be gobbled up by some other power. Still others pointed out that Philippine prosperity depended on free trade with the United States, which took three fourths of Philippine exports. If the Philippines were independent,

MANUEL QUEZON *taking the oath as president of the Philippine Commonwealth,*
November 15, 1935. Quezon had been the principal Filipino leader for twenty-five
years. (Keystone View Company)

most of their products would be shut out of the American market by
our high tariffs. These arguments had such weight that Presidents
Harding, Coolidge, and Hoover firmly opposed setting any date for
giving the islands their independence.

Beginning in 1929 new arguments in favor of independence began
to be heard. Possession of the islands had not increased our trade with
China and other parts of the Far East. Governing and defending the
islands was a heavy expense to the United States. Many Filipinos were
coming to California, and labor unions wished to put an end to this by
making the Philippine Islands foreign territory. Besides, Philippine sugar, tobacco, and cocoanut oil competed with American products. If
the Philippines were a foreign country, the United States could shut
out their products by placing a high tariff on them. There was also a
feeling that we had finished our task of preparing the Filipinos for self-
government and that we had no right to refuse them the freedom
for which they longed.

The Philippines become a commonwealth. In 1934 Congress passed
an act providing that the Philippines should become independent on
July 4, 1946. Meanwhile the islands were to be self-governing except
in foreign affairs. This offer was quickly accepted by the Filipinos.
They held a convention and adopted a constitution for the Common-

wealth of the Philippines. In 1935 they made Manuel Quezon their first president.

Congress realized that the new Commonwealth would need time to adjust itself to the loss of the American market. So the Independence Act said that a certain amount of Philippine sugar, cocoanut oil, and other products would be admitted duty-free each year until 1946.

The Philippine Commonwealth was but six years old when the islands were attacked by Japan. Just before the fall of Bataan, the president and vice-president escaped to Australia. They later came to the United States, where they set up a government-in-exile. President Quezon signed the United Nations Pact, making the Philippines the twenty-eighth member of the United Nations.

What the United States did for the Philippines. Americans may take pride in what the United States did for the Philippines while they were under its rule. Between 1901 and 1935 the Philippine Islands made more progress than had been made in the previous three centuries. Under Spanish rule modern improvements were almost unknown, while most of the people could neither read nor write and lived in hopeless poverty. Under American rule highways, railroads, and telephone and telegraph systems were built. Many fine public buildings were erected. Thousands of free public schools were opened. The number of people unable to read and write dropped from 85 per cent to 37 per cent. Modern methods of agriculture were introduced, greatly increasing the output of the farms and plantations. Foreign trade increased to six times what it had been. The masses of people had more to eat and wear and better houses in which to live. One of the most important improvements was made by American public health workers. In every village safe water was provided. This controlled many diseases spread by impure water. Smallpox was wiped out by vaccination. Good health rules were taught to all the people. Sickness and death decreased remarkably.

Perhaps the best thing we did was to help the Filipinos become a nation capable of democratic self-government. We made this possible by educating the people and allowing them to take responsibility for their government. Along with our language they learned our ideas of democracy and the rights of the common man. As a result of our encouragement and their own desire for self-rule, they made themselves ready for independence in the short space of about thirty-five years.

Other American possessions. The largest of our possessions is Alaska. With twice the area of Texas, it has about two hundred thou-

AN ELEMENTARY SCHOOL IN THE PHILIPPINES. *English is taught in the schools and today about one quarter of the Filipinos can speak English. Many of the Filipino teachers have studied in the United States.* (Keystone View Company)

sand people — one to every three square miles. Scientists tell us that Alaska could support at least five million people. It is rich in minerals, lumber, furs, and fish. About half of the territory is suitable for grazing, while in some sections crops can be grown. The climate is like that of Norway and Sweden. After living in southern Alaska for many years, a scientist wrote, " Had the Pilgrim fathers settled in Sitka instead of in Plymouth, they would have found milder climate, better soil and timber, and more game, furs, and fish." Alaska became an incorporated territory in 1916. In 1958 Congress voted to admit Alaska as a state.

We own a number of small islands in the Pacific, valuable as naval or airplane bases. The average American had never heard of them until we went to war with Japan. American Samoa lies about 1500 miles south of Hawaii. (See pages 457–458.) Wake and Guam, stepping stones between Hawaii and the Philippines, were taken by Japan soon after her sneak attack on Pearl Harbor. We also own the Midway Islands northwest of Hawaii and Howland, Palmyra, and Jarvis islands south of Hawaii. A few tiny islands near the equator are claimed by both the United States and Great Britain. As air transportation develops, the value of such islands will no doubt increase. Except for American Samoa and Guam, almost no one lives on these islands.

In 1916 Denmark sold us the Virgin Islands in the West Indies. There are about fifty islands in the group, but only three are large enough to have any importance. These three contain about twenty-five thousand people. We bought these islands during World War I because we feared that Germany might take them. Since they are only a thousand miles from the Panama Canal, we could not afford to let them go to an unfriendly nation. The people of the Virgin Islands are extremely poor, for most of the land is not suited to farming, and there are no other natural resources. Our government has spent large sums there for public health and education and for the development of industries to employ the people. The Virgin Islands have a governor appointed by the President.

To identify: Aguinaldo, Moros, Manuel Quezon.

To explain or define: incorporated territory, pagan, unincorporated territory.

Subjects for Talks or Written Reports

1. Life in the Hawaiian Islands. 2. Life in the Philippine Islands. 3. The Filipino rebellion against the United States after the Spanish-American War. 4. Life in Alaska. 5. Conditions in the Virgin Islands.

Questions for Understanding the Text

1. (*a*) What was the chief issue in the presidential campaign of 1900? (*b*) Which side did the Republicans take? The Democrats? (*c*) Which party won the election? 2. Contrast the government of Puerto Rico before and after July 4, 1952. 3. Why do only a fourth of the Puerto Ricans speak our language? 4. Why are most Puerto Ricans so poor? Of what do they complain? 5. Tell what you know about the Hawaiian Islands and their people. 6. Would you favor having Hawaii and Alaska admitted to the Union as states? Why or why not? 7. Tell what you know about the Philippine Islands and their people. 8. (*a*) Why did the Filipinos rebel against the United States? (*b*) Do you think we should have given them their independence at that time? 9. State the new arguments in favor of independence for the Philippines which were heard during the 1930's. 10. Give the main features of the Philippine Independence Act. 11. Outline the progress made in the Philippines while they were an American colony. 12. Tell about the climate and products of Alaska. 13. Of what importance are the small islands we own in the Pacific? 14. Why did we buy the Virgin Islands? 15. Tell about conditions there.

CHAPTER 35

THE PANAMA CANAL

arly interest in a canal. From the time Balboa crossed the Isthmus of Panama and discovered the Pacific Ocean (1513), men dreamed of digging a canal across this narrow strip of land. The United States first showed its interest in a canal across the isthmus in 1846, the year in which the Oregon question was settled and in which we seized California. Having suddenly reached the Pacific, we needed an easy water route from the East to the West. So a treaty was drawn up with Colombia, to which Panama belonged, giving the United States a right of way across the isthmus. Soon after, gold was discovered in California, and the "Forty-niners" started their famous rush to the "diggings." The journey overland or around Cape Horn was long and dangerous. People realized that a canal was greatly needed.

Great Britain, too, was interested in digging a canal across Central America. But we did not wish her to have full control of it. In 1850 the United States signed a treaty with England agreeing that any canal connecting the two oceans, built by either country, should be controlled by both. Further, the canal should not be fortified and should be open to the use of all nations. No canal was dug then, however. After the transcontinental railroads were built, Americans lost interest in a canal.

A French company begins work. In the early 1880's a French company began a canal across Panama. Americans were somewhat alarmed, and President Hayes declared that "the policy of this country is a canal under American control." This did not discourage the French company. Its head was Ferdinand de Lesseps, who had won world-wide praise as the builder of the Suez Canal. De Lesseps toured the United States in order to make friends for his company. He appointed an advisory board of distinguished Americans. In addition he sold stock in his company to American as well as to European investors. The result was that American objections to the project died down.

De Lesseps figured that his canal would cost one hundred and seventy million dollars. But construction of the canal proved unexpectedly difficult. After some five years of work he had spent three hundred million dollars and had completed only one third of the task. Tropical diseases struck down the engineers and workmen. Thousands of them died every year from yellow fever and malaria. It looked as if the work could not be completed until medical science discovered some way to control these sicknesses. Unable to raise any more money, the company went bankrupt and digging stopped.

American interest revives. When the French company failed, no group was more disappointed than our Western farmers. For years they had been complaining of railroad freight rates. They believed that cheap water transportation from coast to coast would force the railroads to cut down their charges for hauling freight.

American manufacturers, too, were eager to have the canal completed. More and more they looked on the whole United States as their market. Cheaper transportation would help them to sell goods in all sections of the country.

After we got Hawaii and the Philippines the need for a canal was plain to nearly everyone. We saw new trade opportunities in the Far East, but to make the most of them our shippers had to have a short, cheap route from the Atlantic to the Pacific. Besides, we needed the canal in order to defend our new possessions. Unless the canal was dug, we would have to build and maintain two navies — one in the Atlantic and one in the Pacific.

A new treaty with England clears the way. American military leaders insisted that if we dug a canal it ought to be entirely under our control; also, it should be fortified. But this was impossible under the terms of the treaty we had made with England in 1850. Our Secretary of State, John Hay, took up the problem with the British ambassador at Washington, and a new treaty was drawn up. The British government gave up its rights under the old treaty and agreed that the United States might build a canal which was to be under the control of the United States alone, with the understanding that all nations could use it on equal terms.

Congress selects a route. The canal could be dug either through Panama or Nicaragua. The French Panama Company, which was eager to sell its rights and equipment to the United States, naturally wanted Congress to decide in favor of the Panama route. However, Nicaragua is nearer to the United States. Besides, engineers said it would be easier and cheaper to dig a canal through Nicaragua than through Panama. In January, 1902, the House of Representatives voted in favor of the Nicaraguan route. Greatly alarmed, the French Panama Company swung into action. Hoping to keep the Senate from agreeing with the House, lobbyists for the company tried to persuade the senators that volcanoes in Nicaragua would interfere with the digging and the operation of a canal. They did not make much progress until May, when a Nicaraguan volcano became active. This led the Senate to decide in favor of the Panama route. Congress then agreed to pay the French Panama Company forty million dollars. The President was instructed to get from Colombia control of a strip of land across Panama. If satisfactory terms could not be arranged, the canal was to be built across Nicaragua.

Colombia refuses our offer. For a strip of land six miles wide across Panama, the United States offered Colombia ten million dollars at the start and a yearly rent of a quarter of a million dollars. Colombia refused the offer. The rights of the French Panama Company would expire in a little more than a year, and when this happened Colombia could take over the company's property and obtain the forty million dollars which the United States was willing to pay for it. Why, Colombian leaders asked, should their government accept the small sum of ten million dollars for one of its greatest resources?

President Roosevelt pretended that he had no patience with Colombia's attitude. He said that Colombian politicians were greedy and dishonest. He hinted that the United States might take the needed strip of land by force.

Panama breaks away from Colombia. Roosevelt was in a hurry to start digging the canal before the next election. The French company, too, wanted immediate action. And leaders in Panama feared that if the United States did not soon begin the canal there, it would be built in Nicaragua instead. The idea occurred to all of them that Panama might declare itself an independent nation and then accept the terms offered by the United States. Panama had once been independent, and since joining Colombia it had tried several times to secede. It would gladly try again if the United States would give it protection.

On October 10, 1903, President Roosevelt wrote a personal letter to his close friend, the editor of the *Review of Reviews*, in which he said: "Privately, I freely say to you that I should be delighted if Panama were an independent state, or if it made itself one at this moment; but for me to say so publicly would amount to . . . [stirring up a] revolt, and therefore I cannot say it." Soon after, the *Review of Reviews* had an article entitled "Will Panama Declare Independence?"

"THE NEWS REACHES BOGOTA." *Immediately after Panama became independ-ent, Roosevelt prepared to start work on the Panama Canal.* (From the cartoon by W. A. Rogers in the *New York Herald*, November 15, 1903)

Meanwhile officers of the French company were busy here and in Panama raising funds for bribery and organizing a small army at Panama City.

President Roosevelt ordered several warships to Panama, with instructions to prevent the landing of Colombian troops. This made the success of the uprising sure. As soon as the American vessels arrived, the tiny republic proclaimed its independence. A minister from Panama was received in Washington at once; he happened, oddly enough, to be an officer of the French company and a French citizen. Only fifteen days after the bloodless revolution a treaty was signed by which the United States guaranteed the independence of Panama. In return for a strip of land ten miles wide, we agreed to pay Panama ten million dollars down and a quarter of a million dollars every year.

Roosevelt's action causes ill will. Some years later Theodore Roosevelt remarked:

If I had followed . . . [ordinary] methods, I should have sent a dignified state paper of probably two hundred pages to the Congress, and the debate would be going on yet; but I took the Canal Zone and let Congress debate, and while the debate goes on, the canal does also.

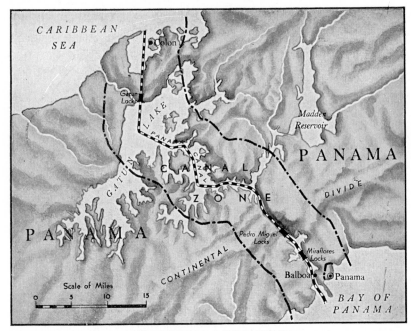

THE PANAMA CANAL ZONE

Roosevelt's direct methods probably speeded up the building of the canal by at least a few months, but he has been severely criticized for his action. The American minister to Colombia said that the friendly relations existing between the two countries were "changed suddenly and unexpectedly when President Roosevelt denied to Colombia the right to land troops upon her own soil to suppress a threatened revolt." The President's action not only offended Colombia but also aroused the distrust of all Latin America. Hoping for friendlier relations, in 1921 the United States paid Colombia twenty-five million dollars. This was a way of saying "We are sorry."

The canal is completed. The United States Army engineers began work on the canal in 1904. The first task was to provide safe living and working conditions in a rainy, tropical land where typhoid fever, yellow fever, and malaria constantly threatened all the inhabitants. Fortunately medical science had made much progress since the 1880's. Colonel William Gorgas of the Army Medical Corps did a remarkable job in controlling these dangerous diseases. To prevent yellow fever and malaria, which are carried by mosquitoes, he ordered the screening of living quarters and the draining of swamps where mosquitoes breed.

To prevent typhoid, he saw to it that water and food supplies were made safe from infection. He succeeded in making the Canal Zone the healthiest strip of land under tropical skies, with a death rate actually lower than that of an average American city.

In 1907 Colonel George W. Goethals was placed in charge of the project. After that, progress was very rapid. Goethals was generous in praising the work already done by the French company and by the American engineer whom he replaced, yet his accomplishments were far greater. No engineering problem was too hard for him to solve. When rock slides filled Culebra Cut as fast as it was dug, he went right on digging. He was most considerate of the welfare of the thousands of men who worked under him. He visited them constantly, trying to make sure that they were well fed and comfortably housed and that they had suitable recreation. He spent part of every day hearing complaints from the workmen. No complaint was too unimportant for his attention. He had a high standard of honesty and permitted no politics in filling positions and no graft in buying supplies. Although the canal and its fortifications cost almost half a billion dollars, the taxpayers got all they paid for.

The cutting of the canal is the greatest work of engineering ever attempted. Thirty-five thousand men labored on it for ten years. A mountain was removed at Culebra Cut. Another mountain was built to dam the Chagres River and form Gatun Lake. Huge locks were built to lift vessels eighty-five feet and lower them again to sea level. The vast undertaking has been called "the greatest liberty man has ever taken with nature." The canal was opened to ships in August, 1914, just at the beginning of World War I.

Protecting the canal. The canal has greatly benefited the commerce of the United States and of the world. It has also increased the usefulness of our Navy and in this way strengthened the defenses of the entire Western Hemisphere. Our enemies would pay a high price to destroy it. To protect it from attack is one of the main tasks of our armed forces.

Protection for the canal is also one of the main purposes of our foreign policy. For example, we purchased the Virgin Islands in 1917 in order that no unfriendly nation could seize and use them to threaten the canal. In 1940 we obtained the right to establish naval bases in several British possessions in the Caribbean in order that no enemy fleet may approach the canal.

The possibility that an enemy might sometime succeed in making

COLONEL GOETHALS AND PRESIDENT TAFT *in the Canal Zone. The President had come to inspect the vast construction project then under way.* (Keystone View Company)

"THE CONQUERORS OF YELLOW FEVER." *Dr. Lazear inoculating Dr. Carroll by means of an infected mosquito, August 27, 1900. Twenty-one volunteers, several of whom lost their lives, submitted to the experiments, which were first suggested by Dr. Carlos Finlay, a Cuban, and directed by Major Walter Reed.* (From the painting by Dean Cornwell. Copyright by Wyeth, Inc., Philadelphia)

the canal useless has caused military leaders to urge the building of a second canal. If a second canal is ever built, it will probably go through Nicaragua. In 1939 Congress seriously considered the question of building a Nicaraguan canal but decided against it. Instead the lawmakers directed that another set of locks be built for the Panama Canal. The new locks were to be much larger than the old ones. Work on the project was stopped in 1942, soon after the United States entered World War II. The construction has never been resumed.

To identify: Balboa, George W. Goethals, William Gorgas, John Hay, Ferdinand de Lesseps.

To explain or define: graft, isthmus.

SUBJECTS FOR TALKS OR WRITTEN REPORTS

1. How Balboa discovered the Pacific Ocean. 2. Traveling across the isthmus in the time of the gold rush in California. 3. The digging of the Suez Canal. 4. The French company's work on the Panama Canal. The difficulties that arose. 5. The conquest of yellow fever. 6. Panama revolts against Colombia. 7. The life of Colonel William Gorgas. 8. The life of Colonel George W. Goethals. 9. The digging of the Panama Canal. 10. How the Canal Zone is governed.

QUESTIONS FOR UNDERSTANDING THE TEXT

1. When did the United States become interested in digging a canal across the isthmus? 2. What agreement did we make with England in 1850 concerning the control of any canal across Central America? When was this agreement changed? 3. Tell of the attempt made by the French company to dig the Panama Canal. Why did the effort fail? 4. (*a*) Why were farmers eager to have a canal across the isthmus? (*b*) Why did the manufacturers want it? (*c*) Why did the Navy Department want it? 5. Why did Congress decide to build the canal through Panama instead of Nicaragua? 6. (*a*) What terms did we offer Colombia for a strip of land across Panama? (*b*) Why did Colombia refuse the offer? 7. (*a*) How did President Theodore Roosevelt encourage the uprising in Panama? (*b*) How did other Latin-American countries feel about this? (*c*) What did we finally do to remove some of Colombia's resentment? 8. What unfavorable conditions had to be overcome before work on the canal could begin? 9. How did Colonel Gorgas make possible the building of the canal? 10. Why do we honor the memory of Colonel Goethals? 11. Discuss the digging of the canal. 12. What have we done to protect the canal?

CHAPTER 36

THE CARIBBEAN SEA BECOMES AN
AMERICAN LAKE

aribbean America. The flags of sixteen nations fly over the mainland and islands that make up the region known as Middle, or Caribbean, America. Twelve are the flags of republics, while four fly over possessions of the United States, Great Britain, France, and the Netherlands. The United States has always had a strong interest in Caribbean America, for its safety requires that no unfriendly power shall ever gain a foothold there.

Our Caribbean policy. Through the years the United States has developed certain ideas, or principles, that guide us in dealing with our Caribbean neighbors. *First*, of course, there is the Monroe Doctrine. In 1823 President Monroe declared that the Western Hemisphere was no longer open to colonization by European nations and warned European governments not to interfere with its political affairs. *Second*, there is the principle that all possible canal routes through Central America shall be controlled by the United States. We have made treaties with various Central American countries to assure us that no corporation and no country except the United States shall be allowed to dig a canal through Central America. *Third*, there is the principle that no outside nation may intervene in — that is, enter by force — any country of the Western Hemisphere for the purpose of collecting debts or protecting property owned by its citizens. Our Caribbean policy rests on these three principles.

Debt troubles of the Caribbean republics. The Caribbean republics (except Cuba) freed themselves from European rule more than a hundred years ago. Although they have constitutions similar to ours, the masses of their people are poor, uneducated, and unprepared for self-government. Many of their presidents have been military leaders who seized the government by force and remained in power until overthrown by force. Foreigners are sometimes hurt and property owned by foreigners is often damaged during these disturbances. The foreigners may then claim damages, which they ask their home governments to collect.

Other foreign debts arise because dishonest officials borrow money in the name of their government for their own use. Sometimes a Caribbean president has used his office to make himself rich. Not satisfied with what he could get through taxation, he has put his country into debt by borrowing money — often at extremely high interest rates — from European and American bankers. When driven from office, such a president usually has skipped the country, taking with him everything in the public treasury and leaving his successor to worry about repaying the country's foreign debt.

Weak nations owing debts to strong ones stand in danger of having their countries occupied by foreign troops. This is how it happens. When a banker finds he cannot collect a loan made to a weak country, he calls upon his government to collect it. His government then warns the weak country to pay its debt. The weak country is likely to reply that it received only a part of the money or none at all and, anyway, has no funds with which to pay the sum demanded. The strong country may then send an armed force to collect the money. When this happened in Africa and Asia, European governments took possession of the weak countries and made them into colonies. The United States, too, has sometimes occupied a weak country in order to collect a debt, but afterward it has always withdrawn its troops and returned the country to its people.

The Caribbean republics have had many disputes with European governments in regard to debts or claims for damages. These countries would have lost their independence years ago had the United States not prevented European countries from taking possession of them. One incident of this kind happened in Venezuela, and Theodore Roosevelt, who was President at the time, worked out a solution. Another happened in Santo Domingo (also called the Dominican Republic).

Venezuela's debt troubles. In 1902 Venezuela refused to pay foreigners for losses which they claimed they had suffered during a revolution. Great Britain, Germany, and Italy then sent warships to blockade the ports of Venezuela, seize the customhouses, and collect the Venezuelan duties. The people of the United States wanted this to be stopped and called upon President Theodore Roosevelt to act. The feeling of many Americans was expressed in a newspaper verse

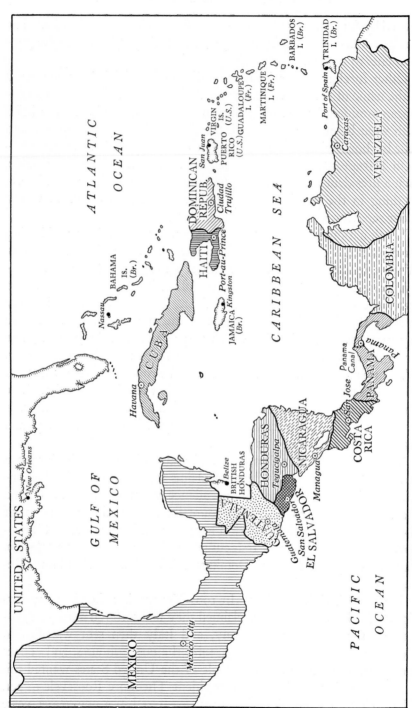

THE FLAGS OF SIXTEEN NATIONS FLY OVER CARIBBEAN AMERICA

which speaks of Admiral Dewey, commander of the United States
Navy:

> Yankee Dewey's near La Guayra,
> Yankee Dewey Dandy.
> Maybe just as well to have our
> Yankee Dewey handy.

Roosevelt urged the different governments to settle the dispute by
arbitration — that is, to let a committee of men from different countries act as judges and tell how to settle it. When Venezuela agreed
to this, the European powers also did so. The Venezuelan claims were
then settled at The Hague, where courts of this kind are held. The
court said that of the thirty-eight million dollars claimed, less than
eight million should be paid.

Santo Domingo's debt difficulties. In 1904, after years of local wars
and bad management of the country's money, Santo Domingo found
itself bankrupt. It owed money to foreign countries and could not
even pay the interest. There were rumors that the European creditors
intended to collect their debts by force.

President Roosevelt believed that since the Monroe Doctrine would
not allow outside powers to keep order in Caribbean America, the
United States itself must do so. In his annual message to Congress in
1904 he said it was the duty of the United States to intervene in the
affairs of its neighbor republics in case of long-continued wrongdoing
or mismanagement. This interpretation of the Monroe Doctrine is
known as the "Roosevelt corollary." It meant that the United States
would force its neighbors to pay their bills in order to prevent any
outside power from doing so.

Roosevelt put his corollary into effect by taking charge of Santo
Domingo's finances. The Dominican president agreed that the United
States should collect his country's customs, turning over part of the
money to his government for its regular expenses and using the rest to
pay off the debt. An American financial adviser was appointed, who
succeeded in doubling the country's revenue and cutting in half the
claims of the European and American creditors. With the customhouses in American hands revolution was less profitable than before,
and the little republic settled down to enjoy some peace and prosperity.

The United States occupies Santo Domingo. In 1916 there was
fear in Washington that Germany might take possession of a fine harbor on the eastern end of Santo Domingo. To prevent this, American
forces occupied the country. Because of disorders there they did not

leave when danger of German seizure was past, and for eight years they ruled the country. During this time many schools and roads were built, and sanitary conditions were greatly improved. Yet the natives tired of American interference and longed for their freedom. The neighboring countries criticized the United States for keeping Santo Domingo under its control. In 1924 the United States returned the government to the people of Santo Domingo and withdrew the American soldiers. However, the Dominican government agreed that an American official should continue to watch over Santo Domingo's finances and that she would not borrow any more money without the approval of the United States.

The dollar becomes a diplomat. Americans with money used to find plenty of chances to invest it in home industries. They seldom invested money abroad. But as their fortunes grew to great size, America's rich men began to look for chances to invest some of their money in foreign countries. After 1900 our foreign investments grew very rapidly.

President Taft, who followed Theodore Roosevelt in the White House, thought Americans should be encouraged to invest their money abroad. He particularly wanted to encourage American investments in Caribbean America, for he believed that if the Caribbean nations would borrow money from Americans instead of from Europeans, there would be less danger of Europeans meddling in their affairs. He also thought that the Caribbean nations would benefit from closer contact with the United States. At the same time American investors could make a profit from developing Caribbean industries. Taft did all he could to persuade the Caribbean countries to pay off their debts to Europeans and to borrow from Americans. This policy has been called "dollar diplomacy." It has continued to some extent ever since Taft was President.

Trouble in Nicaragua. The United States has a special interest in Nicaragua, not only because it is near the Panama Canal but because it contains the best route for a second canal. At the time Taft was in the White House, Nicaragua had passed through one revolution after another and was heavily in debt. Taft thought the little country would become more orderly if its finances were straightened out. He took advantage of the fact that a new dictator had just come into power in Nicaragua to bring pressure upon the new government. He let the dictator know that his government would not be recognized by the United States until it got a loan from American bankers with which to pay off its European debts. Taft also insisted that Nicaragua should have an American financial supervisor, for he expected that revolutionists would be discouraged if the customhouses were under American control and thus out of their reach.

Unfortunately Nicaragua's affairs did not straighten out as Taft had hoped. Disturbances soon broke out again, and the American bankers who had lent money there demanded that the United States government protect their investments. Marines were landed in 1912 and remained there nearly all the time until 1933. Nicaraguan guerrillas fought them all the while.

Trouble in Haiti. In 1915 terrible disorders broke out in Haiti, and many people were murdered. At the same time the country's finances were badly mixed up, and it was rumored that Germany planned to step in to collect a debt. The United States took the island republic under its protection, landed United States marines there, and restored order. The Haitians then elected a president acceptable to the United States and unwillingly signed a treaty giving the United States almost complete control of the government. Under American occupation the debt was reduced and revenues increased. Roads, sewers, water systems, schools, and hospitals were built. For the first time the health of the people received attention. As a result of changes in the prisons, the death rate of prisoners dropped from 65 per cent a year to less than 2 per cent. In spite of these and other improvements, many Haitians wanted their freedom. Through the nineteen years of occupation, more than two thousand Haitians were shot for resisting American officials. Starting in 1930, during the Presidency of Mr. Hoover, the marines moved out, and in 1934 the Haitian government took over control.

Cuba becomes an American protectorate. When Congress instructed President McKinley to free the people of Cuba from Spain, it promised that Cuba should be independent. American forces remained in the island only until a democratic Cuban government could be set up. During this period yellow fever was stamped out, a public school system established, and many public works constructed.

Congress was afraid to let the young Cuban government stand entirely upon its own feet, so it passed the Platt Amendment, to which Cuba was obliged to agree. The Platt Amendment stated that (1) Cuba was not to permit a foreign power to secure partial or complete control of the island, (2) it should not borrow too much money (this might result in foreign interference), (3) it should sell or lease to the

THE CAPITOL, HAVANA, CUBA. *This modern building is one of the most beautiful capitols in America.* (Publishers' Photo Service)

United States coaling or naval stations on the Cuban coast, and (4) the United States should have the right to enter Cuba to preserve the island's independence and to preserve order. These terms were intended to protect Cuba and to insure orderly government, yet they limited Cuban independence, and the Cubans accepted them only because they had to.

Early in 1902 the United States withdrew, leaving the Cuban government in full charge of the island's affairs. For four years everything went well. Then stormy times began. The United States intervened four times (1906, 1912, 1917, and 1920) to restore order and protect American property. Cuban patriots hated this interference. They claimed that Gerardo Machado, who ruled from 1925 to 1933, remained in office only because he had American support. In 1934 the United States made a new treaty by which it gave up its rights under the Platt Amendment.

Americans have invested large sums in Cuban sugar plantations, sugar mills, railroads, mines, and public utilities. Most of the banking there is in the hands of one New York City bank. Cubans often complain because American investors have so much influence in island affairs. They say that the island cannot be really independent while most of its industry and commerce and much of its best land is in the hands of foreigners.

The Mexican problem. Because of Mexico's larger population and stronger national spirit, the United States did not try to deal with her by the same methods used in the small Caribbean nations. Yet heavy American investments in Mexico and the beginning of a long period of civil war in 1911 caused the United States to watch what was happening there very carefully.

To understand the civil war that broke out in 1911 we must look back over Mexican history. From 1823 to 1876 Mexico had one civil war after another. Porfirio Diaz seized control of Mexico in 1876. Crushing all opposition, he held power until 1911, while the common people of Mexico groaned beneath his rule. He parceled out among his own friends vast areas of land which belonged to the Indian villages or to the nation. This changed the villagers into landless *peons*, as they are called, scarcely better off than slaves. Diaz cared as little for the rights of industrial workers as he did for the rights of the villagers. Industrial workers suffered from long hours and miserable wages. If they tried to strike, they were shot down by government troops. When foreign mineowners could not get enough laborers, local officials arrested Indians on fake charges and compelled them to work in the mines. Diaz gave away the nation's mineral resources to rich foreigners. The foreigners invested money to develop the mines and oil fields. By 1910 Americans had invested nearly a billion dollars there, and owned 80 per cent of the railroad and mining property and 70 per cent of the oil property of Mexico. Rich Britishers and Germans also had large investments in Mexico. Huge profits were made from these investments, but the Mexican people did not benefit from them. It was said, "Mexico is rich, but the Mexicans are poor."

When Diaz began his eighth term as president, Francisco Madero led a revolt against him. Madero came from a cultivated and well-to-do family. He was a sincere democrat, eager to restore his country to the common people. The United States let him use Texas as a base, and in 1911 he succeeded in overthrowing Diaz and in making himself president of Mexico. Madero allowed Mexican workers and peons to organize and took away some of the privileges enjoyed by rich foreigners. Before he could bring about further reforms, General Huerta started a rebellion against him. Huerta got arms from Americans and other foreigners with investments in Mexico. Too late, President Taft prohibited the export of arms from the United States to Madero's enemies. Madero was overthrown and murdered less than two years after taking office. Most of his reform program was still only on paper.

Wilson tries "watchful waiting." Although other nations quickly

MEXICAN REFUGEES *boarding a train at Vera Cruz in April, 1914. The United States fleet had seized the city and the Mexicans expected war to follow.* (Courtesy of National Archives)

recognized the Huerta government, the United States refused to do so. President Wilson announced a new principle to guide American foreign relations — the United States would not recognize governments founded on force. The President did not plan to intervene in Mexico; he hoped that the Mexican people would rise against the murderous Huerta. "My ideal," he said, "is an orderly . . . government in Mexico; but my passion is for the submerged 85 per cent of the people who are now struggling for liberty."

Civil war broke out between the followers of Huerta and the Constitutionalists (those who had followed Madero). President Wilson sent his own representative to Mexico City to urge Huerta to resign. Huerta scornfully refused. Then Wilson lifted the arms embargo so that the Constitutionalists might get arms from the United States. For this and for not recognizing Huerta, the President was savagely criticized at home and abroad. Persons with investments in Mexico wanted Huerta to rule because they thought he could bring order to the country; they were more interested in the safety of their money than in the welfare of the Mexican masses. They made fun of Wilson's policy of "watchful waiting." European investors took the same attitude as American investors. The German Kaiser said, "Morality is all right, but what about dividends?"

In April, 1914, Wilson learned that a German ship was on its way to Vera Cruz with munitions for Huerta. To prevent the delivery of this cargo, he ordered the American fleet to seize the port. This cost the lives of eighteen Americans and nearly two hundred Mexicans. War fever swept both the United States and Mexico. At this point Argentina, Brazil, and Chile offered to help settle the quarrel by appointing mediators — that is, diplomats who study a dispute and propose a peaceful solution. Wilson gladly accepted the offer. When the mediators sided with the United States, Huerta thought it wise to leave Mexico. Carranza, a leader of the Constitutional party, then declared himself President. Wilson recognized him and called our troops out of Vera Cruz. All Latin America was glad that we had not gone to war with Mexico and that we had let other Latin-American countries help us in settling the dispute.

Carranza was no sooner in office than Villa led a revolt against him. After a year of bloody fighting Villa retired to the mountains in northern Mexico, where he lived as a bandit chief. Since he blamed the United States for Carranza's victory, he wanted revenge on the "gringos," as he called the Americans. Early in 1916 a band of his followers killed sixteen American citizens. American newspapers now angrily demanded that we "clean up" Mexico. A few weeks later Villa raided a town in New Mexico, killing sixteen more Americans. President Wilson sent General Pershing into Mexico with sixteen thousand troops and orders to capture Villa "dead or alive." Although Carranza agreed to let the American soldiers come, he did nothing to help them and soon showed a very unfriendly attitude toward them. This led a good many Americans to clamor for war. To avoid trouble Wilson recalled Pershing, leaving the Mexicans to deal with Villa.

Mexico's quarrel with foreign oil companies. Under old Mexican laws everything beneath the surface of the soil belongs to the nation; a landowner has no right to minerals found beneath his land. Diaz paid no attention to this law; as we have seen, he gave away most of Mexico's mineral lands to foreigners. In 1917 Mexico adopted a new constitution declaring that oil pools and other mineral deposits belong to the nation. The government then decided that the oil companies should no longer get their oil absolutely free, but should pay the government 5 per cent of the value of every barrel produced. The big American and English oil companies objected loudly. They tried hard to get the United States government to interfere. President Wilson steeled himself against this pressure. "I have to remind myself," he said to his secretary, "that I am President of the United States and not of a small group of Americans with vested interests in Mexico." However, the complaints of the oil interests were not overlooked. When General Obregon became president of Mexico in 1920, the United States refused to recognize his government until he agreed that the 1917 constitution would not apply to oil properties obtained by foreigners before 1917.

General Obregon's promise pleased the foreign oil companies but not the Mexican people. Within two years a new land law was passed, stating that those who then owned Mexican minerals could keep possession for fifty years but after that the minerals should belong to the nation. The larger oil companies were very angry about this, and while Coolidge was President our State Department sent some strongly worded notes to the Mexican government. In 1927 President Coolidge chose Dwight W. Morrow to be American ambassador to Mexico, and Morrow persuaded the Mexican government to back down. But the Mexican people still believed that all minerals found beneath their soil should belong to the nation.

In 1937 there were serious labor troubles in the oil fields. The Mexican government appointed a commission to investigate. The commission reported that the oil companies were making large profits and should pay higher wages. When the Mexican government ordered them to pay higher wages, the oil companies protested fiercely and called upon their home governments to back them up. These protests offended the Mexicans, who claimed that the oil companies had no respect for the Mexican government. President Cardenas sent word to the American ambassador, "If our petroleum is an obstacle . . . [to our national self-respect] we will burn the oil wells."

Cardenas made up his mind that the power of the great oil companies must be broken. In 1938 he nationalized — that is, took possession of — the property of seventeen of the largest British and American companies. The oil companies were furious, but Secretary of State Cordell Hull said that the Mexican government had acted within its rights, provided that it paid a fair price for the property it had taken. After a long dispute with the American companies, Mexico agreed to pay some twenty-four million dollars for their claims. The attitude of the United States during this affair pleased and surprised the whole of Latin America. We sent no soldiers to protect the oil companies. We respected Mexico's independence and did not try to prevent her from solving the oil problem in her own way.

Our influence over other Caribbean governments. The United States government has interfered very little with the governments of

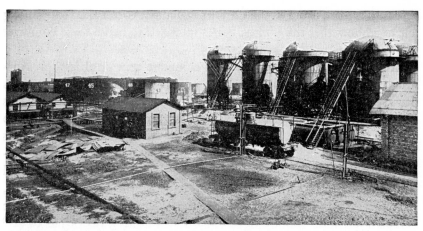

PETROLEUM REFINERY AT TAMPICO, MEXICO. *Diaz unlawfully gave away Mexico's oil fields to foreigners. Later the Mexican government had a hard time getting the oil fields back.* (Courtesy of Pan American Union)

any Caribbean nations except Santo Domingo, Nicaragua, Haiti, Cuba, Mexico, and Panama. Yet all the Caribbean countries are under our watchful eye. Without the protection of our fleet they would doubtless have been conquered long ago. Because they need our protection, they want to have friendly relations with the United States; and they are guided by the United States in their relations with foreign nations.

American economic influence in the Caribbean. While the Caribbean countries are politically independent, they have little economic freedom. Most of them are heavily in debt, chiefly to American bankers. Furthermore, American investors own most of their plantations, mines, railroads, and other businesses. As a natural result American bankers and investors have a strong influence in these countries. This is most plainly seen in Honduras, the so-called "banana republic." A single American fruit corporation owns the railroads and plantations of Honduras and has great influence in the government of the country. No president unfriendly to the company is likely to stay in office. Economic control by one or more foreign corporations is, of course, no more welcome to a nation than control by a foreign government. So far only the Mexican government has been strong enough to free itself, in part, from this kind of control.

What Latin Americans think of our Caribbean policy. Latin Americans long feared and distrusted the United States. This fear and distrust reached a new height when Theodore Roosevelt helped Panama to separate from Colombia. The practice of sending American armed forces to restore order in the Caribbean countries created a fear among our neighbors that the United States intended to make these countries into colonies.

Ever since 1927, when President Coolidge sent Ambassador Morrow to Mexico, the United States has tried to show Latin Americans that we want to be a good neighbor. In 1930, while Mr. Hoover was President, our State Department gave up the Roosevelt corollary to the Monroe Doctrine. (See page 487.) In 1933 the United States joined with all the other Latin-American nations in a treaty saying that "No state has the right to intervene in the internal or external affairs of another." In 1934 Congress repealed the Platt Amendment, which had given us special rights to interfere in Cuban affairs. As the "Good Neighbor" policy developed, Latin Americans began to feel much friendlier toward the United States.

Recent British-American co-operation in the Caribbean. Since 1940 England and the United States have been co-operating to promote the welfare of the people in Caribbean America. This co-operation began when the British gave us the use of naval bases on several of their islands in the Caribbean. One of the first problems that arose was how to protect the health of American soldiers and sailors stationed on these islands. A great deal of work had to be done to reduce sickness among the island people in order to guard the health of our military men. In this work the British and American governments co-operated.

When German submarines became active in the Caribbean in 1941-43, it was necessary for the Caribbean countries to produce more food so that they might get along without the supplies they formerly got from the United States, Canada, and Newfoundland. American and British experts worked out plans for growing more food and for increasing the catch of fish. All the Caribbean countries joined in making plans for more trade in food among themselves.

In March, 1942, the United States and England set up the Anglo-American Caribbean Commission. In 1946 France and the Netherlands became members. The purpose of the Commission is to study conditions in the Caribbean area and recommend ways for improving the welfare of the people. Upon the Commission's advice the Caribbean countries have taken steps to cut sugar production and to grow a variety of crops, especially foods for home use. Much has also been done to improve communication between different parts of the region and to encourage the building of roads, water systems, and electric plants. Efforts are being made to promote industrial development.

To identify: Cardenas, Carranza, Diaz, gringos, Huerta, Madero, Dwight W. Morrow, Obregon, Platt Amendment, Roosevelt corollary, Villa.

To explain or define: arbitration, intervene, mediator, nationalize, peon.

Subjects for Talks or Written Reports

1. How Haiti won its freedom from France. 2. The history of The Hague court. 3. Our occupation of Santo Domingo. Changes made during the occupation. The attitude of the people toward our interference. 4. American intervention in Nicaragua. 5. Haiti during the American occupation. 6. Cuba under Gerardo Machado. How Machado was overthrown. 7. The life of Francisco Madero. What he wanted to do for Mexico. 8. How Mexico finally regained possession of her oil fields.

Questions for Understanding the Text

1. What countries have possessions in the Caribbean area? 2. Why will the United States always be interested in Caribbean America? 3. State three ideas that guide our State Department in dealing with affairs in the Caribbean. 4. State two ways in which the Caribbean republics have sometimes got into debt to foreigners. 5. (*a*) When a weak country owes money to a strong one what is likely to happen? (*b*) What did this lead to in Africa and Asia? (*c*) What has saved the Caribbean nations from being seized by European nations? 6. (*a*) What happened to Venezuela in 1902? (*b*) How was the trouble settled? 7. What did Theodore Roosevelt's corollary to the Monroe Doctrine mean? 8. Why did American forces occupy Santo Domingo in 1916? 9. Did our control please the people of Santo Domingo and their neighbors? 10. (*a*) When did Americans begin to invest large sums of money in foreign countries? (*b*) Why did President Taft try to encourage American investments in Caribbean America? 11. Why were United States marines kept in Nicaragua most of the time from 1912 to 1933? 12. (*a*) Why did we take control of Haiti in 1915? (*b*) Did the Haitians like to have our forces there? 13. (*a*) State the terms of the Platt Amendment. (*b*) Is Cuba now fully independent? Explain. 14. Describe conditions in Mexico which led to the overthrow of Diaz in 1911. 15. Who helped Huerta to overthrow Madero? 16. Was Wilson's policy of "watchful waiting" popular among persons with investments in Mexico? Explain. 17. (*a*) Why was General Pershing sent to Mexico? (*b*) What was the result? 18. (*a*) Under Mexican law who owns minerals found beneath the surface of the soil? (*b*) What happened when Mexico tried to enforce this law? (*c*) When did the Mexican government actually take possession of the oil fields owned by the larger British and American companies? (*d*) What did Secretary of State Hull say about this? 19. What is meant by saying that the Caribbean countries have little economic freedom? 20. State the purposes of British-American co-operation in the Caribbean.

CHAPTER 37

THE UNITED STATES IN WORLD WAR I

War breaks out in Europe, 1914. In July, 1914, war broke out in the Balkan countries. Soon most of the European nations were in the fight. In the United States the first idea was to keep out of the conflict. "Peace-loving citizens of this country," said the *Chicago Herald*, "will now rise up and tender a hearty vote of thanks to Columbus for having discovered America." That was a joking way of expressing America's attitude toward the war: "Thank heavens we are not mixed up in it."

The United States tries to be neutral. President Wilson issued a proclamation (August, 1914) saying that the United States would stay neutral. At the time nearly everyone here agreed with the President. Even the vigorous Theodore Roosevelt said, "We should remain entirely neutral."

Yet Americans could not be indifferent to the struggle. Millions of them were of foreign birth or foreign parentage. Groups of German-Americans, Italian-Americans, Polish-Americans, Russian-Americans, Irish-Americans, and others began to organize and to demand that their adopted country help their homelands. Feeling between the pro-Ally and the pro-German sympathizers grew very bitter. This is amusingly shown in a rhyme published by the *New York Sun* describing the writer's experience in a barber shop:

> The barber to the right of me was hoching for the Kaiser.
> The barber to the left of me was hacking for the Czar.
> A gentleman from Greece was shearing off my fleece,
> While very near a swart Italian stropped his scimitar.
> And when presently discussion, polyglot and fervid,
> On political conditions burst about my chair,
> I left the place unshaven — I hope I'm not a craven,
> But I sort of like to wear a head beneath my hair!

President Wilson urged Americans to be neutral "in thought as well as in action," not letting themselves be "thrown off balance by a war with which we have nothing to do, whose causes cannot touch us."

GERMANY DECLARES WAR ON RUSSIA;
FRANCE PREPARES TO JOIN HER ALLY;
ITALY QUITS THE TRIPLE ALLIANCE

BRITISH ULTIMATUM TO GERMANY;
JOHN BURNS QUITS THE CABINET;
GERMANS ADVANCE THROUGH BELGIUM

HEADLINES *announcing the outbreak of World War I in Europe. At the time few Americans dreamed that our country would be drawn in; nevertheless they followed the war news with great interest.*

But this advice was impossible to follow. "Only persons mentally paralyzed," said one editor, "could be neutral in thought."

The majority of Americans sympathized with England, France, Belgium, and the other Allies. A hundred ties of language and culture bound us to the British. Memories of French aid in the Revolution bound us to the French. Believing that the United States owed a debt of gratitude to France, some prayed, "Forget us, God, if we forget the sacred sword of Lafayette." Thousands of Americans enlisted under the British and French flags.

On the other hand, the majority of Americans had little sympathy with Germany and the other Central Powers (Austria-Hungary, Bulgaria, and Turkey). For many years our relations with Germany had not been particularly friendly, for we had disapproved of her ambitions in the Pacific, in China, and in the Caribbean. When the Germans tore up a solemn treaty and invaded Belgium, our distrust turned to anger. We applauded Belgium for her heroic resistance and condemned the Germans for their savage treatment of Belgian civilians. We began to realize that we should not like to live in a world in which Germany was the strongest power. We hoped that the "Beast of Berlin," as his enemies called the German Kaiser, would be soundly beaten. However, we did not want to get into the fight ourselves.

The British interfere with our neutral rights. Each side interfered with our neutral right to trade with the other side. The situation was much like the one we faced during the Napoleonic wars, which led us into the War of 1812. At first Great Britain's actions bothered us more than those of Germany. This was natural, since Britain had control of the seas and intended to prevent Germany from getting war supplies and even foodstuffs from abroad. German ships were quickly driven from the sea lanes. If neutral ships could also be kept from taking supplies to Germany, Germany might be seriously weakened.

Great Britain published a list of articles which neutrals must not send to the enemy. Besides war materials the list included many other things useful in modern war, such as leather, cotton, wool, rubber, chemicals, and even foodstuffs. In order to carry out this rule, she forced American merchant ships bound for Europe to enter British ports, where they could be examined at leisure. This practice angered American shippers, in spite of the fact that the British paid good prices for any cargoes they took. Our government sent Great Britain note after note of protest but aside from that did nothing. We did not want to take any steps that might lessen our profitable trade with the Allies. Besides, President Wilson privately believed that England was fighting our fight. He told his secretary that he would never "take any action to embarrass England when she is fighting for her life and the life of the world."

German submarines interfere with our rights. German interference with our neutral rights was more serious because it caused a loss of life. Early in 1915 Germany proclaimed that all the waters around Great Britain were a war zone and that her submarines would destroy every enemy ship found there. Neutral ships might be sunk by mistake, and Germany warned them to keep out. Germany also stated that she might be unable to provide for the safety of crew and passengers on destroyed vessels.

Under the old rules of international law a warship could sink a merchant ship only after searching it and rescuing its passengers and crew. But the submarine was small and, at that time, not heavily armed. If it came to the surface near an enemy vessel, the submarine might be rammed or sunk by a shell. The only way it could operate safely was to torpedo the enemy ship without warning. It could not stop to save the lives of those on board. Germany insisted that the old law did not apply to the submarine, but President Wilson refused to accept this view. He announced that the United States would hold the German government strictly to account for all acts endangering the lives of American citizens.

AMERICAN CARTOONISTS ANGRILY DENOUNCED *an advertisement by the German Embassy which appeared the day before the* Lusitania *sailed, warning Americans not to travel on Allied ships. The one on the right, entitled "Vell, Ve Varned 'Em," was printed in the* New York Herald, *May 8, 1915. The one on the left, entitled "The Announcer," appeared in the* Brooklyn Eagle *one year later.*

In spite of Wilson's notes, the Germans carried out their threat. Several Americans were drowned when submarines sank British freighters and an American tanker in the war zone. Then an event took place which shocked the civilized world. On May 7, 1915, the British liner *Lusitania* was torpedoed off the Irish coast. The great ship sank in eighteen minutes. Of the nearly two thousand persons on board, some twelve hundred were drowned, among them one hundred twenty-eight Americans. A wave of horror and anger swept over the United States. For the first time the American public began to think of making war on Germany. Theodore Roosevelt raised his voice for war. He said it was unthinkable that we should refrain from action: "We owe it not only to humanity but to our own national self-respect."

President Wilson did not listen to those who called for war. He knew that most of the people, except in the East, did not want to fight Germany. Besides, the country needed time to prepare for war. Wilson sent a series of sharp notes to Germany protesting against the sinking of passenger ships and asking that no merchant ship be sunk without warning. Finally, in February, 1916, Germany said she was sorry for the loss of American lives in the *Lusitania* sinking and agreed to pay damages. She also ordered her submarine commanders to spare all passenger ships. In May, after another strong note from Wilson, she promised that neither merchant nor passenger ships would be sunk without warning and without protecting the lives of their crews and passengers. Wilson's patience had won a diplomatic victory. A leading senator said:

> . . . without orphaning a single American child, without widowing a single American wife, without firing a single gun, without shedding a single drop of blood, he [Wilson] has wrung from the most militant [warlike] spirit that ever brooded above a battlefield an acknowledgment of American rights and an agreement to American demands.

That fall with the help of the slogan, "He kept us out of war," the President was elected for a second term.

The United States enters the war. Early in 1917 the Germans announced that they would adopt all-out submarine warfare. The British blockade was beginning to strangle them, and they had decided to stake everything on winning an early victory. By sinking all ships, enemy or neutral, approaching the British Isles, they expected to starve Britain within a few months and force her to ask for peace. They knew that the sinking of American ships would bring the United States into the war, but they were not afraid of that. Our army was pitifully weak, and the war would be over, they thought, before we could raise a sizable force and take it to Europe.

President Wilson at once broke off relations with Germany. The Senate approved the action by a vote of seventy-eight to five. War could now be avoided only if Germany did not sink our ships. Within a few weeks eight American ships were sent to the bottom. This made it clear that Germany was at war with us. On April 2 the President went before Congress to ask it to declare war. In one of the great speeches of all history he stated America's war aims. He explained the war as a crusade or mission to insure peace.

> We are now about to accept . . . battle with this natural foe to liberty and shall, if necessary, spend the whole force of the nation to check . . . its power. . . . *The world must be made safe for democracy*. . . . We have no selfish ends to serve. . . . We are but one of the champions of the rights of mankind. We shall be satisfied when these rights have been made as secure as the faith and freedom of nations can make them. . . .
> It is a fearful thing to lead this great and peaceful people into war,

into the most terrible and disastrous of all wars, civilization itself seeming to be in the balance. But the *right is more precious than peace,* and we shall fight for the things which we have always carried nearest our hearts — for democracy, for the right of those who submit to authority to have a voice in their own governments, for the rights and liberties of small nations, for . . . such [a union] of free peoples as shall bring peace and safety to all nations and make the world itself at last free. To such a task we dedicate our lives and our fortunes, everything that we are and everything that we have, with the pride of those who know that the day has come when America is privileged to spend her blood and her might for the principles that gave her birth and the peace which she has treasured. God helping her, she can do no other.

The nation is united but unprepared. Now that war had come, the vast majority of Americans loyally supported the government. The nation was more firmly united than it had been at the start of any previous war. Disloyal groups were fewer and weaker than in the War between North and South, and they were not able to interfere seriously with the war effort.

Although united, the country was still unprepared to fight a well-armed enemy. We had less than three hundred thousand soldiers, including the National Guard (volunteer militia). Even the regular army was not trained for the sort of fighting demanded by the European war. There was a serious shortage of trained officers. We were also short of machine guns, planes, big guns, and a thousand other articles needed by a modern army. It is no wonder that German experts ranked the military strength of the United States between that of Belgium and Portugal.

Few Americans were troubled by our lack of preparedness. Most of them thought the part of the United States in the war would be to furnish money, food, ships, and munitions to the Allies and to use our excellent navy to fight the submarine. Many thought that Germany was on her last legs and would soon be beaten. The President himself did not think our army would have to go to Europe.

The United States decides to send an army overseas. Within a few weeks of our declaration of war Great Britain and France told our government that the Allies were in grave danger of defeat. German submarines were destroying Allied ships at a terrible rate. For three years there had been a powerful German army in northern France, and the Allied armies were not strong enough to drive it out. Germany had conquered Belgium, Serbia, and Rumania. Russia was go-

GENERAL PERSHING AT LAFAYETTE'S TOMB, *June, 1917. This tribute from the leader of the American army gave new heart to the exhausted French nation.* (Harris and Ewing)

ing through a revolution, and her armies were close to collapse. Italy was tottering. The French army had suffered frightful losses and was losing heart. British and French leaders begged us to send at least a small force overseas at once. Its arrival, they said, would give their people courage to go on.

The President sent General John J. Pershing to France with twelve thousand men. He visited the tomb of Lafayette, an act which thrilled liberty-loving people everywhere. On July 4 Pershing's little army paraded through Paris to thunderous applause. An American writer has pictured the scene.

> There was the crowd sweeping along the street below the great iron fence of the Tuileries, from curb to curb, with no order, men, women, children trotting along, hot, excited, trying to keep up with the slender column of our khaki-clad regulars, who marched briskly along. French soldiers in their light blue trotted beside them, as closely as they could get, looking at them with almost childish interest and wonder, as boys trot hurrying beside a circus parade. Our soldiers were covered with flowers — and always the steady roar of the crowd and now and then cries of *Vive l'Amérique!* (Long live America!)

Pershing decided that three million American soldiers were needed to defeat Germany. He at once set about preparing for them. In the ports assigned for American use channels had to be deepened and docks

SOLDIERS WEARING GAS MASKS *for protection against poisonous gas. The Germans introduced the use of poison gas early in World War I.* (Courtesy of United States Signal Corps)

built. A thousand miles of railroads must be built to carry our men and supplies. A hundred thousand miles of telegraph and telephone lines had to be strung. Training camps, supply depots, and hospitals had to be established. It was a gigantic undertaking, accomplished with a speed that amazed the Europeans.

The United States raises and trains an army. How should the United States recruit the millions of men needed for the army? Should it rely on a call for volunteers, or should men be drafted? America did not like the idea of drafting soldiers. The one time it was tried, after two years of the War between North and South, riots had broken out. Army leaders convinced the President that a draft was necessary, and after a hard fight he persuaded Congress to pass the Selective Service Act.

Careful thought was given to ways for making the draft as democratic as possible. Instead of having Army officers list the young men and take them from their homes, the whole process was carried out by civilians. All men of draft age were asked to register at the voting place nearest their home. A local board of civilians decided who should be excused from service because of dependents, physical disabilities, or home duties. No one was allowed to hire a substitute. The final choice was then made by lottery and the men notified to report to duty by a post card from their local board. Nearly three million men were drafted before the war came to an end. The draft machinery worked well, and disturbances were almost unheard of.

The recruits had to be trained, but first they had to be provided with quarters. With lightning speed sixteen soldier-cities were built for the Army (the drafted men) and sixteen others for the National Guard. Each training camp housed forty to fifty thousand men. Each had its own water system, sewers, electric light plant, paved streets, laundries, kitchens, bakeries, hospitals, libraries, and theaters. The camps cost nearly as much to build as the Panama Canal.

The average soldier spent six months in a training camp learning the ABC's of military life and toughening himself for life at the front. Some of his instructors were British and French officers fresh from three years' experience in the battle zone. Then he went overseas for two months' more training, followed by a month in a "quiet" section of the front. After another month of training behind the lines, he might go into an active sector where battles were in progress.

The United States transports the army to France. The problem of getting American soldiers and their supplies to France was so hard that the Germans thought the United States never could solve it. To carry millions of men was difficult, still more so the vast quantities of materials they had to have for living and fighting. For every American soldier overseas there had to be provided daily *fifty pounds* of equipment, munitions, and other supplies. The United States did not have the ships to do this. Its Allies did not have them, for submarines were sending their ships to the bottom two or three times faster than new ones could be built. The United States started a vast shipbuilding program, but no ships could be produced until shipyards were built and until hundreds of thousands of shipyard workers were recruited and trained. In view of these facts American military leaders thought that they could not attempt large-scale operations in Europe until 1919.

As 1917 drew to a close, defeat stared the Allies in the face. They desperately needed more soldiers. America had less than two hundred thousand men in France, none of them yet in combat. General Pershing cabled: "The Allies are very weak and we must come to their relief this year, 1918. The year after may be too late. It is very doubtful if they can hold on until 1919 unless we give them a lot of support this year." Making a tremendous effort, America speeded up the shipment of men. By June, 1918, nearly three hundred thousand a month were going overseas. By November there were about two million American soldiers in France. Half of these men went overseas in ves-

JAMES MONTGOMERY FLAGG *painting a recruiting poster in front of the New York Public Library, July, 1918.* (Courtesy of National Archives)

sels that the British managed to spare from the work of carrying food to their civilian population.

The transports sailed in formation, guarded by destroyers. At night every glimmer of light was hidden, and the ships speeded ahead in blackness. Lookouts watched every inch of the sea for the ripple of a periscope or the trail of a torpedo. To the doughboys packed in the crowded hold, the voyage meant homesickness, seasickness, and fear of sudden death. Fortunately very few of the soldiers going to Europe were lost at sea.

The home front. The winning of the war demanded the help of the entire people. Production of every kind of war goods — guns, planes, ships, chemicals, clothing, food — had to be increased with all possible speed. Thousands of war plants had to be built. Steel, copper, fuel, lumber, cotton, wool, fats, and other raw materials had to be turned out to the limit of the nation's capacity. All this must be accomplished in spite of the absence of almost five million men in the armed forces. Said the President, "It is not an army we must shape and train for war — it is a nation." To accomplish this the government had to exercise vast powers.

1. Increasing production. The making of all kinds of war materials had to be speeded up. The government became dictator over industry, labor, and agriculture. It took over the railroads and the telegraph

and telephone lines. It fixed the prices of a number of raw materials. It constructed giant shipyards and munition plants. It brought about a 40 per cent increase in coal production and a 20 per cent increase in the nation's industrial capacity.

2. Doubling food exports. When the United States entered the war, Great Britain and France were close to actual hunger. So many of their ships had been sunk by submarines that none could be spared to bring food from distant Argentina and Australia. Unless the Allies could get greatly increased quantities of grain and meat from North America, they would be forced to surrender. The United States, then, had to expand its production of food at the very time when much of the man power on its farms had gone into the army or into war industries.

Herbert Hoover was named Food Administrator. With remarkable energy and efficiency, Hoover threw himself into his task. He appealed to the farmers to plant more grain and raise more hogs. He asked every family to make a war garden. He asked people to use substitutes for meat, sugar, and wheat, to observe certain days of the week as "meatless" and "wheatless" days, and to avoid all waste of food. Everywhere, before all eyes, in newspapers and magazines, on posters and bulletin boards, appeared the slogan, "Food will win the war!" The result of Hoover's program was the doubling of American food exports to Europe. Without this additional food the Allies could not have fought on.

3. Raising money for the war. The war cost the United States fifty million dollars a day. How this huge amount of money was raised is one of the most romantic stories of the war — a story of the co-operation of rich and poor, of Wall Street and Main Street. The people accepted taxes far heavier than Americans had ever dreamed of. In addition they bought "liberty bonds" to a total of twenty-one billion dollars. Over twenty million persons bought bonds in the fourth war loan drive — a most amazing record when we stop to consider that before the war not more than three hundred thousand Americans were in the habit of buying stocks and bonds.

4. Making the nation war-conscious. How this peace-loving nation, with its millions of foreign-born, was made war-conscious, how it was led to support the war with all its strength, is another romantic story. It is the story of a remarkable advertising man, George Creel, whom the President appointed head of the wartime Committee on Public Information. As Creel saw it, his chief job was to arouse en-

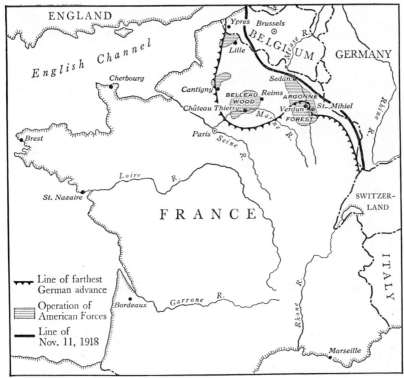

AMERICAN OPERATIONS ON THE WESTERN FRONT

thusiasm for the war. To do it, he said, would be the world's greatest adventure in advertising. He set out to acquaint Americans with every phase of their country's war effort and to thrill them with the President's statement of war aims.

Creel published seventy-five million pamphlets. He enlisted seventy-five thousand volunteer speakers known as "Four-minute men," who spoke in factories during the lunch hour, at every theater and motion-picture show, at restaurants, on the trains — everywhere, in fact, where they could find an audience. He called on the nation's most gifted artists to make posters. He recruited song leaders to lead patriotic singing by theater audiences. He asked the advertising men of the country to help make America war-conscious. As a result of this vast patriotic campaign the nation was stirred as it never had been before. Every man, woman, and child wanted to help win the war. All were uplifted in the belief that the war was a crusade for democracy, a war to end wars, injustice, and oppression.

AMERICAN "DOUGHBOYS" *on the battle line in France. The soldiers lived and fought in trenches. Although they give added protection from the enemy, life in trenches is very hard and uncomfortable.* (Courtesy of United States Army Signal Corps)

The Germans take the offensive, 1918. German leaders knew they had to win the war before American troops arrived in large numbers. Russia had collapsed, releasing forty divisions of fresh German troops to fight in France. In high hopes of victory the Germans made ready to take the offensive in the spring of 1918. They had two hundred divisions to oppose one hundred sixty-two divisions of French and British.

Late in March, 1918, the Germans began a strong attack on the southern end of the British line, near the point where it joined the French line. Within eight days the enemy swept forward thirty-two miles, capturing ninety thousand prisoners and threatening to separate the British and French armies. The crisis forced the Allies for the first time to appoint a commander in chief. General Ferdinand Foch was chosen.

A few days later the Germans began a second drive against the British line. General Haig called on his troops to fight to the last man: "With our backs to the wall, and believing in the justice of our cause, each one of us must fight on to the end." The situation was so grave that Pershing postponed his plan for an independent American army and offered all his resources to Foch. American troops rushed to the front to serve with British and French units at weak spots in the line

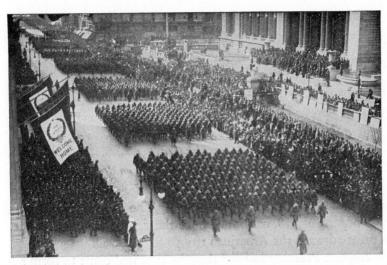

HOME–COMING OF VETERANS FROM OVERSEAS, 1919. *Through wildly cheering crowds men of the American Expeditionary Force marched along Fifth Avenue, New York.* (Acme)

A third German drive began late in May. It was finally stopped on the banks of the Marne, within fifty miles of Paris. At Château-Thierry the French were too weak to make a stand, and the Americans blocked the German advance. Afterward, in a fierce counterattack, American marines drove the Germans out of Belleau Wood. The German command was surprised to discover how well the Americans could fight.

On July 15 the Germans thundered across the Marne in another powerful drive. They were successful everywhere except when they ran into the fresh American divisions. American resistance was so stubborn that the German chief of staff complained, "The Americans appear inexhaustible." By July 18 the strength of the German attack was used up. Foch called upon the Americans to counterattack, and they drove a deep wedge into the German lines. "The tide of war," said Pershing, "was definitely turned in favor of the Allies." Later the German chancellor wrote:

At the beginning of July, 1918, I was convinced that before the first of September our adversaries would send peace proposals. . . . That was on the 15th. On the 18th even the most optimistic among us knew that all was lost. The history of the world was played out in three days.

THE ARMISTICE *ending World War I began on November 11, 1918.*

A separate American army is formed. The Allied counteroffensive, which began July 18, continued until the signing of the armistice. In this great advance the American troops fought well.

In August, Pershing insisted that the time had come to form a separate American army, so the scattered American troops were brought together. They were given the task of pinching off a dent in the Allied front known as the "Saint Mihiel salient." Over half a million American soldiers were in this battle, which freed seventy French villages from German occupation.

France is cleared of the enemy. Late in September, Foch ordered an attack along the entire Allied line. The task of the American army, which by this time included one million, two hundred thousand men, was to push the Germans out of the Argonne Forest. The sector was strongly fortified, and in addition its ridges and deep ravines, all densely wooded, made it hard to take and easy to defend. The battle was the greatest and longest in American history. It raged for forty-seven days, with heavy losses on both sides. Step by step the Germans were forced back a distance of about thirty miles. The battle ended with the capture of Sedan, an important railroad center. Farther to the west the British and French armies were also advancing. Part of Belgium and nearly all of France had been cleared of the enemy. By the second week of November the German army was in danger of destruction.

The armistice, November 11, 1918. Germany's allies had already surrendered. Revolution threatened in Germany; the Kaiser was about to flee. And now the German high command faced the greatest military disaster in history. To avoid this, the Berlin government asked for an immediate armistice; and five days later, November 11, at eleven in the morning, firing ceased.

To identify: Allies, Central Powers, Committee on Public Information, Ferdinand Foch, Food Administrator, Herbert Hoover, Lafayette, *Lusitania*, John J. Pershing, Selective Service Act.

To explain or define: armistice, liberty bond, pro-Ally.

SUBJECTS FOR TALKS OR WRITTEN REPORTS

1. The Navy's part in World War I. 2. Fighting the German submarine in World War I. 3. Women's part in American war industries, 1917–18. 4. New weapons used in World War I (especially poison gas, the airplane, the tank, the submarine, long-range guns). 5. What trench warfare was like in World War I. 6. Life aboard a troop transport in World War I. 7. Popular songs in World War I. 8. The work of the Red Cross in World War I. 9. Animal heroes in World War I.

QUESTIONS FOR UNDERSTANDING THE TEXT

1. What causes of complaint against Great Britain did the United States have in the early days of the war? 2. Compare the violations of neutral rights of the United States before it entered World War I with those that led to the War of 1812. 3. Why did Wilson adopt a firmer tone toward Germany than toward England when writing notes complaining of interference with American neutral rights? 4. Should the United States have gone to war after the sinking of the *Lusitania?* 5. (*a*) Why did Germany decide on all-out submarine warfare? (*b*) When did this begin? 6. Why did the United States go to war with Germany? 7. Show that President Wilson considered the part of the United States in the war a crusade or mission. 8. What features of the draft in World War I may have helped prevent draft riots like those of the War between North and South? 9. What did Wilson mean by saying, "It is not an army we must shape and train for war — it is a nation"? 10. Why was it said, "Food will win the war"? 11. How did the United States manage to double its food exports to Europe after it entered the war? 12. How did the United States obtain money to finance the war? 13. What was responsible for the remarkable patriotic spirit that developed after the United States entered the war? 14. Why did the German high command think it must win its spring and summer offensive of 1918 or lose the war? 15. Why did not Pershing plan on large-scale operations in France in 1918? What caused him to change his plans? 16. Is it true, as Hitler claimed, that the German armies were not defeated on the field of battle in World War I? 17. Is it true that the United States was responsible for the defeat of Germany? 18. Turn to page 569 and discuss the relative cost of World War I to the United States, Russia, France, the British Empire, and Italy.

CHAPTER 38

THE UNITED STATES FAILS
TO WIN THE PEACE

The United States becomes a world leader. Entrance into World War I gave the United States a position of leadership in world affairs. President Wilson wanted to use our influence (1) to promote democracy in Europe, and (2) to establish an association, or league, of nations to keep the peace. Just as communities have courts to settle disputes between individuals and to punish lawbreakers, he thought that nations should band together to have a world court and to see that quarrels between nations were settled justly and peaceably. In this way the nations could create a system of *collective security* in which even the smallest would be safe from attack.

President Wilson made it plain that the United States had no selfish war aims — it desired no territory or war damages. It was not seeking revenge; it did not want to crush Germany, but only to destroy the undemocratic German government. "We have no quarrel," Wilson said, "with the German people." We were fighting, he repeated again and again, for a world order of peace and justice.

Wilson hoped to persuade the Allied leaders to accept the same war aims as the United States. Early in 1918 he outlined his program for a peace without revenge. There were fourteen points, the more important being (1) an end to secret treaties, (2) freedom of the seas in peace and in war, (3) the removal of barriers to world trade, (4) reduction of armaments, (5) self-government for subject peoples (minorities), and (6) an association, or league, of nations to keep the peace and insure the independence of all. The remaining points had to do mainly with the return of conquered territories in Europe to their peoples and the adjustment of boundaries and colonial claims for the benefit of the population concerned. It was a program worthy of a great democratic nation. For the time being it made Wilson the moral leader of the world.

The world looks to Wilson for a just and lasting peace. George Creel used Wilson's peace program as a weapon against the enemy. He showered Germany and Austria-Hungary with leaflets containing the Fourteen Points. A great many of the enemy were stirred by these leaflets. Peace on Wilson's terms looked so attractive that they began to wonder why they should go on fighting. In the end the governments of both countries crumbled. The Germans asked for peace based on the Fourteen Points and set up a democratic government. The unhappy minorities within Austria-Hungary refused to go on fighting to keep alive an empire in which they had no freedom.

The Fourteen Points were studied not only in the enemy countries but throughout the world. To millions of war-weary people they brought new hope — hope that a day was at hand in which the nations would live together in peace and justice. Wilson began to be thought of as a kind of world savior. In southern and eastern Europe the peasants put up pictures of Wilson beside images of the saints.

Wilson goes to the Peace Conference. In the armistice agreement with Germany the Allies promised to make a peace treaty based on the Fourteen Points. At the same time the Allies got President Wilson's consent to a point of their own — that Germany should pay for the damage done by her armed forces to civilians and their property. With these very general ideas on how the peace treaty would be written, the war came to an end.

The Peace Conference was called to meet in Paris on January 18, 1919. Delegates from thirty-two countries opposed to the Central Powers would be there, but none from the Central Powers or Russia. Some of the countries represented were eager for spoils, and some wanted to crush Germany so completely that she could never rise again. Would the American peace program be carried out if Wilson was not there to insist upon it? Could any other American sent to Paris speak with the authority of the President? Wilson thought not, so he decided to go to Paris as the head of the American Peace Commission. The decision offended many Americans. Some believed the President should never leave American soil. Others thought his trip was due to a wish to be in the spotlight. He was further criticized because he appointed three Democrats and only one Republican to the Peace Commission. He left for Paris in a storm of criticism, most of it from Republican newspapers.

The President received a wonderful welcome in Europe. He was the guest of honor at great celebrations in France, England, and Italy.

Crowds cheered him wherever he went. It is easy to understand their feelings. Wilson stood for justice, and the people of every country thought their own particular demands were just. Besides, he stood for democracy and peace. An Italian workingman remarked to an American reporter:

> They say he thinks of us — the poor people; that he wants us all to have a fair chance; that he is going to do something when he gets here that will make it impossible for our government to send us to war again. If he had only come sooner! I have already lost my two sons. Do you believe he is strong enough to stop all wars?

Wilson was deeply touched by the faith shown in him by the common people of Europe. Yet he knew they expected too much. On the way to the Peace Conference he said to George Creel:

> I am wondering if you have not unconsciously spun a net for me. It is to America that the whole world turns, not only with its wrongs but with its hopes and grievances. . . . Yet these ancient wrongs, these present unhappinesses, are not to be remedied in a day or with a wave of the hand. What I seem to see — I hope I am wrong — is a tragedy of disappointment.

The work of the Peace Conference. Never had a peace conference faced so many difficult problems. Border fights were still going on in eastern Europe. There was famine in the defeated countries, and Communism threatened to spread over them. Order must be restored with all possible speed. Germany and Austria must be made harmless. The boundaries of the new republics — Poland, Finland, Czechoslovakia, Yugoslavia, Estonia, Latvia, and Lithuania — must be established. The amount to be paid by Germany for war damages must be considered. There were scores of other troublesome questions to be taken up.

The conference divided into a number of commissions, each responsible for making recommendations on certain problems. The recommendations were studied by the "Big Three" — Lloyd George, the British prime minister; Clemenceau, the French prime minister; and President Wilson. Those recommendations accepted by the Big Three were then presented to the entire conference. The agreements reached by the conference became treaties when signed by the countries concerned.

The most important agreement was the Treaty of Versailles (named for the suburb of Paris where it was signed). This treaty declared Ger-

FOUR LEADERS AT THE PEACE CONFERENCE. *From right to left, they are President Wilson, Premier Clemenceau of France, Prime Minister Lloyd George of Great Britain, and Premier Orlando of Italy.* (Courtesy of United States Signal Corps)

many guilty of starting the war, forced her to disarm, took away all her colonies, and required her to pay war damages, or reparations, to the limit of her ability. The terms were harsh, though less so than those Germany had imposed on Russia in 1917. Wilson finally agreed to them because there was no other way to get the support of Clemenceau and Lloyd George for the project nearest his heart — the League of Nations. Wilson thought that the League would have power to correct any injustices and mistakes contained in the treaties, and he felt sure that in time it would do so.

The League of Nations. The idea of an association of nations was not new. For years statesmen on both sides of the Atlantic had been saying it was needed. In 1914 former President Taft outlined a plan for a League of Nations to Enforce Peace. A year later many leading Americans of both parties formed an organization to work for this league. As the terrible war dragged on, the common people of America and Europe became interested in the idea of an association of nations to prevent war. Wilson spoke for them when he insisted that the Covenant (constitution) of the League of Nations be made part of the Treaty of Versailles.

The League of Nations came into being in January, 1920. Its duties were (1) to enforce the peace treaties made at Paris, (2) to promote international co-operation, and (3) to work for collective security. Membership was open to all self-governing nations, including Canada, Australia, and the other dominions in the British Commonwealth of Nations.

The League was governed by an Assembly and a Council. The Assembly, in which every member nation had one vote, had power to take up any matter that concerned the peace of the world. It met once each year. On most questions it could decide nothing without a unanimous vote. It could not force a member to take any action against its will. It was far from being a superstate or world government.

The Council acted as an executive committee for the Assembly. It had from three to five permanent members and from four to eleven others chosen by the Assembly for three-year terms. Had the United States joined the League, it would have received one of the permanent seats on the Council. Decisions of the Council did not become final until approved by the Assembly. In emergencies, however, the Council could act without waiting for the Assembly to come together, provided that all members of the Council were agreed.

Each member of the League pledged itself not to interfere with the territory and independence of the other members and to defend them from attack. This was stated in Article X of the Covenant, which Wilson called the "heart of the League." Members also promised to place their disputes before the Council, the World Court, or a board of arbitrators. In case one of the parties in a dispute should refuse to settle it peaceably and should go to war, then the members of the League were pledged to make it stop fighting. This was Article XVI. The steps to be taken against an aggressor (a nation guilty of starting a war) were to be decided by the Council. The Council might ask all members of the League not to trade with the aggressor. If this failed to stop the fight, the Council might then ask the members to use their armed forces against the aggressor. If the members really lived up to their obligations under Articles X and XVI, any war could be stopped. Time proved that some members of the League were not ready to compel an aggressor to keep the peace. That is how the plan for collective security broke down. Had the United States been a member of the League, and had it used its great influence to support Articles X and XVI, the story of the League might have been very different.

While the League failed to prevent war, it carried on a great deal of useful work. It promoted international co-operation in such fields as public health, education, transportation, communication, and the care

TERRITORIAL LOSSES

░░ by Russia

▨ by Germany

▒ by Austria-Hungary

■ by Bulgaria

----- Boundaries of 1914

——— Boundaries of 1923

NORWAY

SWEDEN

FINLAND

SOVIET UNION

ESTONIA

LATVIA

LITHUANIA

NORTH SEA

DENMARK

ENGLAND

Danzig

EAST PRUSSIA

NETH.

BELGIUM

GERMANY

POLAND

CZECHOSLOVAKIA

FRANCE

SWITZERLAND

AUSTRIA HUNGARY

RUMANIA

ITALY

JUGOSLAVIA

Serbia

Monte-negro

BULGARIA

BLACK SEA

CORSICA

SARDINIA

BALEARIC IS.

ALBANIA

GREECE

TURKEY

MEDITERRANEAN SEA

SICILY

CRETE

TERRITORIAL CHANGES IN EUROPE, 1918–1923

COUNCIL WING OF THE LEAGUE OF NATIONS PALACE *at Geneva, Switzer-land. This large and beautiful structure was completed in 1938.* (From *The Palace of the League of Nations,* by Louis Cheronnet. Published by *L'Illustration,* Paris)

of refugees. It gathered information and published reports on all kinds of international problems. It established the World Court, which set-tled a number of disputes between nations. The World Court was successful in every case where both parties to the dispute were willing to have it settled peaceably.

The fight against the treaty in America. When Wilson returned to the United States in July, 1919, he laid the Treaty of Versailles, includ-ing the League Covenant, before the Senate. At that time a clear ma-jority of the American people seem to have favored signing the treaty and thereby joining the League. Thirty-two state legislatures had gone on record in favor of the League. A poll of newspaper editors showed that most of them believed we should join the League. Even in the Senate a majority was ready to vote for the treaty and the League. Wilson did not doubt that he could win the support of the two thirds necessary to ratify a treaty.

Senator Lodge of Massachusetts, a prominent Republican and a bit-ter enemy of the President, was chairman of the Senate Committee on Foreign Relations. He made up his mind to take out of the treaty the very parts which Wilson thought most important, especially Article X of the League Covenant. His committee was packed with men un-friendly to the League. They decided to keep the treaty from reaching the Senate floor until public opinion could be turned against it. For weeks they held hearings, at which every imaginable argument against the treaty and the League was brought forward. Then Lodge and a few others made a vigorous fight against the treaty on the floor of the Senate. They attacked the League as a superstate which would order American boys to fight anywhere in the world where trouble happened to break out. They claimed that the League might interfere with purely home affairs, such as the tariff and immigration. They repeated over and over again that England would have six votes in the League to our one — an argument which led millions to oppose the treaty. (The statement was based on the fact that each of the British dominions had a vote in the Assembly.)

Wilson was asking the American people to turn their backs on the old policy of nonentanglement with European affairs. This policy had been laid down by Washington, Jefferson, and Monroe; to depart from it, said Wilson's enemies, was un-American. The Hearst papers took as their slogan "One hundred per cent Americanism"; they considered a "one hundred per cent American" to be one who opposed the treaty and the League. The advertisement of an anti-League meeting in Boston is an example of the attacks made on the League:

AMERICANS AWAKE!!

Shall we bind ourselves to the War Breeding Covenant?
It impairs [injures] American Sovereignty!
Surrenders the Monroe Doctrine!
Flouts [disregards] Washington's warning!
Entangles Us in European and Asiatic Intrigues [Quarrels]!
Sends Our Boys to Fight throughout the World by Order of a
 League!
"The evil thing with a holy name!"

Such appeals to fear, hate, and national pride gave a false idea of the League's actual power, which, as we have seen, was extremely limited. The strong feelings aroused prevented clear thinking about America's place in world affairs.

Wilson appeals to the nation. Led by Senator Lodge, the Republicans in the Senate planned to "Americanize" the treaty by adding reservations, or amendments, to it. Most of the reservations had to do with Articles X and XVI of the League Covenant. Wilson thought that the changes proposed would make the League helpless to prevent war.

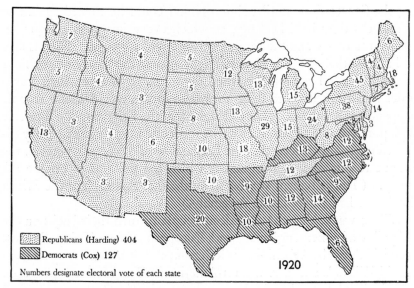

Republicans (Harding) 404
Democrats (Cox) 127
Numbers designate electoral vote of each state

1920

THE PRESIDENTIAL ELECTION OF 1920

He decided to make a nationwide tour to explain the treaty directly to the people. When they understood it, he felt they would support him in his struggle against the politicians. Paying no attention to the advice of physicians and friends (for he was sixty-three and worn out from the strain of the past six years), he started a speaking trip that might have exhausted the most vigorous man. Wilson knew the risk he was taking and said he would be glad to give his life to save the League.

East of the Mississippi his audiences were lukewarm, but as he went farther west they received him with more and more enthusiasm. In Seattle, San Francisco, and Pueblo, Colorado, there were great demonstrations in his honor. It seemed that his efforts to rally the people were succeeding. But after giving nearly forty speeches, he reached the end of his strength. He collapsed in Colorado and was rushed back to Washington. For the rest of his term he lay in the White House, a shattered old man. Without his leadership the fight for the treaty was lost. In March, 1920, the Senate finally rejected the treaty and the League.

The election of 1920. Wilson did not know the fight was lost. He still hoped that public opinion would force the Senate to accept the treaty without serious changes. He declared that the presidential election of 1920 would give the people a chance to vote on the League.

The Democrats nominated Governor Cox, of Ohio, who came out strongly for the League. The Republicans chose Senator Warren Harding, of Ohio. He promised peace and quiet — "normalcy" — and avoided taking a clear-cut stand either for or against the League. Former President Taft and some other well-known Republicans supported Harding as the surest way of getting into the League; others supported him as the surest way of keeping out. It was very confusing, and by this time the average voter had lost interest in the whole question. He was tired of hearing about international problems which he did not understand. On election day a landslide swept Harding into office.

The election cannot be considered a vote on the League. The Republican victory was due to many causes, some of them going back to the beginning of Wilson's Presidency, when he attacked big business. If the election meant anything, it meant that the voters were tired of Democratic rule and Wilsonian idealism. They wanted a change. The good-natured, easygoing Harding, with his offer of a return to normalcy, was just the man to suit them at that particular time.

We return to isolationism. The fight over the treaty was between two groups of Americans — the *internationalists*, who thought the United States should use its influence to establish a system of collective security, and the *nationalists*, or *isolationists*, who thought we could safely turn our backs on world affairs. The 1920 election convinced Harding that the isolationists spoke for the people. As President he had nothing to do with the League of Nations and did his best to isolate the United States from the rest of the world, especially from Europe.

For the first time in its history, the Republican party stood for isolation. Ever since the War between North and South it had tried to expand our territory and our influence, but now it tried to follow a policy laid down when the nation was small and helpless. This policy kept America from taking any real responsibility for world affairs. A sizable section of the Democratic party also favored isolation. The result was that throughout the 1920's and 1930's the United States had as little as possible to do with Europe and the League of Nations.

We see now that by supporting the League we might have strengthened those groups in Europe who believed in justice and collective security. By refusing to support the League, we strengthened other groups of Europeans who wanted to conduct international affairs by the old methods that time after time had led to war. Collective security did not receive a fair trial. The new world order of peace and justice was never built. That is how we lost the peace.

❀ ❀ ❀

Names to identify: Big Three, British Commonwealth of Nations, Clemenceau, Lloyd George, Warren Harding, Senator Lodge, Treaty of Versailles, World Court.

Words to explain or define: aggressor, armament, collective security, covenant, dominion, internationalist, isolationist, reparations.

Subjects for Talks or Written Reports

1. Mistakes made by Wilson in 1918–1919 which weakened his influence in the United States. 2. Wilson's struggle at the Peace Conference with (*a*) Clemenceau, (*b*) Lloyd George, and (*c*) Orlando. 3. The rebirth of Poland at the Peace Conference, with an explanation of the Polish Corridor. 4. Territory taken from Russia at the Peace Conference and what was done with it. 5. What became of the territory of Austria-Hungary? 6. What was done with the German colonies? 7. Senator Lodge's battle against Wilson. 8. What the League of Nations accomplished in promoting international co-operation. 9. How the League of Nations was supported and how much it cost. 10. The personality and ideals of President Harding compared to those of President Wilson.

Questions for Understanding the Text

1. (*a*) Outline Wilson's peace program. (*b*) Why did it make him the moral leader of the world? 2. (*a*) How did Wilson's peace program influence the Germans? (*b*) The Austro-Hungarians? 3. (*a*) Why did Wilson decide to attend the Peace Conference? (*b*) What did critics say of his decision? Of his appointments to the Peace Commission? 4. What grave problems faced the Peace Conference? 5. How did the Peace Conference carry on its work? 6. Name the principal terms of the Treaty of Versailles. 7. (*a*) What were the three duties of the League of Nations? (*b*) In which was it most successful? 8. How was the League of Nations governed? 9. (*a*) Show that the League of Nations was not a superstate or world government. (*b*) Show that it could not take any important steps without the consent of all its members. 10. What did Articles X and XVI of the League Covenant require the members of the League to promise? 11. (*a*) Outline the main arguments against the League of Nations. (*b*) Which arguments were based on a faulty understanding of the League? 12. (*a*) Tell about Wilson's speaking tour in 1919. (*b*) Had he been able to use the radio, how might it have changed the outcome of his struggle with the Senate? 13. Discuss the presidential campaign of

1920. Why did Harding win?   14. (*a*) How did the Republican party try to expand American territory and influence in the years between 1865 and 1912?   (*b*) Did it continue this policy after World War I?   Explain.

ACTIVITIES FOR UNIT EIGHT

1. Show by a pictograph or bar graph the comparative area, population, and national wealth of Alaska, Hawaii, the Philippines, and Puerto Rico.
2. Draw a cartoon to show the main results of the Spanish-American War.
3. Appoint committees to prepare an illustrated book on United States possessions. Cover their history, resources, people, living conditions, industries, government, and their feelings about American rule.
4. Make a model or a panoramic painting of the Panama Canal.
5. Develop a panel discussion on the question of whether or not the United States was justified in intervening in the affairs of the Caribbean nations that were unable to pay their debts.
6. On outline maps show (*a*) the principal events of the Spanish-American War, (*b*) American possessions, with the date when each was obtained, (*c*) Europe before and after World War I, (*d*) the farthest Russian and the farthest German advances on the eastern front during World War I, (*e*) the farthest German advance on the western front and the German line at the time of the armistice.
7. Hold an exhibit of relics and pictures of World War I. Prepare a catalogue explaining each item and telling who lent it to you. Invite other classes to view the exhibit.
8. Make an outline of the principal events between the outbreak of World War I and the declaration of war by the United States.
9. Have the class sing some of the best songs of World War I.
10. Write an illustrated report on the use of the aircraft in World War I.
11. Make a chart showing the material and the human cost of World War I to the United States and to the warring nations as a whole.
12. Make a table in which you list in two columns the differences between World War I and World War II.
13. List in two columns the possible advantages and disadvantages to the United States had it joined the League of Nations in 1920.

READINGS FOR UNIT EIGHT

(Stars indicate the easier books)

GENERAL ACCOUNTS

Beals, Carleton. *The Crime of Cuba*. Lippincott.
*Bond, A. R. *Inventions of the Great War*. Appleton-Century.
*Finger, C. J. *Our Navy*.
Fish, C. R. *The Path of Empire*. (Chronicles)

Franck, H. A. *Roaming in Hawaii.* Stokes.
Hayes, C. J. H. *A Brief History of the Great War.* Macmillan.
*Nida, Stella M. *Panama and Its "Bridge of Water."* Rand McNally.
Reck, Daisy. *Puerto Rico and the Virgin Islands.* Farrar & Rinehart.
*Rolt-Wheeler, Francis. *The Boys' Book of the World War.* Lothrop.
Sears, L. M. *A History of American Foreign Relations.* Crowell.
Slosson, P. W. *The Great Crusade and After, 1914–1928.* (A. L. S.)
*Stefansson, Evelyn. *Here Is Alaska.* Scribner's.
Sullivan, Mark. *Our Times, 1900–1925,* 5 vols. Scribner's.
*Thomas, Lowell. *Raiders of the Deep.* Doubleday, Doran.
*Thomson, J. E. *Our Atlantic Possessions.* Scribner's.
*———. *Our Pacific Possessions.* Scribner's.
*Verrill, A. H. *Panama of Today.* Dodd, Mead.
Wood, William and Gabriel, Ralph H. *In Defense of Liberty.* (Pageant)

BIOGRAPHY

Dodd, W. E. *Woodrow Wilson and His Work.* Doubleday, Doran.
*Fast, Howard M. *Goethals and the Panama Canal.* Messner.
*Judson, Clara. *Soldier Doctor; the Story of William Gorgas.* Scribner's.
McCracken, Harold. *Pershing, the Story of a Great Soldier.* Brewer and Warren.
Parkman, M. R. *Fighters for Peace.* Appleton-Century. (Statesmen)
Pershing, John J. *My Experiences in the World War.* Stokes.
Seymour, C. *Woodrow Wilson and the World War.* (Chronicles)
Simonds, F. H. *They Won the War.* Harper. (Leading generals)

FICTION

*Abbott, W. J. *Blue Jackets of 1918.* Dodd, Mead.
Cather, Willa. *One of Ours.* Knopf.
*Driggs, L. L. *The Adventures of Arnold Adair, American Ace.* Little, Brown.
Gerould, G. H. *Filibuster.* Appleton-Century. (War in Cuba)
Haines, D. H. *The Dragon-Flies.* Houghton-Mifflin. (Aviation)
Kantor, MacKinlay. *Cuba Libre.* Coward-McCann. (Cuba, 1899–1914)
*Lamprey, Louise. *Days of the Leaders.* Stokes. (Stories about war)
Nordhoff, C. B. and Hall, James Norman. *Falcons of France.* Little, Brown. (Air warfare in World War I)
*Paine, R. D. *Ships Across the Sea.* Houghton Mifflin. (Short stories)
*Rolt-Wheeler, Francis. *Wonders of War in the Air.* Lothrop.
*———. *The Wonder of War on Land.* Lothrop.
*Thompson, A. R. *Gold-seeking on the Dalton Trail.* Little, Brown.
Thompson, C. G. *Terry, a Tale of the Hill People.* Macmillan. (The Philippines, 1900–1902)

UNIT NINE

DOMESTIC AFFAIRS (1920–1940)

After World War I the people of the United States seemed weary of hardships and self-sacrifice. Many wanted to give their whole attention to making money, often through speculation and sometimes through fraud. Others gave themselves to the pursuit of pleasure. Idealism was out of style.

The country appeared to be remarkably prosperous. There was a lively demand for luxuries. The stock market was booming. City land and real estate soared. Careful observers, however, saw signs of coming disaster, for the farmers were having hard times and in the cities unemployment was gradually increasing.

The crash came in October, 1929. Millions lost the savings of a lifetime. As spending stopped, unemployment grew. By 1932 the country was in the depths of a fearful depression, the worst and longest in its history. The people blamed the party that was in power and that fall the Republicans suffered a crushing defeat. For the first time since Woodrow Wilson, a Democrat was elected President.

The new President, Franklin D. Roosevelt, got Congress to vote huge sums to relieve the needy and to make jobs for the jobless. He also launched a remarkable program of reform, which won the approval of most progressives and members of labor unions. This reform program was interrupted by the outbreak of World War II.

THE CRAZE FOR GAMBLING IN STOCKS. *From 1925 to mid-October, 1929, stock prices moved rapidly upward. Millions of people who had no experience in the buying of stocks were attracted to the stock market in the belief that any security they bought would rise in value. Some bought a great deal of worthless paper from crooked promoters. Often they borrowed money to pay for securities on which they expected to make a fortune. The whole nation seemed to be living in a fool's paradise.* (**Drawn** by Fitzpatrick for *Collier's Weekly*, 1929)

CHAPTER 39

DISASTER FOLLOWS THE "MAD TWENTIES"

Why the twenties are called "mad." A letdown in morals and ideals followed World War I. Most Americans were tired of idealism, both in foreign affairs and at home. They had lost interest in reform, so they turned their backs on Wilsonism and the whole progressive movement. More than ever before they busied themselves in making and spending money. A craze for speculating led to land booms here and there, and later to a most remarkable boom in the stock market. There was a great deal of lawlessness. Crooked stock promoters fleeced the public of billions of dollars. Respectable citizens disobeyed the prohibition laws. Bootleggers and racketeers flourished. Politics had seldom been more corrupt. The idea that government should let business alone again became popular. National feeling was very strong, and it was often shown in undesirable ways.

A period of nationalism. The strong nationalism of the years following the war was commonly expressed in such slogans as "America first," and "One hundred per cent Americanism." It caused the United States to remain outside the League of Nations and the World Court. It led to the passage of strict immigration laws, which closed the doors to most European and all Asiatic labor. Nationalism also showed itself in dislike of foreigners and of anyone who criticized the American way of life.

After the Bolshevik revolution in Russia (October, 1917), men of wealth everywhere feared the spread of Communism. The next year Congress passed an Alien Act under which foreigners could be deported for their opinions. In carrying out this Act the Department of Justice rounded up thousands of aliens thought to have radical ideas and deported them without the benefit of a regular trial. The Act was repealed in 1921.

During the twenties anyone who criticized business or the government was considered un-American and suspected of being a "Red." Socialists, although they believed in peaceful and constitutional meth-

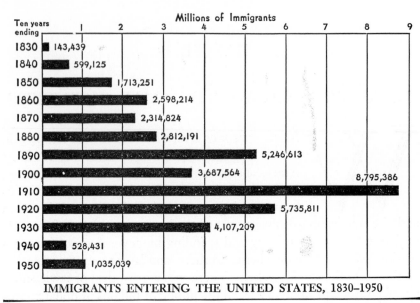

IMMIGRANTS ENTERING THE UNITED STATES, 1830–1950

In 1921 Congress limited the number of immigrants to be admitted annually from any one country. The Immigration Act of 1924 carried this policy further by reducing the total number of immigrants to be admitted to 164,667. In 1927 this number was set at 150,000. After 1930 the Immigration Service let in very few immigrants.

ods of change, were thought to be dangerous radicals. Progressives and pacifists were looked on with suspicion and sometimes had difficulty in securing a public hall for their meetings. Most of the states passed laws intended to force people to be loyal to the American political and economic system. In some states teachers were required to take an oath to uphold American institutions.

A new Ku Klux Klan sprang up to fight so-called "un-American" ideas. It was directed mainly against Catholics, Jews, foreigners, and Negroes. Adopting the disguise and the methods of the Klan of Reconstruction days (see pages 331–332), it spread terror over a large part of America. Where the Klan was strong, newspapers and politicians feared to lift their voices against it, and business and professional men had to join or lose their customers and clients. At its peak in 1925 the Klan had over five million members. In 1928 it helped defeat the Democratic candidate for President, Alfred E. Smith, mainly because he was a Catholic. The Klan expressed a kind of national feeling ill-suited to a land of liberty. The "one hundred per cent Americans" who led it cared nothing for our great traditions of freedom and justice for all. Fortunately the Klan lost much of its influence by the end of the twenties.

A period of lawlessness. In 1919 the Eighteenth, or Prohibition, Amendment was added to the Constitution. In spite of the fact that the Amendment was approved by forty-six of the forty-eight states, and probably at least two thirds of the people wanted it to succeed, prohibition was a failure. Those who wanted liquor were determined to have it, even at a very high price. The profits from selling liquor illegally were so great that sellers were willing to pay large bribes to the officers responsible for enforcing the law. Almost every city of any size had "speakeasies" and numerous bootleggers. Some of the liquor was brought in by smugglers, or rumrunners; some of it was made illegally within our borders. Much of this lawless business was in the hands of powerful and well-organized gangs of criminals. Often one gang stole liquor from another gang, this practice being known as "hijacking."

Gangsters sometimes used the money they made in the liquor business to branch out into other kinds of crime, particularly kidnaping and racketeering. A "racket" usually consisted of forcing businessmen to pay the gang for so-called "protection." In the dry-cleaning business, for example, it was necessary to buy "protection" to keep the gangsters from secretly placing acids in the cleaning fluids.

Gradually most of the friends of prohibition became discouraged. They began to think that perhaps it would be best to return the control of the liquor business to the states and to try, by education of the young, to solve the drink problem. By 1932 the Democratic party dared to take a firm stand in favor of repeal, and a year later repeal was voted.

Business is given a free rein. For twelve years, 1921 to 1933, the government was in the hands of conservative, or "Old Guard," Republicans. Harding, Coolidge, and Hoover, who occupied the White House in turn, believed that "the business of the United States is business." They wished to free private enterprise from government control and also to assist it in every possible way. They neither enforced the antitrust laws nor did anything else to limit the growth of big business.

Congress was equally friendly to big business. It voted large sums of money, or *subsidies,* to aviation companies and shipowners. It helped nationwide advertising by keeping the postage rate for magazines below the cost of the service. In 1922 it raised the tariff to the

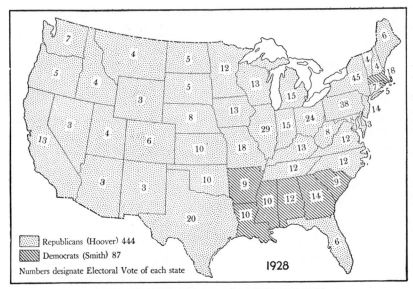

THE PRESIDENTIAL ELECTION OF 1928

Republicans (Hoover) 444
Democrats (Smith) 87
Numbers designate Electoral Vote of each state

1928

highest level yet reached, and eight years later raised it still higher. Congress also reduced income and corporation taxes again and again, shifting much of the tax burden from the shoulders of the rich to those of the middle class and the poor.

The public in general seemed satisfied to have the government help big business. The old fear of the great corporations had largely disappeared. This change was partly due to the fact that since the war millions of Americans had bought industrial stocks. In part it was due to the new comforts and luxuries made possible by large-scale production. As automobiles, radios, mechanical refrigerators, and other conveniences came into common use, people felt that the companies who made them were doing a public service and deserved every consideration from the government. Big business helped to encourage this way of thinking.

Progressives attack the power trust. A few voices could still be heard urging control of big business. They were particularly concerned about the electric power industry. This had now become one of the nation's largest and most necessary industries. Like other public utilities, it was in need of strict regulation. The states were unsuccessful in their efforts to bring the industry under control because so much electric power crossed state lines.

In 1920 Congress set up the Federal Power Commission to license hydroelectric plants on navigable rivers. Since nine tenths of the nation's electricity was produced in steam plants, and many of the hydroelectric plants were not on navigable streams, the Commission had control over only a small part of the electric industry. Throughout the twenties a little group of progressives in Congress tried to get federal regulation of all power companies doing business across state lines. They were backed by several state governors, including Alfred E. Smith, of New York, and his successor, Franklin D. Roosevelt.

Some progressives urged government ownership as the only way to get low rates for small users. They pointed out that publicly owned hydroelectric plants in Canada were selling electricity to consumers at less than half the price charged by private companies in the United States. Senator Norris, of Nebraska, was the leader of this group. For years he fought to keep the government from selling its big power plant at Muscle Shoals in Alabama. This had been built during World War I to supply power for two government-owned nitrates plants and had been idle since the war. Presidents Harding, Coolidge, and Hoover favored selling both the power plant and the nitrates plants to private companies at their own price. Each time the proposal was made, Norris succeeded in blocking it. In 1928 he persuaded Congress to pass a bill directing the government to operate the plants. Coolidge vetoed the bill. In 1931 Congress passed a similar bill which Hoover vetoed in ringing words.

Business prospers and grows bigger. After a brief depression in 1920–21, business boomed until almost the end of the twenties. There was a tremendous demand for automobiles, radios, electrical appliances, tractors, trucks, and farm machinery. Industries grew bigger year after year, and turned out ever greater quantities of goods. Profits were generous. Between 1922 and 1929 the 2046 leading manufacturing companies of the United States made an average profit of more than 11 per cent a year.

The stronger corporations in each industry grew larger. Railroad mergers went on until a few large systems controlled almost all of the rail lines. Electric power lines and plants came under the control of a handful of holding companies. Food manufacturers were combined into large firms. Chain stores grew rapidly; by 1929 the largest grocery chain had seventeen thousand, five hundred branches. Most theaters, newspapers, magazines, and radio stations were bought up by chains. Much of the best farm land passed into the hands of corporations. In nearly every field of work most of the business was done by a few concerns. By 1929 the two hundred largest business corporations (not including banks or insurance companies) owned as much wealth as their three hundred thousand competitors. In fact, these same two hundred giants owned nearly one fourth of the nation's total wealth.

Business sells to the masses. Mass-production industries need a wide market. They must sell to the masses or else shut down. That is why national advertising developed so rapidly during the twenties. By 1929 two billion dollars a year was being spent on advertising — five times as much as in 1915. Advertising quickly created a demand for new comforts and luxuries. Every American family began to dream of owning a new car, a radio-phonograph, modern plumbing, and modern home furnishings. Millions of families bought these things, usually on the installment plan, that is, they paid so much each week or month.

During the twenties our industries increased their output by about 50 per cent. The earnings of the masses of people rose too slowly to enable them to buy all the additional goods being produced. For a time the surplus was sold abroad. When our export market fell off, the surplus stayed in the warehouses. Yet only one of every two American families had any sort of car; only one in twenty had a mechanical refrigerator; and even in cities nearly half the homes were without such comforts as electric lights and furnace heat. It took a terrible depression to make clear the simple fact that the masses of people in the United States had too little buying power to keep mass-production industries running full time.

The stock market boom. The years 1922 to 1929 brought the greatest business prosperity the nation had ever known. Although farmers were going through hard times and there were never less than two million unemployed wage earners, the earnings of businessmen and stockholders and many industrial workers were rising. This created a spirit of rosy optimism.

The spirit of optimism and the fact that large profits were being made in industry led to a boom in the stock market. From 1925 to mid-October, 1929, prices rose with scarcely any serious interruption. Investors were making fortunes. As the news got around, millions of people who had never before owned stock began to gamble in the stock market. Promoters took advantage of their ignorance to issue and unload vast quantities of almost worthless stocks. Both sound and un-

CALVIN COOLIDGE *was President from 1923 to 1929. This painting was made by De Witt Lockman in 1931, two years before Coolidge died.* (Courtesy of New York Historical Society)

HERBERT HOOVER *on the White House lawn, June 17, 1932, soon after his renomination by the Republican convention. He is holding his pet Norwegian elkhound.* (Associated Press)

sound stocks kept going up as more and more people rushed to buy. The country had never seen such a boom in stocks.

Many gamblers on the stock market borrowed money to buy securities. By 1928 borrowings for this purpose were so large that several leading bankers grew fearful. However, President Coolidge and Secretary of the Treasury Andrew Mellon declared that all was well. No President before had ever given advice about the stock market, but the people felt sure that Coolidge knew what he was talking about. They kept on borrowing to buy stocks. Whenever the stock market dipped, the President and the Secretary of the Treasury sent it soaring again with a statement that business was sound.

Hoover promises the end of poverty. President Coolidge declared that he did not "choose to run" for another term. He helped his Secretary of Commerce, Herbert Hoover, win the 1928 nomination for President. Hoover believed thoroughly in letting business alone. He thought the growth of big business helped the whole nation. The country's prosperity in the twenties was due, he firmly believed, to Republican policies. In his acceptance speech he claimed that his election would mean continued prosperity. He promised to lead the nation to yet undreamed-of plenty, saying:

We in America today are nearer to the final triumph over poverty than ever before in the history of any land. The poorhouse is vanishing from among us. We have not yet reached the goal, but given a chance to go forward with the policies of the last eight years, we shall soon, with the help of God, be in sight of the day when poverty shall be banished from this nation.

Hoover wins the election. The Democrats nominated Governor Alfred E. Smith, of New York. He was a progressive and had given New York a remarkably good government. He was extremely popular among city wage earners in the Northeast. However, many rural Democrats objected to him because he wanted to repeal the Prohibition Amendment and because he was a Catholic.

The campaign of 1928 was the first in which the radio played an important part. Millions who had never before heard a presidential candidate heard Smith and Hoover over the air. Mr. Smith criticized the Republicans for doing nothing for farm relief, and he also tried to stir up interest in the problem of electric power. But the public was more interested in (1) his attack on prohibition, and (2) the question of whether a Catholic ought to be permitted to become President. Although Smith received the largest popular vote ever given a Democrat, Hoover carried forty states. Four Southern states that had been Democratic since the end of reconstruction went for Hoover.

The bubble bursts. Early in 1929 there were signs that business was slowing up. Building had fallen off, and steel and automobile production was dropping. Between two and four million wage earners were unemployed. Bank and business failures were increasing. Yet few paid any attention to these warning signs. Hoover's inauguration caused stock prices to climb faster than ever. In two days in early March one bank stock rose nine hundred fifty dollars a share, and a single individual made thirteen million dollars on this stock alone. Stories of such winnings started a new wave of gambling which went on furiously until fall. Insiders, however, were now selling rather than buying.

On October 24, 1929, the market dropped sharply. This started a stampede of selling. On October 29 occurred the greatest panic in the nation's history, with stock prices slumping by fourteen billion dollars. Some stocks dropped 80 per cent that day; for others no buyers at all could be found. By the end of the year the loss in stock values came to forty billion dollars. Millions of people had lost their life savings. Scores killed themselves. There was gloom everywhere.

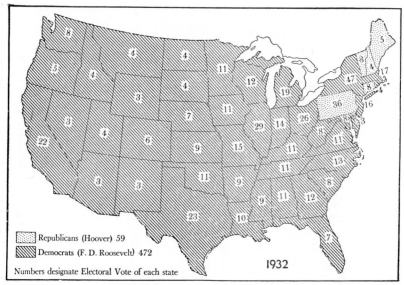

THE PRESIDENTIAL ELECTION OF 1932

For the next three years the market coasted slowly down, sometimes rising a little only to sink again. In September, 1929, the average price of 240 representative stocks was $312; by July, 1932, it had dropped to $34.

A terrible depression follows. President Hoover and many others thought that the economic system would soon adjust itself. They were mistaken. The stock market crash was followed by the worst and longest depression in American history.

The millions who had lost their savings naturally began to spend less freely, especially for things like automobiles and refrigerators. This led to severe unemployment in those industries. Unemployment cut buying power and led to still more unemployment. By the end of 1932 there were probably some thirteen million unemployed. This was about 40 per cent of the country's usual force of wage and salary earners. Most of those who still had jobs had taken wage cuts or were working part time. From their shrunken earnings workers had to support their unemployed relatives.

The relief problem. For about a year after the crash relief for the needy was left to private charity. City governments gradually had to take over most of the burden. Unfortunately hundreds of small cities and scores of large ones, including New York, Chicago, Philadelphia,

FORECLOSURE OF A CORN–BELT FARM IN 1932. *State troopers were needed to control the angry farmers who might otherwise stop the sale.* (Acme)

Detroit, Boston, and others, were close to bankruptcy. (One reason for this was that many property owners could not pay their taxes.) As a result the relief furnished the needy was often barely enough to keep them alive. In Detroit, for example, relief was, for a time, limited to seven and a half cents a day for each person. In many places the only relief to be had was in the bread line. By 1932 most of the state governments were spending money for relief, yet in large sections of the country the relief supplied was still of the scantiest sort. City and state officials claimed that the federal government ought to help carry the relief burden.

The farm problem. Ever since 1920 farmers had been pinched because of the low prices for what they had to sell and the high prices for the industrial products they had to buy. After the crash the difficulties of the farmers grew worse. Prices of farm products dropped so low that most farmers could not pay the interest on their mortgages or even meet their taxes. Between 1929 and 1933 hundreds of thousands of farms were sold at auction for nonpayment of taxes and debts. In 1932 Midwestern farmers banded together to prevent auction sales or else saw to it that the foreclosed farms were sold for a dollar or two and returned to their former owners. These actions remind us of Shays' Rebellion one hundred and fifty years earlier. (See page 97.)

Hoover tries to restore confidence. President Hoover expected the depression to be brief. The chief thing needed, he thought, was to restore public confidence in our economic system. He failed to realize or did not make public the true seriousness of the situation. From time to time he made optimistic statements, suggesting that prosperity was just around the corner. He asked employers not to cut wages or discharge their workers, and he asked the state governments to spend more money for public works in order to create jobs. Neither request had much effect. Late in 1931 he decided that the federal government should take action to speed recovery. Upon his recommendation Congress set up the Reconstruction Finance Corporation to lend federal money to large banks, railroad companies, and insurance companies which were close to failure. Congress also made small appropriations for public works, aid to distressed homeowners and farmers, and loans to the states for relief. These steps were continued on a larger scale after Franklin Roosevelt became President.

President Hoover objected to the proposal that the federal government take on the relief burden. He was also against any large-scale spending on federal public works. When a group of liberal congressmen tried to push through a bill providing two billion dollars for a public works program, he described it as "the most gigantic pork barrel ever proposed." Although conditions were getting worse, to the end of his term he clung to the idea that the depression would soon be over.

Why the depression was so severe. Ever since America became an industrial nation there had been occasional periods of hard times, always followed by a return to prosperity. Each time recovery was due to natural causes and not to action by the government. The depression which began in 1929 lasted so long that the people finally insisted on the government's taking action. Why was it so long and so severe?

In the first place the nation's capacity to produce was greater than its capacity to consume. A surplus of goods piled up which the masses were unable to buy. This was mainly because a large part of the national income was going to a small part of the population. In 1929, for example, one tenth of 1 per cent of the families in the United States received as much income as the 42 per cent of the families at the bottom of the income scale. Sixty per cent of the families of the nation earned less than $2,000 a year, an amount too little, at 1929 prices, to enable a city family to live under decent and healthful conditions. Had every family received an income of at least $2,000, all the surplus goods could have been used and much more besides. In fact, unemployment would have disappeared.*

In the second place, beginning in 1925, there was too much money to invest. The very well to do could not spend all the money they received. They saved more than could be used for new capital goods (factories, railroads, machines, trucks, office buildings, and the like). The excess savings flowed into foreign loans and the stock market. One result was the great boom in stock prices, followed by collapse.*

In the third place the nation's big businessmen followed a course which resulted in great unemployment. In earlier depressions when supplies piled up, prices dropped until consumers could buy again. This started the wheels turning, provided jobs, and led to recovery. But in this depression big business cut output instead of cutting prices. For example, the production of farm implements and of motor vehicles was cut 80 per cent, while their prices dropped only a little. On the other hand, the prices of farm products, leather, and crude oil fell 50 per cent or more, while production remained almost as large as usual, for these items are sold by a great number of competing producers who could not easily unite to control prices and cut output.

There were other reasons for the severity of the depression, among them: (1) the almost total loss of our foreign market after passage of the Smoot-Hawley Tariff Act in 1930; (2) weaknesses in the banking system which appeared in the failure of thousands of banks in 1930, 1931, and 1932; and (3) taxes which fell heavily on the masses, cutting their buying power, while doing little to prevent the further growth of large fortunes.

The depression spread to the whole world in the early thirties. President Hoover said that unsettled world conditions held back American recovery. This explanation did not satisfy those who thought that the time had come for far-reaching reforms at home.

The nation goes Democratic. The Old Guard who controlled the Republican party still fought reform. They renominated President Hoover on a conservative platform. The Democrats nominated a progressive — Governor Franklin D. Roosevelt, of New York. The outcome of the campaign was never in doubt. Roosevelt promised a "new deal" that would help the "forgotten man." He carried forty-two states and received nearly seven million more popular votes than Hoover. Both houses of Congress went Democratic by a large majority.

* The statistics and conclusions are from reports of the Brookings Institution.

To identify: Bolshevik, Calvin Coolidge, Federal Power Commission, Herbert Hoover, Andrew W. Mellon, Senator Norris, Reconstruction Finance Corporation, Alfred E. Smith, Wilsonism.

To explain or define: bootlegger, buying power, excess savings, hijacking, hydroelectric plant, mass production, national income, nitrates plant, racketeer, radical, socialist, stock promoter, subsidy, teacher's oath.

Subjects for Talks or Written Reports

1. The "Red" scare in the early twenties. 2. The activities of the Ku Klux Klan during the twenties, especially in your state. 3. Land booms during the twenties. 4. How the Federal Bureau of Investigation helped in stamping out rackets. 5. How national prohibition contributed to lawlessness and corruption. 6. Why there was a demand for repeal of the Prohibition Amendment. 7. Immigration laws passed by Congress during the twenties. 8. The march of the "bonus army" to Washington in 1932. How the marchers were treated. 9. The farmers' holiday movement in the early thirties. 10. The problem of migrant boys during the depression. 11. Life in a Hooverville. (Hooverville was the name given to shacks built by the jobless on a vacant lot out of discarded lumber.

Questions for Understanding the Text

1. Is it fair to call the twenties "mad"? Why or why not? 2. How was nationalism shown after World War I? 3. Contrast the attitude toward big business held by Theodore Roosevelt, Taft, and Wilson with that of Harding, Coolidge, and Hoover. 4. Name some of the ways in which Congress helped big business. 5. Why did the progressives urge federal regulation of the power industry? 6. (*a*) What did Senator Norris want done with the government plants at Muscle Shoals? (*b*) What did Presidents Harding, Coolidge, and Hoover want done with them? 7. Discuss the growth of big business during the twenties. 8. Why did manufactured goods begin to pile up in the warehouses months before the crash? 9. (*a*) Account for the boom in stocks during the late twenties. How did Coolidge and his Secretary of the Treasury help the boom? (*b*) How did Hoover's inauguration affect the stock market? 10. Tell about the presidential campaign of 1928. 11. Why did insiders begin to sell out their stock holdings in mid-1929? 12. (*a*) Describe the stock market crash. (*b*) How much paper wealth (measured in stock values) was lost by the close of 1929? (*c*) Was any real wealth (measured in physical property and goods) destroyed in the crash? 13. Did the crash cause the depression? Explain. 14. How were the needy cared for during the Hoover administration? 15. What did Hoover do about the depression? 16. Was the depression due, as many businessmen said, to overproduction? 17. Why was this depression unusually severe?

CHAPTER 40

THE "NEW DEAL"

F*ranklin D. Roosevelt: background and personality.* Franklin D. Roosevelt, a distant cousin of Theodore Roosevelt, came from an old and well-to-do New York family. After graduating from Harvard, he studied law. In 1910, when he was twenty-eight, he decided to go into politics. He ran for state senator on the Democratic ticket in a district which only once in over fifty years had sent a Democrat to Albany. Greeting the farmers at work in their fields, speaking wherever he could collect half a dozen listeners, he covered the district from one corner to the other and won by a large majority.

In Albany the young senator led a successful revolt against the state political boss. This made him a recognized leader among New York progressives. He helped manage Woodrow Wilson's successful campaign in his state and in return was appointed Assistant Secretary of the Navy. In 1920, as the Democratic candidate for Vice-President, he carried on a vigorous fight for the League of Nations. When he was stricken with paralysis a few months later, his promising political career seemed to be over. For the next seven years he struggled to regain his health. Meanwhile he studied American history and government and exchanged letters with leading thinkers here and abroad.

In 1928, still crippled, Roosevelt was elected governor of New York. He gave the state progressive leadership and was re-elected in 1930 by the biggest majority in the state's history. Because of his popularity in his home state, and because New York has a large number of electoral votes, he was now in line for nomination for President.

Roosevelt was probably the most gifted Democratic leader in the country in 1932. He knew the American past and was unusually well-informed about world affairs. Like his cousin Theodore, he had broad interests and enjoyed and got along well with people in all walks of life. Also like his cousin, he had enormous energy and a cheerfulness that spread to those around him.

Roosevelt's inauguration. On March 4, 1933, when Roosevelt became President, the depression was at its worst. Throughout the coun-

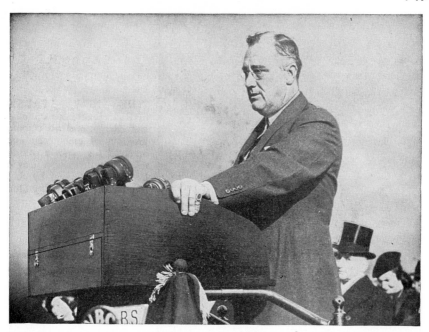

PRESIDENT FRANKLIN DELANO ROOSEVELT *was the first President to make frequent use of the radio to explain his program to the people. President Roosevelt had an effective speaking voice.* (Courtesy of United States Department of the Interior)

try most of the banks were closed. Between thirteen and fourteen million workers were unemployed. State and local relief funds were nearly exhausted. Many cities and towns were bankrupt, without money to pay schoolteachers and other public servants. Millions of farm families were penniless. Panic gripped the country. There was a growing feeling that forceful measures were necessary to restore confidence and prosperity.

In this grave hour Roosevelt's inaugural message renewed the nation's courage. Democratic government, he said, would endure; prosperity would return. "The only thing we have to fear is fear itself — nameless, unreasoning, unjustified terror. . . . Plenty is at our doorstep, but a generous use of it languishes [fails] in the very sight of plenty." The President promised prompt action to relieve poverty and want; to prevent foreclosure of small farms and homes; to put people to work; to raise farm prices; and to regulate transportation, communication, and other public utilities.

The first hundred days. Roosevelt's first acts as President were to order the closing of all the banks in the country and to call Congress

"THE NEW LEADER-
SHIP." *Roosevelt's optimism
and energy, and his vigorous
program of emergency laws
renewed the nation's courage
when the depression was at
its worst.* (Drawn by S. J.
Ray for the *Kansas City Star*)

into special session on March 9, 1933. The hundred following days
were unlike any in the history of Congress. With the aid of experts —
the so-called "Brain Trust" — the President had prepared a series of bills
to meet the emergency. He placed these before Congress one after
another, and they were all promptly passed. Even the Republican
congressmen for the most part supported the President.

The Emergency Banking Act was passed the day that Congress met.
Within five days the banking crisis was under control. Later in the
session Congress strengthened the banks permanently by creating the
Federal Deposit Insurance Corporation. Congress also established the
Civilian Conservation Corps (the CCC), under which three hundred
thousand young men, housed in well-built camps, were set to work on
the public lands making trails, cutting fire lanes, planting trees, and
building brush dams across gullies. Before the CCC was discontinued
in 1942, it gave work and training to three million jobless youths and
completed a vast number of useful conservation projects. Another act
created the Federal Emergency Relief Agency and provided federal
funds to help the states care for the needy.

Before the end of this remarkable hundred-day session Congress also
created the Tennessee Valley Authority, passed the Agricultural Ad-

justment Act, gave the President power to manage the nation's currency, and brought the sale of securities under federal control. Congress also came to the aid of the railroads, made legal the sale of light wines and beers as an easy way of raising revenue, and passed the National Recovery Act to help business and at the same time protect the rights of labor. A first appropriation of three billion, three hundred million dollars was made for public works to create jobs. During the next year or two the money was spent for building highways, bridges, dams, low-cost housing units, schools, hospitals, and other federal and local projects.

The main outlines of the "New Deal" were laid down in these hundred swift-moving days. For the time being the President's program was approved by nearly every group in the country; party and class differences were forgotten; almost everyone hailed the President as a great leader. The program had restored the nation's faith in democracy.

Important New Deal reforms. The New Deal was made up in part of measures for relief and recovery and in part of measures for reform. The reform measures had to do chiefly with (1) agriculture, (2) labor, (3) social security, (4) electric power, (5) housing, (6) regulation of communication industries (radio, telephone, telegraph), (7) regulation of the stock market, (8) banking and currency, and (9) the lowering of tariffs by trade agreements with other countries. All of these were important, but we shall take up only the first four here. Trade agreements will be discussed in the next chapter.

1. Agriculture. The farm depression began in 1920, when Europeans reduced their heavy wartime purchases of American farm products. The price of farm products then dropped so low that few farmers could make a good living. Every year during the twenties many farmers lost their farms because they could not pay interest and taxes. However, the worst was yet to come. Unemployment cut the home market, with the result that between 1929 and 1933 farm prices fell 62 per cent. Prices of manufactured articles purchased by farmers fell only half as much. On this account farmers had only half as much buying power in March, 1933, which was the lowest point in the farm depression, as they had had four years earlier.

In order to raise prices, the President wanted the farmers to raise less food. But a farmer cannot afford to cut down his production. If he should, his expenses would wipe out his earnings. Therefore the New Deal proposed to pay farmers to produce less until prices rose.

The Agricultural Adjustment Act of May, 1933, provided benefit payments to those who cut their production of certain crops — cotton, corn, hogs, rice, tobacco, and others in which there was a large surplus. The farmers co-operated well; by 1934 more than forty million acres of farm land had been taken out of cultivation. Farm prices rose; in addition the farmers received several hundred million dollars from the government.

In 1936 the Supreme Court set aside the Agricultural Adjustment Act. Congress then passed a second and better farm-relief law — the Soil Conservation Act of 1936. This provided that the government would pay farmers to use part of their lands for "soil-conserving crops," such as clover and alfalfa. These crops enrich the soil; they also have a soil-binding effect which prevents loss of the valuable topsoil by washing, gullying, and dust storms. By 1940 nearly six million farmers had joined in this program and were receiving benefit payments averaging more than a hundred dollars each. Farm income was more than double what it had been in 1932. But not until World War II did farmers have as much buying power as they had had in the five years before World War I.

The New Deal took a number of steps to provide farmers with cheap credit. A Farm Mortgage Relief Act helped farm owners avoid the foreclosure of their farms. A Farm Security Administration was set up to make small loans to needy tenant farmers for the purchase of equipment and work animals. A Farm Tenancy Act provided money to help thousands of tenant farmers buy farms. On the whole, Congress showed little interest in the tragic situation of the millions of sharecroppers, subsistence farmers — that is, farmers with nothing to sell, producing only for their own families — and migratory farm laborers, who move from place to place in search of work. Roosevelt tried to awaken the nation to the needs of these groups of forgotten men, but did not get very far.

2. Labor. Before the New Deal, labor legislation had been left to the states. The states were not very successful in regulating labor conditions, since industries could move from places with strict labor laws to others where labor was less protected. The New Dealers favored federal laws to regulate wages and hours and to protect workers in their right to form unions for the purpose of bargaining with their employers.

The National Recovery Act of 1933 attempted, among other things, to spread work, shorten hours, raise wages, and end child labor. It

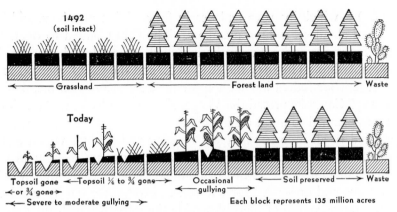

1492
(soil intact)

←——— Grassland ———→ ←—————— Forest land ——————→ Waste

Today

Topsoil gone ←—Topsoil ¼ to ¾ gone—→   Occasional   ←—— Soil preserved ——→ Waste
←—or ¾ gone—→   ←—gullying—→
←— Severe to moderate gullying —→   Each block represents 135 million acres

EXTENT OF SOIL EROSION IN THE UNITED STATES

Half of our land suitable for farming has lost one fourth to three fourths of its topsoil.
(Courtesy of Soil Conservation Service)

also guaranteed to workers the right of collective bargaining. (When a union makes an agreement with the employer, the process is called *collective bargaining*.) In 1935, when the Supreme Court declared the Act unconstitutional, big business began a powerful drive against labor unions. The drive might have succeeded had not Congress the same year passed the Wagner Labor Relations Act. This Act set up a National Labor Relations Board to prevent unfair labor practices. The Act prohibited employers from interfering with the right of workers to organize or to bargain and stated that employers must not support company unions. Many employers expected the Act to be declared unconstitutional. However, the Supreme Court upheld it, declaring that workers have a right to organize and that unions are necessary to give workingmen the chance to deal on an equal basis with their employers.

During its first five years the National Labor Relations Board handled nearly 27,000 labor disputes. It prevented 869 strikes, settled 2161 strikes which had already been called, and ordered employers to take back 21,163 workers who had been dismissed for union activities. That it improved labor relations is shown by the fact that it greatly reduced the time lost through strikes.

Labor unions grew rapidly under the New Deal. The American Federation of Labor (A.F. of L.) increased its membership from two million in 1933 to about eight million in 1952. A new labor organization sprang up in 1935 — the Congress of Industrial Organizations

(C.I.O.) — which by 1937 had nearly four million members, and by 1952 had about six million members. The C.I.O. aimed to organize entire industries and included both skilled and unskilled workers in its membership. (In 1955 the A.F. of L. and the C.I.O. merged into one large labor federation with approximately 16,000,000 members.)

In 1938 Congress passed the Wagner Wages and Hours Act. The Act was planned to put a ceiling over hours and a floor under wages. It applied to all industries, except farming and fishing, which make products sold across state lines. It fixed forty cents an hour as the normal minimum wage and forty hours as the normal working week, with "time and one-half" for overtime. Products made by children under sixteen could not be sold outside the state in which they were made. While a minimum wage of sixteen dollars a week was scarcely sufficient even at that time, the Wages and Hours Act was considered to be an important forward step for American labor. (See page 637.)

3. Social security. Until 1935 security for the jobless, the aged, and the disabled was left to the states. A few states had old-age pensions and assisted the needy blind and the disabled, but only one state had unemployment insurance. It was clear that federal action was needed. At the insistence of the President, Congress passed the Social Security Act of 1935, one of the greatest achievements of the New Deal.

Under the Social Security Act the federal government promised to aid states having a pension system for needy persons of sixty-five years of age or older. Up to three fourths of the cost of the pension, if not more than a certain size, is paid by the federal government. To lessen the need for pensions, the Act also created a system of old-age insurance, paying benefits to the retired worker whether or not he is in need. The cost of old-age insurance is met by small regular payments by workers and their employers. To persuade the states to establish compulsory unemployment insurance, the Act provided for a federal tax on pay rolls. Ninety per cent of the tax collected in a state is returned to that state if it has a satisfactory program of compulsory unemployment insurance. The Act also provided that the federal government would match funds set aside by the states to help crippled children, the needy blind, needy mothers, and disabled workers. By 1938 all the states had adopted old-age pensions and unemployment insurance and had increased their aid to crippled children, the blind, the disabled, and needy mothers.

In 1939 Congress added survivors' insurance to old-age insurance. This protects children under eighteen and wives over sixty-five in the

FRANCES PERKINS, *the first woman ever to hold a post in the Cabinet. She became Secretary of Labor on March 4, 1933. She had to deal with unemployment on a vast scale, the rapid growth of labor unions, the split of the labor movement into A.F. of L. and C.I.O., sit-down strikes, and labor in the defense program.* (Painted for *Fortune* by Arthur Szyk. Courtesy of the artist)

event of the father's or husband's death. Until the law was revised in 1950 only three in every five workers were covered by old-age and survivors' insurance. About ten million additional workers were made eligible for it in 1950.

4. Electric power. President Roosevelt was eager to bring the benefits of cheap power to everybody. The usual rates to small users were far too high; in fact they averaged some fifteen times the cost of producing and distributing the current. One way to get lower rates was through federal regulation. Another way was to set up publicly owned plants as "yardsticks" to show how cheaply electricity could be supplied and how much its use in the home and on the farm could be increased.

The President and his advisers worked out a plan for using the power plant at Muscle Shoals as a yardstick. (See page 533.) Congress approved the plan in May, 1933, when it created the Tennessee Valley Authority (TVA). The TVA is a public corporation managed by three directors appointed by the President. Congress gave it the right to produce, distribute, and sell electric power; build dams, reservoirs, and power lines; improve navigation; control floods; and promote the social and economic welfare of the Tennessee Valley region. The region includes parts of seven states — Alabama, Georgia, Kentucky, Mississippi, North Carolina, Tennessee, and Virginia.

The TVA built seven dams to control floods and to run power plants. It carried on a valuable program of reforestation and soil conservation. It built thousands of miles of power lines. The current produced is sold to consumers by private companies, by co-operatives, and by towns and cities, at rates approved by the TVA. These rates are about half the average rate to small users in other parts of the United States. The use of electricity on homes and farms in the region has grown remarkably. Many village industries have developed to take advantage of the cheap power. The entire region, which was one of the poorest in the country, is gradually growing prosperous.

In 1937 the President proposed seven similar projects for other parts of the country. Congress took no action, partly because of the strong opposition of the private electric companies, and partly because of an unwillingness to increase the President's powers. However, the Public Works Administration (PWA), which Congress established in 1933, built large hydroelectric plants at Hoover Dam on the Colorado River (started under President Hoover), at Grand Coulee and Bonneville dams on the Columbia, and at Fort Peck Dam on the Missouri. The PWA also lent money to towns and cities wishing to build electric plants and distribution systems. The private power interests opposed the public ownership of electric plants. They argued that the government should not compete with private business. But for the time being their objections were cast aside.

The power interests received another blow in 1935 when Congress passed the Public Utility Act. This directed the Federal Power Commission to regulate all companies sending power across state lines. It stated that electric holding companies must not "milk" the companies under their control — that is, they must not make the controlled company pay a high price for the services performed by the holding company. The Security and Exchange Commission was given power to do away with any electric holding company when this appears to be in the public interest. The power interests felt sure that the Supreme Court would find the Public Utility Act unconstitutional.

Conservatives complain. At first there was little opposition to the New Deal. Almost everyone realized that far-reaching reforms were necessary to save the nation. As soon as times grew better, conservatives in both parties began to complain that the New Deal was destroying personal liberty. Among them was the President's former friend, Alfred E. Smith, who had turned conservative. Former President Hoover said that the policies of the Roosevelt administration were totally un-American, that they strangled private enterprise in a mass of governmental controls. Financial and industrial leaders criticized the administration for encouraging organized labor, for throwing away public money on relief, and above all for bothering business with unnecessary regulations. Wealthy people often accused the President of Communistic leanings. They also declared that he was making himself a dictator, that he was forcing Congress to do as he said, and that he was deliberately encouraging class hatred.

The campaign of 1936. As criticism of the New Deal grew, Republicans looked forward hopefully to the 1936 election. They selected Governor Alfred M. Landon, the "Coolidge of Kansas," to run against Roosevelt. Leaders of finance and industry gave heavily to the Republican campaign fund. Two thirds or more of the newspapers joined the "stop-Roosevelt" movement.

Roosevelt had the support of organized labor and most of the farm organizations. In fact the common people generally were for him. Forty-six million men and women voted — a record-breaking number. The result was a triumph for Roosevelt and the Democratic party. The Republicans carried only two states — Maine and Vermont. The Democrats increased their majority in both houses of Congress. Democratic governors were elected in most of the states. It was the most sweeping political victory since 1820, when Monroe was elected President for the second time.

The fight over the Supreme Court. Roosevelt's second inauguration took place on January 20, 1937. (The Twentieth Amendment, adopted in 1933, had done away with the custom of inaugurating the President on March 4.) In his inaugural speech he said that the United States had means to provide a comfortable living for all, yet one third of the people were ill-housed, ill-fed, and ill-clad. He pledged himself to go on fighting for reform.

New Dealers wondered whether further reforms were possible, in view of the attitude of the Supreme Court. The Supreme Court had found a large number of New Deal laws to be unconstitutional. Four of the justices, who were very old and very conservative, nearly always found that any given reform was contrary to the Constitution.

The more important were (1) a new Agricultural Adjustment Act, to control production and storage of basic crops, (2) the Bituminous Coal Act, to bring order into the coal industry, (3) the National Housing Act, appropriating money to help local governments build modern, healthful living quarters for low-income families, (4) the Food, Drug, and Cosmetic Act, strengthening the old Pure Food and Drug Act passed in 1906.

In 1938 Congress also appointed a Temporary National Economic Committee (TNEC) to study the problem of monopolies and large corporations. President Roosevelt said that the study should be welcomed by all "who sincerely want to preserve the system of private enterprise for profit." He added, "No people, least of all a democratic people, will be content to go without work or to accept some standard of living which obviously and woefully falls short of their capacity to produce." In 1940 the TNEC issued a long series of reports showing that many changes were needed to save and strengthen our economic system. Had the times been peaceful, these reports might have led to important new laws. But war had already started in Europe, and no one knew how long we could stay out. Just as Wilson's reform program was interrupted by the threat of war, so was Roosevelt's. Further reform must wait for the return of peace.

The election of 1940. In 1940 the Republicans chose Wendell Willkie to be their standard-bearer. Mr. Willkie was new to politics. As president of a large electric holding company, the Commonwealth and Southern, he had been an outspoken critic of the TVA experiment. He attacked the New Deal for being inefficient and extravagant, yet showed sympathy with most of its basic ideas. He owed his nomination, not to the Republican party bosses, but to the rank and file of the party, who wanted a progressive candidate.

The Democratic party broke the two-term tradition by nominating President Roosevelt for a third term. The campaign showed that the people did not regard the third-term question as very important. A majority of the voters feared to entrust the nation at that critical time to a new and untried leader. The result was the re-election of Roosevelt. The no-third-term tradition at last was broken.

Appraisal of the New Deal. We are still too close to the New Deal to pass final judgment on it. That serious mistakes were made is certain. That the New Deal failed to solve the unemployment problem is equally sure. On the other hand the New Deal made great advances in reducing the surplus of farm products; in providing easy credit for

tives in both parties began to complain that the New Deal was destroying personal liberty. Among them was the President's former friend,
Alfred E. Smith, who had turned conservative. Former President
Hoover said that the policies of the Roosevelt administration were totally un-American, that they strangled private enterprise in a mass of
governmental controls. Financial and industrial leaders criticized the
administration for encouraging organized labor, for throwing away
public money on relief, and above all for bothering business with unnecessary regulations. Wealthy people often accused the President
of Communistic leanings. They also declared that he was making himself a dictator, that he was forcing Congress to do as he said, and that
he was deliberately encouraging class hatred.

The campaign of 1936. As criticism of the New Deal grew, Republicans looked forward hopefully to the 1936 election. They selected
Governor Alfred M. Landon, the "Coolidge of Kansas," to run against
Roosevelt. Leaders of finance and industry gave heavily to the Republican campaign fund. Two thirds or more of the newspapers
joined the "stop-Roosevelt" movement.

Roosevelt had the support of organized labor and most of the farm
organizations. In fact the common people generally were for him.
Forty-six million men and women voted — a record-breaking number.
The result was a triumph for Roosevelt and the Democratic party.
The Republicans carried only two states — Maine and Vermont. The
Democrats increased their majority in both houses of Congress.
Democratic governors were elected in most of the states. It was the
most sweeping political victory since 1820, when Monroe was elected
President for the second time.

The fight over the Supreme Court. Roosevelt's second inauguration took place on January 20, 1937. (The Twentieth Amendment,
adopted in 1933, had done away with the custom of inaugurating the
President on March 4.) In his inaugural speech he said that the United
States had means to provide a comfortable living for all, yet one third
of the people were ill-housed, ill-fed, and ill-clad. He pledged himself
to go on fighting for reform.

New Dealers wondered whether further reforms were possible,
in view of the attitude of the Supreme Court. The Supreme Court
had found a large number of New Deal laws to be unconstitutional.
Four of the justices, who were very old and very conservative, nearly
always found that any given reform was contrary to the Constitution.

"THE LAST OF A LONG LINE." *During Franklin Roosevelt's first term many New Deal laws were killed by the Supreme Court. Early in 1937 few expected that the Wagner Labor Relations Act and the Social Security Act would survive.* (From the *Washington Post*)

Two of the remaining justices often lined up with these four. Three usually upheld reform, taking the position that the Constitution was intended to serve the welfare of all the people. In most of its decisions, therefore, the Court split six to three, or five to four.

Early in February, Roosevelt startled the country by proposing a reorganization of the Supreme Court. He recommended that when a judge passed the age of seventy without retiring, the President should have the power to appoint an additional judge to share his work. Under this plan the membership of the Court might, if necessary, be increased to fifteen.

The proposal led to a storm of protests from conservatives and some liberals. The President was charged with planning to "pack" the Court. Critics of the Court replied that it was already packed, and the problem was to unpack it. The debate raged for months. Even the experts on constitutional law disagreed with one another about the President's proposal.

Meanwhile the Court began to take a more liberal view of the Constitution. In March, by another five-to-four decision, it upheld a Washington minimum-wage law, although a year earlier it had set aside a similar law passed in New York. In April it changed the definition of interstate commerce (commerce between the states) that had led it to throw out the National Recovery Act. As a result the Wagner Labor Relations Act was upheld. In May the Court upheld the Social Security Act, upsetting a ruling laid down when the Agricultural Adjustment Act was set aside. Friends of the President felt he had won his battle over the Court, although Congress did not pass his reorganization plan. After this no important New Deal law was found unconstitutional.

In June the aged Justice Van Devanter retired. The President at last had a chance to appoint a liberal to the Supreme Court. A few months later another of the conservative justices retired. By 1941 Mr. Roosevelt had been able to make seven appointments to the Court. The decisions of the Court showed the change in its membership. The Court was now more inclined to interpret the Constitution in such a way as to carry out the will of Congress. To the ordinary citizen it seemed as if the Court had a new interest in the rights and needs of the common people.

Unemployment remains an unsolved problem. The New Deal did not solve the problem of unemployment. Between 1930 and 1941 the number of persons able and willing to work but unable to find jobs was never less than seven million. By 1940 business had fully recovered; industrial output was greater than in 1929; yet unemployment was still a major problem. At the beginning of 1941, despite huge orders for war and defense materials, there were still seven or eight million workers who could not find jobs.

Congress was obliged to keep on appropriating money for relief. In 1935 the relief of *unemployables* — that is, people unable to work — was turned over to the state and local governments. The federal government was to supply work relief to the needy who were able to work. That year the Works Progress Administration (WPA) was set up to furnish useful work not requiring much expense for materials. A wide variety of useful projects was carried on by WPA workers. Many unemployed women were put to work making garments for the needy. Unemployed writers, artists, musicians, actors, and teachers were put to work on projects making use of their special skills. The National Youth Administration (NYA) was established in 1935 to give part-time work to needy high school and college students that they might continue their education. By 1940 the federal government had spent sixteen billion dollars for relief and seven billion dollars on public works to create jobs.

The reform program is interrupted. During 1937 and 1938 Congress passed several reform measures which should be mentioned.

The more important were (1) a new Agricultural Adjustment Act, to control production and storage of basic crops, (2) the Bituminous Coal Act, to bring order into the coal industry, (3) the National Housing Act, appropriating money to help local governments build modern, healthful living quarters for low-income families, (4) the Food, Drug, and Cosmetic Act, strengthening the old Pure Food and Drug Act passed in 1906.

In 1938 Congress also appointed a Temporary National Economic Committee (TNEC) to study the problem of monopolies and large corporations. President Roosevelt said that the study should be welcomed by all "who sincerely want to preserve the system of private enterprise for profit." He added, "No people, least of all a democratic people, will be content to go without work or to accept some standard of living which obviously and woefully falls short of their capacity to produce." In 1940 the TNEC issued a long series of reports showing that many changes were needed to save and strengthen our economic system. Had the times been peaceful, these reports might have led to important new laws. But war had already started in Europe, and no one knew how long we could stay out. Just as Wilson's reform program was interrupted by the threat of war, so was Roosevelt's. Further reform must wait for the return of peace.

The election of 1940. In 1940 the Republicans chose Wendell Willkie to be their standard-bearer. Mr. Willkie was new to politics. As president of a large electric holding company, the Commonwealth and Southern, he had been an outspoken critic of the TVA experiment. He attacked the New Deal for being inefficient and extravagant, yet showed sympathy with most of its basic ideas. He owed his nomination, not to the Republican party bosses, but to the rank and file of the party, who wanted a progressive candidate.

The Democratic party broke the two-term tradition by nominating President Roosevelt for a third term. The campaign showed that the people did not regard the third-term question as very important. A majority of the voters feared to entrust the nation at that critical time to a new and untried leader. The result was the re-election of Roosevelt. The no-third-term tradition at last was broken.

Appraisal of the New Deal. We are still too close to the New Deal to pass final judgment on it. That serious mistakes were made is certain. That the New Deal failed to solve the unemployment problem is equally sure. On the other hand the New Deal made great advances in reducing the surplus of farm products; in providing easy credit for

A WORK–RELIEF PROJECT. *Under the New Deal the federal government under-took to provide useful employment for all the needy who were able to work. The picture shows a sewer-building project near Utica. New York.* (Courtesy of Works Progress Administration)

farmers; in conserving soil, forests, and water power; in bringing order into the stock market; and in safeguarding small investors and savings bank depositors. Much progress was also made in lowering the cost of electricity to small users; in bringing electric holding companies under control; and in protecting purchasers of food, drugs, and cosmetics. Some progress was made in reviving our foreign trade by means of trade treaties. (See page 564.)

The New Deal caused Americans to give more thought to their government than they had given in many years. They became aware of serious economic and social conditions that, if not corrected, might destroy our democracy. As the editors of the *London Economist* said: "Mr. Roosevelt may have given the wrong answers to many of his problems. But he is, at least, the first President of modern America who has asked the right questions."

To identify: American Federation of Labor, Brain Trust, Civilian Conservation Corps, Congress of Industrial Organization, Federal Deposit Insurance Corporation, National Labor Relations Board, National Youth Administration, Tennessee Valley Authority, Wagner Wages and Hours Act, Wendell Willkie, Works Progress Administration.

To explain or define: collective bargaining, migratory farm laborer, "milk," sharecropper, subsistence farmer, unemployable.

SUBJECTS FOR TALKS OR WRITTEN REPORTS

1. The Federal Communications Commission — its history and accomplishment. 2. The housing problem in America and what the New Deal did toward solving it. 3. The work of the Farm Security Agency. 4. The work of the National Youth Administration. 5. The work of the National Resources Board. 6. The work of the Rural Electrification Agency. 7. The importance of soil conservation to the United States. 8. The problem of farm tenancy in the United States; what has been done to solve it. 9. Mrs. Franklin Roosevelt — her personality and her work for reform. 10. Frances Perkins — her life and work. 11. Wendell Willkie — his life and teachings. 12. Conditions necessary for full employment in time of peace.

QUESTIONS FOR UNDERSTANDING THE TEXT

1. What experiences helped prepare Franklin Roosevelt for the Presidency? 2. Sketch economic conditions in the United States in early March, 1933. 3. (*a*) What was unusual about the first hundred days of Roosevelt's administration? (*b*) Name the principal laws passed during this time. 4. What were the aims and accomplishments of the Civilian Conservation Corps? 5. (*a*) Why was there a farm depression throughout the twenties? (*b*) Why did it grow worse after 1929? 6. (*a*) Why was government action necessary to reduce crop surpluses? (*b*) What action was taken? 7. What groups of farm people received little consideration from Congress? 8. How did labor benefit from the New Deal? 9. (*a*) Discuss the work of the National Labor Relations Board. (*b*) How did it succeed in bettering labor relations? 10. How was the membership of the C.I.O. unlike that of the A.F. of L.? 11. Outline the main features of the Social Security Act. 12. What is the difference between old-age pensions and old-age insurance benefits? 13. (*a*) Discuss the work of the TVA. (*b*) How was it to serve as a "yardstick"? 14. Outline the main features of the Public Utility Act. 15. Mention some of the frequent criticisms of President Roosevelt and the New Deal. 16. (*a*) What change was made in the date for inaugurating the President? (*b*) In what year was this change first put into effect? 17. (*a*) How did President Roosevelt propose to reorganize the Supreme Court? (*b*) Why did he propose this? Did he accomplish his purpose? 18. (*a*) What task was given to the Temporary National Economic Committee? (*b*) Why did its work bring no immediate reforms? 19. (*a*) Why did Roosevelt run for a third term? (*b*) Account for Willkie's defeat. 20. What would you say for and against the New Deal?

ACTIVITIES FOR UNIT NINE

1. Continue work on the classbook, *American Hall of Fame*, and on the history of your community.
2. Appoint a committee to interview various well-informed persons on the question, "Is there a liquor problem in your community?"
3. Investigate the success or failure of prohibition in your community.
4. Investigate the history of the Ku Klux Klan in your community and your state. A near-by newspaper may be able to help you.
5. On an outline map of the United States show on each state the names of any of our Presidents who came from that state. How do you explain what you find?
6. Make a map showing the distribution of our foreign-born whites by states. Consult the *World Almanac*.
7. Interview a member of the Department of Public Welfare and the secretary of the Family Welfare Society in your community to obtain information on the number needing relief each year of the 1930's.
8. List the projects carried out in your community with the aid of federal funds in an effort to relieve unemployment during the 1930's.
9. Each student might ask his parents to tell how the depression affected them. Write as much of the story as they are willing for you to write and hand it in without using names or any means of identification. A committee might go over the papers, reading interesting portions aloud in class and tabulating such facts as the proportion of fathers who were unemployed for a year or more, the proportion who lost their businesses, farms, and homes, and the proportion who moved to a smaller dwelling and suffered other serious cuts in their scale of living.
10. Make a list of economic problems not solved by the New Deal which are likely to be important in the years to come. Do you think the solution should be sought through private, state, or national action?
11. Each student might ask several well-informed adult acquaintances to tell him what they consider to be the good and the bad effects of the New Deal. Appoint a committee to tabulate the replies.

READINGS FOR UNIT NINE

(Stars indicate the easier books)

GENERAL ACCOUNTS

Allen, Frederick L. *Only Yesterday*. Blue Ribbon.
——. *Since Yesterday; the Nineteen-Thirties in America*. Harper.
Beard, Charles A. and Smith, George H. E. *The Old Deal and the New*. Macmillan.
*Chase, Stuart. *The Economy of Abundance*. Macmillan.

*Chase, Stuart. *Rich Land, Poor Land*. McGraw-Hill. (Conservation)
*Coyle, David C. *Roads to a New America*. Little, Brown.
Daniels, Jonathan. *A Southerner Discovers the South*. Macmillan.
Davie, M. R. *World Immigration, with Special Reference to the United States*. Macmillan.
Fay, Bernard. *Roosevelt and His America*. Little, Brown.
High, Stanley. *Roosevelt — and Then?* Harper.
Hoover, Herbert. *The Challenge to Liberty*. Scribner's.
*Huberman, Leo. *Man's Worldly Goods*. Harper.
Lane, Marie and Lane, Steegmuller. *America on Relief*. Harcourt, Brace.
Lindley, E. K. *Roosevelt Revolution; First Phase*. Viking.
Lord, Russell. *Behold Our Land*. Houghton Mifflin.
Orth, Samuel P. *Our Foreigners*. (Chronicles)
Perkins, Frances. *People at Work*. Day.
Slosson, P. W. *The Great Crusade and After, 1914–1928*. (A. L. S.)
Symes, Lillian and Clement, Travers. *Rebel America: The Story of Social Revolt in the United States*. Harper.
Wiese, Mildred and Reticker, Ruth. *The Modern Worker*. Macmillan.
Wright, C. M. *Here Comes Labor*. Macmillan. (Labor's objectives)
Wright, Richard. *12 Million Black Voices*. Viking.
Yates, R. F. *Machines Over Men*. Stokes.

BIOGRAPHY

Adams, S. H. *Incredible Era*. Houghton Mifflin. (Era of Harding)
Charnley, M. V. *The Boys' Life of Herbert Hoover*. Harper.
Coolidge, Calvin. *Autobiography*. Cosmopolitan.
Irwin, Will. *Herbert Hoover*. Appleton-Century.
Johnson, Gerald W. *Roosevelt: Dictator or Democrat?* Harper.
Ludwig, Emil. *Roosevelt, a Study in Fortune and Power*. Viking.
*Moses, Belle. *Franklin Delano Roosevelt*. Appleton-Century.
White, William A. *Calvin Coolidge*. Macmillan.

FICTION

Fairbank, Janet A. *The Lion's Den*. Grosset. (Congressman's life)
Glasgow, Ellen. *Vein of Iron*. Harcourt, Brace. (Southern depression)
*Lawrence, Josephine. *Sound of Running Feet*. Stokes.
*——. *If I Have Four Apples*. Grosset. (The depression)
Merrick, Elliott. *From This Hill Look Down*. Putnam's. (Depression)
Thomas, Dorothy. *The Home Place*. Knopf. (The depression)
Watts, Mary S. *The Fabric of the Loom*. Macmillan. (American life)
*Widdemer, M. C. *In the Shadow of the Skyscrapers*. Harcourt, Brace.
Yeager, D. G. *Bob Flame, Rocky Mountain Ranger*. Dodd, Mead. (Problems of conservation; the CCC)

UNIT TEN

THE END OF ISOLATIONISM

After World War I the United States tried to return to its old policy of isolation. On some matters, of course, it co-operated with other nations, but most of the time it preferred to go its way alone. When signs appeared of another war in Europe, Congress passed laws intended to keep the United States neutral.

Meanwhile we were following the "Good Neighbor" policy in Latin America. We tried to overcome the distrust that the Latin-American republics felt toward us. We agreed that the Monroe Doctrine was their concern as much as ours and that they should have an equal voice with us in enforcing it.

Trouble appeared in the Pacific in 1931, when Japan seized Manchuria. A few years later Japan attacked China as part of a plan to bring all Asia under her control. This placed the United States in danger, although few Americans realized this until Japan attacked American bases in the Pacific on December 7, 1941.

When the United States went to war with the Axis, all Europe lay under Hitler's heel. Great Britain was in danger of being crushed. Latin America was threatened with invasion. German U-boats almost controlled the Atlantic. Democracy was fighting for its very life. How the United States threw all its resources into the fight, how the tide finally turned against the Axis, is one of the great chapters in human history.

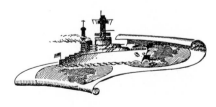

UNITED NATIONS FOOD CONFERENCE. *This important meeting took place at Hot Springs, Virginia, in the spring of 1943. The delegates made plans for supplying food to undernourished and hungry people in the occupied countries after the enemy was driven out. A few months later the United Nations Relief and Rehabilitation Administration was set up to organize relief on a global scale.* (Courtesy of *Life*)

CHAPTER 41

ISOLATION PROVES IMPOSSIBLE

Two conflicting ideas about foreign policy. After World War I most Americans were weary of international responsibilities. They did not want to be disturbed by events abroad. They thought the United States could have peace by turning its back on world affairs. They wanted to return to the policy of *isolation* followed when the nation was young. Some Americans, however, thought that this policy was completely out of date. They wanted the United States to work with other nations to promote world prosperity and to remove the causes of war. They favored a policy of *international co-operation.* Between the end of World War I and the start of World War II, American foreign relations were influenced by both groups. Sometimes the United States co-operated with other nations and sometimes it refused to do so.

STEPS TOWARD INTERNATIONAL CO-OPERATION

While Congress and the people usually moved toward isolation, the President and the State Department often tried to move in the direction of international co-operation. Some of the efforts toward co-operation failed; others succeeded. We shall discuss only a few of them.

The Washington and London naval conferences. During World War I the United States made plans to build the strongest navy in the world. Britain and Japan also began to enlarge their navies. When the war ended, most of the new warships were not yet finished. Each power went on with its building program, partly because of national pride and partly because of the fear that a new war was brewing in the Far East.

Americans wanted to stop the naval race. Some thought that big navies might actually make war more likely. Others thought that the building of warships was a foolish waste of taxpayers' money. In 1921, therefore, the United States asked eight other countries to join us in a conference at Washington.

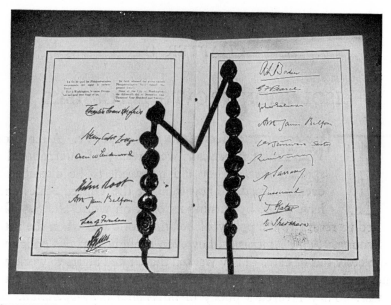

SIGNATURES ON THE NINE–POWER TREATY. *This pact, made at the Washington Conference in 1921, bound nine governments to respect China's independence
and the principle of the "Open Door."* (Keystone View Company)

Secretary of State Hughes startled the delegates on the very first
day by proposing that sixty-six battleships be scrapped, including
thirty American ships then under construction and thirty-six British
and Japanese ships. The Secretary's speech, said a British reporter,
"sank more ships than all the admirals of the world have sunk in a cycle
of centuries." The Secretary recommended that the strength of the
American, British, and Japanese navies in capital ships (those of over
10,000 tons) be kept at the ratio of 5 to 5 to 3, respectively, and that
no new capital ships be built for ten years. The British accepted the
proposal at once, but the Japanese hesitated. They finally consented
when the United States agreed not to strengthen its naval bases in the
Aleutians and the Philippines and on Samoa and Guam. This meant
that the Japanese navy, though smaller, would be supreme in Far Eastern waters, since the American navy did not have adequate bases there.
The conference reached other agreements intended to end the fear of
war in the Pacific, and these were no less important than the naval
agreement. (See pages 585–586.)

At a conference held in London in 1930, the United States, Great
Britain, and Japan made a new naval treaty. No capital ships would
be built until 1936, and the building of smaller ships would also be lim-

ited. Five years later, when this agreement was about to expire, another naval conference met in London. The Japanese now insisted on the right to build a navy equal to any in the world. When the United States delegates refused to consent to this demand, the Japanese delegates walked out. The naval race among the world powers then began all over again.

The Pact of Paris. During the 1920's a small group of influential Americans suggested that the world should make war illegal. In 1927 the foreign minister of France, Aristide Briand, backed the idea by suggesting that France and the United States agree never to make war on one another. War between the two countries would thus be outlawed. Secretary of State Kellogg believed that all the nations should be invited to sign such an agreement. He and Briand drew up the famous paper known as the Pact of Paris. In 1928 nearly all the nations on earth signed this pact, which pledged them to settle every dispute by peaceful means.

The treaty had no teeth. Secretary Kellogg himself said, "The only enforcement behind the pact is public opinion." Yet many hailed it as a great forward step in the direction of world peace. They thought that somehow the pact would enforce itself. They did not discover for several years that the pact was only a gesture, an expression of the popular wish for peace.

Co-operation with the League of Nations. The League of Nations was organized to promote international peace, justice, law, disarmament, and every kind of international co-operation likely to benefit mankind. The United States believed in these great ideals. In fact, for some twenty years before the League was founded, the United States had taken a leading part in efforts to develop international co-operation. Statesmen in other countries naturally expected the United States to join the League. Its failure to do so disappointed all those everywhere who believed in international co-operation. It seemed unlikely that the League could succeed without the weight of American influence behind it.

Almost from the start, however, the United States government found that American interests required its co-operation with the League. In 1923 the State Department began to send "unofficial observers" to meet with League committees concerned with nonpolitical matters, such as health regulations and commerce. Official American delegates were sent in 1924 to a conference on the opium problem After that the United States was represented at most League confer ences of a nonpolitical nature. Early in the 1930's the United States co-operated with the League in dealing with certain political matters. For instance, a representative of the American government met with the League Council in 1931 while it was considering what to do about the Japanese invasion of Manchuria. Again in 1935, when the League was considering the Italian invasion of Ethiopia, the United States showed its willingness to co-operate. But as long as it was not a member of the League, there was little the United States could do to strengthen it or to encourage its members to take a firm stand.

The "Good Neighbor" policy. The United States had a special responsibility for promoting co-operation in the Western Hemisphere. Yet American interference in the affairs of certain Latin-American countries caused all of them to fear the United States. (See Chapter 36.) Presidents Coolidge and Hoover took the first steps to correct this situation. The fuller development of the "Good Neighbor" policy came under President Franklin D. Roosevelt. What was done to win the friendship of Latin America and to promote inter-American co-operation will be told in the following chapter.

The Trade Agreements Act. The United States showed little willingness to co-operate with other nations in economic affairs until 1934, when Secretary of State Hull persuaded Congress to pass the Trade Agreements Act. This Act gave the President power to make special trade agreements with other countries without submitting them to the Senate. He was also given the right to lower our tariff rates as much as 50 per cent for nations willing to lower their tariffs on United States products. By 1940 Secretary Hull had made trade agreements with twenty-one nations. These treaties lowered the duties on over four hundred imported products, about one eighth of those covered by the tariff. As a result the United States bought more goods from other nations, and they in turn bought more goods from us. The trade agreements removed some of the ill will felt toward the United States because of its high tariffs.

STEPS TOWARD ISOLATION

At the same time that the United States was co-operating with other nations in some matters, there were other matters in which it did not co-operate. President Roosevelt, for example, was responsible for the failure of the London Economic Conference of 1933. Congress showed its desire for isolation by refusing to join the League of Nations and the World Court, by passing strict immigration laws, by refusing to cancel the war debts, and by passing rigid neutrality laws.

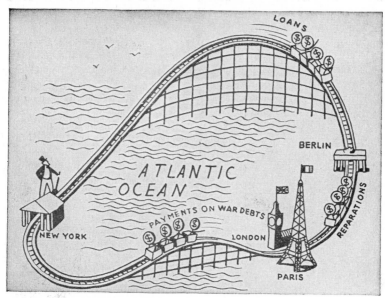

UNCLE SAM'S ROLLER COASTER. *When Americans stopped lending money to Germany, the Allies could no longer pay their war debts to us.* (From "Battles without Bullets," *Headline Series.* By permission of Foreign Policy Association)

The war debts–reparations problem. World War I changed the United States from a debtor to a creditor nation. Instead of owing money to foreigners, foreigners now owed money to us. This change was mainly due to the fact that during and right after the war, our government lent the Allies about ten billion dollars. Seventy per cent of the money was spent for military supplies, and the rest for supplies needed in reconstruction. Nearly all of the money was spent in the United States, with great benefit to American business.

The Allies wanted the United States to cancel these debts. They argued that the loans were a contribution to the common cause — the defeat of the Central Powers. The United States had given almost no military aid to the Allies for a whole year after it entered the war, and American losses in killed and wounded were very small compared to their losses. Besides, their total expenditures for the war effort and their property losses were far greater than those of the United States, while their resources were less. Simple justice, they felt, required the United States to forgive their debts.

The debtor nations did not have the cash to pay off their debts. There was not enough gold in all Europe for this purpose, and what gold there was, was needed to keep the national currencies on a sound

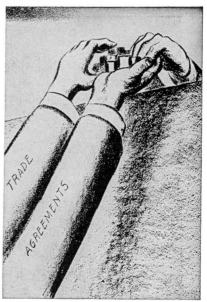

"WHY NOT GET TOGETHER?"
(Drawn by Fitzpatrick for the *St. Louis Post-Dispatch*)

"HANDS ACROSS THE TARIFF WALLS." Drawn by Fitzpatrick for the *St. Louis Post-Dispatch*)

"BALL AND CHAINS THAT DRAG." *A British cartoonist of the 1920's pointed out that world trade was hindered by reparations, war debts, and heavy expenditures for armaments.* (From *The News of the World,* London)

basis, because the paper money in European countries, like that in the United States, was payable in gold. Some European countries suggested that the United States should accept goods instead of money in payment for the debts. After all, they had received goods from America, not money.

The United States did not want goods. It feared that a flood of European goods might close its factories. As early as 1920 Congress rushed through an emergency tariff bill intended to shut out foreign products. President Wilson vetoed the bill, saying:

> If there ever was a time when America had anything to fear from foreign competition, that time has passed. If we wish Europe to settle her debts — governmental or commercial — we must be prepared to buy from her. Clearly this is no time for the erection of high trade barriers.

Wilson's advice was not heeded. Two years later a tariff law was passed raising duties to the highest level in the country's history. The law made it impossible for European nations to pay their debts to the United States in goods and led to new requests for cancellation.

If the debtor nations did not pay what they owed, the American taxpayer would have to shoulder the burden. So Congress insisted on payment. Agreements were drawn up with the debtor countries, providing for repayment over a period of sixty-two years and reducing the original interest rate of 5 per cent to an average of about 2 per cent.

England, France, Italy, and Belgium planned to collect reparations from Germany to pay what they owed the United States. They suggested that if the United States would forgive their debts, they would forgive Germany an equal amount of reparations. But the United States government refused to see any connection between debts and reparations. For a time Germany was able to pay reparations with money borrowed from American investors. When the depression came, these investors stopped lending money abroad. Then reparation payments dried up; and soon after, Allied debt payments to the United States came to an end. By 1934 all the debtors, except Finland, had stopped making payments. No one thought that the debts would ever be paid.

The debtors felt that the American attitude toward the war debts-reparations problem was selfish. Students of international affairs thought it was shortsighted. They argued that the attempt to pay war debts and reparations in money caused serious hardships in Europe and helped prepare the way for the rise of the Nazis and Fascists. **If this** is so, the United States was indeed "penny wise and pound foolish."

The Neutrality Act of 1935. American desire for isolation was strengthened by the failure of the European countries to pay their debts and by signs that another war was in the making. Americans wanted to make sure that when war came the United States would stay out. There was a widespread feeling that the United States had made a mistake in getting into World War I and that if it were careful, it could avoid making such a mistake again.

In 1934 the Senate appointed a committee, headed by Senator Nye, of North Dakota, to make a study of the munitions industry. The committee gave special attention to the period 1914–17. It was shown that in those years American munitions manufacturers had made large profits by supplying the Allies and that they expected even more profits should the United States enter the war. It was also shown that before the United States declared war, American bankers had lent nearly three billion dollars to the Allies for the purchase of war supplies. If the Allies had been defeated, as appeared likely early in 1917, they would not have been able to repay what they had borrowed. The committee's inquiry led many people to conclude that these economic ties between the United States and Europe had been one of the chief causes for our entry into the war.

Soon after the report of the Nye Committee there appeared a crop of magazine articles, books, and broadcasts denouncing the "merchants of death," who sold munitions, and the international bankers. There were also many novels and moving pictures showing the horrors of war and suggesting that all wars are evil. Numerous pacifist organizations were formed, and thousands of college students and other young people signed pledges not to go to war.

Pacifists and liberals joined with isolationists in demanding a law to prohibit the sale of munitions to all countries at war. Such a law, it was thought, would help the United States to stay neutral. The State Department, seeing that conflicts were likely to arise between aggressor nations and their victims, wanted a law enabling the President to stop the shipment of munitions to the aggressor, while allowing shipment to the nation that had been attacked. Congress was unwilling to give the President such power. It passed the Neutrality Act of 1935, forbidding the sale or transport of munitions to any nation at war.

Application of the Neutrality Act in Ethiopia and Spain. Late in 1935 Italy attacked Ethiopia. The President quickly enforced the

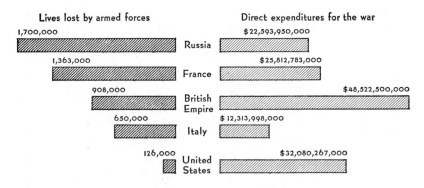

COST OF WORLD WAR I TO THE UNITED STATES
AND FOUR OF THE ALLIES

Neutrality Act by forbidding the shipment of munitions to either nation. He had no power to prevent Americans from filling Italian orders for such important war materials as cotton, copper, scrap iron, rubber, and oil. But he promised that if the League of Nations chose to blockade Italy, the United States would not interfere. The League Council then considered asking Great Britain and France to use their fleets for a blockade of Italy. Mussolini declared that he would fight Great Britain and France rather than submit to a blockade. These nations, partly because they knew they could get no munitions from the United States if Italy attacked them, voted against a blockade. Italy then had no trouble conquering the unarmed people of Ethiopia. After this no weak country could expect protection from the League. Our neutrality law had helped to destroy Woodrow Wilson's dream of collective security.

In 1936 civil war began in Spain. The rebels, led by General Franco, wanted to set up a Fascist dictatorship. They received considerable help from Italy and Germany. The "loyalists," those who supported the government, received some help from Russia. Roosevelt applied the Neutrality Act to this civil conflict. The embargo hurt the "loyalists" because Franco could get munitions from Italy and Germany. Franco finally triumphed. The application of the Neutrality Act in the Ethiopian war and the Spanish Civil War caused many of its supporters to realize that the act might hurt a cause they wanted to succeed. However, this did not check the trend toward isolationism.

The Neutrality Act of 1937. Congress passed another and stronger neutrality act in 1937. Upon the outbreak of any war the President

"PEACE STRIKE" *of students at the University of California at Los Angeles. More than a thousand students left the campus to take part in a nationwide demonstration called by the United Student Peace Committee. In the 1930's many college students in the United States, Canada, and Great Britain, believing that all war is evil, were pacifists.* (Press Association, Inc.)

was directed to forbid the sale of munitions and also the loan of money to either side. In addition the President was given the right to forbid the sale of *important raw materials* to countries at war, unless the purchaser paid cash and took them away himself. This was the so-called "cash-and-carry" rule. It had two purposes: (1) to keep American ships out of war zones where they might be sunk, and (2) to prevent the sale of supplies on credit to countries at war, since this might give the United States an interest in the success of one side rather than the other. The object of the Act was to keep the United States out of all wars. The Act was passed at the peak of American isolationism.

The Neutrality Act of 1939. Within two years a good many Americans began to doubt that isolationism was a safe policy. Hitler's Panzer divisions burst into Poland (September 1, 1939), and France and England then declared war on Germany. The democracies were not well armed, yet they could not buy a single cartridge in the United States. President Roosevelt called for a special session of Congress to revise the neutrality law. He urged Congress to repeal the arms embargo and also to give him power to prohibit American ships from sailing into danger zones.

For the next six weeks there was a stormy debate in Congress, in the newspapers, and over the radio. Isolationists approved of keeping American ships out of danger zones but argued that repeal of the arms embargo would surely cause the United States to be drawn into the war. Those favoring repeal argued that as long as the arms embargo was in force America was really helping Hitler. According to a Gallup poll, 56 per cent of the people favored repeal. Early in November, Congress passed the Neutrality Act of 1939. The arms embargo was lifted and *all trade* with belligerents placed on a cash-and-carry basis. This meant that as long as France and England controlled the seas, and as long as they had ready cash, they could buy in the United States anything they wanted. The new law also gave the President power to bar American ships and passengers from danger zones. Thus the Act looked two ways at once — toward partial co-operation with France and England on the one hand, and toward isolation on the other hand.

Conclusion. The foreign policy of the United States between 1918 and 1940 wavered between complete isolationism and limited co-operation with other nations. The American people were not ready for wholehearted international co-operation, either to promote world prosperity or to settle quarrels between nations. They had little faith in the possibility of preventing war by combining with other nations against an aggressor. They did have faith in the old policy of isolation. This, they thought, would keep the United States at peace.

Signs of another war appeared in Europe. Americans imagined that it would be no concern of theirs; Congress passed strict neutrality laws. By late 1939, when France and England were in danger, our people began to see their mistake. They did not want Hitler to triumph. They wanted to help the democracies fighting for their lives. Isolation had once more proved to be impossible.

❁ ❁ ❁

To identify: Briand, Fascist, Good Neighbor policy, Hull, Kellogg, Neutrality Acts, Nye Committee, Pact of Paris, Trade Agreements Act, Washington Conference.

To explain or define: aggressor nation, arms embargo, belligerent, capital ships, creditor nation, isolationism, reparations.

Subjects for Talks or Written Reports

1. The conquest of Ethiopia. What the League of Nations did about it.
2. Civil war in Spain. How it began. Intervention by Italy, Germany,

and Russia. Why Franco won. 3. A typical trade agreement between the United States and another nation. 4. Why much of the world's supply of gold came to the United States before 1933. Why still more came here afterward. 5. After the world-wide depression began, Germany prohibited all imports unless the seller would take his payment in German goods. Why did Germany take this step? How did this system of international barter work in practice? 6. The findings of the Nye Committee and their effect on public opinion. 7. American co-operation in the nonpolitical activities of the League of Nations. 8. The story of efforts to get the United States into the World Court. 9. Conditions in Germany which prepared the way for a dictator. 10. How President Franklin D. Roosevelt wrecked the London Economic Conference of 1933.

QUESTIONS FOR UNDERSTANDING THE TEXT

1. (a) Why was isolationism so popular after World War I? (b) When did it reach its peak? 2. Why are our Presidents and Secretaries of State more likely than members of Congress to believe in international co-operation? 3. (a) What was the purpose of the Washington Conference called in 1921? (b) What did it accomplish? 4. (a) What was done at the London Naval Conference of 1930? (b) Of 1935? 5. (a) What was the purpose of the Pact of Paris? (b) Why did it fail? 6. Why and how did the United States co-operate with the League of Nations? 7. (a) What was the Trade Agreements Act? (b) What did it accomplish? 8. How did World War I change the United States from a debtor to a creditor nation? 9. Give the arguments for the cancellation of the Allies' war debts to the United States. 10. (a) Give the arguments for and against American high tariffs after World War I. (b) How did the American tariff policy interfere with payment of the war debts? 11. Why did reparations payments dry up when the depression came? 12. What events led to the passage of the Neutrality Act of 1935? 13. (a) What kind of neutrality act did the State Department favor in 1935? (b) What kind of act was passed? 14. Did the Neutrality Act of 1935 protect American interests during the invasion of Ethiopia? During the Spanish civil war? Explain. 15. Did the Neutrality Act of 1937 protect American interests when war broke out in Europe in 1939? Explain. 16. How did the Neutrality Act of 1939 really favor France and England although no countries were named?

CHAPTER 42

INTER–AMERICAN CO-OPERATION

THE SLOW GROWTH OF CO-OPERATION AMONG THE AMERICAN REPUBLICS

The beginning. In 1826 Simon Bolivar, the great Latin American patriot, called a conference of all the nations of the Western Hemisphere. He hoped the American republics would band together in a great federation to defend themselves from European interference and to promote trade with one another. Our Congress debated so long over sending delegates that they did not arrive until the conference was ended. The Latin-American countries were so busy with local problems that they did not give active support to this scheme. Only four of them had delegates at the meeting. Thus the conference seemed to have failed.

In 1889 the United States took the lead in reviving the idea of inter-American co-operation. Secretary of State Blaine invited the other republics to join us in the first International Conference of American States at Washington. All but one of the Latin-American republics accepted the invitation. The main purpose of the conference was to promote trade between the American republics. The delegates created the Bureau of American Republics, to encourage peace, commerce, and friendship between its members.

The Union of American Republics. In 1910 the Union of American Republics was organized. It includes the twenty-one independent countries of the Western Hemisphere. (While Canada is practically an independent nation, it has so far not been invited to join the Union.) The organization's work is carried on by the Pan American Union, which has headquarters in Washington in a beautiful building given by Andrew Carnegie. The Pan American Union is controlled by a board of governors. The diplomatic representative from each of the American republics is a member of this board. Each member country pays a share of its expenses. The Union is a clearinghouse for infor-

HEADQUARTERS OF THE PAN AMERICAN UNION, *Washington, D. C. Twenty-one American republics are members of the Union, the purpose of which is to promote co-operation throughout the Western Hemisphere. This building, given by Andrew Carnegie, is designed and furnished in Spanish style. It is one of the show places of Washington.*

mation about the American republics. It makes arrangements for holding inter-American conferences, and works constantly for greater co-operation among the various American countries.

Why inter-American co-operation proved difficult. The development of inter-American co-operation has not been easy. The Latin-American countries have felt a closer relationship to Europe than to the United States or to one another. Although they cut their political ties with Europe long ago, just as we did, they are still bound to Europe by ties of culture and trade.

Travel and communication between the Latin-American countries and between them and the United States has always been difficult. The lofty Andes Mountains and the dense tropical jungles have kept the people of the various countries apart. Besides, the lack of capital has delayed the building of railroads, highways, and telephone lines to connect the various countries. There has even been a shortage of steamship service between the ports of North and South America. Until recently, travelers from some parts of South America reached the United States by way of Europe.

Another difficulty in developing co-operation among the American republics lies in their differences in language, religion, and customs.

For instance, neither Spanish nor English is understood in all parts of North and South America. The Brazilians speak Portuguese; most of the people of Paraguay speak an Indian tongue; while there are some communities of Latin America where German or Italian is the principal language heard.

Perhaps the biggest difficulty in developing co-operation between Latin America and the United States is Latin-American distrust of us. Latin America remembers our taking of Texas and half of Mexico; the Panama Revolution of 1903, which deprived Colombia of an important province; the annexation of Puerto Rico; and our frequent interference in the affairs of countries around the Caribbean. Fear of the United States reached its height between 1905 and 1925. A well-known Latin-American journalist said in 1913: "To save themselves from Yankee imperialism, the American democracies would almost accept a German alliance or the aid of Japanese arms. Everywhere the Americans of the North are feared." A little of this feeling still lingers, particularly in Argentina.

How Latin Americans felt about the Monroe Doctrine. The Monroe Doctrine has, in the past, caused much ill will toward the United States. It is true that Latin Americans did not object to it at first. They realized that it was a much-needed shield against European interference. But after we took New Mexico and California from Mexico in 1846, Latin Americans began to fear that the United States might be planning to get control of the entire hemisphere. This fear increased when Theodore Roosevelt added his famous corollary to the Monroe Doctrine. (See page 487.) The Doctrine now seemed not a shield so much as a cloak behind which Latin America was to be strangled by the United States. Fear of the Monroe Doctrine was partly quieted in 1930, when the State Department declared that the corollary was no longer in force.

The Good Neighbor policy. Late in the Coolidge administration our relations with Latin America began to improve. Our long quarrel with Mexico over the oil question was smoothed over (see pages 493–494), and we called our marines out of the Dominican Republic. Hoover continued the good work. As President-elect he made a goodwill tour of Latin America. He did not interfere when Salvador and the Dominican Republic stopped paying interest on their debts to American investors. He called the marines out of Nicaragua and arranged for them to leave Haiti as well. When Hoover left the White House, our relations with Latin America were better than they had been at any time in the past thirty years.

President Franklin D. Roosevelt built on the foundation laid by Coolidge and Hoover. In his first inaugural address he said: "I would dedicate this nation to the policy of the good neighbor." He and Secretary of State Hull lost no time in putting the Good Neighbor policy into practice. In 1933 the United States and the Latin-American republics signed a pact declaring: "No state has the right to intervene in the internal or external affairs of another." To prove that we meant what we said, we soon after gave up our right to intervene in Cuba. In 1936 we made a new and fairer treaty with Panama. Secretary Hull also made trade agreements to promote business between the United States and Latin America. The Department of State set up a Division of Cultural Co-operation to encourage a better knowledge and understanding among all the American republics. Most important, in 1936, at a special Inter-American Conference held at Buenos Aires, the United States agreed that the Monroe Doctrine was the concern of all the American republics, and each should have an equal voice with us in helping to enforce it. As late as 1923 the United States had claimed that the Monroe Doctrine was the concern of no American nation except itself. Its new attitude therefore pleased Latin America.

THE AXIS THREAT TO LATIN AMERICA

The Axis seeks control of Latin America. Axis leaders knew that Latin America has vast natural resources — mineral deposits, oil fields, tropical forests, and rich farm land. They laid careful plans to get possession of these riches. Their plans included (1) the spreading of propaganda, (2) the use of Axis nationals who had migrated to Latin America, (3) economic control of Latin America, (4) control of Latin-American air lines, and (5) the use of armed force.

1. The spreading of Axis propaganda. In 1933, when Hitler came to power in Germany, the Nazis started a propaganda campaign in Latin America. They were especially eager to stir up fear and distrust of the United States, for they wanted to end our influence in Latin America.

The Nazis supported a newspaper in almost every important city of Latin America. They supplied all newspapers with free news services which colored the news to suit Nazi purposes. They sold at very low prices radio sets built to pick up only Berlin broadcasts. They furnished daily radio programs to Latin-American stations. They gave thousands of free scholarships to Latin Americans wishing to study in German universities. They sent visiting professors to give courses in

Latin-American universities, paying their entire salary and expenses. They organized young people's societies, or Bunds, like those in Germany, for developing loyalty to Nazi ideas. They also established a large number of schools taught in German by German teachers.

The Italian Fascists carried on propaganda in Latin America in much the same style as the Nazis. They did just as much harm to the cause of inter-American co-operation.

Propaganda carried on by the Spanish Falange (the party which helped destroy the republic of Spain) was even more successful than that of the Nazis and Italian Fascists. It had the tremendous advantage of being Spanish. Many patriotic Latin Americans who would not think of joining a German or Italian organization became members of the Falange. Thus they came under Axis influence.

2. The use of Axis immigrants in Latin America. There are about two million German nationals, or immigrants, in Latin America, most of them in Brazil, Argentina, and Chile. They live in groups and try to preserve their German culture unchanged. Many of them believed in Nazi ideas and gladly undertook to help the Nazi agents. Others were forced to help by threats that otherwise their relatives still in Germany would be made to suffer. The Axis also obtained help from some of the three million Italian immigrants and from some of the half million Japanese immigrants in Latin America.

3. Axis attempts to get economic control. The Axis nations, particularly Germany, tried to get economic control over Latin America by the same methods that they used so successfully in the Balkans. They bought large quantities of Latin-American raw materials, which they paid for with manufactured goods rather than money. When this barter method of payment was first outlined, it sounded attractive. However, it worked out to the disadvantage of the Latin Americans. The Nazis used it to unload inferior manufactured goods which they did not want and which often were of little value to their customers. Furthermore, Latin-American firms doing business with Axis firms were asked to dismiss their Jewish employees and to hand over important business posts to Axis agents. Thus the Axis nations gradually got a strangle hold over their customers.

The Axis countries gave money to their agents for starting all kinds of businesses in Latin America. Axis agents also bought a large number of established businesses, especially banks, utility companies, plantations, mines, and stores. They used the businesses they controlled for four purposes: (1) to obtain markets for their manufactured products, (2) as a blind for their undercover activities, (3) as an excuse for buying land valuable for airfields and for military purposes, and (4) as a means of gaining political influence in the countries of Latin America.

4. Control of Latin-American air lines. Air tranportation is unusually important in Latin America because of the great distances and the lack of adequate railroads and highways. Realizing this, Germany and Italy built many airports there and operated many air lines. They chose some routes for strategic reasons and not for their commercial value. For instance, many of their airports were located in places near the Panama Canal and the bulge of Brazil. We did not see that this situation was very dangerous until after the Nazis had overrun Europe in 1939 and 1940. Then we suddenly realized that the Nazis could use their airports to get control of the Panama Canal, the Caribbean region, and most, if not all, of South America.

5. The use of armed force. We now know that the Axis intended to get outright military control of Latin America. They offered to help our neighbors fight "Yankee imperialism" (1) by selling them warships, warplanes, arms, and ammunition, and (2) by sending them, free of cost, German military and naval officers to train their armed forces. The officer class of several republics became pro-German.

The Nazis made ready to take over Brazil, Argentina, Uruguay, and several other Latin-American countries. They secretly, and in some countries openly, drilled their Bunds and storm troops in preparation for the day when they would be needed. Their agents hid large stores of arms and ammunition ready for use.

Danger to the United States. Had the Axis succeeded in getting control of any part of South America, they could quickly have seized possession of the airports, seaports, and means of communication throughout the continent. They could then have challenged our power in the Caribbean, and very likely could have put the Panama Canal out of commission. Damage to the canal would so interfere with our navy that we might have found it impossible to defend ourselves and our neighbors in a two-ocean war. Thus, the whole Western Hemisphere would have been in danger.

MEETING THE AXIS THREAT TO THE AMERICAS

The Lima Conference, December, 1938. The Eighth Conference of American States met in Lima, Peru, in the closing days of 1938. A new world war appeared to be just ahead, and our State Department was eager to line up the twenty-one American republics in a solid front against the Axis. Some of the delegates did not realize how well the Axis was succeeding in its plans to gain control of Latin America, and perhaps a few felt more friendly to the Axis than to the United States. At any rate, the Conference did not take any strong steps. However, it adopted resolutions condemning racial and religious persecution, stating the loyalty of the Americas to republican government, and providing that the American republics would consult together in case any one of them was in danger of attack by a foreign nation.

The foreign ministers meet at Panama, September, 1939. The outbreak of war in Europe in September, 1939, opened a new chapter in inter-American relations. Having agreed to consult together promptly in an emergency, the twenty-one republics sent their foreign ministers to a meeting in Panama. The ministers drew up a Declaration of Neutrality and formed an Inter-American Financial and Advisory Committee to sit in Washington for the duration of the war.

The foreign ministers meet at Havana, July, 1940. The fall of the Netherlands and France brought a new meeting of the foreign ministers. They had to decide how to prevent Germany from getting the French and Dutch possessions in the Caribbean area. They agreed that if any European possessions in the New World should be handed over to the Axis, the American republics would take these possessions under their joint control. This agreement was a milestone in inter-American co-operation.

Another urgent problem was what to do about Axis spies and fifth columnists. Just before the Havana meeting a plot to set up a Fascist government in Uruguay was uncovered. Hoping to prevent similar plots in other republics, the delegates arranged to exchange information about illegal activities of Axis agents. This led most of the countries to take strong steps to prevent such activities.

Co-operating for economic defense. Normally about 55 per cent of Latin-American exports go to western Europe. With most of Europe in Axis hands and a British blockade to keep merchant ships from reaching the Axis, Latin America had lost its biggest market. Unless prompt and large-scale action were taken, the Latin republics faced economic misery. In their distress the people might be easily misled by Axis propaganda. The economic defense of the Western Hemisphere was, then, no less important than its military defense.

Plans to prevent an economic breakdown in Latin America were drawn up by the Inter-American Financial and Economic Advisory Committee. The plans had four main objects: (1) to stimulate the

NAVAL OFFICERS FROM LATIN AMERICA *on a mission to the United States in the spring of 1941. They were photographed on the steps of the Pan American Union Building in Washington.* (Courtesy of Pan American Union)

development of mining; (2) to encourage the production of rubber, quinine, oil-bearing seeds, and other products that would be needed in large quantities if the United States went to war; (3) to promote trade between the Latin-American countries; and (4) to help Latin America find a market for products which could no longer be sold in Europe.

Most of the money needed in carrying out the plans was lent by the United States through the Export-Import Bank. The Latin republics spent much of the money in the United States for mining machinery, rails, locomotives, and other things needed to develop their industries. Congress also made large appropriations for the purchase of defense materials from Latin America.

Co-operating for military defense. After the fall of France the Americas were in the greatest danger in their history. (See page 597.) The United States needed and received the co-operation of the Latin republics in order to protect the Western Hemisphere from attack. All of them strengthened their defenses, usually with the aid of loans from the United States. Our army and navy officers helped train their fighting men. Many of their highest officers came here to study our methods of defense and to consult with our military leaders. Brazil and Panama gave us air bases on their soil. Thus our neighbors helped us get ready to meet the expected Axis attack.

To identify: Axis, Blaine, Bolivar, Bund, Falange, Pan American Union.
To explain or define: imperialism, nationals.

SUBJECT FOR TALKS OR WRITTEN REPORTS

1. Simon Bolivar. Why he is called the "George Washington of Latin America." What he tried to do and what he accomplished. 2. The military and naval strength of the Latin-American republics. 3. Economic conditions in any one Latin-American republic. Its economic relations with the United States. 4. How the Axis worked to get economic control of South America. 5. Co-operation between the United States and Canada for the defense of North America. 6. The area, population, and industrial development of Latin America compared with that of the United States.

QUESTIONS FOR UNDERSTANDING THE TEXT

1. (*a*) Who called the earliest conference of American republics? (*b*) What was his purpose? What was accomplished? 2. (*a*) What was accomplished at the first Pan-American Conference in 1889? (*b*) Where was it held? (*c*) How many have been held since? 3. (*a*) What is the work of the Pan American Union? (*b*) How is it governed and supported? 4. Discuss the main difficulties in developing inter-American co-operation. 5. (*a*) Name some of the steps taken to improve our relations with Latin America. (*b*) Which Presidents deserve credit for this improvement? 6. (*a*) Why did Latin Americans formerly object to the Monroe Doctrine? (*b*) What was done at the Buenos Aires Conference in 1936 to overcome their objections? 7. (*a*) Discuss Axis propaganda activities in Latin America during the 1930's and 1940's. (*b*) Were these a danger to hemispheric safety? Explain. 8. How did Axis agents make use of Axis nationals living in Latin America? 9. (*a*) How did the Axis pay for Latin-American products? (*b*) Why was this method of payment bad for Axis customers? (*c*) In what other ways did the Axis try to get economic control of Latin America? 10. Why did Germany and Italy seek control of air lines in Latin America? 11. How did the Nazis work to get control of the armed forces of the Latin-American republics? 12. (*a*) State the economic difficulties of Latin America due to the outbreak of war in Europe. (*b*) Name some of the steps taken to improve the situation. 13. Why did the fall of France cause fear for the safety of the Western Hemisphere? 14. Discuss the co-operative defense of the Western Hemisphere.

CHAPTER 43

TROUBLE IN THE PACIFIC

American interests in the Far East. Americans became interested in the Far East soon after the Revolutionary War, when New England merchantmen started to trade with China. For many years Canton was the only Chinese port open to foreigners, but in the 1840's China made treaties opening several other ports. The United States obtained the right to trade in these ports in 1844. It also received the privilege of *extraterritoriality*, which meant that American citizens in China were governed only by American law and could be tried only by American officials. Other nations obtained similar privileges.

Japan barred foreigners from her shores until 1853–54, when Commodore Matthew C. Perry sailed into Japanese waters with a fleet of warships and persuaded Japan to make a treaty with the United States. This was the first treaty Japan had ever made. It opened Japanese ports to American trade and started Japan on the road to becoming a modern nation.

American interest in the Far East grew rapidly after Hawaii, Samoa, Wake Island, and the Philippines (1898–99) were acquired. Possession of the Philippines made the United States a near neighbor of China and Japan. American businessmen thought it would now be easy to develop a brisk trade with the vast population of China.

The Far Eastern grab bag. While the United States was occupied with the Spanish-American War and its settlement, England, France, Russia, Germany, and Japan were getting ready to gobble up the Chinese Empire. Each had forced the weak Chinese government to give it certain privileges, including the lease of seaports. Each was insisting that it should have economic control over a portion of Chinese territory chosen as its "sphere of influence." China had also been forced to give up some of its possessions outright. Britain had taken Burma. France had taken Indo-China. Japan had taken Formosa and Korea. The United States, the only great power that had seized neither terri-

THE *SIERRA NEVADA in Hong Kong harbor about 1860.* *This American clipper
ship sailed to many foreign lands.* (Painted by a Chinese artist. Courtesy of Charles
D. Childs Gallery, Boston)

tory nor a sphere of influence from China, was in danger of being shut
out of the Chinese market.

The "Open Door" policy. The United States government wished
to protect its commercial interests in China and also to prevent any further seizures of Chinese territory. In 1899 John Hay, the Secretary of
State, sent a note to each of the great powers asking them to help preserve freedom of trade and equal commercial opportunities in China
for all nations — that is, to maintain an "Open Door." Great Britain
promptly and heartily agreed, but some of the other powers agreed
only halfheartedly and after months of delay. Early in 1900 Hay announced that the Open Door policy had been accepted by all the powers concerned. His statement was more hopeful than accurate. Time
was to show that most of the powers gave lip service to the Open Door
idea but did not intend to put it into practice.

The Boxer uprising. A few months after Hay's announcement a
Chinese society known as the "Boxers" rose up against the "foreign
devils." The Boxers wanted to drive all foreigners out of China.
After a series of violent actions against foreigners and their property,
they surrounded the foreign legations at Peking (now Peiping). An
international army of eighteen thousand French, English, German,
Italian, Portuguese, Russian, Japanese, and American soldiers hurried

AMERICAN TROOPS *on the Temple of Agriculture grounds at Peking, China, in August, 1900. The United States sent soldiers to protect the lives and property of American citizens from the attacks of the Boxers.* (Courtesy of National Archives)

to the rescue. The United States supplied two thousand, five hundred troops — a sign of its new responsibility as a world power.

Secretary Hay feared that the other great powers would use the Boxer uprising as an excuse to seize more Chinese territory. He stated that it was the purpose of the United States to uphold the territorial integrity (wholeness) of China. This statement had the desired effect. The only penalties imposed on China were the punishment of the Boxer leaders and the payment of an indemnity (damages) for injuries and losses suffered by foreigners during the uprising. The indemnity demanded was very heavy, but it might have been still worse had Secretary Hay not tried to protect Chinese rights.

Our share of the indemnity was twenty-four million dollars. When it was found that the losses to American citizens and the cost of sending soldiers to Peking amounted to only eleven million dollars, Congress ordered the difference returned to China. This friendly action won the good will of the Chinese people. China used the money to create a fund for sending Chinese students to American colleges.

A cloud comes between the United States and Japan. For half a century after Commodore Perry's visit, American relations with Japan were friendly. The United States took pride in Japan's rapid development into a modern industrial nation. When the Japanese tried to drive Russia out of Manchuria in 1904, American sympathies were with Japan. Japan defeated the Russians and became the strongest power in the Far East. Then American feelings changed, and the United States began to take note of Japan's growing strength.

In 1905 Japan asked President Theodore Roosevelt to arrange peace terms with Russia. The peace conference of the Russo-Japanese War was held at Portsmouth, New Hampshire. The peace treaty did not give Japan everything it wanted, and for this the President was blamed. The Japanese felt they had been cheated of some of the fruits of their victory. This was the first cloud to come between the United States and Japan.

Japan attempts new conquests during World War I. Since 1902 Japan had been a military ally of Great Britain. When Britain went to war with Germany in 1914, Japan also declared war on Germany. Japan seized the peninsula of Shantung, which had been a German sphere of influence in China. Japan also took the Caroline, Marianas, and Marshall islands — German possessions in the South Pacific. There are about 1400 of these little islands, with a total area of some 830 square miles. A Japanese admiral called them "natural aircraft carriers." They were to be useful to Japan in her attempt to win control of the Pacific in the 1940's.

In 1915 Japan insisted that China agree to twenty-one demands. These were intended to turn China into a Japanese sphere of influence. The United States protested, and China took courage to resist. Japan then postponed most of the demands "for further discussion." Once again the United States had shown a willingness to protect China, short of going to war.

The Far Eastern settlement at the Washington Conference. After World War I, relations between the United States and Japan were somewhat strained. The Japanese did not like our refusal to let them come to the United States. They did not like the laws of some of the states in the Far West which prevented Japanese from owning land. Besides, they felt that the United States was blocking their ambitions in China. The United States, on its part, had become highly distrustful of Japan. The Hearst papers talked continually about the "yellow peril." Sensational books, with such titles as *The Menace of Japan*, *The Rising Tide of Color*, and *Must We Fight Japan?* were widely read. Many Americans thought that war with Japan was bound to come. Others thought the differences could be straightened out if the United States really tried to be friendly with Japan.

In 1921 President Harding called the Washington Conference for two purposes: (1) to end the naval armaments race, and (2) to find a way to keep peace in the Far East. (See pages 561–562.) The Conference also produced the Four-Power Treaty and the Nine-Power Treaty.

The alliance between Great Britain and Japan was replaced by the Four-Power Treaty. This bound Japan, Britain, France, and the United States to respect one another's possessions in the Pacific and to consult together if these possessions were threatened by any other power. In the Nine-Power Treaty the same four powers and five others (Belgium, Holland, Portugal, Italy, and China) agreed not to interfere with China's independence and to maintain the Open Door in China. The signers did not agree to defend China's independence by force; they merely agreed not to attack it. China's request that the powers give up extraterritoriality and other special privileges within her borders was not granted.

Exclusion of Japanese immigrants creates new ill will. The Washington Conference resulted in somewhat better feeling between the United States and Japan. The naval race was stopped. The United States agreed that Japan should be the strongest naval power in the Far East. (See page 562.) Japan promised to uphold the Open Door. Some two years later, when Tokyo was destroyed by an earthquake, Americans quickly raised a large relief fund. For a little while there was real friendliness between the two nations. However, new friction was soon to develop over the immigration question.

Following the Russo-Japanese War, thousands of Japanese settled in California. The Californians demanded that Japanese immigrants be excluded. (Chinese laborers had been excluded since 1882.) Not wishing to hurt the pride of a sensitive nation, President Theodore Roosevelt did not want Congress to pass an act to prevent Japanese immigrants from entering the United States. Instead, he got the Japanese government in 1908 to make a "gentlemen's agreement" not to give passports to laborers wishing to come to the mainland of the United States. Japan observed the agreement faithfully. Yet when the Immigration Act of 1924 was passed, Congress, against the advice of President Coolidge and Secretary of State Hughes, insisted on excluding all members of the Mongolian race, Japanese as well as Chinese. The proud Japanese people regarded this as an insult. They thought Congress should have given Japan an immigration quota, as was done for other nations. Japan's quota would have been only a hundred immigrants a year. By shutting them out completely, we aroused the lasting resentment of the Japanese people.

Growth of Chinese nationalism. While American-Japanese relations were growing cooler, American sympathy for China continued
to increase. The republican movement in China, which began about
the turn of the century, pleased Americans. They were pleased, too,
by the growth of national spirit in China.

Hundreds of Chinese students after 1900 went abroad each year to
study. Thousands more went to missionary colleges in China, where
they were taught by European and American instructors. These students came to realize that if China was to take its place in the world, it
must adopt Western science and industrial methods, and must develop
a strong and democratic government. They wanted to make China
strong and free. This aim was also held by many Chinese businessmen
in the port cities, who had been influenced by Western ideas. They
joined with the educated youth of China to found the National People's party. (The Chinese name is Kuomintang [gwō′ min täng].)
Its aims were nationalism, democracy, and livelihood (a living for the
people). Its leader, Dr. Sun Yat-sen, hoped to free his people from the
injustices they suffered from their own rulers and at the hands of foreign nations.

The first revolution took place in 1911. It drove out the Manchus
(the family which had ruled for three hundred years) and set up the
republic of China. But the people were not yet ready for self-government, and the feeling of national unity was still very weak. For the
next fifteen years the country was in the grip of Chinese war lords,
who set up their own governments in the provinces and defied the central government. Foreign powers supplied arms to the war lords in
return for special privileges.

After World War I the National People's party appealed to the
United States, Great Britain, Japan, and other powers for help, but got
none. Finally they turned to Soviet Russia, which had given up the
special rights and privileges obtained by imperialist Russia. With the
help of advisers from Moscow, Sun Yat-sen reorganized the People's
party and began to build an army. Many Russians migrated to China
and carried on Communist propaganda. After Sun Yat-sen's death in
1925, the leader of the army, Chiang Kai-shek (Chē äng′ Kī′ shek′),
became the head of the People's party. He led China's second revolution, 1926–28, and founded the Nationalist Government of China.

The Manchurian crisis, 1931. Manchuria was a valuable Chinese
province north of China proper. The great bulk of the population
was Chinese, but most of the business and industry of the province be-

"DON'T FAIL US," *pleaded the Chinese to the League of Nations during the Japanese advance in 1938. This picture shows a mass demonstration in Canton.* (Acme)

longed to the Japanese. Japan wanted to control Manchuria. In September, 1931, Japanese agents blew up a section of the Japanese-owned South Manchurian Railway and accused the Chinese of the crime. Using this incident as an excuse, the Japanese army went into action. While China appealed to the League of Nations for help, the Japanese conquered Manchuria. They set up there a so-called Chinese government. However, it was wholly under Japanese control, and for this reason became known as a "puppet" government. Japan renamed the province "Manchukuo." The United States did not recognize it.

Japan did not then have large stores of war materials, and her war industries were not yet strong. It is likely that if the rest of the world had stopped trading with Japan, she would have been forced to yield. With this in mind, our Secretary of State, Henry L. Stimson, informed the Council of the League of Nations that the United States would co-operate with it fully to stop the war. Stimson urged the Council to use "all pressure and authority" within its power. The Council promptly invited the United States to send a delegate to sit with it while the situation in Manchuria was being considered. The United States did so. Great Britain and France were unwilling to take any strong steps against Japan. Then, too, it was uncertain whether our Congress would approve any strong steps. So the Council did nothing except appoint an investigating committee.

After a year of study the League investigating committee found that Japan had been in the wrong. When the report was accepted by the League, Japan resigned. She remained in control of Manchukuo. It now appeared safe for any government to defy the League of Nations and to ignore the Pact of Paris — as Hitler and Mussolini certainly noted. Convinced that they had nothing to fear from the United States or the League, Japanese military leaders made ready for new conquests. Manchuria, with its rich farm land, oil fields, and coal and iron deposits, supplied new materials for war. Japan hastened to make Manchuria a base for war industries.

Undeclared war in China. In 1937 Japan sent armies into North China. She did not declare war, but within eighteen months she occupied the five provinces and most of China's seacoast farther south. It appeared that Japan might soon control the whole of China.

Americans were sympathetic toward the Chinese. Yet they did not intend to risk war with Japan in order to help China. In October, 1937, when President Roosevelt declared that aggressor nations should be "quarantined," the public gave him little support. The idea of collective security was no more popular than it had been in Woodrow Wilson's time.

Under the Neutrality Act of 1937 the President was required to forbid the lending of money and the exporting of munitions to countries at war. Since no declaration of war had been made, Roosevelt did not apply the law to China and Japan. With Manchuria's resources at her command, Japan could make her own arms, warships, and airplanes, while China must buy them from other countries. Besides, China needed to borrow money to buy arms. Under the conditions it seemed best not to enforce the Neutrality Act.

Japan joins the Axis. China proved hard to conquer. Japan held the coastal region, containing most of China's industries, railroads, and large cities, but could not force the Chinese to surrender. Even in the occupied areas, Chinese guerrillas continued to worry the invaders. When war began in Europe in September, 1939, the war in China was at a standstill.

South of China lay rich lands which were weakly defended — French Indo-China, British Malaya, Burma, and the Netherlands Indies. In the summer of 1940, with France and the Netherlands crushed and Britain fighting for her life, Japan saw new opportunities

FOREIGN SPHERES OF INFLUENCE IN CHINA, 1914

European countries, as well as Japan, sought to control portions of Chinese territory. In the treaty ports the foreign powers maintained soldiers and warships.

for conquest. She was willing to join the Rome-Berlin Axis in exchange for a free hand in southeastern Asia and the South Pacific. In September, 1940, Japan, Germany, and Italy signed an alliance. The three powers promised to come to one another's aid if any one of them should be attacked by any country then a neutral — a threat clearly aimed at the United States. Germany and Italy agreed to let Japan establish a "New Order of Greater East Asia." In return Japan secretly promised to make war on Britain and the United States when the time was ripe. This promise was soon known to our State Department.

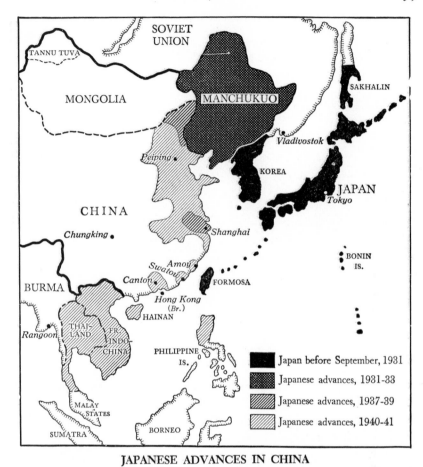

JAPANESE ADVANCES IN CHINA

Japan seized control of China's seaports and her richest provinces. The areas occupied by Japan contained most of China's industries, mines, and railroads.

The United States sent re-enforcements to Hawaii and the Philippines and warned the seventeen thousand American citizens in the Far East to come home. Japan's next move was the landing of troops in Indo-China. The governor of Indo-China begged us for planes and artillery, but we were unable to spare any. He appealed to Australia, only to learn that it, too, had no arms that could be spared.

In July, 1941, the Japanese completed their occupation of French Indo-China and made ready to seize the Netherlands Indies. Our government "froze" Japanese assets (money and other property) in the United States — putting a stop to all trade between the two countries.

DESTRUCTION OF THE BATTLESHIP *U.S.S. ARIZONA at Pearl Harbor, December 7, 1941. Japan intended to cripple the main American Pacific fleet and did so. Eighteen of our ships were sunk or damaged in this attack.* (H. Armstrong Roberts)

Meanwhile Japan was apparently trying to reach an agreement with the United States. Between March and December, 1941, the Japanese ambassador in Washington, Admiral Nomura, had no less than sixty talks with Secretary Hull.

In November, claiming that it was a last effort to maintain peace, Japan sent one of its veteran diplomats, Mr. Saburo Kurusu, to help Nomura. Kurusu brought Japan's offer to withdraw from Indo-China and to stop her advance in southeastern Asia if the United States would agree to Japanese control of China. On November 26 our government gave its reply: Japan must withdraw all troops from Indo-China and also from China. The Japanese answer was given on December 7, 1941. It took the form of a sneak attack on the American naval bases at Pearl Harbor and Manila. On the following day Congress declared war against Japan.

To identify: Boxers, Chiang Kai-shek, Four-Power Treaty, John Hay, Kuomintang, National People's party, Nine-Power Treaty, Open

Door policy, Commodore Matthew C. Perry, Russo-Japanese War, Henry L. Stimson, Sun Yat-sen.

To explain or define: extraterritoriality, gentlemen's agreement, guerrillas, immigration quota, indemnity, puppet state, sphere of influence.

SUBJECTS FOR TALKS OR WRITTEN REPORTS

1. The story of American missions in China and Japan. 2. Commodore Perry's two trips to Japan. 3. Discriminations against the Japanese by some of our states before 1939. 4. Japan's rapid industrial development after Perry's visits. 5. Japanese rule in Korea and Manchuria. 6. Why Chinese nationalism grew so slowly. 7. Decline of the Kuomintang.

QUESTIONS FOR UNDERSTANDING THE TEXT

1. (*a*) Why were Americans interested in the Far East? (*b*) When did their interest begin? (*c*) What event increased their interest? 2. (*a*) Explain what is meant by the Open Door policy. (*b*) When was it announced? 3. (*a*) What was the Boxer uprising? (*b*) What action was taken by the interested powers? 4. Why did so many Chinese students come to the United States after 1900? 5. (*a*) What brought about the Russo-Japanese War? (*b*) How did it change our attitude toward Japan? Japan's attitude toward us? 6. (*a*) When did Japan gain control of the Caroline, Marianas, and Marshall islands? (*b*) Of what value were they to her? 7. (*a*) What was the gentlemen's agreement regarding Japanese immigration to the United States? (*b*) Did Japan observe the agreement? 8. Why did Japan resent the Immigration Act of 1924? 9. (*a*) What two groups formed the National People's party of China? (*b*) State the three aims of the party. (*c*) Who was its leader? 10. (*a*) What was accomplished by the first Chinese revolution in 1911? (*b*) Why was a second revolution necessary? (*c*) Who led it? 11. In Manchuria political control followed economic control. Explain. 12. (*a*) How did Secretary Stimson think that Japan might be forced to give up Manchuria? (*b*) What did the League Council do? 13. How did control of Manchuria aid Japan in further conquests? 14. What events proved that the American people were unwilling to use troops to enforce the Open Door policy? 15. In your opinion should the Neutrality Act have been applied to the war between Japan and China? 16. What was the agreement made in 1940 between Japan, Germany, and Italy? 17. (*a*) What terms did Japan propose to prevent war with the United States? (*b*) What was the American reply? 18. (*a*) In your opinion would Congress have voted to go to war to drive Japan out of Indo-China and China? (*b*) Why did we go to war with Japan?

CHAPTER 44

DEMOCRACY IN PERIL

he rise of Hitler. Germany did not recover from the effects of World War I for many years. Unemployment was a serious problem throughout the 1920's and early 1930's. Besides economic difficulties, Germany suffered from feelings of national shame. She had been defeated in 1918; she had lost all her colonies; she had been compelled to disarm; and she was expected to pay heavy damages. When a leader arose who promised to bring back her prosperity and her national pride, the Germans flocked to his banner. Hitler soon destroyed representative government and set up a military dictatorship. From then on he ruled Germany with an iron hand.

Hitler prepares for world conquest. Hitler began at once a tremendous program of rearmament. He took Germany out of the League of Nations. He refortified the Rhineland, which had been demilitarized by the Treaty of Versailles. He built up a huge air force and a mechanized army such as the world had never before seen. He made an alliance with Mussolini, forming the so-called Rome-Berlin Axis. In 1936–38 Hitler and Mussolini helped Franco achieve power in Spain. In return they expected the use of Spanish bases and other help in case of war. Japan became a member of the Axis in 1940. Together the three Axis nations expected to dominate the world.

Hitler seizes Austria, Czechoslovakia, and Poland. In 1938 Hitler took Austria by force. Soon after, he demanded the Sudetenland from Czechoslovakia. The British and French prime ministers went to Munich to beg Hitler not to touch the helpless little republic. When he refused, they yielded rather than go to war. Hitler told them he wanted no further territory. "It is peace in our time," said Prime Minister Chamberlain of Great Britain on his return from Munich, but Winston Churchill said, "Britain and France had to choose between war and dishonor. They chose dishonor. They will have war."

HITLER ADDRESSING A THRONG *of two million Germans, May 8, 1934. Hitler and other Nazi leaders taught that Germans are a master race who deserve to rule the world. This belief led the Nazis to set out on a program of world conquest.* (Acme)

Like the United States, Great Britain had a large number of isolationists, who thought they could have peace if their government would only mind its own business. Ever since Hitler and Mussolini began their aggressions, British isolationists had favored "appeasement," which meant giving in to the dictators in the hope that they would then be quiet. After Munich the British saw that appeasement was a threat to their own safety. Yet they were not prepared for war.

In March, 1939, Hitler took the rest of Czechoslovakia. The same month he seized Memel from Lithuania. Then Mussolini, who by this time had finished mopping up Ethiopia, took Albania. Shortly after, Hitler began to thunder at Poland for the return of Danzig and the Polish Corridor. In August, Hitler surprised the world by signing a nonaggression pact with Russia. Then he suddenly ended discussions with Poland and hurled his armies across the Polish frontier. While the Nazis quickly overran the western half of Poland, the Russians occupied the eastern half.

France and Britain expected Hitler to attack them next. On Sep-

tember 3, 1939, they declared war on Germany. Within a few days
most of the British dominions also declared war.

Congress revises the neutrality law. As the Neutrality Act of 1937
required him to do, the President promptly prohibited the export of
arms and munitions to the belligerents — Germany, Russia, Poland,
France, Great Britain, and the British dominions. This did not hurt
Germany, which was armed to the teeth, but it threatened defeat to
the poorly armed democracies. As we have seen (pages 570–571),
the President at once called a special session of Congress to revise the
neutrality law, and after a hot debate Congress repealed the arms
embargo.

Hitler conquers western Europe. In the spring of 1940 the Germans swiftly conquered Denmark, Norway, the Netherlands, Belgium, and Luxemburg. The invaders then crossed into northern
France. Within four weeks they destroyed the French army and
drove the British army out of France. Meanwhile Italy entered the
war, attacking France from the southeast. On June 22 the French
were forced to sign an armistice. German troops occupied two thirds
of the country. The unoccupied remainder was at Hitler's mercy.
Its government, located at Vichy, had no choice but co-operation
with the Axis.

The United States realizes its danger. In the summer of 1940 Hitler's
army, poised for invasion, stood on the shores of the English Channel,
less than twenty miles from England. England had no land defenses to
speak of. Her air force was still far from strong. Her army, heroically
rescued from Dunkirk, had left all its equipment in France. Skilled
military observers in Europe thought that within a few weeks England
"would have her neck wrung like a chicken." Even if England somehow managed to resist invasion, she was still in terrible danger. Hitler
was pressing the Vichy government to bring France into the war on
the side of the Axis or at least to place the French fleet and the French
colonies in Africa at his service. The combined French, German, and
Italian fleets might seize control of the Atlantic and quickly reduce the
British to starvation.

The American people realized for the first time that the Western
Hemisphere was in danger. If Britain fell, the United States would be
left alone to defend North and South America against an enemy with
the economic and military might of all Europe at his back. From Da-
kar in French West Africa, only sixteen hundred miles from the bulge
in Brazil, the Axis could easily launch an attack against Latin America.

"INFERIOR DECORATION." *An English cartoonist's idea of paper-hanger Hitler's "New Order" for Europe in 1941.* (From the *Daily Dispatch,* Manchester, England)

If the Axis got control of any of the French, Dutch, and English possessions in the Caribbean area, our Panama life line could be cut and our sea power made ineffective. (See page 578.)

The Americas were safe only while the British fleet controlled the Atlantic. The United States had but a one-ocean navy, and for years we had kept most of our ships in the Pacific to safeguard our western coast and our Pacific outposts. Because Japan might attack us, we could not now bring our fleet back to the Atlantic.

Destroyers for bases. From bases in Norway, Denmark, the Netherlands, Belgium, and France, German submarines and aircraft stepped up their attack on British shipping. The number of ships sunk or damaged was staggering. In July, 1940, over four hundred thousand tons of British and Allied shipping went to the bottom, and this rate of loss continued for many months. Unless the British could cut down these losses by giving their freighters better escort protection, defeat was certain.

In September, 1940, Roosevelt announced that he had given the British fifty overage American destroyers. Built in World War I, they had been out of commission for years. In return the British made us a free gift for ninety-nine years of bases in Newfoundland and Bermuda and leased us six bases in the Caribbean. We needed these bases for the naval and air defense of the Western Hemisphere. About the same time the United States and Canada made plans for the joint defense of North America.

The United States gets ready for battle. Congress had begun to strengthen our navy, army, and air forces in 1937, but three years later the United States was still far from ready to resist an attack. This became clear after the spectacular Nazi victories in the spring of 1940. In September, Congress made all male citizens between the ages of twenty-one and thirty liable for a year's military training. This was the first peacetime draft in the history of our country. By fall Congress had voted almost eighteen billion dollars for defense. The plans called for a two-ocean navy, a large army, and an air force second to none.

The Lend-Lease Act. In November, 1940, Roosevelt was re-elected for a third term. Sure of popular support, he pushed ahead vigorously with his program for strengthening national defense and aiding Great Britain. In a "fireside chat" late in December he said, "The United States is determined that the Axis powers are not going to win this war." Nothing but an Allied victory would ensure the kind of world in which nations could live in security. "We must be the great arsenal of democracy," said the President.

England's cash reserves were almost used up. She would soon be unable to pay cash for her heavy purchases in this country. If we lent her billions of dollars, she could never repay us in money. The President suggested that we lend goods instead of dollars and expect repayment to be made in goods. Accordingly, a "Lend-Lease" bill was placed before Congress early in January, 1941. The bill would give the President power to lend defense materials and war equipment to foreign nations "whose defense the President deems vital to the defense of the United States."

Congress passed the Lend-Lease Act in March, 1941. A London magazine called it the "Declaration of Interdependence." It made us a nonshooting ally of Great Britain and the other nations fighting the Axis.

Guarding the sea lanes. It was foolish for the United States to export war material that would only go to the bottom of the Atlantic. So as soon as the Lend-Lease Act was passed, the President took steps to protect Lend-Lease cargoes. He transferred ten Coast Guard cutters and twenty mosquito boats to the British for convoy service. He took the Danish colonies of Greenland and Iceland under American

"A STRANGE RACE HORSE." *While Hitler flies down the track on his Axis mount, Uncle Sam's horse is pulled two ways by the dispute between interventionists and isolationists.* (Drawn by C. C. Hungerford for the *Pittsburgh Post-Gazette*)

protection for the duration of the war to prevent their use as bases for Axis submarines. He instructed the air force to patrol the Atlantic as far as Iceland in order to warn British ships of the presence of enemy submarines. By early summer he ordered American warships to convoy British merchantmen from the United States to Iceland. The toll of ship losses began to decline.

The invasion of Russia. In the fall and winter of 1940–41 Hitler forced Hungary, Rumania, and Bulgaria to join his "New Order." In April, when Yugoslavia and Greece refused to join, they were invaded and crushed. Hitler then drove the English from the island of Crete. Military experts guessed that he would next launch a drive to get control of the Suez Canal, the Red Sea, and the Near East. Instead, Hitler suddenly hurled his armies against Russia (June 22, 1941).

Only three powers stood between Hitler and the domination of the entire world — the United States, the British Empire, and the Soviet Union. Hitler wanted to crush Russia for three reasons: (1) to make sure her military power would not be turned against Germany, (2) to gain control of Russian raw materials, industrial strength, and man power for use in further conquests, and (3) to open a gateway to India and beyond.

The war in Russia raged along a two-thousand-mile front. By the

WENDELL L. WILLKIE, *Republican candidate for President in 1940, speaking in support of the Lend-Lease bill to members of the Senate Committee on Foreign Relations, February 11, 1941. Willkie believed the United States could best protect itself by aiding the nations fighting the Axis.* (Press Association, Inc.)

middle of November, 1941, the Germans had advanced over five hundred miles and had conquered five hundred thousand square miles of Russian territory — almost three times the area of Germany. Then the Russians stopped the German drive and slowly pushed the Germans back.

Hitler may have expected his attack on Russia to divide the people of the democracies, since so many of them hated Communism. If so, he was disappointed. Stalin was welcomed as an ally against Nazism. Both England and the United States sent supplies to Russia.

The Atlantic Charter. The growing partnership of the United States and Great Britain was highlighted in August, 1941, when Roosevelt and Churchill met at sea. The two statesmen drew up the "Atlantic Charter" — a statement on which they wanted the peace settlement to be based. There were eight points in this agreement:

1. The United States and Britain seek no additional territory.
2. Territorial changes should only be made according to the wish of the population concerned.
3. All peoples should be allowed to choose their own form of government.

4. All nations should have access to the trade and raw materials of the world.
5. The United States and Britain will encourage international co-operation to improve labor standards and social security.
6. The peace should give all peoples freedom from want and freedom from fear.
7. The seas should be free to all in time of peace.
8. Aggressor nations should be forced to disarm until a permanent system of international security can be established.

The Atlantic Charter cheered liberals and gave new hope to the conquered peoples of Europe. It seemed to pledge the United States to the defeat of Hitler and the establishment of a democratic peace.

The shooting begins. During 1941 German and Italian submarines sank several American merchantmen. In September a German submarine off Iceland fired at the United States destroyer *Greer*. Roosevelt then announced that our patrols would attack any Axis raider found within American defense areas. This meant the beginning of an undeclared naval war. Soon after, one American destroyer was damaged and another sunk by U-boats.

In November Congress passed an act permitting the arming of our merchant ships as a defense against submarines. Congress also repealed parts of the neutrality law so that our ships could carry Lend-Lease cargoes direct to countries fighting the Axis. The American people no longer wished to keep our ships out of these danger spots, because they wanted to give the greatest possible aid to the countries fighting the Axis.

War is declared. American leaders realized that at any time the Axis might take some step that would force us to declare war. When the expected action came, it was in the Pacific. The Japanese attack on Pearl Harbor united the American people behind the government as nothing had yet done. The day after the Pearl Harbor attack Congress declared war on Japan. Germany and Italy then declared war on the United States. We were, as the President said, "in it all the way."

To identify: Atlantic Charter, Chamberlain, Churchill, Rome-Berlin Axis.
To explain or define: appeasement, arsenal of democracy.

Subjects for Talks or Written Reports

1. The life of Adolf Hitler. 2. How the Nazis kept themselves in power in Germany. 3. Why the Sudetenland was so important to Czechoslovakia. 4. The Russian war with Finland. 5. Why Russia made a nonaggression pact with her known enemy, Hitler. 6. The evacuation of Dunkirk. 7. The Battle of Britain. 8. The Battle of the Atlantic. 9. How the Vichy government was forced to aid Hitler. 10. The Battle of Russia.

Questions for Understanding the Text

1. How do you account for Hitler's rise to power? 2. (*a*) Why did Hitler and Mussolini want a sympathetic government in Spain? (*b*) How did they obtain it? 3. Why did Hitler want control of the Sudetenland? (Look at a physical map of southeastern Europe.) 4. Why and when did Britain and France declare war on Germany? 5. Why and when did Congress repeal the arms embargo? 6. Outline Hitler's gains in the spring of 1940. 7. (*a*) Why was Great Britain in peril after the fall of France? (*b*) How was the Western Hemisphere threatened? 8. (*a*) Why did Great Britain need our old destroyers? (*b*) Why did we hesitate to transfer them? 9. (*a*) Why did we need additional bases in the Atlantic? (*b*) How did we get them? (*c*) Why does one nation rarely permit another to establish bases on its territory? 10. (*a*) When did the United States begin to take seriously the task of preparing for war? (*b*) What plans were made? 11. What steps did the United States take to protect Lend-Lease cargoes? 12. (*a*) What gains did Hitler make in the period just before he invaded Russia? (*b*) Why did he want to conquer Russia? 13. (*a*) Briefly state the eight points of the Atlantic Charter. (*b*) When and where was it drawn up? 14. When did we begin undeclared naval war on the Axis? 15. When and why did Congress decide to approve the arming of our merchant ships? 16. Why did Japan attack the United States?

CHAPTER 45

THE UNITED STATES IN WORLD WAR II

The United Nations Pact. In December, 1941, when the United States went to war with the Axis, we were far from ready for war. Besides, our navy had been seriously weakened during the surprise attack on Pearl Harbor. Fortunately, the United States did not have to fight alone. On January 1, 1942, representatives of twenty-six governments met at Washington to take the title of "United Nations" and to sign an agreement accepting the Atlantic Charter and promising not to make a separate peace.

The United Nations pool their resources. The defeat of the Axis called for the combined efforts of all the United Nations working in close co-operation with one another. Their military resources — men, ships, machinery, raw materials, foodstuffs — were placed in a common pool for use wherever needed. Joint planning boards were set up in Washington. In addition, there were frequent conferences between the leaders of the various nations.

Latin America helps, too. The Japanese attack on Pearl Harbor awakened Latin America to its danger. Nine of the Caribbean countries declared war on the Axis as soon as we did. Most of the other American nations broke off relations with the Axis within a few weeks. By August, two others had gone to war with the Axis. Those that did not go to war made no claim to being neutral; instead they gave full use of their ports to any American nation that was at war.

A number of Latin-American countries took unusual steps to show their friendship for the United States. The Central American republics gave us bases for use in defending the Panama Canal. Colombia said that the United States might establish bases anywhere within her borders — a remarkably generous offer. Brazil and Mexico co-operated with us in every possible way.

ICELAND

SHETLAND IS.

NORWAY

SWEDEN

FINLAND

BALTIC SEA

ESTONIA

Leningrad

UNION OF
SOVIET
SOCIALIST
REPUBLICS

DENMARK

LATVIA

LITHUANIA

Moscow

GREAT
BRITAIN

IRELAND

NETH.

Berlin

WHITE
RUSSIA

Farthest
Axis advance

London

BELGIUM

GERMANY

POLAND

ATLANTIC

Paris

CZECHO-
SLOVAKIA

Kiev

Kharkov

Stalingrad

OCEAN

FRANCE

SWITZ.

HUNGARY

UKRAINE

Rostov

Vichy

YUGOSLAVIA

RUMANIA

Sevastopol

CORSICA

Rome

ALB.

BULGARIA

BLACK SEA

Caucasus Mts.

CASPIAN SEA

SPAIN

PORTUGAL

SARDINIA

MEDITERRANEAN SEA

GREECE

TURKEY

Gibraltar
(Br.)

Algiers

Tunis

SICILY

CRETE

CYPRUS

SYRIA

Teheran
IRAN
(PERSIA)

Casablanca

TUNISIA
(Fr.)

Alexandria

IRAQ

FR.
MOROCCO

El Alamein

SUEZ
CANAL

Cairo

RIO DE ORO
(Sp.)

ALGERIA

LIBYA
(It.)

EGYPT

RED SEA

SAUDI
ARABIA

FRENCH WEST AFRICA

FRENCH EQUATORIAL AFRICA

ANGLO-
EGYPTIAN
SUDAN

ERITREA

GAMBIA
(Br.)

FR. SOM.
BR. SOM.

PORT.
GUINEA

SIERRA
LEONE
(Br.)

GOLD COAST
(Br.)

NIGERIA
(Br.)

LIBERIA

CAMEROONS

ETHIOPIA

RIO MUNI
(Sp.)

UGANDA
PROT.
(Br.)

KENYA
(Br.)

IT. SOMALILAND

CABINDA
(Port.)

BELGIAN
CONGO

TANGANYIKA
TERR.
(Br.)

INDIAN

OCEAN

ANGOLA
(Port.)

NORTHERN
RHODESIA

MOZAMBIQUE

SOUTHWEST
AFRICA

BECHUA-
NALAND

SOUTHERN
RHODESIA
(Br.)

MADAGASCAR

Axis and Occupied Areas

French Territory
controlled by Vichy

TERRITORY HELD BY THE ROME–BERLIN AXIS, 1942

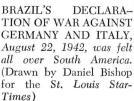

BRAZIL'S DECLARA-
TION OF WAR AGAINST
GERMANY AND ITALY,
*August 22, 1942, was felt
all over South America.*
(Drawn by Daniel Bishop
for the *St. Louis Star-
Times*)

MOBILIZING THE RESOURCES OF THE UNITED STATES

The United States had a far more difficult job ahead of it than in World War I, and that was difficult enough. Our enemies had spent years getting ready for war. Their people had been taught to sacrifice everything for the sake of the nation. Their civilians had given up all leisure and comfort in order that the nation's whole strength might be used for battle. Their people thought that the people of the United States were too soft and pleasure-loving to make a similar effort.

Most Americans had little notion of the great strength of our enemies. They expected that business would go on almost as usual in spite of the war. They did not dream of the great changes that must be made on the home front during a "total war."

1. Obtaining man power. When we declared war, we had almost two million men in the Army and Navy. Our military leaders believed that a total force of nearly eleven million would be needed. Congress passed a law requiring all men between the ages of eighteen and sixty-five to register, and making all those between the ages of twenty and forty-five liable to service. In the autumn of 1942 it was decided that men past the age of thirty-eight would be deferred, while those of eighteen and nineteen would be drafted. By that time draft boards

were already calling up married men without children. By early 1944 many fathers were being called up. Fifteen per cent of the entire population served in the armed forces during the conflict.

The drafting of millions of men and the employment of other millions in war industries resulted in a shortage of labor. The shortage was worst in low-paid occupations, such as farming. To meet the scarcity, employers hired people who in ordinary times do not easily find jobs — housewives, inexperienced young people, the aged, and the handicapped. In December, 1942, the War Manpower Commission was set up to work for the wisest possible use of the nation's labor supply. Rules were made to prevent employers in war industries from grabbing one another's workers, and to discourage workers from shifting from one job to another. Steps were taken to persuade millions of women to become wage earners.

2. Shifting industry into war production. To produce the vast quantities of ships, tanks, planes, guns, and other things needed for war, it was necessary to stop producing many things desired by civilians. For instance, automobile factories had to make army trucks, jeeps, and tanks instead of cars for civilian use. Factories that used to make washing machines, refrigerators, radios, electrical appliances, phonographs, pianos, and the like had to make war equipment instead. Nearly every industry had to shift wholly or partly into war production. In January, 1942, the War Production Board was created to take charge of the changes in the nation's industries.

3. Saving raw materials. The production of war supplies demanded huge amounts of rubber, metal, oil, and other raw materials. Early in the war, Japan cut us off from the places where we formerly got nearly all our rubber and tin. We were not producing enough and could not import enough aluminum, copper, steel, leather, wool, fat, or pulpwood to meet the wartime need. It was necessary for the War Production Board to decide how our scant supplies of raw materials could best be used. A system was worked out by which the most important war industries had first call on any material. Under this system many industries making goods for civilians had to shut down or use substitutes.

Vigorous efforts were made to increase the production of raw materials within the United States, and also in Canada and Latin America. In addition, people were asked to collect scrap rubber, metal, tin cans, cloth, paper, and fat for use in war industries. Volunteer workers conducted scrap drives in every community. The pupils of our high schools and elementary schools helped make these drives a success.

"THE USUAL FAMILY SQUABBLE." *Everyone agreed that inflation ought to be prevented, yet many wanted higher wages or higher prices for what they produced. This condition made price control very difficult.* (Drawn by Hutton for the *Philadelphia Inquirer*)

4. Rationing scarce goods. Many kinds of goods wanted by civilians became scarce. Those that were most in demand, like coffee, sugar, meat, canned goods, butter, shoes, and tires were rationed so that the supply might be fairly divided. Without rationing, scarce goods would have gone to those able to pay the highest prices. The rationing system placed every consumer on his honor. Some, of course, tried to get more than their share by buying on the "black market," buying without coupons, or using ration books and coupons that did not belong to them. But the great mass of Americans accepted rationing good-naturedly and did not cheat.

5. Raising money for the war. The war cost the United States 340 billion dollars, or twenty times as much as World War I. This sum was equal to seven-eighths of the entire national wealth. It amounted to about 2400 dollars for every man, woman, and child in the country. The money was raised by taxation and by borrowing. Taxes were higher than ever before. They fell heavily on all classes of the population. In 1944, for example, a family with two children and a net income of $3000 paid an income and victory tax of $212. A family with a net income of $100,000 paid an income and victory tax of about $68,000. Besides paying heavy wartime taxes, everyone with an income was asked to put at least a tenth of it into war bonds.

6. Controlling prices. Even after paying high taxes and buying bonds, most civilians had more money to spend than ever before. Yet there was a shortage of nearly every kind of goods and services used by civilians. The small supply and the heavy demand meant that prices were bound to go up. The rise started long before we entered the war. In April, 1941, Congress established the Office of Price Administration (OPA) to keep prices in check.

The task of holding prices down was very difficult. Farmers, who had suffered so long from low prices, insisted that farm prices should be allowed to rise, and Congress listened to their pleas. As food prices went up, workers demanded higher wages, and higher wages led to higher prices for whatever they produced. Manufacturers and store-keepers complained that they must get higher prices to cover the increased cost of doing business. Some individuals declared that the price-control program was un-American. Yet the ordinary house-wife, who even with more money to spend found it hard to make ends meet, was thankful for price control. Although the cost of living rose at least 25 per cent above what it had been in 1939, it would certainly have risen much more had prices not been regulated.

AFTER MANY LOSSES THE ALLIES GAIN THE INITIATIVE

Japanese advances in the Pacific. When the Japanese made their treacherous attack on our naval base at Pearl Harbor, Hawaii, their aim was to cripple our main Pacific fleet. They succeeded in sinking or damaging eighteen ships, including eight battleships. This was one of the worst naval disasters in modern times.

Another Japanese aim was to deprive us of air and naval bases in the Pacific. They took Guam on December 12 and Wake Island on December 23. They destroyed our air force in the Philippines and within a month captured our naval base at Manila. Small American and Filipino forces on Bataan and Corregidor continued to resist the Japanese heroically until spring; then Japan got control of the Philippines.

The day after Pearl Harbor, the Japanese sank two British warships on duty near Malaya. The Japanese navy was now stronger than the combined Pacific fleets of the United States, Great Britain, and the Netherlands. The Japanese soon conquered Malaya; on February 15 they captured the great British naval base at Singapore. The loss of Singapore was a terrible blow to the nations fighting Japan, for it deprived them of the best base in the South Pacific and opened the way for additional Japanese conquests.

UNITED STATES SUBMARINE *destroying a Japanese trawler in enemy waters, April 28, 1943. American submarines were very active in the Pacific.* (Official Navy Photo from Acme)

The Japanese began their invasion of Burma before the fall of Singapore. The object was to cut off the Burma Road, over which supplies were sent to China, and to get a base for the invasion of India. By the end of April all Burma was in Japanese hands, and Japanese planes were bombing cities in India. Meanwhile, the Japanese had invaded and conquered the Netherlands Indies, the world's richest storehouse of raw materials, especially oil, tin, and rubber. This was serious for us, since nearly all our rubber came from the Indies. The Japanese now had all the resources they needed for a long war.

The threat to Australia. The Japanese push into the Indies placed Australia and New Zealand in grave danger. These two British dominions together have little more than eight million people — about one thirteenth of Japan's population. If Japan seized Australia, the United Nations would lose almost the last remaining bases from which they might start a drive against Japan.

The United States was determined to keep the enemy out of Australia. Every ship that could be spared was used to carry men and munitions to the land "down under." In May, 1942, a Japanese fleet appeared in the Coral Sea, just off the northeast coast of Australia. In a five-day battle American planes sank or damaged twenty Japanese ships and drove the others off. The Battle of the Coral Sea saved Australia from immediate invasion. It was our first real victory of the war.

The threat to Hawaii. Early in June the Japanese moved eastward. They occupied several of the Aleutian Islands, from which they might attack Alaska and our Pacific coast, and from which we might have attacked their shipping. They also sent a strong naval force toward Hawaii. Our planes met the Japanese fleet near Midway Island, damaging it severely. The Battle of Midway was a turning point in the Pacific war. The threat to Hawaii was ended. The Japanese fleet was still powerful, but it was no longer master of the Pacific.

The Battle of Guadalcanal. Late in the summer the Japanese again turned southward. They began to build an airfield on Guadalcanal in the Solomon Islands. It threatened our supply lines to Australia and New Zealand. American Marines seized the airfield in August and held it through one of the most exhausting campaigns of the war. In November a large Japanese naval force approached Guadalcanal. It was routed in a fierce three-day battle. After that the United States held the initiative in the Pacific.

Shipping losses. In the first year after we entered the war, Allied shipping losses were worse than ever. Japanese submarines raided shipping along our Pacific coast. German submarines were active in the Caribbean Sea, the Gulf of Mexico, and the North Atlantic. Italian submarines did great damage in the Mediterranean. On the average, ten Allied ships were sunk each week, making a total of twelve million tons of shipping sunk in 1942. This was more than the output of all British and American shipyards put together. Furthermore, by the end of 1942, Axis submarines were being built twice as fast as they were being destroyed. Unless ways could be found to defeat the U-boats, the United Nations would lose the war.

The war in Russia. During the winter of 1941–1942 the Russians had succeeded in pushing the Germans back, but in May, 1942, the Germans took the offensive again. Hitler used the bulk of his forces against the Russians in an effort to knock the Soviet Union out of the war. The Nazis captured the Crimea, and, after a nine-month siege, the great Soviet naval base at Sevastopol. Early in September they laid siege to Stalingrad, a big industrial city on the Volga. If they occupied this city, they could stop the Russians from using the Volga River, then the principal north-and-south supply line for the Russian armies. In three months of fierce hand-to-hand fighting, the Russians hurled back one German attack after another. Late in November the Russian forces suddenly began to encircle the ruined city. When Hitler ordered his men not to retreat, they were trapped and destroyed.

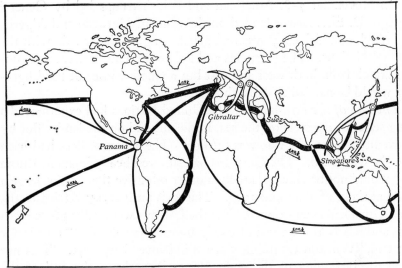

THE AXIS PINCERS THREATEN WORLD–WIDE SHIPPING

The Axis planned to control the world's principal shipping lines by seizing Gibraltar, the Suez Canal, Singapore, and finally the Panama Canal. (From *The Background of Our War,* Farrar & Rinehart)

Meanwhile another German army had driven into the Caucasus. This army had three objectives: (1) to capture the rich Caucasian oil fields, (2) to cut Russia off from the Black Sea, and (3) to open a pathway into Iran and the Middle East. For a time the Germans made important gains, but by late November they were forced to retreat. The Russians had the offensive and were able to keep it throughout the winter.

The war in North Africa. The only place where the British and Americans met the Germans in land fighting in 1942 was North Africa. In June the German army in Libya defeated the British and drove into Egypt. It seemed that the Nazis would get control of the Suez Canal. This would have made the Mediterranean an Axis lake and prepared the way for a German push into the Middle East and India.

Tanks and planes from the United States and fresh British troops brought from the Middle East saved the British from disaster. In October the Axis armored columns were stopped at El Alamein. The British then forced General Rommel to retreat. The Germans were driven from Egypt, then across Libya and into Tunisia.

On November 7–8, American and British troops led by General Dwight D. Eisenhower landed on the coast of Morocco and Algeria. A French colonial army was organized to fight side by side with the United Nations. The Germans and Italians in Tunisia were now under attack from both west and east but a whole winter of hard fighting would be needed to drive them out.

The end of the beginning. The United Nations had experienced a long series of disasters on the sea, in the air, and on the land. But by November, 1942, the tide was turning. The Japanese fleet had been greatly weakened. The Germans had suffered heavy losses in Russia and would not be able to launch another offensive there on as large a scale as those of 1941 and 1942. The Axis push across Africa to the Suez Canal had been stopped. Yet the U-boats were still a grave menace, and nearly three years of costly fighting lay ahead. "This is not the end," Winston Churchill warned in November, 1942. "It is not even the beginning of the end. But it is, perhaps, the end of the beginning."

VICTORY IS WON IN EUROPE, 1943 — MAY 7, 1945

Ship sinkings are sharply cut. During the early part of 1943, Allied shipping losses in the Atlantic continued to be heavy. By spring the situation improved. By summer U-boats were being sunk at the rate of one a day. By the autumn of 1943 the Battle of the Atlantic had been won. The Axis was losing submarines as rapidly as the Allies were losing merchant ships.

Victory in Africa. In the winter of 1943 the Allied forces in North Africa made little progress because of rain, mud, and supply troubles. But once the Allies gained superiority in the air, it was the Axis forces in Tunisia who could no longer get supplies. Early in May the Axis lines began to crumple, and within a few days all resistance ended.

The whole of Africa was now held by the Allies. Their supply lines through the Mediterranean were safe. They could bring pressure on Spain and Turkey to stay neutral. From Tunisia they could strike either at Italy or the Balkans — what Churchill called the "soft underbelly of the Axis."

The invasion of Italy. Eisenhower promptly got ready to move against Italy. In June he attacked Italy's islands in the Mediterranean. The island fortress of Pantelleria surrendered after a terrific bombardment from the air and the sea. In July troops of the United Nations landed on the southeastern coast of Sicily. Early in September they

AN ANTIAIRCRAFT BATTERY *on guard near Venafro, Italy. In World War II, as in other wars, Negro servicemen have made an important contribution.* (Acme)

landed in southern Italy. Five days later a group of high Italian officials imprisoned Mussolini and announced Italy's surrender. Soon after, the Italian fleet was turned over to the United Nations. Hitler rushed a large force southward into Italy, occupying the country as far south as Naples.

The campaign for the control of Italy was long and difficult. For several months the Allies were not able to get beyond Cassino. On January 22, 1944, they secured a beachhead at Anzio, twenty-five miles south of Rome. The Germans threw in strong re-enforcements and it was not until June 4 that the Allied armies marched triumphantly through Rome. Then they pushed on toward the north. The Germans fell back, fighting all the way, until they reached the Arno River. Here they entrenched themselves in the so-called Gothic Line. They held northern Italy until the end of the war.

The air war on Germany. During 1942 the production of planes in British and American factories increased tremendously. At the end of May the British were able to send a thousand planes against the industrial city of Cologne. Several more raids of this size took place during the remainder of the year.

The air war on Germany really went into high gear in the spring of 1943. By this time the United States had a large air force based in the

British Isles. Five hundred to a thousand British and American planes could now attack Germany almost any day when the weather was suitable.

Month by month the Anglo-American air raids did more damage. So many German planes and aircraft factories were destroyed that by spring of 1944 the Nazis were not able to put more than four hundred fighter planes into the air to meet an attack. As many as six thousand Anglo-American planes were now attacking European targets in a single day. They bombed airfields, docks, railway junctions, and freight yards from the British channel to the far Baltic coast.

The liberation of France. The long-awaited second front was opened June 6, 1944, when the Allies landed an army on the Normandy coast of France. The world waited anxiously to see the outcome. Would the fighting men wading ashore on those beaches get through the Nazi shore defenses — the big guns planted close together, behind concrete ten feet thick; the miles of mine fields and tank traps; the jungles of barbed wire; the endless hedgerows lined with machine guns? Or would most of the soldiers perish in a heroic but useless attempt to establish beachheads?

For hours before the landings an Allied fleet — the greatest fleet ever assembled — blasted the Nazi defenses. Hundreds of sky trains moved paratroopers behind the enemy lines to seize bridges and destroy communications. When the landings started, swarms of American and British fighter planes crisscrossed the skies overhead to prevent German planes from interfering. Far behind the beachheads Allied bombers pounded bridges, railroad depots, and oil dumps in order to keep enemy re-enforcements from reaching the battle area. These mighty and complicated operations were a success. By the end of a week the Allies held a narrow strip sixty miles long on the French coast.

The Germans fought fiercely to drive the Allies out. Above all they wanted to keep our forces from obtaining seaports where heavy equipment could be landed. By the end of June the Allies got possession of Cherbourg, although the Germans had wrecked the famous port so badly that weeks went by before it could be used. A few days later the Allies took Caen, a still more important port. With these two ports in our hands, the Germans could no longer hope to throw back the invaders. A German newspaper told its readers: " Everything is at stake. . . . Every man who can carry a gun must take to arms."

LANDING IN NORMANDY, JUNE 6, 1944

LEND–LEASE SUPPLIES *on the way to Russia.   A United States truck train makes a rest stop somewhere in the Persian Corridor.* (Acme)

In mid-August the American Seventh Army landed in southern France. We had almost as many men in the air alone as the Nazis had on the ground. Almost half the men in the Nazi ranks were Russians, Czechs, and Poles — fighting only because they were forced to do so. By the fifth day more than a hundred thousand Americans were ashore. They moved quickly northward through the Rhone Valley to join the Allied troops pouring east from Normandy.

Meanwhile the French Army of the Interior (the Maquis), the members of which had fought underground for so long, gave invaluable help to the Allies. With arms brought to them by Allied airplanes, they freed large areas of France from the Nazis.

Paris was liberated late in August. By early September the Germans were in headlong flight from France. In four days the Allies took an area in northern France that had been fought over for four years in World War I. Then they swept into Belgium and the Netherlands. A high-placed Nazi spokesman admitted that Germany was beaten, but called on his countrymen to fight on in order to force the Allies to give better terms than "unconditional surrender."

The Russian counterblitz. During the winter of 1943 the Russians won back all the territory they had lost in the preceding summer. Hitler, despite heavy losses already suffered by his armies in Russia,

LEADERS AT THE TEHERAN CONFERENCE, *November, 1943. President Roosevelt is seated between Premier Joseph Stalin of Russia and Prime Minister Winston Churchill of Great Britain. At this history-making conference further plans were made to destroy the German forces and to establish a lasting peace.* (Press Association, Inc.)

made one more attempt to force the Soviet Union out of the war. Compared with his offensives of 1941 and 1942, this one was on a small scale. Begun in July, it petered out in ten days. Then the Russians struck back with amazing speed and power. Although Hitler ordered his men to resist to the end, the Germans had to keep on falling back.

The last of the Nazis were driven from the Ukraine in the summer of 1944. Then the Russians swept across Poland and into East Prussia. In September Finland, which had been fighting Russia ever since the end of 1939, agreed to lay down her arms. During the autumn the Russians destroyed most of the Germans trapped in the Baltic countries — Estonia, Latvia, and Lithuania.

At the same time the Nazis were being pushed out of the Balkans. Russia conquered the German forces in Rumania, Bulgaria, and Hungary. Meanwhile in Czechoslovakia, Yugoslavia, Greece, and Albania, the people were doing their best to drive out the Nazis. By the end of 1944 the Germans had lost nearly all the Balkans. This meant the loss of man power, oil, minerals, foodstuffs, and industrial products, all of which Germany sorely needed. Moreover, the Balkans had become a base from which the Soviet Union made ready to launch a great winter drive into Austria and southeast Germany.

Final months of the Battle of Germany. In mid-December of 1944, as the Anglo-American forces drew near the Rhine, the Germans began a strong counteroffensive, now known as the Battle of the Bulge. It was a desperate gamble by which they hoped to split and disorganize the invading armies. Striking in the region of the Belgian frontier with all their strength, they drove a deep wedge into the Allied lines. After a fortnight of hard fighting the Allies stopped the German thrust. The Germans had so weakened themselves that they could now do little to hold back the invasion.

The Allied plan for crushing Germany was a pincers attack from the east and from the west. Ten million Allied soldiers stood on or near the borders of the Reich. The first attack opened in the east on January 13. The Red Army pushed across the Vistula and in three weeks advanced three hundred miles to the Oder River, the last of Germany's eastern defense lines. Here, forty miles from Berlin, they paused to regroup.

On February 28 the Allied armies launched a great drive from the west. All along the front they broke through the German defenses and gathered at the Rhine. On March 7 and 8 American forces gained a solid foothold on the eastern bank of the river south of Cologne. Allied soldiers were now able to cross the river in mass. They encircled and captured an army of 350,000 Germans in the Ruhr Valley. On April 12 they crossed the Elbe River and pushed into Bavaria, where Hitler had hoped to make his last stand.

The Russians crashed the Oder River barrier on a wide front late in March. Two Russian armies then encircled Berlin. While they fought their way into the blazing city, American and Russian forces linked up (April 25) at the little town of Torgau in central Germany. Here the Supreme Command ordered the Anglo-Americans to halt their advance. On the same day Italian patriots, or Partisans, rose against the Germans in northern Italy. The Italian front collapsed, leaving the way open for a possible Allied drive into Austria and southern Germany.

On May Day a German radio station announced that Hitler had died in his flaming capital and that Grand Admiral Doenitz had succeeded him. The next day all the German forces in Italy and Austria — over a million men — surrendered. Three days later a million Ger-

man soldiers in Holland and Denmark laid down their arms. On
May 7 the German High Command signed formal papers of unconditional surrender. The war in Europe was over after five years, eight
months, and six days of bloodshed and destruction.

The death of President Roosevelt. Roosevelt did not live to see the
victory of the United Nations. Exhausted by his heavy wartime duties, he passed away on April 12, 1945, at Warm Springs, Georgia,
where he had gone for a brief rest. Vice-President Harry S. Truman
succeeded him. As millions of people throughout the world mourned
Roosevelt, the new President promised to work for the same domestic
and international ideals which the dead leader had held dear.

VICTORY IS WON IN THE PACIFIC, 1943 — AUGUST 14, 1945

Allied advances in the Pacific. Besides protecting Australia, the
United Nations had two principal aims in the Pacific: (1) to obtain
strong naval and air bases from which to attack Japan, and (2) to destroy Japan's great system of bases and supply lines. This would require the capture of many groups of islands held by Japan.

Throughout 1943 Australians, New Zealanders, and Americans
were slowly pushing the enemy from the Solomons and from New
Guinea. The gains were limited and won at extreme cost. In July,
far to the north, the enemy was driven from the Aleutians, ending the
threat to Alaska. In November American forces moved into the Gilbert Islands in the Central Pacific, winning Tarawa after terrible
fighting.

In 1944 the war against Japan was fought on many fronts. The Allied forces under General MacArthur now had the upper hand in the
Solomons, the Admiralties, New Britain, and New Guinea. However, there was much mopping up to be done. During the spring and
summer MacArthur's forces struck at various points in the Netherlands Indies, and at the end of October made a surprise landing at
Leyte in the central Philippines. In December, while the last resistance was being cleared from Leyte, MacArthur began the occupation
of Mindoro. This cut the Philippines in two and prepared the way
for the invasion of Luzon.

In the Central Pacific, Admiral Chester Nimitz was working to
clear the seas for a safe convoy route from Hawaii to the Philippines.
In the winter he took possession of the Marshall Islands. Saipan, a
big air base in the Marianas, was taken in July. Guam, another island
in the same group, was recaptured in August, and we began at once to

THEATER OF WAR IN THE FAR EAST AND THE PACIFIC

make it into a powerful naval and air base from which to attack Japan.
The next month Nimitz invaded the Palau Islands, six hundred miles
east of the Philippines.

At the end of October the American fleet finally met the main Japa-
nese fleet in the Philippine Sea. In the most decisive naval battle since
Midway the Japanese fleet was crippled and routed. The United
States now had control of the Pacific. Before the end of the year

our Superfortresses had begun to bomb industries and communications in Japan itself.

Defeat stares Japan in the face. As 1945 began, the outer defenses of the Japanese empire were crumbling. Moreover, cities in Japan's home islands were being destroyed by Superfortresses based on the Marianas. The bulk of the Japanese navy had been put out of action. American forces were supreme on the sea and in the air.

On January 9 General MacArthur's troops landed on Luzon, the largest of the Philippines. Seven weeks later (February 23) they captured Manila. Except for mopping up, the United States now had control of the Philippines.

On February 19 our Marines landed on Iwo Jima, a volcanic island only seven hundred miles from Tokyo. Iwo was needed as a base for fighter planes and a refueling station to aid in the bombing of Japan. It was won after twenty-six days of bloody fighting. The Ryukyus, a chain of islands at the doorstep of southern Japan, were invaded on April 1. There followed a long and costly struggle for Okinawa, one of the Ryukyus and a base from which we could invade Japan's home islands. Okinawa fell on June 21. Meanwhile British troops were advancing rapidly in Burma, and Chinese troops were winning battles against the enemy in South China. The Japanese in the Dutch East Indies were gradually being wiped out.

Week by week the bombing attacks grew fiercer. By July as many as six hundred Superfortresses took part in a single raid. Smaller planes based on Iwo Jima and Okinawa pounded airfields and harbors day after day. Planes from British and American carriers cruising near the home islands added to the destruction. In addition, American and British warships bombarded Japanese coastal cities, meeting little resistance. How much longer could Japan hold out?

Japan rejects the ultimatum of July 26. In mid-July a Big Three conference met at Potsdam, Germany. One of the questions taken up was how to hasten the surrender of Japan. It was decided to outline the surrender terms and publish them in an ultimatum calling on the Japanese to surrender or be completely destroyed. The terms were published on July 26. Four days later Japan turned them down.

Japan is forced to give up. By this time nearly all shipping to and from Japan's home islands had been choked off. Millions of Japanese were both homeless and hungry. As a warning of worse things to come, on August 1 our B-29's carried out the greatest air raid ever made. Over eight hundred Superforts took part and only one of

UNLOADING OPERATIONS *in the South Pacific. Mud often added to the difficulties of moving supplies.* (H. Armstrong Roberts)

them was lost. The commander of the United States Army Air Forces announced that the United States alone would soon have seventy-five hundred bombers and fighter-bombers which could be sent out in a single raid.

Japan still refused to surrender. The United States then made use of a secret and terrible weapon, the atomic bomb. The first was loosed on Hiroshima on August 6. In a few moments it wiped out 60 per cent of a city of 318,000 people. The whole world was stunned by the news.

For weeks Russia had been moving men and supplies to the Manchurian border. On August 8 she declared war on Japan. Her troops swiftly overran Manchuria, where they took thousands of Japanese prisoners.

On August 9 American flyers dropped the second atomic bomb. Most of the city of Nagasaki was pulverized. On the same day President Truman told Japan to surrender or be wiped out. A few hours later the Japanese government announced that it would accept the Potsdam terms if the emperor could remain in power. On August 14 Japan surrendered.

The occupation of Japan began late in August. General MacArthur took up residence in Tokyo as Allied Supreme Commander. On September 2 the papers of surrender were signed on the battleship

Missouri in Tokyo Bay. "From this day," declared President Truman in a radio broadcast, "we move toward a new and better world of peace and international good will and co-operation. . . . This is a victory of more than arms alone. This is a victory of liberty over tyranny."

To identify: Eisenhower, Gothic Line, MacArthur, Maquis, Nimitz, Okinawa, Rommel, United Nations.

To explain or define: beachhead, counterblitz, news commentator.

SUBJECTS FOR TALKS OR WRITTEN REPORTS

1. How the United States solved the problem of raw materials for war production. 2. How the United States solved the problem of man power. 3. The Burma Road. What its loss meant to the Chinese. 4. The Ledo-Burma Road. What its opening meant to China and her allies. 5. How air power helped in the liberation of Europe. 6. The contribution to victory made by the Russians. 7. The contribution to victory made by the Latin-American countries. 8. The activities of the French underground before and during the liberation of France. 9. The reconquest of the Philippines; of the Netherlands Indies. 10. The human and the money cost of World War II to each of the principal participants.

QUESTIONS FOR UNDERSTANDING THE TEXT

1. What resources did the members of the United Nations place in a common pool? 2. Name some of the ways in which Latin-American countries helped the Allies. 3. How did the United States obtain enough man power to supply both the armed forces and essential industries? 4. (*a*) What kinds of raw materials were particularly scarce in the United States? (*b*) What was done to conserve these raw materials? 5. (*a*) Why was rationing necessary? (*b*) Was it a success? 6. How did the United States raise money to pay for the war? 7. (*a*) Why was price control necessary? (*b*) Why was it so difficult? 8. (*a*) What was the aim of the Japanese attack on Pearl Harbor? (*b*) Was it accomplished? 9. Why was the Japanese conquest of the Netherlands Indies so important? 10. Why did the United States military leaders think that the defense of Australia was necessary for our own safety? 11. What was the importance of the Battle of Midway? 12. How did the Russian victory at Stalingrad change the course of the war? 13. Had the British failed to stop the German drive into Egypt in 1943, what might have happened? 14. (*a*) Why did Russia keep calling on Britain and the United States

to open a second front in Europe? (b) Why was the opening of the second front so long delayed? (c) When was it opened? 15. How did the victory in North Africa help the United Nations? 16. Name the principal objectives of the United Nations in the Pacific. 17. Describe the Russian counterblitz in 1943 and 1944. 18. Describe the steps in the liberation of France and the conquest of Germany. 19. Why was the capture of Iwo Jima and Okinawa of great importance? 20. Describe Japan's situation just before the first atomic bomb was dropped. 21. What were the terms for the surrender of Japan?

ACTIVITIES FOR UNIT TEN

1. Make a chart entitled "Foreign Relations of the United States between the Two World Wars." List the important events in four columns headed respectively: The United States in World Affairs, European Affairs, Pacific Affairs, and Inter-American Affairs.
2. Make a time line on a chart or on the blackboard of the events mentioned in this unit that are most worth remembering.
3. Prepare an illustrated article on some section or country of Latin America. The articles might be combined to make a classbook.
4. Make a classbook on the war in the Pacific, illustrated with maps and pictures. Do the same for the war in Europe and Africa.
5. Using wall or desk outline maps show (a) the principal products of Latin America, (b) the principal mineral deposits of Latin America, (c) the distribution of population in Latin America, (d) the principal airways connecting the United States with Latin America, (e) the Pan-American Highway and the railways of Latin America, (f) foreign spheres of influence in China before the Japanese invasion, (g) areas held by Japan at the height of its power, (h) principal battles and campaigns in the Pacific after 1939, and in Europe after 1943.
6. Hold an exhibit of relics and pictures of World War II.
7. List the effects of World War II on (a) the United States, (b) Latin America, (c) China, (d) Russia, (e) Germany, (f) England.

READINGS FOR UNIT TEN

(Stars indicate the easier books)

GENERAL ACCOUNTS

Abend, Hallet. *Ramparts of the Pacific.* Doubleday.
*Coe, Douglas. *Road to Alaska.* Messner.
*Commager, Henry S., editor. *Pocket History of the Second World War.* Pocket Books.

Cousins, Norman. *Modern Man Is Obsolete*. Viking.

Crow, Carl. *Meet the South Americans*. Harper.

Davis, Forrest. *The Atlantic System: The Story of Anglo-American Control of the Sea*. Reynal & Hitchcock.

Davis, Forrest and Lindley, Ernest K. *How War Came: An American White Paper*. Simon and Schuster.

Deuel, Wallace R. *People under Hitler*. Harcourt, Brace.

*Floherty, John J. *The Courage and the Glory*. Lippincott.

*Goetz, Delia. *Half a Hemisphere: The Story of Latin America*. Harcourt, Brace.

Gollomb, Joseph. *Armies of Spies*. Macmillan.

*Hersey, John. *Hiroshima*. Knopf.

*Lefferts, Walter. *Neighbors North and South*. Lippincott.

Lengyel, Emil. *America's Role in World Affairs*. Harper.

Nevins, Allan. *America in World Affairs*. Oxford University Press.

*O'Connor, Tom. *Atoms and You*. Reynal & Hitchcock.

*Peck, Anne M. *Pageant of South American History*. Longmans.

Reves, Emory. *The Anatomy of Peace*. Harper.

Roberts, S. H. *The House That Hitler Built*. Harper.

*Seeger, Elizabeth. *Pageant of Chinese History*. Longmans.

Sommerfield, John. *Volunteer in Spain*. Knopf.

Stowe, Leland. *While Time Remains*. Knopf.

Vernadsky, George. *A History of Russia*. Yale University Press.

Waln, Nora. *Reaching for the Stars*. Little, Brown. (Nazi Germany)

*Williams, Chester S. *Ways of Dictatorship*. Row, Peterson.

BIOGRAPHY

Davis, Kenneth S. *Soldier of Democracy*. Doubleday. (General Eisenhower)

*Hersey, John. *Men on Bataan*. Knopf. (General MacArthur)

*Nicolay, Helen. *MacArthur of Bataan*. Appleton-Century.

Perkins, Frances. *The Roosevelt I Knew*. Viking.

Sheean, Vincent. *Personal History*. Doubleday.

van Loon, Hendrik. *The Life and Times of Simon Bolívar*. Dodd, Mead.

FICTION

Bromfield, Louis. *Until the Day Break*. Harper. (Occupied Paris)

Felson, Gregor. *Struggle Is Our Brother*. Dutton. (Russian guerrillas)

Hobart, Alice T. *Oil for the Lamps of China*. Bobbs-Merrill.

*Savery, Constance. *Enemy Brothers*. Longmans. (About a Nazi child)

*Shiber, Etta. *Paris Underground*. Scribner's.

Sowers, Phyllis A. *Sons of the Dragon*. Whitman. (Wartime China)

*Williamson, T. R. *Beyond the Great Wall*. Bobbs-Merrill.

UNIT ELEVEN
THE UNITED STATES AS A
WORLD LEADER

Once the Axis powers were defeated, the United States hastened to return to peacetime pursuits. The armed forces were quickly demobilized. Industries resumed the production of civilian goods. Wartime economic controls were soon abandoned, for people were tired of them and thought them no longer necessary. Inflation doubled the cost of living.

Foreign relations overshadowed domestic affairs in importance. The United States found itself with many international responsibilities on which it could not turn its back. Isolationism had become impossible. Instead the nation had to assume the position of a leader in world affairs. It took an active part in the work of the United Nations. It helped the nations of western Europe to rebuild their ruined cities and industries. It gave military aid to Greece and Turkey to prevent their falling under Communist control. It entered a military alliance with the countries of western Europe and supplied them money to strengthen their defenses. It intervened, on behalf of the United Nations, to repel a Communist attack on South Korea. At the mid-century, Americans feared that once again the democratic nations of the world were in danger of conquest by a combination of totalitarian powers.

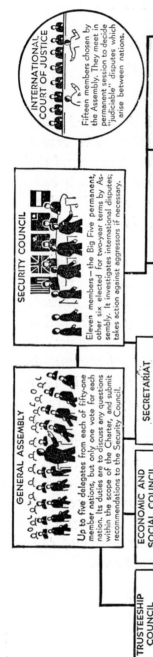
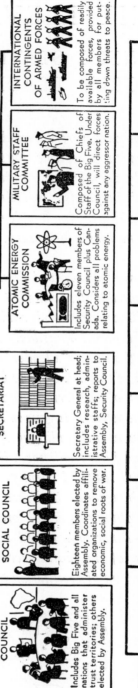

INTERNATIONAL COURT OF JUSTICE

Fifteen members chosen by the Assembly. They meet in permanent session to decide "judiciable" disputes which arise between nations.

GENERAL ASSEMBLY

Up to five delegates from each of fifty-one member nations, but only one vote for each nation. Its duties are to discuss any questions within the scope of the Charter, and submit recommendations to the Security Council.

SECURITY COUNCIL

Eleven members—the Big Five permanent, other six elected for two-year terms by Assembly. It investigates international disputes; takes action against aggressors if necessary.

SECRETARIAT

Secretary General at head; includes research, administrative staffs; reports to Assembly, Security Council.

TRUSTEESHIP COUNCIL

Includes Big Five and all nations that administer trust territories; others elected by Assembly.

ECONOMIC AND SOCIAL COUNCIL

Eighteen members elected by Assembly. Coordinates affiliated organizations to remove economic, social roots of war.

ATOMIC ENERGY COMMISSION

Includes eleven members of Security Council plus Canada. Considers all problems relating to atomic energy.

MILITARY STAFF COMMITTEE

Composed of Chiefs of Staff of the Big Five. Under Council, will direct forces against any aggressor nation.

INTERNATIONAL CONTINGENTS OF ARMED FORCES

To be composed of readily available forces, provided by all members for putting down threats to peace.

EDUCATIONAL SCIENTIFIC AND CULTURAL ORGANIZATION

Organized to foster world intellectual cooperation through education, science and culture.

FOOD AND AGRICULTURAL ORGANIZATION

Research and study organization; endeavors to raise world food and nutrition standards.

INTERNATIONAL LABOR ORGANIZATION

Includes labor-management delegates; to raise world employment, welfare standards.

INTERNATIONAL CIVIL AVIATION ORGANIZATION

Deals with the complex economic and legal problems in commercial air transportation.

INTERNATIONAL BANK

Established by the Bretton Woods agreement. Provides loans for reconstruction and development.

INTERNATIONAL MONETARY FUND

Also part of Bretton Woods plan, to be used by members to help stabilize currencies.

WORLD HEALTH ORGANIZATION

Will serve as research organ and as an information center on world medical developments.

INTERNATIONAL REFUGEE ORGANIZATION

Being organized. Successor to UNRRA, will care for refugees; resettle displaced persons.

Graphics Institute for the New York Times

THE STRUCTURE OF THE UNITED NATIONS

CHAPTER 46

DOMESTIC AFFAIRS,
1945-1953

THE PERIOD OF DEMOBILIZATION
AND RECONVERSION, 1945-1948

The wish for "normalcy." Once Japan had surrendered, a mood of war weariness swept over the United States. People were tired of wartime sacrifices and wartime restrictions. They wanted the servicemen and servicewomen to come home at once. They wanted an end of rationing and of high wartime taxes. Businessmen desired that price controls be abolished. Landlords wanted an end of rent control. There was a general wish that the country return to "normalcy."

The period between V-J Day and the election of 1948 brought demobilization and the reconversion of industry to peacetime production. It also brought inflation, labor unrest, a severe housing shortage, and a crisis in education due to the overcrowding of school buildings and the scarcity of qualified teachers. Democrats and Republicans disagreed on the best way to meet these problems. So did factions within each party. The first three years after the war were therefore marked by an unusual amount of political wrangling.

Demobilization and the armed services. Within a year of the defeat of Japan, more than twelve million members of the armed services were returned to civilian life and nearly all the troops overseas at the time the war ended were back in the United States. Within two years the Air Force was reduced from 85,000 to 9,000 planes, the Army from 89 to 12 divisions, and the Navy had withdrawn hundreds of ships from active service.

In 1947 Congress passed an act merging the Army, Navy, and Air Force under a Secretary of Defense. This important official has Cabinet rank. The Departments of the Army, Navy, and Air Force are each headed by a secretary who is not a member of the Cabinet.

The President asked for the adoption of universal military training. The proposal was favored by military leaders and by many veterans.

The public generally was opposed to it for four reasons: (1) the program would be costly, (2) military training was thought to be a waste of time for men who would not be called upon to fight, (3) it might lead other nations to question our peaceful intentions, and (4) it would give our military leaders more influence than they have ever had in peacetime. The proposal received little attention in Congress.

Congress authorized the maintenance of about two million men in the armed services. Hoping to obtain enough men by voluntary enlistment, Congress raised the pay of servicemen and took other steps to make the military life more attractive. But enlistments lagged, and in 1948 Congress reluctantly passed a peacetime draft law. The law required the registration of all men between eighteen and twenty-six years of age. Until 1950, however, few men were drafted.

Aid to veterans. Veterans found their return to civilian life made easier by the Servicemen's Readjustment Act, which Congress passed in 1944. The act is popularly known as the "G.I. Bill of Rights." Its generous provisions included: (1) a year of unemployment compensation for veterans unable to find jobs, (2) government-guaranteed loans to help ex-servicemen set themselves up in business or on farms, (3) government-guaranteed loans to help veterans to buy homes, (4) pensions and hospitalization for those disabled in war, and (5) benefits for veterans wishing to continue their education. The G.I. Bill enabled many veterans to go into business, to become home owners, to go to college, or to take apprenticeship training.

The Atomic Energy Commission. Not quite a year after the first use of atomic weapons, Congress passed a bill creating the Atomic Energy Commission, a board of five civilians. The establishment of a civilian rather than a military board is in harmony with the democratic belief that final authority over the nation's military power should rest in civilian hands. The commission was instructed to carry out research on both the military and nonmilitary uses of atomic energy. It took charge of four national laboratories for nuclear research that had been operated by the War Department during the war (at Oak Ridge, Los Alamos, Chicago, and Berkeley) and established others at Brookhaven, Hanford, and elsewhere. In these laboratories scientists are working to improve atomic weapons, to find out how atomic energy can be used to power ships and industrial plants, and to test the value of radioactive substances in medicine, biology, and other fields.

Industry reconverts to peacetime production. When the fighting

SCENE AT THE URANIUM PILE, *Oak Ridge, Tennessee. Radioactive material, which has just been removed from the uranium pile, is held at the end of the long rod. The woman worker is measuring the radioactive strength of the sample to check the safety of handling it.* (F. R. Williams, Monsanto Chemical Co.)

stopped in 1945, there was a shortage of consumer goods throughout the world. Furthermore, there was a scarcity of raw materials, fertilizer, steel, machinery, railroad equipment, and ships, which seriously interfered with efforts to raise the output of consumer goods. Even in the United States the supply of certain raw materials, especially lumber, wood pulp, oil, and steel, was not sufficient to meet the nation's needs. Yet people in devastated areas throughout the world looked to the United States for help. For several years we exported more goods that we had ever sent abroad in peacetime.

The demand of our own people for goods was also larger than ever before. Billions of wartime savings were ready to be spent on automobiles, radios, refrigerators, washing machines, and other things that civilians could not purchase during the war. To satisfy the huge demand, our industries converted rapidly to peacetime production.

The widespread unemployment that many had predicted would occur after the war did not develop. Returning veterans and workers discharged from war plants soon found jobs. The number of employed persons rose from about fifty-four million in 1945 to over sixty-one million in 1948.

The high cost of living. Through 1946, 1947, and part of 1948 prices kept climbing. The purchasing power of the dollar declined, and as a result the *real* income of many Americans was lower than it had been during the war. The steady rise of prices was caused by a number of factors, including: (1) the war-created scarcity of consumer goods and the inability of producers in the first three years after the war to supply the heavy demand, (2) the spending by consumers of their wartime savings, (3) the weakening of price controls in 1946, before production had caught up with demand, (4) the heavy exports to foreign countries, and (5) a series of wage increases to workers.

The tax burden. During the war federal taxes reached an all-time high. The tax burden weighed heavily on people of all levels of income. At the end of the war many taxpayers demanded that this burden be lightened. Congress adopted a tax cut within a few weeks after V-J Day. The excess profits tax was abolished, corporation taxes were lowered, and a modest cut in all income taxes was allowed. Economists argued that a further cut would be unwise in view of the need to reduce the enormous public debt. Furthermore, high income taxes would be a check on inflation, since they would reduce the amount of money in the hands of consumers. In spite of these arguments taxpayers continued to ask for relief. Early in 1948 Congress passed a bill to lower taxes over the President's veto.

The Twenty-second Amendment. In March, 1947, Congress submitted the Twenty-second Amendment to the states for ratification. This amendment provides that "no person shall be elected to the office of President more than twice, and no person who held the office of President for more than two years of a term to which some other President was elected, shall be elected to the office of President more than once." Ratification of this amendment by three fourths of the states was completed in 1951.

The Presidential Succession Act. In 1947 Congress, responding favorably to a suggestion of President Truman, modified the Presidential Succession Act of 1886. In the event of the death or incapacity of the President when there is no Vice-President, the Speaker of the House of Representatives is to succeed to the Presidency. Next in line of succession is the president *pro tempore* of the Senate, and then the Cabinet members, beginning with the Secretary of State.

Labor unrest; the Taft-Hartley Law. During World War II, largely because of the opportunities for overtime work (paid for as time and one half and sometimes as double time), millions earned more than ever before. The end of the war put a stop to nearly all overtime work. Thus wage earners, particularly those who had been in the war industries, found that their take-home pay was sharply reduced.

Most groups of organized workers soon demanded higher hourly wage rates. They said that wages must go up because of: (1) the increased cost of living, (2) the loss of overtime pay, and (3) the necessity for maintaining the buying power of wage earners in order to prevent another depression. The refusal of employers to meet the wage demands led to strikes in the automobile, steel, coal mining, electrical goods, meat packing, railroad, and other basic industries.

The numerous work stoppages produced a demand for labor legislation that would check the power of the unions and make them more fully responsible for their actions. Congress passed the National Labor Relations Act of 1947, better known as the Taft-Hartley Act. The new law replaced the National Labor Relations Act of 1935 (the Wagner Act) and was bitterly opposed by organized labor. President Truman vetoed it, but Congress passed it over his veto.

The Wagner Act was confined to limiting the unfair labor practices of employers. The Taft-Hartley Act forbade labor unions to engage in various unfair practices, such as jurisdictional disputes, the fixing of excessive fees for admission to the union, and coercing employees in choosing a collective bargaining agency. The act outlawed the closed shop — that is, one in which persons not members of the union may not be hired. Labor unions were forbidden to spend union funds to influence elections to political office. The act also required labor unions to file a notice of intention to change or terminate a contract sixty days before the contract's expiration. In addition it stated that a union wishing the services of the National Labor Relations Board must file an affidavit from each of its officers saying that he does not belong to the Communist party.

Supporters of the new law claimed that it restored equality of bargaining power between labor and management. Labor leaders declared that the act tipped the scales on the side of management and wiped out gains which labor unions had won over a long period of painful struggle. In the election of 1948 some of the Congressmen who had voted for the Taft-Hartley Act were defeated through the efforts of organized labor. Congress held hearings on proposed changes in the measure, but no agreement had been reached when the Republicans took over the government in 1953.

The housing shortage. One of the nation's most serious postwar problems was the shortage of houses. In 1945 it was estimated that at

PRESIDENT GARDENS, *a postwar housing development at Kansas City, Missouri. Built by a group of local businessmen at a cost of $2,500,000, it has a shopping center and five playgrounds. When it opened in 1946, a one-bedroom unit rented for $65 monthly.* (Wide World Photos)

least a million families were doubling up on living quarters because they could not find places of their own, while at least seven million families were living in dwellings that did not meet minimum standards of health and safety. The situation grew worse when veterans came home and tried to find places to set up housekeeping.

The shortage of houses continued for several years after the war in most of the nation's cities and towns. Often it was impossible for a family, especially one with children, to find an apartment or house for rent. A large number of families went heavily into debt because they had to buy homes in order to have a place to live.

In 1948 a boom got under way in the house construction industry. Most of the houses built sold for over $10,000 or rented for over $80 a month. Students of the housing problem urged Congress to do something to promote the building of houses for families in the low- and middle-income groups.

Ever since the end of the war the President had advocated a federal program to stimulate the construction of low-cost housing. Some Republican leaders, including Senator Taft, favored federal action, but most Republicans believed that the housing problem could be solved by state and community action and by private enterprise. The Eightieth Congress did not pass a housing bill, although the President again urged it to do so in the special summer session of 1948.

The crisis in education. The high birth rate of the 1940's led to a marked rise in the number of children attending school. Soon after World War II the flood of "war babies" began entering the first grade. Some would reach the junior high school by 1952. The postwar period brought a record number of babies as well. For this reason the enrollment in both elementary schools and high schools would be at an all-time peak throughout the 1950's and most of the 1960's.

The rise in the number of children of school age led to a shortage of classrooms. In most places throughout the nation school buildings were overcrowded. The size of classes was increased. In many places the schools operated on a half-day schedule, with one group of pupils attending in the morning and another group in the afternoon. Some communities erected new school buildings adequate to end the overcrowding. Other communities were either unwilling or unable to spend sufficient money for this purpose, and millions of children continued to attend school in obsolete and crowded buildings.

A scarcity of teachers developed. It began during the war when many left the profession to enter the armed services or to take better paid work in business or in the government. Rural schools were particularly hard hit and a large number of them closed. In both the city and the country many schools were kept open by lowering the requirements for teaching certificates. Conditions did not improve much until several years after the war. In 1954 there was still a lack of elementary teachers and a severe shortage of classrooms.

The educational crisis was particularly severe in the poorer communities. It seemed clear that these places could not support good schools or pay adequate salaries to teachers. Outside help was needed. Educational leaders asked for federal aid to the schools.

The question of federal aid for education. Most states give money to local communities to help maintain their public schools. The purpose of state aid is to insure that schools in the poorer districts shall not fall below certain minimum standards set by the state. State aid works well in a state with a high per capita income, for such a state can raise enough tax revenue in the more prosperous communities to permit substantial help to the poorer communities. But in a state with a low per capita income, state aid to schools is bound to be on a small scale. The only way that the schools in some states can obtain funds to meet a worth-while minimum standard is through federal aid.

In 1917 Congress passed the Smith-Hughes Act, which provides federal aid for vocational education. Ever since this law was passed, educational organizations have urged Congress to provide *general* aid for schools. General aid would not be limited to a particular kind of school or a particular kind of curriculum as is aid furnished under the Smith-Hughes Act.

After World War II a number of bills authorizing general aid to education were introduced in Congress. The most important differences in these bills concerned the method of distributing the funds to the states. Some Congressmen from wealthier states objected to the use of federal taxes to improve schools in the poorer states. A number of Congressmen objected to the use of federal money for school systems which maintain segregated schools for Negro children. Many legislators felt that federal aid should be limited to pupils in public schools; others felt that all children should benefit, whether in public, private, or parochial schools. Some held that the use of public money to help church schools in any way, even for bus transportation or health services, violates the principle of separation of church and state. The question of whether federal funds should be used to aid nonpublic schools aroused so much controversy that Congress did not pass any of the educational aid bills it was considering. (See page 693.)

THE ELECTION OF 1948 AND THE PERIOD OF THE FAIR DEAL, 1949–1953

The Republicans expect to elect a President. The year 1948 was one of prosperity. As the time for the national conventions drew near, Republicans were confident of victory in the November election. In the mid-term election of 1946 their party had won a majority of seats in the House of Representatives and had also gained control of the Senate. Republicans hoped that passage of the Taft-Hartley Act and a tax reduction bill over the President's veto would win the approval of many voters. Moreover, Republicans expected that the President's support of civil rights legislation in the 1948 session of Congress would split the Solid South.

Still another reason for Republican confidence was the fact that former Vice-President Henry A. Wallace had left the Democrats and was running for President as a candidate of the Progressive party. It was thought that Mr. Wallace would draw more votes from the Democrats than from the Republicans.

The Republicans nominated Governor Thomas E. Dewey of New York as their candidate for President. They adopted a platform praising the American system of free enterprise, calling for less government control over business, and urging that more responsibility for housing, public health, and social welfare be left to the states.

The Progressive party campaign. Henry Wallace had been asked to resign as Secretary of Commerce in 1946 because of a speech in which he condemned the administration's "get tough with Russia" policy. Wallace said that this policy would lead to a third world war. He advocated a large-scale program of economic aid to underdeveloped areas throughout the world, including the Soviet Union. At home he favored measures to extend the New Deal. When the Communist party endorsed him and became active in his campaign, many liberals withdrew from the Progressive party. Instead of the four or five million votes Mr. Wallace expected to gather, he received only a few more than a million votes.

The Democratic campaign. Republican chances for victory looked so promising and Democratic chances looked so poor that many prominent Democratic leaders abandoned Mr. Truman altogether. Instead they tried to rally the party behind some other candidate with more obvious popular appeal. An attempt was made to persuade General Dwight D. Eisenhower to accept the Democratic nomination but he refused to be drafted into politics. Finally, at a spiritless convention, the Democrats nominated Mr. Truman.

Largely at Mr. Truman's insistence, a civil rights plank was included in the platform. It called for guarantees of "these basic and fundamental rights: (1) the right of full and equal political participation, (2) the right of equal opportunity of employment, (3) the right of security of employment, and (4) the right of equal treatment in the services or defense of our nation." The adoption of the civil rights plank led some of the Southern delegates to walk out of the convention. These "Dixiecrats," as they were called, held a separate convention and nominated Governor Thurmond of South Carolina as their candidate for President.

Few thought that Mr. Truman could win. All pre-election polls predicted victory for Governor Dewey. Many Democratic leaders did not think it worth while to help the President in his campaign. Almost single-handed, Mr. Truman put up a valiant fight. He toured the country, speaking from his train at hundreds of stops along the way. He blamed the Eightieth Congress for its failure to enact housing and anti-inflation laws and called it the worst the country had ever had. He promised to fight for repeal of the Taft-Hartley Act. He advocated federal development of river valleys, additional federal

PRESIDENT TRUMAN *on his ten-thousand-mile tour in 1948. During a brief stop in Pittsburgh, the President chats with the citizens from the rear platform of his special train.* (Acme)

power projects, a different type of farm price supports in order to lower the cost of food to the consumer, laws to guarantee civil rights, extension of social security benefits, compulsory health insurance, and federal aid for housing and education.

The election returns came as a surprise to almost everyone. While the popular vote was close, Mr. Truman had a clear majority of the electoral votes. The Dixiecrats carried only four states. The Democratic party recaptured control of both houses of Congress and won many state and city elections as well.

The "Fair Deal." In his inaugural address in January, 1949, President Truman gave the name "Fair Deal" to his program of action. It was in large part an expansion of the New Deal. Since Congress (1949–1953) was controlled by the Democrats, there seemed a good chance that much of the program would be enacted. But the President's party was badly split. Parts of the Fair Deal did not appeal to Southern Democrats or to conservative Democrats from other regions. These anti-Truman Democrats combined with Republicans to defeat many of the President's proposals.

Congress did not repeal the Taft-Hartley Act. Nor did it enact the revised system of farm price supports (the "Brannan plan") desired by the President. A Senate filibuster killed an anti-poll tax bill and a fair employment practices bill; other parts of the civil rights program did not come to a vote. A bill for compulsory health insurance was bottled up in committee. A measure providing federal aid

DISPLACED PERSONS *seen through a porthole. The seven-year-old perched on his luggage has just arrived in New York on his way from Austria to Ohio.* (Acme)

to education passed the Senate but was defeated in the House. A proposal to establish a new Department of Public Welfare was rejected, as was a bill to create a Columbia Valley Authority similar to the Tennessee Valley Authority. The St. Lawrence Seaway was not approved. All of these were items in the Fair Deal.

Congress adopted these parts of the program:

1. Raising of the minimum wage from forty to seventy-five cents an hour. The change made up for the rise in the cost of living since 1938, when the forty-cent figure was adopted.

2. Admission of displaced persons. The Eightieth Congress had authorized the entry of 205,000 displaced persons over a two-year period. Critics of this law felt it discriminated against Catholics and Jews. The Eighty-first Congress corrected the defects in this measure and doubled the number of displaced persons to be admitted.

3. Extension of federal rent control. Congress voted to continue rent control, in places where it was still in force, until June, 1951, provided the local community wanted it.

4. Establishment of the National Science Foundation. This agency is to encourage scientific research by granting federal funds for selected research projects.

5. Extension and strengthening of the Reciprocal Trade Agreements Act. A majority in the Eighty-first Congress agreed with the nation's economists on the necessity for (1) promoting freer trade and (2) increasing American imports.

6. Provision for housing. The Housing Act of 1949 authorized a program of public housing and slum clearance. It provided for the building of as many as 135,000 units of low-rent public housing each year for six years. The federal government would pay a subsidy to make up the difference between the cost of operating these projects and the rents which low-income families could afford to pay for living in them. The act authorized a billion dollars in loans for slum clearance and a fourth of a billion in loans for improving rural homes.

In 1950 Congress passed another housing bill, authorizing 3.5 billions for loans and mortgage insurance to encourage private builders.

7. Granting of federal aid for building schools in districts where federal activities had caused overcrowding.

8. Granting of loans for extension of rural telephone service.

9. Expansion of the social security system and increase in benefits. In 1950 Congress voted to make some ten million additional workers eligible for old age and survivors' insurance. Benefits to the aged and to their survivors were increased by an average of 77 per cent. The increase was barely enough to compensate for the rise in the cost of living since the benefits were originally fixed. The new act also provided aid to needy persons who are totally and permanently disabled.

The recession of 1949–1950. By 1948 production had almost caught up with demand. In the second half of the year food prices dropped slightly. So did clothing prices. In 1949 some manufacturers of durable goods such as refrigerators, furniture, and automobiles announced small price reductions. It appeared that most of the postwar shortages were at an end. In clothing and some other lines surpluses began to appear.

During the first half of 1949 a recession, or business decline, set in. Between four and five million workers were unemployed during the first half of 1950. Americans began to fear that growing unemployment would lead to a serious depression. The fear vanished in mid-1950 when the Korean crisis forced the United States to step up expenditures for national defense.

The nation rearms. The Korean War made clear that the United States must build up its military strength. When South Korea was invaded, our military man power was at its lowest ebb — 1,458,000 —

since 1941. The three armed services were receiving about 13.3 billion dollars a year and in order to live within their appropriation were still scaling down in size.

In July, 1950, shortly after the United States went to the defense of the Republic of Korea, the Army, Navy, and Air Force began to call back reservists and to encourage voluntary enlistments. Draft boards started to induct men. Plans were made to increase military personnel to three and one half million men and women.

Some training camps were reopened. The Navy took ships "out of mothballs." The Air Force removed planes from storage. Producers of tanks, planes, and other military equipment received large orders. The stockpiling of critical materials, which had gone on slowly since V-J Day, was hastened. The nation's military budget was more than tripled.

Taxes are raised. In the spring of 1950 Congress was considering a further cut in taxes, particularly of the wartime excise taxes on furs, jewelry, cosmetics, admissions, transportation, and telephone service. When fighting broke out in Korea the tax reduction bill was rewritten and became a bill to raise taxes by 4.5 billion dollars. In 1951 Congress enacted still higher taxes.

The inflation spiral. Within ten weeks after the conflict in Korea began, the wholesale prices of twenty-eight basic raw materials advanced an average of 25 per cent. As the cost of living started to go up, organized labor asked for higher wages. Automatic increases were granted to the few unions with contracts that base wages on changes in the consumer price index. Some companies voluntarily paid higher rates. Strikes and strike threats caused many other employers to hike wages. The 1952 steel strike and a drought in the same year intensified the problem of the rising cost of living.

The Defense Production Act. Shortly after the Korean war began the President asked Congress for powers to impose wartime controls on the economy. Six weeks later Congress sent to the White House an economic controls bill — the Defense Production Act of 1950. It gave the President the power to control the use of essential materials, to restrict credit to consumers, to set up a war labor board, to punish hoarding, to ration consumer goods, and to curb prices and wages.

The Defense Production Act gave enormous emergency powers to the President. It left him to decide whether to use the powers and how to use them. As it has always done in time of danger, Congress entrusted the President with far more authority than usual.

Rearmament, inflation, high taxes, the Korean War, and international problems dominated the closing years of the Truman administration. As the twenty-year period of Democratic control came to an end on January 20, 1953, there was every reason to believe that the Truman administration would be remembered chiefly for its actions in the field of international relations. (See Chapter 49.)

❀ ❀ ❀

To identify: Dixiecrat, Smith-Hughes Act of 1917, Taft-Hartley Act.

To explain or define: closed shop, consumer price index, deficit financing, general aid to schools, jurisdictional dispute, left-wing group, metropolitan area, per capita income, real income, recession.

SUBJECTS FOR TALKS OR WRITTEN REPORTS

1. Changes in the cost of living since 1915. 2. Changes in the federal debt since 1915. 3. The current system of farm price supports. 4. Report of the President's Committee on Civil Rights. 5. Work of the (Hoover) Commission on the Organization of the Executive Branch of the Government. 6. The platform and membership of the Progressive party of 1948. Its later history. 7. Arguments for and against compulsory health insurance. 8. Arguments for and against a federal fair employment practices law.

QUESTIONS FOR UNDERSTANDING THE TEXT

1. How is the drastic postwar reduction of the armed services to be explained? 2. What arguments were advanced against universal military training? 3. Outline the chief provisions of the G.I. Bill of Rights. 4. Would a democracy be likely to give control of the manufacture of atomic weapons in peacetime to military leaders? Why or why not? 5. Account for the rise in prices from 1945 to 1948. After June, 1950. 6. Why did the administration oppose tax reduction in 1947 and 1948? 7. Why did Congress have little success in reducing federal expenditures after World War II? 8. Mention some features of the Taft-Hartley Act. Who opposed it? 9. Why did the housing boom of the late 1940's fail to overcome the housing shortage? 10. What evidence pointed to the existence of a crisis in education after the war? How do you account for the crisis? 11. Why is there a demand for federal aid to education? What controversy interfered with passage of a federal aid bill? 12. Explain the pre-election confidence of Republicans in 1948. 13. What ideas led Henry A. Wallace to start the Progressive party? 14. Outline the parts of the Fair Deal which Congress adopted. 15. Describe recent changes in the social security program. 16. List the powers given the President in the Defense Production Act of 1950.

CHAPTER 47

NATIONAL CONCERN
OVER COMMUNISM

pposition to communism grows. Ever since the Bolshevik (Communist) Revolution in Russia in 1917, many Americans have been afraid that communism would spread. In the 1920's and 1930's a number of states and cities took various steps to restrict Communists and hamper their activities. After World War II fear of communism became more intense. Congress and the state legislatures placed new curbs on Communists and their sympathizers. Labor unions ousted Communists from office and even from membership. Communism was attacked as the enemy of democracy, religion, and liberty.

The number of Communists in the United States was small. Why then was the party thought to be a menace? To answer this we must know something about the ideas of Karl Marx, the party's leading prophet, and about the history of the party here and abroad.

COMMUNISTS SEIZE CONTROL IN RUSSIA
AND ESTABLISH THE COMINTERN

The teachings of Karl Marx. Karl Marx was a German scholar who lived in the nineteenth century. The son of a lawyer, he became active in the working class movement while a university student. After being exiled from Germany and later from France, he settled in England, where he earned a bare living as a writer. Two of his writings have had a tremendous influence. One was a pamphlet, *The Communist Manifesto*, by Marx and Friedrich Engels, which appeared in 1847. The other is a three-volume work, *Das Kapital*. The latter describes the system of capitalism as it was in Western Europe in Marx's day, telling how it developed, what he thought was wrong with it, and what its future would be.

Marx maintained that the type of economic system which exists in any period of history contains within it the causes of its own destruction. For example, Marx argued that the economic system of the ancient world was based on slavery, and that it broke up because slavery weakened society to the point where it could not defend itself against invaders. The slave system was followed by the feudal system, in which most of the people were bound to the land as serfs. It broke up with the rise of the middle class, which demanded freedom to engage in commerce and industry. Thus the feudal system was replaced by industrial capitalism.

Capitalism, said Marx, also had weaknesses which would destroy it. The capitalists wanted the largest possible profits. Therefore they would pay the lowest possible wages. The workers would not be able to buy the products of the factories and this would cause periodic depressions. The struggle for foreign markets, raw materials, and new fields of investment would bring nations into conflict with each other, leading to frequent wars. The result, said Marx, would be ever greater misery for the working class, or *proletariat.*

Marx argued that the fall of capitalism was bound to come; that it would give way to socialism, a system in which the means of production (mines, land, factories, railroads, stores, etc.) would be owned and operated by the workers themselves; that a classless society would result, bringing in a new age of plenty, individual freedom, and world peace. However, this Utopia would not arrive until capitalism had been overthrown. Meanwhile there would be a bitter class struggle between the workers and the owners of the means of production (often called the *bourgeoisie*).

Since no ruling class, said Marx, ever gives up its power and privileges voluntarily, the workers will have to use force in taking over the property of the capitalists. A dictatorship of the proletariat will then be established. But the dictatorship is to be a temporary stage, lasting only until the enemies of the proletariat are crushed. After that, said Marx, the state (by which he meant the government) will gradually wither away, until the people have greater freedom than ever before.

What Marx did not foresee. Time has exposed many shortcomings in Marx's teachings. His philosophy was materialistic and antireligious. He did not foresee the rise of powerful labor unions able to force employers to pay higher wages and establish sick benefits and pension systems, and strong enough to obtain laws for the benefit of the working class. Nor did he think that great American corporations would sometimes pay higher wages than they were compelled to do, because they wanted to increase the nation's purchasing power.

Marx knew little about the workings of democratic government. He did not think it could serve the interests of all classes. Since he believed that every government is run for the benefit of a small ruling class, he could not imagine a government which, for example, would impose a steeply graduated tax upon incomes and inheritances to obtain money to help the whole nation. He did not dream that a democratic government would use its taxing power to finance a school system for all the people, or a program of social security, slum clearance, public improvements, and a host of other measures to "promote the general welfare," while it preserved the "blessings of liberty." He did not foresee that a democratic government might even own and operate some public utilities. In short, Marx did not believe that in a democratic government the people would be able to bring about whatever changes they considered necessary.

Communists and socialists. The idea of a new social and economic organization was not invented by Marx. It had been advocated by visionaries for centuries. Marx's followers called these forerunners "Utopian" socialists and regarded themselves as "scientific" socialists. Since Marx's time other thinkers have contributed to socialistic ideas and there have been different factions within the socialist movement.

As time went on, many socialists came to think that socialism could be brought about gradually and peacefully. They often called themselves "Social Democrats" to emphasize that they believed in democratic methods and not in violent revolution. There were Social Democratic parties in every country in Europe and in many non-European lands. In Great Britain and its dominions the group was known as the Labor party. In the United States the main group called itself the "Socialist party." Like other Social Democrats, American socialists uphold constitutional methods of change.

In czarist Russia the socialists had to work underground. The government was so oppressive there seemed little hope that reforms could be made without a revolution. In 1903 the Russian Social Democratic party split. The majority, who were followers of Nicolai Lenin, took the name "Bolsheviks." They believed that revolution was near and when it came a small, well-disciplined group should be ready to seize control and set up a dictatorship of the proletariat. The minority, who favored a more moderate program, were called "Mensheviks." After the Bolsheviks seized power in October, 1917, they adopted the name "Communists."

The Russian Revolution. World War I revealed the inefficiency and corruption of the czar's government. The terrible losses suffered at the front and the hunger and misery at home made the people so desperate that they could no longer be silenced by the use of force. The czar gave up his throne in March, 1917, and a group of moderate reformers, headed by Alexander Kerensky, took over the government. Although the people were utterly war weary, Kerensky tried to continue the war. Meanwhile, the Bolsheviks gained support by promising to make peace with Germany and by encouraging the peasants to seize the land of the big landholders. Kerensky was driven out. Lenin and other old Bolsheviks proceeded to establish what they called the "dictatorship of the proletariat." In fact the real power was kept in the hands of the Communist party, which has never included more than three or four per cent of the people.

The Communists, or "Reds," met tremendous opposition from the former privileged classes, from the Russian Orthodox Church, and from those who hoped to establish a democratic government. Foreign countries sent troops and supplies to help the "Whites," or anti-Communists. Some believe that foreign intervention did much to assure the victory of the Communists by making them appear to be patriots fighting against the nation's foreign enemies. The civil war ended in 1921, leaving great devastation and bitterness. Although the war was over, the Communists continued to fight the church. In the next twenty years a large proportion of church buildings were closed or taken over for nonreligious uses.

After Lenin's death (1924), Stalin, who was secretary-general of the Communist party, became the most powerful man in Russia. He launched a series of five-year plans to industrialize the country and make it secure against attack. To pay for this gigantic program of industrialization and armament, the standard of living of the people, which had always been very low, was further reduced.

Far from withering away, the government became more and more powerful. The people were permitted even less liberty than they had enjoyed under the czar. No criticism of the government's policies was permitted. Those who opposed the government were given long terms of forced labor or were executed. Even in the fields of literature, music, art, and science, individuals had to conform to the "party line." Both Lenin and Stalin changed or "reinterpreted" some of Marx's ideas, and today Communists refer to their basic theories not as Marxism but as Marxist-Leninist-Stalinism. Every Communist is expected to be faithful to these ideas in even the small details. "Deviation" from the party line is punished ruthlessly. At times even a prominent party leader may be "purged."

Under Stalin's leadership (1924–1953) Russia entered World War II and emerged as a strong military and industrial power. Russia dictated the policies of several satellite countries in Europe, and saw communism triumph in China and extend its influence in other parts of the Far East. Stalin died in March, 1953. Malenkov succeeded him as leader in Russia, while Western observers speculated on the possibility of a struggle within Russia for control of the government.

International communism. Lenin thought the Russian revolution would be a starting point for a world-wide revolution. In 1919 he organized the Communist International, or Comintern, to lead the Communist parties then being formed in many parts of the world. From the beginning the Comintern was controlled from Moscow, and Communists everywhere followed the same "party line." It is interesting to note that the Communists in every country were more hostile to the Social Democrats and other advocates of moderate reform than to those who opposed reform altogether.

For a time there was a strong Communist party in Germany, but Hitler suppressed it when he came to power in 1933. Elsewhere in Europe and in America communism attracted a small group of devoted followers, and had the support of some intellectuals. The Comintern also devoted considerable effort to stirring up revolutionary movements in the Orient. Colonial and semicolonial peoples were urged to struggle for independence.

With the rise of Hitler, who made no secret of his desire to fight Russia, Communists throughout the world began to emphasize the dangers of fascism. They urged a program of collective security to keep the Axis from carrying out a program of world conquest. The Soviet Union tried to have the League of Nations take action to prevent Fascist aggression in Ethiopia, Spain, and elsewhere. The Communists expressed a willingness to work with democratic and social democratic groups in a Popular Front against fascism. As a result the Communists increased their influence in France and other countries which felt menaced by Hitler and Mussolini.

The purges that took place in the Soviet Union in 1937 and 1938 shocked democratic nations and weakened the Popular Front movement. When the Soviet Union signed the treaty of nonaggression and friendship with Germany in 1939, the Popular Front movement was abandoned, and the Comintern lost still more of its influence. In

1943, as a sign of good will to Russia's allies, Stalin dissolved the Comintern. It was revived in a disguised form in 1947 as the Communist Information Bureau, or Cominform. (See pages 669, 670.)

Communism in the United States. In 1919 a number of former socialists organized the American Communist party. They joined the Comintern and praised the Russian revolutionary program. They provided leadership in several unsuccessful strikes in the years 1926–1929, but at that time the Communists failed to capture control of any established union. In 1929 the Comintern ordered them to start organizing new unions under Communist leadership. The policy did not meet with much success, since few American workers were willing to join unions led by known Communists.

The severe depression which existed in the United States in the early 1930's helped the Communists. They organized demonstrations by the unemployed. They talked and wrote about Russian achievements under the First Five-Year Plan, boasting that Russia would soon surpass the American standard of living. When Franklin D. Roosevelt became President, they said he was a Fascist. Party membership increased from about 7500 in 1930 to about 25,000 in 1934.

In 1935 the American Communists changed their policy of organizing new unions and set about winning influence in established unions by "boring from within." The party also worked hard to gain control of liberal organizations by planting in each a secret "cell" of Communists. The strategy of boring from within was based on a simple formula — the handful of Communists in the organization worked harder than the other members, always came to meetings, volunteered to do the difficult or unpleasant jobs that other members did not want to do, and stood for a bold rather than a timid policy. When an important vote was to be taken the Communists would often succeed in delaying it until most of the other members had gone home. Thus a few Communists could exert influence out of all proportion to their numbers.

During the period of the Popular Front, the party formed a number of organizations to promote special causes such as minority rights, world peace, friendship with the Soviet Union, or adult education. Many non-Communists joined these organizations, often without knowing that they were controlled by Communists. The name "transmission belt" or "Communist front" was applied to a group of this type. The phrase "fellow-travelers" has been used to describe those who supported the Communist program and party line without actually joining the party.

Meanwhile the Communists had begun to support Roosevelt, particularly in his effort to make Americans aware of the dangers of fascism. By 1939 the party claimed a membership of 100,000. If the claim was true, this is the largest number of actual members that the party ever had at any one time. Many who joined it grew disgusted with its undemocratic methods, its strict discipline, and its shifting policies and dropped out. There were others who supported the Communist party line but did not become party members.

After the Stalin-Hitler pact the party declared that the war in Europe was not between democracy and dictatorship but between the rival imperialisms of France and England on the one side and Germany on the other. The party denounced Roosevelt as a warmonger and supported the isolationists. This sudden change in the official party line cost it a large number of its members and sympathizers. The party line shifted again when Hitler attacked Russia in 1941; and once again the party lost members and "fellow-travelers."

Fascist groups are organized in the United States. The 1930's saw the organization of many groups which had Fascist ideas. In general they were opposed to Catholics, Jews, Negroes, aliens, Communists, labor leaders, pacifists, and liberals. Some had patriotic names like "Defenders of the Constitution" or "League to Protect Freedom." Others, frankly admitting their Fascist tendencies, took names like "Silver Shirts" or "Black Legion." Some of these organizations had a following in different parts of the country.

The Un-American Activities Committee. The growth of un-American activities, both on the left and on the right was a threat to democracy. In 1938 the House of Representatives set up the Committee on Un-American Activities. During its investigation it uncovered much useful information. However, prior to and during the war little serious attention was given to the Committee's activities. Indeed, the Committee was criticized by many who regarded Communist agitation as not sufficiently important to receive serious attention. The Committee was frequently denounced as "fascist" and "engaged in witch hunts," "thought control," and "red baiting." Its influence was weakened by the headline-catching utterances of several members of the Committee, and by its tendency to pin the Communist label

THE UN–AMERICAN ACTIVITIES COMMITTEE *and the press listen intently to the testimony of former Under Secretary of State Sumner Wells.* (Associated Press)

onto movements that received Communist support, yet were entirely American in their aims and methods. It was even argued that the Committee itself was un-American and should be discontinued.

In the postwar years public indifference toward communism and toward the activities of the House Committee began to disappear. Events abroad, particularly in Poland, Czechoslovakia, Italy, Germany, and China revealed that Communist parties in foreign countries were in reality the agents of a foreign government. In the United States, too, Communist literature and Communist-front organizations persistently supported the policies of Russia and criticized those of the United States. A series of events helped to confirm the belief that Communist and Communist-front organizations were subversive.

a. In Canada it was discovered that a Communist spy ring had secured important secrets for transmission to Russia (1946).

b. A number of former members of the Communist party published accounts of their experiences and testified in court about their activities. Two of them, Elizabeth Bentley and Whittaker Chambers, claimed that they had acted as agents for the collection of information to be sent to Russia.

c. Acting upon evidence collected by the House Committee and the Federal Bureau of Investigation (F.B.I.), the Attorney General published a list of organizations which the Department of Justice described

SPY PROBE WITNESS *refuses to answer questions about his accuser, Elizabeth Bentley (right), or to say whether or not he is a Communist.* (Harris and Ewing)

as subversive (1946). Most of these organizations were charged with supporting the Communist party line; others were Fascist organizations.

d. It became known that some Communists or fellow-travelers had worked their way into influential positions in the government, labor unions, the entertainment field, and the press. In March, 1947, President Truman established a Loyalty Review Board to check the loyalty of present and prospective employees of the federal government. In the meantime labor unions "cleaned house." The A.F. of L. and C.I.O. expelled Communist-dominated unions and got rid of officers who were regarded as Communists or Communist sympathizers.

e. Whittaker Chambers, a former Communist, claimed that Alger Hiss had been a member of a Communist spy ring in 1938 and had supplied Chambers with State Department documents for transmission to Russia. Hiss had had a brilliant career in the federal government, including responsible positions in the State Department. Hiss denied the charges and later was indicted for perjury. In the first trial the jury disagreed, but in the second trial Hiss was found guilty and sentenced to a five-year term in prison.

f. In 1949 the federal government tried eleven well-known Communist leaders. They had been indicted on charges that they had violated the Smith Act of 1940, which made it a crime to teach or advocate the overthrow of the government of the United States by force. In this long trial, which lasted from January to October, 1949, the government produced testimony based on the writings, speeches, and meetings of Communists over a period of years. Government witnesses included former Communists, and secret agents of the F.B.I. who had posed as Communists to gather evidence. The jury found the eleven guilty. Similar trials in other parts of the country led to the conviction of other Communist officials.

g. Early in 1950 Dr. Klaus Fuchs, a German-born scientist who had become a naturalized British citizen, was arrested in England as a Communist spy. Dr. Fuchs confessed that while working in America on atomic energy research he had transmitted atomic secrets to Russian agents. A little later, a few Americans were arrested and either confessed or were found guilty of similar activities. Two of these, Julius and Ethel Rosenberg, suffered the death penalty in 1953.

These events finally convinced the great majority of Americans that the Communist party and its activities were a serious threat to the United States.

The Internal Security Act, 1950. In September, 1950, Congress passed a new measure designed to protect the United States against subversive activities. The McCarran-Wood Act, or Internal Security Act, provides that Communist and Communist-front organizations must register with the Attorney General, file financial statements, and properly identify their literature. If the law is evaded, the Attorney General may file charges with a new Subversive Activities Control Board, which has power to conduct hearings. The decisions of the Board are subject to review by the courts. Aliens who are members of Communist organizations may be deported, and persons who ever belonged to a Communist or any totalitarian party may not enter the country. The law declares that it is unlawful to conspire to establish a totalitarian dictatorship or to conceal membership in Communist organizations when seeking government employment. The law also provides that in the event of an emergency proclaimed by the President, Communists may be placed in detention camps. In a vigorous message President Truman vetoed the bill, declaring that it was hostile to civil liberties and too general to be enforced. He called the registration clause "about as practical as requiring thieves to register with the sheriff." He added that the law would set the government up in the "thought control business" and would "harass all of our citizens in the exercise of their right of free speech." Congress, however, repassed the bill over the veto by large majorities.

How the Communist party differs from other parties. In 1950 the Supreme Court had before it a case which tested the constitutionality of part of the Taft-Hartley Act. The part tested was the clause that if a union wishes the services of the National Labor Relations Board, the officers of the Union must swear that they are not members of the Communist party. The Court upheld this provision. In writing his opinion Associate Justice Robert H. Jackson made the following comparison between the Communist party and other political parties:

(1) The goal of the Communist party is to seize powers of government by and for a minority rather than to acquire power through the vote of a free electorate. . . .

(2) The Communist party alone among American parties past or present is dominated and controlled by a foreign government. . . .

(3) Violent and undemocratic means are the calculated and indispensable method to attain the Communist party's goal. . . . In not one of the countries it now dominates was the Communist party chosen by a free or contestible election; in not one can it be evicted by any election. The international police state has crept over Eastern Europe by deception, coercion, *coup d'état,* terrorism and assassination. . . .

(4) The Communist party has sought to gain this leverage and hold on the American population by acquiring control of the labor movement. All political parties have wooed labor and its leaders. But what other parties seek is principally the vote of labor. The Communist party, on the other hand, is not primarily interested in labor's vote, for it does not expect to win by votes. It strives for control of labor's coercive power — the strike, the sit-down, the slow-down, sabotage, or other means of industrial paralysis. Congress has legalized the strike as labor's weapon for improving its own lot. But where Communists have labor control, the strike can be and sometimes is perverted to a party weapon. . . . This labor leverage, however, usually can be obtained only by concealing the Communist tie from the union membership.

(5) Every member of the Communist party is an agent to execute the Communist program. What constitutes a party? Major political parties in the United States have never been closely knit or secret organizations. Anyone who usually votes the party ticket

is reckoned a member, although he has not applied for or been admitted to membership, pays no dues, has taken no pledge, and is free to vote, speak, and act as he wills. . . .

Membership in the Communist party is totally different. The party is a secret conclave. Members are admitted only upon acceptance as reliable and after indoctrination in its policies, to which the member is fully committed. . . . Each pledges unconditional obedience to party authority. Adherents are known by secret or code names. They constitute "cells" in the factory, the office, the political society, or the labor union. For any deviation from the party line they are purged and excluded.

The problem of preventing Communist infiltration and safeguarding civil liberties. In trying to find a satisfactory way of dealing with communism, the American people were equally interested in safeguarding the fundamental rights of free speech and free assembly. Consequently there was much concern over the growing practice of demanding "loyalty oaths" from teachers, over the scrutiny of textbooks for "un-American" or unpopular ideas, and over the tendency on the part of some groups to label ideas or proposals they do not like as "red," "Communistic," or "subversive." There was also considerable discussion of the fairness of applying the principle of "guilt by association" to those who had once been members of front organizations or who expressed sympathy for a particular reform that happened to have Communist approval.

Senator Joseph R. McCarthy, Wisconsin Republican, was particularly vocal in hinting that a number of prominent people were friendly to communism or sympathetic to Communist causes. He accused the Truman administration of not being vigilant in weeding out Communists and claimed that the State Department harbored a number of Communists. A Senate committee investigated Senator McCarthy's charges and declared that they were without foundation. Senator McCarthy countered that the committee had "whitewashed" the charges and kept up his attack. The phrase "McCarthyism" came into use to describe reckless and unsupported charges of "guilt by association" or "sympathy with communism."

Senator McCarthy claimed that the coinage of the word "McCarthyism" was part of a "smear" campaign to discredit him and to distract attention from his charges. It was pointed out that Communist infiltration and espionage was an alarming and unpleasant fact. Many who denounced communism denounced "McCarthyism" as well and expressed the fear that if "McCarthyism" spread, it would tend to stifle all freedom of thought. Already, these critics said, there was a tendency to regard unorthodox or unpopular ideas as synonymous with communism. On the other hand, many supported Senator Mc-Carthy, even though they disagreed with his tactics. They argued that he had kept the issue of Communist influence and infiltration in the public eye. McCarthy's supporters often found fault with his critics. They claimed that these critics, by emphasizing the evil effects of "McCarthyism," were aiding the Communist cause, for they appeared to be engaged in an "anti-anti-Communist movement."

Communist infiltration and "McCarthyism" were issues in the 1952 presidential campaign. McCarthy was re-elected to the Senate and continued to claim that government officials were lax in exposing individuals with Communist leanings. In 1954 the Department of the Army filed charges against McCarthy, claiming that he had promised to "go easy" in investigating alleged Communist infiltration in the Army if special favors were granted to a former member of his staff. The dramatic Senate hearings on these charges were televised. After study by a special committee, the Senate condemned McCarthy by a vote of 67 to 22. The hearings and the Senate vote markedly weakened his influence, even before his death in 1957. Though congressional committees continued to investigate possible Communist activities, their methods were less spectacular than formerly. President Eisenhower discontinued (1953) the Loyalty Review Board established by President Truman and directed that each department head was to be held responsible for the loyalty of his staff.

❁ ❁ ❁

To identify: Comintern, Cominform, *Communist Manifesto, Das Kapital,* Friedrich Engels, Alexander Kerensky, Nicolai Lenin, Karl Marx.

To explain or define: bourgeoisie, coup d'état, imperialism, McCarthyism, means of production, proletariat, saboteur, Utopia.

Subjects for Talks or Written Reports

1. Conditions in Russia leading to the abdication of the czar. 2. The civil war in Russia, 1917–1921, and its effects. 3. Economic history of Russia since 1917. 4. Religious history of Russia under the Communists. 5. The history and platform of the American Socialist party. 6. The history of the Communist party in the United States. 7. The activities of Fascist organizations in the United States during the 1930's. 8. The work of the Subversive Activities Control Board. 9. The American tradition of

freedom of speech, press, and assembly. 10. The trial of the "Eleven," 1949. 11. Malenkov as Stalin's successor. 12. The influence of Senator McCarthy.

QUESTIONS FOR UNDERSTANDING THE TEXT

1. What explanations can be given for American fear of Communists in the United States? 2. Summarize the main teachings of Karl Marx. Do you think he would approve the government of Russia today? Why or why not? 3. Explain some of the shortcomings in Marx's teachings. 4. How did the Bolsheviks come into power in Russia? What groups opposed them? 5. What was the effect of foreign intervention against the Reds in Russia? 6. When was the Comintern established? What was its purpose? The Cominform? Its purpose? 7. Explain the purpose of the Popular Front movement. What two developments destroyed it? 8. Trace the history of the Communist party in the United States up to World War II. 9. Explain what is meant by "boring from within." How is it done? 10. What is meant by a "transmission belt" or "Communist-front" organization? 11. What methods were used to prevent the employment of Communists by the federal government? 12. Do you think that a person who has ever been a Communist should be barred from government employment? Why or why not? 13. What is the history of the House Committee on Un-American Activities? 14. Discuss the influence of Communists in the American labor movement. 15. According to Associate Justice Jackson, how does the Communist party differ from other political parties? 16. Why did President Truman veto the McCarran-Wood bill? Have any of his fears proved to be justified? 17. In restricting Communists, many Americans wondered whether our traditional civil liberties would be endangered. What can be said for and against this position?

CHAPTER 48

THE UNITED NATIONS MEETS WITH
SUCCESSES AND FAILURES

THE UNITED STATES HELPS ESTABLISH A WORLD ORGANIZATION

Plans for a new world security organization. Even while the people of the Allied countries threw their whole energies into winning the war, they thought about how another war could be prevented. The only hope seemed to lie in a system of collective security. There was a new interest in the teachings of Woodrow Wilson and much discussion of why the League of Nations had failed.

In the late summer of 1944 representatives of the United States, the Soviet Union, Great Britain, and China met at Dumbarton Oaks, Washington, D.C. They prepared the outline for an organization similar to the League of Nations but much stronger. All members of the United Nations were asked to study the proposals.

The San Francisco Conference. In February, 1945, Roosevelt, Churchill, and Stalin met at Yalta for their second and last conference. Among other things, they decided to summon all the United Nations to meet at San Francisco for the purpose of writing the charter of the new world security organization.

On April 25, shortly after the death of President Roosevelt, representatives of fifty nations met at San Francisco. The conference continued for two months. The charter which finally emerged from the meeting gave more voice to the smaller nations than did the Dumbarton Oaks proposals. However, most of the power was to lie in the hands of the Big Five (the United States, the Soviet Union, Great Britain, China, and France).

The United States ratifies the charter. In appointing six delegates to the San Francisco Conference, Roosevelt had wisely selected four Congressmen, including Arthur H. Vandenberg, one of the Senate's foremost Republicans. Vandenberg, once an isolationist, had become a staunch advocate of international co-operation and gave full support to the charter. His influence counted heavily. Early in August,

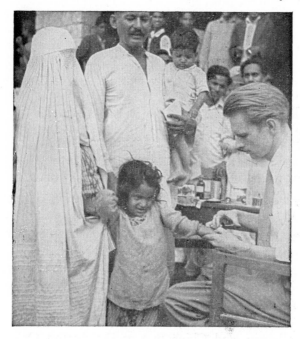

DANISH DOCTOR *gives tuberculin test to child in Karachi, Pakistan, while her parents and brother look on. The International Tuberculosis Campaign was made possible by the World Health Organization of the U.N.* (Acme)

1945, the Senate ratified the charter by a vote of 89 to 2. By the end of 1945, fifty-one member nations had ratified, and plans were being prepared to launch the new world organization.

Purposes and structure of the United Nations. In the words of the preamble of the charter: "We the peoples of the United Nations, determined to save succeeding generations from the scourge of war . . . to promote social progress and better standards of life in larger freedom . . . have resolved to combine our efforts to accomplish these aims. . . ." The organization seeks to settle disputes between nations, provide collective security against armed attack, promote justice, increase the general welfare, and establish human rights. It has six major organs: the General Assembly, the Security Council, the Economic and Social Council, the Trusteeship Council, the International Court of Justice, and the Secretariat.

The General Assembly meets at least once a year. Every nation has one vote, although it may send five representatives. Decisions on important questions are reached by a two-thirds vote. The Assembly may make recommendations to the members on any problem related to world peace and the improvement of international relations.

The Security Council was given the responsibility for preventing war. It has eleven members; the Big Five are permanent members and six others are elected by the Assembly for two-year terms. The Council may discuss any question which any seven of its members wish to bring before it. But in order to take action on a matter of importance, seven members, including each of the Big Five, must vote "Yes." Thus each of the Big Five has a veto over any important action of which it does not approve. The frequent use of the veto by the Soviet Union (by mid-1958 it had used the veto eighty-five times) weakened the Security Council. At the same time the General Assembly grew stronger and more important. In November, 1950, the General Assembly adopted a resolution, proposed by the United States, known as *United Action for Peace*. This resolution provided that if the Security Council, because of lack of unanimity of the permanent members, fails to deal promptly with a threat to peace, the General Assembly may consider the matter immediately. If the General Assembly is not in session, it may be called in a special emergency session within twenty-four hours on the request of any seven members of the Security Council. This resolution also created a Peace Observation Committee to observe and report on any area where international tension exists, and a Collective Measures Committee to report on the methods and resources, including armed forces, which might be used by the United Nations in case of a breach of the peace.

The Economic and Social Council is the third important organ of the United Nations. It is a board of eighteen nations, elected by the Assembly for three-year terms. Its purpose is to help the entire world achieve better living conditions and thus to remove the economic and social causes of war.

The Economic and Social Council has a number of committees and commissions at work on various problems. Thirteen specialized agencies are affiliated with it, among them the United Nations Educational, Scientific, and Cultural Organization (UNESCO), the International Refugee Organization (IRO), the International Labor Organization (ILO), the International Bank for Reconstruction and Development, and the World Health Organization (WHO). Each specialized agency holds conferences, gathers information, publishes reports, and takes other steps to solve international problems in its particular field. These agencies are doing a great deal of useful work.

The fourth body of the United Nations is the Trusteeship Council. It supervises territories taken from the defeated nations after World Wars I and II and given to some of the victors to administer. The country made responsible for such a territory does not own it out-

DAG   HAMMARSKJOLD,
*who succeeded Trygve Lie as
Secretary General of the
United Nations in 1953, lis-
tens to a session of the General Assembly.* (Wide World)

right, but acts as a trustee, or guardian, for it. The charter says that
the people in a trust territory may look forward to independence.

The International Court of Justice is the fifth major organ of the
U.N. It resembles the World Court established by the League of Nations and, like that court, meets at The Hague. Any nation may
agree to accept the Court's jurisdiction — that is, to take disputes to
the Court and promise in advance to abide by its decisions. The
Court handles legal questions only and not political disputes, which
are handled by the Security Council. The Court hears only cases
which are brought to it with the consent of the parties concerned.

The sixth organ of the U.N. is the Secretariat, the actual working
force which carries on at the headquarters. It is directed by a Secretary General, who is nominated by the Security Council and elected
by the Assembly for a five-year term. Mr. Trygve Lie of Norway
was chosen as the first Secretary General. He served until 1953,
when he was succeeded by Dag Hammarskjold (ham'mar shield) of
Sweden. The Secretariat is made up of about three thousand workers
from all parts of the world — economists, statisticians, stenographers,
translators, and others.

Achievements in restoring peace. Examples of the way in which
the United Nations works to restore peace are the cases of Palestine,
Indonesia, and Kashmir. When the British withdrew their troops

from Palestine in May, 1948, war broke out between the new Jewish state of Israel and the neighboring Arab states. The General Assembly appointed Count Bernadotte of Sweden as mediator. When Bernadotte was assassinated in Israel, the task of mediation was taken over by his deputy, Dr. Ralph Bunche of the United States. An armistice was arranged between Israel and its Arab neighbors. The Assembly established the Palestine Conciliation Commission to assist Israel and the Arab nations in drawing up formal peace treaties. In 1950 Dr. Bunche was awarded the Nobel Peace Prize for his services.

Another example of successful action by the U.N. to restore peace was in the war between the Netherlands and its possession, Indonesia. Fighting broke out when the Dutch returned to Indonesia after the defeat of Japan and attempted to put down the independence movement. The Security Council appointed a Good-Offices Committee for Indonesia. As a result of the committee's work, Dutch and Indonesian representatives met on board the *Renville*, a United States naval transport, to work out armistice terms. In January, 1948, the Dutch signed a truce with the Indonesians and agreed to the establishment of the United States of Indonesia. At the end of 1948 fighting broke out again and the Dutch conquered a large area. The Security Council condemned the Dutch military action as contrary to the *Renville* agreement and called upon the Netherlands to withdraw its forces to their original position. The outcome was recognition by the Dutch of the independence of Indonesia.

Early in 1948 India and Pakistan sent troops into Kashmir. It was feared that all of India would be engulfed in a religious war between Hindus and Moslems. The Security Council issued a cease-fire order and asked for a plebiscite (vote) to find out whether the people of Kashmir wished to join India or Pakistan. Fighting stopped but neither side was willing to withdraw its troops. In 1957 India said it would not agree to a plebiscite.

TENSION BETWEEN THE SOVIET UNION AND THE UNITED
STATES THREATENS TO WRECK THE UNITED NATIONS

The work of the United Nations and its agencies was greatly hampered by friction between the Communist and non-Communist states, and especially between the United States and the Soviet Union. At times there was doubt whether the United Nations could survive.

Why did tension develop? World War II reduced the strong nations of the world to two — the U.S.S.R. and the United States.

Each possessed immense resources and military might. Each differed from the other in its form of government, its economic system, and its attitude toward human rights. Yet the two governments might have got along peaceably had the U.S.S.R. been willing to co-operate in carrying out the purposes of the United Nations.

The Soviet Union gave evidence of imperialistic ambitions at the end of World War II, when it annexed Latvia, Lithuania, Estonia, and large portions of Poland and Rumania. It justified the seizure on the ground that this territory had once belonged to Russia. However, if the people in the annexed areas had been free to express themselves, it is doubtful that a majority would have chosen annexation. During the next two years the Soviet Union established governments it could dominate in Poland, Rumania, Hungary, Bulgaria, Albania, Yugoslavia, and Czechoslovakia. In each case it accomplished this result by giving aid to the native Communist party. Once the Communist party had control of the government it suppressed all opposition. Henceforth the country was a Russian satellite, since its leaders listened to Moscow's bidding. (Only in Yugoslavia did the dictator, Marshal Tito, insist on putting his own country's interests first and those of the U.S.S.R. second. Moscow has been trying ever since to oust Tito.)

The Soviet Union continued to promote the Communist movement throughout the world, either because of hope of dominating the world or because of zeal for spreading the Communist system. After World War II Communists were especially active in Greece, Italy, Germany, France, and in the Middle and Far East. Their activity led non-Communists to fear that the Soviet Union would gradually get control of most of Europe and all of Asia.

World unrest favors the spread of communism. The Communist movement gained strength in places where the people were discontented and restless. Following World War II there was unrest in most parts of the world. It was due to a number of causes.

(1) The war disrupted normal ways of living and destroyed human and material resources on a vast scale. Millions of families were broken. Millions of homes were destroyed. Millions of individuals became displaced persons.

(2) The war quickened the industrial revolution in countries like India and Brazil. While industrial revolution brings many benefits, it also creates grave insecurity by causing people to leave the farms and go to live in cities.

(3) In Eastern Europe, Asia, Africa, and Latin America the population was growing rapidly. The rising population created a heavy pressure upon supplies of food and raw materials. The Food and Agriculture Organization of the United Nations, after a survey of food production in seventy countries, reported that the world's food output ought to be doubled within twenty-five years.

(4) The spirit of nationalism was growing stronger in colonial areas. Dependent peoples in Asia and Africa were demanding self-government. Burma, India, Indonesia, Jordan, Israel, Korea, Pakistan, and the Philippines all received their independence in the period 1945–1950. The desire of colonial peoples for national independence threatened to destroy the English, French, and Dutch empires.

(5) The human rights movement was creating a demand among minority groups and submerged peoples for a larger measure of freedom and dignity as well as for a share in their government.

The unrest that existed everywhere, and particularly in the poverty-stricken areas of the world, favored the spread of revolutionary ideas. Underprivileged peoples wanted more opportunity for themselves and their children. Would they embrace democracy or communism? In country after country that was the crucial question.

The Soviet Union conducts world-wide propaganda. Russian leaders took full advantage of world unrest. They sent agents to help and watch over the activities of native Communists in all countries.

Through its control of Communist parties everywhere, the Soviet Union directed a world-wide campaign of propaganda. It told underprivileged peoples in non-Communist lands that they are the victims of capitalist exploitation. It claimed that under the Communist system all individuals could get shares of land and housing without discrimination on the basis of class, color, or religion. It argued that the personal liberties which democratic leaders talk about have no meaning for poor people. It taught that the Communist system would bring a higher standard of living and greater opportunities for education, recreation, and medical care. It stated also that a Communist revolution is sure to come in every country and that when all countries have adopted communism there will be no more war. These arguments and promises had a powerful appeal to three groups of people: (1) those who have suffered much from war, (2) those living in economic misery, and (3) those who have endured great discrimination because of their color or religion.

Lack of communication between East and West. There was

"WHAT NOW, MR. SCIEN— TIST?" *The control of atomic power is perhaps the biggest problem mankind has ever faced. Atomic power may mean either worldwide prosperity or world- wide destruction.* (Drawn by Fitzpatrick for the St. Louis *Post-Dispatch,* March 27, 1946)

scarcely any way by which people in the Soviet Union and its satel- lites could learn the truth about events beyond their borders. There seemed to be an "iron curtain" stretched between the Communist states and the rest of the world. The people of these countries were forbidden to listen to non-Communist broadcasts, such as Voice of America, or to travel in non-Communist lands. For the most part, they were not permitted to read foreign publications. Few foreign visitors were permitted to enter the Soviet Union or the nations un- der its control. The movements of foreign newsmen and representa- tives of foreign governments were greatly restricted.

Failure to obtain international control of atomic weapons. Fear of the atomic bomb magnified the tension between the Soviet Union and the United States. Hoping to assure the world of our peaceful in- tentions, President Truman declared soon after the defeat of Japan that the new weapon should be placed under international control. Representatives of the United States, Great Britain, and Canada, which had worked together in producing the bomb, met at once to discuss a method for international control.

When the General Assembly met early in 1946 it created the Inter- national Atomic Energy Commission, consisting of the eleven mem- bers of the Security Council plus Canada. At the commission's first meeting our representative, Bernard Baruch, announced the American plan for international control of atomic weapons. The plan called for setting up an Atomic Development Authority responsible to the United Nations. The authority was to own all uranium deposits and all atomic plants. Thus it would have complete control over all atomic activities everywhere. It would have to operate by majority rule. The United States offered to destroy its existing atomic bombs and to release its atomic secrets to the new world authority as soon as an effective system of control was in operation. This was an astonishingly generous offer.

Russia presented a different plan. It called for a treaty to outlaw atomic weapons. All those in existence were to be destroyed at once. Each nation was to conduct its own atomic activities. There would be an international control agency, but its actions would be subject to the veto.

The commission adopted a plan based largely on the American proposals. When this plan was laid before the Security Council, nine members approved it. The Soviet Union defeated it by not voting. For three years the commission tried to find a compromise plan but the effort was fruitless. The Russians refused to abandon the veto and to accept an effective system of inspection. In November, 1948, the General Assembly recommended the adoption of the American plan by a vote of 48 to 6. It rejected the Russian counter proposal. The deadlock over the international control of atomic weapons has continued.

On September 23, 1949, President Truman announced, "We have evidence that within recent weeks an atomic explosion occurred in the U.S.S.R." Thus it became known that the United States no longer had a monopoly of atomic weapons.

The hydrogen bomb. Toward the end of 1949 it was announced that physicists thought they could produce a new weapon, the hydrogen bomb, many times more destructive than the bomb dropped on Hiroshima. Soon after, the President ordered the Atomic Energy Commission to go ahead with its research and to make the hydrogen bomb as soon as possible. Since that time a special plant has been constructed near Aiken, South Carolina. A thermonuclear (hydrogen) explosion took place in a test late in 1952. Some nine months later Russia also conducted a thermonuclear explosion. (See page 697.)

Disputes over membership. Lack of co-operation between the Soviet Union and the Western powers was repeatedly shown in voting on new applications for membership in the U.N. After a series of vetoes, the long deadlock over the admission of new states was broken in 1955 when sixteen nations were admitted to membership — Albania, Austria, Bulgaria, Cambodia, Ceylon, Finland, Hungary, Ireland, Italy, Jordan, Laos, Libya, Nepal, Portugal, Rumania, and Spain. Four of these — Albania, Bulgaria, Hungary, and Rumania — belong to the Communist bloc. More nations were admitted in 1956.

The Soviet walkout. In January, 1950, the Security Council voted on the question "Should the delegate from the Nationalist or from the Communist government of China be seated on the Council?" Five members voted in favor of the Communist representative. Six members voted for the Nationalist representative. The Russian delegate, Joseph Malik, walked out of the Security Council, declaring that his government would not take part in meetings of the Council so long as Nationalist China held a seat. He returned in August, 1950.

Russia blocks the work of the Korean Commission. Korea, which was liberated from Japanese control in 1945, was divided into two zones. The northern zone was occupied by the Soviet Union, the southern zone by the United States. In September, 1947, the United States asked the General Assembly to take steps to establish a national government for Korea. The Assembly created the Korean Commission and instructed it to hold free elections in both zones. Russia refused to let the commission enter its zone and established there a Communist government, the People's Republic of Korea. Russia withdrew its occupation troops at the end of 1948, but left a large number of officers and men to train the North Korean army.

The Korean Commission supervised an election in the American zone, as a result of which the Republic of Korea was organized. The United States recognized it on January 1, 1949, and withdrew the last of its occupation forces six months later.

The Security Council takes decisive action in Korea. On June 24, 1950, North Korean tank columns moved south across the border. The invaders were well equipped with Russian tanks, guns, and planes. They were far stronger than the ill-equipped army of South Korea. It looked as if all Korea would shortly be united under a Communist government imposed by force.

At the request of our State Department, the Security Council met the day after the invasion began. By a vote of 9 to 0 (Russia being absent and Yugoslavia not voting), the Council called on the North Koreans to "cease hostilities" and withdraw their invasion forces.

NORTH KOREAN REFUGEES *fleeing from Chinese Communist forces. Carrying their few possessions in bulky bundles, the refugees are using this frail craft to cross the ice-choked Chongchon River. One woman is carrying a bundle on her head and her child strapped to her back.* (Associated Press)

Three days later American planes went into action to help the South Koreans. Within a few hours the Security Council took the strongest action of its history. It recommended "that the members of the United Nations furnish such assistance as may be necessary to the Republic of Korea to repel the armed attack and to restore international peace and security in the area." The following week the Council requested the United States to take charge of the U.N. forces.

For the first time the United Nations had armed forces fighting under its banner. Sea and air power and military equipment were supplied chiefly by the United States. Sixteen nations made some contribution to the fighting forces, but the United States and South Korea furnished the overwhelming majority of the troops. The Korean War dragged on for three years until July, 1953, when an armistice was signed which left neither side the victor. It was hoped, however, that by intervening with armed force in order to preserve the independence of the Republic of (South) Korea, the United Nations had been strengthened and Communists taught that aggression does not pay. (See Chapter 49.)

❁ ❁ ❁

To identify: Bernard Baruch, Ralph Bunche, Dag Hammarskjold, Trygve
   Lie, Joseph Malik, Marshal Tito, Secretariat.

To explain or define: "iron curtain," mediator, plebiscite, satellite, veto.

SUBJECTS FOR TALKS OR WRITTEN REPORTS

   1. The work of UNRRA (the United Nations Relief and Rehabilitation Administration).   2. The work of the World Health Organization,
the Food and Agriculture Organization, International Labor Organization, or any other specialized agency of the U.N.   3. Work of the International Bank for Reconstruction and Development.   4. Work of the
Trusteeship Council.   5. Arguments for and against the admission of
Communist China to the U.N.   6. The situation in Korea.   7. Progress
in settling the dispute over Kashmir.   8. Conditions in any country behind
the iron curtain.   (Consult *Readers' Guide.*)   9. The future of the U.N.

QUESTIONS FOR UNDERSTANDING THE TEXT

   1. Why was it thought best to establish a world security organization
before the war ended?   2. What are the six major organs of the United
Nations?   State the functions of each.   3. Why is the General Assembly
able to accomplish more than the Security Council?   4. Which is more
democratic in its procedures, the Security Council or the General Assembly?   Explain.   5. Explain the resolution of the General Assembly known
as "United Action for Peace."   6. How may the work of the Economic
and Social Council contribute to world peace?   Name some of the council's subdivisions.   7. Account for the tension between the U.S.S.R. and
the United States which developed after World War II.   8. What conditions produced world-wide unrest after World War II?   9. To what
groups of people does Communist propaganda have most appeal?
10. What was the usual manner in which Communists came to power in
Eastern Europe?   11. What were the principal differences between the
American and the Russian plans for control of atomic energy?   12. What
reason did the Soviet delegate give for walking out of the Security Council in January, 1950?   When and why did his walkout end?   13. How did
Russia block the work of the first Korean Commission?   14. What action
did the Security Council take when the North Koreans invaded South
Korea?   What circumstances made this action possible?

CHAPTER 49

THE NATION WORKS OUT A NEW FOREIGN POLICY

THE UNITED STATES USES ITS ECONOMIC STRENGTH TO CHECK COMMUNIST AGGRESSION

Difficulties in writing the peace treaties. Friction between the Soviet Union and her recent allies, Great Britain, France, and the United States, began to develop shortly after the defeat of Germany and Japan. Because of the strained relations among the Big Four the process of writing peace treaties with the nations defeated in World War II was extremely difficult. After many conferences, the four conquerors agreed on peace treaties for Italy, Hungary, Rumania, Bulgaria, and Finland. All five lost territory, were required to pay reparations, and had to limit their military forces to the size laid down in the peace treaties. The treaties with Rumania and Hungary provided that Russia might keep troops in those countries along its line of communication to Austria until a peace treaty with Austria should go into effect. These peace treaties were signed at Paris early in 1947.

At the Yalta Conference (February, 1945), Roosevelt, Churchill, and Stalin outlined a plan for dividing both Germany and Austria, after their defeat, into four occupation zones. Each of the Big Four was to occupy one of the zones. Vienna and Berlin, the capitals of Austria and of Germany, were also to be divided into four sections. When the plan was put into effect, the unco-operative attitude of the Soviet Union caused endless difficulties.

A government for the whole of Austria was set up late in 1945. It was given considerable power over domestic affairs. In 1953 the country was still under occupation because the Big Four had not been able to agree on a peace treaty. In the case of Germany and Japan the four conquerors were unable to agree on a peace treaty.

Goals of our new foreign policy. For a time after World War II American leaders hoped for friendly relations with the U.S.S.R. But this hope was gradually abandoned as efforts to reach an agree-

JAPANESE PEOPLE *of Hiroshima. Notice their faces as they stand on the street waiting for their first look at the emperor.* (Horace Bristol from Black Star)

ment with Russia about such problems as the control of atomic energy, the government of Germany, and peace treaties for Austria, Germany, and Japan came to nothing. Americans began to realize that Russian leaders preferred to keep the world in a state of unrest in order to promote the growth of communism.

As relations with the Soviet Union grew worse, the United States adopted a new foreign policy. It had three related aims: (1) to stop Soviet expansion, (2) to weaken the Communist movement in non-Communist lands, and (3) to strengthen democracy and promote private enterprise in non-Communist lands. These goals were endorsed by leaders in both major parties, although there was disagreement at times on the best way of advancing toward them.

The Truman Doctrine for Greece and Turkey. Our first effort to check Soviet expansion came in 1947, when we began to give military aid to Greece and Turkey. A civil war was going on in Greece, and it seemed likely that the Communists would seize the government, as they had already done in Poland, Rumania, Bulgaria, Yugoslavia, and Hungary. (See pages 660–661.) Greek Communists were receiving aid from Bulgaria, Yugoslavia, and Albania, all three of which were then dominated by Moscow. Russia was bringing pressure on Turkey for control of the Dardanelles, the straits that connect the Black Sea with the Mediterranean. If Communist designs in Greece and

Turkey succeeded, the Soviet Union would dominate the eastern Mediterranean and could interfere with traffic through the Suez Canal. In a special message to Congress in March, 1947, President Truman asked for $300,000,000 for military and other aid to Greece and $100,000,000 for military aid to Turkey. The President said that the United States should use its resources to check Communist expansion — a policy that became known as the "Truman Doctrine."

After much debate, Congress voted the money which the President asked. American military missions were sent to Greece and to Turkey to help in training their armed forces. The Greek and Turkish armies were supplied with modern equipment. A network of military roads was built in Turkey. Fighting in Greece came to an end in the summer of 1949. The military and economic aid which we gave to Greece and Turkey amounted to 1.5 billion dollars. It strengthened them and made them allies of the West. (See page 673.)

The European recovery program (the Marshall Plan). In June, 1947, Secretary of State Marshall made a speech calling attention to the widespread misery in Europe and the urgent need of a program to bring about economic recovery there. He suggested that the European nations hold a conference to list their economic needs and resources, to work out a blueprint for aiding one another, and to decide how the United States could help them to help themselves.

Marshall's proposal led to the Conference for European Economic Co-operation, which met at Paris in July, 1947. Sixteen nations were represented, including Greece and Turkey. At first Russia acted as though it would take part in the conference; but it withdrew from participation and directed its satellite nations to do likewise.

The conference spent twelve weeks in planning a four-year European recovery program. A report was drawn up which showed how the participating countries could help one another and the kinds of goods they must have from the United States and elsewhere in order to feed their people and rebuild their basic industries. It was estimated that a credit of about twenty billion dollars would be needed to carry out the plan and that sixteen billion should come from the United States.

The Cominform opposes the European recovery program. In September, 1947, there was a conference in Poland of the chief Communist leaders in nine countries — Russia, Poland, Hungary, Rumania, Yugoslavia, Bulgaria, Czechoslovakia, France, and Italy. The conference decided to establish a Communist Information Bureau, known as the "Cominform." The Cominform declared war on the Marshall Plan, stating that it was a scheme by which the United States would undermine the independence of the nations taking part in it.

The Molotov Plan. To console its satellites for not taking part in the Marshall Plan, the Kremlin offered the "Molotov Plan." This led to the formation of a Council of Economic Mutual Aid by the Communist countries. The council encouraged the exchange of goods between its members and linked them more firmly to the Soviet Union. But Russia could not give its satellites the aid which they might have received under the Marshall Plan.

Congress approves the European recovery program. At the beginning of 1948 the President asked Congress to vote money for the European recovery program. There was much opposition to this request. Many Americans saw no reason why they should be taxed to help Europe. Had it not been for the strong support of Senator Arthur Vandenberg, chairman of the Senate Committee on Foreign Relations, the measure would probably have been defeated. In the end Congress passed the Economic Co-operation Act, with an appropriation of 5.3 billion dollars for the first year of the program. The act said that it is "the policy of the people of the United States to encourage the unification of Europe." Soon the Economic Co-operation Administration (ECA) was shipping large quantities of food, raw materials, and industrial and agricultural machinery to the co-operating European nations. This aid undoubtedly checked the spread of communism in Western Europe.

The European recovery program (ERP) was successful in restoring industrial and agricultural production. European industrial activity caught up with and surpassed that of the prewar years. The political effects of Marshall Plan funds were also important. In Italy the Communists suffered a severe defeat in the spring elections of 1948. The influence of Communist parties was weakened, not only in Italy, but also in France and other countries of Western Europe. The ERP also led to the organization of the North Atlantic Alliance and to plans for economic and political cooperation among the countries of Western Europe.

The Berlin crisis. In 1948, France, Britain, and the United States made plans to merge their zones in West Germany and to establish there a Federal Republic of Western Germany. Shortly after these plans were announced, the Soviet Union, which controlled the roads and railroads leading out of Berlin, cut off all traffic to that city from

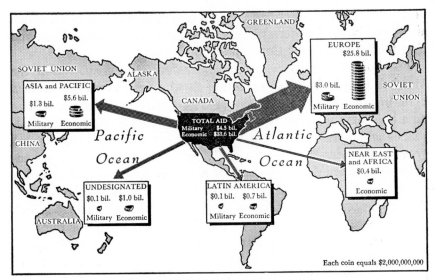

MILITARY AND ECONOMIC AID

From the end of World War II to the end of June 1952, the United States sent abroad approximately 38 billion dollars in military and economic aid. (The New York Times)

the west. As an excuse Russian leaders said that they objected to a proposed currency reform in Berlin. The real purpose of the block-ade was to force the Western powers out of the city, to make them abandon their plans for the West German Republic, and eventually to bring all of Germany under Communist control.

Berlin is about a hundred miles inside the Russian zone of occupa-tion. The two million people in the American, British, and French zones of the city were dependent on imports from West Germany. Britain and the United States answered the blockade by using air-planes to supply these people with food and fuel. The U.N. Security Council discussed ways of ending the blockade, but no action could be taken because of the Russian veto.

The "airlift" was a spectacular success. When it had continued for nearly a year the Russian delegate to the United Nations began to talk with representatives of the other occupying powers about a uni-form currency for Berlin. As a result of these conversations the blockade was brought to an end.

Soon afterwards the Soviet Union established the East German Democratic Republic. Controlled by the Communist party, it is re-ally a puppet government. The Russians have continued to give support to the National German Front, a Communist organization which aims to make the Western powers leave Berlin and to unite West and East Germany under a Communist government.

The Point IV program: aid to under-developed areas. After the Marshall Plan had been in operation about a year, President Truman in his inaugural address (January, 1949) declared: "We must embark on a bold new program for making the benefits of our scientific advances and industrial progress available for the improvement and growth of under-developed areas." Since this suggestion in his address was Point IV, the program of aid to under-developed areas has come to be known as the Point IV program. Congress delayed more than a year before appropriating about thirty million dollars to launch the program. In October, 1950, the first project — one for rural improvement in Iran — got under way with an allocation of $500,000. Since that time other projects have been started in different parts of the world, particularly in Asia, Africa, and Latin America.

In the meantime, the United Nations began a program of technical aid to countries wishing to improve their agriculture, industry, transportation, health, and education. Supporters of the United Nations Technical Assistance program, and the Point IV program, argue that they are an effective weapon for fighting Communist propaganda in impoverished areas where the people might be misled into accepting Communism as a way of improving their lot.

Economic aid to the allies of the United States and to neutral countries threatened with Communist subversion became an arm of American foreign policy. Congress however regarded military aid as more important than aid designed to promote economic progress. In the 1950's the great bulk of the annual appropriations for foreign aid went for arms and other military needs rather than for developmental assistance.

The United States Information Service. Shortly after World War II Congress created a new agency — the Office of International Information (OII). Its purpose is to spread correct information about the United States, especially in countries under Communist control or where Communists are gaining influence. The OII conducts radio broadcasts known as the Voice of America, some of them beamed at countries behind the "iron curtain." It also distributes printed material and motion pictures, conducts information centers and libraries of American publications in several foreign capitals, and supplies news releases to foreign newspapers.

The North Atlantic Treaty. The Berlin crisis of 1948–1949 dramatized the danger that German Communists, with Russian support,
would seize control of all Germany. If this happened, France and
Italy, in each of which there was a large Communist minority, would
probably soon find themselves in the Communist fold. The remaining countries of Western Europe, under Communist pressure from
without and within, might then become Communist states. Great
Britain and the United States believed that their safety depended on
saving Western Europe from communism. Accordingly, they proposed that the countries fringing the Atlantic join in a mutual defense
pact. The United States Senate (July, 1948) adopted a resolution
favoring such a pact.

A year later the Senate ratified the North Atlantic Treaty, which
made the United States a military ally of Canada, Great Britain,
France, Belgium, the Netherlands, Luxemburg, Norway, Denmark,
Iceland, Italy, and Portugal. Norway joined the pact in spite of So-
viet pressure, but Finland and Sweden thought it safer not to do so.
(Greece and Turkey became members of the North Atlantic Treaty
Organization, NATO, in 1952.)

The nations which signed the treaty pledged themselves to settle
all international disputes peacefully and to refrain from the threat or
use of force. They also agreed to consider that an attack against one
of them is an attack against them all and to assist the one attacked.
The treaty established the North Atlantic Council on which each
member state is represented by its foreign minister.

In the summer of 1950 the State Department called upon the other
members of the Atlantic Alliance to expand their defense programs
and to make plans for the joint defense of Western Europe. The
North Atlantic Council agreed to a greatly increased program of rearmament. Because most of the NATO countries were impoverished
by World War II, Congress appropriated several billion dollars to
assist them to rearm. General Dwight D. Eisenhower was summoned
from retirement to become the commander-in-chief of the military
forces of the countries of the North Atlantic Pact.

The European Defense Community (EDC). In May, 1952, five
NATO countries (France, Italy, Belgium, the Netherlands, and Lux-
emburg) together with West Germany signed a treaty organizing the
European Defense Community. By this treaty the six countries stated

GENERAL MATTHEW RIDGWAY (*left*), *supreme commander of Allied Forces in Europe, inspects the guards of honor of seven nations in the courtyard of the French castle of Fontainebleau. When General Ridgway became Army Chief of Staff in 1953, he was succeeded in the European post by General Gruenther.* (Wide World)

that aggression against one is aggression against all and agreed to establish a six-nation army. The same six countries also organized the European Steel and Coal Community, to unite all of their coal and steel industry into one free market. Leaders in the movement which brought about these developments outlined a plan to unite the six nations under a single constitution. In 1954 France decided not to ratify the treaty creating EDC. However, the six nations did succeed in establishing Euratom. (See page 697.) They also made plans for a common European market. A political union may lie far in the future.

A "peace contract" with West Germany. By 1949 the Berlin crisis and other developments made it clear that agreements could not be reached with Russia which would make it possible to write a peace treaty for a united Germany. Therefore, the United States, along with England and France, encouraged the organization of a West German Federal Republic, while Russia established the East German Democratic Republic. The West German Federal Republic, whose first chancellor was Dr. Konrad Adenauer, appears to have achieved a fairly stable democratic government and to have made a remarkable economic recovery.

The United States declared the end of a state of war with Germany late in 1951. The next spring the United States concluded a "peace contract" with West Germany, in spite of protests from Russia. The

United States Senate ratified the West German peace contract on July 1, 1952. At the same time the Senate indicated that it would approve a mutual defense treaty with the six countries of the European Defense Community.

Germany, particularly Berlin, remains the most delicate and sensitive point of contact between East and West, between Russia and the United States. In the summer of 1953, a few months after Stalin's death, there were serious anti-Communist riots in East Germany. The immediate cause was a shortage of food. These riots were interpreted as a sign that Russian control was weaker than had been thought. The United States volunteered to give food supplies to the people in East Germany in the hope that this demonstration of good will might encourage them in further resistance to the Russians.

THE UNITED STATES PERSUADES THE UNITED NATIONS TO USE ARMED FORCE TO CHECK COMMUNIST AGGRESSION IN ASIA

While the nations of the Western World were worried about how and when and where they might be harassed by Russia, it was in Asia that the actual clash of armies challenged the world leadership of the United States and the effectiveness of the United Nations.

Postwar developments in Southern Asia. Shortly after World War II England gave up her dominant position in southern Asia. Burma withdrew from the British Commonwealth of Nations and became an independent nation (January, 1948). The great Indian subcontinent was divided into two self-governing dominions — India and Pakistan (1947). Both India and Pakistan remained within the British Commonwealth of Nations, and both agreed to accept the good offices of the United Nations in settling a dispute over Kashmir. Prime Minister Nehru of India emerged as an important world figure. He tried to be a mediator between the East and West.

Through the good offices of the United Nations, the Netherlands finally recognized the independence of the rich and populous islands that make up the Republic of Indonesia. (See page 660.)

In the states, or provinces, of French Indo-China, an area inhabited by approximately thirty million people, there has been an intermittent and bitter civil war. As in Burma, Indonesia, and India the people want independence. In Vietnam, one of the provinces, the movement for independence is sponsored by the League for the Independence of Vietnam, and is known as the Vietminh. The Vietminh is controlled by Communists and receives supplies from Red China.

FRENCH TROOPS IN FRENCH INDO–CHINA. *In the summer of 1953 French units arrived to bolster the Laos defenders.* (International News Photos)

Its leader is Ho Chi-minh. The Vietminh has acquired control by armed rebellion of large portions of Vietnam and have threatened to invade the provinces of Laos and Cambodia. Although the United States has given financial aid and military supplies, the French government has been unable to suppress the Communist uprising. Many observers believe that if Indo-China is to be saved from Communist control, France must be willing to make sweeping concessions to the demand of the Indo-Chinese for independence. They believe that unless this is done the Communist-dominated Vietminh, with the aid of Red China, and powerful Communist groups in Burma, Thailand, and Indonesia, might succeed in bringing all or nearly all of southeast Asia within the Communist orbit. In spite of minor political reforms made by France, the fighting continued, and French forces were defeated. Finally, after nearly eight years of fighting, France (1955) agreed to the withdrawal of troops and to the partition of Vietnam.

The peace treaty with Japan. Russia had a voice in the Commission which supervised the Allied occupation of Japan. However, Russia did not have much influence because the occupation troops were largely American and because General Douglas MacArthur exercised a vigorous and almost dictatorial authority in Japan. MacArthur disarmed the Japanese, weakened the power of the militarists, large landlords, and business leaders, secured a law for the redistribution of land on easy terms to tenant farmers, and restored civil liberties. He sponsored a revised constitution for Japan, which reduced the authority of the emperor and established a parliamentary government similar to that of England.

After 1948 the United States thought it was time to prepare a Japanese peace treaty. Russia opposed this course of action, but in 1950 the United States announced that it would not tolerate a "perpetual veto" on the conclusion of a peace treaty with Japan. The Truman administration turned over the task of working out a peace treaty to John Foster Dulles, who later became Eisenhower's Secretary of State. In September, 1951, at a conference at San Francisco, forty-eight nations agreed to the terms of the Japanese peace treaty. The treaty reduced the territory of Japan to the home islands. Japan gave up Korea, Formosa, and many other islands formerly under her control. Japan was allowed to rearm for defense purposes. By a separate agreement the United States retained the privilege of keeping some troops and air bases in Japan. In 1952 the Senate ratified the peace treaty and also a mutual security agreement with Japan.

Agreements with the Philippines, Australia, and New Zealand. The Senate in 1952 also ratified two other mutual security pacts, one with the newly independent nation of the Philippines, and another with Australia and New Zealand (referred to as ANZUS). The United States is the only nation which is a member of all three mutual security pacts. These agreements have been regarded by some as the possible nucleus of a Pacific Treaty Organization similar to NATO.

The Communists acquire control of China. When World War II ended, the Nationalists and Communists resumed their struggle for mastery of China. The United States gave military supplies to the Nationalists, but a large amount of this material fell into the hands of the Communists, as one Nationalist regiment after another went over to the enemy. In 1946, General Marshall, sent as special envoy to China, tried to end the fighting and to get the Nationalists and Communists to co-operate politically in a program of reform. After the failure of General Marshall's mission, the United States began to withdraw its support from the Nationalists. Many observers claimed that the Nationalist regime was weakened by inflation, black market operations, graft, internal rivalries, and the failure to introduce long-needed agrarian reforms. Under the leadership of Mao Tse-tung (mä'ó dzŭ' dŏong') the Communists forced the Nationalists to abandon one stronghold after another.

In August, 1949, the Department of State published a White Paper which reviewed American policy in China. The White Paper declared that the two billion dollars spent to support the Nationalists since the defeat of Japan had accomplished nothing because of the inefficiency and dishonesty of the Chiang government, and that it would be futile to spend any more.

Toward the close of 1949, Chiang Kai-shek was forced to withdraw the remnants of the Nationalist army, about 500,000 men, to the island of Formosa. The government he set up there claimed to be the real government of China. But in China proper Mao Tse-tung and the Communists were in actual control. The Communist government of Mao Tse-tung was recognized by England, India, Russia, and several other countries. The United States refused to recognize Mao Tse-tung. Russia protested that the "People's Republic of China" and not Nationalist China should be represented in the United Nations. To emphasize her protest Russia refused to take part in the deliberations of the Security Council between January and August, 1950. (See page 664.)

Political controversy over America's China policy. Critics of the Truman administration vigorously attacked the State Department for its "China policy," because there was alarm over the success of Mao Tse-tung and fear that Communist influence might spread to nearby Asiatic countries. The controversy over American aid to Chiang Kai-shek had been going on within and without the State Department even before the defeat of Japan. Congressional investigations and reports dealt with the part that pro-Communist sympathizers and a China lobby supporting Chiang may have played in shaping American public opinion and American policy.

The beginning of the Korean War. We have already noted that the three years' war in Korea was a test of the United Nations. The war began early in the morning, Sunday, June 25, 1950 (Far Eastern time and date). The North Koreans were well prepared and equipped for a lightning campaign of conquest; the South Koreans were prepared only to repel border raids. If the Republic of Korea were allowed to fall unaided, the consequences might be disastrous. Our leaders believed that the men in the Kremlin regarded Korea as a test of what the United States would do to prevent further Communist aggression. If we did nothing they could go ahead with their plans to help native Communists set up Communist governments in one Asiatic country after another. President Truman and his advisors decided to send help to the Republic of Korea.

The United States did not act alone. The day after the invasion began, the Security Council called upon all members of the United Nations to give aid to the Republic of Korea. (See page 665.) On Tuesday, June 27, President Truman informed the Senate and House of Representatives that he had ordered the United States sea and air forces to give cover and support to the retreating South Korean troops. The Korean War, or "Police Action" as it has been called, expressed the determination of the United Nations and the United States to use armed force to check aggression.

The fighting in Korea, July, 1950–November, 1950. A few days after the outbreak of hostilities, General Douglas MacArthur was designated as the Supreme Commander of the United Nations forces in Korea. During July and August the North Koreans forced United Nations troops into the southeastern corner of the peninsula. There a small beachhead around Pusan was maintained. During September and October the United Nations forces began to counterattack. As a result of a brilliant amphibious landing at Inchon (September 15, 1950), the United Nations forces recaptured Seoul, the capital of South Korea, and drove the enemy back to the 38th parallel (the line dividing North and South Korea). There was delay in taking advantage of these successes while diplomats debated the wisdom of pursuing the enemy into North Korea. Finally, MacArthur was given authority to move his troops into North Korea. During October and November a large portion of North Korea was occupied by U.N. forces. Some troops even reached the Yalu River on the border between Manchuria and Korea.

Red China intervenes. Late in November, MacArthur ordered a general advance. But with dramatic suddenness the war changed. Chinese troops had crossed the Yalu River from Manchuria late in October, 1950. On November 26, two days after MacArthur launched his offensive, the Chinese opened a big counteroffensive. The powerful Chinese thrust split the U.N. forces in two. Within a few weeks the Chinese troops recaptured Seoul and pushed the U.N. forces below the 38th parallel. In late January and February, 1951, the U.N. forces checked the enemy attack and began a series of cautious advances. By the end of March, 1951, they had reached the 38th parallel for the second time.

The MacArthur controversy. General Douglas MacArthur became the central figure in a controversy over the basic objectives of the Korean War, and over the way it should be fought. When the Chinese entered the war in large numbers MacArthur argued that the character of the war had changed. He chafed under instructions not to bomb the Chinese bases and supply routes in Manchuria. By public statements he appealed to public opinion in the hope that there might be a reversal of official policy. MacArthur wanted permission to bomb the enemy bases north of the Yalu, to blockade the China coast, and to use the Chinese forces on Formosa. President Truman and his advisers feared that if China was attacked on its own soil, Russia might go to its defense. We would then have to fight a global war. On April 11, 1951, President Truman relieved MacArthur of his command, declaring that, "We do not want to see the conflict in Korea extended. We are trying to prevent world war, not start one. . . . A number of events have made it evident that General MacArthur did not agree with this policy. I have, therefore, considered it essential to relieve General MacArthur so that there would be no doubt or confusion as to the real purpose and aim of our policy."

The dramatic dismissal of MacArthur clearly revealed that the United States accepted the point of view of important leaders in the United Nations that the Korean War should not be conducted in such a way as to force a decisive victory. It was equally clear that the United States, having checked the Communist invasion, was determined to use its ground troops, its air power, and its navy to maintain the independence of South Korea.

Armistice negotiations and stalemate. In June, 1951, the Russian delegate to the United Nations made the surprising statement that the war could be ended. By July an armistice commission was appointed. Discussions over the terms of a truce dragged on for more than two years. One of the principal stumbling blocks was the Red demand that all prisoners be repatriated, even against their will. Many prisoners taken by the U.N. had surrendered in the belief that they would be protected from the Communists. If forced to return to Communist territory they would be killed. Every now and then there were indications that the armistice commission might reach an agreement, but each time the Communists caused new postponements, new quarrels, and new interruptions.

For a few months there was a lull in the ground fighting but later, when the armistice talks seemed to be getting nowhere, fighting was renewed. Both sides sought to retain or capture strategic hills and ridges. The air war stepped up in intensity. Occasionally the United States bombed targets that it had formerly refrained from attacking. More Russian-built planes were in the air than ever before. The jet-propelled airplane and other new weapons of attack and defense were being tested in Korea.

The stalemate in Korea became a major issue in the presidential campaign of 1952, and was probably a factor in the defeat of the Democratic candidate. The new administration gradually let it be known that unless a truce were concluded in a reasonable time, it would resort to other means to put an end to the stalemate. Stalin died in March, 1953, and the new Russian leaders temporarily adopted a more conciliatory tone toward the West. Whatever the cause, armistice negotiations were resumed, and there was a surprisingly quick agreement on the exchange of sick and wounded prisoners. Early in July a compromise on the exchange of prisoners who did not want to be repatriated was worked out. It provided that each nation, under the supervision of a neutral commission (India, Switzerland, Sweden, Poland, and Czechoslovakia), would have a limited time in which to persuade the unwilling prisoners to change their mind about repatriation.

An armistice was finally signed late in July, 1953, and the fighting ceased — whether temporarily or permanently remains to be seen. The war had devastated South Korea and inflicted over a million casualties. The United States casualties were approximately 140,000, including 25,000 dead and 13,000 missing or captured. It was a great tribute to the progress of medical science that more than eighty per cent of the 103,000 wounded American troops were returned to duty. It is estimated that the financial cost of the war to the United States was more than twenty-two billion dollars.

The Korean War ended in stalemate. In Europe and America there was satisfaction, but little rejoicing, over the signing of the truce. The United Nations and the United States fought for a limited objective — to save the Republic of (South) Korea. They achieved it. President Eisenhower warned the American people that they had "won an armistice on a single battleground, not peace in the world.

We may not now relax our guard nor cease our quest. We and our United Nations allies must be vigilant."

To identify: European Defense Community, Marshall Plan, Molotov Plan, NATO, Truman Doctrine, White Paper on China.

To define or explain: thermonuclear explosion, thirty-eighth parallel, unilateral action.

SUBJECTS FOR TALKS OR WRITTEN REPORTS

1. Accomplishments of the European recovery program. 2. The reciprocal trade agreements program since 1945. 3. The membership and activities of the Cominform. 4. Political and economic developments in Germany since 1945. 5. The Inter-American Treaty of Mutual Assistance (1947). 6. Arguments for and against the termination of United States aid to China in 1949. 7. Work of the Office of International Information. 8. The American program of aid to underdeveloped areas. 9. Progress of Japan since V–J Day.

QUESTIONS FOR UNDERSTANDING THE TEXT

1. What may explain Russia's failure to agree on a peace treaty for Austria? Germany? 2. What conditions led the United States to give military aid to Greece and Turkey? 3. Who drew up the European recovery plan? What did it cover? What did Congress do to put it into operation? 4. Why did European nations experience a dollar gap during the recovery program? 5. Why did the Soviet Union and its satellites not participate in the European recovery plan? What plan did Moscow offer as a substitute? 6. What conditions led Great Britain and the United States to propose the Atlantic Alliance? 7. What nations joined the Atlantic Alliance? Account for the failure of Finland and Sweden to join. 8. Why did Congress vote money for helping the members of the Atlantic Alliance to rearm? 9. Why and when did Russia blockade Berlin? What did the other occupying powers do then? 10. Account for the fact that much of the material we gave to the Chinese Nationalists was used by the Communists. 11. What was the outcome of General Marshall's mission to China? 12. Account for the rapid progress of the Chinese Communist armies in 1949. 13. Why did the United Nations go to the aid of the Republic of Korea? 14. Why was a United States fleet sent to Formosa in 1950? 15. Why did the President relieve General MacArthur? 16. How did the armistice commission compromise the dispute over the repatriation of war prisoners? 17. Why is French Indo-China a potential danger spot?

CHAPTER 50

THE RETURN OF THE REPUBLICANS
TO POWER

THE PRESIDENTIAL CAMPAIGN OF 1952

The Democrats nominate Stevenson. President Truman remained silent throughout 1951 about his intention to seek re-election in 1952, though rumors circulated that he did not desire renomination. Many Democratic leaders tried to persuade Governor Adlai E. Stevenson of Illinois to seek the nomination. Their efforts in his behalf were rewarded; the Democratic Convention nominated him on the third ballot. The convention chose Senator John Sparkman of Alabama as his running mate.

The selection of the Alabama senator for the second place on the ticket represented a determined effort on the part of Democratic leaders to keep the "Solid South" in line. "States rights" Democrats or "Dixiecrats" had bolted the 1948 convention over the civil rights issue. At the 1952 convention older, more conservative politicians successfully maneuvered to avoid an open break with the Southern delegations. It was hoped that the nomination of a Southerner for the Vice-Presidency would give the Democratic party the electoral votes of the Solid South.

The Republicans turn from Taft to Eisenhower. The outstanding Republican leader during the Truman administration was the able and forthright Senator Robert A. Taft of Ohio. Taft had lost the 1948 presidential nomination to Governor Dewey of New York, but his re-election to the Senate in 1950 by a large majority made him the logical candidate for the nomination in 1952. Taft became known as "Mr. Republican." However, some Republican governors and senators, particularly in the East, tried to persuade General Dwight D. Eisenhower to seek the Republican nomination.

General Eisenhower, then Supreme Commander of NATO, was in Europe throughout 1951. The general remained silent concerning his intentions, but his friends organized and campaigned for him. Early in 1952 Mr. Eisenhower announced that he would accept the nomination. He was nominated on the first ballot. In thus turning away from "Mr. Republican" the Republicans chose a newcomer to politics, but a man who was genuinely popular and greatly admired and respected abroad. Youthful Senator Richard M. Nixon of California became the vice-presidential nominee.

Eisenhower is elected. Both General Eisenhower and Governor Stevenson conducted vigorous campaigns. The general sought to take advantage of the friction between Northern and Southern Democrats and became the first Republican presidential candidate to campaign in the South. Democratic governors in some Southern states publicly announced that they would not support the Stevenson-Sparkman ticket. Governor Stevenson supported the Truman record and tried to avoid alienating either the liberal or the conservative wing of his party.

The election resulted in an overwhelming victory for Eisenhower. Eisenhower carried 39 states with 442 electoral votes; Stevenson carried 9 states with 89 electoral votes. Eisenhower swept every section of the country except the South. Even there he won an unusually large popular vote and captured the electoral vote of three states — Florida, Virginia, and Texas.

The election was an Eisenhower landslide, it should be noted, rather than a Republican landslide. Eisenhower generally ran ahead of the Republican candidates for governor, Congress, or local offices. In the Eighty-third Congress (1953–1954) the Senate was almost evenly divided between Republicans and Democrats; the Republicans obtained a small majority in the House of Representatives. Even this small Republican margin was wiped out two years later, in the Eighty-fourth Congress (1955–1956), when both the Senate and the House of Representatives had Democratic majorities.

EISENHOWER'S FIRST TERM

The end of an era. Eisenhower's inauguration on January 20, 1953, marked the end of twenty years of Democratic control of the national government. The election seemed to indicate that the people, as Eisenhower had urged during the campaign, wanted a change. But just what change the election of a Republican President would bring was not clear as the Eisenhower administration got under way. The social and economic adjustments resulting from New Deal and Fair Deal legislation on agriculture, labor, and welfare were well rooted and popular. In regard to them the Eisenhower administration did not attempt any basic changes. The major outlines of the foreign policy developed by Roosevelt and Truman were continued. The new administration was committed to economy in government and a reduction in taxes. Nevertheless there was no scuttling of the social welfare programs of the New Deal and the Fair Deal. Indeed as time passed the Eisenhower administration sponsored increased expenditures for housing, roads, education, and improvements in the social security program. The new administration made cuts in foreign economic and military aid. The international situation was such, however, that no drastic changes were made.

The new President's Cabinet. Mr. Eisenhower broke with precedent by naming shortly after his election the men he intended to appoint to the Cabinet and to other important positions. With few exceptions the men he selected were new to national politics. They were recruited for the most part from the fields of banking and industry. Mrs. Oveta Culp Hobby, named as Federal Security Administrator, became the first Secretary of the new Department of Health, Education, and Welfare. As time passed the chief storm centers of the Eisenhower administration were John Foster Dulles as Secretary of State, Charles E. Wilson as Secretary of Defense, and Ezra Taft Benson as Secretary of Agriculture.

The budget, the national debt, and taxes. In the one area in which campaign pledges urgently called for action, the Eisenhower administration moved with caution. Although Congress was in a mood to reduce taxes, President Eisenhower argued that taxes should not be reduced until the budget was balanced. (It was not until the fiscal year of 1956 closed that a balance was achieved.) In 1953 the President, with the help of Senator Taft, prevailed upon Congress to extend the excess profits tax. In subsequent years the Eisenhower administration endeavored, without too much success, to prune the amount spent for defense and foreign aid. The Republicans put through minor but not substantial changes in the tax structure.

Economic controls are lessened. In February 1953 wage controls adopted during the Korean War were lifted. Gradually price controls were removed from various items. Rent controls were dropped except in specified areas which had a serious housing shortage. The Defense Production Act of 1950, which had been enacted to strengthen the national economy to support the Korean struggle, was allowed to expire. The Reconstruction Finance Corporation, which

DRILLING AN OIL WELL *in the offshore waters near Freeport, Texas.* (Courtesy of Humble Oil and Refining Company)

had functioned throughout the depression and the war, terminated its activities.

The states receive control of offshore oil deposits. In the first months of Eisenhower's administration Congress passed a law giving the states control of offshore, or Tidelands, oil deposits. President Truman had vetoed similar bills on this controversial topic which had become an issue in the campaign of 1952.

The discovery of oil deposits in the area off the coast of California and of some of the Gulf states had raised the question as to whether such offshore deposits belonged to the states or to the federal government. The states, claiming ownership, wanted to lease the deposits to private companies and to use the royalties so obtained to reduce taxes and finance public improvements. Advocates of national ownership wanted the oil deposits held as a national resource, to be used as a source of federal revenue and as a reserve for Navy use. In 1947 the Supreme Court held that the federal government rather than the states had paramount rights to the three-mile area along the coast and "full dominion over the resources of the soil under that water area, including oil." In 1953 Congress enacted a law to the effect that the states could lease and collect royalties on oil deposits within the "historic seaward boundaries" of the states. In the case of most states this phrase meant three miles out to sea. But in the case of Texas and Florida it meant ten and a half miles to seaward, because when these two states were admitted to the Union they had the right to exercise jurisdiction ten and a half miles to seaward. This same law gave Congress control of offshore oil deposits "beyond the historic boundaries of the states."

The St. Lawrence Seaway and Power Project. For a quarter of a century the proposal to connect the Great Lakes with the Atlantic by way of the St. Lawrence River had been the subject of controversy. The construction of the seaway also involved the construction of hydroelectric power plants. Three Presidents — Hoover, Roosevelt, and Truman — all had urged the project and conducted negotiations with Canada. Congress, however, had failed to take action. Finally, in 1953, Canada announced that it would proceed without American approval. President Eisenhower then persuaded Congress to give the state of New York the right to co-operate with the Province of Ontario in building dams and hydroelectric power plants at the International Rapids. The electric energy generated is to be divided between New York and Ontario, with the understanding that New York will make some of the energy available to nearby states.

In 1954 Congress authorized construction of the St. Lawrence Seaway jointly by the United States and Canada. To make the St. Lawrence navigable between Montreal and Ogdensburg, N.Y. — a distance of 120 miles — it will be necessary to construct six locks. The estimated cost of construction is about $273,000,000, of which the United States agreed to contribute $91,000,000. The seaway will convert such inland cities as Milwaukee, Chicago, Buffalo, Cleveland, Detroit, and Toledo into seaports.

Controversy over TVA. From its beginning TVA has been the subject of controversy between those who favor government-sponsored power projects and those who believe that the government should not compete with private power companies. After the war the Atomic Energy Commission needed additional electric power for some of its projects. The question then arose as to whether the needed steam-generated electric power plant should be built by the TVA with federal funds or by private companies. Finally in 1954 the Eisenhower administration awarded a contract — known as the Dixon-Yates contract — to private companies to build a steam plant at West Memphis, Arkansas. The Democrats criticized the Dixon-Yates contract as an administration measure designed to weaken TVA. They charged the Republicans with being too concerned with promoting the welfare of private interests. When the city of Memphis, Tennessee, announced that it would build the power plant, the administration canceled the Dixon-Yates contract.

Other successes and failures. In general, President Eisenhower pursued a middle-of-the-road policy. Not infrequently a combination of moderate Republicans and moderate Democrats gave him the majority he needed. Thus, despite opposition from members of his own party, the Reciprocal Trade Agreements were extended, first for one year, then for a three-year period, till June, 1958. In 1958, they were again extended. Congress increased the number of people covered by the Social Security program and also its benefits. This program, first inaugurated in 1935 during the days of the depression, now provides old age and survivors insurance for more than 80 per cent of all gainfully employed workers. In 1953 Congress created the Small Business Administration to protect the interests of small businesses and to make loans to them. In 1954 Congress raised the minimum wage rate to one dollar per hour (page 637). It liberalized the insurance and mortgage features of the Housing Act to encourage home ownership and it provided for the construction of 45,000 low-cost housing units.

In 1956 the Congress approved a gigantic appropriation for the construction of highways. The Federal Highway Bill of 1956 provided for building, during the next thirteen years, a national network of superhighways designed to connect most cities with a population of 50,000 or more. Twenty billions was allocated to the states to help pay for the highways. In addition, the law appropriated two and a half billion dollars — to be matched by the states — for the construction of primary, secondary, and rural roads. To help pay the cost of this program Congress raised the federal gasoline tax.

In 1952, Congress had passed the McCarran-Walter Immigration and Nationality Act over the vigorous veto of President Truman. Under this law the total number of quota immigrants that might be admitted each year was slightly over 154,000; no quota restrictions were placed upon persons born in the countries of the Western Hemisphere or on the alien husbands and wives of American citizens. Truman based his veto on the ground that the law was discriminatory. Congress liberalized immigration restrictions in 1953 to permit the admission of 214,000 immigrants above the normal quota during a three-year period (1953–1956). This temporary modification was intended primarily to provide for the admission of displaced persons

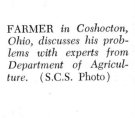

FARMER *in Coshocton, Ohio, discusses his problems with experts from Department of Agriculture.* (S.C.S. Photo)

from countries behind the "iron curtain." There were also a few minor amendments to the law in 1954. Many people continued to argue that the whole immigration policy of the country needed a complete revision.

AGRICULTURAL DISTRESS PROVOKES CONTROVERSY

Prosperity is general, except among farmers. During President Eisenhower's first term the country enjoyed four years of rather general prosperity. There was a record number of employed persons; industrial production increased each year; wages remained high, and the cost of living was fairly stable. However, as during the 1920's, this industrial prosperity did not extend in equal degree to the farmers. Farm prices and farm income continued to decline. The Democrats tried to make political capital out of the decline in farm income. They directed their fire at Secretary of Agriculture Benson.

How the support program helped the farmer. The principle of "parity payments" to help farmers was inaugurated as part of the New Deal. The price support program works as follows: the farmer may borrow money from the federal government on certain storable crops. The amount of the loan is based on the support price, which is a percentage of the "parity price" of the crops the farmer is raising. A "parity price" is a government-determined price designed to keep the farmer's purchasing power at a certain level. If, when the crop is harvested and ready for sale, the market price should be higher than the support price, the farmer sells his crop at the market price, repays his loan, and keeps the profit. If the market price is below the support price at that time the government stores the farmer's crop and cancels his loan. Thus, in effect, the farmer sells his crop to the government at the support price. Later the government may sell the stored crop at a profit or loss depending on market conditions. Under this price-support program the government at times has become the owner of more surplus agricultural products than it could store or distribute. The government gave part of the surplus food to subsidize school lunch programs. It also allowed part of it to spoil or be destroyed. Since food prices were high and the drain on the Treasury considerable, the whole support program came under attack.

Rigid vs. *flexible price supports.* The Hope-Aiken Law of 1948 fixed price supports for basic commodities at 90 per cent of the parity price for a two-year period when a *flexible* rather than a rigid price support program was to be introduced. Later this law was amended to postpone the flexible support program. The question became a matter of debate in the presidential campaign of 1952.

Secretary of Agriculture Benson stoutly championed flexible supports, claiming that the decline in farm prices and income resulted from the surpluses that had piled up during the Truman administration. He argued that the 90 per cent parity program had been in effect too long, and that the Truman administration had failed to apply satisfactory acreage controls when surplus supplies began to accumulate. In 1954 price supports on wheat, cotton, corn, rice, and peanuts were put on a sliding scale of 90 to 75 per cent of parity. Secretary Benson sharply cut acreage allotments on wheat and cotton, the surpluses of which were a burden to the Treasury. However, farm prices and income continued to fall. The Democrats argued that rigid price supports at 90 per cent of parity should be re-established in order to help the farmer.

The Farm Bill of 1956 compromises the issue. Mr. Benson succeeded in getting Congress to approve a compromise farm bill in the spring of 1956. The act established a "soil bank" of 1.2 billion dollars to be used to compensate farmers for withdrawing part of their acreage from cultivation. The bill retained flexible supports for wheat, corn, cotton, rice, and peanuts, and raised the price support on feed grains from 70 to 76 per cent of parity. If farm prices improved, both sides could argue they had helped put it through. Even before the soil bank measure became law, farm prices had begun a slow upward climb. There were many who believed that the farm problem, however, was a "hardy perennial." (See page 701.)

CIVIL RIGHTS AND "DESEGREGATION" BECAME SERIOUS ISSUES

"To Secure These Rights." In 1947 a distinguished committee, appointed by President Truman to review the treatment accorded minority groups, submitted a significant report, under the title *"To Secure These Rights."* This report, which was circulated widely, reviewed discriminatory practices of employers and labor unions and restrictions on voting and on the ownership of property. The committee indicated that the problem of discrimination was not sectional, but national, in scope and that it had many aspects. While various minority groups — Indians, Jews, Catholics, those of Oriental descent, and others — are frequently subject to discrimination, the unequal treatment of the Negro was found to be most serious. The report recommended a federal Fair Employment Practices Committee and federal laws against poll taxes and lynching. The committee's recommendations are commonly referred to as a program of "civil rights legislation."

Gains in the promotion of civil rights. During World War II, President Roosevelt, by executive order, set up a federal Fair Employment Practices Committee (FEPC). Its function was to provide to minority groups, especially Negroes, equal opportunities for work in factories having war contracts. The FEPC demonstrated that whites and Negroes could work side by side without serious friction. Although Truman urged creation of a permanent committee it was discontinued when the war ended. In 1945 New York passed the Ives-Quinn law, which set up a Fair Employment Practices Committee for that state. This committee has had marked success in overcoming discrimination based on race and religion. Several other states have created similar committees.

President Truman's support of a civil rights program led to the "Dixiecrat" revolt from the Democratic party in 1948 (page 635). Although several civil rights bills passed the House of Representatives, filibusters by Southern Democrats blocked their passage by the Senate. The chief argument used against these bills was the old one that federal legislation would be an unwarranted interference with the rights of the states. Others argued that the problem of prejudice and discrimination could be solved only through education and persuasion, not through legislation.

In spite of the failure of Congress to act, there were notable gains throughout the country in furthering the basic ideal of equality for all in the enjoyment of civil rights. The number of lynchings has declined markedly, from 119 in the 1930's to 29 in the 1940's. The poll tax is now a condition for voting in only five states. Today few labor unions still exclude Negroes. The armed forces have gone a long way toward integrating whites and Negroes. Various localities have taken steps to end discriminatory practices in employment and in schools, public conveyances, restaurants, and theaters. Public housing projects in some parts of the country are open equally to whites and Negroes.

The Supreme Court supports civil rights. In recent years the Supreme Court has made several important decisions dealing with civil rights. It held that private restrictive agreements prohibiting the sale of property to certain groups, while not illegal, cannot be enforced in federal or state courts (*Shelley* vs. *Kraemer*, 1948). The Court sustained the right of Negroes to take part in Southern primary elections (*Smith* vs. *Allwright*, 1944); it held that segregation in railroad dining cars was improper (*Henderson* vs. *the United States*, 1950). In 1953 the Court ruled that restaurants in the District of Columbia could not legally refuse to serve meals to Negroes.

The most far-reaching decisions deal with discrimination in public education. In 1896 the Supreme Court had ruled (*Plessy* vs. *Ferguson*) that laws which required segregation of races in schools and public conveyances were constitutional if "equal facilities" were provided for all. In recent years the Court began to apply the doctrine of separate but equal facilities with extreme care. Thus in 1950 (*Sweatt* vs. *Painter*), the Court ruled that Texas could not exclude Negroes from the all-white University of Texas Law School since the Texas State Law School for Negroes did not provide "equal" facilities. In deciding the facilities of the two schools were not equal, the Court took into consideration such factors as the size of the library, scholarship funds, the number of students and teachers, and the prestige of the university. The Supreme Court also ruled in 1950 (*McLaurin* vs. *Oklahoma*) that the University of Oklahoma Graduate School could not require Negro students to use special seats in the classroom, library, and cafeteria. Since 1950 many Southern colleges have opened their graduate schools to Negroes.

The Supreme Court rules against segregation in schools. These decisions were in a sense preliminary to the important historical decision rendered by the Supreme Court in 1954. The decisions of several lower courts upholding segregation in public schools were appealed to the Supreme Court. The legal briefs presenting these appeals claimed that the fundamental issue was not the nature of the facilities provided for whites and Negroes, but the basic fact of segregation itself. These cases attacked head-on the 1896 doctrine of "separate but equal facilities." In a unanimous decision (May 17) the Supreme Court reversed the doctrine of *Plessy* vs. *Ferguson* and ruled that segregation itself violated the Fourteenth Amendment, arguing that "separate educational facilities are inherently unequal." The Court, realizing that its decision would involve a drastic social revolution in several areas, indicated that it would accept briefs from interested parties as to when and how the decision would be implemented. A year later the Court ruled that states and communities should comply with the decision "within a reasonable time." It also directed that the lower federal courts should be used by parties seeking compliance with the desegregation ruling.

Some communities, including the District of Columbia, immediately began to plan for desegregation of their school systems. On the other hand, some states indicated that they would not comply with the decision. Some governors, senators, and representatives supported this defiance of the Supreme Court. They invoked the old doctrine of states' rights. Once again arguments that had been advanced at the time of the Virginia and Kentucky Resolutions and of the Lincoln-Douglas debates became the subject matter of editorials, speeches, and heated exposition in prosegregation and antisegregation rallies.

The desegregation ruling of the Supreme Court and its aftermath focused the attention of the whole country on the fundamental issue of civil rights. International relations were affected by subsequent developments; so, too, were national and local politics. Some progress toward desegregation was made in many areas; however, in other areas, defiant opposition provoked violence and a series of moves and counter-moves by state and federal authorities. (See pages 703–705.)

Federal aid for schools is defeated. The Eisenhower administration attempted to obtain federal aid for schools by avoiding the issues that had prevented action in the past. (See page 634.) It proposed that the federal government should allocate funds to help states and localities build school buildings. Since new schools were greatly

A MODERN SCHOOL, *typical of the well-lighted, spacious buildings being built to-day.* (Lockwood Schools, District #26, Yellowstone County, Montana)

needed, this bill had bipartisan support and seemed sure of passage. However, an amendment was added to the bill providing that states which refused to "desegregate" in compliance with the Supreme Court decision would not receive federal funds. To the great disappointment of many, the amended bill failed of passage. Federal aid to education, like the farm problem and civil rights, is likely to be an issue for some time to come. (See page 702.)

The principle of separation of church and state. The question of the separation of church and state, which was a factor in the debate over federal aid, has come before the Supreme Court in various ways. Oregon once required all children between the ages of eight and sixteen to attend public schools. In 1925 the Supreme Court (*Pierce* vs. *The Society of Sisters*) declared the Oregon law unconstitutional on the ground that it was contrary to the provision of the Fourteenth Amendment which forbids a state to deprive a person of liberty without due process of law. In this case the court held that the Oregon law was an unreasonable interference with the liberty of parents to direct the education of their children.

More recently many states have enacted laws permitting children to be released from schools one hour a week to receive religious instruction in their own faith. The nature of the released-time program varies in different parts of the country. In Champaign, Illinois, the Board of Education allowed the different religious denominations to use the school building during the released hour to instruct in their own faith those children whose parents requested such instruction. In *McCullom* vs. *the Board of Education* (1948), the Supreme Court (8 to 1) declared this local practice unconstitutional on the ground that so to use school property for a religious purpose was contrary to the principle of separation of church and state as expressed in the First Amendment. However, in 1952 the Supreme Court (*Zorach* vs. *Clauson*) ruled that the released-time program in New York City was constitutional. New York City children did not receive religious instruction on school property but in churches or private property located near the school building. In this case Mr. Justice Douglas, writing the majority opinion, stated:

> We are a religious people whose institutions presuppose a Supreme Being. We guarantee the freedom to worship as one chooses. . . . When the state encourages religious instruction or co-operates with religious authorities by adjusting the schedule of public events to sectarian needs, it follows the best of our traditions. For it then respects the religious nature of our people and accommodates the public service to their spiritual needs. . . . We cannot read into the Bill of Rights . . . a philosophy of hostility to religion.

THE COLD WAR TROUBLES THE EISENHOWER ADMINISTRATION

New faces appear, but the old issues remain. Stalin died in March, 1953. His successor, Georgi Malenkov, resigned in February, 1955, when a new group of leaders took over control of affairs in Russia. Nikita S. Khrushchev became party boss, Nikolai Bulganin, Premier, and Georgi K. Zhukov, Minister of Defense. The friction between East and West continued. New trouble spots and new crises developed, but the basic difficulties remained. Many Americans believed that the United States no longer had pre-eminent power in atomic weapons and that Russian industrial and technical strength had made great progress. Russia began to compete with the United States in extending economic and military aid and trade opportunities to certain countries, particularly those which were neutral in the "cold war."

We have already noted (page 681) that an armistice, but not peace, was achieved in Korea. North and South Korea were not united. After civil war, fostered by Communists from within and without, had ravaged Vietnam for a few years, French troops there were defeated; France was forced to permit Communists to acquire control of North Vietnam. The issue of the admission of Red China to the

United Nations was not settled. The Chinese Nationalists remained in control of Formosa, in spite of Red China's expressed determination to dislodge them. Early in 1955 the possibility of hostilities in this area was so acute that President Eisenhower asked Congress to authorize the use of force to prevent Red China from invading Formosa. Although some argued that such a use of force would lead to a third world war, Congress gave approval by a vote of 85 to 3 in the Senate and 409 to 3 in the House of Representatives. Possibly because of this overwhelming indication that the United States was ready to fight, Red China took no action against Formosa.

In attempting to woo the "neutralist countries" of the Far East and Near East, Russia alternated aid and promises with threats. Secretary Dulles countered some of the Soviet threats by bringing into existence the Southeast Asia Treaty Organization (SEATO). Its members were Pakistan, Thailand, the Philippines, Australia, New Zealand, Great Britain, France, and the United States.

In 1955 Russia at long last agreed to a peace treaty with Austria, thus ending ten years of occupation. However, Russia remained deaf to all pleas for a union of East and West Germany. The United States countered by strengthening the ties between West Germany and the West. West Germany became a member of NATO (see page 673) and was permitted to rearm. While Chancellor Adenauer based his policy on alliance with the West, his opponents urged a united and neutral Germany.

In the Near East the Soviets made the most of the continuing rivalry between the Israelis and the Arabs and began to supply military and economic aid to Egypt and other members of the Arab League. Shortly after the United States announced that it would not help finance the construction of a projected dam in Egypt, Prime Minister Gamel Nasser "nationalized" the Suez Canal. His action created international tension and led to a series of international conferences and negotiations.

In October, 1956, Israeli forces invaded Egypt, occupying the Gaza strip and the Sinai peninsula. England and France forcefully landed troops in Egypt in an effort to compel Nasser to restore the international status of the Suez Canal. The United States condemned these actions and supported the decision of the U.N. to send an international police force to Egypt. Reluctantly the Israelis, the French, and the English agreed to withdraw their units when U.N. troops were ready to take their place. Strangely enough the United States, in criticizing its allies, England and France, had the support of Russia, which endeavored to use the Suez crisis to increase its prestige in the Middle East. The U.N. troops in Egypt succeeded in their mission.

Eisenhower advocates "atoms for peace." Efforts to achieve agreement on the international control of atomic energy remained deadlocked. In December, 1953, speaking before the General Assembly of the United Nations, President Eisenhower proposed that all nations, including Russia, should co-operate to develop the peacetime uses of atomic energy. The Soviet Union found fault with his proposal of an international atomic stockpile to make nuclear materials available for research purposes. Yet it indicated that it would be willing to study the idea. By the Atomic Energy Act of 1954 Congress authorized the President to join with other nations in creating an international atomic pool for peaceful purposes. Without Russian consent or participation in the general plan, the United States gave fissionable materials to several NATO nations. To co-operate in peaceful atomic research six small European countries established an organization known as "Euratom."

A conference "at the summit" raises hopes. England's Prime Minister Winston Churchill, as early as 1953, strongly urged a face-to-face meeting of the heads of states engaged in the "cold war" as a way of easing world tension. The new Russian leaders, the United States, and France all accepted the suggestion. The meeting "at the summit," as it was called, was held at Geneva in July, 1955. Outwardly there was cordial good will and seemingly a determination on the part of all present to find a satisfactory method of "co-existence." President Eisenhower dominated the Geneva Conference. He captured the imagination of the world by proposing that Russia and the United States frankly exchange their military plans and permit mutual aerial inspection of their respective military installations. The conference adjourned in apparent good spirits, leaving to a conference of foreign ministers discussion of the unification of Germany and the aerial inspection of military installations.

The Russians attack the "cult of Stalinism." The foreign ministers' conference failed to maintain the "spirit of Geneva" or to bring about any real settlement of outstanding issues. It became known that while Russia was pretending to be interested in peace and disarmament, it was shipping munitions to the countries of the explosive Middle East. In spite of the failure of the conference, there were evidences that Soviet strategy or tactics had changed. Russia apparently adopted a "soft policy," either to lure the West to let down its guard or to win neutralists to its side.

In the summer of 1955 there began an exchange of visitors between the "East" and the "West." Russian agricultural experts were allowed to visit the United States; American farmers traveled in Russia. Meanwhile a limited number of other foreign visitors were permitted to visit Russia. General Twining accepted Russia's invitation to be present at a special exhibition of Russian aerial strength in the summer of 1956. Russian leaders made good will tours to the countries of Southeast Asia as well as to Yugoslavia. Marshal Tito of Yugoslavia was feted in Russia. Russian "smiles and wiles" puzzled the statesmen of the West.

Still more puzzling was the action of Khrushchev and other Russian leaders in openly criticizing Stalin's regime at the Twentieth Congress of the Communist party in Russia (February 1956). Stalin's leadership of Russia was repudiated; Stalin himself was painted as a brutal, bloody, and dictatorial tyrant. This shift from worship of Stalin to complete downgrading shocked the Communists in other countries. But gradually the "faithful" began to accept the "new party line," to the effect that any of the failings of communism, either within or outside of Russia, should be attributed to the ruthless tyrant Stalin and not to communism itself. The "new line" seemed to say to the world, "Rejoice with us that the evil Stalin is dead, and co-operate with us in promoting peace and democracy in the world."

While the West closely watched these internal maneuvers, Western leaders did not let down their guard, for they doubted that the new line indicated any fundamental change in Russian policy. In June 1956 the Central Committee of the Communist party, reviewing the reactions in different countries to Russia's denunciation of the "personality cult," frankly warned:

> Let the bourgeois ideologists concoct fables about "crimes" of communism, and about "confusion" in the ranks of the Communist party. We are used to hearing such incantations by the enemies. Their forecasts always burst like soapbubbles. Luckless forecasters like these have come and gone, but the Communist movement, the immortal and life-giving ideas of Marxism-Leninism, triumphed and are continuing to triumph. This will also be the case in the future. No foul, slanderous attacks of our enemies can stop the irresistible trend of the historical development of mankind toward communism.

In November, 1956, the Communists once again gave evidence to the world of the determination expressed in this quotation. At that time Russia ruthlessly intervened with tanks and troops to crush the efforts of Hungary to free itself from the Soviet yoke. Thousands of Hungarians sought refuge in Austria, but many were deported to Russia. The United States agreed to admit 21,500 Hungarian refugees. The General Assembly of the United Nations condemned Russia's actions. Even Tito of Yugoslavia, though apparently restored to favor in Russia, criticized Russia. So, too, did some of the "neutralist" nations like India. A few Communists in Western countries resigned from the party in protest against its policy in Hungary. There was some speculation that events in Hungary might force Russian leaders to return to "Stalinism."

PRESIDENT EISENHOWER *thanks Republican Committee workers for their efforts in the 1956 campaign.* (*United Press Photo*)

EISENHOWER IS ELECTED TO A SECOND TERM

The Republicans depend on Eisenhower for victory. Republican party leaders believed that their success in 1956 depended on Ike's willingness to seek a second term. Their hopes fell in September, 1955, when the President suffered a heart attack. The President made a slow but steady recovery and party leaders were jubilant when he announced early in 1956 that he would run again. They were worried again in June, 1956, when the President had to undergo abdominal surgery. His normal recovery from this second illness reassured them, and by the time of the Republican Convention, Republican leaders were confident that Ike would be re-elected.

The President's illness directed attention to Vice-President Richard M. Nixon, who did not have the whole-hearted support of Republican leaders. But the President expressed confidence in Nixon, who let it be known that he wanted to run a second time. The Republican Convention at San Francisco nominated both men unanimously.

The Democrats select Stevenson and Kefauver. In 1955 Adlai E. Stevenson announced that he would again seek the Democratic nomination; Senator Estes Kefauver of Tennessee also wanted the nomination. Both men campaigned for delegates to the Democratic Convention in states which held presidential primary elections. Kefauver won a few delegates, but was defeated by Stevenson in such key states as Oregon and California. The Chicago Convention of the Democratic party selected Stevenson as their presidential nominee on the first ballot. After a close contest with Senator John F. Kennedy of Massachusetts, Kefauver was selected as the vice-presidential nominee.

Eisenhower is re-elected. Stevenson and Kefauver waged a vigorous campaign appealing to local interests in different sections of the country. Mr. Stevenson tried to arouse national enthusiasm by urging elimination of the draft and discontinuance of hydrogen bomb tests "as soon as practicable." These suggestions boomeranged in the last days of the campaign when developments in Poland, Hungary, and Egypt aroused fears that the cold war might become a hot one. The President limited his campaign to a few key speeches; Nixon did the heavy campaigning for the Republicans.

As in 1952, the outcome of the 1956 election was an overwhelming endorsement of Eisenhower, but not the Republican party. Eisenhower's landslide victory did not result in the election of a Republican Congress. The voters gave control of both houses of the Eighty-fifth Congress (1957–1958) to the Democratic party.

What happens if the President is too ill to serve? More than any other President, Mr. Eisenhower had encouraged the Vice-President to become actively identified with the policies of his administration. The illnesses of the President focused attention on the constitutional question concerning the succession to the Presidency in the event of the President's incapacity. This problem was not definitely resolved, although President Eisenhower, and President Truman before him, urged that the matter be clarified either by Congressional action or by constitutional amendment. It was argued that the precise point where executive authority rested during the temporary or prolonged incapacity of the President was too important to be left to chance.

JUNEAU, ALASKA. *The newest state capital. Congress passed the Alaska State-hood Bill in 1958, and early in 1959 President Eisenhower proclaimed Alaska the 49th state.*

An economic recession develops. An economic decline began in 1957 and continued into 1958. Layoffs in industrial plants made unemployment a serious problem. Creeping inflation added to the nation's economic woes. To check the economic down-turn, the administration took steps to make credit more easily available, encouraged federal housing projects and private home building, extended weekly unemployment insurance benefits, and increased federal expenditures for defense. The administration, however, did not support the proposal of many business and political leaders for tax reduction. One exception to the gloomy economic picture in 1957 and 1958 was the improvement in farm income.

At the time of the mid-term elections of 1958, signs were beginning to appear that the economic recession had run its course, and that the country with a population of 175,000,000 was on the way to another period of prosperity. However, inflation continued to be a matter of grave concern.

The Eighty-fifth Congress. Although controlled by Democrats, the Eighty-fifth Congress accepted a large part of President Eisenhower's program. Appropriations for foreign aid were continued in substantial amounts. The Reciprocal Trade Program was extended for a four-year period. Social security benefits were increased. Congress provided for the admission of Alaska as the forty-ninth state. It also yielded to the President's request for power to streamline the military establishment, more clearly defining the powers and functions of the Secretary of Defense, the Joint Chiefs of Staff, and the three branches of the armed forces. Congress also created a civilian National Aeronautics and Space Administration charged with the responsibility for co-ordinating programs and research into outer space.

The Civil Rights Bill. Probably the most important legislation of the first session of the Eighty-fifth Congress was the enactment of a civil rights law (1957). This law set up a bipartisan Civil Rights Commission, and also provided for an additional Assistant Attorney General to assist the Commission in dealing with the legal aspects of civil rights. The Civil Rights Commission was authorized to investigate instances of the denial of the right to vote or of interference with "equal protection of the law," because of race, color, religion, or national origin. In effect, the Civil Rights Act of 1957 established procedures which would safeguard the voting privileges and civil rights of citizens.

Federal aid to education. The second session of the Eighty-fifth Congress appropriated large sums, for a four-year period, to assist education. The National Defense Education Act of 1958 was somewhat different from earlier proposals for federal aid to education. The act appropriated funds to be given to the states, usually on a "matching" basis, to strengthen science, mathematics, and foreign language instruction, to improve guidance, counseling, and testing services, to help in the identification and encouragement of able students, to experiment in the use of television, radio, and motion pictures for educational purposes, and to improve the statistical services of state educational agencies. The law also provides fellowships for graduate study and permits colleges to arrange for students to borrow up to $1000 a year, to a total of $5000 for tuition, books, and living expenses. Although the loan fund is available to all students, colleges are urged to give consideration to able students who plan to teach or who show special ability in science, mathematics, engineering, or modern foreign languages. Loans can be repaid in a ten-year period, beginning one year after graduation; if a student goes into teaching, up to fifty per cent of the loan is canceled at the rate of ten per cent per year.

CONGRESS INVESTIGATES BASEBALL. *Casey Stengel testifies before a congressional subcommittee looking into possible violations of the Anti-Trust Act by major league baseball. Mickey Mantle and Ted Williams are ready to back up his statements.*

Investigating committees. Congressional investigating committees, which have become an important part of the legislative process, attracted public attention. One, under the chairmanship of Senator McClellan, investigating labor and management relations, unearthed some unsavory practices in a few labor unions.

Another Congressional committee revealed that Bernard Goldfine, a New England industrialist, had been lavish with gifts apparently in the hope that he might obtain government favors. Mr. Sherman Adams, Assistant to the President, admitted that his acceptance of Mr. Goldfine's gifts had been "imprudent" but denied any wrongdoing. Mr. Adams resigned as Presidential Assistant on the ground that his continuance in office would hurt the election campaigns of Republican candidates for office.

Desegregation. One of the most important domestic issues of Mr. Eisenhower's second term was the series of incidents surrounding the implementation of the Supreme Court rulings of 1954 and 1955 concerning desegregation in the schools. As noted earlier some school districts which had maintained separate schools for whites and Ne-

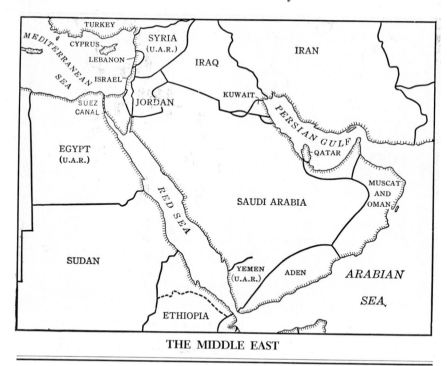

THE MIDDLE EAST

groes proceeded to provide for "integrated" schools. Some did it forthwith; others developed moderate and gradual plans. Some refused to take any action at all. A dramatic crisis developed in Little Rock, Arkansas. There the school board provided for the admission of a few Negro students to the Central High School for September, 1957. However, Governor Faubus called out the Arkansas National Guard to prevent the admission of the Negro students, claiming that this action was necessary to avoid violence and disorder. Regarding the action of Governor Faubus as a direct challenge to federal authority, President Eisenhower ordered federal troops to Little Rock, Arkansas, to maintain order and to protect the Negro students attending Central High School. He also ordered the National Guard of Arkansas into federal service. Throughout 1957–1958 federal troops remained in Little Rock and the Negro students attended Central High School. As the school term closed federal troops were withdrawn. As the September 1958 school term approached, Governor Faubus sought through various court actions to prevent the return of Negro students to Central High School. He lost three court battles, one of which involved a decision of the Supreme Court to the effect that there should be no delay in proceeding with integration at Little Rock. However, school was not reopened on schedule. Private school corporations were hurriedly organized to operate schools, but were denied the right to use public school facilities.

Elsewhere in the South "desegregation" provoked tension, disorder, and court actions. Four years after the Supreme Court decision of 1954, confusion and uncertainty prevailed as to when and how school integration would become a reality in several communities.

The Eisenhower Doctrine. Foreign affairs continued to command a great deal of attention during Eisenhower's second term. We have already noted (pages 696–697) that serious trouble developed in the Middle East where Russian propaganda, along with financial and military aid, strengthened the leadership of Colonel Nasser, the strong man in Egypt and the Arab world.

As the Suez crisis of 1956 quieted down, President Eisenhower asked Congress for authority to send troops to any nation threatened by international communism, provided the threatened nation requested such help. After considerable debate, Congress approved what has come to be called the Eisenhower Doctrine. The situation in the Middle East remained tense and uncertain. Nasser organized the United Arab Republic consisting of Egypt, Syria, and Yemen, and forged closer ties with Russia. By these actions, Nasser hoped to undermine the influence of the nations associated in the Baghdad Pact — Iraq, Turkey, Pakistan, Iran, and Great Britain. In 1958 it was an-

THE NUCLEAR–POWERED USS SKATE *explored the Arctic Ocean under the polar ice. The Navy is now building nuclear-powered surface ships, which will sail for years without refueling.*

nounced that Russia would lend money to help Nasser finance the construction of the Aswan Dam. American withdrawal from the financing of this project was one of the factors which had precipitated the nationalization of the Suez Canal and the crisis of 1956.

Soviet versus American prestige. International communism suffered a temporary setback by the denunciation of the "cult" of Stalinism in February, 1956, and by uprisings in Poland and Hungary in the fall of 1956 (page 699). The ruthless and brutal suppression of the revolt in Hungary by Russian troops temporarily weakened Russian influence in neutralist countries. As time passed, Russia through increasing propaganda, and financial and military help, seemed able to regain and extend its influence. Khrushchev emerged as the "boss" of Russia and, through force, the mutual exchange of "state visits," trade agreements, and financial aid strengthened the Russian "bloc."

The Suez crisis, along with Russia's growing military, industrial, and scientific strength, had its effect on the NATO alliance. France, weakened by defeats in Indo-China, by the Egyptian fiasco, and by continued disturbances in Algiers, was torn by internal dissension. In the summer of 1958 France accepted the leadership of General Charles de Gaulle who proceeded to organize the Fifth French Republic. England, too, was chagrined by events in the Middle East, and was alarmed by Russia's developing military and economic strength.

Russian success in launching the first artificial satellite in 1957 awakened Americans from their lethargy. Hostile demonstrations greeted Vice-President Nixon in Peru and Venezuela while on a "good-will" tour of South America in 1958. Americans began to realize that their prestige in different parts of the world was at low ebb, and that vigorous action was necessary to win the respect and confidence of people in many areas.

The Middle East crisis of 1958. In July, 1958, a violent revolution in oil-rich Iraq led to the assassination of the King and the quick establishment of a government friendly to the Pan-Arab nationalism of Colonel Nasser of Egypt. It appeared as though Nasser was succeeding in weakening the influence of the Baghdad Pact, and that the revolution might spread to nearby Lebanon and Jordan. Upon the request of the Lebanese President, the United States landed marines in Lebanon. England flew troops into Jordan. Nasser and Khrushchev accused the United States and England of armed aggression

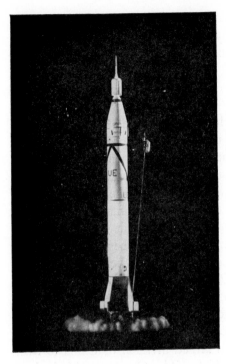

A JUPITER–C *rocket launches the tiny Explorer I satellite. By the end of 1958 the United States had put into orbit a 4½ ton satellite, by far the largest to that date.*

and demanded the immediate withdrawal of American and British forces. The crisis was referred to an emergency session of the General Assembly which met in mid-August, 1958. President Eisenhower suggested the following proposals: the United Nations should take adequate measures to preserve peace in Lebanon and Jordan, and to check indirect aggression from without; a comprehensive program of regional economic development should be developed; and the United Nations should take measures to check an arms race in the Middle East. Rather surprisingly, the Arab States proposed an acceptable compromise, stating that they would accept the services of a U.N. observer team in the Middle East and would not resort to force to compel the withdrawal of American and British forces. For their part England and the United States agreed to withdraw their forces as soon as practicable. By late October 1958 American troops were withdrawn from Lebanon, and England had withdrawn from Jordan.

The Quemoy crisis in the Far East, 1958. Tension over the Middle East had scarcely subsided, when, on August 23, 1958, Chinese guns on the mainland began a heavy bombardment of the island of

Quemoy. Matsu and Quemoy are small islands a few miles off the China coast which were held by Chinese Nationalist forces under Chiang Kai-shek. The main stronghold of Nationalist China was the island of Formosa (or Taiwan). In the 1955 crisis in the Far East, Congress had voted approval to the use of force to prevent Red China from invading Formosa. The bombardment of Quemoy in 1958 raised the question as to whether the United States would use force to prevent the seizure of the small off-shore islands by Red China. While there seemed to be general agreement that the islands of Quemoy and Matsu were not strategically important to Nationalist China or to the United States, it was argued that the abandonment of these small islands under the threat of force might mark the beginning of the end of American influence in the Far East; it was believed that Red China, at some time in the future, would begin an aggressive attack on Formosa itself, and that the way was being prepared for ultimate domination of the Far East by Red China.

The United States reaffirmed its support of Formosa, but suggested that Chiang Kai-shek should reduce his forces on Quemoy and also secured a public announcement from Chiang Kai-shek that he did not plan to use Formosa to launch an armed invasion of China to overthrow the government of Red China. The Quemoy crisis had not subsided, when Khrushchev shifted the scene of tension by demanding the withdrawal of American and British forces from West Berlin. The Suez crisis, the Middle East crisis, the Far East crisis, and the new Berlin crisis were all regarded as aspects of the tensions resulting from the cold war between East and West.

The mid-term election of 1958. The trend to the Democratic party revealed by the capture of control of the Eighty-fifth Congress in 1956, in spite of Eisenhower's overwhelming victory, was emphasized by the mid-term elections of 1958. The chief issues, apart from special local issues, were the economic recession and foreign affairs. The Democrats won a resounding triumph, obtaining control of the Eighty-sixth Congress, 1959–1960, by a wide margin; in the Senate the Democrats would have 64 members to 34 for the Republicans; in the House, the Democrats would have 283 members to 153 for the Republicans. The Democrats were jubilant and looked forward to success in the presidential campaign of 1960.

❁ ❁ ❁

To identify: Ezra Taft Benson, John Foster Dulles, Mrs. Oveta Culp Hobby, Estes Kefauver, Nikita Khrushchev, Colonel Nasser, "Mr. Republican," Adlai E. Stevenson.

To explain or define: civil rights, desegregation, economic controls, excess profits tax, flexible price supports, offshore oil deposits, St. Lawrence Seaway, "separate but equal facilities," soil bank.

Subjects for Talks or Written Reports

1. The way delegates to national nominating conventions are selected.
2. The factions within the Republican party in 1952 and since. 3. The factions within the Democratic party in 1952 and since. 4. History and management of the federal debt. 5. The functions of the Department of Health, Education, and Welfare. 6. The Eisenhower campaign in the South in 1952. 7. Stevenson's campaigns in 1952 and 1956. 8. The career and influence of Senator Taft. 9. The conference at the summit. 10. "Atoms for Peace." 11. Egypt's "nationalization" of the Suez Canal. 12. "Neutralism" in the cold war. 13. The revolt in Hungary. 14. Earth satellites. 15. Presidential incapacity.

Questions for Understanding the Text

1. Why was Senator Taft regarded as the "logical" candidate for the Republican nomination in 1952? 2. Why did some members of his own party object to him as a candidate? 3. Why did the Republicans turn to General Eisenhower rather than to some other prominent Republican? 4. How do you account for General Eisenhower's voting strength in the Solid South in 1952 and 1956? 5. Why was the election of 1952 an Eisenhower rather than a Republican victory? 6. What disposition did Congress make of the offshore oil controversy? 7. Why did the Dixon-Yates contract provoke controversy? 8. Describe the St. Lawrence Seaway and Power Project. 9. What gains have been made in the promotion of civil rights? 10. What was the effect of the decision of the Supreme Court in 1896 concerning "separate but equal facilities"? 11. What was the decision of the Supreme Court in 1954 concerning segregation in the public schools? In 1955 concerning the implementation of this decision? 12. What have been the effects of these decisions? 13. Explain the provisions of the farm legislation of 1956. 14. What social welfare laws were sponsored by the Eisenhower administration? 15. How did the Communist "party line" shift after the death of Stalin? 16. What new crises in the cold war developed during Eisenhower's administration? 17. What

were the issues in the presidential campaign of 1956? 18. What were the provisions of the Civil Rights Act of 1957? Of the National Defense Education Act of 1958?

ACTIVITIES FOR UNIT ELEVEN

1. Prepare an exhibit on our trade with the rest of the world and discuss its importance to our own and other nations' prosperity.
2. Prepare a list of the chief foreign problems faced by the United States today. Discuss possible solutions for each problem you list.
3. Make diagrams or charts to illustrate changes in the national debt, the cost of living, the national income, the cost of national defense, the cost of foreign military and economic aid, the size of the armed services in the past ten years.
4. Have two different committees draw up a list of items they would like to see in Republican and Democratic platforms.
5. Hold a panel discussion on the influence of Senator McCarthy.
6. Debate the question of retaining the veto power in the Security Council.
7. List the mutual security pacts of which the United States is a member. Explain the reasons for each pact.
8. Investigate and report on the details surrounding the dismissal of General MacArthur. Evaluate the reasons for his dismissal in the light of the facts available at the time (April, 1951), and in the light of the facts available at the time the class holds its discussion.
9. On an outline map of the world indicate the "hot spots" where tension has developed in the cold war.
10. Arrange a display of cartoons dealing with current foreign and domestic problems. Explain each cartoon and discuss its effectiveness.
11. Investigate and report on compliance with the Supreme Court ruling on desegregation.
12. Investigate and report on the peacetime developments in the field of atomic energy. Developments in the exploration of outer space.
13. Formulate the arguments for and against a program of general federal aid to education. Did the National Defense Education Act of 1958 provide an answer to these arguments?
14. Hold a panel discussion on developments toward the international control of nuclear weapons.
15. Summarize the gains made by labor since the close of World War II.
16. Outline the important social and economic changes that have taken place in the United States in the past ten years. What issues or problems have developed as a result of these changes?

READINGS FOR UNIT ELEVEN

Stars indicate the easier books.

Allen, F. L. *The Big Change, America Transforms Itself: 1900–1950.* Harper.

*Arne, Sigrid. *United Nations Primer: The Key to the Conferences.* Rinehart.

Bailey, T. A. *America Faces Russia.* Cornell University Press.

Baxter, J. P. *Scientists against Time.* Little, Brown.

Bush, Vannevar. *Modern Arms and Free Men.* Simon and Schuster.

Chase, E. P. *The United Nations in Action.* McGraw-Hill.

Dietz, David. *Atomic Energy in the Coming Era.* Dodd, Mead.

*Donovan, R. J. *Eisenhower: The Inside Story.* Harper.

Dulles, F. R. *America's Rise to World Power, 1898–1954.* Crowell.

Fischer, John. *Why They Behave Like Russians.* Harper.

*Gitlow, B. *The Whole of Their Lives; Communism in America.* Scribner.

Gunther, John. *Behind the Curtain.* Harper.

——. *Inside Russia Today.* Harper.

*Higgins, Marguerite. *The War in Korea: The Report of a Woman Combat Correspondent.* Doubleday.

Hoover, J. Edgar. *Masters of Deceit: The Story of Communism in America and How to Fight It.* Holt.

Kennan, G. F. *American Diplomacy, 1900–1950.* University of Chicago Press.

Leyson, B. W. *Atomic Energy in War and Peace.* Dutton.

Lilienthal, David E. *This I Do Believe.* Harper.

*Martin, J. B. *Adlai Stevenson.* Harper.

Mills, C. W., and Schneider, H. *The New Men of Power: America's Labor Leaders.* Harcourt, Brace.

Oliver, R. T. *Why War Came in Korea.* McMullen.

Petrov, Vladimir. *My Retreat from Russia.* Yale University Press.

*Philbrick, H. A. *I Led Three Lives.* Grosset.

President's Commission on Civil Rights. *To Secure These Rights.* Simon and Schuster.

**Primer on Communism.* Anti-Defamation League of B'nai B'rith.

Roosevelt, E., and Ferris, H. *Partners: The United Nations and Youth.* Doubleday.

*Rovere, R. N., and Schlesinger, A. M. Jr. *The General and the President.* Farrar, Straus.

Wahlke, J. C., editor. *Loyalty in a Democratic State.* Heath.

White, T. H. *Fire in the Ashes: Europe in Mid-Century.* Sloane.

APPENDIX

DECLARATION OF INDEPENDENCE

IN CONGRESS, JULY 4, 1776

A Declaration by the Representatives of the United States of America, in Congress Assembled

When, in the course of human events, it becomes necessary for one people to dissolve the political bands which have connected them with another, and to assume, among the powers of the earth, the separate and equal station to which the laws of nature and of nature's God entitle them, a decent respect to the opinions of mankind requires that they should declare the causes which impel them to the separation.

We hold these truths to be self-evident: That all men are created equal; that they are endowed by their Creator with certain unalienable rights; that among these are life, liberty, and the pursuit of happiness. That, to secure these rights, governments are instituted among men, deriving their just powers from the consent of the governed; that, whenever any form of government becomes destructive of these ends, it is the right of the people to alter or to abolish it, and to institute a new government, laying its foundation on such principles, and organizing its powers in such form, as to them shall seem most likely to effect their safety and happiness. Prudence, indeed, will dictate that governments long established should not be changed for light and transient causes; and accordingly all experience hath shown that mankind are more disposed to suffer while evils are sufferable, than to right themselves by abolishing the forms to which they are accustomed. But when a long train of abuses and usurpations, pursuing invariably the same object, evinces a design to reduce them under absolute despotism, it is their right, it is their duty, to throw off such government, and to provide new guards for their future security. Such has been the patient sufferance of these colonies; and such is now the necessity which constrains them to alter their former systems of government. The history of the present King of Great Britain is a history of repeated injuries and usurpations, all having in direct object the establishment of an absolute tyranny over these states. To prove this, let facts be submitted to a candid world.

He has refused his assent to laws the most wholesome and necessary for the public good.

He has forbidden his governors to pass laws of immediate and pressing importance, unless suspended in their operation till his assent should be obtained; and, when so suspended, he has utterly neglected to attend to them.

He has refused to pass other laws for the accommodation of large districts of people, unless those people would relinquish the right of representation in the legislature, — a right inestimable to them, and formidable to tyrants only.

He has called together legislative bodies at places unusual, uncomfortable, and distant from the depository of their public records, for the sole purpose of fatiguing them into compliance with his measure.

He has dissolved representative houses repeatedly, for opposing, with manly firmness, his invasions on the rights of the people.

He has refused, for a long time after such dissolutions, to cause others to be elected, whereby the legislative powers, incapable of annihilation, have returned to the people at large for their exercise; the state remaining, in the mean time, exposed to all the dangers of invasions from without and convulsions within.

He has endeavored to prevent the population of these states; for that purpose obstructing the laws for the naturalization of foreigners, refusing to pass others to encourage their migration hither, and raising the conditions of new appropriations of lands.

He has obstructed the administration of justice, by refusing his assent to laws for establishing judiciary powers.

He has made judges dependent on his will alone for the tenure of their offices, and the amount and payment of their salaries.

He has erected a multitude of new offices, and sent hither swarms of officers to harass our people and eat out their substance.

He has kept among us in times of peace standing armies, without the consent of our legislatures.

He has affected to render the military independent of, and superior to, the civil power.

He has combined with others to subject us to a jurisdiction foreign to our constitutions and unacknowledged by our laws, giving his assent to their acts of pretended legislation:

For quartering large bodies of armed troops among us;

For protecting them, by a mock trial, from punishment for any murders which they should commit on the inhabitants of these states;

For cutting off our trade with all parts of the world;

For imposing taxes on us without our consent;

For depriving us, in many cases, of the benefits of trial by jury;

For transporting us beyond seas, to be tried for pretended offenses;

For abolishing the free system of English laws in a neighboring province, establishing therein an arbitrary government, and enlarging its boundaries, so as to render it at once an example and fit instrument for introducing the same absolute rule into these colonies;

For taking away our charters, abolishing our most valuable laws, and altering, fundamentally, the forms of our governments;

For suspending our own legislatures, and declaring themselves invested with power to legislate for us in all cases whatsoever.

He has abdicated government here, by declaring us out of his protection and waging war against us.

He has plundered our seas, ravaged our coasts, burned our towns, and destroyed the lives of our people.

He is at this time transporting large armies of foreign mercenaries to complete the works of death, desolation, and tyranny already begun with circumstances of cruelty and perfidy scarcely paralleled in the most barbarous ages, and totally unworthy the head of a civilized nation.

He has constrained our fellow-citizens, taken captive on the high seas, to bear arms against their country, to become the executioners of their friends and brethren, or to fall themselves by their hands.

He has excited domestic insurrection among us, and has endeavored to bring on the inhabitants of our frontiers the merciless Indian savages, whose known rule of warfare is an undistinguished destruction of all ages, sexes, and conditions.

In every stage of these oppressions we have petitioned for redress in the most humble terms; our repeated petitions have been answered only by repeated injury. A prince whose character is thus marked by every act which may define a tyrant is unfit to be the ruler of a free people.

Nor have we been wanting in our attentions to our British brethren. We have warned them, from time to time, of attempts by their legislature to extend an unwarrantable jurisdiction over us. We have reminded them of the circumstances of our emigration and settlement here. We have appealed to their native justice and magnanimity; and we have conjured them, by the ties of our common kindred, to disavow these usurpations, which would inevitably interrupt our connections and correspondence. They, too, have been deaf to the voice of justice and consanguinity. We must, therefore, acquiesce in the necessity which denounces our separation, and hold them, as we hold the rest of mankind, enemies in war, in peace friends.

We, therefore, the representatives of the United States of America, in General Congress assembled, appealing to the Supreme Judge of the world for the rectitude of our intentions, do, in the name and by the authority of the good people of these colonies, solemnly publish and declare, That these united colonies are, and of right ought to be, free and independent states; that they are absolved from all allegiance to the British crown, and that all political connection between them and the state of Great Britain is, and ought to be, totally dissolved; and that, as free and independent states, they have full power to levy war, conclude peace, contract alliances, establish commerce, and do all other acts and things which independent states may of right do. And, for the support of this declaration, with a firm reliance on the protection of Divine Providence, we mutually pledge to each other our lives, our fortunes, and our sacred honor.

CONSTITUTION OF THE UNITED STATES
OF AMERICA

(The headings in heavy type are inserted for the reader's convenience)

PREAMBLE

The people, voting by states, establish the Union. We the people of the United States, in order to form a more perfect union, establish justice, insure domestic tranquillity, provide for the common defence, promote the general welfare, and secure the blessings of liberty to ourselves and our posterity, do ordain and establish this CONSTITUTION for the United States of America.

Article I. Legislative Department

Section I. CONGRESS

Congress consists of two houses. All legislative powers herein granted shall be vested in a Congress of the United States, which shall consist of a Senate and a House of Representatives.

Section II. HOUSE OF REPRESENTATIVES

1. The people elect their representatives. The House of Representatives shall be composed of members chosen every second year by the people of the several States, and the electors in each State shall have the qualifications requisite for electors of the most numerous branch of the State Legislature.

2. Who may be representatives? No person shall be a Representative who shall not have attained to the age of twenty-five years, and been seven years a citizen of the United States, and who shall not, when elected, be an inhabitant of that State in which he shall be chosen.

3. Representation in the House is based on population. Representatives and direct taxes [1] shall be apportioned among the several States which may be included within this Union, according to their respective numbers, which shall be determined by adding to the whole number of free persons, including those bound to service for a term of years, and excluding Indians not taxed, three fifths of all other persons.[2] The actual enumeration shall be made within three years after the first meeting of the Congress of the United States, and within every subsequent term of ten years, in such manner as they shall by law direct. The number of Representatives shall not exceed one for every thirty thousand, but each State shall have at least one Representative; and until such enumeration shall be made, the State of New Hampshire shall be entitled to choose three, Massachusetts eight, Rhode Island and Providence Plantations one, Connecticut five, New York six, New Jersey four, Pennsylvania eight, Delaware one, Maryland six, Virginia ten, North Carolina five, South Carolina five, and Georgia three.

4. Vacancies in the House are filled by election. When vacancies happen in the representation from any State, the Executive authority [3] thereof shall issue writs of election to fill such vacancies.

5. The House selects its speaker; it alone has power to impeach. The House of Representatives shall choose their Speaker and other officers; and shall have the sole power of impeachment.

Section III. SENATE

1. The Senate represents the states. The Senate of the United States shall be composed of two Senators from each State, chosen [by the legislature thereof,] [4] for six years; and each Senator shall have one vote.

2. One third of the senators are chosen every two years. Immediately after they shall be assembled in consequence of the first election, they shall be divided equally as may be into three classes. The seats of the Senators of the first class shall be vacated at the expiration of the second year, of the second class at the expiration of the fourth year, and of the third class at the expiration of the sixth year, so that one third may be chosen every second year; [and if vacancies happen by resignation or otherwise, during the recess of the legislature of any State, the Executive [5] thereof may make temporary appointments until the next meeting of the legis-

---

[1] Modified by the Sixteenth Amendment.
[2] The phrase "other persons" refers to slaves. The word "slave" appears nowhere in the Constitution. The three-fifths rule ceased to be in force when the Thirteenth Amendment was adopted.

[3] Governor.
[4] Repealed in 1913 by the Seventeenth Amendment.
[5] Governor.

lature, which shall then fill such vacancies.] 6

3. **Who may be senators?** No person shall be a Senator who shall not have attained the age of thirty years, and been nine years a citizen of the United States, and who shall not, when elected, be an inhabitant of that State for which he shall be chosen.

4. **The Vice-President presides over the Senate.** The Vice-President of the United States shall be President of the Senate, but shall have no vote, unless they be equally divided.

5. **The Senate chooses its other officers.** The Senate shall choose their other officers, and also a President *pro tempore,* in the absence of the Vice-President, or when he shall exercise the office of President of the United States.

6. **The Senate alone has power to try impeachments.** The Senate shall have the sole power to try all impeachments. When sitting for that purpose, they shall be on oath or affirmation. When the President of the United States is tried, the Chief Justice shall preside: and no person shall be convicted without the concurrence of two thirds of the members present.

7. **Conviction may result in removal from office.** Judgment in cases of impeachment shall not extend further than to removal from office, and disqualification to hold and enjoy any office of honor, trust or profit under the United States: but the party convicted shall nevertheless be liable and subject to indictment, trial, judgment and punishment, according to law.

Section IV. Election and Meetings of Congress

1. **Regulation of elections.** The times, places and manner of holding elections for Senators and Representatives shall be prescribed in each State by the legislature thereof; but the Congress may at any time by law make or alter such regulations, except as to the places of choosing Senators.7

2. **Congress must meet once a year.** The Congress shall assemble at least once in every year, and such meeting [shall be on the first Monday in December, unless

they shall by law appoint a different day.] 8

Section V. Organization and Rules of the Houses

1. **Each House may refuse to seat a member.** Each house shall be the judge of the elections, returns and qualifications of its own members, and a majority of each shall constitute a quorum to do business; but a smaller number may adjourn from day to day, and may be authorized to compel the attendance of absent members, in such manner, and under such penalties, as each house may provide.

2. **Each House makes its own rules of procedure.** Each house may determine the rules of its proceedings, punish its members for disorderly behavior, and with the concurrence of two thirds, expel a member.

3. **Each House must keep and publish a record of its proceedings.** Each house shall keep a journal of its proceedings, and from time to time publish the same, excepting such parts as may in their judgment require secrecy; and the yeas and nays of the members of either house on any question shall, at the desire of one fifth of those present, be entered on the journal.

4. **Both Houses must agree regarding adjournment.** Neither house, during the session of Congress, shall, without the consent of the other, adjourn for more than three days, nor to any other place than that in which the two houses shall be sitting.

Section VI. Privileges of and Prohibitions upon Congressmen

1. **Congressmen receive a salary from the United States and have certain privileges.** The Senators and Representatives shall receive a compensation for their services, to be ascertained by law and paid out of the treasury of the United States. They shall in all cases except treason, felony and breach of the peace, be privileged from arrest during their attendance at the session of their respective houses, and in going to and returning from the same; and for any speech or debate in either house, they shall not be questioned in any other place.

2. **A Congressman must not hold any**

---

6 Repealed in 1913 by the Seventeenth Amendment.
7 This is to keep Congress from naming the meeting places of the state legislatures.

8 Repealed in 1933 by the Twentieth Amendment.

other federal civil office. No Senator or Representative shall, during the time for which he was elected, be appointed to any civil office under the authority of the United States, which shall have been created, or the emoluments whereof shall have been increased, during such time; and no person holding any office under the United States shall be a member of either house during his continuance in office.

Section VII. Method of Making Laws

1. **Money bills must originate in the House of Representatives.** All bills for raising revenue shall originate in the House of Representatives; but the Senate may propose or concur with amendments as on other bills.

2. **The President has a veto power.** Every bill which shall have passed the House of Representatives and the Senate, shall, before it become a law, be presented to the President of the United States; if he approve he shall sign it, but if not he shall return it with his objections to that house in which it shall have originated, who shall enter the objections at large on their journal, and proceed to reconsider it. If after such reconsideration two thirds of that house shall agree to pass the bill, it shall be sent, together with the objections, to the other house, by which it shall likewise be reconsidered, and, if approved by two thirds of that house, it shall become a law. But in all such cases the votes of both houses shall be determined by yeas and nays, and the names of the persons voting for and against the bill shall be entered on the journal of each house respectively. If any bill shall not be returned by the President within ten days (Sundays excepted) after it shall have been presented to him, the same shall be a law, in like manner as if he had signed it, unless the Congress by their adjournment prevent its return, in which case it shall not be a law.

3. **All resolutions or votes go to the President for his approval.** Every order, resolution, or vote to which the concurrence of the Senate and House of Representatives may be necessary (except on a question of adjournment) shall be presented to the President of the United States; and before the same shall take effect, shall be approved by him, or being disapproved by him, shall be repassed by two thirds of the Senate and House of Representatives, according to the rules and limitations prescribed in the case of a bill.

Section VIII. Powers Granted to Congress

Congress has certain enumerated powers:

1. **It may lay and collect taxes.** The Congress shall have power to lay and collect taxes, duties, imposts, and excises, to pay the debts and provide for the common defence and general welfare of the United States; but all duties, imposts and excises shall be uniform throughout the United States;

2. **It may borrow money.** To borrow money on the credit of the United States;

3. **It may regulate foreign and interstate trade.** To regulate commerce with foreign nations, and among the several States, and with the Indian tribes;

4. **It may pass naturalization and bankruptcy laws.** To establish an uniform rule of naturalization, and uniform laws on the subject of bankruptcies throughout the United States;

5. **It may coin money.** To coin money, regulate the value thereof, and of foreign coin, and fix the standard of weights and measures;

6. **It may punish counterfeiters.** To provide for the punishment of counterfeiting the securities and current coin of the United States;

7. **It may establish a postal service.** To establish post offices and post roads;

8. **It may issue patents and copyrights.** To promote the progress of science and useful arts by securing for limited times to authors and inventors the exclusive right to their respective writings and discoveries;

9. **It may establish inferior courts.** To constitute tribunals inferior to the Supreme Court;

10. **It may punish crimes committed on the high seas.** To define and punish piracies and felonies committed on the high seas and offences against the law of nations;

11. **It may declare war.** To declare war, grant letters of marque and reprisal,[9]

---

[9] Letters given to private citizens in time of war authorizing them to capture enemy ships.

and make rules concerning captures on land and water.

12. **It may maintain an army.** To raise and support armies, but no appropriation of money to that use shall be for a longer term than two years;

13. **It may maintain a navy.** To provide and maintain a navy;

14. **It may regulate the Army and Navy.** To make rules for the government and regulation of the land and naval forces;

15. **It may call out the state militia.** To provide for calling forth the militia to execute the laws of the Union, suppress insurrections, and repel invasions;

16. **It shares with the states the control of the militia.** To provide for organizing, arming and disciplining the militia, and for governing such part of them as may be employed in the service of the United States, reserving to the States respectively the appointment of the officers, and the authority of training the militia according to the discipline prescribed by Congress;

17. **It makes laws for the federal district.** To exercise exclusive legislation in all cases whatsoever, over such district (not exceeding ten miles square) as may, by cession of particular States, and the acceptance of Congress, become the seat of government of the United States,[10] and to exercise like authority over all places purchased by the consent of the legislature of the State, in which the same shall be, for the erection of forts, magazines, arsenals, dock-yards, and other needful buildings; — and

Congress has implied powers:

18. **It may make laws necessary for carrying out the enumerated powers.** To make all laws which shall be necessary and proper for carrying into execution the foregoing powers, and all other powers vested by this Constitution in the government of the United States, or in any department or office thereof.[11]

Section IX. POWERS DENIED TO THE UNITED STATES [12]

1. **The full control of Congress over immigration is postponed until 1808.** The migration or importation of such persons

10 The District of Columbia.
11 This is the famous "elastic clause."
12 For other powers denied to the United States see Amendments I–X.

as any of the States now existing shall think proper to admit shall not be prohibited by the Congress prior to the year 1808; but a tax or duty may be imposed on such importation, not exceeding $10 for each person.[13]

2. **Congress may suspend the writ of "habeas corpus" [14] only in case of rebellion or invasion.** The privilege of the writ of *habeas corpus* shall not be suspended, unless when in cases of rebellion or invasion the public safety may require it.

3. **Attainders [15] and "ex post facto" [16] laws are forbidden.** No bill of attainder or *ex post facto* law shall be passed.

4. **Direct taxes must be apportioned according to the population.** No capitation, or other direct, tax shall be laid, unless in proportion to the census or enumeration herein before directed to be taken.

5. **Export duties are forbidden.** No tax or duty shall be laid on articles exported from any State.

6. **Congress must not discriminate against any port in regulating commerce.** No preference shall be given by any regulation of commerce or revenue to the ports of one State over those of another: nor shall vessels bound to, or from, one State, be obliged to enter, clear, or pay duties in another.

7. **Public money may not be spent without an appropriation by Congress.** No money shall be drawn from the treasury, but in consequence of appropriations made by law; and a regular statement and account of the receipts and expenditures of all public money shall be published from time to time.

8. **Titles of nobility may not be granted.** No title of nobility shall be granted by the United States: and no person holding any office of profit or trust under them, shall, without the consent of the Congress, accept of any present, emolument, office, or title, of any kind whatever, from any king, prince, or foreign state.

13 This refers to the foreign slave trade. The words "slave" and "slavery" are not used in the body of the Constitution.
14 The writ of *habeas corpus* enables a person under arrest to obtain an immediate examination in court to find out whether he is being legally held.
15 A bill of attainder is the condemning and sentencing of an individual by a special legislative act without giving him the opportunity of defending himself in the courts.
16 An *ex post facto* law fixes punishment for acts committed before the law was passed.

Section X. POWERS DENIED TO THE STATES

Absolute prohibitions on the states:

1. **The states are forbidden to do certain things.** No State shall enter into any treaty, alliance, or confederation; grant letters of marque and reprisal; coin money; emit bills of credit; make anything but gold and silver coin a tender in payment of debts; pass any bill of attainder, *ex post facto* law, or law impairing the obligation of contracts, or grant any title of nobility.

Conditional prohibitions on the states:

2. **The states may not levy duties without the consent of Congress.** No State shall, without the consent of the Congress, lay any imposts or duties on imports or exports, except what may be absolutely necessary for executing its inspection laws: and the net produce of all duties and imposts, laid by any State on imports or exports, shall be for the use of the treasury of the United States; and all such laws shall be subject to the revision and control of the Congress.

3. **Certain other federal powers are forbidden the states except with the consent of Congress.** No State shall, without the consent of Congress, lay any duty of tonnage, keep troops or ships of war in time of peace, enter into any agreement or compact with another State, or with a foreign power, or engage in war, unless actually invaded, or in such imminent danger as will not admit of delay.

Article II. Executive Department

Section I. PRESIDENT AND VICE-PRESIDENT

1. **The President is the chief executive.** The executive power shall be vested in a President of the United States of America. He shall hold his office during the term of four years, and together with the Vice-President, chosen for the same term, be elected as follows:

2. **The President is chosen by electors.** Each State shall appoint, in such manner as the legislature thereof may direct, a number of electors, equal to the whole number of Senators and Representatives to which the State may be entitled in the Congress; but no Senator or Representative, or person holding an office of trust or profit under the United States, shall be appointed an elector.

It requires a majority of the electoral votes to elect. [The electors shall meet in their respective States, and vote by ballot for two persons, of whom one at least shall not be an inhabitant of the same State with themselves. And they shall make a list of all the persons voted for, and of the number of votes for each; which list they shall sign and certify, and transmit sealed to the seat of government of the United States, directed to the President of the Senate. The President of the Senate shall, in the presence of the Senate and House of Representatives, open all the certificates, and the votes shall then be counted. The person having the greatest number of votes shall be the President, if such number be a majority of the whole number of electors appointed; and if there be more than one who have such majority, and have an equal number of votes, then the House of Representatives shall immediately choose by ballot one of them for President; and if no person have a majority, then from the five highest on the list the said house shall in like manner choose the President. But in choosing the President the votes shall be taken by States, the representation from each State having one vote; a quorum for this purpose shall consist of a member or members from two thirds of the States, and a majority of all the States shall be necessary to a choice. In every case, after the choice of the President, the person having the greatest number of votes of the electors shall be the Vice-President. But if there should remain two or more who have equal votes, the Senate shall choose from them by ballot the Vice-President.] [17]

3. **Congress decides the time of choosing electors.** The Congress may determine the time of choosing the electors and the day on which they shall give their votes; which day shall be the same throughout the United States.

4. **Who may be President?** No person except a natural-born citizen, or a citizen of the United States, at the time of the adoption of this Constitution, shall be eligible to the office of President; neither shall any person be eligible to that office who shall not have attained to the age of thirty-five years, and been fourteen years a resident within the United States.

[17] Repealed in 1804 by the Twelfth Amendment.

5. In case of the President's death or disability the Vice-President succeeds him. In case of the removal of the President from office or of his death, resignation, or inability to discharge the powers and duties of the said office, the same shall devolve on the Vice-President, and the Congress may by law provide for the case of removal, death, resignation, or inability, both of the President and Vice-President, declaring what officer shall then act as President, and such officer shall act accordingly, until the disability be removed, or a President shall be elected.

6. The President receives a salary. The President shall, at stated times, receive for his services a compensation, which shall neither be increased nor diminished during the period for which he shall have been elected, and he shall not receive within that period any other emolument from the United States, or any of them.

7. The President takes an oath of office. Before he enter on the execution of his office, he shall take the following oath or affirmation: — "I do solemnly swear (or affirm) that I will faithfully execute the office of President of the United States, and will to the best of my ability preserve, protect and defend the Constitution of the United States."

Section II. POWERS OF THE PRESIDENT

1. The President has important military and civil powers. The President shall be commander in chief of the army and navy of the United States, and of the militia of the several States, when called into the actual service of the United States; he may require the opinion, in writing, of the principal officer in each of the executive departments, upon any subject relating to the duties of their respective offices, and he shall have power to grant reprieves and pardons for offences against the United States, except in cases of impeachment.

2. The President may make treaties and nominate officers of the United States. He shall have power, by and with the advice and consent of the Senate, to make treaties, provided two thirds of the Senators present concur; and he shall nominate, and by and with the advice and consent of the Senate, shall appoint ambassadors, other public ministers and consuls, judges of the Supreme Court, and all other officers of the United States, whose appointments are not herein otherwise provided for, and which shall be established by law: but the Congress may by law vest the appointment of such inferior officers, as they think proper, in the President alone, in the courts of law, or in the heads of departments.

3. The President may fill vacancies during the recess of Congress. The President shall have power to fill up all vacancies that may happen during the recess of the Senate, by granting commissions which shall expire at the end of their next session.

Section III. OTHER POWERS AND DUTIES OF THE PRESIDENT

Messages; extra sessions; receiving ambassadors: execution of the laws. He shall from time to time give to the Congress information of the state of the Union, and recommend to their consideration such measures as he shall judge necessary and expedient; he may, on extraordinary occasions, convene both houses, or either of them, and in case of disagreement between them, with respect to the time of adjournment, he may adjourn them to such time as he shall think proper; he shall receive ambassadors and other public ministers; he shall take care that the laws be faithfully executed, and shall commission all the officers of the United States.

Section IV. IMPEACHMENT

Civil officers may be removed by impeachment. The President, Vice-President and all civil officers of the United States shall be removed from office on impeachment for, and on conviction of, treason, bribery, or other high crimes and misdemeanors.

Article III. Judicial Department

Section I. UNITED STATES OR FEDERAL COURTS

The judicial power belongs to the federal courts. The judicial power of the United States shall be vested in one Supreme Court, and in such inferior courts as Congress may from time to time ordain and establish.[18] The judges, both of the Supreme and inferior courts, shall hold

[18] Congress cannot abolish the Supreme Court but may abolish the inferior courts.

their offices during good behavior, and shall, at stated times, receive for their services a compensation which shall not be diminished during their continuance in office.

Section II. Jurisdiction (Authority) of the United States Courts

1. **The kinds of cases which may be heard are listed.** The judicial power shall extend to all cases, in law and equity, arising under this Constitution, the laws of the United States, and treaties made or which shall be made, under their authority; — to all cases affecting ambassadors, other public ministers and consuls; — to all cases of admiralty and maritime jurisdiction; — to controversies to which the United States shall be a party; — to controversies between two or more States; — between a State and citizens of another State; [19] — between citizens of different States; — between citizens of the same State claiming lands under grants of different States, and between a State, or the citizens thereof, and foreign states, citizens or subjects.

2. **In certain cases the Supreme Court has original jurisdiction.** [20] In all cases affecting ambassadors, other public ministers and consuls, and those in which a State shall be a party, the Supreme Court shall have original jurisdiction. In all the other cases before mentioned, the Supreme Court shall have appellate jurisdiction, [21] both as to law and fact, with such exceptions and under such regulations as the Congress shall make.

3. **Trial for crime is by jury.** The trial of all crimes, except in cases of impeachment, shall be by jury; and such trial shall be held in the State where the said crimes shall have been committed; but when not committed within any State, the trial shall be at such place or places as the Congress may by law have directed.

Section III. Treason

1. **Treason is defined.** Treason against the United States shall consist only in levying war against them, or in adhering to their enemies, giving them aid and

comfort. No person shall be convicted of treason unless on the testimony of two witnesses to the same overt act, or on confession in open court.

2. **Congress fixes the punishment for treason.** The Congress shall have power to declare the punishment of treason, but no attainder of treason shall work corruption of blood, or forfeiture except during the life of the person attainted.

Article IV. Relations of the States to One Another

Section I. Credit to Acts, Records, and Court Proceedings

Each state must respect the public acts of the others. Full faith and credit shall be given in each State to the public acts, records, and judicial proceedings of every other State. And the Congress may by general laws prescribe the manner in which such acts, records, and proceedings shall be proved, and the effect thereof.

Section II. Duties of States to States

1. **Citizenship in one state is valid in all.** The citizens of each State shall be entitled to all privileges and immunities of citizens in the several States.

2. **Fugitives from justice must be surrendered by the state to which they have fled.** A person charged in any State with treason, felony, or other crime, who shall flee from justice, and be found in another State, shall on demand of the executive authority of the State from which he fled, be delivered up, to be removed to the State having jurisdiction of the crime.

3. **Slaves and apprentices must be returned.** No person held to service or labor [22] in one State, under the laws thereof, escaping into another, shall, in consequence of any law or regulation therein, be discharged from such service or labor, but shall be delivered up on claim of the party to whom such service or labor may be due.

Section III. New States and Territories

1. **Congress may admit new states.** New States may be admitted by the Congress into this Union; but no new State shall be formed or erected within the jurisdiction of any other State; nor any State

---

[19] The Eleventh Amendment restricts this to suits by a state against citizens of another state.

[20] Original jurisdiction means that a case must commence in the Supreme Court.

[21] Appellate jurisdiction means that a case must commence in an inferior federal court or a state court, from which it may be appealed to the Supreme Court.

[22] "Persons held to service or labor" refers to slaves and apprentices.

be formed by the junction of two or more States, or parts of States, without the consent of the legislatures of the States concerned as well as of the Congress.

2. Congress may regulate federal territory and property. The Congress shall have power to dispose of and make all needful rules and regulations respecting the territory or other property belonging to the United States; and nothing in this Constitution shall be so construed as to prejudice any claims of the United States, or of any particular State.

Section IV. PROTECTION TO THE STATES

Congress guarantees to each state a republican government and protection against invasion and rebellion. The United States shall guarantee to every State in this Union a republican form of government, and shall protect each of them against invasion; and on application of the legislature, or of the executive (when the legislature cannot be convened) against domestic violence.

Article V. The Process of Amendment

The Constitution may be amended by either of two methods. The Congress, whenever two thirds of both houses shall deem it necessary, shall propose amendments to this Constitution, or, on the application of the legislatures of two thirds of the several States, shall call a convention for proposing amendments, which in either case shall be valid to all intents and purposes, as part of this Constitution, when ratified by the legislatures of three fourths of the several States, or by conventions in three fourths thereof, as the one or the other mode of ratification may be proposed by the Congress; provided that no amendments which may be made prior to the year one thousand eight hundred and eight shall in any manner affect the first and fourth clauses in the ninth section of the first article; and that no State, without its consent, shall be deprived of its equal suffrage in the Senate.

Article VI. General Provisions

1. The debts of the Confederation are taken over. All debts contracted and engagements entered into, before the adoption of this Constitution, shall be as valid against the United States under this Constitution, as under the Confederation.

2. The Constitution and federal laws are the supreme law of the land. This Constitution, and the laws of the United States which shall be made in pursuance thereof; and all treaties made, or which shall be made, under the authority of the United States, shall be the supreme law of the land; and the judges in every State shall be bound thereby, anything in the Constitution or laws of any State to the contrary notwithstanding.

3. Federal and state officers are bound by oath to support the Constitution. The Senators and Representatives before mentioned, and the members of the several State legislatures, and all executive and judicial officers, both of the United States and of the several States, shall be bound by oath or affirmation to support this Constitution; but no religious test shall ever be required as a qualification to any office or public trust under the United States.

Article VII. Ratification of the Constitution

The Constitution is in force when conventions in nine states have ratified it. The ratification of the conventions of nine States shall be sufficient for the establishment of this Constitution between the States so ratifying the same.

Done in Convention by the unanimous consent of the States present, the seventeenth day of September in the year of our Lord one thousand seven hundred and eighty-seven and of the Independence of the United States of America the twelfth. In witness whereof we have hereunto subscribed our names.
[Signed by]   G⁰ WASHINGTON
Presidt and Deputy from Virginia

AMENDMENTS TO THE CONSTITUTION [23]

Article I. Religious and Political Freedom

Congress may not interfere with freedom of religion, speech, meeting, and

[23] The first ten Amendments were adopted in 1791. They are frequently called the Bill of Rights.

petition. Congress shall make no law respecting an establishment of religion, or prohibiting the free exercise thereof; or abridging the freedom of speech, or of the press; or the right of the people peaceably to assemble, and to petition the government for a redress of grievances.

Article II.   Right to Bear Arms

The people may bear arms. A well-regulated militia being necessary to the security of a free State, the right of the people to keep and bear arms shall not be infringed.

Article III.   Quartering of Troops

Soldiers may not be quartered on the people. No soldier shall, in time of peace, be quartered in any house without the consent of the owner, nor in time of war, but in a manner to be prescribed by law.

Article IV.   Searches and Seizures

Unreasonable searches are forbidden. The right of the people to be secure in their persons, houses, papers, and effects, against unreasonable searches and seizures, shall not be violated, and no warrants shall issue but upon probable cause, supported by oath or affirmation, and particularly describing the place to be searched, and the persons or things to be seized.

Article V.   Right to Life, Liberty, and Property

The individual is guaranteed certain rights when on trial and the right to life, liberty, and property. No person shall be held to answer for a capital, or otherwise infamous crime, unless on a presentment or indictment of a grand jury except in cases arising in the land or naval forces, or in the militia, when in actual service in time of war or public danger; nor shall any person be subject for the same offence to be twice put in jeopardy of life or limb; nor shall be compelled in any criminal case to be a witness against himself, nor be deprived of life, liberty, or property, without due process of law; nor shall private property be taken for public use without just compensation.

Article VI.   Protection in Criminal Trials

An accused person has important rights. In all criminal prosecutions the accused shall enjoy the right to a speedy and public trial, by an impartial jury of the State and district wherein the crime shall have been committed, which district shall have been previously ascertained by law, and to be informed of the nature and cause of the accusation; to be confronted with the witnesses against him; to have compulsory process for obtaining witnesses in his favor, and to have the assistance of counsel for his defence.

Article VII.   Suits at Common Law

The rules of common law are recognized. In suits at common law, where the value in controversy shall exceed twenty dollars, the right of trial by jury shall be preserved, and no fact tried by a jury shall be otherwise re-examined in any court of the United States, than according to the rules of the common law.

Article VIII.   Bail and Punishments

Excessive fines and unusual punishments are forbidden. Excessive bail shall not be required, nor excessive fines imposed, nor cruel and unusual punishments inflicted.

Article IX.   Concerning Rights Not Enumerated

The people retain their rights even though not here enumerated. The enumeration in the Constitution of certain rights shall not be construed to deny or disparage others retained by the people.

Article X.   Powers Reserved to the States and to the People

Powers not delegated to the federal government are reserved to the states and the people. The powers not delegated to the United States by the Constitution, nor prohibited by it to the States, are reserved to the States respectively, or to the people.

Article XI.   Suits against a State

The federal courts have no authority in suits by citizens against a state. The judicial power of the United States shall not be construed to extend to any suit in law or equity, commenced or prosecuted against one of the United States by citizens of another State, or by citizens or subjects of any foreign state. [Adopted in 1798.]

'Article XII. Election of President and Vice-President

1. **The procedure of the Presidential electors is changed.** The electors shall meet in their respective States, and vote by ballot for President and Vice-President, one of whom, at least, shall not be an inhabitant of the same State with themselves; they shall name in their ballots the person voted for as President, and in distinct ballots the person voted for as Vice-President, and they shall make distinct lists of all persons voted for as President, and of all persons voted for as Vice-President, and of the number of votes for each, which lists they shall sign and certify, and transmit sealed to the seat of government of the United States, directed to the President of the Senate; — the President of the Senate shall, in the presence of the Senate and House of Representatives, open all the certificates and the votes shall then be counted; — the person having the greatest number of votes for President shall be the President, if such number be a majority of the whole number of electors appointed; and if no person have such majority, then from the persons having the highest numbers not exceeding three on the list of those voted for as President, the House of Representatives shall choose immediately, by ballot, the President. But in choosing the President, the votes shall be taken by States, the representation from each State having one vote; a quorum for this purpose shall consist of a member or members from two thirds of the States, and a majority of all the States shall be necessary to a choice. And if the House of Representatives shall not choose a President whenever the right of choice shall devolve upon them, before the fourth day of March next following, then the Vice-President shall act as President, as in the case of the death or other constitutional disability of the President.

2. **The method of choosing the Vice-President is changed.** The person having the greatest number of votes as Vice-President shall be the Vice-President, if such number be a majority of the whole number of electors appointed; and if no person have a majority, then from the two highest numbers on the list the Senate shall choose the Vice-President; a quorum for the purpose shall consist of two thirds of the whole number of Senators, and a majority of the whole number shall be necessary to a choice. But no person constitutionally ineligible to the office of President shall be eligible to that of Vice-President of the United States. [Adopted in 1804.]

Article XIII. Slavery Abolished

Slavery is prohibited. 1. Neither slavery nor involuntary servitude, except as a punishment for crime whereof the party shall have been duly convicted, shall exist within the United States, or any place subject to their jurisdiction.

2. Congress shall have power to enforce this article by appropriate legislation. [Adopted in 1865.]

Article XIV. Limitations on the States

1. **Negroes are made citizens.** All persons born or naturalized in the United States, and subject to the jurisdiction thereof, are citizens of the United States and of the State wherein they reside. No State shall make or enforce any law which shall abridge the privileges or immunities of citizens of the United States; nor shall any State deprive any person of life, liberty, or property, without due process of law; nor deny to any person within its jurisdiction the equal protection of the laws.

2. **When a state limits the franchise, its representation shall be reduced.** Representatives shall be apportioned among the several States according to their respective numbers, counting the whole number of persons in each State, excluding Indians not taxed. But when the right to vote at any election for the choice of Electors for President and Vice-President of the United States, Representatives in Congress, the executive and judicial officers of a State, or the members of the legislature thereof, is denied to any of the

male inhabitants of such State, being twenty-one years of age and citizens of the United States, or in any way abridged, except for participation in rebellion, or other crime, the basis of representation therein shall be reduced in the proportion which the number of such male citizens shall bear to the whole number of male citizens twenty-one years of age in such State.

3. **Certain persons who have been in rebellion are ineligible for federal and state office.** No person shall be a Senator or Representative in Congress, or Elector of President and Vice-President, or hold any office, civil or military, under the United States, or under any State, who, having previously taken an oath, as a member of Congress, or as an officer of the United States, or as a member of any State legislature, or as an executive or judicial officer of any State, to support the Constitution of the United States, shall have engaged in insurrection or rebellion against the same, or given aid or comfort to the enemies thereof. But Congress may, by a vote of two thirds of each house, remove such disability.

4. **Debts incurred in aid of rebellion are void.** The validity of the public debt of the United States, authorized by law, including debts incurred for payment of pensions and bounties for services in suppressing insurrection or rebellion, shall not be questioned. But neither the United States nor any State shall assume or pay any debt or obligation incurred in aid of insurrection or rebellion against the United States, or any claim for the loss or emancipation of any slave; but all such debts, obligations, and claims shall be held illegal and void.

5. **Enforcement.** The Congress shall have power to enforce by appropriate legislation the provisions of this article. [Adopted in 1868.]

Article XV. Negro Suffrage

Negroes are made voters. 1. The right of citizens of the United States to vote shall not be denied or abridged by the United States or any State on account of race, color, or previous condition of servitude.

2. The Congress shall have power to enforce this article by appropriate legislation. [Adopted in 1870.]

Article XVI. Income Taxes

Congress has power to lay and collect income taxes. The Congress shall have power to lay and collect taxes on incomes, from whatever source derived, without apportionment among the several States, and without regard to any census or enumeration. [Adopted in 1913.]

Article XVII. Direct Election of Senators

Senators shall be elected by popular vote. 1. The Senate of the United States shall be composed of two Senators from each State, elected by the people thereof, for six years; and each Senator shall have one vote. The electors in each State shall have the qualifications requisite for electors of the most numerous branch of the State legislatures.

2. When vacancies happen in the representation of any State in the Senate, the executive authority of such State shall issue writs of election to fill such vacancies: Provided that the Legislature of any State may empower the executive thereof to make temporary appointments until the people fill the vacancies by election as the Legislature may direct.

3. This amendment shall not be so construed as to affect the election or term of any Senator chosen before it becomes valid as part of the Constitution. [Adopted in 1913.]

Article XVIII. National Prohibition

The sale or manufacture of intoxicating liquors is forbidden. 1. After one year from the ratification of this article the manufacture, sale, or transportation of intoxicating liquors within, the importation thereof into, or the exportation thereof from, the United States and all territory subject to the jurisdiction thereof, for beverage purposes, is hereby prohibited.

2. The Congress and the several States shall have concurrent power to enforce this article by appropriate legislation.

3. This article shall be inoperative unless it shall have been ratified as an amendment to the Constitution by the legislatures of the several States, as provided by the Constitution, within seven years from

the date of the submission thereof to the States by the Congress. [Adopted in 1919.]

Article XIX.   Woman Suffrage

Women are guaranteed the right to vote. 1. The right of citizens of the United States to vote shall not be denied or abridged by the United States or by any State on account of sex.

2. The Congress shall have power to enforce this article by appropriate legislation. [Adopted in 1920.]

Article XX.   Presidential and Congressional Terms

Presidential and Congressional terms of office begin in January. 1. The terms of the President and Vice-President shall end at noon on the 20th day of January and the terms of Senators and Representatives at noon on the 3d day of January, of the years in which such terms would have ended if this article had not been ratified; and the terms of their successors shall then begin.

2. The Congress shall assemble at least once in every year, and such meeting shall begin at noon on the 3d day of January, unless they shall by law appoint a different day.

3. If, at the time fixed for the beginning of the term of the President, the President-elect shall have died, the Vice-President-elect shall become President. If a President shall not have been chosen before the time fixed for the beginning of his term, or if the President-elect shall have failed to qualify, then the Vice-President-elect shall act as President until a President shall have qualified; and the Congress may by law provide for the case wherein neither a President-elect nor a Vice-President-elect shall have qualified, declaring who shall then act as President, or the manner in which one who is to act shall be selected, and such persons shall act accordingly until a President or Vice-President shall have qualified.

4. The Congress may by law provide for the case of the death of any of the persons from whom the House of Representatives may choose a President whenever the right of choice shall have devolved upon them, and for the case of the death of any of the persons from whom the Senate may choose a Vice-President whenever the right of choice shall have devolved upon them.

5. Sections 1 and 2 shall take effect on the 15th day of October following the ratification of this article.

6. This article shall be inoperative unless it shall have been ratified as an amendment to the Constitution by the Legislatures of three-fourths of the several States within seven years from the date of its submission. [Adopted in 1933.]

Article XXI.   Prohibition Repealed

The Eighteenth Amendment is repealed. 1. The eighteenth article of amendment to the Constitution of the United States is hereby repealed.

2. The transportation or importation into any State, Territory, or Possession of the United States for delivery or use therein of intoxicating liquors, in violation of the laws thereof, is hereby prohibited.

3. This article shall be inoperative unless it shall have been ratified as an amendment to the Constitution by conventions in the several States, as provided in the Constitution, within seven years from the date of the submission thereof to the States by the Congress. [Adopted in 1933.]

Article XXII.   Limitation on Presidential Term

Presidential term is limited. 1. No person shall be elected to the office of President more than twice, and no person who has held the office of President, or acted as President, for more than two years of a term to which some other person was elected President shall be elected to the office of President more than once. But this article shall not apply to any person holding the office of President when this article was proposed by the Congress, and shall not prevent any person who may be holding the office of President, or acting as President, during the term within which this article becomes operative from holding the office of President or acting as President during the remainder of such term.

2. This article shall be inoperative unless it shall have been ratified as an amendment to the Constitution by the legislatures of three-fourths of the several States within seven years from the day of its submission to the States by the Congress. [Adopted in 1951.]

INDEX

Das Kapital (Marx), 641
Davis, Jefferson, 297, 322; portrait, 300; as President of Confederacy, 299, 304, 308, 319, 321
Dawes, William, 63
Dawes Act (1887), 385
Day, Benjamin A., 239
Deane, Elkanah, 22
Debs, Eugene, 376, 441, 442
Debtors, as settlers, 9–10, 11
Debtors' prisons, abolition of, 200, 232
Declaration of Independence, 65–66, 67
Declaration of Neutrality, Latin American (1939), 579
Declaration of Rights and Grievances, 62
Declaration of the Rights of Man, 128
Deere, John, 391
Defenders of the Constitution, 647
Defense, Secretary of, 627
Defense Production Act (1950), 639
De Gaulle, Charles, 706
DeKalb, Baron, 80
Delaware, 3, 16, 44, 100, 315
Delaware River, 100; Washington crosses, 75
Demobilization, after World War II, 627–628
Democracy: in Constitutional Convention, 105–106; direct, 43–44; on frontier, 185; and the Revolution, 86
Democratic party, 289; organization of, 125–126; rise of, under Jackson, 203; after War between North and South, 397–399. *See also* Republican Party, Jeffersonian
Denmark: in North Atlantic Council, 673; in World War II, 596, 618
Departments, federal, 118
Depression of 1929, 536–540
Desegregation, 691–693, 703–705
Detroit: picture of, 97; in Revolutionary War, 80; in War of 1812, 158, 159
Dewey, Admiral George, 463–464
Dewey, Thomas E., 634, 635
Diaz, Porfirio, 491, 493
Dingley tariff, 410
Dinwiddie, Robert, Governor, 53
Disarmament, naval, 561–563
Displaced Persons Act, 637
District of Columbia, slavery in, 283, 287
Dix, Dorothea, 232, 234; portrait, 233
Dixiecrats, 635, 683, 691
Dixon-Yates contract, 687–688
Doenitz, Admiral, 617
Dollar diplomacy, 488
Dominican Republic. *See* Santo Domingo
Donelson, Fort, 312

Douglas, Stephen A., 291–292; debates with Lincoln, 294–296; nominated for presidency, 297, 299; pictured, 298
Draft: peacetime, 628; in Korean War, 640; in War between North and South, 308, 314; in World War I, 505–506; World War II, 598
Dred Scott case, 293–294, 296
Dress, colonial, 28–29
Drugs. *See* Food and Drugs
Dulles, John Foster, 677, 685, 696
Dumbarton Oaks Conference, 655
Dunkirk, 596
Duquesne, Fort, 53–54
Durham, North Carolina, 342
Dutch, in colonial America, 3, 7, 35. *See also* Netherlands
Dutch East Indies. *See* Netherlands East Indies
Dutch Reformed Church, 35
Dynamo, 350

East German Democratic Republic, 671
Economic Co-operation Administration, 670
Economic and Social Council, 657
Edison, Thomas A., 350
Education: coeducation, 365–366; in colonial period, 37–39; desegregation decision, 693; expansion of opportunities, 427; federal aid for, 633–634, 638, 693–694, 702; in Jacksonian Era, 225–231; problems of, after World War II, 633–634; struggle for free public schools, 224, 225–228; of women, 230–231
Eighteenth Amendment, 429, 531
Eire, 664
Eisenhower, Dwight D., 612, 635, 673; presidency of, 683–708
El Alamein, fighting at, 611
Elastic clause, of Constitution, 108
Elector, 108
Electric railways, 360
Electricity, practical use of, 349–350, 363
Elevated railways, 360–361
Eleventh Amendment, 119
Elkins Act (1903), 435
Emancipation Proclamation, 313–314
Embargo Act (1807), 148–149; repealed, 153
Emergency Banking Act (1933), 544
Emerson, Ralph Waldo, 235, 237, 238, 280
Emigrant Aid Society, 292
Emma Willard, 230
Empresario, in settlement of Texas, 248
Engels, Friedrich, 641
England. *See* Great Britain

THE CHALLENGE

OF

THE SIXTIES

1962 SUPPLEMENT

by Frank Freidel

HARVARD UNIVERSITY

President Kennedy and the members of his cabinet assemble at the White House for the first cabinet meeting of his administration. The cabinet, consisting of the heads of the executive departments, meets at least once a week with the President to consider general governmental policies.

THE CHALLENGE OF THE SIXTIES

The New Frontier at Home

A new President and new issues.

In November, 1960, the people of the United States elected a new President, John F. Kennedy. The new President faced many of the same problems in foreign policy that had troubled the United States since 1945. But many of the issues that he faced at home were new ones which had been growing in the past few years. There was the question of "economic growth." Was the country's economy expanding fast enough? There was a continuing unemployment problem. Could new jobs be found for workers in areas or industries not sharing in the general prosperity? There were serious problems facing the cities. Could slums be replaced with adequate housing? Could expressways be built to unsnarl traffic jams? Questions like these, and many other older, unsolved problems were debated during the campaign of 1960. The Republican candidate for the Presidency, Richard Nixon, who had been Vice-President in the Eisenhower administration, proposed one set of answers. The Democratic candidate, Kennedy, proposed another. Kennedy called his program "The New Frontier." In the years after the election, he faced the problem of trying to obtain legislation from Congress to put the New Frontier into effect. It was not easy.

The end of the Eisenhower administration.

One of the most important laws passed in the last two years of President Eisenhower's administration was the Labor Reform Act of 1959. It revised the Taft-Hartley Act to protect workers from dishonest union officials. When a Congressional committee investigated labor racketeering, it found that a few dishonest leaders and some notorious gangsters had been making illegal use of union funds. These funds, which were supposed to be used for the welfare of union members, totaled millions of dollars. Often the rank and file of union members had no control over the money.

John F. Kennedy, at that time a Senator, conducted the committee hearings and framed a bill to protect these union members. Conservative members of Congress, with the approval of President Eisenhower, added to the bill provisions which would further restrict the unions. The resulting Labor Reform Act of 1959 included the following provisions:

A "bill of rights" for the union rank and file. This gave the union members the protection of (1) regulations to safeguard union funds, (2) the right to vote by secret ballot for union officials, (3) the right to a public hearing if they were being disciplined by the union.

Restrictions upon union officials: They must file reports with the Secretary of Labor. They could not hold office if they were Communists or had been convicted of certain crimes.

New restraints against unions: Additional restrictions against secondary boycotting (persuading others not to do business with a firm). The prohibition of picketing to obtain union recognition if an employer had legally entered into an agreement with another union.

Most labor experts thought the effect of the new labor law was like that of the Taft-Hartley Act. It did not hurt strong unions like the Teamsters' Brotherhood which employers feared. It did limit the activities of weak unions and those trying to spread into areas in which there were no unions.

Hawaii becomes a state.

As territories of the United States both Hawaii and Alaska played important roles in our history. Both contributed to the wealth of our country; both served as military outposts for defense. For several years bills had been introduced in Congress for the admission of these territories into the Union as states. Finally, in 1958, a statehood bill for Alaska was passed, as has been seen (see p. 702). Early in 1959 Alaska became the forty-ninth state of the Union. Congress then quickly enacted statehood for Hawaii. In August, 1959, it became the fiftieth state.

The problem of the budget.

Year after year, President Eisenhower had to face the complicated and technical question as to how much the government should spend in order best to provide for the national welfare. Although this question was difficult to understand, it involved the well-being of everyone in the United States. Secretary of the Treasury George Humphrey and his successor, Robert Anderson, both insisted that the government be cautious in its spending, both overseas and at home, both for defense and for the general welfare. The budget must be kept balanced in order to avoid inflation, although at times powerful Congressional leaders thought that more should be spent for defense even if it led to deficits. Several short recessions also led to deficits.

In the fiscal year ending June, 1959, the federal deficit, due to a recession and heavy defense expenditures, was $12,400,000,000. But for the 1960 fiscal year the President proposed a $77,000,000,000 budget which he promised would be balanced by taxes. Northern Democrats attacked it as not large enough, on the grounds that it would not provide the services the nation needed or stimulate growth of the economy. "I am going to fight [big spending] as hard as I know how," President Eisenhower asserted. He succeeded in defeating one measure after another proposed by the Democratic Congress on the grounds that they were costlier than his own proposals. These were bills appropriating money for defense, education and welfare, slum clearance, housing, and other purposes. In the end President Eisenhower won out, and the government ended the 1960 fiscal year with a $1,000,000,000 surplus. He repeated the battle over the 1961 budget.

The debate over the budget between President Eisenhower's supporters and his critics centered around the questions: Was the economy growing fast enough? Was it expanding sufficiently to provide the services the American people needed at home and to maintain on a large scale the enormous defense and foreign aid programs? Could the American economy keep ahead of that of Russia? (Allen Dulles of the Central Intelligence Agency had warned earlier that, while Russian production was still far below that of the United States, the rate of growth was perhaps more than twice as fast.) The problem, which continued after 1961 to baffle the Kennedy administration, was to try to raise the annual level of economic growth from the 3.5 per cent it had averaged since 1945 to perhaps 5 per cent.

The campaign of 1960.

All these questions in the realm of domestic policy, together with even more serious foreign policy problems, became subjects of debate in the campaign of 1960. Through the early months of 1960, Senator Kennedy waged a strenuous battle in state primaries against the liberal Democratic Senator from Minnesota, Hubert Humphrey. After winning the primary in West Virginia, Kennedy gained sufficient support among Democratic politicians to secure the nomination. At the Democratic convention in Los Angeles he was nominated on the first ballot. The leading southern contender for the presidential nomination, Senator Majority Leader Lyndon Johnson of Texas, was nominated for the Vice-Presidency.

By the end of 1959, Vice-President Nixon was so clearly the choice of Republican political leaders that his one rival, Governor Nelson Rockefeller of New York, dropped out of the race for the nomination. At the Republican convention in Chicago, Nixon was nominated without opposition. The vice-presidential nominee was Henry Cabot Lodge, Ambassador to the United Nations.

Both candidates campaigned energetically: Nixon visited every one of the fifty states. Both addressed themselves with seriousness and dignity to the issues of the sixties. Both appeared to foreign observers to be moderate in their approach, with Nixon somewhat more conservative than Kennedy. Millions of people watched intently as the candidates debated each other before television cameras. This had never been done before. In the final days of the campaign, both leaders drew enormous, enthusiastic crowds wherever they appeared. The general agreement among political experts and pollsters was that Kennedy would win, but no one was very sure.

Kennedy won by one of the closest margins in American history — by a fraction of one per cent of the popular vote. Out of nearly 69,000,000 votes cast, he received only 118,000 more than Nixon. His margin of electoral votes was larger: 303 to 219. (Fifteen southern electoral votes were cast for Senator Harry F. Byrd of Virginia.) The President-elect was forty-three years old, and the first Catholic to have been elected to the Presidency.

The Democrats, who had won sweeping victories in the Congressional elections of 1958, as a result of the 1960 election continued to control both houses of Congress by wide margins (64 to 36 in the Senate and 262 to 165 in the House), but lost two Senate seats and 21 House seats to the Republicans.

The New Frontier Begins

President Kennedy takes office.

The closeness of his victory caused President-elect Kennedy to announce appointments and plan a program which would help unify the nation. His actions gave notice even before he took office that his administration would be middle-of-the-road. He intended to please moderates in both the Republican and Democratic parties.

Two of the most important Cabinet appointees were Republicans. One was the Secretary of Defense, Robert S. McNamara, who only a few weeks previously had been named President of the Ford Motor Company. The other was Douglas Dillon to be Secretary of the Treasury. Dillon was a Wall Street banker who had served as Under Secretary of State in the Eisenhower administration. His appointment assured businessmen and bankers that Kennedy would follow conservative financial policies. Through the first year of his administration, President Kennedy continued to appoint Republicans to many of the prominent offices.

For Secretary of State, Kennedy chose a southerner, Dean Rusk, who had been President of the Rockefeller Foundation. Other appointments

Newsmen ask President Kennedy their questions at a news conference.

were designed to win the support of strong political or economic groups. Governor Luther H. Hodges of North Carolina, who had attracted numerous new industries to his state, became Secretary of Commerce. Governor Orville L. Freeman of Minnesota, a tart critic of Eisenhower farm policies, was named Secretary of Agriculture. Stewart L. Udall, a Representative from Arizona, who favored expansion of both recreational facilities and reclamation projects in the West, was appointed Secretary of the Interior. Governor Abraham A. Ribicoff of Connecticut was appointed Secretary of Health, Education, and Welfare. A special counsel of the A.F.L.–C.I.O. and general counsel of the United Steelworkers of America, Arthur J. Goldberg, was named Secretary of Labor.

In a precedent-making action, the President-elect appointed as Attorney General his younger brother, Robert Kennedy, who had managed the presidential campaign. Senator Kennedy broke another precedent in offering a cabinet position, that of Postmaster-General to a Negro, Representative William L. Dawson of Illinois. When Dawson declined, Kennedy named a California insurance executive, J. Edward Day.

When President Kennedy took his oath of office on January 20, 1961, he asserted in his inaugural address, "Let the word go forth from this time and place, to friend and foe alike, that the torch has been passed to a new generation of Americans." In the excitement of the first few weeks of the new administration, it did indeed seem as though a new generation had taken over in Washington. President Kennedy sent an unprecedented number of messages to Congress during its 1961 session — 66 messages calling for 355 specific legislative requests. Some of these messages concerned relatively small matters. The most important of them outlined new large-scale programs: the wiping out of areas of chronic unemployment, the caring for the health of old people, federal assistance to schools, conservation and better use of natural resources, and better development of communities.

Despite these numerous messages, it became apparent as months went by that in domestic matters as well as foreign policy the New Frontier was making no drastic break with the Modern Republicanism of President Eisenhower. (Earlier, as has been seen, Modern Republicanism had represented no sharp contrast to the Fair Deal or New Deal of President Eisenhower's Democratic predecessors.)

Like President Eisenhower, President Kennedy stood for economy in federal expenditures. He wanted to balance the budget whenever possible. Two sorts of crisis could keep him from balancing the budget: (1) the need to spend more money on defense or (2) a recession. At the time that President Kennedy took office, the nation was again suffering from a mild recession. Soon new Russian threats against the western nations forced the government to increase the national defenses. As a result of both of these factors, President Kennedy failed to balance his first budget and the fiscal year ended with a large deficit. Nevertheless, Kennedy insisted upon a balanced budget for the 1963 fiscal year (beginning July 1, 1962). A serious fall in stock market prices in the early summer of 1962 — the worst drop since the great crash of 1929 — carried the threat of a new and far more serious recession. The immediate response of the Kennedy administration was to propose cuts in taxes and new government spending in order to prevent the recession. The spending would again create a government deficit, but the administration considered a deficit less important than the stimulating of the economy.

President Kennedy was able to obtain considerable legislation from the 1961 session of Congress. The Congress was officially Democratic, but in the House of Representatives the coalition of liberal Democrats and Republicans supporting the President was only slightly larger than the coalition of more conservative Democrats and Republicans opposing him. On sixteen out of twenty-three votes in the House, the conservatives blocked bills the President favored. Important pieces of new legislation were:

The Housing Act of 1961, providing over a four-year period a total of $4,900,000,000 in federal grants and loans to develop middle-income housing and local mass transit systems, and to preserve open spaces in cities.

An increase in social security benefits in keeping with the President's recommendations.

An improved minimum wage law, which provided less than Kennedy had requested, but did bring over three and a half million additional workers under its coverage. It provided for a gradual increase of the minimum wage from $1.00 to $1.25 per hour.

Several important laws in the area of national defense and foreign aid.

The conservatives in Congress defeated two of the President's main proposals, bills providing for federal aid for schools and medical aid for the aged.

In his State of the Union message of January 1, 1962, President Kennedy outlined a long-range program which spelled out in greater detail his earlier campaign proposals. He asked once again for federal aid to education, medical care for the aged through the Social Security program, and for

7

measures to strengthen the economy. Because "both equity and common sense require that our nation's urban areas, containing three-fourths of our population, sit as equals at the Cabinet table," he asked for a Department of Urban Affairs and Housing; within a few weeks Congress defeated the proposal. Above all, he asked Congress to empower him to cut tariffs by as much as 50 per cent so that the United States would not be shut out by the newly developing European Common Market. In asking for the tariff reform, he declared:

"Our decision could well affect the unity of the West, the course of the cold war and the growth of our nation for a generation to come. The United States did not rise to greatness by waiting for others to lead. This nation is the world's foremost manufacturer, farmer, banker, consumer and exporter. The Common Market is moving ahead. The Communist economic offensive is under way. The opportunity is ours, the initiative is up to us — and the time is now."

The American Economy in the Sixties

The effects of automation.

The relatively low percentage rates of economic growth at the end of the Eisenhower administration and the beginning of the Kennedy administration should not disguise the fact that America's enormous industrial enterprise had been making notable forward strides both in productivity and in development of new products. Many industries were increasing production through automation. Applied to planning of production this meant feeding vast quantities of complex data into computers, which speedily could give answers it would have taken clerks weeks to find. Through computers, businesses and the government were able to adjust swiftly to economic trends. Automation applied to manufacturing processes meant the coordinating and operating of a series of machines through a single control panel. Thus one operator, in front of push-button controls, could operate enormous rolling machines producing a continuous strip of steel plate.

While automation was increasing productivity, it was also, by 1961, creating serious changes in the working force. More white collar workers and technicians were being needed; fewer unskilled and semiskilled workers were being employed. In 1961, manufacturers were employing 65 per cent more professional and technical workers and 13 per cent more clerks than a decade earlier. At the same time, in an automated industry like automobile manufacturing the number of workers on the production line had dropped 10 per cent since 1947. In textiles the drop was 35 per cent.

Decline in employment due to automation or decrease in demand in industries like automobiles, textiles, and bituminous coal was creating chronic areas of unemployment in time of boom as well as recession. Eight of these industries accounted for between one and two millions of the unemployed. The Kennedy administration sought through the Area Redevelopment Act to bring new industries into the depressed areas and, through the Manpower Training Bill, to retrain unemployed workers for other jobs. Rehabilitation promised to be difficult. Even into the early months of 1962, when the economy had recovered from the recession of a year earlier, approximately 6 per cent of the total American working force was unemployed. This was at a time

An electronic tape control system drills holes in sheets of metal, demonstrating expanding uses of automation in the modern world.

when the number of employed was larger than ever before in American history, and weekly factory wages had reached an all-time high of over $100.00.

A second critical problem was that of trying to achieve national growth at a satisfactory rate without suffering inflation. An upward spiral of wages and prices could seriously injure the nation. Wage increases, said President Kennedy, must be noninflationary. By this he meant that they must not be much more than the 3 per cent a year that national productivity was growing. Under pressure from the administration, the United Steel Workers signed a contract with the companies providing for only a 2½ per cent increase. It was assumed the steel companies would not raise prices. Nevertheless, three days later the United States Steel Corporation raised its prices 3½ per cent, declaring that the increase was necessary to meet rising costs and in order to modernize its plants. Most other steel companies followed. President Kennedy, fearing the price increases

would lead to a new inflationary spiral, declared on television that they "constitute a wholly unjustifiable and irresponsible defiance of the public interest." Defense orders were to be given whenever possible to steel companies that had not raised their prices. Under the pressure, United States Steel and other companies that had announced price increases, lowered them several days later. The episode caused many businessmen to feel that the President was hostile to their interests. When the stock market dropped sharply several weeks later, some people blamed the drop on the President's policies. But President Kennedy, speaking before the United States Chamber of Commerce, declared that he was sympathetic toward the problems of business. He said:

"We seek . . . an economic climate in which an expanding concept of business and labor responsibility, an increasing awareness of world commerce and the free forces of domestic competition will keep the price level stable."

9

Population and individual incomes grow.

The population of the United States was growing far more rapidly than experts had expected a generation earlier. In the 1930's experts had predicted that the 1960 population of the United States would be 140,000,000; but wartime prosperity had brought a boom in the birth rate, and by 1960 the population had passed the 180,000,000 mark. Accompanying this population growth had been a remarkable rise in personal income. By 1959, the median family income was $5,417; this means that half the families received more than this and half of them less. There was still a "hard core of poverty," consisting of 7,500,000 families or single persons who received $2000 or less. But the most typical income was $4600. Translated into living standards it meant that:

96 out of 100 American families had refrigerators
four out of five had television sets
three out of four had at least one car
three out of five owned their own home
one out of ten owned air conditioning.

If economic growth could be continued at the rate of 3.5 or 4 per cent per year through the sixties, President Eisenhower's Secretary of Labor, James P. Mitchell, predicted in a report issued in 1960 that living standards would rise another 25 per cent.

The Ceaseless Struggle Against Communism

The continuing threat from Communist nations.

Into the 1960's the continuing threat from Communist nations cast its shadow over the United States. Both President Eisenhower and President Kennedy had to devote the larger part of their time and energy to strengthening the defenses of the non-Communist world. "In the final choice," President Eisenhower declared in his first inaugural address in 1953, "a soldier's pack is not so heavy a burden as a prisoner's chains." He warned again and again during his eight years as President that the United States must remain strong and vigilant in response to crises. Communist nations were likely to create these crises one after another throughout the foreseeable future. Thus, President Eisenhower declared in 1959:

"As long as the Communist empire continues to seek world domination, we shall have to face threats to the peace of varying character and location. We have lived and will continue to live in a period where emergencies manufactured by the Soviets follow one another like beads on a string."

The nation "in the presence of danger," must not, President Eisenhower admonished, allow itself to "become unhinged by tension and crises." We must "keep our steadiness . . . in meeting this whole business, whether it be in Quemoy or Berlin or anywhere else."

The danger was of a far more complicated sort than the United States had ever faced before. The Director of the Central Intelligence Agency, Allen Dulles, warned in the summer of 1960 that the Communists aimed at nothing short of world domination. Speaking before the Veterans of Foreign Wars, he declared that the policy of the Russian leader, Nikita Khrushchev, centered around five points:

"First, [Khrushchev] proposes to build up Soviet military might based on ballistic missiles which would give him an effective weapon for direct attack on the United States.

"Second, he proposes to build up Soviet industry, the base of Soviet military power. . . .

"Third, he is supporting all elements of extreme nationalism, particularly in Asia, Africa, and Latin America. . . . He is working for chaos in such countries as Cuba and the Congo. And chaos breeds communism.

"Fourth, he is targeting economic and technical aid to the countries in Asia, Africa, and Latin America where the Communists believe they can make the most headway.

"Fifth, he has put into high gear his world-wide subversive apparatus, consisting of local Communist parties, underground and overt, Communist fronts, and all the espionage and propaganda assets of Moscow and its satellite allies."

In this overall program, Dulles pointed out, Russia was receiving the vigorous support of Red China, even though serious differences were developing between the two Communist powers.

Defense spending and the federal budget.

First of all, if the United States were successfully to meet the many Communist challenges, it must be militarily strong. Under the best of circumstances it would be difficult to obtain concessions from Russia; if the United States were relatively weak it would be impossible. Furthermore, the capacity of the United States to launch a devastating retaliatory blow seemed the only real insurance against a surprise attack. American strength precariously balanced Russian force.

From the time he took office, President Eisenhower had to make delicate calculations how best to maintain this balance in the face of recurring threats and crises. Each crisis in one or another part of the world called for difficult sorts of weapons in differing combinations and quantities. For the most part the weapons were new types developed since World War II, so that sometimes it was impossible to know in advance how well they would work. A leading historian, Ernest R. May, explains:

"President Eisenhower, like President Truman, found himself daily in front of issues such as had risen before only in wartime. America stood on the edge of conflict in many theaters: Central Europe, the eastern Mediterranean, the Middle East, India, southeast Asia, Japan, Korea, Africa, and even Latin America. The President was challenged to decide which theater should have priority and what the relative investment should be in readiness at home, in western Europe, and in peripheral areas like Indochina, the Formosa straits, and the Levant (Middle East), where the stakes were lower but the chances of conflict greater.

"These questions involved others, for each threat required a different set of weapons — big bombs, B-52's, missiles, and atom-powered submarines for all-out reprisal; infantry, marines, air transport, cargo vessels, and carriers for limited wars; advisory groups, psychological warfare teams, and economic aid funds for competition short of war. Eisenhower faced the challenge of fixing priorities among arms as well as among theaters.

"Both sets of issues were made all the more intricate by ingenuity of scientists and military technicians. Since development and construction of a given vessel, plane, or missile might take three to seven years, action could not follow immediately upon decision. Weapons in which were invested much time, skill, and money, such as the B-70 bomber and liquid-fueled Atlas missile, began to appear obsolete even before they were workable. A war game called 'Sabre Hawk,' enacted in southern Germany in February, 1958, revealed that one of the standing assumptions of American war plans was wrong: warfare with tactical nuclear weapons (that is to say, small ones) would require more, not fewer, ground troops. . . . Not only weapons but assumptions, calculations, and definitions proved as changeable as the weather. Yet [President Eisenhower as] Commander in Chief was compelled to peer far into the future and to take greater gambles with the people's money and lives than any of his predecessors." [1]

President Eisenhower was determined to maintain defenses strong enough to deter the Communist threat yet not so expensive that they would cause a federal deficit. President Kennedy inherited these same military and budgetary questions in 1961. Before the end of his first year in office he declared, "In terms of total military strength, the United States would not trade places with any nation on earth."

The threat of nuclear war.

The United States had to be strong in its military defenses. During the Eisenhower administration, despite some easing of tensions at the 1955 Geneva Conference, the next several years brought crises in the Middle East, East Asia (see pp. 706–708), and Berlin. What made these so dangerous was the continuing threat that local conflict could grow into a nuclear war. Both sides seemed to be aware of this danger. At times Russia appeared to be anxious to negotiate some sort of reduction in armaments. At other times (presumably when Russia had just developed some new weapon giving it an advantage), the Communists would destroy the negotiations and embark upon renewed tough tactics.

At the beginning of 1957, the United States seemed to be ahead of Russia in development of guided missiles with nuclear warheads. Consequently the Russians seemed interested in arriving at disarmament agreements at United Nations subcommittee meetings being held in London. These agreements would stop the testing of nuclear weapons and establish controls over nuclear devices, long-range missiles and satellites. Conventional armaments also were to be cut. Then, the Russians deadlocked the conference over the question of aerial inspections.

The reason seemed to be two spectacular Russian technical advances. In the summer of 1957, Russia successfully tested an intercontinental ballistic missile more powerful and with a longer range than American missiles. Then in October, 1957, came an even more spectacular coup (see p. 706). The Russians launched a "sputnik," the first successful satellite. Khrushchev, who had just succeeded in strengthening his own position in the Kremlin, used these triumphs to try to threaten western nations and impress the neutrals.

The effect upon the United States was powerful. Three months elapsed before the United States was able to launch its own, smaller satellite. Within the United States there spread a re-evaluation, perhaps overestimation, of Russian missile strength and technical skill, and of the merits of the Russian educational system. An overhauling of the American educational system got underway, and the government began to provide large subsidies to improve the teaching of

[1] E. R. May, editor, *The Ultimate Decision: The President as Commander in Chief* (New York, George Braziller, 1960), pp. 215–216. Quoted with permission.

science and to further scientific research. Also, President Eisenhower in January, 1958, called upon Congress to strengthen the nation's defenses and provide further aid to underdeveloped countries.

The race into outer space.

By building a rocket booster engine much larger than any the United States had felt it needed for military purposes, Russia obtained a lead in the race into outer space which it was able to maintain well into the sixties. At least, it was able to maintain a lead in the size of its exploits, and in the propaganda use to which they were put. "You send up oranges while we send up tons," Khrushchev boasted in 1959. Nevertheless, in scientific achievements the United States quickly pulled abreast of Russia, and in some respects even surpassed it.

The Russians launched only about a third as many space shots, and seemed less interested in systematically exploring space. The United States in less than four years after the Russian launching of Sputnik I had launched forty-six earth satellites and space probes compared with fifteen for the Russians. Thereafter, the tempo of American launchings increased sharply.

Some of the American space firsts were:

Pioneer V, in solar orbit, radioed the earth from 23,000,000 miles, demonstrating that communication between the planets was practical.

Tiros I televised pictures of cloud formations from an altitude of nearly five hundred miles, foreshadowing an enormous advance in understanding and predicting weather.

Transit 1-B and 11-A were forerunners of a highly accurate world-wide navigational system which would operate in bad weather as well as good.

Midas II was the forerunner of a system of satellites to warn of the approach of enemy missiles.

Above all, Americans and their well-wishers throughout the world rejoiced wildly in February, 1962, when Colonel John Glenn orbited the earth

Aurora 7, with flotation gear attached, awaits rescue after orbital flight of astronaut Carpenter.

three times in the Friendship 7. Colonel Glenn's flight, following the first successful Russian orbiting of a man by only 10 months, indicated how rapidly the United States was advancing in the race into space. More important, in contrast to Russian secrecy, the United States allowed the entire world to follow Glenn's flight from the time his capsule was launched by an Atlas-D missile from Cape Canaveral, Florida, until the Friendship 7 parachuted into the Atlantic Ocean near the Bahamas. Some 135 million people watched the launching on television; countless more listened to Glenn's voice while he was speeding around the globe at more than 17,000 miles per hour. Colonel Glenn's flight was duplicated four months later by Lieutenant Commander M. Scott Carpenter, who also orbited the earth three times. These flights were a clear indication that although the United States could not as yet launch as large a spacecraft as the Soviets, it was scientifically and militarily abreast of the Russians in most respects.

The one frightening aspect of the Russian space program was the ability of the Soviet scientists to send five-ton capsules into orbit. The mighty rocket thrust this required illustrated that Khrushchev was not boasting idly when he warned that Russia had the power to rain missiles upon American cities. The destructive force of missiles if they should set off thermonuclear explosions, would be enormous. The Congressional Joint Committee on Atomic Energy warned in August, 1959, that an attack of this sort upon the United States might kill fifty million people and seriously injure another twenty million. It would ruin crops and destroy, or contaminate for months, half the nation's dwellings. A retaliatory blow from American missile bases and atomic-powered sub-

marines would wreak the same sort of destruction upon an aggressor. Thus the United States and Russia were maintaining a precarious "balance of terror."

This appalling prospect of such wholesale destruction led President Eisenhower to assert in August, 1959, "I don't believe anyone is stupid enough to want a general war." And in Moscow the following month, Khrushchev declared, "In our time only a madman can start a war and he himself will perish in its flames." Only the Chinese Communists gave the impression that they would not flinch from an atomic war. While it might kill several hundred million of their own people, there would be several hundred million more left, and China might emerge as the strongest nation in the world.

Khrushchev did not bother to disguise the Communist aim of dominating the world; he had predicted to Americans in a 1957 television broadcast that their grandchildren would live under "socialism." But he and other Russian leaders seemed to be sincere in wanting to obtain their goals by other means than nuclear war. In an age when missiles could be started on their way by pushing a button, the danger that a devastating war might come by accident was too grave to overlook.

A first step toward limitation of nuclear weapons was taken in 1958 when Russia and the United States temporarily stopped their tests. President Eisenhower announced that the United States would stop its testing on a year-to-year basis if Russia would enter into a workable treaty providing suitable controls against secret testing. Also he wanted to be sure the Russians would seriously negotiate toward a reduction in armaments. Representatives of the three nuclear powers, the United States, Great

Britain, and Russia, met at Geneva beginning in October, 1958, and undertook long but inconclusive negotiations.

In the spring of 1961 it became apparent to the American delegation at the Geneva negotiations that the Russians had lost all interest in reaching an agreement. It was six months before the reason became apparent, that behind the shield of the negotiations, Russia was engaging in the lengthy and elaborate preparations necessary to undertake a new series of nuclear tests. Suddenly, in the fall of 1961, Russia began a series of about fifty tests, mostly of relatively small weapons, but culminating in the explosion of a bomb of over fifty megatons. The tests created more radioactive fallout, later deposited throughout the northern hemisphere, than all previous testing combined. Khrushchev warned that Russia possessed even bigger bombs, of 100 megatons in size, but the significance of these weapons seemed to be in their capacity to frighten people, since earlier nuclear weapons were already of such deadly destructiveness. The more important aspect of the tests was that the testing of the smaller weapons seemed to American experts to give Russia a lead in nuclear armament, and forced the United States to return to its own program of development and testing. In the ever-increasing tempo of the atomic race, it was essential that the United States match Russian advances in developing missiles that could destroy satellites and intercept and destroy missiles before they could reach this country.

In announcing that the United States would undertake relatively small-scale atmospheric tests in the Pacific, President Kennedy pointed out:

"Every alternative was examined. Every avenue of obtaining Soviet agreement was explored. We were determined not to rush into imitating their tests. And we were equally determined to do only what our own security required us to do. . . . No single decision of this Administration has been more thoroughly or more thoughtfully weighed. . . .

"In the absence of a major shift in Soviet policies, no American President — responsible for the freedom and safety of so many people — could in good faith make any other decision."

Eisenhower and Khrushchev.

In 1958, Premier Khrushchev began to pressure President Eisenhower to participate in a second summit conference. What Khrushchev's motives might be was not certain. Perhaps he also was alarmed over the threat of atomic warfare; perhaps there were other gains he thought he could obtain at a conference. In any event, the President was wary about meeting Khrushchev again unless some positive achievement for the United States was likely. The thaw in the cold war resulting from the first summit conference at Geneva in 1955 had led to no agreements to reduce armaments. At the same time the relaxation of tensions (the so-called "Geneva spirit") had made the peoples of the United States and western Europe more reluctant to build strong defenses against Russia.

Against this background Khrushchev, in November, 1958, created a new crisis over the status of Berlin. He gave notice that in six months he would sign a separate peace treaty with the government of East Germany, turning over to it the Russia sector in Berlin and the 110-mile corridor through which West Berlin received its supplies. The United States countered by standing on its treaty rights. Khrushchev tried to use the issue to force a summit meeting, but the United States would agree only to a foreign ministers' meeting at Geneva in May, 1959. Once again the delegates could reach no agreement.

The only slight hope of fruitful negotiations seemed to be for President Eisenhower again to meet Premier Khrushchev face to face. In August, 1959, the President invited Khrushchev for a visit to the United States "to see what Americans are like" so that he could learn face to face with the American people their "basic conviction . . . on the major issues of the day."

The thirteen-day visit was enlightening to both Americans and Russians. Though Khrushchev had obviously planned it to obtain the maximum propaganda benefit within the United States and throughout the rest of the world, he did see something of the enormous size and prosperity of the United States. Through televised reports in Russia, millions of Russians shared his glimpses. More important, the American people had the opportunity, through watching Khrushchev repeatedly on television, to learn much more accurately the nature of the Russian premier. They saw for themselves the dogged insistence with which he pressed his views. Americans did not again succumb to the Geneva spirit, but they hoped that with care and patience it might be possible to bargain with Russia.

At Camp David, the President's week-end camp in the Maryland mountains, Khrushchev and Eisenhower engaged in long private talks. Khrushchev agreed to drop the deadline for settling the Berlin question, but would make no other concessions. He did say, as he had previously, that "all outstanding international questions should be settled not by the application of force but by peaceful means through negotiations." He talked afterwards of the "Camp David spirit," but there was no indication that this meant anything more than the earlier "Geneva spirit."

Khrushchev, in addressing the United Nations in New York, dramatically proposed that all nations totally disarm within four years. This proposal created relatively little excitement since Russia had previously refused to agree to every American suggestion for gradual disarmament. And so, indeed, after disarmament negotiations resumed in Geneva in March, 1960, the Russian and American delegates once more rejected each other's plans.

In December, 1959, the United States, Great Britain, and France finally agreed to meet with Russia in a new summit conference in May, 1960. As the date for the conference approached there seemed little likelihood that it would be fruitful. It was in this atmosphere, less than two weeks before the summit conference was to meet, that Khrushchev announced that an American high-speed, high-altitude reconnaissance plane, a U-2, had been shot down over Russia.

When President Eisenhower arrived at Paris for the summit conference, he announced he had stopped the U-2 flights. Khrushchev, pounding the table in a rage, demanded that Eisenhower in addition apologize for the flights and punish those responsible for them. When the President refused to accept these harsh terms, the conference disbanded.

Why did Khrushchev wreck the summit conference which he had labored so long to obtain? The consensus of experts was that the Soviet premier, facing the prospect of returning to Russia empty-handed, exploited the U-2 episode to try to shift the blame for failure to the United States. He also thus drew attention away from the fact that, despite the boasted military power of Russia, the United States for several years had been able to send reconnaissance flights across Soviet territory.

Americans were amazed that Khrushchev's next major maneuver after reviling President Eisenhower in Paris was to sail to New York in September, 1960, to attend the General Assembly meeting of the United Nations. Khrushchev was not treated as an honored guest, and during his stay of nearly a month he was confined, with one exception, to the limits of Manhattan Island. President Eisenhower carefully avoided seeing him. The presence of Khrushchev and the heads of most of the satellite nations was a fascinating spectacle for the people of New York but was vastly more important for the delegations from smaller neutralist nations. Fifteen new African nations were admitted to the United Nations at the meeting.

Khrushchev concentrated his attention upon the delegates from new nations in Africa and Asia, trying to give them the impression that Russia was the foe of colonialism. Western opponents of Khrushchev pointed equally firmly to Russia's own "colonial empire" extending over the satellite nations of Eastern Europe. Nevertheless, delegates from neutral nations listened with enthusiasm to Khrushchev's demands for liberation of colonies and reduction of armaments. On the other hand, many of them were repelled by his attacks upon the popular Secretary-General of the United Nations, Dag Hammarskjold, and his constant clowning and posturing — climaxed when he pounded the desk with one of his shoes.

After his return to Russia, Khrushchev spent weeks in a so-called "Red summit" conference at which Russian views seemed to prevail over the more extreme ones of Communist China. After the American election of November, 1960, he called upon President-elect Kennedy to meet him in a new summit conference to settle the questions of Berlin and disarmament. Also he continued to pose as champion of underdeveloped countries.

President Kennedy takes over.

All these foreign problems seemed so acute that President Kennedy, unlike any of his predecessors, seemed to direct his inaugural address on January 20, 1961, as much to the rest of the world, as to the people of the United States. "In the long history of the world, only a few generations have been granted the role of defending freedom in its hour of maximum danger," he asserted. "I do not shrink from this responsibility — I welcome it."

Firmly the new President stated the national purpose:

"Since this country was founded, each generation has been summoned to give testimony to its national loyalty. The graves of young Americans who answered that call encircle the globe.

"Now the trumpet summons us again — not as a call to bear arms, though arms we need — not as a call to battle, though embattled we are — but a call to bear the burden of a long twilight struggle, year in and year out, 'rejoicing in hope, patient in tribulation' — a struggle against the common enemies of man: tyranny, poverty, disease and war itself."

Before many weeks had passed, Premier Khrushchev began a direct testing of the new President; from the outset, Kennedy prepared to meet the Russian challenge in underdeveloped areas. Russia's courtship of the former colonies in Africa and Asia that were emerging as independent nations posed a serious threat. Ignorance and extreme poverty in many of these areas made them receptive to Communist aid and susceptible to Russian propaganda. Most of these new nations, as their voting record at the United Nations in the early sixties indicated, preferred to remain neutral in the struggle between Russia and the West. They were preoccupied with their own economic problems and those of their sister nations. Thus, the new African nations tended to vote as an "African bloc."

A drawn-out crisis in the Congo dramatized the difficulties in Africa. In the summer of 1960, Belgium gave up its control over the area without having trained the Congolese for self-government. When the new president of the nation could not put down rioting he asked for United Nations troops to maintain order. Backed by these troops, he was able to evict from the Congo numerous Russian "technicians," and after several months to depose the pro-Russian premier (who was later murdered). Trouble continued over the secession of the richest of the provinces of the Congo, Katanga, which led to fighting between U.N. forces and Katanga armed forces, led by European mercenary soldiers in 1961 and 1962. Many American conservatives favored the Katanga secessionists; the Kennedy administration, backing the U.N. troops, claimed that behind the Katanga government were Belgian mining interests, and that without Katanga, the Congo would break up and become booty of the Communists.

In earlier years it had been American policy to oppose neutralism on the part of underdeveloped countries and to try to enlist their active support for the western powers. By the end of the Eisenhower administration, the United States was ready to accept their neutralism, and to help these na-

tions partly out of cold war necessity and partly out of historic humanitarian tradition. President Eisenhower year after year emphasized the defense and humanitarian value of the Mutual Security program. President Kennedy immediately developed the same theme in asking Congress for continued funds.

To expand the foreign aid program, President Kennedy in 1961 established the Peace Corps to recruit and train volunteers and send them to underdeveloped countries where they could serve as teachers, public health aides, agricultural helpers, and in other such capacities. Within the first year, more than fifteen thousand persons had applied to serve in the Peace Corps and over five hundred had already been trained and sent to areas all over the globe.

One of the major purposes of all the foreign aid programs was to try to increase productivity in poverty-stricken areas. The United States and other western powers could best keep underdeveloped nations out of the Communist orbit by raising their living standards. They were indeed giving much aid. Unfortunately the introduction of even simple medical and sanitary reforms helped contribute to an explosive increase in population. It then became difficult to bring about an increase in productivity that could keep up with the growing population. It was necessary for the rate of production to increase faster than the population in order to improve living standards.

The world's population had increased from five hundred million in 1650 to two and a half billion in 1950, but was increasing so rapidly that it would double to five billion well before the end of the twentieth century. The population of most of the underdeveloped countries would increase at least by half between 1960 and 1980.

A Peace Corps volunteer leads a game at a school in the Philippines. The Peace Corps extends U. S. aid in many ways throughout the world.

Yet already half of the world's population (and two thirds of that of Africa, Asia, and South America) were undernourished and living in misery. Per capita yearly income as of 1950 was $1,100 per person in North America as compared with $50 in Asia.

The only way to lessen the extreme poverty was through large-scale aid to bring about economic development at a more rapid rate than the population was increasing. President Eisenhower's Commission on National Goals recommended in 1960 that the United States and the western industrial nations increase their yearly investment by about half, in order to double in the following five years the economic growth of poverty-stricken areas. Only in this way could living standards be raised and tendencies toward communism be stemmed.

Asia struggles with many problems.

The nature of the competition between the United States and Russia in the aid they gave underdeveloped countries was clearly illustrated in India. The United States up to 1960 had provided over two billion dollars in assistance, touching almost every aspect of Indian life: modernization of agriculture, building of irrigation systems, construction of many sorts of factories, and improvement of public health. None of this was as spectacular as the typical Russian program, which, while it involved only a fraction as large an expenditure, involved building a steel mill that could turn out a million tons a year. Certainly the American program was of far more benefit to the people of India; perhaps the Russian program was of greater propaganda effect. The complexity of American relations with India was illustrated at the end of 1961 when India suddenly abandoned its long-standing hatred of armed force and invaded the Portuguese colony of Goa, incorporating it into India. While the United States was severely critical, the Russian government gave India its hearty support.

Throughout much of the rest of Asia, Communist China complicated

19

American policy. Half of the people of Asia lived under Communist governments. Many of the others lived in the shadow of communism, frightened by the warlike Chinese leaders. This was especially true in Southeast Asia, in countries like Thailand, Laos, and South Vietnam. President Kennedy, alarmed at advances of Communist guerrillas in Laos, declared in 1961 that the United States would not stand idly by, and emphasized his wish to see neutrality maintained in Laos by international agreement. Later he decided not to back his words with troops, and accepted from Khrushchev an agreement to a truce in Laos. In the spring of 1962, trouble flared anew as Communist forces broke the cease-fire agreement, threatening to take over the entire country. To protect the neighboring countries, the United States rushed troops into Thailand and strengthened the military mission in South Vietnam. Unless the Communist guerrilla fighters could be countered, large additional areas might be lost.

Difficulties in Latin America.

During the 1930's, through the good neighbor policy President Roosevelt built a great reservoir of cordial relations with Latin America (Chapter 42). After World War II, on the surface at least, the relations remained cordial. The United States and the nations to the south entered into new treaties providing for mutual defense and economic cooperation. The most important of these was the Inter-American Treaty of Reciprocal Assistance, drafted at Rio de Janeiro in 1947. It was implemented in 1948 by the establishment of an Organization of American States.

As the cold war began to take shape after 1945, Latin America began to be neglected. American aid and attention poured into the troubled areas of Europe and Asia where the immediate threat from Communist coups was greatest. The nations to the south received only a tiny fraction of American funds with which to combat acute economic problems.

Soldiers of the Laotian Army patrol a jungle road as part of guerrilla defense against Communist advances.

Soviet artillery on parade in Havana, Cuba, advances past giant portraits of Castro and Lenin on the third anniversary of Castro's revolution.

The vital economic interrelationship between the United States and Latin America complicated the issues. Latin America accounted for a quarter of the exports and a third of the imports of the United States; eighty per cent of the foreign capital invested in Latin America came from the United States. The peoples of Latin America on the one hand wanted more economic aid, and on the other protested against what they claimed was exploitation by American investors. Also they claimed that it was American policy to support despotic dictators if they were friendly toward the United States and not to aid more liberal regimes. In some respects these charges against the United States were inconsistent. Yankees were attacked if they intervened and were criticized if they did not. Basically, the problem was as it was in other parts of the world: the troubles of a rapidly increasing population revolting against poverty.

It was a situation ready-made for Communist agitation. In many Latin American countries, militant Communist parties capitalized upon the undeniable misery of the masses. These conditions and the Communist challenge came to the shocked attention of the American people in 1958 when Vice-President Nixon was attacked by rioters in Lima and Caracas. Immediately the State Department intensified efforts already under way to increase aid to Latin American nations. In keeping with one of Nixon's suggestions, the United States also turned to a policy of giving no more than a correct handshake to dictators but offering a warm embrace to democratic leaders.

This was the background of the crisis over Cuba. Americans had cheered when Fidel Castro at the beginning of 1959 had overthrown the corrupt dictatorship of Fulgencio Batista. But Castro and his followers rapidly took their government further and further to the left, indulging in increasingly bitter and wild tirades against the United States. For many months the United States did not retaliate economically, although in February, 1960, Russia signed a treaty with Cuba, extending a credit of $100,000,000 and agreeing to purchase a million tons of sugar a year for five years. Relations with the United States rapidly worsened as the Cuban government systematically seized American properties. The United States retaliated by ending its purchase of Cuban sugar at an artificially high price, and later by putting an embargo upon all American goods other than medical supplies bound for Cuba. Finally, in January, 1961, when Castro insisted that the American embassy staff in Havana be cut to a handful of employees, President Eisenhower severed diplomatic relations.

When President Kennedy took office, he found that the Central Intelligence Agency was aiding Cuban exiles to train in preparation for an invasion, which according to plans was to have air support by United States planes. After much deliberation, President Kennedy allowed the exiles to land in Cuba in April, 1961, but did not provide them with air cover or other assistance. Within a few hours Castro crushed the invasion, thus delivering a stinging setback to the United States. Before the end of 1961, Castro was openly proclaiming himself a Marxist, and the United States was trying without much success to persuade Latin American nations to take joint action against him. Some people feared Cuba would serve as a Soviet base against the United States. What was more dangerous was the way in which it was serving as a center for the spreading of propaganda to try to start Castro-style revolutions in other Latin American countries.

In 1960, President Eisenhower used the Navy to prevent Cuban intervention in Guatemala, Nicaragua, and Costa Rica; in 1961, President Kennedy sent naval vessels to protect the people of the Dominican Republic after they had overthrown a dictatorship of long duration.

President Kennedy sought to develop a positive program to help remedy the long-standing economic difficulties of Latin America. In his inaugural address he promised "a new alliance for progress — to assist free men and free governments in casting off the chains of poverty." But he also warned, "this peaceful revolution of hope cannot become the prey of hostile powers." Two months later, Kennedy put into action his Alliance for Progress program by proposing that the United States provide large-scale aid for ten years "if the countries of Latin America are ready to do their part." In December, 1961, when he visited Venezuela and Colombia, he was warmly cheered by the crowds.

Khrushchev challenges Kennedy over Berlin.

The new President had only a few scant weeks to begin developing policies toward underdeveloped nations before he was sharply challenged by Premier Khrushchev. He agreed to meet Khrushchev in Vienna in June, 1961, in order to make clear to him American firmness in cold war policies. Khrushchev was tough too, and informed him that the Russian decision to sign a peace treaty with East Germany in December was firm and would not be changed. As soon as the treaty was signed, the question of access to West Berlin was to be handled by the East German government. President Kennedy, like his predecessors, held firm to the position that the right of the United States, Great Britain, and France in West

SECTEUR

An East Berlin border guard leaps over barbed wire as he defects to freedom in West Berlin where his family had fled in an earlier escape from communism.

Berlin rested upon their military victory in World War II. Kennedy was ready to negotiate concerning Berlin and other questions, but he had no intention of making large concessions in return for little or nothing. "You have offered to trade us an apple for an orchard," he subsequently told the Russian ambassador. "We don't do that in this country." To the American people, the President declared, "We do not want to fight, but we have fought before. We cannot and will not permit the Communists to drive us out of Berlin either gradually or by force."

In August, 1961, the Russians suddenly walled off East Berlin from the western sections of the city to prevent the heavy flow of refugees from Communist rule. Along the new barriers a number of ugly incidents took place which seemed likely at any time to grow into serious fighting. The United States began strengthening its armed forces, increasing the draft, and calling 165,000 reservists back into active service. Many Americans began planning or building shelters to protect themselves from fallout. It was the worst war scare since the Korean conflict. Then in the following months tensions eased somewhat, and Khrushchev's December, 1961, deadline came and went without the status of West Berlin having as yet been changed. The impasse did not explode, but it did continue to smolder.

The balance-sheet in the sixties.

As the Berlin scare faded away, the American people had no need to be unduly worried in measuring the strengths or the successes of their nation in comparison with Russia. While the Communists had the power to launch a devastating thermonuclear blow against the United States, the United States could deal an equally devastating counter-blow. It was in order to maintain this balance that President Kennedy had had to order a resumption of nuclear tests. While this balance could be maintained, the danger was less from a global thermonuclear war than from revolutions like Castro's in Cuba and guerrilla advances like that of the Communists in Southeast Asia. President Kennedy was determined to counter this sort of "nibbling" through aid to areas threatened or under attack. Through training anti-guerrilla forces and improving foreign aid programs, he hoped to counter the Communists.

Moreover, the Communist world was suffering from troubles aplenty. President Kennedy told a journalist, Stewart Alsop, in 1962:

"I'm not so much impressed by the challenge of their system. The most impressive thing they've done is their achievement in space. But there is a lot that is not so impressive — East Germany in bad shape, famine in China, the farm shortages in Russia itself. They've poured millions into Cuba, and the people there are still miserable. They can exploit all the misery in the world, but I don't think their system is so impressive."

What lay ahead for Americans? The Communists had "the advantage of a dictatorship, an authoritarian system," President Kennedy pointed out to Alsop. "They can say do this, do that and it's done." As for the people of the United States, "We are a free society, and we have a long, long struggle ahead, a tough competition. And we here in America have to bear the main weight of the burden." Even as he had declared in his inaugural address, theirs was the challenge to carry on successfully the "long twilight struggle, year in and year out . . . against the common enemies of man: tyranny, poverty, disease and war itself."

Following the approval in both houses of the 87th Congress (June, 1960) the twenty-third amendment to the Constitution of the United States was submitted to the states for ratification. The required three-fourths majority of the states had completed its ratification in March 1961. The amendment was declared a part of the Constitution on April 3, 1961.

Amendment XXIII

Section 1. The District constituting the seat of Government of the United States shall appoint in such manner as the Congress may direct:

A number of electors of President and Vice-President equal to the whole number of Senators and Representatives in Congress to which the District would be entitled if it were a State, but in no event more than the least populous State; they shall be in addition to those appointed by the States, but they shall be considered, for the purposes of the election of President and Vice-President, to be electors appointed by a State; and they shall meet in the District and perform such duties as provided by the twelfth article of amendment.

Section 2. The Congress shall have power to enforce this article by appropriate legislation.